The Joan Palevsky    Imprint in Classical Literature

In honor of beloved Virgil—

"O degli altri poeti onore e lume . . ."

—Dante, *Inferno*

The publisher gratefully acknowledges the generous contribution to this book provided by the Jane K. Sather Professorship in Classical Literature Fund.

 SATHER CLASSICAL LECTURES

Volume Seventy

Reimaging Greek Tragedy
on the American Stage

# Reimagining Greek Tragedy on the American Stage

# Reimagining Greek Tragedy on the American Stage

Helene P. Foley

UNIVERSITY OF CALIFORNIA PRESS
*Berkeley   Los Angeles   London*

University of California Press, one of the most distinguished university presses in the United States, enriches lives around the world by advancing scholarship in the humanities, social sciences, and natural sciences. Its activities are supported by the UC Press Foundation and by philanthropic contributions from individuals and institutions. For more information, visit www.ucpress.edu.

University of California Press
Berkeley and Los Angeles, California

University of California Press, Ltd.
London, England

© 2012 by The Regents of the University of California

Library of Congress Cataloging-in-Publication Data

Foley, Helene P., 1942–.
  Reimagining Greek tragedy on the American stage / Helene P. Foley.
     p. cm. — (Sather classical lectures ; 70)
  Includes bibliographical references and index.
  ISBN 978-0-520-27244-6 (cloth, alk. paper)
  1. Greek drama—History and criticism.  2. Theater—United States—History.  I. Title.  II. Series: Sather classical lectures ; v. 70.

PA3131.G554  2012
792.1'20973—dc23                                                    2012000823

Manufactured in the United States of America

21  20  19  18  17  16  15  14  13  12
10  9  8  7  6  5  4  3  2  1

In keeping with its commitment to support environmentally responsible and sustainable printing practices, UC Press has printed this book on Cascades Enviro 100, a 100% post consumer waste, recycled, de-inked fiber. FSC recycled certified and processed chlorine free. It is acid free, Ecologo certified, and manufactured by BioGas energy.

*For all the friends, colleagues, and family members
who kept me company at so many productions
and adaptations of Greek tragedy*

CONTENTS

| | |
|---|---|
| *List of Illustrations* | ix |
| *Preface* | xi |
| INTRODUCTION | 1 |
| CHAPTER ONE.  GREEK TRAGEDY FINDS AN AMERICAN AUDIENCE | 27 |
| 1. Setting the Stage | 28 |
| 2. American Theater Makes Greek Tragedy Its Own | 42 |
| CHAPTER TWO.  MAKING TOTAL THEATER IN AMERICA: CHOREOGRAPHY AND MUSIC | 76 |
| 1. Hellenic Influences on the Development of American Modern Dance | 80 |
| 2. American *Gesamtkunstwerke* | 99 |
| 3. Musical Theater | 107 |
| 4. Visual Choreography in Robert Wilson's *Alcestis* | 116 |
| CHAPTER THREE.  DEMOCRATIZING GREEK TRAGEDY | 122 |
| 1. *Antigone* and Politics in the Nineteenth Century: The Boston 1890 *Antigone* | 125 |
| 2. Performance Groups in the 1960s–1970s: Brecht's *Antigone* by The Living Theatre | 132 |
| 3. The 1980s and Beyond: Peter Sellars's *Persians, Ajax,* and *Children of Heracles* | 138 |

4. Aeschylus's *Prometheus Bound* in the United States:
   From the Threat of Apocalypse to Communal Reconciliation — *154*

CHAPTER FOUR.  REENVISIONING THE HERO:
AMERICAN OEDIPUS — *160*

1. Oedipus as Scapegoat — *162*
2. Plagues — *170*
3. Theban Cycles — *175*
4. Deconstructing Fatality — *179*
5. Abandonment — *183*

CHAPTER FIVE.  REIMAGINING MEDEA AS AMERICAN OTHER — *190*

1. Setting the Stage: Nineteenth-Century Medea — *193*
2. Medea as Social Critic from the Mid-1930s to the Late 1940s — *200*
3. Medea as Ethnic Other from the 1970s to the Present — *210*
4. Medea's Divided Self: Drag and Cross-Dressed Performances — *224*

EPILOGUE — *229*

*Appendix A.* Professional Productions and New Versions of Sophocles' and Euripides' *Electra*s — *239*
*Appendix B.* Professional Productions and New Versions of *Antigone* — *249*
*Appendix C.* Professional Productions and New Versions of Aeschylus's *Persians*, Sophocles' *Ajax*, and Aeschylus's *Prometheus Bound* — *259*
*Appendix D.* Professional Productions and New Versions of *Oedipus Tyrannus* — *265*
*Appendix E.* Professional Productions and New Versions of Euripides' *Medea* — *277*
*Appendix F.* Professional Productions and New Versions of Euripides' *Iphigeneia in Aulis* and *Iphigeneia in Tauris* — *295*
*Appendix G.* Other Professional Productions and New Versions — *303*
*Notes* — *309*
*References* — *343*
*Index* — *363*

ILLUSTRATIONS

1. Lavinia (Alice Brady), Christine (Alla Nazimova), and Orin (Philip Foster) in Eugene O'Neill's 1931 *Mourning Becomes Electra*   16
2. Elektra (Pamela Reed) in Ezra Pound's *Elektra*   23
3. Electricidad (Zilah Mendoza) in Luis Alfaro's *Electricidad*   24
4. George Riddle as Oedipus in Sophocles' *Oedipus Tyrannus*   33
5. Point Loma Greek Theater, San Diego, California   39
6. Athena, Apollo, and Orestes with the chorus of Furies in Aeschylus's *Eumenides*   45
7. The Furies after being persuaded by Athena in Aeschylus's *Eumenides*   46
8. Margaret Anglin as Medea in Euripides' *Medea* and as Iphigenia in Euripides' *Iphigenia in Aulis*   55
9. Margaret Anglin as Sophocles' Electra   57
10. Margaret Anglin in Sophocles' *Electra*   58
11. Four scenes from the souvenir program for the Chicago Little Theatre's tour of Euripides' *Trojan Women*   65
12. Chorus in Euripides' *Trojan Women*, choreographed by Margaret Gage   86
13. Chorus in an unidentified Greek tragedy, choreographed by Margaret Gage   87
14. Scene 3 (Herdsman Scene) in Harry Partch's *Revelation in the Courthouse Park*   103
15. Polynices (Jamyl Dobson) and Eteocles (Benton Greene) in Will Power's *Seven*   106
16. The chorus performs "Wild Women Attack!" in *The Rockae*   115

17. Caroline Burlen as Antigone in the Saturday Morning Club of Boston's Sophocles' *Antigone*   128
18. Three chorus members in the Saturday Morning Club of Boston's Sophocles' *Antigone*   129
19. Darius (Ted van Griethuysen) consoles Atossa (Helen Carey) in Ellen McLaughlin's version of Aeschylus's *Persians*   143
20. Waterwell's *Persians,* a new version of Aeschylus's *Persians*   145
21. Ajax (Shawn Fagan) bones a fish in *Ajax: 100% Fun*   150
22. Oedipus (Kenneth Welsh), Shepherd (Oliver Cliff), and guards (Wilberto Rosario and Douglas Hamilton) in *Oedipus the King,* adapted by Anthony Burgess   163
23. Oedipus (John Campion) mistakenly celebrates his apparent release from guilt with Jocasta (Stephanie Roth-Haberle) in Sophocles' *Oedipus*   174
24. Teiresias (Jeffrey Baumgartner) in Frank Galati's *Oedipus Complex*   182
25. "The Modern Medea" (Margaret Garner) by Thomas Satterwhite Noble   197
26. Nathaniel McQueston (Walter Abel), Oparre (Katharine Cornell), and Faith Ingalls (Ruth Matteson) in Maxwell Anderson's *Wingless Victory*   206

PREFACE

A lover of Greek tragedy since I played Antigone in high school, a passionate theater buff, and a scholar of Greek drama, I began to think about this project from the time I moved to New York to teach in 1979. Starting in the late 1960s, but mushrooming from the 1980s to the present, Greek tragedy, both performances of the originals in translation and adaptations and new versions, began to make increasingly regular appearances on the New York stage. The same phenomenon on a smaller scale was taking place in other major cities, including Boston, Chicago, Los Angeles, Minneapolis, New Haven, Philadelphia, San Francisco, Seattle, Washington, D.C., Atlanta, Berkeley, Dallas, and Kansas City. My Greek drama in translation courses increasingly included more attention to modern productions, while our students at Barnard and Columbia were performing the plays in Greek almost annually. When the Berkeley Classics Department generously offered me the chance to give the Sather Classical Lectures, this project seemed made for me.

Scholarly study of both the ancient and modern performance and the reception of Greek tragedy has developed extensively as well, especially in Europe. In the United Kingdom, the Archive of Performances of Greek and Roman Drama at Oxford, which includes links to other important websites and databases, has played a critical role in collecting data (www.apgrd.ox.ac.uk). Edith Hall, Oliver Taplin, Fiona MacIntosh, and their colleagues at Oxford and Lorna Hardwick at the Open University have served as catalysts and editors for a number of volumes mainly focusing on British, European, and African productions. Erin Mee and I have expanded the range of the series with our own *Antigone on the Contemporary World Stage* (2011). Efforts by many others in Europe, too numerous to mention here, have been equally important. On the American side, Karelisa Hartigan's pioneering attempt to create a comprehensive picture of important U.S. productions from 1882 to 1993, *Greek Tragedy on the American Stage* (1995), was preceded by the more specialized book-length study by Marianthe Colakis, *The Classics in the American Theater of the 1960s and Early 1970s* (1993), and followed by the 2003 study of African American versions of Greek tragedy by Kevin Wetmore Jr., *Black Dionysus: Greek Tragedy and African American Theater,* and, since my lectures, by E. Teresa Choate's 2009 work, *Electra USA.* My own essay-length attempt to study Aeschylus's *Agamemnon* on the U.S. stage (2005) provoked many questions, to which I respond in this book. Yet these efforts, supplemented by a growing number of articles and another book in progress that has emerged from a project at Northwestern, have barely scratched the surface on the American side.

Hartigan's study was based largely on newspaper reviews in a limited number of major cities and thus emphasized, above all, the reaction of critics to the productions that she included. It also focused primarily on productions and close adaptations of the original plays, rather than including the full range of new versions. My own study emphasizes as much as possible productions where I have been able to get a more substantial picture of both script and the production itself. The views of critics are rarely catalogued in detail, although I draw wherever I can on their reports to recapture the productions themselves. I do not offer my own critical reactions to the many plays I have seen myself. That would be another project. This book attempts instead to recover what we can of a frustratingly ephemeral set of efforts and to locate them in a larger artistic and cultural continuum from the nineteenth century to the present.

To this end, I have chosen to address the full range of performances of Greek tragedy from translations of the original plays to adaptations and new versions. This choice seems to me to be true to the tradition that I am studying, which began in Athens as a competition to reenvision Greek myths on stage for a changing audience over time. In many later periods, including ancient Rome, new versions have been the major form of reception of these plays onstage. In my view, inevitably so. Varied attempts at "authenticity," a goal that is in any case impossible given our slim and still-evolving knowledge of ancient Greek productions and the mediation of translation, to say nothing of our unreliable knowledge of the ancient context and many aspects of the texts themselves, have generally proved unsuccessful on the professional stage in the United States, if not on college campuses.

Embodying a Greek tragedy on stage must involve taking a potentially controversial and deliberate position that communicates something to a contemporary audience. If we want to understand why certain plays have proved repeatedly engaging on the American stage, rather than simply on the page, or why and how people have chosen to perform or reinterpret them in certain periods and what kinds of cultural work these productions have performed, we need to include performances of the originals in translation, adaptations, and new versions (sometimes called "remakings" in this book), because they provide different modes of access to these questions. Experimental versions that some viewers might view or have viewed as travesties of the original plays—not "Greek" or "failures"—perform this cultural work differently from but as significantly as those that aim to reinvigorate "high culture" with them.

Theater artists who perform and/or revise Greek tragedy pour immense physical and intellectual energy into an ephemeral attempt to make a challenging work speak to its audience at a specific moment in time (or even afterward, in the memory of the viewers who give a play its meaning). These artists inevitably ask some different questions of the texts than scholars. Seeing performances of the plays or talking to their creators can lead a scholar back to reinterpreting the Greek original or recalibrating what is potentially powerful or controversial about a play. But more important, theater artists' imaginations aim to bridge past and present and open new avenues for considering what these plays have meant or can mean to Americans in different periods. (In this book I confine the term "American" to people in the United States.)

Classical Greek audiences formed a community that experienced tragedy first on stage rather than on the page. Performance at any period can give plays cultural authority and potentially generate new communities. We understand differently when we use our eyes, ears, and body together in a specifically constructed space. Current theater makers and audiences for theater come with diverse backgrounds and diverse responses, and scholars and critics can overprivilege their own reactions. This book has often relied on conversations with both artists and audience members, including devoted family members, students, friends, and colleagues who have seen far more versions of Greek tragedy with me than they might have liked over more than thirty years. This book includes both productions much reviewed in major theatrical venues and small, economically marginal efforts. My access to the resources and special collections of the New York Public Library for the Performing Arts, Lincoln Center, as well as to the archives of various theater companies, including many tapes of productions, has been equally invaluable.

From the nineteenth century, Greek tragedy has served as a fount of form and tradition in the American academy; on the professional stage it became in the early twentieth century a vehicle for some of the most innovative aesthetic developments in the history of U.S. theater and dance and later for the heroic efforts of both well-known and less-familiar artists to explore and confront a range of cultural and political issues. This book tries to explore the ultimately successful struggle of Greek tragedy to find a place on an American stage from the nineteenth century to the present and to isolate, to the degree possible, how the United States has reinterpreted it through its own concerns. The book shows how various plays resonated repeatedly in different periods both with efforts to revitalize

American theater and with specific U.S. controversies about war, slavery, race, the status of women, religion, identity, and immigration.

I originally imagined compiling a carefully contextualized history, comparing theatrical and scholarly reactions to the texts in various periods, and theorizing and evaluating extensively what I discovered. The performances themselves proved far more numerous and open to study than I had envisioned from the scholarship already available. I came instead to view my role as that of pioneer, clearing the way for later study by sharing the most basic historical and aesthetic patterns and thematic trends that my evidence often surprisingly offered me, and allowing the shape of the study itself to delineate my methodology. I chose to eliminate much of my original agenda, excluding college and university productions unless they intersected with the professional theater world, and selected heavily from an enormous body of performances. Many individual plays are not discussed (I myself have written about *Hippolytus*, *Agamemnon*, and a number of other plays elsewhere); *Medea* and *Oedipus Tyrannus* have been pervasive enough on the American stage to warrant separate consideration in this book. Although generic issues play a role in this book, since American artists often pointedly resist what they conceive of as traditionally "tragic," or seek to erode the borders between "tragedy" and "comedy," I entirely neglect generic categories closely related to tragedy, such as opera. I have also eliminated questions of translation in favor of a focus on the relation of productions to a social, aesthetic, cultural, or political context, although, unlike Europe, the United States largely resisted confronting both political power and democracy through the plays until the late 1960s. In order to preserve a sense of the larger picture, I have been unable to treat single productions in the detail they deserve, have risked offering perhaps too many examples in order to establish broader trends, and have relegated most basic production details to the appendices. Balancing goals has been a struggle. The book will offer a more extensive version of Greek tragedy's story on the American stage than before but will still be only a beginning. My goal is to leave behind a set of questions and projects for future exploration.

The book is far more extensive than my original lectures and could not have been written without the support of my husband, son, colleagues, and students. I thank Lynn Kozak and Rachel Lesser, who served as research assistants, and Robert Davis, Pantelis Michelakis, and Rachel Kitzinger for reading some early drafts. Several conversations with Yopie Prins proved invaluable. Robert Davis and Caroline Winterer also offered important assistance on nineteenth-century sources; Julie Malnig provided a script of *Electra Speaks*. At the behest of the Theosophical Society in Pasadena, Ed Lingham provided me with copies of materials that I had requested from the library, as well as relevant parts of his dissertation. The Houghton Library's Theatre Collection at Harvard permitted me to view tapes of *Alcestis* and Wilson's production notebooks. The following theater practitioners provided scripts, interviews, images, and/or access to other resources: Carey Perloff, Will Power, Cara Reichel, Cynthia Rosenthal, Ellen McLaughlin, Arian Moayed and Waterwell, Ellen Beckerman, Touchstone Theatre, Robert Woodruff and the American Repertory Theater, Joanna Settle and Anne DeAcetis, D. W. Jacobs, Frank Galati and the Goodman Theatre in Chicago, Michael John LaChiusa, William Missouri Downs (formerly Bill Streib), Sung Rno, Yubelky Rodriguez and Fluid Motion Theater & Film, P. Seth Bauer and Elysa Marden, and John Epperson. I owe additional thanks to Caroline Winterer and Mary Louise Hart, to Eric Schmidt and Cindy Fulton of University of California Press, to my copy editor Marian Rogers, and to my indexer David Prout. Audiences at Berkeley, Stanford, UC Davis, UCLA, Claremont Graduate School, Bucknell, Northwestern, Classical Association of New England Summer School at Dartmouth, Johns Hopkins, Drew, Wellesley, Wesleyan, University of Toronto, Columbia, and Radboud University, Nijmegen, Netherlands, have offered valuable responses to lecture versions of parts of this material. Research leave from Barnard College and a grant from the Loeb Classical Library Foundation gave me the time to research and write both the lectures and the larger book version. The hospitality and support of the Berkeley Classics Department was critical in allowing me to pursue an ambitious project that has reintroduced me both to my own country and to the plays that I love.

# Introduction
## Americanizing Greek Tragedy

*This is a society dedicated to the proposition that all men can be other than they are created.*
—CHRISTOPHER BIGSBY AND DON B. WILMETH, *THE CAMBRIDGE HISTORY OF AMERICAN THEATRE*

*What the American public wants is a tragedy with a happy ending.*
—WILLIAM DEAN HOWELLS TO EDITH WHARTON

For Americans, "human possibility," the effort to repair and remake the world, stands "as an animating faith."[1] Greek tragedy as a genre, however—and above all Sophocles' *Oedipus Tyrannus*, paradigmatic owing to Aristotle's *Poetics*—has frequently appeared to the American mind to represent fatality, a sense of overdetermination on multiple levels, inimical to the nation's Horatio Alger–oriented mythology. With the exception of new versions of Euripides' *Medea*, Greek tragedy in nineteenth-century America largely met with indifference or resistance on the professional stage. Nevertheless, a growing interest in reading and studying the texts both within and outside colleges and universities, and in viewing Athenian democracy as a precursor to America's own, began to pave the way for a greater receptivity. No longer an image of mobocracy, Athens came in the second half of the nineteenth century to serve as a corrective to Jacksonian-era corruption, materialism, and anti-intellectualism in a fashion that emerged with particular clarity in the 1890 *Antigone* discussed in chapter 3.1 of this book.[2]

At the same time, reviews of the limited number of successful United States professional productions in the second and third decades of the twentieth century continued to dwell on thematic tensions between Greek tragedy and American ideology. The revenge theme central to Sophocles' *Electra*, the most successful Greek original in this period, was also pronounced anachronistic. After World

War II, America came of age as the protagonist on the world stage. Yet it took a series of events in the late 1960s and 1970s, starting with the Vietnam War, Watergate, racial conflicts, feminist politics, and changes in the relation between theater and American society, to inaugurate a longer-term interest that persists until today in the complex relations among individuals and families and the larger community central to Greek tragedy.

United States audiences have generally had a narrow view of Greek tragedy, a form that in fact evolved and varied over the fifth century B.C.E. Tragedy was not limited to "the bleakest form of metaphysical pessimism" and human estrangement, as George Steiner argued.[3] Gods and fate, as opposed to family history or politics, play a fairly reduced role in many plays, and tragedies can end in survival and at least partial resolution as well as suffering. Tragic protagonists meet overdetermined situations head-on; they are generally not passive victims. Although Greek tragedies confront abuses of power and justice and misjudgments by leaders, the costs of imperial victory, and even post-traumatic stress, Athens' democratic audience itself preferred keeping tragic suffering or disaster at arm's length through myth-based plots and through approaching the present through heroes and heroines from locations outside Athens. Tragedies set in Athens or related to Athens with Athenian leaders like Theseus (not the central tragic figure in, e.g., Sophocles' *Oedipus at Colonus*) or future Athenian leaders like Ion in Euripides' *Ion* avoid disaster. Yet, as we shall see in more detail, Greek tragedy poses a number of additional problems for an American audience. Tragic individuals are fundamentally inseparable from their social world; domestic tensions among its elite characters are observed by choruses that preserve a public dimension to the action. Character is illuminated through public speech, difficult choices, and action; protagonists struggling to live a moral life take responsibility for outcomes that can be imposed on them for a range of reasons from within and without. The plays are not didactic; there is no clear triumph of good over evil; many plays arguably lack a firm sense of closure. The questions they pose are not resolvable, but confronting the past and cultural memory is critical to moving forward. In addition, American theater cannot reproduce the direct engagement between a large citizen audience and citizen actors and chorus members central to Greek tragedy. Drama in the United States is not a public political and religious event, and the composition of its audiences has narrowed over time. Unfamiliar myths, verse drama, choral performance, off-stage violence, and long rhetorical confrontations can make the plays both inaccessible or in the last case suspect. Recapturing a form of total theater like Greek tragedy, which included music, dance, and song along with masks and costumes that required nonnaturalistic acting, demands considerable investment of time and money.

In many respects, then, important American engagements with Greek tragedy on stage might seem more surprising than its periodic failure to take hold in the theatrical repertoire. Yet the evolving relation between the plays and the U.S. stage also reflects and illuminates important changes in the country's sense of itself. Greek tragedy has generally served progressive aesthetic, cultural, and political agendas, from transforming outmoded theatrical conventions to serving identity politics or promoting peace. This book will try to define and isolate central developments in the history of America's ambivalent relation to Greek tragedy on the professional stage from the nineteenth century to the present and to explore particular plays, themes, and changes in theatrical practice that best encapsulate them. Understanding the place of "legitimate" (involving high cultural, "refined" aspirations in contrast to popular, "light", or "vulgar" amusement) theater in the United States at different periods is critical to this process, since successful efforts to produce Greek tragedy are repeatedly tied to efforts at theatrical innovation and at expanding the American theatrical repertoire to include more ambitious plays.

I begin this book with a brief outline of this historical background. The introduction then concludes with an examination of how in the case of one popular play, Sophocles' *Electra*, the United States has reinterpreted or "Americanized" this tragedy to address important issues during the twentieth century. Western theater is international, and both plays and players have been crossing oceans through the entire period addressed in this book. My attempt to isolate particular American developments in the reception of Greek tragedy on the professional stage may in many cases be only a question of emphasis. Yet this book will argue that America particularly favors Greek tragedies that permit an exploration of the struggle to establish a self in a world that can appear to encourage and allow self-determination but can finally betray that effort in different ways. New U.S. versions and productions of *Electra*, *Medea*, and *Oedipus* discussed in this volume have also tended to leave behind larger political issues to focus on a confrontation with individual identity. Moreover, when the plays do address controversial cultural and political issues relating to national identity, directors have needed to negotiate productions carefully to be heard.

## TRAGEDY IN AMERICAN THEATER

Important productions of Greek tragedy and of new versions of the plays began to take place on the European stage in the sixteenth century. Greek tragedy made a brief and ephemeral debut on the U.S. stage in the nineteenth. The precolonial period was marked by a Puritan suspicion of theater, which could be viewed as a distraction from more important work, a waste of money, and a source of moral corruption. Theater was in any case not a high cultural priority.[4] Theater troupes largely composed of actors at least originally from England joined stock theater companies in larger American towns starting in the 1790s.[5] Most of the plays performed in the nineteenth century were also of European origin, partly because of America's postcolonial sense of inferiority. Romantic verse dramas, history plays, and public tragedies performed using neoclassical acting styles and featuring patrician military or political heroes from Rome, Greece, or later periods, such as James Sheridan Knowles's *Virginius* (1820) or John Howard Payne's *Brutus or the Fall of Tarquin* (1818), played a role in the repertoire and were popular with male audiences until 1865;[6] Shakespeare was a perennial favorite with all classes.[7] Operas and operettas,[8] pantomime, melodramas, comedies of various kinds, farces, burlesques, variety acts, circuses, vaudeville, minstrel shows, medicine shows, musical revues, and Wild West shows proved increasingly popular.

Until the mid-nineteenth century, all kinds of shows could be performed in venues that attracted a mixed-class audience (largely excluding respectable women) relegated to different parts of a theater.[9] The middling and working classes populated the pit on hard benches; wealthier patrons occupied the first two tiers of boxes, and prostitutes the third tier; a mixed group of those of modest means occupied the gallery. In the major cities some theaters began to specialize in performances attractive to either bourgeois or working-class audiences. In New York the Astor Place Opera House, built in 1847, for example, marked a shift from an inclusive audience to one dominated by the bourgeoisie; the pit was "aristocratized" into a parquet with fixed seats sold by subscription, and poorer, more respectable patrons were relegated to the gallery or amphitheater above the boxes for the wealthy.[10] The Bowery Theatre, by contrast, remained popular with the working classes.[11] Theatrical class division hardened after the collapse of more inclusive theatrical stock companies in the 1870s. Spectators from the industrial bourgeoisie, including increasing numbers of women (eventually outnumbering men), then became the major audience for social comedy and legitimate drama.[12] Over the nineteenth century, American theater responded to political shifts in power from a colonial elite to a Jacksonian democracy to a growing business class; plays, including those performed in various languages other than English, gradually incorporated ethnic, identity, urban, frontier, and economic themes that partly reflected patterns in immigration.[13] Yet ideological tensions between an uncertain age and a stage eager to provide upbeat or morally satisfying entertainment continued to define American theater. Bruce McConachie even goes so far as to argue that because "the entertainment industry was satisfied to deliver an upbeat version of life and the times . . . tragedy as a dramatic form [gradually] lost its voice and purpose in the nineteenth century."[14]

Of critical importance from a generic perspective, melodrama, the most emotionally powerful American theatrical form from at least the 1820s, both overlapped with and diverged from much of Greek tragedy.[15] For democratic America (as for postrevolutionary France, where it first became popular) theater that celebrated the moral superiority of the marginalized or powerless, including the poor, the enslaved, and the immigrant, and challenged the oppression, corruption, and villainy of the powerful proved perennially attractive. The exciting but temporary suffering of many melodramatic characters did not require tragic sacrifice but affirmed social justice and a moral order and helped to create a sense of social identity in an otherwise turbulent social and economic environment.[16] The internal conflicts and ambiguities central to tragedy and other legitimate drama could be projected outward to reflect anxiety about various forms of authority, whether aristocratic, paternal, or religious,[17] while melodrama's exemplary heroes and innocent, embattled women doggedly pursued virtue and integrity. Starting in the mid-1840s, for example, moral reform melodramas such as Henry J. Conway's wildly popular *Uncle Tom's Cabin,* William H. Smith's *The Drunkard,* and Charles H. Saunders's *Rosina Meadows* famously promoted abolitionism or temperance and punished the loss of female virtue. In the post–Civil War industrial age domestic melodramas served the agenda of the business classes by uniting families from different social backgrounds or rewarding hard work.[18] In contrast to tragedy, stylized acting, gestures, and facial expressions could serve in these plays to counter linguistic ambiguity. Tableaux and freezing of the action distilled and underlined specific emotional moments; music helped to define character and heighten tension and pathos.

Over time the genre flexibly incorporated darker themes including unnerving displays of female passion. Among plays that overlapped to a greater degree with tragedy, the heroic melodrama of the Jacksonian era (1830s–1850s), such as Robert Montgomery Bird's play about the Roman slave revolt led by Spartacus, *The Gladiator,* modified the conflict between family and civic duty central to tragedies of the early nineteenth century like the paternalistic *Virginius*. Heroic melodrama's charismatic heroes were called by God to lead a revolt against an oppressive political or social order that ended in their martyrdom. "Apocalyptic melodramas" popular with the working classes during the period 1835–50 focused on honor and revenge in a world on the verge of collapse; the dramatic version of Edward Bulwer-Lytton's *Last Days of Pompeii,* for example, ended in the explosion of Vesuvius. The more tightly structured "sensation melodrama" of the later nineteenth century emphasized themes of chance that reflected the economic and social tensions and uncertainties of the age and featured considerably more active and often ethnic (Jewish or Irish) heroines who could defend attacks on domestic happiness and family with passionate ferocity.[19]

Melodramatic plots perhaps superficially appeared, like some late plays of Euripides, to offer "tragedy with a happy ending." Augustin Daly, author of popular sensation melodramas, even claimed that "it is not impossible that the 'sensational melodrama' may sublime itself to be tragedy."[20] By introducing themes of sacrifice, tyrannical repression and alienation, revenge, chance and uncertainty, and (especially female) passion and by giving the central role to actresses by the turn of the century,[21] melodrama may have helped set the stage for the gradual emergence of Greek tragedy in the twentieth. Yet even when a greater sense of dramatic irony developed in the most sophisticated melodramas, "perhaps the American dramatic sensibility is essentially progressive, seeing the world in comedic or tragicomic rather than through tragic terms."[22] As we shall see, in the nineteenth century, only new versions of Greek tragedies that were colored by the national taste for melodrama, like *Medea*, appealed. In the late nineteenth and early twentieth centuries, the lingering taste for plays that rescue beleaguered female heroines like Sophocles' Electra also betrayed the influence of melodrama. Even after 1970, performances modifying Sophocles' Oedipus to make him a scapegoat who departs Thebes to save his city from the plague at the conclusion of *Oedipus Tyrannus* turned him into a descendant of the (Christianized and martyred) heroes of heroic melodrama. Moreover, given the wide-ranging social status of dramatic characters, the preference for realistic acting and less poetic and distanced language, and the generic blurring of the tragic and the comic in many plays on the later American stage, it is arguably the case that in the United States "any attempt to write [or adapt or perform] tragedy today is likely to produce melodrama instead."[23]

## THE ECONOMICS OF AMERICAN THEATER

Stock repertory theater companies established in major American cities in the nineteenth century increasingly depended on tours by various European, and above all British or formerly British, stars. Many of these stars performed major Shakespearean and other tragic roles, but, especially before the Civil War and despite public interest in reading Greek drama, which began as early as the 1820s–1830s, versions of Greek tragedy were rarely among these performances (see chapter 1.1). Owning and defining "legitimate" theater in America involved a long struggle. Edwin Forrest, subject of the famous Astor Place riots in New York, which broke out following the British star William C. Macready's performance at the Astor Place Opera House in 1849, was the first native-born American actor to achieve star status in tragic roles/heroic melodrama in the 1830s; Charlotte Cushman, the first American actress to do so, achieved stardom only in 1845.[24] American actresses such as Cushman and Matilda Heron proved successful in inaugurating a new focus on female passions (especially in defense of self or family) that arguably served to affirm the need for male domination of women.[25] Before the Civil War Heron had a significant success with the French playwright Ernest Legouvé's passionate, highly beleaguered Medea, and after the Civil War a number of (usually) European actresses followed in her wake with tours of a range of new European *Medea*s (see chapter 5.1 on *Medea*).

The economic decline of stock theater companies in the 1870s was partly provoked by the advent of "combination companies" led by star actors who brought their own (in their view superior) supporting players with them on tours organized in New York.[26] Booking agencies began to reorganize theatrical tours more efficiently along the ever-expanding railroad network across the country. These agencies evolved into the Theatrical Syndicate of 1896, which soon monopolized booking in first-class theaters nationwide. Starting in 1910, the Shubert brothers challenged and displaced the Syndicate by obtaining the same monopoly. By and large most professional productions, whether native or tours by European stars, were then packaged for national distribution in New York City, where the theatrical center was relocated from Union Square to Times Square/Broadway, and moved across the country to other major cities on the "road." Despite critics who claimed that theatrical monopolies discouraged the quality of American acting and native or legitimate drama, this was not entirely the case. As noted above, nineteenth-century theater had "remained subservient to the popular taste and reinforced the dominant morality of the nation."[27] Theater monopolies did homogenize taste by bringing isolated American "island communities" into a larger, more impersonal national and commercial culture; audiences became more passive and attracted to spectacle,[28] but they also expanded their theatrical experience.[29] Occasional visiting European productions of Greek tragedy in the late nineteenth and early twentieth century did appear in major New York venues along with tours by European stars, even though Broadway remained generally reluctant to back even the occasional American production. The 1882 professional production of *Oedipus* was financed by Daniel Frohman, brother of Charles Frohman, who represented the Syndicate in New York and Boston. Its relative failure was important in inaugurating this trend (see chapter 1.1). In fact, none of the successful native productions of Greek tragedy from 1910 to the early 1930s discussed in chapter 1 of this book were initially generated on Broadway.[30]

The period from the 1880s to the 1920s saw various developments that affected theater culture. Competition produced an oversupply of theaters, unionization spread, railroad and labor rates increased following World War I, and the theatrical "road" became increasingly imperiled.[31] These developments allowed a less expensive local alternative theater culture responsive to European art theaters to emerge. The American Little Theatre movement, named after Maurice Browne's Little Theatre in Chicago (1911), was founded by amateurs to raise the quality of cultural experience/American leisure and to create cohesion in local communities in American cities.[32] They aimed through a subscription system to establish resident companies, experiment in staging techniques, and maintain a repertoire of ambitious European and new American drama. These groups, along with other independent producers discussed in chapter 1.2, often made a point of including Greek tragedy in their repertoire.

The Depression, however, dealt a staggering blow to theater. In 1929 there were 75 Broadway theaters and 233 new productions; in 1959 only 34 theaters and 56 new productions. Costs had skyrocketed. By the 1960s it took eight months to recoup investment that had taken only three months to realize in the 1920s.[33] In 1935–39 the short-lived Federal Theatre aspired to include the classics along with new, often political plays, dance, children's theater, and performances by Negro theater groups. The sole representative of Greek tragedy among the many works performed, however, was a 1938 dance piece entitled *Trojan Incident,* based on Euripides' *Trojan Women* with a prologue inspired by Homer (see chapter 2 for further discussion).[34]

In the 1950s, an interest in modernism, ambitious poetic theater, and new American and European plays previously central to the alternative theater of the second and third decades of the twentieth century reemerged. In New York, Off Broadway (from 1947), and eventually also Off-Off-Broadway (starting in 1958), replaced Broadway as the primary generator of legitimate drama, including new plays and classical revivals.[35] Before the brief period 1935–39, the U.S. government had not financed theater and the arts. Subsidies for ambitious theater became available for the first time through money from the Ford (from 1959) and Rockefeller foundations, and the financial support of these foundations, along with the founding of the National Endowment for the Arts in 1965 (followed by state and local equivalents), also helped encourage the creation of important regional theaters across the country. By and large, Off and Off-Off-Broadway, regional theaters of various sizes, and college and universities remain the dominant source of new American versions and performances of Greek tragedy in translation today, though visiting productions from Europe and more recently other parts of the world have continued as well (sometimes on Broadway). From the late 1960s new versions of Greek tragedy produced for an educated audience in both alternative and regional theaters mushroomed.[36] Michael Cacoyannis's production of Euripides' *Trojan Women* at New York's Circle in the Square, which pointedly responded to the Vietnam War, promoted this trend in New York starting in 1963. Translated by Edith Hamilton and starring Mildred Dunnock, Claire Bloom, and Rod Steiner, the play had over 600 performances until 1964 and was filmed by Cacoyannis with different actors in 1971.

## THEATRICAL TRANSITIONS

These economic transitions helped influence important developments in the performance of Greek tragedy in the United States: choice of plays, production styles, and target audiences. In the nineteenth century, performances of the Greek originals in translation (which were rare on either side of the Atlantic in any case), as opposed to new versions, failed to get a responsive audience except (from the 1880s) on college campuses. More successful and theatrically innovative early twentieth-century productions on the professional stage were largely limited to a familiar group of plays—*Electra, Medea, Oedipus*, and *Trojan Women*—and, despite occasional exceptions, a larger repertoire for the professional stage emerged only in the 1980s.[37] The only two new American versions of Greek tragedy written in the nineteenth century were not produced on stage (see chapter 1.2, chapter 3, and chapter 5), but Eugene O'Neill's 1931 *Mourning Becomes Electra,* which attempted to define an American version of the tragic, set the stage for the emergence of new versions of Greek tragedy, which have proliferated since the late 1960s (see chapter 1.2).

Since the late 1960s, several theatrical developments have helped generate performances and new versions of Greek tragedy. First, avant-garde performance groups such as The Living Theatre, The Performance Group, the Open Theater, Mabou Mines, and others often preferred to adapt texts from the past, which were more readily available for transformation, fragmentation, and improvisation than modern plays and offered bridges to theatrical traditions linked with myth, ritual, and a Dionysian liberation of mind and body. These groups were concerned with creating performances through collective improvisation, which also aimed to break down the boundaries between actors, roles, and audience, disrupt theatrical illusion, and actively engage the audience in the performance. A focus on representing ideas through images and the body led to a deemphasis on, if not exclusion of, the language and unified action so central to Greek tragedy itself. On the one hand, plays like The Living Theatre's Brecht's *Antigone* or The Performance Group's new version of Euripides' *Bacchae, Dionysus in 69,* tried to reauthorize the role of the chorus, tragic ritual, and the bonds to a democratic society central to Greek tragedy, and in many ways successfully linked their age to the stage (see chapters 2 and 3). On the other hand, as C. W. E. Bigsby has argued, "performance art is not a tragic art."[38] These groups' celebratory concern with freedom to express the senses, with communitarian impulses and personal transcendence (often relying on Freudian psychology),[39] made serious confrontation with American wars and materialism complicated despite their desire to stage political resistance.

In the 1980s, identity politics concerning gender, race, and nationality played an increasingly central role in American theater. U.S society came to be viewed as a "mosaic" rather than a melting pot.[40] (Earlier ethnic theater in the United States could include Greek tragedy, but these productions were generally less influential beyond their target audiences; see further, chapter 1.1 and chapter 3.)[41] While the treatment of women and barbarians in Greek tragedy provoked criticism in this period, the plays' openness to staging and examining gender conflict and constructed social identities, as well as to neutral casting and varied settings, nevertheless led to many productions and new versions focused on issues of identity. Moreover, since Greek tragedies did not belong to any one modern culture, they were more readily appropriated to explore controversial questions.[42] Feminist and gay theater and various ethnic groups have increasingly made the plays their own (see especially chapters 2 and 5), though issues relating to race and gender played a role in new versions of Greek tragedy from the nineteenth century.

Finally, America's increasingly powerful, central, and controversial role in world history gradually loosened its theater's resistance at many earlier periods to confronting contemporary politics through Greek tragedy. With the exception of Euripides' *Trojan Women*, politically engaged theater from 1910 through the 1930s failed to choose Greek tragedy as a vehicle for addressing political issues. The post–World War II period (despite the Korean War) was largely preoccupied with recovery and material and military advancement. Important playwrights like Arthur Miller and Tennessee Williams were more concerned with depersonalization and individual alienation; the McCarthy-era witch hunts discouraged former New Dealers' pursuit of political and social change.

The era of the Vietnam War proved a turning point, and since the late 1960s and the 1970s Greek tragedy has continued to play a role in that developing story. As we shall see, contemporary theater deconstructs, remakes, and performs a much larger range of the original texts to respond in new ways to current issues and has perhaps come closest of any period in U.S. theater history to reproducing the public questions that Greek tragedy asked of its original audience (see especially chapter 3 and the epilogue). The appropriation of world theater performance traditions, disruption of linear narrative structures, often with forms of pastiche, reconstruction of audience-performer relations and theatrical spaces, nonpsychological characterization, resistance to emotion-based acting, physical styles of performance, distrust of language, cross-dressing, absurdist theater, and tragicomedy have all continued to play a role in the process.

This book will focus on periods and plays that are central to the reception of Greek tragedy on the U.S. stage. Chapter 1.1–2 first examines the nineteenth century's general failure to adopt Greek tragedy in the repertoire of the professional (as opposed to university) stage and make it its own, and then developments that led to a number of important and relatively successful and aesthetically innovative productions in different contexts in the early twentieth century (through 1932). Artists of the latter period aimed to adapt important new aesthetic approaches to theater in Europe for the American context in order to revitalize its theatrical tradition and cultural identity. Chapter 2 examines American attempts to capture Greek tragedy as a form of total theater through consideration of developments in American dance (choreography), music, and visual effects. Chapter 2.1 significantly overlaps in time with the early twentieth-century productions discussed in chapter 1 before moving on to later productions. As in chapter 1, aesthetic innovation has repeatedly proved critically related to American engagement with Greek tragedy.

Chapter 3 addresses through a wider range of plays from the late nineteenth century to the present how American theater has, despite a general reluctance at many periods, addressed public and political issues through Greek tragedy in a fashion that often tries to contain, resist, or reimagine the original plays for a very different democracy. Chapters 1, 2, and 3 aim in different ways to provide an expanded framework for understanding aspects of performances in the thematically organized case studies of chapters 4 and 5, which address two of the most popular tragedies on the U.S. stage from the late nineteenth century to the present: *Oedipus Tyrannus* and *Medea*. (The equally popular *Electra* is addressed more briefly below, but the increasingly ubiquitous *Trojan Women* is addressed only selectively.) These two chapters examine the changing reception of central Greek tragic heroes and heroines and how their stories have served above all to address issues relating to American anxieties about identity. Oedipus's confrontation with an irresistible fate has continually posed the issues with which this introduction opened (chapters 1 and 2 deal with earlier productions of the play); from the 1970s on, which is the focus of chapter 4, American Oedipus has become above all a figure for the individual struggling to remake himself or change/reinterpret his story in a challenging environment. From the nineteenth century to the present, the dangerous Medea, on the other hand, faces and resists social and political restraints as a figure for multiple versions of "the other" in a nation that aims but often fails to be a melting pot. Finally, the epilogue attempts to capture through a brief discussion of Euripides' Iphigeneia plays more recent trends in the U.S. response to Greek tragedy.

As a whole, then, the book has three central areas of investigation, which are interwoven with different degrees of emphasis in each chapter. First, while broadly outlining developments in the reception of Greek tragedy on the American professional stage, it gives primary attention to two periods during which the most significant and numerous productions occurred, the period from 1910 up to the Depression, and that from the 1970s to the present. Second, while similar aesthetic innovations in staging promoted Greek tragedy on the European stage, American contributions in this area emphasized in chapters 1 and 2 have been important, distinctive, and often more successful than native representation of the spoken texts. Third, American theater has tended to respond to Greek tragedy and its central figures in an idiosyncratic fashion that reflects its own changing history and ideology and modifies our understanding of the possibilities for and implications of the tragic genre itself in the modern world.

I close here with a brief case study of a single play that will try to introduce the approach to defining the "Americanizing" of Greek tragedy taken in this book as a whole. Previous publications (including shorter studies not mentioned here) have examined U.S. productions of both Aeschylus's *Oresteia* (Foley 2005) and Sophocles' *Electra* (Choate's 2009 book-length study). This gives me a valuable background against which to offer through *Electra* a brief example of the way that American versions of Greek tragedy have responded to particular cultural issues and made those issues—which are also central in different ways to the Greek originals—visible by remaking and staging them for a modern audience.

## AMERICAN ELECTRA

From the late nineteenth century, Electra, and especially Sophocles' Electra, became one of the three most popular Greek tragic figures on the U.S. stage, along with Medea and Oedipus. As the early performances of Margaret Anglin (1913–28) and Blanche Yurka (1931–32) discussed in chapter 1.2 will demonstrate, Electra's multifaceted domination of the stage in Sophocles (and Euripides) makes her a compelling role for actresses. As an oppressed, virginal victim of injustice, her story resonates with melodrama even if American critics frequently resisted what they thought of as the play's anachronistic and repellent revenge theme: vendetta justice by the siblings Orestes and Electra against their mother, Clytemnestra, and her lover/spouse, Aegisthus, for the killing of their father, Agamemnon. "The play is somewhat removed from modern moods and ways of thinking. Revenge as a religious duty does not easily command our sympathy" (*New York Times*, February 7, 1918); "Revenge, even for the murder of a father, does not strike us as weightily tragic" (John Corbin, *New York Times*, February 17, 1918). Instead, the attraction lay in the play's relentless dramatic focus on its war-scarred, dysfunctional family and on Electra's fierce resistance to being silenced and victimized by it.

The general temptation to build new melodramas based on the problematic psychological parent-child relations in the families of both Agamemnon and Oedipus has only increased in the United States since the early twentieth century (promoted above all by O'Neill's 1931 *Mourning Becomes Electra*). Oedipus and Jocasta, however, undertake their fatal choices in ignorance. Escape is impossible; self-knowledge is to some degree achievable. What makes the house of Agamemnon particularly compelling to Americans is the self-consciousness with which characters confront and make often highly overdetermined choices in the context of their dysfunctional family. Agamemnon chooses in the face of conflicting political, religious, and social pressures to sacrifice his daughter Iphigeneia in order to make war on Troy, and Clytemnestra chooses to kill him for it (along with engaging in adultery and later tyranny with Aegisthus). An often-reluctant Orestes has a divine mandate to kill his mother but must face the consequences of his action, including, in Aeschylus's version, madness inflicted by the Furies, painful exile, and trial by jury in Athens.

In versions of the myth by Aeschylus, Sophocles, and Euripides, the choices made by the innocent sisters Electra, Chrysothemis, and Iphigeneia are constrained in a different fashion: they can only resist or submit. Tragic Electras desperately want to avenge their much-adored but often barely known murdered fathers; they are furious at their unfaithful mothers, both for killing their fathers and for mistreating them, and they project all hopes (and nearly incestuous passions) onto their brothers. They can be self-conscious about and fear repeating their mother's own vengefulness but then enthusiastically echo it. They experience a relentlessly corrupted life verging on drudgery in the wake of Agamemnon's murder and struggle with how best to react to the situation. As women with a living though absent brother to play the role of avenger, they are not by ancient Greek standards initially in a cultural position to act,[43] and their humiliating paralyzed lives can push them close to extremity or madness.

Such tragic self-division and sense of entrapment are by no means unique in Greek drama (or in melodrama). The self-division of mature female figures like Medea, Clytemnestra, and Phaedra,[44] or male figures like Agamemnon, has also received considerable attention in various American versions and performances of Greek tragedies, but here marital and erotic issues come into play, and the characters' ability to make autonomous decisions entails a different kind of responsibility for action. By contrast, the immaturity and psychic vulnerability of Agamemnon's children in an increasingly uncertain and oppressive environment can readily reflect forms of victimization familiar through melodrama and in U.S. popular culture and psychology. In particular, the feminist movement's focus (especially in the 1970s and 1980s) on the struggle to develop a female self under patriarchy resonated easily with the problems faced by these virginal daughter figures. New U.S. versions of Greek tragedy focused on Electra have been exceptionally inventive in representing the heroine's self-division and resistance in various dramatic forms. Many have literally split and even multiplied both the heroine and, increasingly after the 1970s, her sister Iphigeneia as well.[45] While Greek tragic heroes like Oedipus and Orestes also face crises of identity and self-division, they tend to recognize and arrive through action at a more stable (if often, and especially in American versions, maimed) sense of self.[46] Electra's future, more circumscribed by family and social roles, is generally less clear.

In an extreme case in point, Yuval Sharon's 2004 *The Mourners*, part of a new version of the *Oresteia* at Theater Faction in New York, confronted a tentative Orestes, who emerged from a sandpit representing Agamemnon's grave in center stage, with no less than four compelling Electras imprisoned in a rec room. In contrast to any Greek version, Orestes disappeared at their urging to kill his haughty mother and never reemerged on stage. Wearing dark glasses, Elektra mourned her father and her situation with excerpts from Aeschylus's *Libation Bearers*, Euripides' and Sophocles' *Electras*, Richard Strauss's *Elektra*, the rap metal band Rage Against the Machine, and a monologue for Electra from the American playwright Charles Mee's *Orestes*, while her choric doubles in sweatpants engaged in Sisyphean efforts to make things happen. Bathtub Electra washed and beautified herself in preparation for no apparent event as she sang Elektra's aria from Strauss's opera, urging Orestes to act; Internet Electra endlessly tried to control and sift communication from the Internet that we see projected from her PC on the back of the stage; and Fitness Electra worked out for the entire play on a power-walking machine. This production's multiple and eclectic Electra literally performed the original's intensity, psychological fragmentation, and multidimensional paralysis.

Scholars have puzzled over the apparently triumphant ending of Sophocles' *Electra,* in which Orestes succeeds in his coolly planned revenge (no Furies or any other negative repercussions are explicitly mentioned), and Electra's dreams are apparently fulfilled. Homer's *Odyssey* holds up Orestes as a heroic model to the young Telemachus, who yearns to destroy the marauding suitors of his mother and recover his household. Is Sophocles' play taking a similar position? If so, why is Electra the central character? Can an obsessively vocal heroine who has lamented her dead father and nurtured a self-destructive hostility to her mother for so many years find genuine liberation and a future? Can her enthusiasm for the matricide fail to have repercussions? A darker view of the play finds Electra so corrupted by her painful experiences that revenge can no longer restore her to a sense of normality. By and large, this darker view has, after Margaret Anglin's initial triumph with a celebratory interpretation of the role (chapter 1.2), predominated on the U.S. stage.[47] Blanche Yurka, also noted in chapter 1.2, set a later trend by making her Sophoclean heroine Euripidean, and hence more pointedly psychologically confused, divided, and uncertain. From the New York production starring Mrs. Campbell in 1908, Hofmannsthal's *Elektra* and Richard Strauss's later opera *Elektra* (based on Hofmannsthal) have influenced the representation of a succession of nearly mad or at least neurotic Sophoclean virgins. Many actresses playing Electra in translations of Sophocles' play have taken this culturally unspecific route to interpreting the role in both the United States and Europe.[48] New American versions have, on the other hand, tended to dramatize more than Sophocles' original Electra's struggle in the face of overwhelming difficulties to recognize and create a self. Eugene O'Neill asserted that "[man's] struggle used to be with the gods, but now it is with himself, his own past."[49] If "fate is hardly domesticated by asserting that what was once external and supernatural is now internal and psychological," this "relentless engagement with the self,"[50] with a conscious role in one's own making, is in my view characteristic of American productions and new versions of Greek tragedy, and similar dramatic interpretations of other characters will emerge in plays discussed later in this book, though not without a sense (O'Neill included) of external cultural forces at work.[51]

Eugene O'Neill's influential 1931 *Mourning Becomes Electra* borrowed from tragic versions of the myth by Aeschylus, Sophocles, and Euripides to make O'Neill's Electra's battered and divided psyche the linchpin of an elaborate trilogy.[52] Yet as Stark Young remarked in his review of the production directed by Philip Moeller at the Guild Theatre in New York, "It is interesting in our confused and feministic epoch that this new employment of the theme gives the play to Electra.

Nowhere in Greek does this happen." As he wrote in his diary, O'Neill wanted to give modern Electra a tragic ending worthy of her character: "In the Greek story she peters out into undramatic married banality [the Euripides version]. Such a character contained too much tragic fate within her soul to permit this—why should Furies have let Electra escape unpunished?"[53] In *Mourning* Lavinia's (Electra) obsessive attachment to her father and Orin's (Orestes) to his mother set the stage for a long line of neurotic, predictably Freudian and often (as in this case) explicitly incestuous siblings who can emerge as seeming doubles of their parents. Or even ancestors: family portraits line the walls of the house of Mannon; the characters periodically project masklike faces that express their entrapment in a social role. O'Neill's shattered, shell-shocked (from the Civil War), guilt-stricken Orin is pointedly not Sophocles' decisive plotter (fig. 1). A character derived primarily from Euripides' *Electra,* whose young and uncertain hero needs to be pressed to act by his intense, vengeful sister and who awakens, along with her, to a postcrime recognition of their terrible act, Orin leaves Lavinia permanently at center stage to pursue her own "tragic fate within her soul."

Persuasive masters of memory, strategy, or resistance, Greek Electras are forced by their female role to rely on words not deeds. Even when Sophocles' Electra thinks that Orestes is dead, she cannot persuade her sister Chrysothemis to attempt revenge with her; when Orestes appears, she at first emotionally delays and then supports his actions with words. Yet O'Neill's active Lavinia moves from trying to replace her absent father in act 1 to reinhabiting her mother, Christine, in the final act. In the opening act, she controls and defines the archetypal house of Mannon. She, not her mother, runs the household; the servants are loyal to and respond to her throughout. Both plotter and detective, she uncovers her mother's adultery, finds out the true identity of Adam Brant, the Aegisthus figure (the son of her grandfather's brother by a French Canuck nurse), discovers that her father has been poisoned by her mother, lures Orin into killing Brant, frightens (along with Orin) her mother into suicide, rejects incestuous advances from her brother, and allows him to commit suicide rather than reveal the family secrets. But unlike the rest of her family, she does not crack under the strain. Ever defeated in love, she closes the play by shutting herself into the doomed family mansion and terminates the family line by rejecting marriage.

In contrast to Sophocles or Euripides, O'Neill's trilogy refuses to leave his Electra figure with either her completed revenge (Sophocles) or a marriage to Pylades announced by a deus ex machina (Euripides). (Aeschylus simply ushers her into silence offstage after her scene with Orestes.) Assuming after the deaths of her parents and Brant that she has done her duty by the Mannons (386), O'Neill's (in this respect highly American) Lavinia tries to move beyond the tortured family past to love and an ordinary life.[54] She gives up imitating her father and begins to adopt, via a trip to the South Seas, her mother Christine's once-hated sensuality. This

FIGURE 1. Lavinia (Alice Brady) and Christine (Alla Nazimova) greet Orin (Philip Foster) on his return from the Civil War in Eugene O'Neill's 1931 *Mourning Becomes Electra,* directed by Philip Moeller, Guild Theater, New York. Photo by Vandamm Studio (1932). Courtesy of Billy Rose Theater Division, The New York Public Library for the Performing Arts.

typically American effort to reject the past proves impossible. The family's simple and unromantic neighbor, Peter Niles, is no substitute for the tortured Adam Brant, who had awakened her passion while pretending to court her in order to conceal his feelings for her mother. Lavinia's imitation of her mother revives Orin's passionate dependency on Christine. The Puritan heritage and history of her family and the repercussions of the Civil War (the plays are set in 1865–66), which split the national psyche, close in on Lavinia. Yet she finally enters a world of family ghosts in a haunted classical-style mansion with a full self-consciousness and sanity that are rare among those U.S. Electras that come after her. Mourning may become O'Neill's Electra, but her mourning is distilled into a permanent recognition of an irrevocable heritage.[55] Electra's name means "the unmarried one." Lavinia comes to embody this name; yet even in defeat she has captured something like a self, for which she takes responsibility in the fashion of more autonomous Greek tragic heroes. Lavinia implicitly answers an important question: what does a beleaguered young heroine *do*, since the model for positive heroism is male? Here she, however desperately, not only takes action in a fashion that had already emerged in melodrama, but fails either to complete a love story or to go mad in the culturally predictable fashion of other stage heroines.

By the 1970s, Electra once again emerged in avant-garde or radical theater as an archetypal split female psyche. Joseph Chaikin's 1974 and 1976 Open Theater *Electra* reduced the play to three characters, Electra, Clytemnestra, and Orestes, who interacted in pairs.[56] The spare, at times poetic text of *Electra* was written by Robert Montgomery and based on the *Electra*s of Sophocles, Euripides, and Hofmannsthal (Sophocles was the basic inspiration). As with O'Neill, the play offered a doomed therapeutic process. Electra's opening monologue was followed by a scene with Clytemnestra that ended with Electra embodying the spirit of Agamemnon, a recognition scene with Orestes that included a rehearsal of Clytemnestra's murder in which Electra played her mother and prodded Orestes (as in Euripides) to act, and the return of Orestes after a matricide that took place offstage. The characters used a rhythmic, ritualized, even eerie chanting to deliver their lines along with guttural, rhythmic noises. As Mel Gussow put it (*New York Times*, May 24, 1974), "Words [are] handled as fresh constructs, as if they were being coined as they are spoken." Bodily movements evoked images of animals; the actors exuded intense concentration (Martin Oltarsh, *Show Business*, June 6, 1974, 7).

The central preoccupation was recognition, with staging moments where a person becomes intensely aware of his/her own or another's being and mortality. In her opening monologue, Electra recognized herself: "You are Electra." "You are the horror your mother lives with." In her scene with Clytemnestra, the two recognized their highly contradictory relation to each other, and Clytemnestra, who is tormented to an untraditional degree by Agamemnon's brutality to his children (not only the murder of Iphigeneia, but the beating of a three-year-old Orestes),

Agamemon's replacement of her with Cassandra, her murder of her husband, and her current fear of retribution, confronted her past. She and Electra shared moments of past victimization and love; they embraced, and Clytemnestra tended Electra's unkempt body:

> How strange.
> Two women
> being here
> at this moment in time
> in this universe
> breathing.

Electra then became Agamemnon, or that part of herself created through his killing, the embodiment of revenge. "I am Electra,/I am Electra,/I am my father's murder," she later said to Orestes. Here Electra rose from a crouched position to full size, a move enhanced by the actress Michelle Collison's exceptional stature.[57] Clytemnestra and Electra stared at each other in horror/hatred. In the scene where Electra rehearsed her mother's murder with Orestes, the son symbolically recognized his mother before committing the act, as he advanced, then withdrew, while Electra played both herself and her mother, whom the audience had already seen played by another actress. This doubling was evoked through repeated gestures. Earlier Electra had leaned her head on Clytemnestra's thigh; now she did the same to Orestes.[58] Electra/Clytemnestra: "I am your mother./Can you take the life/ that gave you life?" Orestes: "I have no mother." Electra/Clytemnestra: "Then you are not there." One critic described Orestes as "like an electric graph measuring Electra's outbursts."[59] Chaikin's Electra was literally divided into a loving/hating daughter of her mother, an embodiment of Agamemnon, and a performer of her mother.

If in Chaikin's play Electra became the lens through which the contradictory process of tragic recognition of familial relations was focused to no ultimate avail, in the 1974 feminist *Electra Speaks* of the Women's Experimental Theatre (WET), the women of the house of Atreus, and above all Electra, emerged as everywoman. In contrast to any Greek version, their Electra was stunted by *both* anger at/dependence on her mother and angry fear of her father's authority, especially his sacrifice of Iphigeneia; she eventually escaped tragic entrapment by learning to "speak" and walking out the door of the doomed house of Atreus.[60] WET, founded by Clare Coss, Sondra Segal, and Roberta Sklar, offered in *The Daughter's Cycle* a theatrical exploration of women in the patriarchal family and the female journey from childhood to maturity. Founded in part out of feminist disenchantment with the sexism of New Left politics in the 1960s and 1970s, the group turned to a collective exploration and deconstruction of the formation and enforcement of gender roles by cultural institutions; it challenged female infantilization and subjugation in the family and the family romance.[61] Women played all the parts in *Electra Speaks* in a deliberate attempt to question fixed gender identities;[62] the performance was designed for the female spectator, and at least once a week the audience was exclusively female to provide for the most unfettered possible response.[63]

Part 1, *Daughters,* explored the complex and ambivalent mother-daughter relation; part 2, *Sister/Sister,* looked at the patterns of alliance and betrayal in relations between female siblings in the family context; part 3, *Electra Speaks,* studied women in the "archetypal family" of the *Oresteia*— Clytemnestra, Electra, and Iphigeneia as mother, daughter, and sister—but included a Cassandra, who tries to persuade Clytemnestra that she is not the "other woman" but a fellow rape victim, and an Athena, a "Daddy's girl," who as a glib lawyer blames the women, including Electra, for all crimes and concludes her defense of Orestes with "I tell you if that woman [Clytemnestra] were alive today I'd haul her into family court." Overall the play posed the question, "Whose interests are served by the institutionalized division between women in the family?"[64] The daughter's perspective remained central. As one critic put it, "All women's rage, confusion, guilt, and inhibition arise from women's cultural inability to see and know what dad has done."[65] "I agree never to know what I want," says Electra with typical self-hatred. "Why does taking care of yourself so often feel like betraying others." Initially Electra laughs, talks too much, does not know what to say, cannot hear, smiles too much, ends her sentences with a question. Finally, she moves tentatively to self-recognition, separation, speech, and survival through observing the experiences of mother, sister, and herself.

Contemporary psychological studies had stressed that because boundaries between women in the nuclear family are fluid, separation is especially difficult for girls.[66] In this play, each performer also assumed Electra's identity at some point, thus defining her as every daughter, who is and plays everyone but herself. Electra discovers that gaining autonomy does not require devaluation of her mother or surrender to her father. After confronting her mother about her acquiescence to men, marriage, female roles, and to Iphigeneia's sacrifice, or even potentially to the sacrifice of Electra herself, Electra says to her father's spirit/the audience: "I don't know how to be any more. I can either be your daughter or my self. I don't know how to act any more. I used to pass. I used to pass well. I can't pass any more . . . If you hesitate for one second, you won't get what you need. Because they don't want that."

Yet finally, she progresses tentatively from sorrow to laughter and a new life. She removes her unfeminine tuxedo jacket and starts to step out of the door:

| | |
|---|---|
| She tugs | She belches |
| She lugs | She is passing air |
| She heaves | She is breathing |

> She hauls          She signals
> . . .                 She has never done this before
> She stands firm.

Whereas Sophocles' Electra, the unquestioning devotee of her father, represents from the first moment the power of speech against Orestes' ability to act, this new, posttragic Electra pointedly moves to both speech and action by reevaluating family ties and moving beyond them. This Electra again journeys toward an (in this case liberated American) self.

O'Neill aside, Chaikin and WET performed Electra's split psyche physically. Ezra Pound's radical translation of Sophocles' original instead expressed the heroine's extreme cultural alienation verging on madness above all through language. In conjunction with the classicist Rudd Fleming, Pound composed the play in 1951, shortly before his better-known *Women of Trachis,* while the poet was incarcerated in St. Elizabeth's hospital in Washington, D.C. (1945–58). Pound did not publish the play, because his confinement was an alternative to a trial for treason, and he did not wish to advertise his sanity by demonstrating his ability to translate Greek.[67] The play received its first production in 1987, directed by Carey Perloff at New York's Classic Stage Company, was published in 1989 and 1990, and restaged in Washington, D.C., at the Round House Theatre by Tom Prewitt in 1992.[68] Like Elektra, Pound himself was at this point an alien and exile in his own country, obsessed with memories and shut out of a post–World War I and II political, cultural, and social world that seemed to have been reduced to competing fragments in a corrupt economy ("Mycene,/center of the gold trade," *Elektra* 5). In Pound's version, Elektra's words and Orestes' action could no longer align convincingly with one another without destroying Elektra's complex self, as they perhaps do at the play's conclusion in Sophocles.

Pound's attempt to write a specifically American version of *Electra* entailed a cacophony of linguistic styles and dialects that expressed a painful (by implication national) failure of communication, in which characters talked past each other, along with something close to comic absurdity. As noted earlier, Sophocles' Orestes focuses on action; Pound's Orestes uses action speak: "Don't start a war,/take a chance, do it yourself:/kinky course, clean in the kill" (6). In his false messenger speech about the supposedly dead Orestes, Orestes' tutor adopts plausible language hinting at Irish blarney. The brash, vulgar Clytemnestra bullies her daughters, including the accommodating, practical Chrysothemis, who thinks Electra has no sense (53).

In this version, only Elektra struggles to communicate with a variety of styles, ranging from colloquial tough talk to heartrending lyric to ancient Greek, a language she alone shares with the maternal witnesses of the chorus. Elektra's split psyche reflects the contradictory world that she inhabits. Her opening lament mixes Greek, lyrical pain, and fierce colloquial resistance (8–9):

> OO PHAOS HAGNON
>   Holy light
> Earth, air about us,
>   THRENOON OODAS
>   POLLAS D'ANTEREIS AESTHOU
> tearing my heart out
> when black night is over
> . . . .
> Split his head with an axe as
> a woodcutter splits a billet of oak,
> and that killed him
> and nobody else in this house seems to mind.
> Well I'm not going to forget it
> and all the stars can shine on it, all of them
> destiny
> tears of hate
> all flaming rips
> of the stars
> tide
> destiny
> and the day can look at it.
> I won't stand it and just keep quiet.

Yet in her initial debate with Clytemnestra, she turns to a pointed succinctness and linearity that she shares with her family (33): "for if blood for blood makes justice, you'll be the first to go."

Elektra's lament over the urn supposedly containing Orestes' ashes bursts into lyrics (marked by the use of "thee" and "thou," which are not used by other characters) not present in Sophocles' original, where the speech is in spoken iambic trimeter (63):

> All that is left me
> my hope was Orestes
> dust is returned me
> in my hands nothing, dust that is all of him,
> flower that went forth.
> would I had died then
> ere stealing thee from the slaughter
> died both together
> lain with our father.

At the moment of her recognition of Orestes, she offers one moving line: "heart, heart, heart, thou art come" (71).

Finally, echoing Orestes' own language, her words to her brother concerning Aegisthus seem to confirm the views of those interpreters of Sophocles who see Elektra the resistant keeper of memory as a figure brutalized and compromised at the very moment of success (88):

> DON'T
> Don't let him get a word in,
> the brute's caught, what good's a half hour?
> Kill him. Kill him.
> and let the sextons cart him out.
> get the stuff out of sight
> and let me forget it.

In Pound's play, Electra's language can both reflect the divided world in which she lives and reach out to a range of speech that no longer has a stable place in it. Her failure to solidify a stable sense of identity reflects a cultural history that in Pound's view had also begun to lack one.

Ming Xie thinks that Pound aimed in his fairly similar *Women of Trachis* at the "pseudo-colloquial" in order to create a dialect that corresponded to the "artificial" [that is, elevated] Greek of the original, to "revivify" Sophocles, and to make the hearer feel the remoteness and alienness of a Greek play.[69] Yet Pound's translation mystified many New York theater critics. In 1987 this 1951 translation seemed "idiosyncratic," "prosaic," or a "dialogue from sublime to ridiculous." Mel Gussow (*New York Times*, November 11, 1987) thought the actors, who were praised by many critics (especially Pamela Reed as Elektra), "capable of handling a more authentic adaptation."

Perloff's 1987 production realized the heroine's self-division and the cultural fragmentation of her world in performance in a particularly legible way in comparison to other American productions of Sophocles' original in translation that had similar goals. For example, the costumes, ranging from "'60s bad taste" to "'80s high fashion" were as mixed as the words, as were the actors from different ethnic and racial backgrounds and the styles of acting that they adopted. Orestes, an African American actor (Joe Morton) who wore cowboy boots and jeans, belonged to the world of melodrama; Clytemnestra (Nancy Marchand) was an elegantly dressed, alcoholic WASP, and the neurasthenic, intense Electra (Pamela Reed) wore close-fitting black with bleached, chopped-off blond hair (fig. 2).

My final example once again offers to an American Electra obsessed with the past a route to a new self that she is unable to adopt. After performances in Chicago and Tucson, Luis Alfaro's *Electricidad* received its most recent and important production at the Mark Taper Forum in Los Angeles in 2005, directed by Lisa

FIGURE 2. Elektra (Pamela Reed) in Ezra Pound's *Elektra*, directed by Carey Perloff, Classic Stage Company, New York, 1987. Photo by Paula Court, courtesy of Carey Perloff.

Peterson.[70] In the gang-infested barrios of Los Angeles, Alfaro's unwashed heroine, Electricidad (Electricity) perpetually grieves over her dead father, Agamemnón Atridas, El Auggie, the former "king" of the East Side Locos, now a corpse rotting before a makeshift shrine in the front yard of the ill-kept family bungalow (fig. 3). An "old-school" *chola* (Hispanic gangsta girl), Electricidad is steeped in near-mythic tales of gang warfare (linked with the Aztec goddess of revenge, Coatlicue):

> I want to live the old cholo ways, Papa.
> Simple and to the point.
> You mess with me, I mess with you back.
> You want to party, party in your own back yard.
> You shoot, I shoot back. (70)

This play echoed WET's question: "Whose interests are served by the institutionalized division between women in the family?" The heroine's failure to escape a tragic destiny reflected an inability to maintain female bonds in a particular patriarchal world. Her mother, the overdressed, chain-smoking Clemencia (Clytemnestra), justifies her killing of her husband by different and in some respects convincing motives. Forced to be a mother too young, beaten by her husband,

FIGURE 3. Electricidad (Zilah Mendoza) mourns over the corpse of her father, Agamemnón Atridas, in Luis Alfaro's *Electricidad,* directed by Lisa Peterson, Mark Taper Forum, Los Angeles, 2003. Photo by Craig Schwartz.

yet desperate for her children's love, she wants to create a better order in the barrio than her husband's brutal regime, and she invites her daughter to join her. "Everyone forgets what a bully he was. He made us think that we couldn't grow and change and make something better than what we are." "Imagine us working together . . . These hombres wouldn't know how to deal with the both of us. They wouldn't be able to ignore us" (75). Agamemnón himself sent Orestes away to be trained as a future leader, and, in contrast to Greek myth, Clemencia has no conflicts with her much-adored son. Without an adulterous relation to an Aegisthus figure, Clemencia's crude attempts to create a new order gain a certain feminist plausibility in a world that ignores and abuses women.

Alfaro also introduced two additional female figures who try and fail to dissuade the heroine from both her mourning and her revenge. Her paternal grandmother, Abuela, a tough, pot-smoking, sexy old woman who lost both husband and sons to gang warfare and once kept knives and joints in her beehive hairdo, feeds Electricidad and tries to lure her back from the dead to life. "It has to stop. All these guns, all these drogas, that's not who we are. Murdering our own, and for what?" (77). After Clemencia burns up Agamemnón's body, Abuela nearly succeeds in her mission. Second, Electricidad's sister Ifi, a once-tough *chola* with a record of multiple arrests, returns from "doing time" at a convent with nuns, from whom she has learned, although she does not fully understand her conversion, principles of Christian love and forgiveness: "'forgiveness is a virtue' . . . I just learned that one. I don't know what the hell it means" (73). This figure derives from Euripides, whose Iphigeneia in Tauris survives her sacrifice, becomes a priestess, and learns through love of her brother to move past revenge to a form of reconciliation.

Finally, a chorus of three neighborhood women, who express both barrio values and a sense that their world is falling apart, make a feeble attempt at cleaning up, as they whisk the neighborhood with brooms, complain about the behavior at the house of Atridas, and give Electricidad a temporary, fast makeover. "This city [Los Angeles] with no center./No heart./All border towns" (74), they remark. The characters speak a barrio Spanglish, which similarly locates them between two worlds. The heartbreaking failure of these women to win Electricidad to a new order and a new conception of power partly derives from the way that their lives have divided mothers from children, sisters from each other. The heroine's brutal sacrifice of her timid, fundamentally unpugnacious brother to her own local sense of revenge becomes even more futile than in Euripides' version, where the siblings consciously share an awakening to their mistake, because in Alfaro's version the vulnerable Orestes truly goes mad after killing his mother, and all the shocked Electricidad can do is hold his bloody body in her arms. "We never learn" (85), comments a chorus member.

Dividing or multiplying Electra reflects her increasingly archetypal status in the United States as an initially innocent female victim of a dysfunctional family in a violent and corrupt political and social world. The focus on Electra's difficulty in establishing and recognizing a self in these new versions remotivates her cultural inability to act in the Greek originals, which might be otherwise hard to make credible in a modern context, and gives point to her suffering in an American environment that eternally hopes that recognition will perform cures. Sophocles' Electra also has a public role as a self-conscious witness and preserver of cultural memory in a hostile political environment. She creates through her resistant mourning a group of initially reluctant supporters, the chorus of Argive women.[71] Productions of *Electra* have occasionally begun by establishing a repressive political environment—the 2010 production directed by Carey Perloff at the Getty Villa in Los Angeles, for example, enclosed its "palace" with prominent wire fences—but this dimension has tended to give way to a focus on familial conflicts as the play develops. The circumscribed life of these new American Electras often makes it hard for them to comprehend larger historical issues or find allies. Electra tends to remain an isolated individual in a domestic world. Ellen McLaughlin's version of Sophocles in *Iphigeneia and Other Daughters* confronts this female isolation from history but cannot restore the heroine herself to it. Her Electra embodies the history of the family; her mother has a relation to history on a larger scale.[72] American Iphigeneias, who can be emotionally engaged in a positive fashion with both parents and who are deceptively set up for a marriage to the Greek hero Achilles, do come face-to-face with history when the Trojan War demands their sacrifice at Aulis (see the epilogue). Iphigeneia too confronts a self-division over her death that has also frequently been literalized by doubling or even multiplying the heroine on the American stage. Sophocles' determined and focused Antigone, by contrast, has often been less popular on the U.S. professional stage, especially since the 1980s, than the French playwright Jean Anouilh's version of the heroine, who struggles more actively with a sense of self-definition.[73]

As later chapters will demonstrate, from a thematic perspective, Americanizing mature heroines like Medea, who bring a different sense of cultural identity with them from the first, or male leaders/heroes like Oedipus, whose full identity remains to be discovered, involves related but different questions. Analyzing how productions of the original plays in translation from the late nineteenth century through the 1930s, including *Electra*, resonate in the American context, by contrast, requires taking a more historical and aesthetic perspective on the nation's search for an artistic identity (see especially chapters 1 and 2). Finally, productions that address political issues through Greek tragedy represent an increasing, if ambivalent, interest in confronting current issues about national identity through a dialogue with a fictional "past."

ONE

# Greek Tragedy Finds an American Audience

By the end of the nineteenth century, American commercial theater was becoming increasingly entrenched in stereotypical modes of production and a limited repertoire that was largely generated in New York before moving on established circuits to other parts of the country. Although twentieth-century scholarship on early American theater has defended a number of nineteenth-century plays and playwrights, Edgar Allan Poe, commenting as early as 1845 on one of the better new American plays, Mrs. Mowatt's *Fashion*, reflected a stream of later critical opinion when he remarked:[1] "It is a good play—compared with most American drama it is a *very* good play"; in the United States "the intellect of an audience can never safely be fatigued by complexity."[2] In any case, two developments began to liberate artists interested in performing a larger range of serious poetic drama from dependence on the theater syndicates that dominated the late nineteenth-century theater world and to invite new audiences to attend Greek tragedy: the growing success of Greek tragedy on college campuses from the 1880s to the 1930s and the establishment of new venues for performance that permitted theatrical experimentation in stagecraft with strong links to Greek theater in the minds of major theorists and practitioners. Outdoor performances across the country, including those in sports stadia and in new amphitheaters often built on college campuses, here complemented the founding of small, innovative regional theaters.

Part 1 of this chapter first considers why nineteenth-century native efforts at presenting Greek tragedy on the professional stage, and especially translations of the original plays, met with an uninspiring reception. It then looks at how a growing number of university productions, along with small touring Anglo-American and American professional groups who primarily performed on college campuses and at other local venues, paved the way for remarkably successful productions in the second decade of the twentieth century. In 1915, the prominent visiting British director H. Granville Barker took advantage of this trend by staging Euripides' *Iphigeneia in Tauris* and *Trojan Women* in eastern college stadia.

Part 2 focuses on four U.S. artists/theater groups that began to put a stronger American imprint on the reception of Greek tragedy, and to win audiences for the original plays in translation that were not merely respectful yet skeptical—often the standard critical reaction—but positively enthusiastic. As leader of the American branch of the International Theosophical Society, Katherine Tingley built the earliest important outdoor amphitheater in the country in San Diego, where she staged performances of Aeschylus's *Eumenides* in 1899–1927 in order to establish a new spiritual and cultural agenda for American theater. In 1910–15 the noted actress-director-producer Margaret Anglin produced innovative Greek tragedies in the outdoor Hearst Greek Theatre in Berkeley, California, before she won a place for the Greek classics on the larger professional stage of major American cities in 1918–27. In 1912, Maurice Browne and his wife, Ellen Van Volkenburg, founded the Chicago Little Theatre, which aimed to establish the place of serious poetic drama including Greek tragedy on the U.S. stage. Their touring performance of Euripides' *Trojan Women* in 1915 was timed to coincide with Barker's and to advocate peace. Barker, Anglin, and Browne/Van Volkenburg attracted enormous audiences that have not been equaled since. These directors increasingly turned away from efforts at "historical authenticity" in the production of Greek tragedy popular on college campuses and in some early professional performances in favor of making the plays resonate with contemporary audiences. All were particularly attracted to creating "total theater" works that imaginatively united words, music, and dance. Although thematic issues were of interest to them, their most important contribution was to communicate the Greek originals through fresh modes of performance and aesthetic vision. Finally, the Provincetown Players, founded by the enthusiastic Hellenist George Cram Cook, paved the way for Eugene O'Neill's famous remakings of Greek tragedy, the 1924 *Desire under the Elms* and the 1931 *Mourning Becomes Electra*. Cook brought his passion for Greece to Provincetown and New York from the Midwest, where he had experienced the Chicago Little Theatre's early efforts at Greek tragedy. By fostering ambitious new plays by American playwrights, the Players ultimately made the creation of new, American versions of Greek tragedy inviting.

1. SETTING THE STAGE

*Nineteenth-Century Commercial Efforts*

Part 2 of this chapter explores one of the two most fertile periods for American productions of Greek tragedy in the United States. The context out of which these important early twentieth-century productions arose is critical to understanding and evaluating them. In contrast to university performances of the original plays, which developed in the United States after the 1880s, nineteenth-century professional productions of Greek tragedy that visited or derived from Europe typically adapted or transformed the originals. The earliest American professional performance known to me was a pantomime, *Medea and Jason,* performed in 1798, 1880, 1801, and 1805; the 1801 performance featured a spectacular Euripidean ascent by Medea with her children (alive or dead?) at its close. *Medea and Jason* was followed by multiple, often compelling new *Medea*s staged by both European and American artists in a number of major cities, which will be addressed in chapter 5. In 1836–77 radically new versions of Euripides' *Ion* also proliferated; at least seventeen probably represented the new British version by Thomas Noon Talfourd.[3] Talfourd's adaptation, which drew on a number of Greek tragedies, apparently appealed to U.S. audiences because of its republican sentiments, which were also central to other plays (including "heroic melodramas") on the American stage in this period.[4] In Talfourd's new version, Ion, a foundling fostered by the priest of Apollo at Argos, discovers that the plague-ridden city's oppressive king, Adrastus, is his father. Adrastus is assassinated, and Ion, following Apollo's command to establish a republic, commits suicide to assure the success of his new constitution, which transfers sovereignty from the monarchy to the Argives themselves. One enthusiastic admirer, Cornelius C. Felton, the Eliot Professor of Greek at Harvard, was oddly reminded, not of Euripides' very different original, but of an unnamed long-lost work of Sophocles.[5]

We know very little about most other early, often European-derived, commercial performances of plays related to Greek tragedy, however. An 1850 New York burlesque of Francis Talfourd's *Alcestis, or the Original Strong-Minded Woman* at Burton's Olympic Theater and Brougham's Theatre, an 1858 New York version of *Electra* at the Academy of Drama, an 1876 *Helen in Egypt* staged at Philadelphia's Chestnut Street Theatre in 1876, an 1887 version of *Electra* at the Arch Street Opera House in Philadelphia, and a production of Goethe's *Iphigenie auf Taurus* at the Academy of Music in Philadelphia in 1867 and 1869, and in New York in 1867, starring the noted Czech actress Francesca Janauschek, remain mere titles.

By contrast, Franklin H. Sargent's better-documented three native performances of Sophocles' *Electra* in March 1889 at New York's Lyceum in collaboration with the famous producer David Belasco and H. C. De Mille served as a vehicle for students from the American Academy of Dramatic Arts, the first acting school in the United States (see chapter 3). Sargent's graduating American Academy students also performed three scenes from *Oedipus Tyrannus* and odes from *Antigone* on February 21, 1893.[6] His Aeschylus's *Libation Bearers* with the American Academy students in 1908 moved George Odell to remark that "Sargent's staging of Aeschylus was the most beautiful, the most moving play I have ever attended."[7]

Sargent also helped with the 1882 Harvard *Oedipus* discussed below, and supervised student productions at Smith and Vassar. The pioneer settlement house worker Jane Addams staged Sophocles' *Electra* with Greek immigrants at Hull House in Chicago in 1892, followed by a better-documented *Ajax* in 1904, discussed in chapter 3.[8] Yet none of these pioneering American productions fall under the rubric of standard commercial performances.

Three native European-influenced attempts at performing Sophocles' *Antigone* and *Oedipus Tyrannus* on the professional stage in the nineteenth-century United States best illuminate why Greek tragedy failed for both theatrical and thematic reasons to continue attracting the support of American producers even though the plays themselves were gaining a broader readership and beginning to attract university audiences at the end of this same period. On April 7, 1845, George Vandenhoff, as producer, director, and chief actor for a performance financed by a New York investor, William E. Dinneford, attempted to copy for the opening of Palmo's Opera House on New York's Chamber Street a fairly successful London production of *Antigone* in Covent Garden in the same year.[9] The English original derived from a faithful translation by W. Bartholemew of the play done at Potsdam in 1841 with music by Mendelssohn-Bartholdy. Although George's father, John Vandenhoff, and his sister Charlotte had succeeded in making the play upstage the music in London,[10] the uneven New York production closed after a few weeks to largely bad reviews, with a consistent exception made for Mendelssohn's score. Odell pronounced the production "a colossal failure"; attendance dropped radically after the first performances.[11] Edgar Allan Poe's review among several others lambasted the small stage; the design, with its "authentic" colonnaded palace facade, three doors, and flaming altar on a raised stage; its inadequate acting; and the unrehearsed chorus of forty, who poured over challenging musical scores sporting ridiculous gray wigs, beards, and, in some cases, glasses. To the delight of the audience, one "wag" hit the center of the black and white rings on a messenger's shield with a "quid plumb" of chewing tobacco.[12] Some other reviews praised the appropriate classical-style costumes of the actors but agreed on the weakness of the acting (Vandenhoff excepted), which relied on classical poses. Worst of all in Poe's view, however, was the imperfection of *Antigone*'s plot, which could not be expected to appeal to the tastes of modern audiences.[13] The review in the *Anglo-American* (April 12, 1845, 595; see also *New World*, April 12, 1845, 233), like many reviews to come, found the themes of Greek tragedy, especially the inexorability of fate, incompatible with the contemporary ethos.

The play was promptly parodied to far greater success at the nearby Mitchell's Olympic Theatre in an "entirely original and unquestionably novel version of the celebrated Lyrical Tragedy, adapted from the Greek to the American stage . . . under the title of ANTIGONE." With the front of Palmo's Opera House as a backdrop, the ever-popular "William Shakespeare" delivered a prologue followed by a chorus of "un-employed *Artistes* of the *Italian Opera*" who made quizzical comments on an action that travestied Vandenhoff's Creon and Miss Clarendon's Antigone (the unemployed Italian artistes apparently objected to the importation of English drama into the United States);[14] a horn player deliberately upstaged his fellow musicians in the orchestra. Such parodies could enhance the popularity of a serious production but apparently did not in this case.[15]

An earlier, little-documented *Oedipus or the Riddle of the Sphinx,* a native (but probably British-inspired) production starring the former British actor Tom Hamblin as Oedipus was performed twice at New York's Bowery Theatre in October 1834 along with two farces, *The Roman Nose* and *Beulah Spa, or Two of the B'Hoys. Peabody's Parlour Journal* (November 1, 1834, 141) pronounced this "melo drama" "founded on an event of exciting interest, and though the plot (the usual case with such productions) is rather common place, the general effort is good. Mr. Hamblin presented the chief character Oedipus, for which his commanding figure well adapted him. The dress he wore on the occasion was one of the most splendid we ever beheld, and throughout he planned his part with ease, judicion, and dignity. He was well supported by Mr. Ingersoll and Mrs. Flynn—we wish we could say as much for all others concerned." This effort also failed to find favor or make money.[16] A retrospective piece in the *New York Clipper* (February 4, 1882, 758) pronounced such efforts "curiosities." The audience for the Bowery Theatre, a mix of working-class men, women, and wealthier patrons, interestingly suggests an unsuccessful attempt to popularize a classical tragedy with an audience anything but exclusively elite.[17]

Finally, the relative failure of the Broadway version of the influential and successful 1881 Harvard *Oedipus* a half century later, in January 1882, ensured the near impossibility of staging native commercial productions of Greek tragedy for many years.

Although performances on college campuses began at least as early as 1838 with an all-male *Philoctetes* at St. Louis University in St. Louis,[18] the Harvard *Oedipus,* performed indoors at the college's Sanders Theatre, was the first of many important late-nineteenth and early twentieth-century college performances in the United States. The production was lavish, and rehearsals extended for an entire college year.[19] At least six thousand spectators attended the five nights of performance, including such luminaries as Oliver Wendell Holmes, Ralph Waldo Emerson, Henry Wadsworth Longfellow, and William Dean Howells, to say nothing of college presidents and professors from all over the country, magistrates, the editors of leading journals, and most of the instructors at Harvard.[20] Ticket scalping was rampant,[21] and the production was financially lucrative.

*Oedipus* was chosen for "being typical of so many elements of Greek thought," for "the significance of its plot to a modern mind, and the adaptability of its scenic details to modern and local conditions."[22] In an approach that was later imitated in other university performances, as well as on the professional stage, the production put the chorus in an orchestra below the main stage that was connected to it by a flight of steps. The set represented a Greek palace with frieze and columns painted on canvas. The walls were gray marble, the central door imitation bronze. Small altars were set before two side doors, and larger ones in the center stage and in the orchestra.[23] The original music, by Prof. J.K. Paine, used modern harmony and was later distributed by a Boston publisher.[24] A chorus of seven tenors and eight basses from the Harvard Glee Club sang in unison (with the exception of one solo), accompanied by an orchestra of forty and a supplementary chorus of sixty.[25] Great efforts were made to create brilliant costumes "authentic" to fifth-century Athens, since "historical accuracy to the period of the mythical figures was not possible" (fig. 4).[26] The play received extensive laudatory reviews;[27] the female students of Smith College paid it the homage of a parody the following year.

Producers Daniel Frohman and F.H. Ober decided on the basis of this success to restage the play at New York's Booth's Theatre (following a preview at Boston's Globe Theatre) in the winter of 1882. George Riddle, Harvard class of '74 and an instructor in elocution from the college, reprised his role as Oedipus in ancient Greek, while the remainder of an entirely new cast performed in English. This "polyglot" performance, an experience from which one reviewer begged to be spared in the future, met with a respectful but largely unsympathetic reception. Some critics admired the elaborate production, including Riddle's Greek (if not his "pump-handle style"),[28] and approved the performance of a nevertheless far-too-youthful Georgia Cayvan as Jocasta as well as Lewis Morrison as Creon. Yet they universally criticized the translation; deplored the execrable singing; gave mixed reviews to Paine's "pretentious" music, which was in one case described as "Wagner diluted"; lampooned the chorus's Boston accents and the mix (following the Harvard model) of Grecian costume for the actors and swallowtail coats for the chorus, who were ranged in front of the footlights; questioned the production's "authenticity"; and found the play, overall, undramatic and boring. The New York *Spirit of the Times* review (April 4, 1882) was devastating: "Whatever it may have been when the Harvard College boys performed it at Sanders' Theatre, the Greek play at Booth's is no more like an ancient Greek play than Barnum's Roman races are like the circus of the ancient Romans." Many spectators left the opening performance after the first hour (*New York Times*, January 24, 1882); fairly sparse later audiences were reportedly heavy with professors, schoolboys, and women who pretended to follow the Greek (*New York Tribune*, January 31, 1882), although the *New York Mail and Express* (February 2, 1882) claimed that the play continued to attract audiences.

The play's repellent moral content and its pessimistic, decidedly un-American view of human fate were also critical to this reaction. In contrast to Britain, whose censor did not permit a commercial performance of *Oedipus* until 1910 because

FIGURE 4. George Riddle as Oedipus in Sophocles' *Oedipus Tyrannus*, directed by John Williams White, Sanders Theatre, Harvard University, 1881. From Norman 1882.

of its incest theme, U.S. critics confined their disgust at its content to paper: "In Sophocles' time, such trifling matters as a man's committing homicide, marrying his mother, and putting out his eyes afterwards was merely an indication of culture, taste and artistic appreciation of the Athenian public to which his pen was devoted."[29] Even famous visiting European versions of *Oedipus* faired less well in this period in the United States than in Europe. Neither Jean Mounet-Sully's by-then-famous French performances of Jules Lacroix's version of *Oedipus,* which visited New York's Abbey's Theatre along with *Antigone* in March 1894, nor Ermete Novelli's Italian-language production of *Oedipus* at New York's Lyric Theatre in 1907 met with much enthusiasm at the time, although in later years critics sometimes held up Mounet-Sully (who had famously inspired Freud) as a standard against which U.S. performances of Greek tragedies fell short. The *New York Times* (March 28, 1894) viewed the music for Mounet-Sully's production as "modest" and the chorus (mostly female) reminiscent of the graduation exercises at a young ladies school. Although Mounet-Sully's bloodstained appearance in the final scene won some favor, William Winter typically found that "he did not rise to the high level of the tremendous subject of 'Oedipus,' either in imagination, mind, spirit, or the capability of suffering."[30] The *New York Daily Tribune* (March 28, 1894) attributed the low attendance to the horrific content of the play.

The enthusiastic Harvard Oedipus, Professor Riddle, went on to give staged readings of Greek tragedy in the New York area,[31] directed a college *Medea* at Bryn Mawr in 1908, and later served as "director" of Margaret Anglin's far more important *Antigone* at Berkeley in 1910 (see below). Yet the New York commercial stage was apparently not yet ready for more native versions of the plays; at best, critics expressed their respect for Greek tragedy as a form that could no longer attract an engaged audience except for scholars. "*Oedipus* in Greek is a beautiful example of the accomplishments of the ancient poets, but in English it is stupid, tedious and utterly wanting in action and picturesqueness, two absolute essentials in modern playwriting" (*New York Dramatic Mirror,* February 4, 1882). Frohman's failure was not lost on his younger brother Charles, who helped found the Theatrical Syndicate, which dominated the entire country's professional stage until 1915.

In 1914, however, Rudolph Christians starred in and directed a native adaptation of *Oedipus* by Adolf Wilbrandt in German at New York's Metropolitan Opera House. The production used a chorus of three augmented by students from Columbia University and a score by Felix von Weingartner that intensified the action; the set was unusually modern. The nearly sold-out production grossed $6,000. Christians's success probably provides some clues as to the relative failure of these other early efforts. Significantly, "the outstanding merit of the performance was the clear rational tone of human action, without the deterrent emphasis of the academic spirit usually noticeable in an approach to the classic drama."[32] Almost certainly inspired by Max Reinhardt's famous and innovative 1910 *Oedipus* in

Munich (also influential in Margaret Anglin's productions), the choral role was aggrandized by extras, and the ensemble scenes were noted for their realism; Oedipus exited through the audience. The performance anticipated the visit to New York in 1923 of the Covent Garden version of Reinhardt's production, translated by Gilbert Murray and starring Sir Martin Harvey, which again met with a far more ambivalent reaction from critics in the United States than in London.[33] Christians's German-speaking audience was probably more receptive to the play than American critics and audiences more generally, who were uneasy about the play's content and repeatedly preferred their Greek tragedy on the page. Probably because of World War I, this was the last German production of Greek tragedy in New York, and German theater, like that of other ethnic groups in the United States, did not necessarily inspire mainstream performances.[34] Nevertheless, one critic thought that the Irving Place Theater Company, which performed Christians's *Oedipus*, was superior to its contemporaries because of its intelligent, intensive, and exacting rehearsal process.[35] From this perspective, the fresh, nonantiquarian spirit of Christians's *Oedipus* served as a harbinger of later successes by the central artists discussed in part 2 of this chapter.

*The Catalytic Role of University Traditions*

Despite the failure of the Harvard *Oedipus* to secure a place for Greek tragedy on Broadway, much of the impulse for performing Greek originals in the post–Civil War United States stemmed from colleges and universities, especially from their classics and speech (precursors to later theater) departments. The curriculum in most private colleges up to this time had emphasized theology, mathematics, and classics as training for future ministers and statesmen. The need to generate interest in Greek after colleges began to drop Greek admissions requirements in the 1880s,[36] and to expand elective curricula and organized sports in order to prepare students for work in a competitive industrial society,[37] was an important motivation for on-campus productions of Greek plays. The renaissance in college productions of Greek drama begun at Harvard almost certainly enabled the first successful professional performances of Greek tragedy, such as Margaret Anglin's *Antigone* at Berkeley in 1910, which played at least in part to an audience already primed by student productions such as *Oedipus Tyrannus* in the same year,[38] and set the stage for numerous and important early crossings between professional and academic worlds.

U.S. productions of Greek tragedy in schools and colleges began to proliferate at almost the same time as they became popular in England.[39] Aeschylus's *Agamemnon* at Oxford in 1880, Sophocles' *Ajax* at Cambridge in 1882, and the Bradfield College school plays closely coincided with the Harvard *Oedipus* of 1881. Although Harvard's production was inspired by Oxford's, the college's Professor Goodwin had already hoped to do a Harvard *Antigone* in 1876.[40] One reviewer, who had also seen the Oxford *Agamemnon,* found the Harvard play far more lavishly produced, archaeologically self-conscious, and "studied."[41] Within ten years, plays (one-third in Greek) were performed at widely different locations, including Notre Dame, Beloit, University of Pennsylvania, Smith, Grinnell, and Swarthmore; the University of Nebraska did *Antigone* in 1892, and the University of the South at Sewanee *Alcestis* in 1893; Albion and Olivet colleges followed with plays in 1895.[42] The number of productions went up 350 percent over the next ten years,[43] and in 1926–36 the number of productions was greater than ever before and took place in more schools. August Pluggé, writing in his dissertation at Columbia's Teachers College in 1938, counted 349 performances in 143 institutions in forty-one states between 1881 and 1936;[44] even more productions have been identified since his account. Among the colleges with productions, Beloit, Bates, Randolph-Macon Woman's College, and UCLA gave the largest number of performances, and women's colleges were unusually well represented.[45] After the turn of the century, speech departments began to produce Greek plays and overtook Greek departments in the period 1926–36, when the former staged 128 plays in contrast to the latter's 62.[46] The use of Greek gradually decreased.[47] Although *Antigone, Iphigeneia in Tauris,* and *Alcestis* remained the most frequently presented, followed in the 1920s by *Trojan Women,* a larger range of plays began to be performed; after 1904 more productions were done outdoors.[48] Moreover, as chapter 3.1 will show, nineteenth-century interpretations of *Antigone* generally found the play, despite Poe, compatible with American ideals; the plots of *Iphigeneia in Tauris* (a favorite in schools) and *Alcestis* offered a release from fatality that may have assured their popularity.

Despite the more adventurous views of some major European classical scholars like U. von Wilamowitz-Moellendorff and Gilbert Murray, who did not support historical fidelity in modern performances,[49] the early college productions of Greek tragedy tended to aim at what was (often mistakenly) viewed as archaeological correctness, with stereotyped illusionistic scenery and costumes that imitated (unlike productions in classical Greece) clothing from fifth-century Athens;[50] only in the late 1920s and 1930s did some college productions begin to be influenced by modern stage techniques (see below) that proved successful in professional productions.[51]

Universities nevertheless shared a number of conditions and goals with independent theater producers in the early twentieth century, since both groups often relied on minimal financing and technical support and aimed to enrich the cultural environment of their audiences.[52] Other early college productions besides the reworked Harvard *Oedipus* kept the bridge between the college and professional worlds open by being staged in commercial theaters; moreover, since major newspapers often reviewed them, university productions continued to register in the public world. For example, an ambitious Vassar production of *Antigone* was put on at the Opera House in Poughkeepsie in 1893,[53] and in 1903 the University of Pennsylvania performed an elaborate all-male *Iphigeneia among the Taurians* for two performances at the Philadelphia Academy of Music.⁵⁴ Both campuses apparently lacked an adequate indoor performance space at the time and reached out to the larger community for support. The all-male Penn performance used professional costumers and scene designers with music composed by Professor H. A. Clarke; the Orpheus Club of Philadelphia assisted the chorus. As at Harvard, the audience included eminent members of the university administration, enthusiastic members of the local Greek community, and classics professors from other universities, including the eminent Basil Gildersleeve of Johns Hopkins.⁵⁵ H. T. Parker of the *Boston Evening Transcript* (May 2, 1903) remarked on Euripides' (and this play's) relative modernity among Greek tragic writers and praised the performance (Iphigeneia excepted) as appealing to its "picked" audience.

### The Role of Outdoor Performances

A growing fashion for a range of outdoor performance in the late nineteenth and early twentieth century led to the construction in the United States of amphitheaters, often loosely based on Greek and Roman models, that started in 1901 but proliferated in the 1920s and 1930s.⁵⁶ Outdoor performance also created new bridges between universities, where many amphitheaters were built, and professional theater groups that toured to communities off the regular theatrical circuit. Women's groups and private individuals on the East Coast, and private clubs such as the San Francisco Bohemian Club, also sponsored outdoor performances of Greek tragedy, in the first case on the lawns of private homes and in small theaters on estates. New amphitheaters modeled closely on Greek or Greco-Roman theaters, such as that at Bradfield College in England, rather than the restoration of older Mediterranean ones for performances (as in France),⁵⁷ were rarer in Europe.⁵⁸

In the view of Sheldon Cheney, an important critic and the founding editor of *Theatre Arts Magazine*, outdoor performances ideally served to democratize theater audiences and build community spirit through productions aimed at large groups;⁵⁹ professional theater was in private hands and driven by commercial goals, whereas outdoor theater had the potential to reach out to and create a larger audience.⁶⁰ "The drama of the indoor stage is unavoidably the art of the few—although designed, perhaps, to stir the many emotionally—whereas outdoor drama is distinctly social, communal and national. In one particular of community participance, the indoor theatre fails to meet the outdoor theatre—and the inspirational possibilities of the latter are infinite.... One may see therein the possibilities of making the drama a significant force in the life of every citizen who retains the primal religious and dramatic instincts."⁶¹ Similarly, Frank Waugh argued for a "direct relation to the redeeming of the country and industrial districts through constructive leisure" and "the founding of outdoor theatre [especially performances of Greek tragedy] for the people."⁶² Since Greek tragedy was originally developed for outdoor performance, those interested in reproducing "authentic" or archaeologically correct productions naturally gravitated outdoors, despite serious acoustical problems in some cases. For example, although Sarah Bernhardt's performance of Racine's *Phèdre* in 1906 and 1911 at the Berkeley Greek Theatre profited from its excellent acoustics, the fact that the great French diva was barely heard beyond the front rows in other outdoor venues on her cross-country tour does not seem to have dampened her audience's enthusiasm.[63] Finally, as another contemporary critic enthusiastically put it, "Tragedy out of doors is helped tremendously by the elements: all nature conjoins to give it a weird, eerie atmosphere."[64]

In California, the exquisite Greek theater built at Point Loma in 1901 under the aegis of the International Theosophical Society (founded in New York by Madame Helena Blavatsky in 1875) anticipated the building of the ambitious Hearst Greek Theatre at Berkeley by two years (fig. 5). It served as the site for a number of Greek revival productions, such as Katherine Tingley's simple-stage production of *Eumenides* (to be discussed below).[65] Professors and students were the first to produce plays at Berkeley, with an opening three-day festival that included a performance of Aristophanes' *Birds* in 1903. Over the next ten years, before Anglin's productions at the Hearst Theatre (to be discussed shortly), Sophocles' *Ajax* (1904), Aeschylus's *Eumenides* (1907), and Aristophanes' *Birds* were performed in Greek, and *Oedipus Rex* (1910) in English.[66] Other colleges, initially on the East Coast, successfully used sports stadia to stage outdoor performances. Harvard's 1906 Aeschylus's *Agamemnon*, for example, twice attracted an audience of around five thousand to the university stadium before the more famous productions of Barker (discussed below).[67] Outside of California, however, the weather often proved problematic for the development of outdoor performances.

*Democratizing Greek Tragedy Outdoors through Touring Groups*

Several professional groups, which often included British or European actors, paved the way for Anglin's and Barker's successful efforts in university settings by collaborating with colleges and universities to present Greek tragedy outdoors, although some of these groups offered a limited number of performances in professional theaters as well. The success of the Ben Greet Players, headed by an Englishman, Philip Ben Greet, anticipated other groups that staged productions of theatrical classics, especially Shakespeare, at colleges, clubs, and private homes on the East Coast in 1902–18, sometimes in multiple companies.[68] Greet shared with many early producers and enthusiasts of outdoor theater an opposition to commercial theater monopolies and drama lacking serious thematic concerns, as well as a taste for minimalist stage decor, aesthetic purity, and lack of artificiality. He directed Shakespeare's *Twelfth Night* for the opening of the Hearst Greek Theatre in 1903 but did not include Greek drama in his touring repertory.

FIGURE 5. Point Loma Greek Theater, San Diego, California, built by Katherine Tingley. Photo courtesy of the Theosophical Society Archive, Pasadena, California.

A rival American theatrical group, Charles Douville Coburn's Coburn Players, brought outdoor productions of Shakespeare and several Greek tragedies, especially during the summers of 1911–17, to colleges, schools, and clubs particularly in the Midwest and South. Many of the venues on these tours had yet to build indoor theaters, and the Coburn Players apparently had a direct influence on the development of midwestern amphitheaters.[69] The productions generally played before small audiences without music or scenery, with little stage action, and uneven acting.[70] In New York City itself, the Coburn Players got a relatively positive reception for Gilbert Murray's translation of Euripides' *Electra* (accompanied in the first case by Blanche Shoemaker Wagstaff's version of *Alcestis*) in the winter of 1910, which followed an outdoor version in the summer of 1910 at Columbia University under the auspices (as was also typical elsewhere) of the English Department; Isadora Duncan's brother Augustin directed. *Theatre Magazine*'s review approved the venture more for its value as "an educational cult" than as a gripping theatrical venture, although the actors received some sympathetic reviews for their diction, naturalness, and freedom from "theatrical claptrap." The Coburns' stunning Hudson Theatre set, with its four enormous ivy-clad Ionic columns, almost dwarfed the production of a company more accustomed to simple outdoor venues as the Players' attempted to reproduce the newly fashionable sculptural or "plastic" stage set thought to be appropriate for Greek drama (see below).[71] Both *Electra* and, after 1913, *Iphigeneia in Tauris* (*IT*) became a stable part of the Coburns' touring repertoire. A review (*New York Dramatic Mirror*, August 6, 1913) of Murray's translation of *IT* before a large audience at Columbia University in 1913 appraised the play as an "ancient thriller" and noted the splendid diction and "poesy" of the production.[72] Other Coburn actors formed spin-off groups whose productions also aimed to introduce new theatrical techniques to the provinces. Thomas Mitchell and Frank Peters's Art Drama Players mounted a *Medea* on August 2, 1915, and John Kellerd went on from his role as messenger in the 1910 *Electra* to play Oedipus for four New York performances in August 1911 and with a different cast in February 1913.[73]

### Harley Granville Barker's Tour of Eastern College Stadia

England's noted actor/director Harley Granville Barker, however, outshone all the native East Coast efforts discussed so far (but not those in part 2) with a single touring production of Euripides' *IT* and *Trojan Women* in 1915 that was staged for enormous audiences in the often newly built stadia at Yale, Harvard, University of Pennsylvania, City College in New York, and Princeton. (An additional performance at the Piping Rock Country Club on Long Island had a smaller audience.) An estimated 60,000–100,000 people saw the plays.[74] H. H. Asquith, the British prime minister, encouraged Barker's American winter season sponsored by the Stage Society of New York at Wallack's Theatre as part of the war effort. Barker and his wife, the noted actress Lillah McCarthy, who had played Jocasta in the celebrated 1912 production of Max Reinhardt's *Oedipus Rex* at London's Covent Garden, and Iphigeneia in Barker's London *IT* the same year, organized the subsequent campus tour partly to promote interest in Greek tragedy and partly to experiment with choral performance, which had up to this point frustrated Barker. He wanted to create tragedy on a scale unavailable to him before, with monumental performances in the large outdoor spaces for which the plays were originally designed.[75]

In May 1915 Barker performed his close friend Gilbert Murray's translation of *IT* before 15,000 people at the Yale Bowl in New Haven; indeed it was a visit to the Bowl that initially inspired the tour.[76] A committee of professors and administrators had been established to coordinate the tour, with Harvard's George Pierce Baker, noted for his important playwriting workshops, as chair.[77] Yale's Professor David Stanley Smith wrote music played by an orchestra of fifteen to support ambitious choreography; the Yale Classics Department's Thomas D. Goodell was called on to praise the translation; and the university went to great lengths to attract and prepare an audience thought to be unfamiliar with staged Greek tragedy, using press releases, pictures of the beautiful McCarthy, and comparisons between Greek drama and football. (In fact a track meet took place directly outside the stadium during the performance; at Harvard a baseball game interrupted the play.)[78] As noted earlier, *IT* was one of the most performed Greek tragedies on college campuses in the early twentieth century and may have been more familiar to its audience than *Trojan Women,* which was produced with it on the rest of the tour specifically to make an antiwar statement.[79] *Trojan Women* was first established as the quintessentially antiwar Greek tragedy on both sides of the Atlantic around this period. For once the choice of plays received critical praise: "There are passages in Euripides that are utterly modern in spirit, discussions of war and feminism that might have been written today."[80]

For *IT,* the stage was marked out in the center of the Yale stadium, facing one end, with a 100-foot circular ground cloth laid out before an austere monumental set of wood and canvas 100 feet wide and 40 feet high; later used for both plays, this set had a narrow wooden *skene* (stage) reached by five steps and three sets of doors; the central door was gold with black markings. The acoustics at Yale were perfect, and the play was timed to close at sundown as a gold and crimson statue of Athena rose spectacularly above the temple wall (her lines were intoned through a megaphone from the central door below). Barker aimed not at historical authenticity (though many aspects of the production did draw on Greek sources), but at an innovative nonnaturalistic theatrical effectiveness that appealed to many, if not all, critics. His attempt to treat Euripides in many respects as a playwright of the modern theater coincided with those of Margaret Anglin and Maurice Browne.

The cast mixed British and American actors. Reviews praised Murray's translation and the recognition scene, questioned the production's inconsistent tone, and noted stately formal performances by McCarthy as Iphigeneia and Ian Maclaren as Orestes; Claude Rains as the herdsman "bounced a good deal, but the real fire was there," while the barbarian king Thoas "rumbled thunderously" (*New York Times,* May 16, 1915). A chorus of twenty dressed in black and orange and led by the American Alma Kruger took advantage of the geometrical designs on the drop cloth to establish their positions and employ circular rotations, and "sang to the accompaniment of simple melodic music of very ancient flavor"; "their movements were rhythmical and intelligently ordered" (S. W., *Nation* 100, June 3, 1915, 634). The Yale program describes the music as "mostly melody, slow and chant-like, through which the lines may be declaimed with greater emotional intensity and effect than would be possible if they were merely spoken. The melodies are based on ancient Greek scales that were later adopted by the Christian Church and called Gregorian modes. For support of the voices an orchestra of violins and instruments is used."[81] For some critics, however, the musical accompaniment was viewed as thin, the choral chants meager, and the choruses insufficiently visually arresting.

The British designer Norman Wilkinson's "wildly decorative" and colorful costumes, especially those for the barbarian characters, disconcerted many, however.[82] Soldiers wore "union suits of black and white adorned with whisk-brooms of the hue of tomato bisque. There is no describing Thoas himself with his ornithological scepter [ten feet tall], his checkered robe, and his scarlet beard," which provoked laughter from the audience (*New York Times*, May 16, 1915). Iphigeneia's dishabille was considered by the same critic inappropriate for her virginal character (in fact her costume imitated statues of maidens on the Acropolis).

Barker's *Trojan Women*, despite its timely topic, fared somewhat less well as a production. The double bill met with worse acoustics and mixed weather at the other stadia, especially at City College, where the two plays served to inaugurate the Lewisohn Stadium for an audience of five thousand on May 29, 1915, that included students from city high schools who were required to attend. Francis Hackett (*New Republic*, June 5, 1915, 127) lamented the behavior of the professors, "who spent much of their time ruminating mournfully on the piled up spectators behind them, as if feebly contemplating an escape." The play itself was praised not only for its treatment of war, but for its theatrical modernism, its choral movement, and its creation of powerful female roles. The *New York Times* (May 30, 1915) found Chrystal Herne as Cassandra and Edith Wynne Matthison (see chapter 2.1) as Andromache moving but criticized McCarthy, despite "a certain heroic quality," for her "inflexibility, the formalism, and the intense artificiality of her delivery"; the *Nation* (June 3, 1915, 634) found her unheroic and lacking in the grand manner. McCarthy's elaborate, richly colored costume, including a tiara, certainly emphasized her youth and queenly status, not her humiliating woes. The *Nation* (633) also criticized the opening scene, where invisible voices spoke for wooden statues of Poseidon and Athena, but the symbolic final scene, with flaming braziers issuing dark smoke to indicate the fall of Troy and the chorus huddled in misery before them, impressed many. The inspiring program note by Gilbert Murray described the play's conclusion in optimistic terms that have not always met with agreement among classicists and may not have reflected the ending of the performance itself: "No friend among the dead, no help in God, no illusion anywhere, Hecuba faces That Which Is and finds somewhere, in the very intensity of Troy's affliction, a splendor that cannot die. She has reached in some sense not the bottom but the crowning peak of her fortunes.... But they [the Trojan women] have seen in their nakedness that there is something in life which neither slavery nor death can touch."

## 2. AMERICAN THEATER MAKES GREEK TRAGEDY ITS OWN

### Katherine Tingley

Barker's productions, despite their Anglo-American cast, represented a European effort to initiate new theatrical approaches to Greek tragedy in outdoor American settings. Part 2 deals with important native efforts in a similar vein. The

International Theosophical Society's outdoor Greek theater at Point Loma, California, served as the site for a number of Greek revival productions that included Aeschylus's *Eumenides* and philosophical "symposia" along with performances of Shakespeare. While less well known to the theater world than those of Barker, Anglin, and Browne, Katharine Tingley's more amateur productions anticipated all three in appropriating avant-garde European theatrical approaches to Greek tragedy. (The theosophical movement had in fact influenced the development of avant-garde theater in Europe.)[83] In addition, she alone represented the views of an innovative religious and educational movement that developed its own American identity.[84] Her *Eumenides,* staged earlier in New York City at the Carnegie Lyceum and at the Music Hall in Buffalo, New York in 1898, was performed twice outdoors at Point Loma in 1899, with a cast of two hundred, and possibly several times before 1922 (with revivals in 1925 and 1927),[85] including at San Diego's Fisher Opera House in 1901.[86] The choice of *Eumenides* was clearly linked to the Theosophical Society's interest in the "revival of the lost mysteries of antiquity."

Tingley served as leader of the Universal Brotherhood and Theosophical Society from 1896 to 1929; at Point Loma she established the School for the Revival of the Lost Mysteries of Antiquity in 1897 and in 1901 dedicated an outdoor theater seating 500 people in which performances offering insight into these mysteries were to be presented. In 1901 she also purchased the Fisher Opera House in San Diego (renamed the Isis Theatre), which had a seating capacity of 1,400. Tingley's organization pursued humanitarian causes (including war relief and provision of housing for starving women) with the idea that such pursuits could move neophytes toward a recognition of a divine connection (based on the immortality of the soul) that unites all human beings. Drama and the arts, including studying and performing Greek tragedy and Shakespeare, played a central role in the education of children at the Raja-Yoga School in Point Loma, which aimed to develop the body, mind, and soul together, build character, and promote self-control.[87]

The Theosophical Society was founded in the United States in 1875 by Helena P. Blavatsky, W. Q. Judge, and Henry S. Olcott in order to discover universal esoteric truths from the religious and occult traditions of many world cultures.[88] Tingley, who succeeded Judge in an increasingly splintered movement and moved the Society to California, emphasized the goal of "Universal Brotherhood" in order to eradicate "the evils caused by barriers of race, creed, caste, or color, which have so long impeded human progress."[89] She was also conscious of the difficulties posed by her forceful female leadership of the movement; one 1901 production at the Isis Theatre, *The Wisdom of Hypatia,* which explored the teachings of the fourth-century C.E. philosopher and mathematician murdered by Christians, apparently hinted broadly at a similar experience of persecution for Tingley's untraditional sect, and its leader's strong female influence over men and children.[90] During Tingley's ultimately successful suit against the *Los Angeles Times* for slander, the paper's defense attorney, Mr. Shortridge, took the lead in making the full range of such accusations.[91] Not surprisingly, wise women of antiquity such as Diotima in Plato's *Symposium* and Pericles' inspiring concubine Aspasia, in addition to Athena in *Eumenides,* played a role in the school's symposiastic performances. Tingley took the role of Aspasia in the 1923 production of her *Aroma of Athens;*[92] she also made a point of lecturing to all female groups.

As the program to the December 3, 1898, performance of *Eumenides* at the Music Hall in Buffalo put it,[93] Tingley's Isis League of Music and Drama (founded by herself) aimed to "accentuate the influence of Music and the Drama as vital educative factors" and "to educate the people to a knowledge of the true philosophy of life by means of dramatic presentations of a high standard." Tingley, who viewed most contemporary theater as mercenary trash, later argued: "True drama points away from the unrealities to the real life of the soul. As such, true drama should lead and guide the public taste, providing it with ideals towards which it can aspire.... The facilities at Point Loma for dramatic work are unsurpassed anywhere in the world. We are within sight of the day which will once more restore the drama to its rightful position as one of the great redemptive forces of the age."[94]

The 1898 Buffalo program presented *Eumenides* as follows:

THE REVIVAL OF ANCIENT DRAMA
AS AN EDUCATIVE FACTOR IN MODERN LIFE...

It is known that among the people of ancient Greece a higher general culture existed than has since been reached in Europe.... [Greek] drama reflected, less than does ours, the common life of the people; but it dealt much more than ours with great philosophical and mystical tenets, and with esoteric teachings concerning the origin and destiny of man that appear to have been at that time matters of deep interest and discussion.... They were presented in the form of magnificent tragedies and spectacular performances wherein persons and events, half historical, half mythical, served in part to embody and illustrate the profound philosophy that the Grecian dramatists often desired to convey.... What is of value, whatever is noble and elevating in the drama that flowered in the civilization and thought of earlier nations, should still be accessible, and should be more and more so as the general consciousness and dramatic taste of to-day rises to the level of the past.... The first of these works selected for this purpose is the "Eumenides," the famous drama of Aeschylus.

Mme Blavatsky's *Secret Doctrine* served as inspiration for Tingley's interpretation of *Eumenides,* and the art and writing of Richard Wagner (viewed by Tingley as part of a mystical tradition) defined her aims for the ambitious production.[95] The initial New York and Buffalo productions used the 1873 translation by Anna Swanwick;[96] the choice of translation may be another sign of Tingley's preference for female authors and thinkers who shared her active social goals.[97] Tingley directed her student actors accompanied by music (provided in Buffalo by an organ) composed by Wenzel A. Reboch that had an "archaic ring";[98] he included

FIGURE 6. Athena, Apollo, and Orestes with the chorus of Furies in Aeschylus's *Eumenides,* directed by Katherine Tingley, Point Loma Greek Theater, 1922. Photo courtesy of the Theosophical Society Archive, Pasadena, California.

the recently discovered "Hymn to Apollo" found at Delphi in 1893 by the French Archaeological School.[99] Professor H. Fletcher Rivers provided "intricate choric figure dancing."[100]

At Point Loma, where the first performance was given outdoors April 13, 1899, during the Congress of the Historical Society, the Theosophical Society's Woman's Exchange and Mart created elaborate Athenian-style costumes with embroidered borders, an orchestra played the music, and the group's Aryan Press did advertising and programs.[101] For Tingley, Aeschylus's Furies represented the human capacity to transcend spiritual limitations and a "lower passional nature" through free will after being touched "by the vibration of higher thought" in the person of Athena, who arrived in a chariot, decked with a brilliant helmet and breastwork.[102] The Furies' conversion would ideally lead the audience to adjure the violence of war, materialism, and cruelty in favor of peace.[103] (Tingley was an active, if moderate, member of the peace movement before and during World War I.)[104] The 1922 production of *Eumenides* at Point Loma dramatically captured the play's move from darkness to light when the Furies threw off their black, hooded gowns to reveal lovely, garlanded maidens in white holding chains of flowers (figs. 6 and 7).[105] These "fair maidens" represented "truth and virtue moving to the rhythm of

FIGURE 7. The Furies without their black robes after being persuaded by Athena in Aeschylus's *Eumenides,* directed by Katherine Tingley, Point Loma Greek Theater, 1922. Photo courtesy of the Theosophical Society Archive, Pasadena, California.

sweet melody in silence . . . a wonderful factor . . . in nature."[106] The play's closing procession, which seems to have included many costumed members of the school, was enormous. According to one reporter, Ray Stannard Baker, local newspaper reporters spied on the performances of *Eumenides* in the Greek theater from afar and interpreted the play as (presumably dangerous) secret, occult rituals.[107]

Tingley's other major Greek-inspired production, *The Aroma of Athens: Athenian Flower Festival,* a symposium envisioned as responding to the Attic Anthesteria and first presented in 1911, included elaborate Athenian-inspired costumes, the "Ode to Colonus" from Sophocles' *Oedipus at Colonus,* excerpts from epic and archaic poets as well as Aeschylus, hymns to Apollo, pseudo-Platonic dialogues on truth, goodness, and beauty and discourses on the glories of Periclean Athens by Pericles, Aspasia, Phidias, Euripides, Thucydides, and others; songs such as the Greek Swallow Song, children's games, and a closing torch-lit procession with music by votaries in brilliant red.[108] In *The Promise,* a philosophical dialogue written by a student at Point Loma for the school's series of symposia, Aeschylus (a putative mystery initiate himself) even advocated reincarnation of souls.[109] In the same dialogue a priestess of Apollo predicted that the ancient mysteries, which had disappeared for centuries, would reappear during a new golden age at

Lomaland.¹¹⁰ Although reviews of Tingley's productions were generally respectful of the plays' production values and more reserved about the amateur acting,¹¹¹ her efforts caught the attention of Walter Damrosch, a New York composer and conductor who worked with both Isadora Duncan and Margaret Anglin and visited Point Loma in 1916, and partly inspired the work of Henry Bertram Lister in San Francisco during the 1920s and 1930s, whose plays (see chapter 3.2 and chapter 4.3) also showed a joint interest in Shakespeare and Greek tragedy.

*Margaret Anglin*

Despite other significant early performances, the inspiration and passionate dedication of one specific actress, Margaret Anglin, ignited the greatest interest in Greek tragedy on the American stage during the first quarter of the twentieth century and defined standards of performance for the production of the original plays in her era. Anglin, whose Irish father was speaker of the Canadian House of Commons at her birth, left Catholic school in Toronto at age seventeen for a course in dramatic elocution at Nelson Wheatcroft's Empire Theatre Dramatic School in New York City. Her Scottish Catholic mother supported her aspirations, which continued to be opposed by her father. Within a year Anglin was launched on an increasingly successful professional career in the United States. She was not only repeatedly celebrated for her intensity and power as an emotional actress and for her outstanding voice and graceful stage movement, but recognized as a cultured and articulate woman who intensively researched her productions, wrote articles in newspapers and magazines about her aspirations, and became a popular authority on interpreting Greek tragedy; she even received a degree from Notre Dame in 1927 honoring her classical scholarship.¹¹² Anglin served as adapter and rewriter of her own scripts, as producer, as both de facto and formal director of her plays, and on one occasion she revised the music for a performance of *Hippolytus*.¹¹³ She supervised the integration of music into her productions, approved the set design, lighting, and costumes, and oversaw both the casting and training of actors and the work of electricians, painters, and stage crew. Like Barker, she became an avid promoter of new, initially European approaches to stagecraft inspired by Gordon Craig, Max Reinhardt, and Adolphe Appia.¹¹⁴ Her talents at publicity were also exceptional. Synopses and even whole tragic texts appeared beforehand in local newspapers; she encouraged journalistic feature articles on Greek tragedy and her own preparations for her plays; she lured major papers into printing photos and sketches; she promoted talks by prominent lecturers to schools, colleges, theaters, and women's clubs and other social organizations.¹¹⁵

Unlike many other actresses of her generation, Anglin was a serious student of every role and play that she undertook. She began to study *Antigone* intensively with the encouragement of her agent, Alice Kauser, in 1909, a year before her first performance of the play in the Hearst Greek Theatre at Berkeley.¹¹⁶ For this performance she also acquired Professor George Riddle of Harvard as her academic adviser/nominal director; no doubt his 1882 New York performance as Oedipus in ancient Greek drew him to her attention. She spent three years studying Sophocles' *Electra* for a second Berkeley performance in 1913, and she later learned ancient Greek and offered dramatic and other readings in the original.[117] As her career in performing Greek tragedy developed, she toured Europe, attending Max Reinhardt's famous 1910 *Oedipus* in Munich and visiting relevant museum collections and the sites where the plays that she performed were located, as well as the Greek theater at Epidaurus,[118] where she recited the big speeches of Medea and Electra in the original for her husband, Howard Hull.[119] Following forty-five performances (thirty-six as Sophocles' Electra) viewed by over 200,000 people in Berkeley, New York, St. Louis, Philadelphia, Ann Arbor, and Providence,[120] she retained an interest in Greek tragedy throughout her life and was often characterized as America's foremost tragic actress.[121] Anglin's extraordinarily ambitious triple bill of performances of *Iphigeneia in Aulis, Electra,* and *Medea* over a three-week period in 1915 at the Greek Theatre even produced a published collection of sonnets by a poet named Charles Phillips among others.[122]

Like most serious actresses of her day, Anglin had ambitions to become a noted interpreter of Shakespeare. What set her apart was her equally intense interest in the major female roles of Greek tragedy. She aimed with her Berkeley productions to restore prestige to American theater;[123] the Greek tragic roles fulfilled her "desire to gain breadth and depth of expression," and led her to remark: "The mountain peaks are at last in sight."[124] As early as 1904 she expressed interest in performing *Lysistrata* while playing the lead in a contemporary play that she saw as "somewhat based on" Aristophanes, Robert Misch's *Eternal Feminine;* a letter from an enthusiastic critic then urged her to try Electra.[125]

Anglin used the proceeds from her many successful countrywide tours with contemporary melodramas and comedies to finance her move to acting the classics. She had developed a particularly close connection to San Francisco from an early date; San Francisco critics appropriated her as their own, and even claimed to have discovered her true brilliance before the rest of the country; her California summer season in 1903 was the first in which she was fully featured as a star.[126] Her positive reception in the city, along with a letter from her business manager expressing her interest, led to her first invitation from the Music and Dramatic Committee headed by Professor William Dallam Armes of the English Department to perform a Greek tragedy at the Hearst Greek Theatre at Berkeley. The space itself, which Anglin pronounced "the most beautiful theatre in the world," partly provoked her interest.[127] Indeed, Anglin later had a model of the theater built replete with accessories that she could move about to envision a production.[128] The size and scope of the outdoor audience at Berkeley was certainly another enticement; nearly 8,000 had attended a student production of Sophocles' *Oedipus* in 1910.[129]

All but one of Anglin's productions at Berkeley had audiences ranging from 7,000 to 10,000 attendees with increasing numbers being turned away as time went on. Anglin had the voice and presence to reach a large audience, and she was not shy about attempting to do so. (The New York Metropolitan Opera House, the site of Anglin's 1927 triumph, was about the only indoor space that could accommodate very large audiences at the time.)[130] She remarked:

> I take great personal joy in the Greek Theater at Berkeley. It represents to me an unusual experience, for it was in that amphitheater that I came under the spell of an audience vaster than any theater can hold. The swaying movement of the chorus as it partly chants and partly speaks the interpretative lines, the dominant magnitude of love or hate or jealousy or revenge of the principal characters, and all the presence of that vast audience, all act like magic on me. One realizes why Greek drama is potent, why it is of undying quality, why it is actable before modern audiences. No actress could find parts more dramatic, more inspiring and more demanding of the best that is in her.[131]

Anglin's efforts to achieve brilliant performances knew no bounds. In a fashion that was to become standard for her, she began rehearsals for *Antigone* during a cross-country tour of *The Awakening of Helena Richie*. George Riddle joined her in Denver, and her rehearsals in California took place between midnight and 3:00 a.m., after her evening performances.[132] She cast Riddle's student Howard Hull, whom she married soon thereafter, as Haemon. Although night performances in outdoor theaters were viewed as controversial at the time, Anglin insisted on holding hers then, and the lighting using gas calciums was viewed as especially effective.[133] "Night is the most poetic and beautiful parcel of hours. I shall present beautiful plays in the most beautiful way I can, and night and the stars will come to my aid."[134] Antigone's exit to death, described as the "Ode to the Tomb," was singled out as the high point of the production by one of a number of critics who traveled considerable distances specifically to see it. Riddle commended Anglin's mastery of the grand manner of tragedy such as no other actress on the American stage could have done.[135] When silence fell at the conclusion, Clayton Hamilton reported in *Vogue* that a friend standing in the wings heard Miss Anglin say to herself: "I've failed,—My God, I've failed!" "Then," Hamilton continued, "after an appreciable pause, there came a noise like the rushing of a tide at Mont Saint Michel. . . . Then, suddenly the stage itself was assaulted by hundreds and hundreds of clamorous spectators. They swarmed Miss Anglin and strove to touch her fingertips."[136] The remarkable and unexpected success of this production (the first native U.S. professional production of Greek tragedy in translation to win such acclaim) was celebrated in reviews throughout the country, but above all by the *New York Times*, which helped to promote Anglin's effort to make this a major theatrical event.[137]

The staging of *Antigone* was more marked by the current fashion for historical "authenticity" than Anglin's later productions. She narrowed the stage from 133 to 80 feet by planting thirty cypresses around a large oak door (partly to hide her orchestra); the set consisted of an altar, some benches, and three steps down from the central door. Costumes (minus the traditional masks) were colorful, and preclassical in style, with bold, geometric borders.[138] The music was sung by a chorus of forty-five male voices accompanied by an orchestra of seventy-five. Riddle recommended for *Antigone* the 1841 appropriately "classical" musical setting of Felix Mendelssohn-Bartholdy (conducted by Professor Fred Weile of the Berkeley Music Department); he modified the blank-verse translation of Edward Hayes Plumptre, which appeared in the Harvard Classics, through forays into Richard Jebb's translation and commentary. Movement included attitudes that one critic described as "like the women of St. Gaudens come to life."[139] Anglin had lined up the chorus against the back wall of the stage to create the effect of a Greek bas-relief.[140]

After *Antigone*, Anglin seems to have developed a greater reserve about academic influences on her productions, even though she continued to read intensively about all aspects of Greek culture, consult many translations, and solicit the views of classicists such as Benjamin Wheeler and Charles Gayley at Berkeley and a Professor Andreades of the University of Athens; prominent translators such as Edith Hamilton and William Alfred also sought her advice and shared their translations with her.[141] As she put it,

> In rehearsing Greek tragedy I have made this relentless rule: that neither I nor my company shall pass a line without understanding its full significance, in so far as study and research can aid us.... The Greeks held inviolable certain religious, civic, and social rites, and these rites are held inviolable in the dramas. Only by understanding what these rites are will we be able to understand the motives to certain actions.
>
> In presenting Greek tragedy I do not pretend to justify every action to accord with scholarship. But I do seek to reach the essential spirit of the whole.... I suppose the modern scholar might claim I have no justification for many things I do. The only authority I rely on is the underlying humanity of the text. The modern actor should approach Greek tragedies with the conviction that they have been left too long in the clutch of the venerable.... The Classics were written for the people and they should always be for the people.[142]

A Greek play, Anglin noted, is "a classic because it is as interesting now as it was 2400 years ago."[143]

Indeed, Anglin went to increasing lengths to assure the general public that she aimed at entertainment not an academic exercise.[144] Apparently to resist too much academic interference, she rejected invitations from Harvard and Yale to do another *Antigone* under their auspices, and even though she did *Antigone* at Berkeley again in 1928 and at Ann Arbor in 1930, she was in each case directed, to her partial dissatisfaction, by Professor Charles von Neumayer of the Berkeley Speech Department, who frequently did student productions, and by Robert Henderson, who later staged a rival performance of *Electra* starring Blanche Yurka in 1932.[145] By 1915 Anglin confirmed her growing sense of artistic independence by writing in *Hearst's International Magazine* 28 (July 1915):

> There is no reason for us to retain the rigid conventions of Greek drama, for we may rest assured that were the Greek dramatists alive today, they would be the first to utilize, from the modern playhouse, whatever would best serve Greek theater as they saw it. I shall never forget a discussion I had with one of my directors [Riddle] at the time of giving the "Antigone" of Sophocles. A very inexpressive bier had been made to bring on the dead body of *Haemon*. Think of this in the face of the great elemental forces employed by the author of the play! Of course the director intended to use it in place of the "funeral car" of the Greeks, but both of them I discarded, the one as archaeologically restrictive, and the other as dramatically ineffective. In their places *Creon*, King of Thebes, entered, bearing in his arms the body of his son, the last of his race, an infinitely more moving spectacle, surely, than any mechanical device.

This choice later became commonplace and was used by George Tzavellas in his 1961 film *Antigone*. Both could have been inspired by the scene in Shakespeare's *King Lear* in which Lear carries in the dead Cordelia.

In an era that was beginning to celebrate the centrality of the theater director's vision, Anglin applied her stardom to producing and eventually openly directing her own plays. In fact, her biographer, John LeVay, refers to her as the "last of the great actor-producers of the American Stage."[146] Anglin mixed severe simplicity with the pageantry and huge crowds of the *Oedipus* production by Austrian director Max Reinhardt, whom she had met in 1913. She noted: "Reinhardt agreed with me that superfluous accessories distract from, rather than enhance, the dignity of a performance. Although valuable when used with discretion, they should never be obtrusive. The best way to make a play effective is to act it."[147] From Reinhardt, Anglin "learned another thing: the acting in Greek tragedy must be illuminating, interpretative, not merely recitative; that there must be variation in the color of emotion, and where that is impossible—for Greek tragedy is either of such a dull red or white heat that its identifying color is unmistakable—there must be variation of action. In no other drama can an actress find such opportunity for studying shades of emotion that are so nearly alike and yet so subtly different."[148] Walter Anthony, writing in the *San Francisco Chronicle*, compared Anglin's performances to those he had recently seen in Europe. Anglin's were in his view not only far more human but in them "everything not directly contributing to the dramatic effectiveness of the works as they were to be viewed with modern eyes, was discarded. Pedantry yielded in every instance to poetry; affectation to effect, history to histrionism, and the triumph of Anglin's modernism was reflected in the wonderful audiences."[149]

The 1913 *Electra* was part of an ambitious venture financed by Anglin that also included four of Shakespeare's plays. She had originally planned to do *Medea*,[150] but eventually chose Sophocles' version of *Electra* because in her view the heroine was more rational than in other versions.[151] Theatrically speaking, Anglin's Greek productions at Berkeley after *Antigone* were far more ambitious, and her continued close collaboration with her lighting and costume designer, Livingston Platt, and her attempt to maintain a company of predominantly American actors devoted to ensemble playing was unusual for the period.[152] Platt followed and in some respects anticipated Craig and Reinhardt in his pathbreaking work with a small touring company in Bruges, Belgium, and at the Toy Theatre, an early American Little Theatre (see below) in Boston. Anglin specifically identified him as an American Gordon Craig or Max Reinhardt *(New York Dramatic Mirror,* June 1913). The 1913 *Electra* was defined by its simplicity of setting, lack of realism, and imaginative use of lighting. In contrast to *Antigone,* no footlights or calcium lights were employed. "There was no 'shaft of light' thrusting itself over your head to render at once the player and illusion obvious. Instead, the lighting was thrown from cornice tops at either side of the stage, and the mechanism was hidden artfully."[153] The play was framed by a move from dark to light, concluding with a return to darkness.[154] The sets were painted in pointillist dots of color that blended at a distance and provided a rich surface that could be enhanced by lighting.[155] The costumes in this and later productions, more "Homeric" than Periclean in style, were made from rich fabric dyed and woven in Platt's New York studio; their colors aimed to capture the play's dominant moods and emotions; Platt imitated the drape of Greek garments on vase painting and sculpture.[156] In *Electra* Anglin herself wore severe dark blue, the chorus shades of gray and dark brown, and Clytemnestra, followed by colorful attendants, scarlet and gold.[157] This time Platt enclosed a group of cypresses planted to reduce the stage with a six-foot wall. Two huge busts of Greek gods surrounded the central oak doors with six cow skulls mounted above them.[158] To secure an effective entrance for Clytemnestra, Anglin had six hundred seats removed from the Hearst Theatre, thus tossing away $1,200, so that fifteen extra steps could be built for the queen's descent.[159] The decadent procession following Clytemnestra might easily have been borrowed from Hofmannsthal's *Elektra*.[160]

Only the choice of music, inspired by Gluck and Debussy and composed and conducted by William Furst, and the Plumptre translation were less adventurous than in later productions. Less obtrusive than Damrosch's later music, Furst's used woodwind, brass, and percussion instead of a full orchestra.[161]

Anglin believed that all Greek tragic roles should be "interpreted in a simple and in a human manner to reach the pure spirit of the character."[162] She moved in a stately, slow manner, "often speaking her lines without much change in the inflection of her stirring voice."[163] "Her movements and flowing gestures always solidified into Greek poses and gestures."[164] As one critic, writing in 1915, put it, "The economy of Miss Anglin's manner and the reticence of her art are the imperial signs of her genius."[165] Anglin even turned her plays into a form of religious ceremony; latecomers were seated in the last row, and no applause was permitted during the performance.[166]

Anglin's instructions to the one hundred college "girls" who played the Greek maidens fleeing in terror from the murder of Clytemnestra indicate the degree to which she was already directing her own plays in a fashion that involved the chorus continually in the action, mingled chorus and characters in the orchestra, and used the chorus to intensify climactic moments. "'You are intelligent young women. I will not tell you what to do. I will simply ask you to express extreme terror by flying from the sight. Go in any way that seems best to you, but, remember, the moving emotion.' The way Margaret Anglin cleared the stage of its chorus, the way the Greek maidens ran shrieking out of the theatre into the surrounding night, is one of the thrilling memories of those ten thousand who filled the theatre."[167]

The ending evoked lyrical responses from several critics. "Demonstrating that she was no mere dreamer translated to another period and manner of life she gave the Greek play an American climax, furnishing it by leaping upward, sword in hand, ferocious, unwomaned by her triumph over fate."[168] "Off stage, there arises, in due time, a cry of agony, and then there comes a silence and a pause. Then from out the portal of the house of Agamemnon is hurled the sword of the vanquished. This token clatters, hurtling down a stairway of enormous length. Electra shudders away from the symbol of defeat. Then stealthily, she climbs down many steps to examine it with anguished curiosity. With a wild cry, she catches up and flings the thing aloft; for she has recognized it as the sword of the hated murderer, Aegisthus. Then, at last, she dashes it beneath her feet, and tramples on it with a tardy sense of triumph. This point of high dramatic tensity concludes the play."[169] This staging, despite the move from light to darkness that haunts both Sophocles' text and the lighting of this production, confirms that Anglin interpreted the play as concluding with a triumphant vindication for the long-suffering Electra.[170] *Electra,* as one critic later remarked, "uncoiled . . . like a steely, terrific snake—a snake a-glimmer with the splendid, poisonous colors of lurid hate."[171]

Anglin's triple bill of *Iphigenia in Aulis* (*IA*), *Electra,* and *Medea* in 1915 was performed as part of the Panama-Pacific International Exposition in San Francisco (fig. 8). Although the programs list a stage manager for *IA* and *Medea,* Anglin essentially directed the plays herself. Because of heavy demand, *IA* was given twice. Each of the three plays was performed in a different style, but all were highly ambitious and monumental efforts. One eyewitness, chorus member Emily Kimbrough, was particularly impressed by the contrasts in voice and posture of the heroine: "Miss Anglin as Iphigenia had a clear rather high voice of a young girl, totally without the organ-like vibrations of Medea. As Electra her voice was strident, harsh in denunciation, tender, loving, yearning toward Orestes, yet quite different from the passionate voice of Medea. Also she moved as a dancer moves, expressing character or emotion—the walk of a young priestess as Iphigenia going toward her immolation, the slinking crouch of an animal in Medea, the heavy weighted walk of sorrow, despair, in Electra."[172]

In contrast to her *Antigone, Electra,* and *Medea,* Anglin thought of *IA* as a melodrama that offered an opportunity for spectacle and pageantry.[173] "Miss Anglin, as Iphigenia, was attired in the white simplicity of the Grecian princess" in contrast to a chorus in lavenders, greens, pinks, and blues. "The lights directed upon her as she made the entrance revealed a face that seemed inspired more with some inner sense of impending sacrifice than with the thought of approaching nuptials."[174] The entrance included a procession with trumpets, slaves, archers, soldiers with lances, and wedding gifts and bridal raiment carried by a score of attendants. She arrived on stage drawn by a four-horse chariot. A large group of shouting Greeks declared the ominous presence of a Greek army ambitious to sail for Troy.[175] The cast included five hundred,[176] many of them students. Anglin heavily reworked Robert Potter's 1781 translation herself.[177] The costumes and pageantry suggest that Anglin relied on the play's move from fictional marriage to sacrifice witnessed by a chorus of youthful sightseers and stressed the social inevitability of Iphigeneia's death by making the army's desire to go to war visible from the heroine's entrance.

Walter Damrosch, the conductor of the New York Symphony, composed the music for both *IA* and *Medea.* "Mr. Damrosch foreswore quantity evidently in favor of a noble quality, distinctly modern, free, strong in tonal coloring. The song of the handmaidens went particularly well, and there were malignant gleams to the strains which accompanied Clytemnestra."[178] The orchestral music in all three productions (critics noted the influence of Gluck and Wagner) underlined climactic moments and supported entrances, exits, openings, and closings. *IA*'s overture accompanied Agamemnon writing a letter; a cello solo marked Iphigeneia's sacrifice; the play closed with a "Battle Hymn Finale."[179] Drumbeats underlined Clytemnestra's death cries in *Electra;* musical themes marked lament, the royal bacchanalia, the mysterious stranger, and blood guilt. Cello and double basses accompanied Medea's search for the children, reed instruments their shrieks, trumpets their murder, and woodwinds their completed demise.[180] For *Medea,* Damrosch's musical themes underlined Medea's three roles as "sorceress, exile, and vengeful lover."[181] Music typically played a more central role than the choruses in Anglin's productions. In this case fifty musicians and thirty singers sang from offstage, concealed by evergreens planted for the occasion.[182] By contrast, the choral odes were cut, the choral lines were divided among individuals instead of being chanted in

FIGURE 8. Margaret Anglin as Medea in Euripides' *Medea* and as Iphigenia in Euripides' *Iphigenia in Aulis,* Hearst Greek Theatre, Berkeley, California, 1915. *Theatre Magazine* 22.175 (September 1915): 116.

unison (a fashion Anglin despised as monotonous and artificial). Although Anglin hired dance specialists to direct the choral movement and occasionally used an additional group of dancers to supplement the chorus, the chorus played a primarily reactive role as they moved rhythmically and gestured and regrouped in poses adapted from Greek friezes, sometimes in a manner inspired by Isadora Duncan.[183] Anglin played the volume and pitch of the chorus's voices against each other; single members of the chorus sometimes delivered lines accompanied by a full orchestra (melodrame).[184]

*Medea*, which used Gilbert Murray's recent translation, was universally viewed as more modern. "Turbulent, terror-striking, Miss Anglin's Medea was positively sublime in her fearfulness. The Greeks of old hated Medea, as Euripides meant they should; but there was no hatred for the Medea who, in the gloom and grey of the Berkeley night, cried out her wrongs to the starry heavens."[185] Indeed, one of Anglin's actors, Alfred Lunt, recalled that she so frightened the two children in the performance, when she used a full, terrifying voice that she toned down in rehearsal, that they were afraid to be dragged offstage by her.[186] On the *Medea* set, braziers burned constantly on either side of the heavy bronze doors of the palace. The outdoor theater permitted the use of a dramatic exit from the palace roof. "While as Medea I was in the chariot on the roof, and flinging a dreadful speech at Jason. But I couldn't see him for the darkness below me. It was like dropping something into a well and hearing its echo."[187]

Anglin's much-photographed costume was particularly striking; the heroine's barbarism was expressed in a green robe and bloodred scarf, a tiger skin attached at one shoulder, one frontal lock gray, earrings, jeweled sandals, and wrist and arm bracelets.[188] Anglin, who already had a reputation for being willing to take on outrageous female roles in other contexts (*Mrs. Dane's Defense* and *The Awakening of Helena Richie*), seems not to have shared the fear of Euripides' infanticide common to many bowdlerized nineteenth-century Medeas (see chapter 5.1), although her exceptional ferocity was mitigated by a powerful plea for justice.[189] Her Medea, in contrast to Van Volkenburg's interpretation, discussed below, seems to have visibly emphasized the heroine's foreign and terrifying dimensions, whereas Van Volkenburg stressed her lucid intelligence.

Anglin's success at Berkeley led to performances of *Electra* and *Medea* at New York's Carnegie Hall in 1918,[190] while she was playing the farce *Billeted* at the Fulton Theatre, and to performances of *IA* at the Manhattan Opera House in 1921, with Anglin as Clytemnestra and Mary Fowler as Iphigeneia.[191] Although sold out (Carnegie Hall held three thousand), these productions once again did not cover Anglin's expenses.[192] Anglin worked thirty-six hours straight before performing the Plumptre translation of *Electra*, since she served as producer as well as starring actress (figs. 9 and 10). Critics in 1918 noted that she acquired an atypical audience for serious plays in wartime.[193] Platt's severe sets were dominated by verticals and

FIGURE 9. Margaret Anglin as Sophocles' Electra, Carnegie Hall, New York, March 1918. *Theatre Magazine* 27.205 (March 1918): 132.

ELECTRA'S INVOCATION TO THE GODS

ELECTRA SUMMONS THE QUEEN AT AEGISTHUS' COMMAND

FIGURE 10. Margaret Anglin in Sophocles' *Electra*, with set by Livingston Platt, Carnegie Hall, New York, March 1918. *Theatre Magazine* 27, no. 206 (April 1918): 211. Photo by Charlotte Fairchild.

primary colors, projected into the auditorium with neoimpressionist brushwork, and used multiple playing levels and nuanced lighting.[194] For example, in *Medea*, crimson light shone eerily through the grillwork gates used instead of doors when Jason arrived after the murder of the children.[195] John Corbin of the *New York Times*, an enthusiastic viewer of the Berkeley *Electra* in 1915,[196] thought Electra's revenge theme outdated—"one of the few themes in antique drama which are alien to our modern mood"—but praised Anglin's splendid, intense, and vital interpretation of Sophocles: "I hold it as self-evident that Miss Anglin is far more nearly right about it [Greek tragedy] than the scholastic world. It is a thing of rich, human vitality and gorgeous color."[197] Citing the color used in painting classical sculpture in support of this view, he goes on to praise Anglin for "the greatest performance we have been permitted to see since Bernhardt." Or, as another critic put it, "A moment of the clanking steel behind the scenes, and then the breathless audience beheld Miss Anglin, alone on the great steps, clad in black, her white arms raised to heaven, drawing her fierce breath of joy at the fulfillment of the long expected moment upon which had centered all the emotion of her life.... We can name none who possess this splendid vitality, pictorial and plastic sense and intellectual vigor.... This achievement in Greek tragedy must mark Margaret Anglin as our greatest American actress."[198] Anglin's New York *Medea*, again viewed as more modern and more interesting as a play than her *Electra*, was in some cases less to critics' taste. Costumes, sets, and music were praised, but Anglin's own performance and that of the chorus received in some cases more mixed reviews than that of the rest of the cast. Yet even parodic reviews (*Brooklyn Eagle*, February 21, 1918) were bowled over by the scene in which Medea rushes off to kill the children and by her green and scarlet costume.

Despite the continuing reservations about the play's harsh theme,[199] perhaps the single greatest critical success of Anglin's career was the *Electra* performed for two nights at the New York Metropolitan Opera House in 1927, followed by thirteen performances at New York's Gallo Theater in December, at the Metropolitan Opera House in Philadelphia under the sponsorship of the Philadelphia Art Alliance, and in Providence, Rhode Island, in 1928, in an outdoor performance attended by a crowd of eight thousand.[200] A version of this *Electra* was also given at the Garden Theater in St. Louis in 1925, at Berkeley in 1926, and in Boston four years later.[201] The New York Met production had the support of the National Community Foundation, whose members included many classicists. Anglin directed her own performance. As one critic commented, "For once Greek drama was paying dividends."[202] "When the Shuberts announced Miss Anglin's *Electra* last week as a regular theatrical attraction, Sophocles came close to being the leading dramatist for the spring season."[203] Indeed, support from major Broadway producers like the Shuberts would up to this time have been unheard-of for a production of Greek tragedy. Although some critics thought Anglin overwhelmed the rest of the cast, she once again won many rave reviews.²⁰⁴ "Trust Miss Anglin to know the value of shaded lights, of grouped figures, of characters weaving themselves into changing pictures against gaunt grey backgrounds, to know the value of flat pastel tones and of incense smells."²⁰⁵ While the occasional critic complained about the lack of authenticity of Anglin's productions, another more typically asserted that "if any professor objects to Miss Anglin's interpretations, so much the worse for him. I am sure Euripides would have enjoyed them. Whatever isn't living isn't Greek."²⁰⁶

Anglin's other productions and efforts to perform Greek tragedy were less successful. Her Berkeley *Hippolytus* of 1923 was thought overproduced, with music (composed in part by herself) that overwhelmed the actors. As Phaedra, Anglin disappeared too early in the play to satisfy her fans.²⁰⁷ A 1922 invitation by King Constantine of Greece for a Greek tour eventually fell through when he was deposed.²⁰⁸ Anglin tried to do a Greek season in Lewisohn Stadium at New York's City College, but her proposal in this case and in the case of her plans for a permanent theater festival to perform classics at Berkeley was thought too expensive.²⁰⁹ She hoped to perform in a Chicago stadium in 1924, but the space proved too large for a stage performance.²¹⁰ By the late 1920s Actors' Equity regulations made it impossible for her to direct and perform in her productions.²¹¹ In her waning years, when she could no longer afford to finance her own productions, she tried to organize a performance of Euripides' *Trojan Women* with herself as Andromache in 1936 and 1937, and again in 1940 and 1942 with herself as Hecuba (along with another *IA*), as well as a *Persians* with herself as Atossa at Berkeley in 1938. For the first time she was motivated by politics; World War II obsessed Anglin as World War I had not.²¹² She also tried and failed to challenge Blanche Yurka, who aimed to rival her Electra in 1931–32 (see below), with a performance of *Electra* in the Hollywood Bowl in 1938.²¹³ In addition to her performances of the Greek originals, however, Anglin starred in two performances of Julia Ward Howe's *Hippolytus*, a new version of the play based on Euripides' *Hippolytus* and Seneca's and Racine's *Phaedras*, at Boston's Tremont Theatre in March 1911 (see chapter 3.1).

Anglin's career intersected in significant ways with many of the other early important American figures in the reception of Greek tragedy on the U.S. stage. Maurice Browne, whose *Trojan Women* and *Medea* marked the advent of professional performance of Greek tragedy in Chicago, later worked for Anglin as a stage manager of her productions of *IA* and *Joan of Arc* in 1921.²¹⁴ Walter Damrosch, who served as composer for several of Anglin's tragedies until he fell out with her in 1921, also worked closely on a major New York season with Isadora Duncan in 1908–9 in which she danced various versions of the Iphigeneia myth. In 1896 Anglin spent twelve months working under James O'Neill; his eight-year-old son Eugene, who often hung around backstage, idolized Anglin.²¹⁵ Although we have recorded only a backstage visit from Eugene O'Neill to Anglin in Portland, Oregon,

O'Neill is said to have wanted to write a play for her, perhaps even (though it came too late in her life) the part of the Electra figure, Lavinia, in *Mourning Becomes Electra*.[216] Certainly by 1931, the date of the O'Neill trilogy's premiere, Electra had become Anglin's signature tragic role, as well as one for which no competition had emerged. Although her Medea was later eclipsed by that of Judith Anderson in Robinson Jeffers's version starting in 1947 (see chapter 5.2), Anglin remains the single most ambitious and successful American actress/director of Greek tragedy on the American stage.

### *The Chicago Little Theatre*

As a whole the American Little Theatre movement, named after the Chicago Little Theatre,[217] which was cofounded by the British Maurice Browne and his American wife and chief actress, Ellen Van Volkenburg, in 1912, both embraced serious modern plays from the European repertoire and promoted plays by contemporary American writers. Above all, however, the movement challenged the values and organization of commercial theater and developed new modes of theatrical representation. These regional repertory theaters were tiny—Browne's theater on the fourth floor of the Fine Arts Building on Chicago's Michigan Avenue, with a stage fifteen feet across and eighteen feet deep, seated ninety-one, and was supported by four hundred elite subscribers and some left-wing radicals, literati, and members of an upwardly mobile middle class.[218] Greek tragedy, among other canonized classics, would have played little role in the movement if it had not been for the ardent Hellenism of both Browne and George Cram Cook, founder of the Provincetown Players in New York (see below). Both the British Browne and native Iowan Cook had studied Greek as undergraduates at Cambridge and Harvard respectively, and the influence of Greek drama on their own conceptions of theater was reinforced by a shared admiration for the Irish Players of Dublin's Abbey Theatre, whose enthusiasm for new modes of theatrical organization, ensemble acting, new scenic practices, local mythological subjects and a national dramatic literature, poetic diction, tragic form, and "ethical idealism" was fostered by the Irish poets Yeats and Synge.[219] The Players' visit to Chicago in 1911 occurred shortly before Browne's production of Euripides' *Trojan Women* in 1913.

Browne, a Wildean aesthete as an undergraduate, and a poet before he became a theater manager, aimed to reestablish the place of poetic drama on the American scene. He expected to discover "plastic and rhythmic drama,"[220] using "a road map . . . concealed somewhere in the Greek chorus: a choreographic map based on the beat of verse; a map of perfectly synchronized mood, movement and speech, a 'dance' with words."[221] Browne's thinking was directly influenced by Walter Pater's argument that "success is defined not by moral conduct but by the intensity of one's aesthetic experience."[222] The founders' statement announces, of works to be produced:

If they are more Greek, or more Hebraic, than anything else, that is only because to the Greeks and to the Jews rather than to the rest it has been allowed to sweep the unessential absolutely aside and return with clear-eyed innocence to the main facts. The directors of the Little Theatre of Chicago ... [aim at] nothing less than a restoration ... of an institution which has been bastardized, perverted and profaned. The theatre, in our generation, is no more that sacred stage where life is purged and winnowed and heightened.... When, in the future, Poetic Drama once more attains the position to which the self-preservative instincts of humanity entitle it, it will be recognized for what it is—the true religious focusing of man's permanent protest against Fate—lifted above the dust of all ephemeral questioning. It will then be seen that in Poetic Drama, rather than in the noblest sacraments of religion, the race must find its orchestral unity, the rhythm of its natural and tragic breathing.[223]

In short, as in Greece, theater was to become a "temple" in which performances served as rituals that regenerated social life.[224]

Despite a tiny budget and largely amateur (and female) actors who received no pay in the first three years of the theater, the 1913 *Trojan Women*, the group's third play, proved such a success that it remained in the repertory for the next five years, until the theater closed; *Medea* followed shortly thereafter, in 1914. In a 1915 tour supported by the Woman's Peace Party, the creation of Jane Addams, as well as the Carnegie Peace Foundation, the company took *Trojan Women* from Chicago's Blackstone Theatre to play to full houses of around 33,000 people in community groups such as women's clubs, on college campuses, and at commercial theaters in thirty-one cities from Baltimore to San Francisco throughout the nation; it introduced many audiences not only to Greek tragedy, but to new theatrical techniques.[225] The Woman's Peace Party was organized in Washington, D.C., on January 10, 1915, as a union of women working toward a warless future who believed that "a new social consciousness must be developed towards war, just as it has been toward slavery." The play was chosen, according to a program note, as "the most poignant and most beautiful illustration of war's utter futility and unmitigated evil, particularly as war effects women and children. The Women's Peace Party sends it, not as an archaic curiosity, but as a direct message, inspiration and appeal, to the men and women of America." Barker and Browne coordinated their antiwar productions of the play in a rare instance, at least in the first two-thirds of the twentieth century in the United States, of a performance of Greek tragedy aiming deliberately to serve a political cause.[226] Subsequent performances of *Trojan Women*, however, beginning with the single performance directed by Alice Chapin to positive reviews at the Punch and Judy Theatre in New York in 1923, have continued to mark U.S. engagement in military conflicts to the present. Reviews of Browne's production, and especially of Van Volkenburg's Hecuba, were consistently strong, though Browne himself felt that his audiences ranged widely, with college audiences being the most attentive.[227]

Despite their dissemination of "The World's Greatest Peace Play" (program note), Browne's company remained largely aesthetic rather than political in its orientation.[228] Browne promoted the Peace Party's political agenda to the Midwest, which with its large German population was more inclined than the East to stay out of the war, and declined to print Gilbert Murray's insert for the program, which outlined his disapproval of a pacifist reading of the play and introduced the play by accusing its audience "of being equally guilty with Kaiser Wilhelm II in the spread of war." Although the company itself had become more politically radical as it developed, Browne's patrons were not keen on political activism, and a number of his patrons were involved in defense contracts. Overall, Browne was apparently more motivated by the financial and touring opportunity than conviction.[229] The play retained a number of lines that could be read as promoting necessary wars, and Van Volkenburg's Hecuba, notable for her lack of self-pity and restraint until the final scene, followed Murray in concluding with a revelation of irrational meaning to be found in the women's suffering at the play's conclusion:[230]

> All is well,
> Had He not turned us in His hand, and thrust
> Our high things low and shook our hills as dust,
> We had not been this splendor, and our wrong
> An everlasting music for the song
> Of earth and heaven!

Moreover, since Browne cut the play's prologue with the gods Athena and Poseidon, the nature of deity in this production remained less specific.[231]

Aesthetically speaking, Browne's ability to win the sustained attention of his audience depended partly on his innovative stagecraft. Influenced by avant-garde artists such as Gordon Craig, Adolphe Appia, Émile Jaques-Dalcroze, Alexander von Salzmann, Max Reinhardt, Harley Granville Barker, Jacques Copeau, and others whose work he observed in Europe, as well as by East Asian arts, Browne and his designer, Raymond Jonson, aimed at a radically simple focused and unified performance that included no object or any meaningless movement of body, voice, or shift of emotion that was not "indispensable."[232] As Browne's friend the journalist Floyd Dell remarked in a review of *Trojan Women* in *Harper's Weekly*, he "set to work with a score of red, amber and blue electric lights, a few yards of colored cloth, a post-impressionist canvas wall and a dozen amateurs, to create in the mind of his audience that emotional state which should predispose them to appreciate most keenly and fully the tragedy of the women of captured Troy."[233] The original set depicted the great wall of Troy with a central, jagged gap through which the Greeks were imagined to have broken through; every attempt was made to make the backdrop (burlap backed with canvas) look thick and massive, rather than simply painted, and by depicting huge stones and extending the wall into the wings, the set aimed to create monumentality in a small space and to reduce the individuality of the actors.[234] Costumes were muted, blended, and low-key. The one near exception to this severity was the lighting; the sky behind the wall reflected, often gradually, a change of time of day and mood and highlighted the silhouettes of the actors in moments of high drama like the conclusion, where the lighting shifted from fiery red to gray. The five chorus members were brought on slowly, one by one, as the dawn broke from a darkness pierced by the sound of a lamenting voice. Cassandra entered to red lighting, Helen to orange.

Trained by a student of Jacques Dalcroze's eurhythmics, Lucy Duncan, the actors moved to fit the space in an unbroken rhythm.[235] Van Volkenburg had previously been a monologist who performed without props. She now became particularly adept at the restrained, even contemplative style of the movement; the rest of the cast received training in acting, but they remained more amateurish than the far more central choral performances.[236] The chorus, "statuary in motion," as Browne described them in a letter to Gilbert Murray, froze for up to fifteen minutes in poses and tableaux during the episodes.[237] Carefully rehearsed, rhythmic dances were sometimes accompanied by light shifts rather than music.[238] Choral odes were half chanted and half sung and moved fluidly from single voices to unison.[239] The tightly restricted vocal range and rhythm could be described as legato, with all the voices pitched between D and F.[240] Browne thought "rhythm [which he believed to originate in dance] . . . a basic principle of all the arts" and believed the "proper utterance of poetry is the first step necessary for the creation of a drama [like Greek drama] with the qualities of folk-song."[241] While some critics viewed this unified and rhythmic restraint of the chorus as tedious,[242] the attempt to move beyond realism to a more symbolic and grand (on a small scale) style made in the view of others a powerful and novel statement. The deliberate break from realistic sets and naturalistic acting, from spectacular stage effects, and from historical authenticity that was also characteristic in different ways of Platt/Anglin, outdoor performances, and much of the Little Theatre movement, set the stage for a performance style that looked back to Greek and Elizabethan theater but reenvisioned it for the modern stage (fig. 11).

Browne even won the approval of Professor Richard G. Moulton of the University of Chicago for eschewing archaeological niceties ("only possible on an open-air stage") in favor of retaining "the essential spirit of Greek drama, which is the harmony of all the arts, beauty of color, flowing draperies, statuesque figures, gliding movements, rhythmic intonations—all were united in lyric harmony."[243] As Browne himself summarized his accomplishment, "We have tried to prove that those people are wrong who say that this country, so far from being a place where poetic drama cannot find an audience, is the real cradle of its renaissance. We have found that by using the right methods, poetic drama can be made as

FORTH TO THE GREEK I GO

BE STRONG, O KING

ALL IS WELL

FORTH TO THE LONG GREEK SHIPS

FIGURE 11. Four scenes from the souvenir program for the tour of Gilbert Murray's translation of Euripides' *Trojan Women*, directed by Maurice Browne, Chicago Little Theatre Company, 1915. Courtesy of Billy Rose Theater Division, The New York Public Library for the Performing Arts.

*interesting* as any other kind of drama. That is our accomplishment. Moreover, we have brought before our audiences some of the best work of the men who are re-creating the drama of the modern world. Best of all, we are making Euripides our contemporary."[244]

Although other theaters, such as the Toy Theatre in Boston, invited Browne to produce *Trojan Women* even before the tour,[245] the Little Theatre's audience never spread much beyond the educated and affluent, including Chicago's social and artistic elite; *Trojan Women* (most successful) and *Medea* (fourth on the list) proved the only box-office successes among Browne's poetic plays.[246] After the Little Theatre closed, Browne, among other efforts, staged a New York production of *Medea* starring Ellen Van Volkenburg at the Garrick Theatre in March 1920 and later stage-managed Anglin's 1921 *Iphigenia in Aulis* in New York.[247] Anglin's monumental performances set a standard and established a definitive tragic style (including her queenly stature and powerful and varied voice projection) hard to match, but Van Volkenburg's Medea, despite reviews praising her formidable intelligence, mellow voice, sense of conviction, and powerful elocution, was thought to lack "skill, pathos, and passion."[248] The chorus of six and the rhythmic movement of the production received high marks for effort and originality, if not for entirely successful execution; Alexander Woollcott (*New York Times*, March 23, 1920), who thought Murray's translation had begun to seem dated, called the chorus "too Delsartian," although G. W. Firkins (*Review* 2, April 3, 1920) interestingly interpreted it as an extension of Medea's psyche. Browne's smaller-scale production of *Medea*, which apparently aimed at achieving a sense of intense psychological intimacy,[249] was physically and conceptually ambitious; Jonson's stark forty-five-foot-high set achieved an epic quality, and the lighting continued to serve a musical function by underlining emotional shifts through the use of spotlights and quick color changes.[250] This *Medea* achieved the distinction of playing four matinees weekly for four weeks (at a loss of $6,000).[251] One reviewer characterized it as a great feminist play, while another objected to its implausible (for contemporary America) content; Browne himself noted that Medea earlier offended a Madison, Wisconsin, audience with her first "feminist" speech.[252] The same issue of the paper in which this review appeared ironically included a story about a New England farmer's wife who burned herself and her children to death in their barn out of jealousy.[253]

Blanche Yurka, in a 1932 Sophocles' *Electra* staged by Robert Henderson, also failed in the view of most critics to match Anglin's standard;[254] even Barker's well-received productions in 1915 were compared by critics to Anglin's to her advantage.[255] The Boston version of the Yurka production in 1931 at Jordan Hall included a dance interlude by Martha Graham that critics found insufficiently integrated into the production;[256] despite mixed reviews it reopened in New York at the

Selwyn Theater and the Hollis Street Theatre in Boston the following year and toured to Princeton's McCarter Theatre and the Academy of Music in Philadelphia (where Katharine Hepburn played a chorus member/"friend"). Isadora Duncan's adopted daughter, Anna, did the New York choreography to better notices for the solo if not group dances (*New Republic* 69, January 27, 1932, 293), but critics thought the chorus a group of separate individuals who spoke but did not perform any odes, the set too anachronistic, and J. T. Sheppard's translation "flat and unmusical" (*Theatre Arts Monthly* 16 [March 1932]: 189).

Yurka, in the view of her main critical defender, attempted a realistic and intimate portrayal that "presented Sophocles in the humanized and realistic fashion of Euripides" suitable to a smaller modern theater.[257] The play was described in the program as an "heroic melodrama." While appreciating a few highly charged moments,[258] most critics found this *Electra* overly realistic and modern. H. T. Parker (*New York Times,* May 24, 1931), who described Yurka's Electra in Boston as "sombre, abased, self-consumed, vindictive, usually on the edge of frenzy, missing the Sophoclean exaltation, pathos, and poetry," nevertheless praised her recognition scene. *Theatre Arts Monthly* (16 [March 1932]: 188–89) criticized Yurka for being "satisfied . . . to mumble into the floor as she swayed to and fro in her realistic private grief." Commenting on Yurka's dirt-covered body, another critic called the play "a most anthraciting performance."[259]

By the time of Yurka's production critics were also returning once more to doubting the possibility of successfully staging Greek tragedy. As the *New York Times* reviewer Brooks Atkinson (January 9, 1932) put it, "The Greek fables are not our fables, nor is fable part of our culture. To understand the history of the drama it is good to have the Greek tragedies staged occasionally. . . . The nobility of the characters is a matter of scholarly instruction rather than emotional recognition." In his view, "Miss Anglin's 'Electra' shown at the Metropolitan Opera House some years ago, goes still unchallenged here. For Miss Anglin succeeded in translating Greek tragedy into modern theatre terms. By the use of spectacle and sound and by the stature of her acting she caught a dramatic sublimity of mood. Unless the acting is exalted and the staging is done on the heroic scale, the translated tragedy of Sophocles lacks meaning in the modern theatre." In short, Anglin's efforts succeeded—for this period—by being intense, modern, public, large scale, heroic, and democratic. Or, as Clayton Hamilton put it, Anglin proved "that there is a large and eager public in this country which is willing to pay money for the privilege of seeing the tragic drama of the Greeks . . . she has discarded the mask . . . but she has preserved the wonder and the sting."[260] Yet despite these tributes, critics of the early 1930s were also beginning to find the Yurka production more interesting to compare to O'Neill's new *Mourning Becomes Electra* in 1931 than for itself.[261]

### George Cram Cook, the Provincetown Players, and the Emergence of Eugene O'Neill

Maurice Browne's *Trojan Women* was witnessed with admiration in Chicago by George Cram ("Jig") Cook and his wife, the future playwright Susan Glaspell, before they moved east and eventually founded the Provincetown Players (originally called The Playwrights' Theater) in 1915.[262] Like other members of the Little Theatre movement, the Players simultaneously pursued theatrical experimentation with limited resources and created a forum for serious new work by American playwrights, most importantly Eugene O'Neill. Under Cook's aegis and despite his ardent Hellenism, the group performed only one classically based drama, Cook's play *The Athenian Women*, based on Aristophanes' *Lysistrata*. The Players performed *The Athenian Women* during their 1918 New York season; a second performance sponsored by the Woman's Peace Party of New York State took place at Bramwell Playhouse, April 13, 1918.[263] When O'Neill's growing commercial success challenged Cook's views (see below) about the aims of the Players, Cook departed for Greece in 1922 with Glaspell. He spent his time there both reading ancient Greek texts, as he had throughout his life, and immersing himself in modern Greek culture. He died and was buried in 1924 at Delphi. Although he and O'Neill had in the end parted company, O'Neill's own descriptions of his work indicate that his pathbreaking turn to creating new, American versions of Greek tragedy with his 1924 *Desire under the Elms* (loosely related to the plot of *Hippolytus*) and 1931 *Mourning Becomes Electra* (based on Aeschylus's *Oresteia* and the *Electra*s of Sophocles and Euripides) responded to but modified the legacy of Cook, including the latter's enthusiasm for the Irish Abbey Theatre and the work of Yeats, and, possibly, for the achievement of Anglin as well.

Despite the fact that Cook was not an original or even a very coherent thinker, he had a powerful catalytic effect on those around him. After studying philosophy and philology at Heidelberg and the University of Geneva as well as at the University of Iowa and Harvard, he drew on sources as diverse as Nietzsche, Schopenhauer, Freud and Jung, the Cambridge anthropologically oriented classicists (Jane Harrison, Francis Cornford, and Gilbert Murray), Haeckel, and Walt Whitman. Above all, Wagner's interest in fostering a new national art for Germany and Yeats's vision for an Ireland that would recreate the civic and cultural ideals of classical Athens played an influential role on Cook's work.[264] Cook "wished to provoke a renaissance in American writing, a resurgence, socialist in spirit and poetic in its ability to generate dramatic images of human unity. The model and inspiration was always the Greek theatre, which dominated his imagination and which led him to stress the correspondence of the arts."[265] Cook linked what he saw as the integrity, heroism, and democracy of Greece with that of pioneer life in America.[266] Theater could play the leading role in replacing commercialism and in uniting economic, political, and artistic worlds to support a life and art derived from the best in America's cultural heritage.

Cook turned away (at least in theory) from the European model of a director who was aesthetically responsible for brilliant performance, which was largely adopted by Anglin and Browne, to a collaborative model. All members of his group needed to understand and participate in all aspects of theater production and redeem society through Dionysian "inspiration and intoxication, not training and craftsmanship."[267] The Players' manifesto, as envisioned by Cook, ran as follows:

> That a closely knit group of creative and critical minds is capable of calling forth from the individuals who compose it richer work than they can produce in isolation is the basic faith of the founder of our playhouse. He knows that the art of theatre cannot be pure, in fact, cannot be art at all, unless its various elements—playwriting, acting, setting, costuming, lighting—are by some means fused into unity. There are two possible ways of attaining it: the way of the director and the way of the group. Unity in the theatre has been attained, especially by Reinhardt, by imposing upon all the necessary collaborators the autocratic will of one mind—the director's—who uses the other minds involved as unquestioningly obedient instruments. This method of attaining unity leaves room for one and only one free spirit in a theatre.
>
> It was not so when drama first came into the world. Primitive drama, the expression of the communal or religious life of the organic human group, the tribe, had spontaneously the unity of pure art. There may be two hundred actors dramatically dancing the conflict of Winter and Spring, but all that all of them do in the drama springs from one shared fund of feelings, ideas, impulses. Unity is not imposed on them by the will of one of their number but comes from that deep level in the spirit of each where their spirits are one. The aim of the founder of the Provincetown Players, as yet imperfectly fulfilled, is to make all hands work from that level and to do it by recreating a group of modern individuals, individuals far more differentiated than primitive people, a kindredness of minds, a spiritual unity underlying their differences, a unity resembling the primitive unity of the tribe, a unity which may spontaneously create the unity necessary to the art of the theatre.[268]

Cook's views (like Browne's) here partly derive from those of the Cambridge school of classicists, who saw Attic drama as evolving out of primitive rituals and tribal performances to serve the far more sophisticated theatrical tradition of its democracy, a tradition that Cook now aimed to recapture.[269] The spiritual unity and social therapy that grew from theater making extended in Cook's mind to the relation between the players and their audience and aimed at an erosion in the barrier between the two. In response to a production he had seen in New York in 1913 of *Lysistrata,* Cook remarked: "There was something in Greek life and is not in ours—something we are terribly in need of. One thing we're in need of is the freedom to deal with life in literature as frankly as Aristophanes. We need a public like his, which itself has the habit of thinking and talking frankly of life. We need the sympathy of such a public, the fundamental oneness with the public which Aristophanes had."[270] He expanded on this point in his "Letter to the Greek Nation," which was published in an Athenian newspaper: "If the Greeks of 420 B.C. had been compelled by their women, not in a poet's dream, but in reality, to stop their war between brothers—my world ... would have inherited the pure intense Greek beauty of Aristophanes, of Aeschylus, of Euripides, of Homer and Hesiod and Sappho.... If the ancient Greek women had been equal to their Aristophanes, then I, born on the Mississippi River in mid-America, two and a half millennia later, would have inherited a world worthy of mankind."[271]

Comedy's overt agenda appears to have especially suited Cook's taste. His *The Athenian Women* drew on Thucydides to reimagine Aristophanes' *Lysistrata* along these lines. Eventually published in a 1926 bilingual edition in Athens, the play relied on an implicit link between World War I and the Peloponnesian War. The iconoclastic courtesan Aspasia, allied at the play's opening in 445 B.C.E. with her later consort, Lysicles, concocts Lysistrata's women's sex strike for peace with the help of Pericles' wife, Kallia. The women of Greece succeed in establishing the temporary Peace of Nikias, but in the process Aspasia reluctantly abandons the communist Lysicles in favor of rebuilding Athens, still desecrated by the Persian Wars, with her new, aristocratic lover, Pericles. (The relation between Pericles and Aspasia bears some similarity to the relation between Cook and Glaspell; he abandoned an earlier marriage to pursue his artistic agenda with the feminist playwright.)[272] Eventually, the embittered Kallia and her new spouse, the comic poet Hermippos, attack Pericles, Aspasia, and his team of artists and intellectuals (especially Phidias and Anaxagoras). Aspasia cannot regroup her female allies to prevent war after the Theban attack on Plataia, and the Greeks move inexorably toward a disastrous Panhellenic conflict. In Cook's mind the ironic failure to preserve peace and the resulting threat to Western culture derived in both ancient and modern contexts from traditional patriarchal ideas. Yet although Cook at times claimed contradictory adherence to forms of socialism, anarchism, mysticism, and feminism (a major concern for his wife and theatrical partner, Glaspell), the theater he helped to produce was in fact relatively apolitical.[273]

*Eugene O'Neill*

Although O'Neill, like Cook, at times considered himself a socialist or anarchist, and his plays criticized the materialism and harshness of their social world, his tragedies did not, partly because of their socially isolated or marginal characters, adopt the strong public, therapeutic, and communitarian dimensions that Cook saw as central to both Greek and a revitalized American drama.[274] Instead, O'Neill took a different approach to defining an American form of Greek tragedy, in which fate, divine justice, and the supernatural were replaced by the heavily deterministic forces of heredity and environment, of psychology, and of an indifferent natural and social world.²⁷⁵ Through his tragic characters, who could be (as in *Mourning*) but often were not members of a social elite, he aimed "to see the transfiguring nobility of tragedy, in as near to the Greek sense as we can grasp it, in seemingly the most ignoble, debased lives."²⁷⁶ His tragic figures were to gain stature by embracing their fate and confronting it, however hopelessly, with the liberating forces of human imagination. "The people who succeed and do not push on to greater failure are the spiritual middle classes. Their stopping at success is proof of their compromising insignificance. How petty their dreams must have been."²⁷⁷ In this sense tragedy, even deliberate self-destruction, could be life affirming and ennobling for both characters and audience.²⁷⁸

Whereas Cook stressed the social value of old comic directness and drama's call to social unity, O'Neill defended the inspiring effect of tragedy on the physical and psychological reality of individuals:

> People talk of the tragedy [in his plays] and call it "sordid," "depressing," "pessimistic"—the words usually applied to anything of a tragic nature. But tragedy, I think, has the meaning the Greeks gave it. To them it brought exaltation, an urge toward life and ever more life. It raised them to deeper spiritual understandings and released them from the petty greeds of everyday existence. When they saw a tragedy on stage they felt their own hopes ennobled in art. . . . Any victory we may win is never the one we dreamed of winning. . . . A man wills his own defeat when he pursues the unattainable. But his struggle is his success! He is an example of the spiritual significance which life attains when it aims high enough, when the individual fights all the hostile forces within and without himself to achieve a future of nobler values. Such a figure is necessarily tragic. But he is not depressing; he is exhilarating! He may be a failure in our materialistic sense. His treasures are in other kingdoms.²⁷⁹

O'Neill's original attempts to Americanize Greek tragedy did not consistently reflect many of the ideals stated above. For example, the characters in *Desire* are motivated more by greed and lust than an aspiration to resist their fate, and they remain mired in self-deception; the characters in *Mourning* (see the introduction) are so absurdly Oedipal in their motivations that the dramatic tension between inner and outer worlds becomes diluted. The excesses of O'Neill's new tragedies verge on melodrama. Although Robert Benchley preferred O'Neill's *Mourning* to Margaret Anglin's *Electra* precisely for this reason, C. W. E. Bigsby criticized *Mourning*'s relentless, melodramatic focus on the self: "Psychopathology is finally not a substitute for the tragic imagination." Raymond Williams similarly argued that O'Neill replaced Greek action with static psychology.²⁸⁰

Yet *Mourning* in particular was responsible for O'Neill's Nobel Prize in 1936 and became a classic taught in American schools regularly through the end of the Second World War.²⁸¹ What is important for my purposes here is that O'Neill's repossession of Greek tragedy for an American world was a watershed both in inspiring further new versions by playwrights and in setting a new and different standard to which later performances of the Greek originals were often compared. His link between human psychology and tragic fate remained particularly influential.

At the same time, the new stagecraft was considerably less central to performance of the tragic for O'Neill than for Anglin and Browne, who relied so heavily on lighting, set, costume, music, voice, and movement to convey meaning. The one exception indicates O'Neill's new sense of direction. He attempted to redefine the mask original to Greek tragedy as a means of revealing the psychological and social conflicts central to his vision: "More and more surely . . . the use of masks will be discovered eventually to be the freest solution of the modern dramatist's problem as to how, with the greatest possible dramatic clarity and economy of means, he can express those profound hidden conflicts of the conscious and unconscious mind which the probing of psychology continue to disclose to us. . . . For what, at bottom, is the new psychological insight into human cause and effect but a study in masks, an exercise in unmasking? . . . One's outer life passes in a solitude hounded by the masks of oneself."[282] Nevertheless, the central characters in *Mourning* project masklike faces rather than relying on the physical mask of Greek tragedy to convey O'Neill's conception of the tragic. As in some late Euripides' plays,[283] O'Neill's masks invite the audience to peer behind the mask rather than allowing it to convey character through performance.

## CONCLUSION

In 1921 Kenneth Macgowan, a theater critic who was drafted to help run the Provincetown Players after Jig Cook departed for Greece, published a book entitled *The Theater of Tomorrow*. The book's focus on what Macgowan views as a contemporary revolution in U.S. theater in fact identifies some of the reasons why Greek tragedy had begun to attract the interest of innovative early twentieth-century artists, even though they faced an uphill battle before audiences addicted to various forms of realistic drama, comedy, and vaudeville and mired in traditional expectations about the performance of classic plays.

Anglin, Browne, and to a lesser degree Cook, were particular enthusiasts of a Wagnerian unity of all the arts.[284] The technical developments in staging discussed above (an area where American theater continued to shine) were one important factor. Under the influence of European designers like Gordon Craig and Adolphe Appia, sets and lighting originally designed to serve opera and/or to "copy" reality in often extensive detail began to be abandoned in favor of simpler, often formally beautiful sets that suggested a place, mood, or atmosphere and attempted to synthesize all aspects of the drama to serve the meaning of the play. Backdrops utilizing false perspective gave way to sculptural, more architectural settings that avoided visual deception and photographic reality such as those of Platt and Browne and his designer, Jonson. A major revolution in lighting, in which both Livingston Platt and Maurice Browne played a critical role, served to highlight both the actors and their movements and emotions and anything else of critical importance to the drama.[285] As with the impressionists, this lighting broke down color to create more powerful visual and atmospheric effects.

Macgowan argues that the new theater design, which in some respects had its origin in Greek and Elizabethan theater, "demands a type of drama fitted, like the drama of the Greeks, of Shakespeare, of Molière, for presentation upon a stage where illusion is not so important as emotional intimacy, directness, clarity."[286] Since new plays that suited the new theater were slow in coming, the pressure to revive the drama of the past remained,[287] even if, as in the United States, both economic and aesthetic (especially the weight of traditional expectations surrounding the plays) factors resisted it. Indeed, one could take Macgowan one step further than he could see in 1921, and argue that new developments in stagecraft, and their links with Greek theater in the minds of major theorists and practitioners (Craig, Appia, Reinhardt, Duncan, Anglin, Browne, Cook, and even to a more amateur degree, Tingley), played a critical role in reintroducing Greek tragedy to the American stage, in part because American theater needed a new cultural vision that could reinvigorate its sense of identity.[288]

Second, directors like the Austrian Max Reinhardt generated an interest in reorganizing theatrical space and transforming the relation between actors and audience. Even though the dominant role of a director was not the established mode in the United States, in their different ways, both Anglin and Browne, among others, were deeply influenced by Reinhardt. Reinhardt's Grosses Schauspielhaus in Berlin, a remodeled circus building (rather like Madison Square Garden), lit the center of the circus and one end where actors made exits and entrances from a severely simple, if highly technologically sophisticated, monumental set. An audience of around three thousand surrounded the acting space. This permitted Reinhardt to create an intimacy between a huge audience and the grandeur and power of his performance; for example, an immense crowd of suppliants besieged Oedipus in the opening scene, and the blind king exited into the audience at the conclusion. In a sense Reinhardt moved the play into the equivalent of an orchestra and attempted to make the audience part of the action and at one with its "universal" themes.[289] Economically, the lower price of admission invited a move beyond the elite and middle-class audiences who were the standard patrons of serious theater in this period. Outdoor and other large-scale performances in the United States, although we cannot be sure of the exact nature of their audiences, apparently did or aimed to do the same. In a somewhat parallel way, the stages used by the Little Theatre movement also dissolved barriers between audience and actors, by removing curtains, dissolving realism and traditional forms of representation, and revising the relation between actors and audience by bringing the action up close and even into the aisles.

Finally, the new theater of this period aspired to going beyond the well-made play with its focus on character and individual psychology to aim at more imaginative and spiritual values that conveyed greatness of soul and transcended individual actions in favor of conveying the spirit of an age. As Macgowan expressed it,

> The drama must seek to make us recognize the thing that, since Greek days, we had forgotten—the eternal identity of you and me with the vast and unmanageable forces that have played through every atom of life since the beginning. Psychoanalysis, tracing back our thoughts and actions into fundamental impulses, has done more than any one factor to make us recover our sense of unity with the dumb, mysterious processes of nature. We know now through science what the Greeks and all primitive peoples knew through instinct. The task is to apply it to art, and, in our case, to the drama. It may be applied generally; it may give us a drama utterly apart from anything we have now, nearer perhaps to the Greek than any other in spirit, yet wholly new in mechanism and method, mysteriously beautiful and visionary.[290]

O'Neill's new American tragedies (already emerging in *The Emperor Jones* and *The Great God Brown*) later in part responded, if in some respects narrowly, to Macgowan's hope.

Macgowan concludes:

> Of the technical qualities which I see already in evidence about us, most are to be found in the great democratic theatres of Greece, of the Middle Ages and of Elizabethan England. They go back of realism to a theatre that had no earthly conception of being representational, to a theatre where actors, costumes, and what there was of setting, were relatively real things in themselves, presenting emotion directly to their audiences, by either naïve or conventional devices, and never aiming to represent men or women and things as actually existing apart from the audience.... The content of the drama of tomorrow, cut off from realism, is clearly united with the content of primitive and democratic drama even while it goes ahead to a range of mental exploration that must be of gathering importance to a broadly democratic culture.[291]

Because of commercial and governmental processes, the democratic revolution for which Macgowan yearned had in his view little hope of existing outside "communal art," and above all outside theater. Yet, after all, he concluded: "There were once, you know, the Greeks."[292]

Macgowan's views of Greek theater, which in various ways captured those of Tingley, Anglin, Browne, and Cook, may strike us now as apolitical and overly romantic; nor did America immediately experience a theatrical/cultural revolution in these terms, in part because of the intervention of the Depression and the Second

World War, which for a time decimated commercial theater while fostering a more political theater through the Federal Theatre Project (FTP).[293] Outdoor theater performances by professional theater groups no longer brought large and diverse theater audiences together to the same degree. Colleges and professional theater artists during the late nineteenth and early twentieth century shared from an early date a sense of the educational and social value of performing Greek tragedy, and their intermittent collaboration produced one new trend. As noted earlier, according to Pluggé's study of college and university drama, the historicist performances at colleges and universities, especially in speech departments, began to catch up in the mid-1920 and 1930s with trends in independent professional theater, including using stagecraft more often in an interpretive fashion that eschewed "authenticity." I will return to these developments in later chapters, especially chapter 2.1, in the discussion of choreography and music in the important work at colleges of figures like Margaret Gage and Eva Palmer Sikelianos.[294]

Nevertheless, Macgowan captures to some degree why Greek tragedy continued to play a role in early twentieth-century professional theater in the United States despite the limited mark these productions left on the contemporary stage. Greek drama's role in potentially fostering a less commercial, more aesthetic, spiritual, poetic, and even religious or ritualistic form of theater that could unify social groups in a democracy and release them from an oppressive nineteenth-century culture was perhaps more talked about than realized. Yet for those involved the image remained a powerful one that in some respects reemerged in another form in the avant-garde theater of the 1960s and early 1970s and finally established a larger and more stable place for Greek tragedy on the American professional stage.

TWO

# Making Total Theater in America
## *Choreography and Music*

Margaret Gage served as the choreographer of Greek tragedies at the all-female Bennett School of Liberal and Applied Arts in Millbrook, New York, from 1920 to 1935. The school's productions regularly traveled to other colleges and occasionally to professional theaters in major cities and were reviewed and discussed with admiration in New York papers and theater journals. Although many other better-known dancers, from Isadora Duncan and Martha Graham to, more recently, Bill T. Jones, have responded to the problem of conceptualizing Greek dance, myth, and drama on the stage, Gage was probably the first truly ambitious American choreographer of full performances of Greek tragedy in the United States. The views she offered in *Theatre Arts Monthly* (August 1929, 569–70) summed up the problem of representing the chorus on the American stage up to that time and, unfortunately, quite often to the present day. According to Gage, the Greek tragic chorus, with its

> half detached, half active connection with the play, has always seemed to the casual eye of the modern reader an encumbrance to the action, a lengthy interruption of the main dramatic theme. Most modern producers of Greek plays have felt the same irrelevance, and not knowing what to do with this puzzling child, the chorus, have put it in the corner, so to speak, and left it there. They have cut the lyrics shamefully and chanted what was left with monotonous precision, perhaps adding a flutter of life by a few meaningless wavings of arms and marchings to and fro. Or in desperation they have tried to make the chorus dramatic by adding its fifteen members to the cast. And the poor things sit, huddled together on stage like uninvited guests, very much in the way—an embarrassment to the producer and a bore to the audience. To

give them some sort of raison d'etre the Leader rises occasionally, lyre in hand—a mute property at that!—and sings one of the choral odes to the accompaniment of inappropriate music. But even this fails to convince anyone that the chorus is not a mistake. Juggling with numbers has also been tried—increasing the perfect fifteen to a hundred or more to make it impressive by mere bulk, or whittling it down to five or six in order to pretend it is not there at all! But to the Greeks this despised chorus was the central interest of the play, the root of all drama.

The Bennett School performances, by contrast, aimed to be "simple without thinness, primitive without pedantry, diversified without loss of unity, whereby to convey to modern audiences the passionate equivalent of an ancient religious and artistic emotion" (*Theatre Magazine,* December 1921, 398).

From antiquity on, Greek tragedy was thought to have originated in choral performance, which remained central to the form throughout the fifth century B.C.E. The elaborate costumes and neutral masks of Greek tragedy were decorous in contrast to those of the satyr play and comedy; acting in the large outdoor setting of the Theater of Dionysus in Athens relied largely on voice (speech, chant, and song) and gesture. Music was provided by a single double pipe or *aulos,* with occasional additions of percussion, in, for example, Euripides' *Bacchae;* the "new music" of the late fifth century was clearly more virtuosic than before, as was the singing of increasingly professional actors, but insofar as we can tell, musical notation followed the poetic meter of lyric sections quite closely and was above all designed to support and enhance the songs and words of chorus or actors. The twelve, later fifteen, male citizen tragic chorus members rehearsed at great length, but we know virtually nothing about their choreography.[1]

The attempt by twentieth-century theater artists to reappropriate or adapt what they viewed as the "total theater" of ancient Greece (its synthesis of poetic, musical, and dramatic arts) was thus bound to be a somewhat romantic (rather than "authentic") return to "origins" that initially involved a resistance to the confining artistic traditions of the nineteenth-century Western stage (see chapter 1). Post-1960s U.S. efforts to revitalize or reenvision the aural and visual dimensions of Greek tragedy for a largely elite audience has increasingly drawn in part on a wider range of eclectic traditions, mixing Western and African American with non-Western and especially Asian theater and dance traditions, such as Noh, Kabuki, Kathakali, and Chinese opera. However we evaluate these attempts, the gap in our knowledge of how the originals were performed invites a different kind of response to representing the plays than translating or reworking our extant texts, since artists must create almost from scratch music, song, and dance that communicate the original text or new versions to a modern audience. At the same time, performance was essential to the ability of tragedy to communicate with and even create its community (the Greek audience initially saw rather than read the plays), and modern performances that dispense with confronting this question seriously, as Gage suggests, are fundamentally "inauthentic." Many productions of Greek drama in the United States have lacked the resources or even deliberately not attempted to create ambitious choreography, music, and related visual effects. Chapter 2 will focus selectively on some productions that did. It will move from innovations in dance that set the stage for later developments to attempts to integrate all of these elements into full dramatic performances.

The reception of Greek art, myth, and culture in the United States is profoundly intertwined with the development of modern dance in America during the first half of the twentieth century. Although ballet and pantomime had already and continued to respond to classical myths and Greek art, modern dance inaugurated a new relation between movement and music that allowed the choral and musical dimensions of Greek tragedy to be reimagined in performance. U.S. performances of the Greek originals have rarely taken full advantage of these developments, and most of the early Greek-influenced dance pieces failed to develop into full-fledged dramas; yet further experiments in the 1960s and later aimed at reinvigorating Greek *choreia* (choreography and music) would have been impossible before modern dance acquired a serious artistic status in its own right.

Part 1 of this chapter will trace Greek influences on the development of American modern dance, from Isadora Duncan to Martha Graham. As we shall see, Duncan's pathbreaking experiments in the early twentieth century with expressing emotion through the unfettered, "natural" body, often using poses inspired by Greek vases, turned out to be best suited in her own case to solo dance; her attempts to produce works including narrative that more closely responded to Greek tragedy proved less successful. Duncan's techniques certainly influenced choreography in some college and early twentieth-century professional productions of Greek tragedy (such as those of Margaret Anglin; see chapter 1.2) but continued to prove less fertile in full-scale tragic performances. Although all early American modern dance responded to Duncan's work, Margaret Gage's intense and eclectic choral training put the chorus at the center of Greek tragedies produced at the Bennett School in 1920–35, and the chorus was also the focal point of two important productions by the internationally known Eva Palmer Sikelianos at Smith and Bryn Mawr in 1934–35. These productions, however, did not extend their innovative approaches toward movement to the spoken scenes of the dramas, which remained more conventional and less integrated into a whole. Helen Tamiris's choreography for *Trojan Incident,* the Federal Dance Theatre's highly political version of Euripides' *Trojan Women* in 1938, was again innovative in its use of music and movement but apparently failed, in the view of critics, to bridge the gap between choral and acted scenes. Martha Graham's ambitious

Greek dances (1946–67), which responded directly to Greek tragedies, finally developed a new version of "tragic" dance theater, even though they almost never used words and transformed the shape of the action in the original plays through the use of flashback and extended focus on particular emotional and subjective moments.

The first part of this chapter closes with an examination of performances in the late 1960s and early 1970s that revitalized *choreia* by focusing on the integration of music, striking visual images, and movement in order to generate new dramatic rituals. The work of Andrei Serban, Elizabeth Swados, and Ellen Stewart at New York's La MaMa, E.T.C. from the late 1960s to the present will serve as the central example. This group followed in Graham's wake, developing a bodily and musical idiom to express tragic ideas and emotions, although it initially relied, until a performance of Aeschylus's *Agamemnon,* on incomprehensible words.

The pathbreaking developments in modern dance omitted, fragmented, or failed to integrate successfully the spoken parts of the Greek originals. Part 2 of this chapter looks at two attempts to revive Greek drama as a modern form of American total theater that respected the primacy of the word but developed new forms of music and dance to support it throughout, including musical and choreographical accompaniment to spoken scenes: the composer Harry Partch's 1952–61 and later productions of *Oedipus Tyrannus* and *Revelation in the Courthouse Park* (a new version of Euripides' *Bacchae*), and Will Power's hip-hop *The Seven,* a 2006 version of Aeschylus's *Seven against Thebes* choreographed by Bill T. Jones.

Part 3 considers works that developed Greek tragedy in specific American musical settings. After a brief look at the much-studied *Gospel at Colonus* by Lee Breuer and Bob Telson, which restaged Sophocles' *Oedipus at Colonus* as a sermon/performance in a Pentecostal church, and at the Chicago Lookingglass Theatre Company's 2005 *Hillbilly Antigone,* part 3 will examine one rock version, Prospect Theater's 2007 rock opera, *The Rockae* (a version of Euripides' *Bacchae*). This chapter will, however, entirely neglect important operatic versions.[2]

In part 4, visual choreography becomes the central means of communicating tragic ideas in Robert Wilson's *Alcestis,* and the dissonant relation between images, words, sounds, and dramatic styles in the performance of this work becomes key to its exploration of the themes of death and renewal on a transhistoric scale.

Chapter 1 has already treated some of the early twentieth-century attempts in the United States by Anglin, Barker, Browne, and others to address with some success the issues central to this chapter in full productions of plays. Because of the recalcitrant nature of the source material—analyzing choreography and music without the full range of images, written discussions, scores, and recordings reduces the scholar to the vagaries of sometimes unsophisticated reviews—the present chapter will discuss a highly selective number of interesting attempts to make the musical and choreographed aspects of Greek tragedy come alive on the United States stage, which I have with rare exceptions either seen live or taped myself.

## 1. HELLENIC INFLUENCES ON THE DEVELOPMENT OF AMERICAN MODERN DANCE

We cannot understand early experiments in the choreography of Greek drama without taking a quick look at the context out of which they arose. In 1872, a young actor named Steele MacKaye introduced to immediate acclaim in America the "Delsarte System of Expression," François Delsarte's theory of the human system (developed originally for actors), which analyzed and promoted the proper relation between mind, body, and soul and categorized body gestures in relation to the spiritual (head), emotional (upper torso), and physical zones (lower torso and legs).[3] From the 1880s to World War I, an eclectic, popularized American version of Delsarte's system came to dominate the training and behavior of middle- and upper-class women. In its American version a system of gestures and postures derived from the fields of elocution and acting merged with exercise systems devised by gymnastic and education movements, as well as with an older tradition of tableaux vivants often based on Greek models (dating to the 1830s) and amateur theatricals and pantomimes that came to be classified as "living statues." This new "physical culture" movement aimed at health, self-expression, self-improvement, and a unity in mental, physical, and moral life that is particularly well expressed in Mary Perry King's 1900 *Comfort and Exercise: An Essay toward Normal Conduct* (among numerous publications).[4] Modifying bodily behavior putatively enabled the soul to "express the highest aims of the individual will"; assuming a pose created a sign of internal feeling and a unified moral being.[5] Amateur theatricals also offered women in particular a chance to act out dreams, express their emotional life, or articulate moral and political principles.[6]

Dance, including a tradition of social dancing promoted for the educated classes, played a growing part in this new, carefully modulated dramatic presentation of self. Most early productions of Greek tragedy on college campuses, however, either eliminated dance or reduced it to the swaying of bodies and simple movements of hands, arms, or feet imitated from vase paintings, statues, and reliefs.[7] Choruses increasingly influenced by the American brand of Delsartianism, such as that of the Saturday Morning Club of Boston, to be discussed in chapter 3.1 (itself influenced by Sargent and Belasco's 1889 *Electra*),[8] were more pictorial than integrated into the production. The pioneers of modern dance, however, had a much more knowledgeable and complex response of their own to Delsarte. One of the pioneers of modern dance, Ted Shawn of the Denishawn dancers, who wrote *Every Little Movement: A Book about François Delsarte*, institutionalized

Delsartian training in Denishawn's and later in his own innovative dance schools, and virtually every serious early modern dancer was familiar with it.

## Isadora Duncan

Isadora Duncan's famous, innovative, and partly neo-Hellenic approach to dance certainly affected the national conception and practice of choreography in Greek tragedies, but, despite Duncan's appearance of spontaneity, the training and conceptualization required for successful application of her methods proved difficult for amateurs to carry off effectively, and her approach was often misunderstood. Moreover, Duncan's one attempt, together with her brother Augustin, to stage a performance of Sophocles' *Oedipus Tyrannus* in New York in 1915 was generally viewed as a dramatic failure, despite strong, if unsuccessfully integrated, dance interludes. In short, Duncan's conception of Greek choral dancing stimulated important changes but ultimately proved incompatible in her own career with tragic production. For this reason, I offer here only a brief discussion of Duncan's much-studied career in the United States, with an emphasis on her direct engagement with versions of Greek drama.

Born in 1877 and a native of the San Francisco Bay Area, Duncan grew up in a middle-class, partly artistic family that lost its money. In 1895 Duncan and her mother left California for Chicago, New York, and then Europe (London, Munich, and Berlin in 1899, and later elsewhere). From around 1901 Duncan's career began to be carefully followed in the U.S. press.[9] The parts of her U.S. career that acknowledged the inspiration of Greek art unfolded in two stages: (1) the 1908, 1909, and 1911 tours organized by Charles Frohman that involved collaboration with the conductor of the New York Symphony Orchestra, Walter Damrosch, in which Duncan was celebrated as the "Barefoot Classic Dancer" and a representative of spontaneity, naturalness, and freedom;[10] and (2) a second period, 1914–18, during which Duncan, who had always envisioned herself as an embodiment of the Greek chorus by uniting dance, music, and drama, embedded solo performances in more elaborate dramatic productions. The central moment of this second phase was the 1915 season at Otto Kahn's Century Opera Company in New York. Newly imagined danced excerpts from Christoph Willibald Gluck's classically inspired operas as well as a collaboration on a full performance of Sophocles' *Oedipus Tyrannus* were among the important productions of this period.

Imitations of Greek art in American dance were hardly new, and Duncan clearly favored the American Delsartian influence of her childhood over the artifice of ballet or the emphasis on bodily display (especially legs) of vaudeville.[11] She shared with Delsartianism an emphasis on the harmony between body, mind, and soul and the universe as a whole. Yet her dancing aimed to liberate the self from within rather than to control and refine it from without in the Delsartian mode.[12] In her early dances, which featured a veiled, carefully desexualized display of an unbound body, energy was sent up from a low-grounded pelvis (solar plexus) into floating arms and a head raised or thrown back Dionysically, and involved a carefully designed, fluid, and seemingly effortless or even improvised series of steps. Her dance emphasized what she saw in Greek art—"emotion taking possession of the body"—[13] and built up its meaning through a series of signs and symbols. She aimed to make her dance spring from the moods of (often romantic) music,[14] rather than working with its rhythms directly. She performed with muted lighting from the wings, a background of tall, blue-gray curtains, and a carpeted stage. Over time, although she studied Greek vases and sculpture at the National Museum in Athens and at the Louvre in Paris, Duncan insisted against popular assumptions that she made no attempt to reconstruct Greek dance, whose movements she saw as derived from nature, but only to draw inspiration from it.[15] "I don't mean to copy it, to imitate it, but to be inspired by it, to recreate it in myself with personal inspiration; to take its beauty with me towards the future."[16]

Duncan attempted to take advantage of nineteenth-century American Hellenism and the revival of the Olympic Games in 1896 to establish dance as a high art. She performed only in concert halls, opera houses, and salons, with the patronage above all of upper-class women eager for prestige and high "culture." In addition, as Ann Daly put it, Duncan, taking advantage as well of an emerging academic and cultural regard for dance, "established the dancing body as a site of cultural debate."[17] These early phases of her career spawned many U.S. imitations, including choruses in performances of Greek tragedy.

Despite her reputation as a solo dancer, Duncan from the beginning attempted to capture or "revive" the communal spirit of the Greek chorus,[18] "its rhythm, the grave beauty of its movements, the great impersonality of its soul, stirred, but never despairing."[19] Dancing, she argued, "must become again the primitive chorus, and drama will be reborn from her inspiration. Then she will again take her place as the sister art of tragedy, she will spring from music—the great, impersonal, eternal and divine wellspring of art."[20] Dance involves a maenadic/Dionysiac loss of self in community: "In the golden lights of the stage I saw the white supple forms of my companions; sinewy arms, tossing heads, vibrant bodies, swift limbs environed me.... When I fell, in a paroxysm of joyous abandon, I saw them."[21] Her adaptations of Gluck's operas *Iphigénie en Aulide* (Paris, 1774; performed by Duncan in 1905–15) and *Iphigénie en Tauride* (Paris, 1779; performed by Duncan in 1914–15), themselves versions of Euripides' originals, offer among the earliest examples of this effort to capture the chorus in solo dance.[22]

The dances largely animated choral episodes, not characters. Drawing on *IA*, Isadora, dressed in a beige chiffon tunic, evoked young maidens playing the double flute and children's games of ball and knucklebones, then strewing flowers for a wedding procession; she carried an offering to a temple and watched and waved to a Greek fleet arriving to the sound of trumpets. Dressed in a red tunic, she performed warrior or Amazon dances (to the "Dance of the Scythians" from *IT*) that included simulations of battle with a victory over an enemy. As the Taurian Iphigeneia, she marched with a raised sacrificial knife to the altar, dragged victims to their death, and met an imaginary arriving chorus.[23] The French author Ovion, who described the dances in *Mercure de France* (March 1, 1910), saw the knucklebone player as influenced by a terracotta from Tanagra, and the Scythian dances by Plato's description of Pyrrhic dance. The Century Opera version of this often-revised piece also included for the first time spoken and sung choruses (by Duncan's own dancers and several actresses organized by Augustin Duncan) written by Witter Bynner for *IT* and Louis Anspacher for *IA*.[24] This innovation proved unsuccessful. Duncan took a loss on the performances, and critics complained in particular about the singing, declamations, and the orchestra.[25]

Despite the fact that Duncan's many students formed the basis of potential choruses, she never developed this potential fully. Instead, Duncan's experience with performing *Oedipus Tyrannus* at New York's Century Opera Company provoked a permanent return to solo dancing in her career.[26] Augustin Duncan took charge of music (with lyric choruses by Percy MacKaye) and management, and Isadora of the chorus, dances, and crowd scenes. Augustin played Oedipus; Margaret Wycherly, Jocasta; and Duncan's students Irma Duncan, Helen Freeman, Sarah Whitford, and Margherita Sargeant were priestesses of Apollo who mounted up and down the steps to a "temple of Apollo" and performed a mourning dance nonexistent in Sophocles. The production was framed by Beethoven's Symphony No. 5 in C Minor. Duncan danced the second movement as leader of the chorus. Critics panned the contrast between an overly colloquial translation and an inflated delivery in spoken scenes but praised the costumes, music, suggestive lighting, groupings, and staging.[27] In contrast to this mixed effort, Duncan's brother Raymond's cross-country tour of a studiously "authentic" *Elektra* first performed in Europe proved quite successful.[28] His *Elektra*'s choreography was closely based on moments of arrested motion imitating dancing figures on Greek vases.

Although Greek tragedy was performed in honor of its theater god Dionysus, tragic dancing (with the exception of the satyr plays that followed the tragedies) more likely aimed to discipline the bodies of its male citizen dancers than to liberate them.[29] The dance of Dionysus's ecstatic female followers in the visual arts may have appeared in revised form in plays that focused on this god; female choruses were central to archaic Greek (though not classical Attic) culture and Greek tragedy. Yet the identity of the tragic chorus—male or female, old or young, Greek or foreigner—was more varied than Duncan's imagination allowed and required different expressions in movement. Duncan's substitution of women performing ritual for *OT*'s chorus of Theban elders was critical to her entire conception of Greek dance. She often imagined her own solo dance as collective, yet what an audience saw was most likely individual self-expression that bore little relation to tragic or public themes. As with Martha Graham's much-criticized attempt to dance an interlude in Blanche Yurka's *Electra* (see chapter 1.2), Duncan's fundamental conception of the chorus, more lyric than dramatic, made it difficult to integrate into full performance of the plays.

### Margaret Gage

The British actress Edith Wynne Matthison, who received respectful reviews for her Euripides' *Electra* directed by Barker at London's Court Theatre in 1906 and played Andromache to great acclaim both in London and in Barker's 1915 *Trojan Women* in the United States (see chapter 1.2), went on, together with her Greek scholar husband, Charles Rann Kennedy, to tour with the Ben Greet Players (see chapter 1.1) and to do sixteen annual productions of Gilbert Murray's translations of Greek tragedy at the Bennett School of Liberal and Applied Arts in Millbrook, New York. They collaborated over a period of eight months on each production with Margaret Gage, a former Bennett School student, and the composer and chair of the Music Department, Horace Middleton. Matthison and Kennedy took the major parts with Gage. After their first year, students were selected from the entire school and received intensive dance training. Middleton "composed music expressing religious passions, stylistically Greek,"[30] modal music updated through harmony, with shifting moods and rhythms and "counter rhythms and syncopations . . . affording intricate patterns for the dancing." Solos, trios, and full choral songs, sometimes in unison, sometimes in parts, were accompanied by piano and Mustell organ.[31] In 1924 the group built an outdoor wooden amphitheater on campus that held up to a thousand people and included a grass-covered orchestra replete with altar leading up three steps to a stage framed with trees and bushes where minimal structures could be erected; each production began with the entrance of a priest of Dionysus accompanied by acolytes who dedicated a bowl of incense at the altar and "hallowed" the theater while singing a dithyrambic fragment from Pindar.[32] Spectators from the entire region were invited to attend spring productions (including *Antigone* in 1920 and 1923; *Electra*, 1921, 1924, and 1931; *Alcestis*, 1922, 1926, and 1934; *Hippolytus*, 1926 and 1928; *Medea* 1927, 1930, and 1935; *Trojan Women* 1929 and 1932; *IT* 1933).

These productions toured to colleges throughout the Northeast (among others, Williams, Amherst, Mt. Holyoke) and elsewhere (New York City; Ardmore, Pennsylvania; the National Theatre in Washington) performing to considerable praise, especially for the choruses.[33] They played a significant leadership role in the contemporary revival of Greek drama in colleges and schools. Reporters from New York newspapers attended regularly. The *Antigone* of 1923, which was presented at New York's Forty-Eighth Street Theatre in three matinees by an almost exclusively female cast (Kennedy excepted), received mixed reviews for the acting, but other responses to their productions, such as the review of the 1921 *Electra* in *Theatre Magazine* (September 1921), were more laudatory.[34] John Martin, the *New York Times* dance critic, in his reviews of the 1931 Euripides' *Electra* and 1933 *IT*, criticized the "grand manner acting" and incomprehensible words but praised the chorus, which showed the influence of the German choreographer Mary Wigman, for its strength, earthiness, and descriptive gesture in the case of *IT*, and for its flowing movement in *Electra*. "Judged entirely as dances, the choruses are enchanting, and their performance is exemplary." He added: "She has therefore succeeded in creating a unique choreographic idiom in which descriptive pantomime has been completely fused in dance movement." Martin also singled out the imaginative integration of the chorus in the dramas and suggested that Gage should in future direct the actors' movement.[35] Elizabeth Selden, writing in *The Dance Magazine* (December 1929), pronounced Gage the "best living post-Duncan choral master of America" and praised the way that the dance rhythms—walking, running, plastic attitudes, flowing and wavelike movement—fit the plays' structure, words, and theatrical space.[36]

Gage herself had minimal dance training. She studied briefly with the "interpretive" dancer Florence Fleming Noyes and the Isadorables (Duncan's adopted children/students). Since she lived in New York City half-time, she followed the work of important dancers such as Martha Graham, Doris Humphrey, Charles Weidman, and Helen Tamiris and developed a long-term relationship with Mary Wigman, who visited the school and its play rehearsals.[37] Since none of these dancers had as yet collaborated on full productions of Greek plays, however, she developed her own style and conception of performance over time. Gage largely rejected (the often popular) pantomime used in tragic performances as too dramatic; she thought it interfered with the distinctive lyric element of the plays. She wanted the play's emotions to "surge up through the fifteen faces like an ever-changing sea, but they must be impersonal, epic emotions rather than individual reactions."[38] Ballet's "sense of technical virtuosity," and "interpretive" (Noyes) or "aesthetic" (Duncan) dancing, proved in Gage's view too "artful" or "artificial" for Greek tragedy; Gage aimed to produce a group personality, rather than draw attention to individual performances, and to "harmonize" the choral dance "with the architecture of the play."[39]

Gage, like other contemporaries, studied Greek vase painting and sculpture, but she tried to reimagine the movements that she saw not only in three-dimensional but in four-dimensional terms, with dynamic ("rhythmic movements in time") rather than static designs, in order to express "something beyond the words of the lyrics." The contemporary tendency to create dance patterns "aimed to suggest ideas heretofore considered beyond the realm of dancing" proved productive in this attempt. Each active chorus must be "based on a solid symmetrical structure"; "no cleverness of external pattern, no mere stringing together of Greek attitudes

FIGURE 12. Chorus in Euripides' *Trojan Women*, choreographed by Margaret Gage, Bennett School of Liberal and Applied Arts, Millbrook, New York, 1929 or 1932. Photo by Wendell MacRae. Courtesy of the Billy Rose Theater Division, The New York Public Library for the Performing Arts.

must make it seem a manufactured thing. The significant groupings must come like rests at the end of a musical phrase, the silence that gives point to the melody that has gone before and the one that will follow after."[40] Extensive photographs by Wendell MacCrae housed at New York's Lincoln Center Library for the Performing Arts show brilliant costumes and wigs (designed by Gage) and fluid patterns, including running, leaping, and diverse groupings (figs. 12 and 13).

Gage tailored her choreography to the "independent development" of each play. As she put it,

> Compare, for example, the choruses in *The Trojan Women* with those in *The Medea*. The latter have a clear psychological connection between them, and deal progressively with a central theme of love from its first crude passion for liberation to the most philosophical speculations concerning the love of children. They mount steadily from vision to vision, maintaining throughout a group-conscious aloofness. They are Woman with a capital W.

FIGURE 13. Chorus in an unidentified Greek tragedy, choreographed by Margaret Gage, Bennett School of Liberal and Applied Arts, Millbrook, New York, ca. 1930. Photo by Wendell MacRae. Courtesy of the Billy Rose Theater Division, The New York Public Library for the Performing Arts.

The choruses in *Trojan Women* are more a part of the dramatic action. At the beginning of the play they are fifteen individual women, soon to sail away from Troy into slavery. Their first song had the distinct, terse quality of dramatic dialogue. But as the action becomes more poignant with the personal agonies of the characters, the choruses become more impersonal, and this is in direct inversion to the intensity of the episodes. They interject less individual anguish into their songs and take refuge in the realm of pure lyric poetry, where ancient woes are clothed in healing beauty. Then the tide turns and the action moves towards the typical "Greek ending" of serene and purged emotion, the members of the chorus slip back into their dramatic roles and finally leave the scene at the ominous sound of a Greek trumpet. Once again they are fifteen broken-hearted women saying farewell to home forever.[41]

One enthusiastic viewer of the 1929 *Trojan Women* commented on Gage's experiment in this particular play with choral drapery, which became ropes with which to drag an imaginary wooden horse or which acted as sails for the departing ships; the goal was to give "rhythmic variety and pattern" to the choral move into "pure lyric poetry," whereas in other plays she balanced using large if not overly symmetrical groupings by breaking her choruses into smaller groups.[42]

### Eva Palmer Sikelianos

The other notable choreographer of Greek tragedy at colleges in this period, Eva Palmer Sikelianos, a Bryn Mawr graduate who had organized two pathbreaking Greek festivals at Delphi with her Greek poet husband, Angelos, in 1927 and 1930, was invited first by Smith College to direct Euripides' *Bacchae* in a prose translation by Frances Sikelianos as its senior play in 1934 and then by Bryn Mawr in 1935. As with the Bennett School productions, Sikelianos's Bryn Mawr production received notices in major newspapers. These outdoor performances were notable not only for their handwoven silk, wool and/or linen costumes, which Sikelianos had already introduced at Delphi, but for their elaborate choral experiments. At Bryn Mawr a single column was set against trees with a receptacle containing burning incense at the base of the column.[43] Inspired by Byzantine chants, Sikelianos composed modal music to the accompaniment of flutes, Oriental drums, tambourines, and cymbals. The musical modes and types of dancing shifted throughout to mark changes of meaning. Faculty from Smith, Bryn Mawr, and nearby colleges played the male roles, but students played Agave and formed five choral groups of ten who trained, especially at Smith, for months before the performance. The choreography was partly inspired by archaic vase paintings, partly by modern and Greek folk dance; at times the chorus danced or spoke as a whole, at times in alternating groups.[44] As with Gage, these productions, again necessarily limited to female choruses, aimed to restore centrality and a concrete identity to the choral role, especially to dance carefully integrated with music, which tended in contemporary performance to take a second place to music and song, by using "circling waves of power that increased in intensity as the drama unfolded."[45]

### Helen Tamiris and Trojan Incident

In 1938, Helen Tamiris (born Helen Becker to a Russian immigrant family in New York's Lower East Side) codirected (with Harold Bolton) and starred in a dance-theater, antiwar (at this time early Fascism) version of Euripides' *Trojan Women* entitled *Trojan Incident* at the St. James Theatre on Forty-Fourth Street; it closed after twenty-six performances. Vassar classics professor Philip H. Davis, husband of Hallie Flanagan, the director of the Federal Theatre Project, adapted the play; Wallingford Riegger, an important American composer who also worked with choreographers Martha Graham, Doris Humphrey, and Hanya Holm, did the score.[46] For Riegger, the music did not simply serve the dance but was of equal importance: "The dance is a vehicle for the interpretation of music and, at the same time, the music as a tonal portrayal of the rhythm and mood of the dance, both interwoven to form an organic unit which was neither pure choreography nor pure music, nor their sum, but a fusion into something else for which we have no name . . . not music plus drama, but music-drama."[47] Tamiris choreographed solo and group dances and played Cassandra/leader of the chorus; a chorus of twenty-three sang from opposing boxes above the audience, and a dancing chorus of twenty-one, with ten speaking roles, supported the actors on stage. The unusual numbers no doubt resulted from the fact that the FTP was required to spend 90 percent of its budget on personnel.[48] The press release asserted that *Trojan Incident*'s "story of what happened to the women and children of defeated Troy is as fresh as this morning's bombing. . . . The production combines the most interesting technique of ancient and modern theater in a fusion of drama, dance movement and music."[49]

Tamiris had studied Duncan-inspired dance with Irene Lewisohn at the Henry Street Settlement, Italian ballet at the Metropolitan Opera, and Russian ballet with Michael Fokine; she did solo dances with the Bracale Opera Company, performed in nightclubs, and founded the Dance Repertory Theatre in 1930, which featured concerts by Martha Graham, Doris Humphrey, Charles Weidman, and herself. From the beginning her eclectic and innovative work had a political, populist dimension: "I have always felt . . . that no artist can achieve full maturity unless he recognizes his role as a citizen, taking responsibility, not only to think, but to act."[50] Hence, it is not surprising that she later urged the formation of the short-lived Federal Dance Theatre, or FDT (1936–37) as a division of Franklin Roosevelt's New Deal Works Progress Administration and gave up her own dance company and school to serve as the chief choreographer for the New York City branch. The FDT aimed to bring socially relevant dance, above all modern dance, to the masses at reasonable prices and to provide employment for dancers during the Depression years. Tamiris produced important pieces that drew on American sources and music such as Walt Whitman (*Salut au Monde*) and Negro songs of protest (*How Long Brethren?*), but these productions ended when the FDT was forced by politically motivated budget cuts to be absorbed into the FTP until it too was closed in 1939.

Despite generating considerable controversy, Tamiris's *Trojan Incident* represented an ambitious new departure in the choreography of Greek tragedy. Theater critics raised on Gilbert Murray's poetic translations viewed Davis's cut version of Euripides as a prosaic desecration of Greek tragedy; they also objected to using Greek tragedies to engage openly with contemporary issues.[51] Gervaise Butler of the *Dance Observer* ("Tamiris and a Tale of Troy," May 5, 1938, 60) criticized the production's dance for arresting the action, and Brooks Atkinson of the *New York Times* (April 22, 1938) questioned its dense choreography: "Is every gesture supposed to have dramatic significance?" Atkinson accused the chorus of behaving "more like 'workers of the world—unite' than the Trojan women who were pretty angry about the marauding Greeks." "Tamiris, the ideological dancer, comes in as Cassandra with a macabre nuptial dance and a sheaf of group abstractions like mad notes of music spinning across a page." Atkinson conceded, however, that the score played by the WPA orchestra and Howard Bay's setting were excellent, Isabel Bonner's Hecuba "heroic," and "the speed, precision and boldness of the dance imagery are frequently exciting and evoke fugacious impressions of fright and resignation." Despite being "plagued by ineptitude," *Trojan Incident* "is more exhilarating to watch than hundreds of plays that are merely dull."

Dance critics, on the other hand, responded positively to both theme and movement. Since the precise choreography cannot be recaptured, their views allow us to come closer to the production's *choreia*. John Martin, the *New York Times* dance critic (May 1, 1938), though pronouncing the script too condensed, the casting weak, and the relation between the two choruses and the action awkward, praised both Riegger's music and Tamiris (above all her solo dance as Cassandra), who in his view offered a far more modern take than the Browne/Van Volkenburg production of *Trojan Women* in 1913–15 (see chapter 1.2): "Only in the choral odes does the production strike fire and touch at all upon emotional excitement." Similarly, Grant Code in *Dance Observer* thought the choreography Tamiris's finest work: ". . . it is a compliment to Tamiris' integration of the dances into the play, that the dances are stronger when supported by the entire action of the play . . . the group dances were about a society distracted by war, and most particularly about the relation of women to life and to destruction. This is an extremely vital and contemporary theme for us as it was for Euripides. . . . Those who lack passion, pity, poetry, faith in life, hatred of destruction would miss *Trojan Incident*. The smart so-what, ashamed of feeling anything real would miss it. I am sure that you who care about dance did not miss it."[52] Pauline Tish, a member of the chorus, recalled exciting maenadic leaps, jumps, runs, and falls around a huge cracked bell surrounded by ramps. Although Tish praised Tamiris's international inspiration and her use of percussive rhythms, she thought the overall production too complex; in particular, the chorus's attempt to speak in unison regrettably reduced them at times to using only arm and hand movements.[53] Paul Douglas ("Modern Dance Forms," *New Theatre*, November 1935, 26–27) emphasized Tamiris's use of modern dance as "a real weapon for the emancipation of culture." He continued:

> Her refusal to adopt bourgeois dance forms is a dialectic negation and in this sense she is the only dancer who is carrying forward the positive tradition of Isadora Duncan. What are the features of her technique? The space through which she moves seems limitless. There is full use of her entire body in flowing rhythm and it is equally as strong in its mellifluous movement as in its contractions. Candidly aware of the beauty of her body, she is unafraid to use it as a valuable asset. Tamiris has seldom sought escape into subjectivism or abstraction. Always conscious of the social forces

which were determining her relationship to society, her forms have never remained static but are in a constant process of change.

The still-extant script at least gives some sense of the overall tone.[54] Davis's version begins with an epic-influenced spoken prologue that replaced Euripides' gods Athena and Poseidon with a cynical human dialogue among members of the Greek army (Odysseus, Agamemnon, Menelaus, and Thersites) that set up the devious strategy of the Trojan horse. The script then followed Euripides in condensed form but reduced Hecuba's extensive lamentations, often shared in the original by the chorus, in favor of creating a stronger, more politically conscious queen—a "respected," "powerful matriarch," as Davis's production notes put it. The chorus, designed by Davis to be "the core of the play," was also individualized and more assertive than in the original. The play's heroine was in this version the prophetess Cassandra, who remained on stage after her first scene as chorus leader/observer perched on the cracked bell. She embodied the play's message that "the only wisdom lies in staying out of war."[55] She asked:

> In Greece, Mother, and in Troy, and in towns and villages far over the sea,
> Women will long be wondering.
> Must they always think of these things too late?
> A day will come when women will be stronger, and
> And their voices heard,
> When men and women will know their world far better than now. (9)

Cassandra and Hecuba ended the play looking to that better future and ready to struggle for it. While Cassandra recognized the coming misfortunes of the Greeks, Hecuba added:

> There is nothing we can do to save ourselves.
> But the sons that you will bear to the Greeks—
> Will they be wiser than we were?
> Will they be wiser than their Fathers?
> Sing women.
> (Then, as SHE indicates the audience)
> They may hear you. (23)

Hecuba closed the play, again urging the women: "Teach them [the sons], only you could do it. . . . Give them, out of your own abused bodies, the courage to understand the world and to shape it" (27). Euripides' play had left the future, even the survival, of its slave chorus very much in doubt and certainly suggested no future political role for them.

Finally, as Code sensed, Davis adapted the choral odes to the play's active choreography by deleting detailed mythological references in favor of versions with clear themes stressing the gods' betrayal of Troy, the horrors of war, and women's role in the disaster. The first major choral dance, for example, developed beyond the original ode the theme of the Trojan horse stressed in the prologue, using rhythmic repetitions to stress this central theme that probably enhanced the dance movement effectively:[56]

> This is the song of the horse
> . . . . . . .
> But when the monster woke that night
> Death poured from his side and filled the town.
> And when the monster woke that night.
> And when the engine rose to strike.
> Then all the streets of Troy were red,
> And Troy was made a fountain flowing
> With blood for the Horse of Greece to drink.
> And all the streets of Troy were wet.
> The Horse—Blood to wash his jaws.
> The Horse—Blood to shine his hooves.
> The Horse—Blood to die his mane.
> The Horse—Baby's blood for him.
> Now there's a corpse in every room.
> A headless corpse and a widow for sale.
> Slaves for the beds of the Greeks! (12–13)

Despite being unable to convince critics that she could integrate dance, music, and spoken scenes in a production with a unified message, Tamiris's attempt to do so represented an ambitious move beyond earlier professional efforts.

### Martha Graham

Among the early modern dancers, Martha Graham created the most extensive and dramatic new dance versions of Greek myth, often closely based on the original tragedies. Graham's quest for the "primitive" through myth, ritual, anthropology, and psychology was strongly linked to her sense of American identity: "For we, as a nation, are primitive also—primitive in the sense that we are forming a new culture."[57] Her turn to Greek tragedy also allowed her to explore female identity. Graham's focus on the psychology of the tragic heroine, to say nothing of Freudian/Jungian archetypes in general, influenced later new versions of Greek tragedy by women.[58] Yet in attempting to represent the truths of the body and its emotions (a "complete physical awareness"),[59] and above all of the female body, Graham wished to project female empowerment and deploy modernist techniques, in contrast to Duncan and other female dancers who were categorized by Graham's contemporaries as "feminine" and "natural."[60] By avoiding the imitative or flowing, curvilinear movement associated with European ballet, Graham's more androgynous style proved generative for later experiments in tragic choreography.

Graham began her career with the Denishawn group, representing the collaboration of Ruth St. Denis and Ted Shawn from 1916 to 1932, which performed several important pieces with a religious or ritual dimension related to Greek myth (*Death of Adonis, Diana and Endymion, Les Mystères Dionysiaques, From a Grecian Vase, Grecian Suite, Greek Scene, The Minotaur, Orpheus, Pan and Syrinx, Pyrrhic Dance,* and *Sappho*).[61] Shawn, who played a seminal role in establishing the respectability of the male dancer in American modern dance, turned to Greek athletics and culture to establish an image of virile masculine beauty. He outraged some by performing Adonis nude. In *Prometheus Bound*, a solo piece that he developed with music by Alexander Scriabin and presented August 6, 1929, at the Lewisohn Stadium, New York, Shawn performed the role of the rebellious culture hero with his right arm bound to a huge "rock" (in fact two large, basically rectangular slabs set at an angle to each other); the program note described the piece as "a study in limitation."[62]

Graham's earlier dances, such as *Prelude from Gluck's Alceste* (1926), *Fragments: Tragedy and Comedy* (1928), *Lamentation* (1930), *Dithyrambic* (1931), *Three Choric Dances for an Antique Greek Tragedy* (1932), and *Tragic Patterns* (1933), sometimes followed in Denishawn's footsteps by responding to Greek themes, although Graham's biography makes clear that she developed an interest in Greek myth in childhood from her father.[63] Her development of mourning gestures in *Lamentation* was particularly influential. Yet it was not until the late 1940s that Graham began to develop increasingly ambitious responses to Greek tragedy, partly because her originally all-female troupe had become coeducational, partly because Graham's late start as a dancer precluded a career entirely focused on solo dances, and partly under the influence of her leading man at the time (also her husband), Erick Hawkins.[64] These dances included *Cave of the Heart* (1946), based on Euripides' *Medea; Night Journey* (1947), based on Sophocles' *Oedipus Tyrannus; Clytemnestra* (1958), based on Aeschylus's *Oresteia; Alcestis* (1960), based on Euripides' play and Theodore Morrison's poem *The Dream of Alcestis; Phaedra* (1962), based on Euripides' *Hippolytus* and Racine's *Phèdre;* and *Cortege of Eagles* (1967), based on Euripides' *Trojan Women* and *Hecuba*.

Here, I simply want to stress some of the important aspects of Graham's work for the American reception of Greek tragedy and its later performance with a few limited examples.[65] First, Graham made bold moves in the direction of "total theater." Her visually arresting dances, like those of other successful contemporaries, relied on ambitious designers, such as the sculptor and multifaceted Japanese American artist Isamu Noguchi, who did Graham's Greek sets, and her imaginative lighting director, Jean Rosenthal; Graham herself often designed the stunning costumes.

Having commissioned a variety of talented musicians to create new scores for each piece, Graham sometimes worked with the music and sometimes in counterpoint to it. As the *New York Times* dance critic John Martin put it, "Her essential quality of movement is neither spatial nor musical, but dramatic."[66] She developed a dance vocabulary to express emotion in a dramatic narrative.[67] Graham's use of bodily contraction and release from the pelvis (inspired in part by Duncan) was particularly notable, but her repertoire included spiral turns, "knee vibrations," flexed feet, and dramatic leaps and falls. At the very least, all these features opened the way for increasingly ambitious productions of the tragic originals, even if later directors rarely had the resources to develop them.

Second, Graham's dances moved modern dance toward drama by visualizing and often psychologizing relations between her tragic characters, including dancers representing the chorus, in an intense nonnaturalistic fashion. I offer here a brief example from the 1946 *Cave of the Heart*. *Cave* reduces *Medea* to a drama of jealousy. In this version a monumentally heroic Jason appears largely preoccupied by his romantic duets with the Corinthian princess for whom he deserted Medea. In contrast to Euripides' agonistic drama, in *Cave* the closest Medea and Jason come to engaging directly, with the exception of fraught passing moments, is an initial three-way struggle at the opening, where Medea reaches for Jason with the princess in between them; Jason turns Medea upside down and then abandons her again for the princess. Instead, Graham develops the heroine's internal struggle and, to a lesser extent, the female bonds, already present in Euripides' original, between the chorus, here played by a single dancer, and Medea. The chorus opens the piece expressing a presentiment of disaster with a soundless shriek and closes it in an arc of despair as Medea mounts a five-pronged sculpture in a moment suggesting near apotheosis, comparable to her departure in the chariot of the sun in Euripides. In between, the chorus follows Medea's situation intensely and physically tries and fails to prevent her disaster. In *Cave*, however, Medea is above all the outsider (see chapter 5), lurking in her black and gold gown in a frame with copper wires radiating from it created by Noguchi, and in the end virtually bonded to it. She gradually becomes the embodiment of revenge, a snakelike figure at first lying on the ground, then emerging from her "cave" to thrust her hips, writhe, and spin with rage; seized with vibrations, she crawls over the stage to Barber's dissonant score; she finally pulls a red ribbon from her dress, wraps it around her body, and spits it from her mouth. Red ribbons suggest blood/revenge in Japanese theater, but Graham expanded her use of the ribbon to visualize the snake of jealousy encompassing the heroine as well.

After this initial experiment, Graham's Greek tragedy-based dances gradually became more comprehensively theatrical. The female chorus, consistently used to underline the ominous developments/moments of emotional crisis for the heroine in the action, becomes by *Cortege of Eagles* a partially active character; there, a group of hooded Trojan women entrap the treacherous Polymestor for Hecuba to blind with her brooch.[68] The ambitious *Clytemnestra* even included a verbal dimension, with fragments of Aeschylus sung or chanted by a man and woman from the sides of the stage, which helped to clarify its complex plot.

Graham's two pieces after *Cave*, *Night Journey* (1947) and *Clytemnestra* (1958), moved even further toward the tragic originals by enhancing the centrality of choice and action, recognition, and/or reversal in the narrative, all three defined as central to tragedy by Aristotle. Even later pieces like *Cortege of Eagles*, which reflect the looser structure of Euripides' originals, maintain a broader tragic consciousness than *Cave*. At the same time, Graham challenged the Greek originals by imagining events through the consciousness of the major female characters and by reconfiguring or eliminating elements of the original narrative through the use of flashback and a focus on moments of high emotional intensity. *Night Journey* opens with Jocasta contemplating suicide, unfolds as an agonizing flashback on her courtship and marriage to Oedipus, and closes with her hanging and a reemergence of the prophet Tiresias, whose appearances underline the characters' inexorable fate. *Clytemnestra* opens with the dishonored but unrepentant queen in Hades, then evolves as a flashback designed to explore and comprehend her past, and closes, unlike Aeschylus's original, with Clytemnestra's forgiveness of her son, Orestes, at his trial, and her psychological release from humiliation. The later *Phaedra*, in contrast to Graham's sources, responded to Euripides' *Hippolytus* by juxtaposing an enactment of the hero's version of the story, in which Hippolytus rejected Phaedra's love, with an enactment of the queen's fiction about her rape by Hippolytus before her enraged husband Theseus, which permitted her to experience the erotic gratification with her stepson forbidden to her in life.[69] The dance's humans became playthings of the divine duo Aphrodite and Artemis, who simultaneously embodied the characters' own desires. Phaedra's tragic lust derived from her mother, Pasiphae, who consorted with a bull and bore the Minotaur; the mother's veil, which falls on her daughter, becomes in Graham's version her suicidal shroud. Hippolytus initially stands behind a column of shutters; in the opening scene Aphrodite periodically reveals parts of his mesmerizing body. *Phaedra* revived the older woman–younger man theme of *Night Journey*, a theme central to Graham's own life as well. In all three dances, Graham's heroines emphatically paid for their passions.

Finally, the agonistic and dialogic elements of Greek tragedy play an increasingly complex dramatic role in Graham's versions of the original plays. Jocasta and Oedipus's ritualized courtship in *Night Journey*, which unfolds around and on a central bedlike sculpture of a man and a woman designed by Noguchi, evolves from brash conquest by a confident Oedipus to mutual passion, then to shared horror.[70] Clytemnestra, herself a consummate actor, engages powerfully with all the major characters in *Clytemnestra*. She recalls the sacrifice of the desperately pleading Iphigeneia, recognizes yet resists recognizing her double in Helen, succumbs to temptation with Aegisthus, faces an extended, suspenseful contest of wills with an arrogant Agamemnon in the famous tapestry scene, and cowers in maternal anguish as a triple-bodied figure consisting of Orestes, Electra, and the ghost of Agamemnon stalk her to enact a psychologically overdetermined revenge.[71] At her best, then, and especially in the extraordinary ninety-minute epic *Clytemnestra*, Graham created a form of sophisticated dance-tragedy that tells its story through music, the body, and an intense focus on emotion rather than words but develops with time a tighter and more complex action. Graham rightly insisted that her new versions of the originals aimed to discover the past through the present,[72] rather than to revive in direct fashion a Greek sense of choreography or narrative. In a sense she reversed the direction explored by those like Gage and Tamiris discussed earlier; she substituted exciting dance versions for the Greek originals. Graham left a legacy in later efforts, however. Amy Greenfield's 1990 film *Antigone/Rites for the Dead,* for example, drew on Graham's tradition by mobilizing five actor-dancers, including former Graham dancers Bertram Ross and Janet Eilber, as well as Greenfield herself as Antigone.

### Revitalizing the Tragic Chorus in the Late 1960s and Early 1970s

New and influential versions of Greek tragedy in the late 1960s and early 1970s, such as Richard Schechner's famous *Dionysus in 69* and Andrei Serban and Elizabeth Swados's *Trojan Women,* made an effort to generate dramatic action from a chorus and to create a receptive audience for Greek tragedy through the process of performance itself, including invented rituals. Since actors could emerge from and return to their choral groups, both Serban and Schechner in a sense generated in a new context the choral group of singers and dancers out of which Greek drama is thought originally to have emerged. The work of both Serban/Swados and Schechner has been much discussed.[73] Here I aim to describe briefly one effort of the Serban/Swados team, *Trojan Women,* as a prelude to addressing their attempt to imbed the techniques that they developed in a full-fledged performance of Aeschylus's *Agamemnon.*

In the early 1970s (1972–74), the Romanian director Andrei Serban produced with composer Elizabeth Swados a set of three remakings of Greek tragedies, *Fragments of a Greek Trilogy.* The plays were performed with new casts at various intervals over the next twenty years at La MaMa, E.T.C. in New York City (four times, including spring 2004) and in a number of other countries.[74] All three of the plays presented new versions of Euripides' *Medea* and *Trojan Women* and Sophocles' *Electra* and used language incomprehensible to the audience (largely Greek and Latin) in performances that closely echoed the shape of the original plots but reduced them to skeletons of the originals. The actors and chorus tried to capitalize on the phonetic force of ancient tongues to create a "ballet for the mouth" and to "inhabit their bodies" with the sound of ancient texts, using every possible human body cavity as a resonator to discover what enabled Greek actors to project and produce intense communication with an audience and its gods in a huge open space.[75] Techniques for integrating voice, body, and movement borrowed from Noh, Kathakali, Kabuki, and Balinese theatrical traditions were used to tap what Serban called the "energy" that produced the ideas of the texts. The music was deliberately drawn from a mix of world traditions. Serban used settings without a proscenium stage, which at times could bring the audience into the play or challenge its relation to it.

The much-revived (four times in New York from 1974 to 2004 as well as on international tours), positively reviewed, and reimagined *Trojan* Women deemphasized the roles of the aristocratic principal characters in favor of enhancing the audience's sense of group suffering.[76] The audience for *Trojan Women* was led in a festal procession into a large rectangular space framed by scaffolding on all four sides, with a platform at the back from which a ramp and stairs could be lowered. In the first performance the theater was initially pitch-black, and members of the audience were soon separated from their friends by soldiers who pushed through the crowd with groups of Trojan prisoners. Scenes—some only partially visible depending on where one was standing—were played on or around carts pushed through the audience by groups of actors, or on the scaffolding on the sides of the theater. Later, the lights went up, and the audience was ushered to sit on the sides of the theater on both levels (floor and scaffolding) to observe scenes played on the upper platform with the ramp, in the central space, or on a lower front platform. The play moved to a close with a gathering of the women on the front platform in a group that began to sway as if in an imaginary ship moving toward Greece, to the music of a sorrowful song. If one knew the plot of *Trojan Women*, versions of Euripidean scenes involving Cassandra, Andromache and Astyanax, Hecuba, Helen, or Polyxena (borrowed from Euripides' *Hecuba*) could be made out, but the distinction between chorus and actor was considerably reduced by the lack of comprehensible language, the brevity of the scenes, the return of actors to the chorus after playing individual roles, and the nearly continuous sounds of voice and music that accompanied the action. The performance itself emphasized with visceral clarity collective over individual suffering. The choral role in each scene was expanded and more active than in the original. For example, the anger of Euripides' chorus at Helen was graphically enacted for the audience. When a triumphant Helen was wheeled in on a cart, the Trojan women tore off her clothes and smeared her naked body with mud and straw before she was humiliatingly raped by a man dressed as a bear and, in contrast to Greek myth, killed.

*Fragments*' use of invented ritual proved particularly riveting to audiences. Julius Novick (*New York Times*, November 17, 1974), while offering enthusiasm typical of many critics for Serban's "landmark in the history of avant-garde theater in our time," concluded:

> Greek tragedy is a perennial temptation to the modern theater, and a perennial frustration. Everybody knows that there is tremendous power in those strange, distant masterworks, but after 2,400 years hardly anyone in the theater seems to know how to release that power. . . . [Serban has] used the techniques of the modern experimental theater to embrace the strangeness and the distance of these plays. . . . Plot, character, the thrust of argument, are all diminished or missing in these productions. Instead, the plays are turned towards their ritual origins, resolved into a series of ceremonials: of grief, of anger, of preparation, of sacrifice, of triumph.

The production's total theater techniques, which Novick described as "releasing the cosmic intensity of the classics," were strongly influenced by Antonin Artaud and Peter Brook. Gerald Rabkin (*Soho Weekly News,* January 8, 1976) aptly quotes Artaud as follows: "The overlapping images and movements will culminate through the collisions of objects, silences, shouts, rhythms in a genuine physical language with signs, not words as its root. . . . And it can be said that the spirit of the ancient hieroglyphs will preside at the creation of this pure theatrical language."

Serban went on to produce Aeschylus's *Agamemnon* using Edith Hamilton's translation in 1977 at the New York Shakespeare Festival at the Vivian Beaumont Theater, Lincoln Center, and again at the Delacorte Theater in Central Park.[77] The play deployed similar techniques to those in *Fragments,* especially in an apparently fairly cryptic forty-five minute prologue that represented through music and movement the mythic background to the house of Atreus, and in the choral sections, which involved almost half of the original text. As Serban put it, "The Chorus makes a bridge between us and higher possibilities: it is the most important element in the play; it will not only tell the story and bear witness to the action, but is the conscience of the protagonists and the receptacle of the life around them. Their shared collective emotion . . . will reverberate to us and, I hope, involve us in their experience. That is what I am searching for in theater."[78] The odes mimed critical moments, such as the sacrifice of Iphigeneia, which left the gagged princess stripped of her clothing while her agonized mother watched her being impaled, high in the air, on a sword. (Graham's *Clytemnestra* had represented this scene in a similar fashion.)

Nevertheless, the mix of Greek and English in the choruses, supported by powerful African, Persian, and Arabic storytelling music and vivid movement, often proved, to the frustration of many critics, incomprehensible.[79] On the visual side, the use of Aeschylean net imagery, starting from a central pit covered with steel mesh and moving on to the representation of Agamemnon's murder in the bath among other scenes, became overly literal, despite its importance in the original play. Integrating the spoken scenes with the choral movement apparently worked better in the less experimental and shorter Delacorte Theater version, which simplified the set and no longer doubled the parts of Clytemnestra and Cassandra (a brilliant Priscilla Smith), and Agamemnon and Aegisthus (Jamil Zakkai), or placed part of the audience in bleachers on stage to break down the stage's traditional fourth wall.[80]

In his mixed review, the classical scholar Bernard Knox, among others, praised *Agamemon* for its pathbreaking attempt to perform the choral odes. It "puts to shame most previous efforts in this line; after this production, there should be no excuse for posturings in the style of Isadora Duncan and pale imitations of plainsong or—the usual alternatives to these genteelisms—aboriginal howlings and primeval jigs."[81] Nevertheless, this ambitious and provocative *Agamemnon* provoked no later imitations. By contrast, *Fragments* had won almost universal acclaim for its ability to generate "tragic" emotions in the audience, its focus on broad communal issues, its high level of energy, and its intensely rehearsed and integrated performances.[82] Performances based on Greek myth by the Great Jones Repertory Company at La MaMa, E.T.C., generally directed by Ellen Stewart with music by Elizabeth Swados, Genji Ito, and Michael Sirotta, and including spectacular use of puppets, masks, and brilliant costumes, continued at least until 2004 the tradition of *Fragments* but tended to evolve as loosely shaped epics or pageants rather than tragedies. These descendants of the Serban/Swados productions no longer attempted to engage with the language and texts of the original plays. Individual scenes based on Greek tragedy can capture confrontations such as those between the seven Theban defenders and seven attackers from the Argive army represented in Aeschylus's *Seven against Thebes*. In the original dialogue between a messenger and King Eteocles, the king posts a Theban patriot at each of the city's seven gates, only to find himself slated to meet his brother at the final one. The Great Jones's version staged each confrontation between the seven pairs of warriors through varied movement and spectacular images. The 2004 performance, for example, included yet another revival of *Fragments* along with *Mythos Oedipus, Seven against Thebes, Dionysus Filius Dei,* and a premiere of *Antigone*.

## 2. AMERICAN *GESAMTKUNSTWERKE*
### Harry Partch's Oedipus *and* Revelation in the Courthouse Park

> The germ of theatre had its beginnings in prehistoric festivals and rituals. And if festivals among comparatively primitive people of the present day show anything, they show that no artifice or talent or formalized device or abstraction of some facet of life is excluded that contributes to the power of the performance. At present and in general, we see nothing like this. If we go to the ballet, we get ballet—and music incidentally. But we do not go to the ballet with any idea of concentrating on the music. If we go to the opera, we do go with this idea—and incidentally we are likely

to get a spectacle. In all probability, we do not get drama. If we go to see a play, ninety-nine times out of a hundred we get just that—a play.

This specialized trend toward a specialized product involving specialized talents is, in my opinion, a form of unconscious starvation. The theater is starved for music and doesn't know it. The opera is starved for drama, even though drama is right in front of them. And ballet all too often is starved for both, not because both are not present, but because they must be subordinated to incidental roles.

We hear people say that the important thing is the dance, or the important thing is the music, or the important thing is the play. In the kind of art I am talking about, they are all important at once.[83]

In this excerpt from the introduction to a radio broadcast of his version of Sophocles' *Oedipus* on station KPFA in California in 1954, the experimental West Coast composer Harry Partch asserted his interest both in recreating the spirit of ancient Greek drama, which combined words, music, and dance, and in following in the wake of Richard Wagner, whose aesthetic writings urged the creation of "total artworks" (*Gesamtkunstwerke*), even if, in Partch's opinion, Wagner's orchestration repeatedly failed to give "drama" a fighting chance.[84] The eccentric and relatively isolated Partch (his unusual biography includes several years as a hobo during the Depression, occasional grants, and temporary university positions) was very likely unaware of earlier twentieth-century performances of Greek tragedy by Anglin and others discussed in chapter 1, which also aimed to unite in a different fashion text, music, and dance, or of the efforts of Tamiris discussed in this chapter; nor was ballet by then the only major concert dance form.[85] Nevertheless, his experiments with performing Greek tragedy in the spirit of the originals, if not in direct imitation of them, represent both an important and unique approach to recapturing the Greek integration of the arts and an experiment in composing music using his own version of ancient and global (East Asian and some African in addition to Greek) musical modes.[86]

In practice, this meant creating a form of ritualized theater and what Partch called "corporeal" music. "I use the word *ritual,* and I also use the word *corporeal,* to describe music that is neither on the concert stage nor relegated to a pit. In ritual the musicians are *seen;* their meaningful movements are part of the act, and the collaboration is automatic with everything else that goes on."[87] (As Partch knew, the Greek *aulos* or double-pipe player also appeared on stage with the chorus in Greek tragedy.) Partch rejected the canonical Western twelve-note equal temperament scale and developed his own Greek-inspired scale or tuning system with up to forty-three microtones or gradations per octave controlled by a ratio of integers ("Just Intonation") in order to follow more effectively the contours of a comprehensible speaking voice.[88] He built twenty-seven visually exquisite instruments—strings such as kitharas and adapted violas and guitars, chromolodeons (reed pump organs), and percussion, including various marimbas, cloud chamber bowls, and gongs—of hardwoods and other found materials to be played on stage during his dance-dramas (the movement of actors and musicians could replace choreography).

During a 1934 visit to England, Partch met with Kathleen Schlesinger, with whom he discussed theories about Greek music as well as examining her replicated kithara, and approached William Butler Yeats with the idea of giving a musical setting to his version of Sophocles' *Oedipus Tyrannus*. Yeats apparently agreed to the proposal, but Partch was unable to fund the project until 1952, when, with the support of the noted designer Arch Lauterer, he presented his first version of the play at Mills College in California. Revised versions of both text (with the help of a Hellenist) and music followed in 1952–54 and 1967, because of the refusal of Yeats's executors to permit Partch's recording to be released.[89] Partch's *Oedipus* was performed in a fashion closely imitative of Yeats's intoning of his own poetry, which aimed to preserve the "natural" inflections of speech. As Yeats put it to Partch, "No word shall have an intonation or accentuation it could not have in passionate speech."[90] Partch's score for the play attempted to enhance the stature and power (or to achieve "emotional saturation, or transcendence")[91] of the drama by accompanying some of the play's intoned text. "In these settings the inflected words are little or no different from ordinary speech, except as emotional tensions make them different. Assertive words and assertive music do not collide. Tone of spoken word and tone of instrument are intended to combine in a compact emotional or dramatic expression, each providing its singular ingredient."[92]

In *Oedipus*, this meant a strict adherence to monophonic (single-voice) renderings even of the choral sections of the play,[93] although the single male chorus leader was accompanied by a female chorus singing nonsense vocal sounds that were intended to convey emotion and magical power ("extraverbal magic").[94] The musical setting developed increasing and ominous force in the play's extended recognition scenes, and the exit featured dance and pantomime as well as music.[95] As Alex Ross described the play's arresting conclusion in a *New Yorker* review (April 18, 2005, 201) of a 2005 production at New Jersey's Montclair State College,

> The screws begin to turn. The chorus of women sings winding laments that devolve into wordless cries; the cello unfolds garments of another long, dark song; the Marimba Eroica emits its mind-bending basement tones; tribalistic dances and sonic rave-ups take over, and, amid the fog of microtones, pure Pythagorean consonances appear like ghosts. The climax is Oedipus' interrogation of the Herdsman, during which he discovers the awful truth. The simplicity of Partch's method—sending words into the listener's brain along all musical channels—creates hair-raising tension, an aria of the uncanny.

Despite a fairly positive reception by some critics, Partch concluded: "The drama of Oedipus, however compelling, was deposited by the mind in an ancient category called *classical*—that it was not brought home to the audience as a here-and-now work."[96] "I have seen many performances of Greek lyric tragedy," he remarked further, "and I have always felt that the audiences could *admire*, in a distant sort of way, but *never*, absolutely *never*, relate. Well this time, in contemplating the *Bacchae* of Euripides, this time—by golly—I decided that the audience *will* relate."[97] Partch's second version of Greek tragedy, the 1961 *Revelation in the Courthouse Park*, first performed at University of Illinois, Urbana-Champaign, interwove translated scenes from Euripides' *Bacchae* (represented with heightened speech) with a parallel contemporary American setting. Partch's cut version of the original was performed in masks and ponchos, long for women, short for men; masks descended from the ceiling when characters shifted to their Greek roles (fig. 14).[98]

Euripides' play represents the entrance of the god of wine and theater, Dionysus, for whom *Bacchae* was first performed, into Thebes, the city where the god was born. His young mortal cousin, King Pentheus, and his mother, Agave, and her sisters refuse to recognize Dionysus's heritage and divinity. The beautiful, androgynous Dionysus maddens the Theban women and sends them to the mountain; in disguise as a mortal he then attempts to demonstrate his unusual divinity through the dance and song of his foreign female followers, the advice of the wise seer Tiresias and Pentheus's grandfather Cadmus, and miracles reported by a messenger. When he fails, Dionysus tempts Pentheus into spying on the Theban women on the mountain, maddens him, dresses him as a woman, and escorts him to the mountain, where Agave and the other Theban women rip him apart. The mad Agave returns with Pentheus's head, regains sanity, and recognizes her deed. She and Cadmus lament the remains of Pentheus and depart for exile.

The contemporary American section of *Revelation* involved the parallel reception of a 1950s-style rock star/charismatic preacher, probably inspired by Elvis and figures like Billy Graham, named Dion ("a symbol of dominant mediocrity")[99] in the courthouse park of a midwestern town replete with a brass marching band, drum majorettes, clog dancers, elaborately rehearsed tumblers and gymnasts, and dancing highlighted by pelvic thrusts. The play's modern Pentheus, the shy, alienated nonconformist and voyeur Sonny, observes the ecstatic reception of Dion especially by his mom ("a symbol of blind matriarchal power")[100] and the town's young women. That evening, drifting among courting couples, the disoriented Sonny eerily imagines his end in a dream as a return in his mother's arms/harms (341). Partch notes that he chose to enact the rituals and foretell Pentheus's doom more explicitly than in *Bacchae*.[101] With the double vision of Euripides' maddened Pentheus, Sonny envisages his mother's breasts as "two moons" (342). Then, following fireworks and a frenetic communal dance, he observes his mother's departure to make love with Dion; in a second dream sequence his mother watches as he ends up being attacked. The piece closes with the Euripidean Agave's realization

FIGURE 14. Scene 3 (Herdsman Scene): Pentheus is tricked into transvestism in Harry Partch's *Revelation in the Courthouse Park,* University of Illinois, Urbana-Champaign, April 11, 1961. Photo by Gary Goodman from *Enclosure Three: Harry Partch* by Philip Blackburn (American Composers Forum/Innova). Courtesy of the Harry Partch Archive and Philip Blackburn.

that she holds in her hand the head of her son Pentheus. She drops both her own and Pentheus's masks and turns downstage to exit to a "crash of percussion" and a musical "Coda," which includes a fading image of Dion. In contrast to the original plays, in both *Oedipus* and *Revelation* Partch pointedly preferred to terminate the action with the final horrific recognition.[102]

Partch's *Revelation* also launched a critique of contemporary America. His Pentheus lacks the tyrannical side of Euripides' young king; Sonny is an innocent observer sacrificed to social conformity.[103] Several critics make the case that Partch identified with Sonny, whom Partch called "a lost soul, one who does not or cannot conform to the world he was born to."[104] The Freudian elements of the American story—the castrating and dominating mother—and its satire of Christianity (Partch's parents had been Christian missionaries in China) were probably biographical as well.[105] The play's choruses in part satirize American evangelical revival meetings, and, since Partch clearly interpreted the *Bacchae* as an attack on the androgynous god and his uncontrolled religious followers, his version of Euripides' choruses, which Partch called "Hymns to Dionysus," trivialize the god's followers.[106] The first American chorus parodies rock concert ritual and what Partch called the "comic book" music of contemporary life,[107] and contains fragments of short phrases expressing mindless optimism and enthusiasm—"right or wrong," "Heavenly Daze (Days) for a million years," "forever ever more," "deep inside, way down I am" (327)—that Partch had heard in daily life. Each "Hymn to Dionysus" captures elements of the Euripidean choruses that link ancient and modern religion. The *Bacchae*'s *parodos* (entrance song), which introduces the god and his myth to Thebes, evolves as short phrases such as "to the mountains" or "holy joy and get ruhligion" (336); Euripides' first *stasimon* (choral ode), praising Dionysus's democratic beneficence, becomes "what the majority believes and does"; Dionysus's birth from the thigh of his father, the god Zeus, is celebrated as "glory to the male womb" (348); the choral desire for escape from Pentheus is celebrated as "Oh, to be free where no man is" (363); and the choral anticipation of Pentheus's punishment begins: "Hell hounds of madness . . . Justice draw close" (370).

The 1987 exquisitely performed revival of the play by the American Music Theater Festival in Philadelphia, conducted by Partch's disciple Danlee Mitchell with the assistance of Alfred Blatter, and directed by Jiri Zizka (on tape at the New York Public Library for the Performing Arts at Lincoln Center), certainly succeeded far more than *Oedipus* as an example of the total theater at which Partch aimed, with music, dance, masks, intoned speech, filmed images of fireworks, and taped as well as live music.

### Will Power's Seven

*The Seven*, a new, hip-hop version of Aeschylus's *Seven against Thebes* by Will Power, was presented January 18–March 12, 2006, at the New York Theatre Workshop, where it was directed by Jo Bonney. The play, originally commissioned in 2001 by Tony Kelly of Thick Description in San Francisco for a run at the 2002 Hip-Hop Theater Festival, became in its New York revised version a vehicle for an extraordinary multicultural cast who could rhyme in character, handle fragments of Aeschylus's original, sing, and dance.[108] Both the acrobatic, street-inspired choreography by the well-known Bill T. Jones of the Bill T. Jones/Arnie Zane Dance Company and the music, a mix of calypso, doo-wop, R & B, funk, jazz, and blues, by Will Power and Will Hammond and produced by Justin Ellington—the one person the group could find who could handle hip-hop for theater—was developed to enhance and serve the production's modern poetic language.[109] As Power, a pioneer in hip-hop theater whose previous *FLOW* was a hit in the same venue, remarked, "Hip-hop [like Greek tragedy] is thick with language."[110] In this sense, Power's *Seven* replicates Partch's agenda, where *choreia* serves song/words in a new fashion; moreover, since hip-hop theater is currently in the early stages of its possible development, the production became as well a generic theatrical experiment in bringing together music, movement and text from similar traditions that had not as yet taken this kind of theatrical form.[111]

Power's *Seven* offers in the first act a version of Aeschylus's missing *Oedipus*, the original second play in a trilogy that concluded with *Seven against Thebes* and began with *Laius*, a play focusing on the father who originally exposed the infant Oedipus and was later killed by his son when he blocked his passage at a crossroads. This encounter at the crossroads between Oedipus and Laius retains a cameo role in *The Seven*.[112] Oedipus, who cursed his sons, the brothers Eteocles and Polynices, for mistreating him, eventually undermines their attempt to foil the paternal curse by sharing the rule of Thebes in alternate years. Eteocles, who rules first, becomes too taken with power ("Man this king thing is hard./My brother doesn't really want this job!" [50]) His Right Hand is a sleazy white politician who fosters his master's ill-disguised evolution toward exploitation of his citizens. The peaceable Polynices, at first nearly adjusted to his withdrawal into nature, yoga, and meditation with a devoted male companion, Tydeus, becomes outraged at his brother's dishonesty and injustice ("I am big like an Amazon/dot com/But I won't buy shit if I'm being conned" [15]). Failing to maintain faith in themselves or each other, the two succumb to a modern version of fate (fig. 15).

Act 2 moves closer to Aeschylus's plot, which set up a confrontation between seven champions who attacked Thebes and seven who defended it, including the brothers, who kill each other and are mourned at the play's conclusion. In *The Seven*, Polynices' Argive army is introduced on stage rather than described in a messenger speech, and Eteocles' reluctant supporters are Thebes' citizens in general rather than a group of individual patriotic warriors. The coed chorus shifts from one role to another. Among the Seven, Capaneus is a West Coast gangsta, Eteoclus a horse breeder who "protects" his neighborhood, the female Parthenopaeus specializes in martial arts, the huge Hippomedon has apparently just left prison, and the talker Amphiarus is a peace lover who will fight "'til my very last breath." On their side, the Thebans capture the fear of war and resistance to the fraternal duel expressed by Aeschylus's chorus but finally successfully defend their city en masse.

Overall, the play evolves from a semisatirical, often humorous analysis of family dynamics and contemporary culture/politics to the tragic battle between brothers and their death. Power exploited the parallels between the myth, with its three generations of accursed males, and the gang-infested African American culture of the Bay Area (the working-class Fillmore district of San Francisco) in which he grew up during the 1980s and 1990s, where so many young people repeated the mistakes of their fore-parents, and semi-Homeric myths of larger-than-life neighborhood bullies and gang leaders abounded in oral street culture.[113] Oedipus is a

FIGURE 15. Polynices (Jamyl Dobson) and Eteocles (Benton Greene) face off in Will Power's *Seven*, a new version of Aeschylus's *Seven against Thebes,* New York Theatre Workshop, New York, 2005–6. Photo by Carol Rosegg.

bejeweled, velvet-suited pimp or "Original Gangsta" (15), both tyrant and abusive father, who deliberately destroys his sons' will to change. Often accompanied by the doo-wopping Funky Fates, he narrates his fatal encounter with Laius by playing both parts, with Laius as a "1930's blues man from the Mississippi Delta" (18). Yet, as Eteocles remarks in a final moment of realization, "And my Daddy starts to look small/His curse just a piece of it all" (62).

Hip-hop itself evolved as a ritualized attempt to mediate street violence with language and stories,[114] and the play offers a pessimistic answer to the question, Can we outgrow violence? Break dancing, which makes an appearance in the choreography, has also served to translate competition into another mode. Ironically, in this production both forms become part of the final confrontation between the brothers that they were originally designed to prevent/circumvent. Overall, *The Seven*'s script "flipped" or remixed the myth in hip-hop style, creating something new by fusing it with the old. The play opens and closes with a DJ who makes this process of flipping transparent.[115] She gives the audience fragments of a recording of Philip Vellacott's 1961 Penguin translation of Aeschylus—"O house of endless tears . . . It is the curse of your father, that bears fruit in you/And the harvest is no blessing"—before opening a dialogue with Power's own version:

Now let me tell ya who I be
The one who make Shakespeare jam with James Brown
Put Snoopy and Snoop in the same dog pound.
I can transform a scratch
Into more than an itch
There are no two worlds
That I can't mix
I am
The DJ
And every record that exists
I play
I picked this one up yesterday, check it out. (2–3)

The following dialogue between Eteocles and Polynices on their resistance to the curse offers an example of this mixing: "E: Until Atlantis sinks to the sea/P: Until my tendon right here, is called Achilles-yo/E: Until the Drachma turns to dough/P: Until Homer is a dad on a cartoon show/E: Until a Trojan rides rolled up next to my nuts? P: Until they do a new dance, and call it the King Tut/E and P: Well, until that time/it will always be" (11–12).

Despite a largely positive response to the production's high-energy experiment, some critics felt that *The Seven* lacked dramatic momentum until the tighter, more active, and "tragic" second half.[116] Others criticized the play's generic shifts in tone.[117] Some thought the music less notable and original than text and choreography. Nevertheless, as with Partch, *The Seven*'s experiment in using music and choreography to support the new version's language may prove influential in future experiments.

### 3. MUSICAL THEATER

Most musical theater in the United States also aims, whether self-consciously or not, at being a form of total theater, although one very different from and at times alien to Greek tragedy. Part 3 will examine a brief selection of U.S. attempts to represent Greek tragedy through forms adapted from musical theater. (*Marie Christine,* Michael John LaChiusa's near-operatic musical version of *Medea,* will be discussed in chapter 5.3); there have also been gospel, bluegrass, and rock versions, including some with multimedia dimensions. These musical forms in themselves invite a dialogue between American culture, where local versions of these modes are popular and pervasive, and Greek tragedy. After briefly contrasting the much-discussed *The Gospel at Colonus* with the little-known *Hillbilly Antigone,* both of which raise important questions about the compatibility of Christian musical traditions and Greek tragedy, I will focus on one of several ambitious rock versions, *The Rockae,* a close adaptation of Euripides' *Bacchae.*

### The Gospel at Colonus: *Sophocles' Oedipus at Colonus as Gospel Musical*

Lee Breuer and Bob Telson's *The Gospel at Colonus* reimagines Sophocles' *Oedipus at Colonus* (*OC*) as a sermon on confronting fate and death from "The Book of Oedipus" performed in a black Pentecostal church. Initially performed at the Brooklyn Academy of Music in 1983, it was presented on public television in its Great Performances series in 1985, revived at the Broadway Lunt-Fontanne Theatre in 1988, and yet again at Harlem's Apollo Theater in 2004; it traveled to various venues in the United States and is still regularly performed by amateur groups. The play has provoked so much critical attention and controversy for its cultural politics—in particular, the attempt to integrate pagan tragedy and Christian Pentecostal service—that any detailed discussion is impossible here.[118] Certainly Sophocles' episodic play, with its unique, royal, irascible, unforgiving blind hero, cursed by the gods from birth and imperiously forcing his polluted Theban body on a sacred Athenian grove of the Furies only to be received as a still potentially wrathful, firmly local, protective civic hero, sits uneasily with *The Gospel*'s concluding cathartic Christian resurrection of a categorically downtrodden collective Oedipus replete with connotations of grace, shared ecstasy, the passion of Christ, and the love of God. Sophocles' *OC* also responds, if obliquely, to contemporary Greek democratic and interpolis politics;[119] by contrast, *The Gospel*'s white authors used the black Pentecostal setting to meditate on the painful internal exile of blacks in American culture and to perform a utopian cultural integration.[120]

Regardless of the controversies provoked by the amalgamation of the *OC* and *The Gospel* (an issue that Breuer himself addressed through the use of metatheater), I want here to remark briefly on the one aspect of *The Gospel* that united critics and viewers: the ability of its remarkable, and relatively apolitical, music and performance to engage and move its audience even as they experience its possible, and perhaps deliberately visible, contradictions.[121] As Breuer put it, "As was the classic Greek performance, the Pentecostal service is a communal catharsis which forges religious, cultural, and political bonds. Should not the living experience teach us something of the historical one?"[122]

More important for chapter 2, *The Gospel at Colonus* is the only adaptation of Greek tragedy known to me that attempted to make the choral engagement in the story grow logically out of a contemporary ritual setting. It deploys a reimagined version of the full mixture of speech, act-dividing song, and shared lyrics between actor and chorus contained in the original. Richard Burton's book on Sophoclean choruses pronounced Sophocles' *Oedipus at Colonus* itself to be the oratorio it in essence became in *The Gospel*.[123] Sophocles' original also included an exceptional degree of choral engagement apparently typical of some of his later plays.[124] The chorus of *Oedipus at Colonus* not only sings four choral odes and five lyric dialogues with actors but engages in rapid stichomythia (dialogue) and initiates and repeatedly tries to participate in the action. Structurally speaking, then, both *OC*'s rapid and fluid movement from event to event and song to song and the gradual transformation of the suffering Oedipus to heroic status made it more adaptable to the Christian context of *The Gospel* in terms of both form and content than other Greek tragedies.

*The Gospel*'s roles were performed by multiple characters, some singers or groups of singers and some speakers, thus creating communal protagonists who ultimately face mortality collectively through Oedipus's story. For example, Oedipus was played by both a gospel group, Clarence Fountain and the Five Blind Boys of Alabama, and the actor Morgan Freeman, who also served as preacher. Actress Isabell Monk spoke as Antigone, but both her role and Ismene's were also sung by members of the J. D. Steele singers. The choral role itself was divided between a large seated African American gospel choir (Brooklyn's Institutional Radio Choir accompanied by Telson's band) that served as the congregation and responded throughout, and a smaller choral group (J. J. Farley and the Original Soul Stirrers) that represented it in direct engagement with the actors and used a mixture of solo and group song. As Barbara Goff and Michael Simpson observed, "The multiplicity of voices, then, in *Gospel*, can be understood as a figure for the social dimension of language and of identity, and the formal qualities of the play thus work towards the same issues of community and integration as are tackled by the drama as a whole."[125] Breuer's adaptation deliberately exploited theatrical elements of the African American religious tradition: elements of Pentecostal church services such as chanted sermons, call-and-response with repetitions, testifying, improvisation, clapping, stomping, shouting, active engagement of the congregation in the service, and the participation of a range of music and musical groups throughout. Historically speaking, African American music, already a cultural amalgam, has found its way in multiple forms into the American musical mainstream even while its creators remain excluded from full participation in the society. The black church's music and rhythmic rhetoric have served as a source of unity and solace for its members, and as a site for creation of new forms of theater and performance, including the gospel musical.[126] As Kevin Wetmore puts it, "It is the theatricality of the church that is used to re-historicize the theatricality of Sophocles' text."[127] The church's white piano thus appropriately serves in *The Gospel* as Oedipus's sanctuary and descends and rises with his death and resurrection. In reconfiguring Oedipus as a representative of African American culture, Breuer aimed at a modern form of tragic catharsis. Yet Telson's and the performers' music in many respects achieved what the text's new version itself, in the view of its detractors, could not.[128]

## Hillbilly Antigone

*Hillbilly Antigone,* a story created by Rick Sims and Heidi Stillman, with book, music, and lyrics by Sims and directed by Stillman, was performed by Chicago's Lookingglass Theatre Company in May–July 2005. The play set Antigone's story in a fictional Hatfield versus McCoy–style feud- and incest-ridden 1920s Appalachian community located on Badd Mountain, "where both sides are wrong and both sides are right" ("The Feudin' Song" and "The Battle of Badd Mountain"). The gun-toting Antigone Flick, already involved in a Romeo and Juliet–style forbidden romance with Harmon [Haemon] Waller, defied corrupt judge and Pentecostal preacher Creon Waller to bury her half-mad brother Amos [Polyneices], whom Creon had strung up as a sinner, partly because he worked for the invasive new railroad. Antigone's blind grandmother, a Holy Roller who spoke in tongues, played the role of Sophocles' Tiresias. Creon tested Antigone's piety with a snake that bit her ("The Ballad of a Snake Bitten Bride"). The play nevertheless inverted Sophocles' conclusion; the (perhaps overly) villainous Creon died, while the righteous Antigone survived.

As in the case of *The Gospel at Colonus,* reviewers criticized the script for allowing Christian spirituality to betray the original's focus on complex public rather than pointedly domestic issues.[129] In one view, the play was "more concerned with personal [religious] demons than head-to-head conflict and tragic inevitability."[130] Antigone's decision to do "what I had to do" ("I Buried My Brother") received relatively little attention, and Creon offered no serious justification for his acts. One song, "God's Plan," expressed the play's central dilemma as follows: "Do you know the will of god?/ Did you take the path of salvation?/ Did you take the fate of your soul in your hands?/Are you sure you've done right when you go to sleep at night and you're walking hand in hand with God's plan? . . . Pray before you act, make sure it's not the devil talking back!"

Again as with *The Gospel,* the songs, inspired above all by the Carter family, met with a positive reception in their own right, as did some of the acting, the vivid country costumes, and a corrugated metal shadow box set surrounded by painted scenes in the style of carnival banners. Music played on acoustic guitar, steel resonator guitar, and autoharp reportedly offered in part a musical homage to the Coen brothers' film *O Brother, Where Art Thou?* Yet the conclusion ultimately reduced Sophocles' play to an unambiguous battle between good and evil that is standard in melodrama.

## The Rockae

Prospect Theater Company's *Rockae,* a rock-opera version of Euripides' *Bacchae,* with music and lyrics by Peter Mills, choreography by Marlo Hunter, and directed by coauthor Cara Reichel, was performed to strong reviews at the Hudson Guild Theatre, New York, September 14–October 14, 2007.[131] King Pentheus, dressed in leather, denim, and a codpiece, confronted a scantily clad '70s metal-rock god, Dionysus, with low hip-hugging black pants, leather straps across his bare chest, and a curly blond wig. The other characters were dressed largely in black, chartreuse, and purple and embellished with decadent nets, fringes, boots, chains, piercings, capes, and corsets. An on-stage band perched on a raised platform that was also used to represent the prison in Pentheus's palace where Dionysus's maenadic followers were temporarily chained, as well as Mt. Cithaeron, where the Theban women maddened by Dionysus were located; the 1980s-style dancing included frenzied jumps, kicks, and slides and often pitted male and female characters against each other. On the musical side, the hard-rock mode shifted at times into folk, funk, and metal. All of this, however well performed and directed, may sound predictable. Defining Dionysus as an androgynous rock star (e.g., Dion in Partch's *Revelation*) is hardly new. What put this performance in a different category was the way that the book and lyrics attempted to capture complex aspects of Euripides' play in a modern version.

As summarized above, Euripides' play represents the entrance of the god of wine (and theater), Dionysus, into his birthplace, Thebes, and leaves his mortal victims shocked at the god's violent punishment of those who rejected him. Dionysus is a hard divinity to comprehend rationally for those both inside and outside the play. The performance of the play must capture the elusive nature of his divinity through music and dance that represents the god's ability to cross boundaries, including those between Greek and foreigner, male and female, old and young, and the beneficent and horrific, and move its audience as well as the actors temporarily into another environment.[132]

*The Rockae*'s script followed Euripides' original quite closely, though it gave names to its three main (African American) maenadic followers of Dionysus—Aeolia, Lydia, and Phrygia—and had them actively madden Thebes' women on stage with a rousing song, "Run to the Mountain," that adapted the *Bacchae*'s *parodos* (opening lyric). This group also substituted for the persuasive blind seer Tiresias in his scene with Cadmus and Pentheus, thus making Dionysus's power to excite his followers actively present on stage from the play's opening moment. Although many sections of *The Rockae* were spoken in prose, Dionysus's prologue and the two messenger speeches (spoken in iambic trimeter in the original) were sung as lyrics that vividly captured the eerie entry of the divine into a secular world. The prologue, which introduced the god and his personal story (the death of his mother Semele, his birth from the thigh of his father, the god Zeus), began as a verse solo, "A God Walks the Earth," that was then joined at its conclusion by the god's three maenads:

> DIONYSUS:
> MOTHER,
> I'VE MADE THE VINES OF IVY
> GROW THICK UPON YOUR GRAVE.
> I STILL REMEMBER
> THE INJUSTICE THAT WAS DONE YOU,
> AND MOURN THE LIFE YOU GAVE.
> ......
>
> DIONYSUS & PHR/AEO/LYD:
> A GOD WALKS THE EARTH,
> STILL HIDDEN FROM MORTAL EYES.
> A GOD WALKS THE EARTH—
> THIS FLESH AND BLOOD A MERE DISGUISE.

The first messenger speech, "Cowherd's Song," was sung to guitar with a slight country flavor but included a choral hymn slowly emerging behind the cowherd's description of the miraculous doings of the Theban maenads on the mountain. A brief dissonant musical interlude suggested the chaotic violence produced when the previously peaceful women were interrupted by herdsmen. The final messenger speech, "Soldier's Song," began with a light drum accompaniment to its description of the early stages of Pentheus's mission in disguise as a woman to spy on the Theban maenads. Euripides' original gives the whole speech to the messenger. Here, as the soldier companion of Pentheus sang, Dionysus and Pentheus interrupted with a dreamy exchange, then duet, in high tenors that suggested a mother/child as well as a more broadly androgynous relation. The passage drew on the mad Pentheus's earlier desire to return home in his mother's arms from the previous Euripidean scene:

> DIONYSUS:
> OH, MY FOOLISH CHILD,
> YOU'LL SEE WHAT YOU WERE MEANT TO SEE
> I WILL CARRY YOU
> HIGH ATOP THE WORLD.
> YOU'LL BE WHERE YOU'RE CONTENT TO BE
> I WILL CARRY YOU THERE.
>
> SOLDIER:
> AND THE SOFT-SPOKEN STRANGER
> TOOK AHOLD OF A PINE TREE'S TOP,
> AND HE EASILY BENT IT,
> BROUGHT IT DOWN TO THE GROUND.
> THEN MY FOOLHARDY MASTER
> SAT ASTRIDE OF THE HIGHEST BOUGH,
> AS THE STRANGER SO GENTLY LET THEM LIFT HIM HIGH

INTO THE SKY.

PENTHEUS:
OH, AT LAST I SEE THE THINGS THAT I WAS MEANT TO SEE

DIONYSUS:
NOW YOU BEGIN TO SEE, MY BEAUTIFUL CHILD . . .

PENTHEUS & DIONYSUS:
YOU (I) HAVE CARRIED ME (YOU)
HIGH ATOP THE WORLD.
I'M (YOU'RE) RIGHT WHERE I WAS (YOU WERE) MEANT TO BE.
YOU (I) HAVE CARRIED ME (YOU) THERE.

MAENADS:
THE DAWN WILL COME AND WE WILL SEE THE WORLD
THROUGH NEW EYES.
THE GLORY OF THE GOD WILL BE UNFURLED
THE SUN WILL RISE.

PENTHEUS:
NOW THE WHOLE WORLD SEEMS TO HOLD ME . . .

DIONYSUS:
NOW ALL OF THE WORLD IS HOLDING YOU . . .

PENTHEUS:
LIKE A MOTHER'S LOVING ARMS.

DIONYSUS:
LIKE A LOVING EMBRACE FROM A MOTHER.

PENTHEUS & DIONYSUS:
AND AS LONG AS I (YOU) REMAIN HERE,
ON THIS HIGH AND HOLY PLANE HERE.
YOU (I) WILL KEEP ME (YOU) SAFE FROM HARM.

Dionysus then summoned his maenads with a powerful male voice, the messenger described Pentheus's musically underlined fall, and Pentheus's eerie childlike voice addressed the mother about to kill him. Here the script refused Pentheus the final futile recognition of his errors found in Euripides:

PENTHEUS:
MOTHER, IT'S YOUR SON.
I KNOW YOU RECOGNIZE THIS FACE YOU SEE,
YOU, WHO CARRIED ME . . .
MOTHER, I WAS SCARED
BUT NOW I'M IN THE SAFEST PLACE TO BE.
YOU WILL CARRY ME HOME.

SOLDIER:
AND AGAVE APPEARED TO UNDERSTAND,
AS SHE TENDERLY TOOK HIM BY THE HAND
AND . . .
LIMB BY LIMB,
SHE STARTED TO RIP HER SON TO PIECES . . .

Earlier songs in different musical styles also served to develop Dionysus's rites as both alluring and alien. The chorus's song "Abandon" had an Eastern flavor (dropped in the rest of the play, which did not establish any clear cultural identity for the chorus); the sultry "Poison in the Veins," sung by Dionysus, the chorus, and a fantasizing Pentheus described Pentheus's gradual and terrifying surrender to Dionysus; "Let the Bedrock Rock" turned Dionysus's hard-rock destruction of Pentheus's palace into a cataclysm that shook the world to its roots; "Wild Game," sung by Agave, her sisters, and the chorus turned the whole group into ecstatic hunters (fig. 16). The final scene included a heartbreaking reconstructed lamentation ("Lament") by Agave and her sisters over the bodily fragments of King Pentheus (largely concealed in a blood-smeared body bag) that has been lost from the manuscript of Euripides' original. Although some critics objected to this shocking transition (a problem arguably inherent in the original text), the earlier songs did anticipate the frightening side of the cult, and this lyrical response to Pentheus's death maintained emotional tension better than a full drop into sanity. The play's final song, "Only Now," shared by Cadmus, Agave, and her sisters Ino and Autonoë, affirmed its uneasy (but never cheap and easy) representation of Dionysiac liberation. The concluding moral offered below was followed by a renewed invasion of Dionysiac music and song.

THERE IS NO MORAL TO THE STORY YOU'VE SEEN HERE,
THIS BLOODY QUARREL 'TWEEN A MAN AND A GOD.

AUTONOË:
THERE IS NO LESSON TO LEARN FROM THIS TURN OF THE TABLES.

INO:
THIS IS NOT AESOP'S FABLES!

CADMUS:
THERE IS NO MORSEL OF GOOD COUNSEL TO GLEAN HERE,
NO PEARL OF WISDOM YOU CAN GREET WITH A NOD.

INO:
NO COMFORT FOR STRIFE.

AUTONOË:
NO SOLACE FOR SORROW.

FIGURE 16. The chorus performs "Wild Women Attack!" in *The Rockae*, a version of Euripides' *Bacchae*, adapted and composed by Peter Mills, directed by Cara Reichel with choreography by Marlo Hunter, Hudson Guild Theatre, New York, 2007. Photo by Gerry Goodstein.

> AGAVE:
> NO PROMISE THAT LIFE WILL BE BETTER TOMORROW.
> NO!
>
> ALL FOUR:
> ONLY NOW, WHAT YOU'RE FEELING AT THIS MOMENT,
> TORN APART, NOT YOUR BODY BUT YOUR SOUL.
> ONLY NOW, RIPPED TO PIECES,
> DOES THE POWER THIS RELEASES
> MAKE YOU WHOLE SOMEHOW

Nearly all U.S. productions of the *Bacchae* have necessarily made serious attempts to represent the worship of Dionysus through extensive music (not necessarily rock) and dance. Other performances of Greek tragedy less obviously amenable to rock treatments have nevertheless produced new versions more loosely connected to the Greek originals, rather than trying like *The Rockae* to capture the ambiguities of the original in a more operatic but also legible mode.[133] One critic, John Beer (*Village Voice*, September 25, 2007), even argued that the vocal performance in *The Rockae* made good "on the premise that rock opera just might be the best way of conveying the intensity of Greek tragedy to a modern audience."

## 4. VISUAL CHOREOGRAPHY IN ROBERT WILSON'S *ALCESTIS*

Robert Wilson's highly choreographed production of Euripides' *Alcestis* challenged its audience to experience a different relation between the visual and oral aspects of tragedy. Greek tragedy itself was presented in an orchestra backed by a stage building with a narrow stage or stage area containing a single door; scenery was minimal; unchanging painted panels on the stage building were complemented at times by altars, statues, or tombs either on the stage or in the orchestra; the use of props was minimal. Wilson's *Alcestis* added a multilayered, imagistic visual script. This production at the American Repertory Theater in Cambridge, Massachusetts, in 1986 has been much and well discussed.[134] Here I would simply like to emphasize the different ways that Wilson's production opened questions about representing Greek tragedy on stage for a modern U.S. audience that often responds more strongly to visual aesthetics than to verbal ones. In contrast to the other efforts at total theater discussed in chapter 2, set, sound, props, movement, language, costumes, and makeup all speak deliberately different languages in Wilson's theater.[135] In the case of *Alcestis,* Wilson followed the major stages of the story of Alcestis's ironically disastrous attempt to save her husband, Admetus, from death by sacrificing her own life. Versions of the major Euripidean scenes included a confrontation between Death, who had come for Alcestis, and Apollo, god of light and supporter of Admetus for his generous hospitality; Alcestis's death scene followed by lamentation; the hero Heracles' inopportune arrival and his deception by Admetus; a confrontation with Admetus's aged father, who had refused to die for his son; Heracles' banquet during Alcestis's burial, his discovery of the truth, and his rescue and return of a silent Alcestis from death. Nevertheless, the production ultimately reinterpreted this script, leaving the audience with a much more uncertain and transhistorical perspective about its (in this case increasingly mysterious) themes of death and rebirth/renewal.

I begin with the setting, since this is where Wilson himself tends to start.[136] Alcestis's individual story expanded into a story of human culture by connecting past and present with vivid metaphors and images.[137] The stage, which Wilson viewed as a mask, was divided into horizontal bands.[138] At the back was a mountain range inspired by Delphi,[139] with an initially blue sky above; before it three cypress trees at stage left were planted in a strip of earth; at the center was a river, invisible but audible when actors walked through it; in front, a paved path. Domestic scenes in the family of Alcestis were played on or from a small platform stage left, and Heracles' banquet took place before the "shadow box" on stage right. On the mountain sat archaeological relics, such as Chinese terracotta funeral figures and the prow of a Viking ship. In the right foreground was a large Cycladic figure. Boulders marking a change in time gradually fell slowly down the mountain onto the stage. Visually speaking, the play evolved as a journey through time and space to a mysterious apocalyptic conclusion. The lighting brought the audience on a parallel journey from morning until dark.[140] In a visible historical shift the three cypress trees burned and became Corinthian columns, then industrial smokestacks that belched fire at the conclusion. A small city appeared on the mountain; death glided backward across the river; a green laser burned an "eye of god" into the mountain, and the sky turned bloodred as the stage darkened.

The script itself included a prologue written by the German playwright Heiner Müller that (coincidentally) revolved around the apparent murder and return of a now-dead woman in a landscape that included many of the play's central images (birds, mountains, trees) and was recited by a wrapped androgynous mummy-like figure suspended stage right.[141] Fragments of this script continued to appear throughout the main text. (Wilson already had his setting and images planned before receiving it.) The production concluded with a seventeenth-century anonymous Kyogen farce, *The Birdcatcher in Hell*, translated by Harvard student Mark Oshima with a score by Laurie Anderson, in which the birdcatcher, Kiyoyori, descends to and escapes death after the underworld god and his demons taste his wares. Euripides' *Alcestis* was originally presented in the slot of a satyr play during the theatrical festival at Athens' City Dionysia and contains a number of comic elements, especially in Heracles' banquet scene. Wilson shifted *Alcestis* into the blacker tragic category, though he did not eliminate humor, and created a new satyric ending with the Kyogen farce.

Wilson's *Alcestis* had eight scenes, each with a different style that disrupted dramatic continuity, including three choral scenes (two, four, and seven) that replaced Euripides' original odes and reflected a movement from life to death. In the first timeless chorus, women washed their hair in the river while peasant men planted rice. The second chorus sacrificed a goat and smeared themselves with blood, accompanied by a frenzied electronic score that ended in verbal cacophony. The third choral scene entailed a procession of formally lamenting women, again using the outstretched arms of the first choral scene, holding branches and accompanied by the clacking of sticks, gull sounds, and the wail of an ambulance.

The nonchoral scenes repeatedly juxtaposed the mythic/remote and the modern. At the opening a youthful Apollo confronted a white, winged, birdlike Death as the two repeatedly paced slowly back and forth. Simultaneously a man lay stage right with a woman in white hovering over him. Alcestis and Admetus in slip and pajamas enacted her death scene on a bed while a radio played in the background, thus bringing together motifs of sex and death;[142] Admetus angrily confronted his father, whose aged, ambiguous status was visualized through his half-naked body covered with a loincloth and stigmata and a transparent life-support system.[143] After the hilarious banquet scene, in which a waiter in tails and glasses slapped a table setting on a table, and Heracles, sporting a lion skin, told bad jokes ("I said to Achilles, for god's sake wear a boot"), several mysterious dead figures—a man with an Egyptian crocodile mask, a matron with hat and veil, a man in evening clothes with a glowing eye and a neon tube growing from his shoulder—remained at the banquet table after Heracles left for Hades.

In Euripides' play, Heracles brings a silent Alcestis back from death as a reward for Admetus's hospitality; in Wilson's version, Heracles returns with not one but three silent, shrouded female figures—Alcestises or Fates—who follow an apparently grieving Admetus and then sit on the darkening stage.[144] Indeed, by interpolating Müller's phrase "perhaps the daily murder of the perhaps daily resurrected woman" into Alcestis's explanation of her sacrifice to Admetus, the play had already ironically underlined Admetus's betrayal of Alcestis in Euripides' original (he had promised not to replace his wife).

Wilson's *Alcestis* contested the primacy of the word in Euripides' text, but not only by establishing a powerful visual language on stage. First, the relation between actors' words and often slow, ritualized movement was disrupted. Actors spoke the text on stage mixed with recordings.[145] Wilson did not like the "ping pong" of dialogue in Greek tragedy;[146] he turned dialogues into disembodied monologues stripped of psychological underpinnings.[147] He fragmented Dudley Fitts and Robert Fitzgerald's translation of *Alcestis,* adding interpolations from Müller or repetitions like the word "nothing," and diffused at times a sense of clear sequence or cause and effect, without in fact losing the general sense and progression of Euripides' text.[148] This was particularly the case in the scene between the dying Alcestis and Admetus, which followed the evolution of the scene from its dreamy opening confrontation with the ferryman of Hades, Charon, to Admetus's last desperate attempt to keep Alcestis among the living. Here the text reduces to a minimum some of the final moments of Euripides' scene between the dying Alcestis and Admetus:

>ALCESTIS:
>I am nothing
>nothing
>speak of me as nothing
>nothing
>me
>
>ADMETUS:
>if not for me
>look at your children
>bargain with the god
>for years for only one more year of youth

> for months, for weeks, for just
> a few more days
> oh not for days! For nights, for just a night
> for one more night, for just this one
> for this
> ...ahh...

By contrast, Alcestis's confrontation with Charon, ferryman of the dead, in Wilson's text comes quite close to the eerie original but enhances images, cuts unnecessary words and grammatical connectives, and blurs the boundaries between husband and wife:

> holding
> calling
> waiting
> I see the lake
> the dark lake
> a boat
> I see the boat on shore
> and Charon
> holding
> a double oar
> calling
> waiting
> why
> why are you waiting Alcestis
> come
> are you holding me back
> listen
> listen
> can you not hear
> him
> listen he is angry
> I hate this angry god and the voyage he is calling
> you for
> What a terrible thing this is for us both
> someone is touching me (laughs) touching touching
> there
> drawing me down to death's house
> it is death himself
> with great wings death
> frowning on me
> such strange journey
> and I am so afraid
> children goodbye you have...

no mother
no

Wilson created in *Alcestis* a total artwork that simultaneously refused to cohere by drawing the viewer's attention to its partly dissonant sights and sounds and its unwillingness to interpret the multiple layers of its conclusion. At the same time, the production aimed at a stunning visual and aural magnitude on a mythic scale that remains consonant with the play's serious if ambiguous treatment of mortality and sacrifice.

## CONCLUSION

Chapter 2 has tried to demonstrate that aesthetic developments in modern dance laid the groundwork, like the developments in stagecraft discussed in chapter 1, for efforts to restore to U.S. performances of Greek tragedy the full range of dimensions it had originally, although in a form more legible to modern audiences. In classical Greece, masked actors had primarily to use voice and gesture to communicate to their audiences. Modern choreography has exposed the body more fully than ancient tragic costume (deliberately) permitted, and has developed movement that expresses and intensifies emotion, if still aiming to retain a level of impersonality, collectivity, and at times, ritualization. Modern dance's interest in ritual and the body gave new energy to choral performance and other aural dimensions of the plays. Yet integrating the lyric and spoken elements of the Greek originals has continued to prove difficult. Music (with dance) that served speech, such as that of Partch, Power, Breuer and Telson (see also LaChiusa in chapter 5.3), and Mills and Reichel, aimed to make a heavily verbal and at times rhetorical theater more compelling to a modern audience. At the same time, drawing on American musical traditions such as gospel, folk, and rock can prove both contradictory and complementary to efforts to capture the religious and conceptual elements of Greek tragedy. Robert Wilson's *Alcestis* serves as a reminder that representation of tragic ideas through visual choreography—even in a sometimes illegible form—may well suit an age that favors communication through multiple kinds of images.

From an aesthetic perspective, American innovation in *choreia* has reflected a sensitivity to eclectic international influences while also responding to developments in dance and music more specific to the United States. From a thematic point of view, Partch, Power, Graham, and Mills and Reichel exploited a theme of self-division stressed in the introduction and in the discussion of *Oedipus* and *Medea* in chapters 4 and 5 in a fashion that can make psychological vulnerability peculiarly heroic. Many of these performances, including those focalizing through the psychology of individual characters in a way that appeals to a modern American audience, also emphasized an increasingly large range of social issues, while maintaining interest in questions relating to gender, race, and violence present from an early date. Over time, like many of the other productions discussed in other chapters of this book, a characteristic American resistance to tragic fatality has gradually given way to acceptance of darker views, such as those represented in Wilson's *Alcestis*, *The Seven*, and *The Rockae*, though they can be undercut or enhanced by humor. Economics perennially undermines ambitious efforts to perform Greek tragedy as total theater, but its intermittent flowering on the U.S. stage has produced a number of significant aesthetic experiments. In many respects the productions discussed in chapter 2, like those treated in chapter 1, represent some of the most innovative American contributions to the modern performance of Greek tragedy.

THREE

# Democratizing Greek Tragedy

*Why stage the declamatory Greeks . . . unless to disguise what one was thinking under a fascist regime?*
—JEAN PAUL SARTRE, *CARREFOUR*, SEPTEMBER 9, 1944

*The very notion of a work created for the expression of a social, political, economic, or moral content constitutes a lie. . . . Once there appears the concern to signify something (something external to art), literature begins to retreat, to disappear.*
—ALAIN ROBBE-GRILLET, "ON SEVERAL OBSOLETE NOTIONS"

Performed at large public festivals for the god Dionysus in Athens before an audience of Athenians (though possibly not women) and visitors from elsewhere, Greek tragedy used a repertoire of Panhellenic myth to create a dialogue between the world of its democratic audience and Greek cultural traditions.[1] Tragedies from Aeschylus to Euripides unquestionably respond to changing social and political realities in the Attic polis, even though from an early date the plays began to be performed in other Greek city-states around the Mediterranean and developed an international following. Yet the plays were rarely overtly topical and probably never deliberately subversive. Aeschylus's *Persians* (472 B.C.E.), which deals with the second Persian expedition against Greece in 480–479 B.C.E., does directly engage with historical reality, however, and his *Eumenides* of 458 B.C.E. also refers to recent changes in the Attic justice system and an alliance with Argos. Yet tragedies that reminded the Athenians of the political sorrows of either themselves or their allies provoked outrage (e.g., Phrynichus was fined for his 493 B.C.E. *Sack of Miletus*, in which the Persians sacked an Ionian colony of Athens). Outside of these early plays, it is challenging to pin down what kind of political statement is being made through tragedy.[2] Questions are easier to identify than answers.

U.S. democracy, which has faced a diverse mingling of peoples and cultures and increasingly less-inclusive theater audiences, has in many respects also resisted the pointed exploration of specific public and political issues through Greek tragedy, at least until the late 1960s. The politics of race, gender, and identity were central both to Greek tragedy itself (with barbarian-Greek relations substituting for race in the classical period) and to versions of Greek tragedy written and performed in the United States from the nineteenth century on. Yet wartime situations did not provoke a turn to Greek tragedy in the United States as often as they did in Europe. The First and Second World Wars produced few instances beyond Euripides' *Trojan Women,* the Korean War none, and the Iraq War and the global violence of the late twentieth and early twenty-first centuries are already well on their way to generating more examples than the war in Vietnam. The United States has generally not deployed Greek drama as a form of covert political resistance, as many other countries have (especially as a way around censorship or tyrannical government), and many productions have not been comfortable even indirectly identifying tragic heroes with American leaders or public figures (see chapter 4) or with the nation as a whole. Tragedies that focus on family drama (often revised to be more melodramatic and private than in the original plays) proved until recently more popular among Americans than those that focus more heavily on potentially controversial public issues.

Non-Greek tragedies on public themes, history plays, and heroic melodramas did bring politics into nineteenth-century theater, but a late nineteenth-century shift to lauding theater's potential role in promoting democracy, cooperation, and even morality in (especially amateur) productions hindered more than facilitated making political statements through the performance of classical drama.[3] As noted earlier, the performance of Greek tragedy was often considered incompatible with American myths that downplay history and the forces of social determinism in favor of optimistic stories of hard work and struggle leading to success as well as with America's utopian self-image as a nation; tragedy's concern with revenge and threats of social upheaval was also viewed with a (perhaps nervous) distaste. In the early twentieth century, theatrical audiences for plays with a political edge were broadly based only during the period of the Federal Theatre Project (1935–39). Since that time, economic and class issues have frequently confined the audience for legitimate drama to the moneyed and educated, who often attend theater to be entertained rather than challenged.

Many studies have documented the active relation throughout Europe between the performance and adaptation of Greek tragedy and various historical and political issues and controversies. The story in the United States has barely begun to be examined. Despite continued interactions between U.S. and European theater at all periods, the difference becomes particularly clear in the reception of theater artists and groups who crossed or are still crossing frequently from one world to another, from British and Continental actors performing in the United States in the nineteenth century to the controversial The Living Theatre in the 1960s or the provocative director Peter Sellars from the 1980s to the present. This chapter will make a point of comparing the reception of latter two on both sides of the Atlantic.

Although all theater performances could be said to be "political" in the general sense of relating to "the polis," this chapter will confine itself to cases where artists made self-conscious choices to perform Greek tragedy in response to a set of specific or in rarer cases general long-term public issues and controversies. Although *Trojan Women* remains the most popular and most frequently performed tragedy for such political reasons, *Antigone* has been more popular in the United States, in contrast to other countries, at colleges and universities than on the commercial stage, especially before 1970. Part 1 of this chapter documents, however, an 1890 production of *Antigone* by American women that reflected a broader cultural and political interest in the heroine during the nineteenth century and set the stage for later feminist interpretations of the play that represent a different perspective. Part 2 looks at the development of politically oriented performance groups in the 1960s–1970s through the lens of The Living Theatre, especially its performances of Brecht's *Antigone*. Part 3 examines productions in the 1980s and beyond through several plays that have been performed fairly rarely: Aeschylus's *Persians*, Sophocles' *Ajax*, and Euripides' *Children of Heracles*. Peter Sellars's productions of versions of these tragedies serve as a focus for evaluating the U.S. reception of different styles of confronting politics through *Persians* and *Ajax* by different theater groups in this period. The larger issue raised by Robbe-Grillet in the quotation above, about the aesthetic problems produced by modernizing or making topical aspects of Greek tragedy, will hover behind this discussion rather than becoming the central question.

Part 4 turns to an important issue thus far barely examined in this book, the divine sphere and what it can come to represent in a world that long ago abandoned these gods. Productions of Aeschylus's *Prometheus Bound* from 1967–1999 highlighted through the medium of divine figures contemporary issues faced by humanity as a group, such as nuclear power or economic catastrophe, even more than problematic wars, political and social conflicts, or heroes/leaders. The final production discussed in part 4 introduces an unusual optimistic resolution to American class and economic tensions through a new version of Aeschylus's partially lost Prometheus trilogy. Overall, recent performances of Greek tragedy conscious of America's ever more controversial role as an overextended world power have made the potentially tragic side of politics more compelling than before. I have addressed elsewhere the way that productions and new versions of Aeschylus's *Oresteia* in the United States responded to a combination of feminist issues, Vietnam, and millennial violence at the turn of the twenty-first century.[4] The epilogue will briefly take note of further recent trends evidenced in productions of Euripides' Iphigeneia plays.

## 1. *ANTIGONE* AND POLITICS IN THE NINETEENTH CENTURY: THE BOSTON 1890 *ANTIGONE*

As far as we can tell, the only self-conscious native attempts in the nineteenth century to respond to current public social or religious issues through Greek tragedy in the United States were made by women. We have already considered Katherine Tingley's 1898 production of *Eumenides* in chapter 1.2 and will turn to Harriette Fanning Read's published 1848 *Medea* in chapter 5.1. Our third example is an 1890 *Antigone* performed by and for women that aimed to make a public statement about women's roles in American democracy through the play. While Greek tragedy increasingly thrived at colleges and universities for students of both sexes under professorial supervision in the late nineteenth and early twentieth century, private groups and clubs also developed an interest in performing Greek tragedy outside the academy. Women often formed close to 80 percent of legitimate theater audiences by the early twentieth century, and, in part because of their lack of higher education, they were eager to promote educational and cultural ventures in all-female or other private groups.[5] Although many amateur performances by women grew out of an upper- and middle-class tradition of performing recitations, tableaux, and pantomimes in the late nineteenth and early twentieth century and promoted a fairly aesthetic cultural agenda, some were more adventurous in spirit if not in theatrical practice. (On the conventions of the period, see chapters 1 and 2.)

In 1890, the Saturday Morning Club of Boston, a group of socially prominent young Boston women (about seventy in number, most unmarried) interested in "general enlightenment and cultivation" (*Boston Daily Advertiser*, March 13, 1890), gave four performances of *Antigone* in Boston's Bumstead Hall after a year's preparation by about fifty amateur actors; tickets were sold to an enthusiastic but exclusively female audience with the proceeds going to charity. The group received limited male help. It paid Charles Copeland to do an initial reading of E. H. Plumptre's translation and consulted with Professor John Williams White of Harvard. B. J. Lang adapted Mendelssohn's music for female voices; Franklin H. Sargent of the American Academy of Dramatic Arts in New York offered a few sessions of professional coaching and lent scenery. The entire cast of *Antigone* also attended Sargent and Belasco's Sophocles' *Electra* at Boston's Hollis Street Theatre in 1889,[6] and a few cast members later attended dress rehearsals of the Smith College *Electra* (1889). No expense was spared on the costumes and "pretty-feminine touches" such as programs of "papyrus" scrolls on double rods tied with yellow ribbons, and tickets shaped like drachmas embossed with the head of Sophocles and the date in Roman numerals.[7] Ticket receipts of $3,521.00 minus expenses of $1,291.61 netted a hefty $2,299.39 for children's causes (the Prevention of Cruelty to Children, the West End Nursery, and The Playgrounds).[8]

The club president, Ellen M. Dennie, was inspired by the ladies of Queen's College, London who performed Euripides' *Alkestis* in 1886. Interest in Greek tragedy and women's causes had played a role in the club's formation. Julia Ward Howe, who founded the club for her daughter Maud, was author of the "Battle Hymn of the Republic" and a noted poet, playwright, essayist, and abolitionist active in various women's movements pursuing both peace and suffrage. Howe, who pronounced the Saturday Morning Club's *Antigone* "pathetic and powerful ... a high feast of beauty and poetry,"[9] had earlier written a verse play *Hippolytus* for the young Edwin Booth, with the even more famous Charlotte Cushman slated to play Phaedra. An 1864 production of Howe's *Hippolytus* at the Howard Athenaeum in Boston was mysteriously canceled much to her disappointment; its "dark" content was apparently thought insufficiently attractive to contemporary audiences, and the manager's wife disliked the role she would have played.[10] In 1910 Margaret Anglin (see chapter 1.2) promised Howe to take on Phaedra with Walter Hampden as Hippolytus; Howe died before the performance in 1911,[11] and Anglin was too overcommitted to bring the play to New York.

Maud Howe's group adopted the principle that all women share a common history. *Antigone* was chosen for its "refinement" and "universality," as well as a "tragic sensibility" and "sense of repose in the face of suffering" derived from a putative Greek closeness to nature. According to the "Memories of Antigone," written by chorus member and later published author, Mary Gray Morrison, the Saturday Morning Club's aim in producing *Antigone* was to urge modern women to celebrate Antigone's particularly female challenge to masculine authority.[12] Females in Morrison's view appropriately represented "the eternal right" against the dictates of a male law ("his own law"),[13] and the play "portray[ed] in the figure of a girl the ideal spirit which appeals to the higher law against the human mandate." Morrison thought the play was ideologically sympathetic because Athens, as an aspiring, young democratic power, was before its [putative] postclassical decline not unlike contemporary America.

Americans of the period frequently resisted pessimistic pagan concepts of fate (see chapter 4), particularly because Christianity valorized suffering through the passion of Christ and the martyrdom of the saints. Morrison challenges the rigidity of this view by asking: "Is our race outgrowing tragedy?" She notes: "The time is long past when the Christian refuses to acknowledge his debt to the distant ages or separates himself from his groping, aspiring brothers of all times." And she goes on to explain:

> Through the Greek play we were led into deeper sympathy and understanding of the pagan world not only on the tragic but on every side. The belief in fate became clear and natural as this familiarity with its surroundings grew more vivid. We saw how this idea of theirs was the easiest and most natural explanation of the problems of life among which the mind of man has groped ever since it became a reasoning

machine. A faith most stern it was in its conclusions; the gentle Master [Christ] had not walked the earth.

The club's production not only defined an assertive symbolic role for women of the period but unified the group during the rehearsal. In describing "what *Antigone* did for us," Morrison asserts that the play's performance "brought an atmosphere of outdoor life into the experience of us whose race has so long lived in dwelling houses." Study of the play led to changes in the cast's view of the characters. "Creon went from being a 'traditional tyrant' to being played with more subtlety and depth." Ismene's "timid conservatism" was understood as "no outgrown thing," and Haemon's "loyal defense of the woman he loves . . . tempered as long as possible by filial affection" represented "an ideal of young manhood [not] to be soon out-grown." In addition, "a Greek play appears to be a good thing to bring out the Christian virtues," which were embodied both in the collective process of performing the play and in the move beyond the "domestic or personal" to a deeper perspective. The group "formed for a time almost an ideal republic." Finally, both rehearsal and performance led to a sense of "repose" derived from contact with the naturalness of a Greek world where "no nervousness is in its atmosphere." To convey this repose, the group used Delsartian poses (some derived from Greek art), which were standard in contemporary manuals for teaching women proper deportment (discussed in chapter 2; Sargent and Belasco's choreography for their 1889 *Electra* also drew on Delsartian poses; see figs. 17 and 18). As one reviewer put it, "The repose of the figures during the exciting passages of the dialogue gave all the more opportunity for pose and expression to do their work upon the mind and heart. The attributes of motionlessness well assumed by the chorus of maidens during the scene in which Antigone bewails her fate gave to the eye the pleasure and to the heart the relief which comes from having some deep, common grief voiced by an artist" (*Boston Daily Advertiser*, March 13, 1890).

*Antigone* was extensively and positively reviewed (presumably exclusively by women) in the Boston papers.[14] On the one hand, the choral performance, with its apparent "ease" of movement and exquisite singing, was thought by one review to outclass that of Sargent and Belasco's recent overly busy *Electra*.[15] The *Boston Post* reviewer (March 13, 1890) thought the performance superior to the 1881 Harvard *Oedipus* (see chapter 1.1), and the *Boston Daily Globe* review (March 13, 1890) thought it might easily have had a "long run." Reviews also lauded the professionalism of the actors, especially Mrs. Alice Kent Robertson's "strong, heroic manner" as a "haughty, stiff-necked" Creon, and Mrs. Caroline C. Burlen as a black-gowned, tender, and determined Antigone.[16] Others remarked on the production's "historical accuracy" and "womanly reserve."[17] A few reviewers lost sight of the production's aims in an absorption with the aesthetic aspects of the performance. Jean Kincaid expressed a bantering curiosity at male exclusion from what

FIGURE 17. Caroline Burlen as Antigone in the Saturday Morning Club of Boston's Sophocles' *Antigone*, Bumstead Hall, Boston, 1890. Photo courtesy of the Schlesinger Library, Radcliffe Institute, Harvard University.

FIGURE 18. Three chorus members in the Saturday Morning Club of Boston's Sophocles' *Antigone*, Bumstead Hall, Boston, 1890. Photo courtesy of the Schlesinger Library, Radcliffe Institute, Harvard University.

she described as a "beauty show": "If admiring fathers and brothers, friends and cousins, could but see how beautiful these same girls are in their Greek garb they would join in irresistible entreaty to banish every other style of dress and Worth and Redfern would go out of business" (*Boston Daily Globe,* March 13, 1890). The *Boston Evening Transcript* (March 13, 1890) also stressed the exclusive femaleness of the whole project and the opportunity to observe female heads without hats, which had to be removed for the performance. Other contemporary accounts responded strongly to the beautiful pastel choral costumes (green, lilac, rose, and crocus), the chorus's ornate sacrificial procession, and picturesque choral groupings in the orchestra below the main stage.[18]

What *Antigone* represented to the women of the Saturday Morning Club of Boston was in certain respects typical of the period. As Caroline Winterer has shown, the period 1840–1900 in the United States cast the heroine as "the incarnation of Victorian ideals of true womanhood," a model for internal self-perfection that domesticated and muted the original's political dimensions.[19] Winterer argues that *Antigone,* along with Greek drama generally, became of increasing interest in American schools and colleges and in popular culture, including women's magazines and fiction, from the 1840s. The study of Greek and classical literature became available to some women in schools during this period as well; *Antigone,* for example, was required for entrance to Bryn Mawr in 1885. Antigone's active spiritual devotion to father, brother, and family, her heroic piety, and her sacrifice of motherhood and wifehood were preserved from being deemed unfeminine or overly aggressive because she is dragged unwillingly into a conflict with a Creon usually defined in this period as tyrannical and corrupted by excessive power, a "patriarch gone awry."[20] As A. T. Murray insisted in a book describing a 1902 Stanford production of the play, "It would have been [impossible] for the high-minded girl, filled with loyalty to her dead brother . . . to have chosen any other course"; by contrast, even a good citizen may resist a Creon who is conventional, shortsighted, and narrow in his views, as well as too personal.[21]

Performing Sophocles' *Antigone* could be linked with the educational aspirations of young women in a manner that preserved traditional female piety. In "The Sacrifice of Antigone," a story by Elizabeth Stuart Phelps published in 1891, Dorothy Dreed of East Omaha, Nebraska, a poor college student who is working her way through college, wins a Greek oration contest as the only woman to compete for the $200 prize by haranguing Creon and then lamenting her death. Found dying of starvation by a professor and a lady benefactor, she dies, willing her prize money to her father and her youngest brother for his college education. As in Morrison's "Memories," Antigone's story was deemed generally compatible with a nonsectarian Christianity and with the aspirations of the American democracy, which was struggling with growing materialism. At the same time, Winterer views this nineteenth-century engagement with *Antigone* as leading to a reinforcement of woman's role in the family and a "retreat from public engagement."[22] The Saturday Morning Club, by contrast, turned its performance into a public gesture, which led the group, at least in its own view, out of domestic confinement to a growing sense of the possibility of an active public role for women, and to a deeper intellectual understanding of their own world that expanded to some degree beyond contemporary clichés.

More female-generated, if apparently less politically conscious, productions followed in the wake of the Boston *Antigone.* A similar performance of Plumptre's translation of *Antigone* by a predominantly female group (six young men were included) at the Hyperion Theatre in New Haven in 1891 commended Greek tragedy in its program as "the highest expression of the moral and religious consciousness of the age"; the *Boston Transcript* reviewer (April 13, 1891) praised some of the acting, if not that of Antigone and Creon, but criticized the weak additional chorus of eighteen young women and the brilliant costumes, which included a messenger in a full suit of armor and a group of Theban elders mysteriously carrying a (Bacchic) thyrsus. In this period revivals of Greek tragedy often included additional voices beyond the chorus that sang accompanied by an orchestra, usually concealed at the side of the stage; in this case the awkward group of supporting singers was in full view. The 1909 performance of *Trojan Women* by the Women's Club of Upper Montclair (New Jersey), directed by Mabel Kay Barrows Mussey on the lawn of Mrs. Julian R. Tinkham's home was likely to have been motivated by the large number of female roles, although politics could have played a role. The production included a cast of six actors, a chorus of sixteen, music by Constance Mills Herreshoff, and fifteen women who inaugurated the performance with dances in honor of Apollo.[23] In 1912 and 1914 Marita Howard staged three performances of Euripides' *Electra* at the Brookside Theatre, an outdoor theatre that she designed and managed on her estate in Mount Kisco, New York. Both performances were reviewed by New York newspapers.[24] As one review of the Boston *Antigone* noted, "It is interesting to see how many of the works of the classic Greek dramatists lend themselves to performances by the English speaking women of today."[25]

Since these early productions (including those of Margaret Anglin, discussed in chapter 1.2, and of Kennedy/Matthison, discussed in chapter 2.1), *Antigone* has continued to reflect female aspirations in the United States, and female directors and playwrights have often played a central role in productions of the play. I offer here three out of a number of examples (others are starred in appendix B) that brought gender and/or political issues to the fore in unusual ways. Martha Boesing's 1983 *Antigone Too*, performed at the ATA Women's Theater Festival in Minneapolis, Minnesota, interwove Sophocles' play with documentary accounts of seventeen courageous American women who defied society for human welfare, and featured a chorus of historical figures, including Mother Jones, Emma Goldman, and Rosa Parks. Boesing and others had just emerged victorious from their June trial for trespassing at Honeywell's local bomb factory. In 1998, Gloria Maddox's Madwoman of the Woods Productions staged *Antigone through Time*, directed by Richard S. Bach at the Connelly Theater, New York, which examined a 1940s camp on a Greek island where some three thousand women were interned for resisting the German occupation of Greece and the Fascist regime and for refusing to sign a declaration of repentance. The women were shot by a firing squad, danced and sang ethnic music by Nana Simopoulos, and donned white veils that suggested ghosts or brides; at various points the performers put on white masks and performed Sophocles' *Antigone*.

The 2004 feminist *Antigone Project* performed at New York's Julia Miles Theater invited five female playwrights, paired with five female directors, to juxtapose short new pieces that responded to the heroine's story (especially in the version by Brecht). The plays were loosely based on various versions of *Antigone*.

## 2. PERFORMANCE GROUPS IN THE 1960s–1970s: BRECHT'S *ANTIGONE* BY THE LIVING THEATRE

As chapter 1.2 showed, Greek tragedy generally played a more important role in the cultural and aesthetic than the political side of new theater initiatives from 1910 into the early 1930s, although both Barker and Browne aimed to advocate peace in their 1915 productions of *Trojan Women* (see chapter 1). The short-lived and often highly political Federal Theatre Project (FTP) of 1935–39 produced the 1938 dance piece entitled *Trojan Incident,* based on Euripides' *Trojan Women,* and discussed in chapter 2.1. Hallie Flanagan, the former director of the FTP, was herself inspired by the democracy and social relevance of Greek theater, especially after a trip to theater sites in Greece in 1934; the FTP motto from an inscription on Delos read: "We let out these works on the vote of the people."[26] Yet the abrupt demise of the FTP proved chastening to those interested in representing political issues onstage, although Off-Broadway and other smaller groups across the country continued to produce some American and European classics.[27] When Flanagan did a reading in August 1945 of Alfred J. Brenner's *Antigone,* a modern version set in an occupied country, the play was simply dismissed as dated.[28] Moreover, during this post-Depression period universities were not as actively taking up the slack. The psychological realism of the 1940s and 1950s, in which playwrights such as Arthur Miller and Tennessee Williams began to reformulate social issues as private traumas, and legitimate theater was dominated by a sense of loss and social disillusion, apparently proved largely incompatible with Greek tragedy, although Miller's attempt at an American tragedy, *Death of a Salesman,* was an important exception, as were a small number of professional performances of the original plays.[29]

Among the avant-garde/experimental and politically oriented theater groups that formed in New York during the late 1950s and especially in the 1960s, Julian Beck and Judith Malina's The Living Theatre, Joseph Chaikin's Open Theater, and Richard Schechner's The Performance Group all performed important new versions of Greek tragedy. The earliest of these groups, The Living Theatre, initially set out, like the Chicago Little Theatre (see chapter 1.3), to revitalize American dramatic performance through the power of poetic language.[30] Part 2 of this chapter will focus only on The Living Theatre for several reasons besides its primacy and its long-standing interest in Greek tragedy, which helped to facilitate its move to what it thought of as aggressively political theater in the late 1960s. Most important, the group developed its later signature style and its production of Bertolt Brecht's *Antigone* in Europe before bringing it to the United States. Among the important politically oriented productions of the late 1960s, The Living Theatre's *Antigone* allows us to compare European and U.S. reactions to a performance style that drew on cultural traditions from both sides of the Atlantic, and thus to contextualize the group's efforts in a broader fashion.

In the formative phases of The Living Theatre, Beck and Malina had deeply admired Katharine Cornell in Jean Anouilh's *Antigone* (1946), Judith Anderson in Robinson Jeffers's *Medea* (1947; see chapter 5.2), and the London Old Vic's visiting performance of Yeats's *OT* with Laurence Olivier (May 1946).[31] New versions of Greek tragedy were central to The Living Theatre's early efforts to promote poetic theater in New York. For example, the California poet, classicist, fellow anarchist, and Orientalist Kenneth Rexroth's trilogy *Beyond the Mountains*, staged by The Living Theatre to negative reviews in New York, December 30, 1951,[32] anticipated the group's fascination with a mythic, semiprophetic sense of preclassical mysteries. This highly formal, three-part, dense and cryptic verse-drama was performed using masks, elaborate costumes, and formal techniques borrowed in part from Noh drama. Play one, *Phaedra*, staged, contrary to Greek and Roman versions, the ultimate sexual capitulation of Phaedra and her usually resistant stepson Hippolytus to each other. Theseus returned, and Hippolytus confessed his "rape" of Phaedra to his father. The practical soldier Theseus had in fact anticipated and even approved this possible romance before his return. Yet the horrified Phaedra and Hippolytus killed themselves. In play two, *Iphigeneia at Aulis,* Iphigeneia and Achilles, again contrary to Rexroth's classical sources, passionately celebrated their love. Iphigeneia, who had also been her father's lover in this version, persuaded Agamemnon to deceive Achilles and permit her sacrifice for the sake of the war at Troy. The final play of the trilogy, which was less related to Greek tragedy, took place at the dawn of the Christian era in the last Greek city remaining from Alexander's empire, in Bactria/Afghanistan. Malina, who also played Racine's Phèdre in a translation by Beck during this period (1955), was riveted by the opportunity to perform these outrageous versions of Phaedra, Iphigeneia, and (in the last play) Berenike. (Later, Brecht's Antigone became her favorite role.) The "poeticizing libertinage" (as Stefan Brecht put it)[33] of this trilogy eventually broadened into a lifelong struggle for The Living Theatre against the forces of social (including sexual) repression, war, and corrupt, tyrannical political power.

In a further stage in the development of its theatrical form, The Living Theatre performed weekly staged readings in 1960 of the entire corpus of Greek tragedy at New York's New School for Social Research and socialized with various New York artists and intellectuals interested in global mythologies, such as the famous Joseph Campbell. It also staged, to bad notices, the first commercial production of Ezra Pound's *Women of Trachis* (June 22, 1960), an idiosyncratic translation/adaptation of Sophocles' play, and John Ashbery's *Heroes*, a modernization of the encounter between Odysseus and Circe that was criticized for its homosexual innuendos.[34] The Living Theatre's production of Pound aimed at "universality" by using a mix of primitive and postclassical costuming and by playing characters in the style of different eras. The group's interest in developing its theatrical style through versions of classical drama continued even after Beck's death in 1985. Judith Malina and

Hanon Reznikov performed (in 1988) Michael McClure's *Vktms*, a version of the Orestes myth in which Hanon played Orestes, *Kassandra* (1988–89), and *Waste*, a 1989 play on the destruction of natural resources by the West that included a reinterpretation of scenes from Aeschylus's *Seven against Thebes*.

In 1964, the Becks were arrested for failure to pay taxes on their New York theater and decamped for Europe. There they developed a number of complex signature theater pieces that they performed to considerable interest all over Europe and later on an extensive U.S. tour in 1968–69. Two of these retained a connection to the Becks' earlier interest in classics and myth: *Mysteries and Smaller Pieces*, which grew out of The Living Theatre's interest in preclassical myth and ritual and the origins of theater, and Bertolt Brecht's *Antigone*, which Malina, a native German speaker, had translated into free verse while in Passaic County Jail for promoting integration in 1964.[35] The group became notorious for its promotion of anarchism, pacifism, and sexual and emotional liberation in its performances; for its active, indeed aggressive engagement with its audiences; and for its constant political confrontations outside the theater. *Antigone* remained the most traditional of its presentations, in that it adhered fairly closely to Brecht's text and put the group's theatrical techniques to a more controlled and formal use than elsewhere. Among The Living Theatre's productions, *Antigone* most closely adhered to the group's initial interest in using language as a mode of arriving at truth and authenticity. Yet, as Beck put it, "We . . . are trying to reach towards some kind of communication of feeling and idea that push toward some other area that is beneath words or beyond words or *in addition to words*. The object was not to destroy language [but] . . . to deepen it and amplify it and to make the communication real rather than a series of lies."[36] Collective improvisation, a radically redefined relation to the audience and among actors, and a new stress on the truth of the body and other nonverbal elements of theater came into play.

Brecht's adaptation of *Antigone*, based on Hölderlin's translation of Sophocles, was first performed in Switzerland in 1948. Brecht's play eliminates the central role of divinity to play out Sophocles' story in human and political terms. The tyrant Creon has engaged in an imperialistic war of aggression to acquire wealth in the form of metal from the mountains of Argos. The patriotic soldier Eteocles dies in the battle with Argos, trampled in pursuit of the deserter Polyneices, who objects to the unjust war and is killed by Creon and his henchmen. Antigone feels justified in breaking Creon's law precisely because it is human. In its first speech, the chorus does not celebrate peace, as does Sophocles' chorus, but greedily anticipates the returning spoils of war. Sophocles' famous choral "Ode on Man" (*Antigone* 332–75) becomes in Brecht's version a meditation on human greed and monstrosity. Brecht's chorus of old men is deeply complicit with his Creon throughout. Instead of giving up its festal celebration of peace at Creon's first entrance, as in

Sophocles, the chorus begins to enter into a celebratory orgy in honor of the god Dionysus that distracts it from loss, mourning, and the absence of the young men, who have not yet returned from battle. After hearing predictions by Antigone and Tiresias about the city's fate, the chorus discovers from Creon that the war is in fact not going as well as it had thought. The elders face the fact that tyrants, as Brecht's Antigone had warned, eventually begin to treat their own countrymen as enemies. But this revelation is too late; a messenger arrives to announce a disastrous defeat of the army and the death of Creon's son Menoeceus; Creon soon returns with the bloody shirt of his dead son Haimon. Despite its disillusionment with Creon, however, the chorus closes the play by vowing to follow its leader, even if from now on the city's course will be all downhill. The play stresses that every character, even those who perform with exemplary motives, like Antigone and Haimon, acts too late, and thus all are complicit in the final disaster: "She who saw it all could only help the enemy." This adaptation, whose relevance to recent events in Nazi Germany hardly needs elaborating, stresses collective cultural responsibility for historical disasters and the role of collaborators and those who passively tolerate imperialistic policies.

The Becks were thoroughly familiar with the details of Brecht's own production of *Antigone* from his published *Modellbuch* on the play (*Antigonemodell 1948*, published in 1949) and borrowed Brechtian distancing techniques, such as announcing the content of each scene directly to the audience. At the same time, "*Antigone* was an experiment to find out if the Artaudian devices were possible with a text that was poetic, political, and classical in origin, though contemporary in application."[37] Under the influence of their interpretation of Antonin Artaud, the Becks used actors' bodies and voices to create a production "staged with total sound" that included chants, laments, shrieks, hums, imitations of wind, and a period of forty-five minutes in which the chorus celebrated Dionysus by dancing to the sound of tongue clacking and thigh slapping.[38] Some postures were adapted from Greek or Egyptian art and the production, perhaps harking back to O'Neill, created visual "masks" for Creon and the chorus—faces imprinted with rigid festive smiles during the Dionysiac celebration.

The Living Theatre's *Antigone*, performed in informal street clothes without sets, props, or lighting, substituted a confrontation between the players, representing Thebes, and the audience, representing Argos, for Brecht's prologue, which shows two German sisters discovering the dead body of their brother, a Nazi deserter. The actors stared with hostility at the arriving audience. Houselights remained on. Creon, accompanied by choral wailing in the background, then physically propelled his army from behind into the audience, where the warring brothers were killed in the laps of the viewers and brought on stage. The chorus also moved into the audience during the "Ode on Man," thus making the viewers complicit with the ode's despairing view of humanity. The final scene also departed from Brecht. Here the entire cast lined up, stared with growing terror at the audience (Argos) and retreated back as if violently attacked; the lights went out.

The body of Polyneices remained on stage throughout the play as a sign of injustice and a stimulus to revolt. He was mourned by Antigone to the point where she lay over the body in a sexualized posture; the body was draped over her back as a burden, literally pushed back and forth, first between the two sisters as they argued in the opening scene and later between Haimon and Creon, and posed with Antigone and Haimon after their deaths. In the end, the last messenger echoed Antigone's pose over Polyneices by standing over Creon as he announced the Theban defeat; Haimon was then draped over Creon's back. As in Sophocles' play, Creon's error burdened him with Antigone's own fate, in this case literally. The complicity of the elders (symbolically "castrated" early on by Creon) with their leader was expressed visibly as the group surrounded Creon when he spoke, or turned or moved at his command; without them, Creon moved without full authority.[39] The "elders" created a throne for Creon from their bodies and hovered angrily over Antigone as she was about to leave for her death. At this point the rest of the chorus embodied the offstage masses reported by Haimon in Sophocles who had more sympathy for Antigone. The chorus as a whole enlarged the confrontation between Antigone and Creon by actively miming to speeches describing action, surrounding Antigone with a human wall as Ismene tried to share the crime with her, and representing a refusal to engage by enacting figures seeing, hearing, and speaking no evil. Tricked into celebrating the Theban victory prematurely, the chorus finally performed a continuous Dionysiac dance while Antigone, a figure who served to stress The Living Theatre's adherence to anarchy, ritual, and refusal of repression and silence, went to her death ignored, as well as when Tiresias, pointedly played by a black actor, spoke.

As Beck put it,

we did antigone in 1967
> so that:
> antigone's example
> after 2,500 years of failure
> might at last move
> an intellectual paying audience
> to take action
> before it is

too late[40]

The Living Theatre meant its performances of the late 1960s, including *Antigone*, to respond especially to the Vietnam War with its growing casualties and unpopularity, and in the 1980s to nuclear war, environmental disaster, and patriarchal oppression.[41] In fact, although Beck at times explicitly imitated Lyndon Johnson and later Richard Nixon in playing Creon in the United States, The Living Theatre's *Antigone* largely maintained, in contrast to its more overtly revolutionary pieces, an oblique relation to contemporary events and deliberately retained Brecht's political pessimism in order to counter its own tendency to "theatrical utopianism."[42]

Although Malina began translating *Antigone* in the United States in 1961, the first public performance took place in Germany. The Living Theatre clearly found that Europe, rather than simply the late 1960s, enabled it to develop its assertive collective political and theatrical style. Beck explained:

> We were very much under the influence—after the war and in the early fifties—of that critical attitude which said: you cannot mix art and politics; you cannot mix art and activist-social thought, they don't go together; they degrade each other. This was an attitude very strong in America at that time, which deeply influenced the art of the era. It was a form of censorship. I don't think that we came to a breakthrough in the theatre until we became frankly political. And when we insisted on saying politically what we wanted to say politically, we felt free to discover breakthrough ways of doing it. Therefore, the plays in Europe have taken on a different character. . . . I have a feeling that certainly in Europe there is much more clarity about the political situation than among radicals in America. It seems to me they are better prepared over there, politically—both feelingly and intellectually.[43]

At the same time, Stefan Brecht (Brecht's son) argued for a specifically American coloring to The Living Theatre's versions of anarchism or of Artaud:

> Their anarchism is modern American, suspicious of moral stricture, indifferent to economics, disdainful of the power of social structure, sociologically nominalist: the State is a state of mind. . . . But they do not moralistically attack the State or Ruling Classes but psychologically attack *repression in the individual*. . . . Their atheist but vitalist metaphysics, an Americanly optimist counterpart to Artaud's paranoid vision of man's desperate stand against a destructively creative, cruelly evil universe, replaces traditional anarchist faith in practical reason, good will & progressive evolution with a trust-against-reason in life's emotions & creative energy.[44]

The ritualized elements of The Living Theatre's productions, the dramatic invitation to join the spiritual community of the company after liberation and purification, even reminded critics of old-time American religion.[45] Robert Brustein remarked:

> I guess it's really a religious movement more than it is a political one. I really think they make a great effort to transform the inner man. And they do a wonderful job of convincing you, me, members of the audience that they themselves have been transformed. . . . But without a god, without some really inspired religious doctrine, I don't see where it can last. You're not going to be converted to it, except when you're in its presence. That's why it's so much like a revival meeting.

Moreover, in the American context, Brustein added, "I say this talk of revolution is romantic rhetoric. Revolution is simply impossible in this country."[46]

The group's performances also consistently provoked more interest and enthusiasm—along with considerable controversy—in Europe than at home.[47] The American tour in 1968–69, which has been chronicled by Renfreu Neff, was a checkered experience, with performances creating excitement, controversy, and ambivalence wherever The Living Theatre went. In the case of *Antigone*, although Dan Sullivan of the *Los Angeles Times* (March 1, 1969) pronounced the play "the most effective weapon the company has in spreading its message of revolution," others objected to the analogy between Nazi Germany and U.S. Vietnam policy or were confused about what role was being established for the play's audience—was it victim or collaborator? Eric Bentley thought that the concept stressed in the production, "If you go out and use violence against your enemies, you will return and use it against your own people," was "just not true historically." Many in the audience even wanted to identify with the Thebans.[48]

By the 1980s, when it returned to the United States, The Living Theatre and its *Antigone* received a far more negative critical reception as dated and theatrically inept.[49] Many other politically oriented productions, including performances and new versions of Greek tragedy, were developed in the United States from the late 1960s through the 1970s. Yet The Living Theatre's controversial relation to its audience, and the contradictions between its aggressive behavior and its utopian aims, proved to be more notoriously problematic. From a theatrical perspective, however, the group's performance style, and the visceral, imagistic quality of its presentation, with its nearly continuous sound and semiritualized movement, proved influential and important for later, less aggressively political productions, including those of Greek tragedy, by others. Joseph Chaikin's closely contemporary 1982 *Antigone* at New York's Public Theatre, translated by John Chioles, was similarly dismissed as typical of the excesses of 1960s experimental theater,[50] "too political," "one man's struggle to keep women out of power," the Vassar girl versus the Old Testament Abraham.[51] (Chaikin was a former actor in The Living Theatre.) By contrast, Richard Schechner's closely contemporary, pathbreaking *Dionysus in 69*, a new version of Euripides' *Bacchae* developed by The Performance Group,[52] deployed avant-garde theatrical techniques but achieved a far better critical reception for a production that was in many ways more socially than politically provocative.

### 3. THE 1980S AND BEYOND: PETER SELLARS'S *PERSIANS*, *AJAX*, AND *CHILDREN OF HERACLES*

By and large, with the exception of pre- or postwar "peace plays" like Euripides' *Trojan Women*, pointedly political, and especially topical, versions of Greek tragedy had until the 1980s often met with an ambivalent or even outright negative or dismissive reception in the United States, as tragedy also did when it became too topical in the Athenian democracy. Since the 1980s (and especially since the 1990s), however, assertive public statements made through Greek tragedy have become increasingly popular, by being less direct in some cases or by defusing some of the tensions produced by more aggressive political drama through humor or by reimagining the relation between ancient and modern texts inserted into a version of the original texts. The director Peter Sellars, another American artist who, like Beck and Malina, has worked very frequently in Europe as well as the United States, has offered topical versions of Greek tragedy that have met with contrasting reactions on both sides of the Atlantic. Each of his three main productions—Aeschylus's *Persians,* Sophocles' *Ajax,* and Euripides' *Children of Heracles*—employed slightly different theatrical strategies from the other two, which help to explain the varied U.S. reception. Part 3 will also contrast Sellars's controversial versions of *Persians* and *Ajax* with slightly later U.S. versions of the same plays that took different approaches and received a more positive critical reception.

*Aeschylus's* Persians

First, I will contrast Peter Sellars and Robert Auletta's version of Aeschylus's rarely performed *Persians,*[53] which reimagined the play in response to the First Gulf War, with two versions provoked by the Second Gulf War, or Iraq War. The 1993 Sellars-Auletta *Persians* received a fairly respectful response at the Salzburg Festival in Austria and the Hebbel-Theater in Berlin but proved increasingly controversial at Scotland's Edinburgh Festival and at the Mark Taper Forum in Los Angeles.[54] An adaptation by Ellen McLaughlin that adhered quite closely to Aeschylus's text was first directed by Ethan McSweeny in April 2003 to considerable acclaim at Pace University's Michael Schimmel Center for the Arts in New York by Tony Randall's National Actors Theatre. It was later performed in Berkeley (2004) under the direction of Barbara Oliver at the Aurora Theatre Company, then at the Shakespeare Theatre, Washington, D.C., in 2006, again directed by Ethan McSweeny, and in 2008 at People's Light & Theatre, in the Philadelphia area, directed by Jade King Carroll. A partially comic, musical version that contained passages from the original play by the Waterwell theater group, written by Arian Moayed and directed by Tom Ridgely, moved from a successful Off-Off-Broadway run in 2003 (Under St. Marks) to Off Broadway (Perry Street Theatre) in 2005. Of the three, Waterwell's *Persians* was overall the best received by critics, a development that may be indicative of evolving American reactions to politics mediated through Greek tragedy on the stage.[55]

Aeschylus's *Persians,* the earliest Greek tragedy preserved for us, was written by a veteran of the Persian Wars. It reimagines, apparently with considerable sympathy, the historical moment of the Persian defeat by the Greeks at Salamis from the perspective of the enemy and, in the view of some scholars, invites Athens to reexamine its own move towards empire through the disastrous experience of the other.[56] Aeschylus's play opens with the Persian queen Atossa's worried approach to her chorus of elderly advisers. Her fears for the Persian expedition led by her son Xerxes against Greece are soon borne out by a messenger speech describing its defeat in the naval battle at Salamis. The despairing Atossa resolves to call on the ghost of her more successful husband, Darius; he appears but has little to offer but regret for his son Xerxes' rash expedition. Xerxes returns and laments the Persian defeat with the elders.

Sellars turned to *Persians* to draw the nation's attention to the damage suffered by Iraqis during the bombing in the First Gulf War (1991). As he put it in his program note,

> The Gulf War was one of the most censored wars in the history of journalism. The Pentagon carefully controlled the flow in information to the outside world. One of the things we rarely saw on television in this war with Iraq was Iraqis. Dead or alive. The term "collateral damage" was used to describe dead sons, daughters, wives, mothers and fathers. The human toll was largely discounted or screened out with ideological or commercial filters.
>
> One of the reasons, possibly, for theater to continue to exist in our technological age is as a kind of alternative public information system that is able partially to humanize the denatured results of our vaunted and costly objectivity. Is it possible to restore a more sophisticated level of outrage and empathy to the history of our own lifetimes? Television permits you to be a spectator, but theater makes you a participant. In the process, might we be encouraged to accept some of the responsibility for this history and for these lifetimes?

Robert Auletta's script for *Persians* follows Aeschylus's plot fairly closely,[57] but it combines an ancient cultural framework replete with traditional rituals, bird omens, gods, and laments with entirely anachronistic references to the Gulf War and the modern world:

> They poured forth from Susa
> . . .
> marching on foot, mounted on horses,
> in warships and skyships,
> riding in mechanized land monsters,
> burning the earth in armored chariots. (12–13)

This opening chorus ends with the bombing of a hotel, which is immediately followed by the entrance of the literally divine (18), yet also (in her own words) nearly hysterical, queen Atossa from retirement in her palace. Auletta substitutes models in Eastern and Western dress for the queen's dream of two Greek and Persian women/horses pulling apart and destroying a chariot. The model in

Western dress whips Xerxes and ruins his royal clothes. The Athenians are "terrorists, you see./Force always seems to work for them./They are experts at applying sanctions—to garotte a country,/cut off its life of trade,/suffocate and humiliate its people" (33). The chorus curses the name of America after hearing of the Persian disaster and pointedly, unlike in the original play, includes excruciatingly detailed descriptions of the bombing and the civilian deaths of women and children in the Gulf War (37). It goes on to wonder: "Who are the men/who invent such weapons,/ who spend their days/modernizing death?" (43–44). "Why don't they put it all on television?" (44). "How long will American power itself last?" (74).

Very likely it was this highly explicit attack on U.S. policy that caused about 100 of the 750 audience members at the Mark Taper Forum to walk out every night from the production.[58] Yet the play by no means exonerated either the "Persians" or Xerxes/Hussein. The megalomaniac Xerxes "enjoyed slaughtering his own people" (47) and was far more interested in defying the United States of America (88) than in lamenting his fellow citizens whom he both loves and despises. In a program interview, Auletta explained the need for a modern audience to "find some psychological basis for the war." Yet this version's heavily psychologized analogy between Xerxes and Hussein failed to win over an audience potentially more inclined to such approaches. Xerxes' character flaws were explained by his father's distant and competitive and his mother's overly indulgent relations to him. The ghost of Darius was evoked largely to confirm his own flawed nature as father and to view the civilian dead rather than to represent a figure of more mature past authority, as in Aeschylus. Darius's final suggestion, to dress Xerxes again as a king, proved fruitless. Xerxes ended the play by slashing open his filthy garments and urging Atossa and the chorus to dress a chorus member in his clothes as king. They do so, thereby ironically accomplishing a result that occurred for Hussein only as a result of the Second Gulf War.

In contrast to the Sellars/Auletta version, Ellen McLaughlin's script for the 2003 *Persians* contained no direct references to the Iraq War nor to the possible parallels between the hubristic Xerxes and his heroic father in twice failing in their attack against Athens/Greece and the Bush father and son's two attacks on Iraq, where the second war was popularly motivated in part as a revenge for the father and also met with unexpected problems because of "failed intelligence." McLaughlin's introduction reflects an Aeschylean delicacy and complexity in handling the relation between friends and enemies effectively for the play's audience. Although both audience and director were well aware of the structural parallels between past and present, "we, for that matter, are neither the Persians nor the Greeks," asserted McLaughlin.[59] This *Persians* was performed immediately after the invasion of Iraq in March 2003, when its full repercussions were as yet unknown. The play's success, as was likely in the case of Aeschylus, apparently derived in part from its ability to capture sympathy for the Persians even while revealing their tragic mistakes.

McLaughlin's version added two important new elements, a description of Xerxes' flogging of the Hellespont, drawn from the historian Herodotus, which enhances Xerxes' hubris, and the reappearance in the final scene of Queen Atossa to greet her shattered son as a suppliant (in the original this meeting did not occur).[60] The latter change permitted Atossa's evolving views to unify the play and to help put Xerxes' humiliation in perspective; McLaughlin here omits the issue of offering Xerxes new clothing in favor of verbal consolation. Both linguistically and visually the elegant costumes (the Atossa of the New York production appeared first in gold, then in simple black), the brilliant red sand of the set, the silent, sudden entrances of both Darius and Xerxes, and the slow, ritualized movement of the characters maintained a stark dignity (fig. 19). Intended as an "antiwar play," the production underlined a sense of loss and collective responsibility derived more from human than divine causes; each chorus member, for example, maintained a particular public position on the situation, and, provoked by the Persian suffering, moved gradually from rage about the war to a sense of the complexity of the conflict. The play's indirect warning for all makers of empire echoed the original play (273):

> *Chairman:* Defeat is impossible.
> *All:* Defeat is unthinkable.
> *Chairman:* We have always been the favorites of fate. Fortune has cupped us in her golden palms. It has only been a matter of choosing our desire. Which fruit to pick from the nodding tree.

The translation followed the general sense of the Greek, and although it did not anachronize sharply, it created an accessible modern version of Aeschylus's text and at times expanded on images in the original to make them particularly vivid. Aeschylus's text, for example, describes the suffering of the waiting wives and children. McLaughlin's expansion makes this experience of absence as specific as the actual loss of life in battle:

> Here a curtain is pulled back
> And a pale face appears at a window.
> Wife or mother
> She looks once again, she can't help it,
> At the bend in the road where she lost sight of him.
> She knows she won't see him there, rounding that curve,
> His shoulders tilted at that familiar angle,
> His gait unique, his alone.
> Once again, he is not there.
> But she can't stop looking for him.
> Just as she can't stop listening for that familiar tread on the stair.
> Can't stop opening the closet once again

FIGURE 19. Darius (Ted van Griethuysen) consoles Atossa (Helen Carey) in Ellen McLaughlin's new version of Aeschylus's *Persians*, directed by Ethan McSweeny, Shakespeare Theatre Company, Washington, D.C., 2006. Photo by Carol Rosegg, courtesy of the Shakespeare Theatre Company.

> To smell his lost body on the clothes he once wore.
> She has come to know him in his absence so much better
> Than she could ever have known him in his presence.
> ... She is haunted by his details now
> And every person she sees who is not him
> Wrenches her with his wrongness.
> ...
> She knows he won't come into view.
> It's impossible. (269)

Margo Jefferson of the *New York Times* found the play a "more than timely ... heart-wrenching and terrifying ... pageant of disaster," a successful attempt that served "the playwright's gifts by refusing to simplify." McLaughlin's *Persians* satisfied Jefferson's view that a "new version ... can't just imitate. Every age has its own rhythms and drives. The classic must make us feel the new acutely" (June 11, 2003).[61] Far from provoking controversy, this *Persians* soon invited further new productions in Berkeley, Washington, and Philadelphia.

In New York, after the Pearl Theatre had independently scheduled its own *Persians* for the fall of 2004, the Off-Off-Broadway group Waterwell staged *The Persians . . . a comedy about war with five songs* in 2005. Waterwell's *Persians* framed sections of Aeschylus's play with a metatheatrical reality TV–style modern context (MTV Persia) punctuated by eclectic contemporary music (classical string music at the opening, then funk, rhythm and blues) and lively choreography in nightclub style. The play's topicality was explicit, but not overemphasized. The actors playing Atossa, Darius, Xerxes, and the messenger (played by the director Tom Ridgely) also played the Ghazis, a modern Iranian family. The tragic characters delivered in a more stylized and distanced fashion Atossa's dream about the Persian and Greek women yoked by Xerxes, Aeschylus's entire messenger speech about the battle of Salamis, Atossa's decision to call on Darius for counsel, and Xerxes' unhappy return. The script described the messenger speech as an "eyewitness report from over 2,000 years ago" (587), and it retained that kind of central authority.

The actors' modern Iranian roles as a mother skilled in popular dream interpretation, a hawkish grandfather, and a son crippled by his overly protective mother stressed themes of revenge and parental disappointment that appear in the original. For example, Atossa (the actress Hanna Cheek) had a skeptical dialogue with herself as Parvein, an Iranian mother skilled in popular dream interpretation: "PARVEIN: Whenever there is a horse or something acting like a horse it is a sign of pocket money coming to you soon. . . . ATOSSA: I don't think that's what it means. I think it means that we're going to lose this war on Greece" (582). The production also played more generally on the actors' own identities/ethnicities. For example, as Darius the African American Rodney King delivered an angry rhythm-and-blues ballad.

Ancient and modern worlds converged in the need for prayer in times of stress and in the theme of blame, or *takhseer* in Farsi. The problem of intercultural translation/mutual recrimination emerged in a song delivered in Farsi with crude English translations on cards, and then in English with cards in Farsi (583). Failed cultural translation had tragic as well as humorous dimensions, as Xerxes/the modern Iranian son (Arian Moayed, an Iranian immigrant) reiterated at the close his *takhseer,* nearly howling as he recited the names of ancient (Persian) and modern (the Iran-Iraq War, the Iraq War) Persian and American fallen in Farsi mixed with English (591; fig. 20). In a final shared speech the chorus closed the play with a pointed mix of light and serious that had shaped the whole:

> Woe upon woe upon woe upon woe upon
> How could you go and bring oh so much woe upon
> Woe upon woe upon woe upon woe upon

DEMOCRATIZING GREEK TRAGEDY 145

FIGURE 20. Waterwell's *Persians,* a new version of Aeschylus's *Persians* by Arian Moayed, directed by Tom Ridgely, Perry Street Theatre, New York, 2005. Photo by Ryan Jensen, courtesy of Waterwell.

> Show some remorse for the choice of your course upon
> Woe upon woe upon woe upon woe upon
> Throw us a bone you been gone for so long upon
> Woe upon woe upon woe upon woe upon
> Lo and behold it was all for the Gloria
> Woe upon woe upon woe upon woe upon
> Lo and behold it was all for the gold upon
> Woe upon woe upon woe upon woe upon
> . . .
> These people paid for a comedy show not for
> Woe upon woe upon woe upon woe upon
> Look high and low but there's nowhere to go upon
> Woe upon woe upon woe upon woe upon
>
> (Blackout)
> . . . . . .
>
> HANNA (ATOSSA/PARVEIN):
> I said Persia, oh Persia

No peace I find
Just an old sweet song
Keeps Persia on my mind.

ALL: Persia on my mind. (591–92)

Waterwell's version tried to preserve the integrity of both the ancient and the modern by juxtaposing them at a moment in U.S./Middle Eastern relations in which, in the group's view, Persian Iran seemed to be becoming by the minute hopelessly more Islamic, yet also absurdly culturally eclectic. The play, which continued to be revived by the group, found no good way out of continual violence or a clear location of blame but saw little point in being wistful, in trying to revive the past; the production suggested that only memory, laughter, and song and dance can allow us to look more carefully at the peculiar binds we are in. And this approach clearly resonated with its audiences.

### Sophocles' Ajax

In Sophocles' play *Ajax*, the second-best Greek warrior in the Trojan War has what might be termed a psychotic break when the arms of the dead Achilles are awarded to the strategist Odysseus rather than to himself. The goddess Athena deflects Ajax's homicidal wrath at the Greek chieftains onto their cattle. Ajax comes to himself and commits suicide, despite attempts by his concubine Tecmessa and his men (the chorus) to dissuade him. The chieftains Agamemnon and Menelaus try to prevent his burial, but Odysseus persuades them to relent and acknowledges Ajax's brilliant, if partially outdated, mode of heroism.

Sophocles' *Ajax* has rarely been produced in the United States, although its first production in 1903 was already linked with cultural politics. In the early nineteenth century, immigrant communities often used theater as a political and cultural statement. In the first known (all-male) production (six performances in 1903) Greek immigrants living near Hull House in Chicago were encouraged by Jane Addams to demonstrate the glory of Greece to ignorant Americans.[62] The amateur actors, drawn from a local population of about seven thousand, many of whom did not speak English, rehearsed in Chicago for seven nights a week for ten weeks; Georgios Metalas was a great success as Ajax. Hull House artists improved the scenery, which depicted ships on the shore; the music was sung in unison to the clarinet.

In 1904 Mabel Hay Barrows, formerly of Hull House, again directed the play with immigrants to considerable success at Clinton Hall in New York's East Side ghetto; she herself played Tecmessa. Costumes in the New York production were Homeric rather than Attic; the music by Willys Peck Kent and the choreography impressed critics as "archaic" in style. Despite the use of Modern Greek, the large (six-hundred-seat) Clinton Hall production attracted a diverse audience; reviews in both Chicago and New York were respectful, and the *New York Dramatic Mirror* (April 2, 1904) was enthusiastic about what "the push-cart industry" could achieve. Given Addams's sensitivity to the immigrants' anguish over the loss of dignity and identity offered by their heritage in a world indifferent to it, it seems unlikely that the choice of play was accidental. A 1904 article by Elizabeth C. Barrows, however, stresses the "unlettered" Chicago actors' interest in the burial theme.

Since the mid-1980s, however, the play has served to explore a fundamental conflict between American concepts of heroism threatened with obsolescence and the ruthless realism of modern, capitalist, and imperialistic politics. The most recent versions focus above all on the catastrophic stress that the battlefield can induce in warriors. Here I will contrast the controversial Sellars-Auletta version of 1985, which met with a generally positive reaction in Europe, with Ellen Beckerman's 2005 *Ajax: 100% Fun* by New York's LightBox Theatre Company. The second production was also pointedly political in its focus but adopted a style of theatrical pastiche that has proved quite successful for a number of other recent politically oriented productions of Greek tragedy in the United States.

Sellars and Auletta had teamed up before *Persians* to offer another controversial political statement through their 1986 production of Sophocles' *Ajax*, first at the La Jolla Playhouse in San Diego and then at the American National Theater at the Kennedy Center in Washington, D.C. It later toured Europe in 1987 (Brussels, Amsterdam, Antwerp, Stuttgart, North Rhine-Westphalia, and Vienna). Sellars had been invited to create a repertory company in Washington, but the production of *Ajax* closed early because of negative local reviews and responses, poor attendance, and cost overruns; the company was dissolved. The play was set in the near future after a successful U.S. attack on a leftist regime in Latin America. At the time Sellars and Auletta cited the recent American bombing of Libya, the sending of troops to Nicaragua, and the general repression of discussion and censorship during the Reagan era as motives for their version of *Ajax*, but Sellars now represents the play as a retrospective on the Vietnam War.[63]

The play was staged at the back entrance of the Pentagon with Athena presiding over a public hearing. Menelaus, Agamemnon, and Odysseus were played as five-star generals, some of whom, in an era before Colin Powell, were African American. Ajax, a wildly successful general with a Native American background, had married the exiled "red" daughter of the Latin American dictator whose regime he had toppled. Tecmessa was played by an Asian American actress (Lauren Tom), however, which brought resonances of Vietnam to the part. The chorus of soldiers/jury members—three blacks, a white, and a Korean dressed in military fatigues—sang blues and funk music and played the messenger, Teucer, Menelaus, and Agamemnon. The script included an evangelical messenger with angel's wings who spelled out Ajax's gospel of serving the spirit of man, not God; a black Athena in a silver evening gown (Aleta Mitchell) who was once raped by Ajax, her favorite, and now delighted in seductively torturing him in the opening scene and presiding over the hearing thereafter; a terrified Tecmessa who cursed God for Ajax's destruction; and ruthless, competitive, media-savvy generals who wanted to deny Ajax burial at Arlington National Cemetery, wipe out his memory, and improve their chances of running for office. In the final scene, the blinds over the windows flew up, exposing the Pentagon as an empty facade.[64] Water continuously flowed over a raked floor as it washed away the blood of the still-living hero and soiled the pristine uniforms of the generals. The public quality of the play was also maintained by the use of microphones by all characters except in the intimate scene between Tecmessa, Ajax, and their son; Sellars saw the microphones as the equivalent of Greek masks.[65]

Although it is not hard to see why this production proved controversial, some reviews outside Washington were in fact quite positive, praising in particular the remarkable performance of the deaf actor Howie Seago as Ajax. The hero's deafness communicated both his inability to see and hear as others do, and the tragic failure of communication between himself and his fellow generals. Seago's lines were spoken either by different chorus members or, in the scene in which he speaks to his son, by Tecmessa; Seago himself used sign language except at one desperate moment when he spoke for himself, saying: "How can you turn away from me now when I need you?" (27) His use of gesture, ranging from his violent movements at the opening, where the mad hero was exhibited laughing insanely in a bloody transparent plastic box, to his fluid and poetic motions as he signed his famous last speech to his wife and followers about the inexorability of time and change, was reinforced in the final scenes by the silent presence of his dead body and of his anguished, politically vulnerable wife.

Manhood gone berserk is a familiar American theme. In creating an Ajax "nailed to a circus of blood," whose violence and pride resonated not only with his Native American warrior ancestry, but with dangerous, marginally civilized, mythic, often antiheroic U.S. film heroes ranging from cowboys to sons of the Mafia, Sellars had in mind roles played by Al Pacino and Robert De Niro.[66] The play asked what this kind of ambiguous figure means to us now, and why he is so firmly lodged in our national imagination despite a reality that ignores him. In this version, Ajax is both the "force and heart of the American army"(22) and the earliest American, who has been replaced by fast-talking, pretentious, and slick later immigrants. He is terrifying, poetic, yet nonverbal, and vulnerable to a dangerous internal collapse. The first half of the play had far fewer modern references, which underlined even more than in the original play the sharp transition from Ajax's complex, isolated world among friends and family to that of his double-speaking, more contemporary fellow generals. The chorus was finally reduced to one person after taking other parts; Tecmessa was silenced, and Teucer bound to a chair. Ajax himself failed to achieve the quick death for which he wished, and was forced to experience the war of words over his drenched, helpless body. Despite the contemporary setting, the play's hypothetical war (Auletta says in his introduction that he deliberately avoided mentioning Vietnam) and the powerful and original portrait of the hero nevertheless permitted this controversial adaptation to retain a more compelling tragic authority for some audience members than *Persians*. Speaking of Shakespeare, Sellars has remarked: "The reason we apply poetry to these questions [contemporary social and political issues] is because in the end it's more interesting than journalism. Shakespeare can go further than *Newsweek*. Shakespeare's equipment is better calibrated to deal with what we are actually facing as a society."[67] In *Ajax*, Sellars came closer to this goal.

A flurry of interest in *Ajax* in more recent years has offered new angles on interpreting the play in the context of the Iraq War.[68] For example, both the New York *Ajax* by Teatro Latea in November 2004 and *Ajax: 100% Fun* by the LightBox Theatre Company in 2005, directed by Ellen Beckerman at the Culture Project in New York, inserted interpolated modern texts (identified in the play's program) into a performance of the original. Beckerman was influenced by similar techniques in the new versions of Greek drama by the American playwright Charles Mee.[69] LightBox's production, on which I will concentrate here, was inspired by episodes of fragging (soldiers turning against and killing their own commanders) in the Iraq War but wished to make, especially through Odysseus's dramatic shift to advocating Ajax's burial at the ending, a larger point: "At a time when so many people in the world are gathering their energy to fight their enemies, it feels important to remind ourselves that 'the enemy' is an identity that is fluid, shifting, and ultimately just a figment of our imagination" (director's note).

The play opened with a scene at stage right in which the actor playing Ajax recalled a fishing trip with his formidable father as he boned a raw fish (fig. 21). The boy, for once, had outclassed his father by catching a legal-sized trout.[70] This recollection set the stage for Ajax's own fear of failing his father, which is central to the original play. This version's interpolated texts had varied functions, some in effect choral in their implications. Excerpts from interrogations of Iraq War prisoners, collected by Amnesty International,[71] framed the opening scene in which Athena displayed the mad Ajax to a terrified Odysseus, and served to provoke questions about the scene by collapsing boundaries between torturer and tortured. The second of these interrogations was accompanied by Christina Aguilera's song "Dirty," which was actually used to induce stress in prisoners. A typical line in the interrogations ran: "INTERROGATOR: We are trying to ascertain who are the good guys and who are the bad guys? Which are you?" ... "INTERROGATED: You have no right to keep me here if you have no evidence. INTERROGATOR: That's just the way it is. You got caught in a war." Another interrogation occurred after Ajax

FIGURE 21. Ajax (Shawn Fagan) bones a fish in *Ajax: 100% Fun*, adapted and directed by Ellen Beckerman, Culture Project, New York, 2005. Photo by Benjamin Heller, courtesy of Culture Project.

departed to commit suicide: "INTERROGATOR: You should be afraid because we are very unsure what to do with you." A final interrogation, which came after Ajax's suicide, turned the hero into the interrogated.

Other excerpts offered modern takes on the reactions of soldiers to combat. For example, Ajax's crewmen imagined the ideal care package for combatants and enumerated what they would like to do to the enemy in a list partly derived from Anthony Swofford's *Jarhead* and partly from Evan Wright's *Generation Kill*. A section with interpolated suicide notes appeared just before Ajax's last speech; the final suicide note and the play's subtitle came from Kurt Cobain: "The fact is I can't fool you. The worst crime I can think of would be to rip people off by faking it and pretending as if I'm having 100% fun. Thank you all from the pit of my burning, nauseous stomach. I don't have the passion anymore, and so remember, it's better to burn than to fade away."[72] Songs, sometimes sung by the actor playing Odysseus to guitar accompaniment and sometimes sung and danced to recorded music by the cast, were interspersed throughout the play to similar effect. Just before the play's final song, the men drew on Jonathan Shay's book *Achilles in Vietnam* in a fragment about the failure to adjust to civilian life by returning veterans.

Running through the whole performance was a series of remarks by the character playing Menelaus/Donald Rumsfeld drawn from *Pieces of Intelligence: The Existential Poetry of Donald H. Rumsfeld* (compiled by Hart Seely), which develops a bizarrely ironic relation to the text. The entire play came to seem as if it were occurring in a vacuum of leadership or authoritative political analysis, in which access to the truth had become increasingly random. This representative text occurred after the first Odysseus, Ajax, Athena scene and before the second interrogation excerpt:

> RUMSFELD (to the audience, friendly):
>
> You're going to be told a lot of things.
> You get told things every day
> That don't happen.
>
> It does not seem to bother people . . . they don't—
> it gets printed in the press
> and the world thinks all these things happened.
> They never happened.
>
> Everyone is so eager to get the story
> Before in fact the story's there
> That the world is constantly being fed
> Things that haven't happened.
>
> All I can tell you is
> It hasn't happened.
>
> It's going to happen.

Overall, Sophocles' tragedy retained its integrity in *Ajax: 100% Fun* through a kind of Brechtian distancing, but it was interrupted, queried, and brought into modern focus by the interpolated texts, which were far more public and sober in tone than in Waterwell's *Persians* and aimed to increase the tragic uncertainties of the original, although they did not try to be exactly analogous to the original scenes. Rumsfeld himself will very likely prove less meaningful as an individual to an American audience in the near future, but the modern experiences of war depicted here will not. Energetic theatrical precision helped to integrate Sophocles' play and the later texts,[73] although this kind of production runs the risk of both representing the ancient text less provocatively or imaginatively than a straight performance of the original play and underlining its "pastness." Not surprisingly,

LightBox's emphasis on battle stress has continued to generate new productions in the United States. Ellen McLaughlin's *Ajax in Iraq*, directed by Scott Zigler at the American Repertory Theater (ART) in Cambridge, Massachusetts, October 9–11, 2008, and revived in 2011, directed by August Schulenburg for the Flux Theatre Ensemble at the Clemente Soto Vélez Cultural & Educational Center in New York, took an analogous approach by juxtaposing scenes from Sophocles' *Ajax* with a parallel story about A. J., an heroic female soldier and military rape victim in Iraq. McLaughlin developed the text after extensive collaboration with Harvard graduate students in theater, who had researched the Iraq War and other wars using sources ranging from personal interviews and websites to published works. In 2010–11, Brian Doerries' Theater of War project presented with considerable success staged readings of his translations of Sophocles' *Ajax* and *Philoctetes* for audiences that include veterans and victims of post-traumatic stress disorder.[74]

### *Euripides'* Children of Heracles

Sellars's third pointedly political production of Greek tragedy, which aimed to address the contemporary refugee problem with productions in Europe (at a Kurdish resettlement center in Germany, and in France, Italy, and the Netherlands) and the United States (at ART in Cambridge in 2005),[75] met with a considerably better reception than his two earlier plays.[76] The difference in approach is telling. This time Sellars embedded Ralph Gladstone's translation of Euripides' rarely performed *Children of Heracles* (only seven productions since antiquity are known, none in the United States)[77] in an evening that opened with a dialogue among refugees, professional human rights experts, and political leaders led by broadcaster and journalist Christopher Lydon, continued with the play and a short meal, and closed with films from countries that recently produced or are producing political refugees. The lobby of the Loeb Drama Center in Cambridge was strewn with images of refugees, and materials documenting their current situation were distributed.

Euripides' play deals with the fate of the children of Heracles, who are exiled after the death of their father and forced to seek sanctuary. Athens at first reluctantly agrees to receive them even at the price of a battle against Heracles' persecutor, the tyrant Eurystheus, who had sent him on his famous labors. Success in battle requires the sacrifice of a virgin; Heracles' daughter heroically steps into the breach to volunteer for death just as Athens is about to back out. After Athens' victory in the battle, in which Heracles' aged supporter, Iolaus, is rejuvenated, Heracles' mother, Alcmene, takes revenge on the prisoner Eurystheus by insisting on his death, despite his status as a prisoner of war. In the ambivalent conclusion Athens finally agrees to this revenge as long as its leader is not directly involved. Attic myth traditionally celebrated the city-state's reception of problematic suppliants, and this particular instance was already famous in Attic funerary orations.

Euripides complicated the story, and thus the whole issue of receiving refugees, by introducing a new role for both Heracles' daughter and the enraged Alcmene.

Sellars had the children of Heracles played by actual refugee children, who sat in often visibly unengaged and thus antitheatrical silence at a raised altar surrounded by a florescent rectangle except when they entered the audience to shake their hands and thank audience members for allowing them into the country. The choral role was played by two speakers sitting at a conference table off stage right who created a bureaucratic atmosphere suggestive of a public hearing or tribunal and by a Kazakh singer of epic in a rich red native costume, Ulzhan Baibussynova, who accompanied her traditional largely minor-key songs about peace, freedom, social unity, and violence on a two-stringed lute, or *dombra*. (Supertitles translated her songs, which were available on the ART website in 2008, www.amrep.org.) The public tone of the play was maintained by the use of microphones, which were moved around the stage for rhetorical emphasis, and the lighting, which could project large shadows of the major figures on the blank back wall. Other images were avoided, in order to separate the stage experience from that created in other visual media, like films or TV. The actors playing Heracles' family spoke in accented English, and their women dressed in discreet clothing suggestive of the Middle East. The same actress played both Heracles' daughter and Alcmene; the virgin, who was sacrificed on stage, thus seemed to give birth to her avenging grandmother. Iolaus was helpless in a wheelchair until his miraculous departure for battle. The humanity of the Athenians and family of Heracles was stressed by spare but pointed instances of close physical contact at critical moments, especially in the case of the Attic king, here president, who was played by a woman in Western dress, as was the aggressive Argive envoy from Eurystheus. The president's care for the refugees was underlined when she turned her back to the audience to attend to them. The ending was made more ambivalent by the appearance of Eurystheus in the bright orange overalls of a Guantánamo detainee as he stood behind a transparent acrylic shield.

By laying the refugee question before the protodemocratic government of Athens in Euripides' play, Sellars wished to provoke a parallel dialogue in a democratic nation founded and enriched by refugees. Regardless of the controversy generated by both refugees and immigration in the United States (or Europe) in many periods, the audience here could hardly fail to recognize the many sides of the issue. As Sellars put it, "The Greeks invented democracy and theater almost at the same moment—and not by accident. They knew you had to have a place where you can discuss difficult questions at a high level. And that will never be the Senate." Sellars continued: "The civil discourse of theatre makes democracy possible because it provides a place where you don't have to be polite, where the gloves are taken off, but where nobody is actually taking the blow."[78] The entire production left considerable room for debate, and the decision to perform an unfamiliar, Greek original that itself included patriotic elements in a complex modern context rather than offer an aggressive, new, and more pessimistic version, as in *Persians* and *Ajax*, may explain in part the different and far more sympathetic reception this play received in the United States. In addition, the refugee problem is an international one, so the play could invite a broader and less-pointed discussion.

## 4. AESCHYLUS'S *PROMETHEUS BOUND* IN THE UNITED STATES: FROM THE THREAT OF APOCALYPSE TO COMMUNAL RECONCILIATION

As a conflict among divinities, Aeschylus's rarely performed *Prometheus Bound* (*PB*) inevitably raises a different set of political issues in the mind of an audience. In *PB*, which may not be by Aeschylus himself, but composed by a fifth-century B.C.E. poet, the god Zeus, recently established as an all-powerful ruler of the universe, has the older-generation god Prometheus, or Forethought, chained to a remote mountaintop by Force, Might, and the reluctant god Hephaestus because of Prometheus's benefactions to humankind, especially his gift of fire, which is the source of the divine tyrant's own power (his thunderbolts) and of the technical skills that enable humans to control nature. Prometheus remains intransigent following a series of visits by a chorus of daughters of Ocean; his father-in-law Oceanus, the human victim of Zeus' lust; the pregnant Io, who has been forced to wander the world as a cow but will one day give birth to a new dynasty in Egypt; and finally Zeus's messenger Hermes, who wants to find out from Prometheus the secret of Zeus's possible future loss of power. Zeus then inflicts further punishment on Prometheus and perhaps as well on the loyal Oceanids (the staging of the play's conclusion is uncertain). This play was very likely part of a now-lost trilogy in which Prometheus and Zeus were eventually reconciled.

Until the late 1960s, U.S. theater expressed little interest in *PB*. The earliest production of the play was staged in Greek in New York as a benefit for the famous Delphi Festival production by Angelos Sikelianos and his wife, Eva Palmer Sikelianos, in May 1930; a 1957 English version starring Blanche Yurka and Clarence Derwent, directed by James Derwent with costumes by Eva Palmer Sikelianos, recreated the famous Delphi production.[79] In 1964 a performance of *PB* at New York's East River Amphitheater by the Group of Ancient Drama attracted little attention; it was reperformed as *Black Titan* in 1970 by the same group in honor of Martin Luther King Jr. In a move toward later politically oriented productions, Klansmen bound John McCurry as Prometheus, and Io was sold as a slave by a white master.[80]

From the late 1960s to the mid-1980s, however, several important new versions used the play to address central issues of the period: imperialism (especially the Vietnam War), the exploitation of women, and the dangers of technology, particularly the possibility of nuclear annihilation. In 1967, with the support of Robert Brustein, who was well known for promoting plays with a political focus, the Yale School of Drama performed a new prose version by the poet Robert Lowell, starring Irene Worth as Io and Kenneth Haigh as Prometheus and directed by Jonathan Miller. Miller's eclectic production, which set the play in the seventeenth century against an unending, imprisoning brick wall and costumed Hermes as an SS officer and Hephaistos as a crippled Negro, was unable to give energy and focus to an already complex and densely worded new version of the original. Reviews responded to the superlative acting of Worth and Haigh but agreed that "it couldn't possibly make it—on Broadway or off."[81]

In Lowell's pessimistic play, an overly intellectual Prometheus is destroyed by the very gift of fire that he gave to humanity, and the rest of the universe will soon join him. In Aeschylus, without the help of the prophetic Prometheus, Zeus is in danger of producing a divine son who will replace him. Lowell's Prometheus confronts a universe no longer structured by the dictates of fate. For the tyrannical Zeus, "no piece of knowledge ever quite turned into wisdom" (52), and he now whiles away his time playing with his thunderbolts and fireworks.

Lowell's humans are described as "people, who are more gaily industrious and disciplined than their neighbors, people who have forced every land and water to be a highway for their daring, who imagine they have left imperishable monuments for good and evil behind them—they will be men who hold elections and know how to obey" (41) and will misuse the gift of fire to create "a blackened trail of motion" on earth (59). The pregnant Io, a female victim of imperialistic violence whose child will be born to no great future "in the muddy shallows of that dismal little Asian backwater" (45), even surrenders voluntarily to Zeus before meeting a horrific death.[82]

Lowell's moral outrage and his broad despair at (democratic) man's and god's betrayal of their intellectual capacities in favor of power, technology, and violence were picked up in a far more topical fashion in Richard Schechner's 1985 production of *The Prometheus Project: Four Movements and a Coda* at his New York Performing Garage, which pointedly equated Promethean fire with the atom bomb and turned Io into a prototypically abused woman.[83] Part 1 featured slides of Hiroshima accompanied by music and watched by a figure in a leather coat, apparently Prometheus regretting both giving fire to humankind and preventing mortals from seeing their doom. The theme of voyeurism linked parts 1 and 2. In part 2 the innovative porn star Annie Sprinkle, was clad in a tight nurse's outfit before she stripped and lectured about sex education to four dirty, hooting old men in raincoats. The audience was asked if they were ashamed to watch, but no one could leave without crossing the stage. In part 3, Sprinkle put on Io's heifer's head and ran back and forth accompanied by "virginally garbed"[84] women, two of whom described sexual assaults by men. In part 4 a naked Prometheus was bound and tied at length by two men and one woman. Prometheus's torture was described, Io and the rest of the cast returned, and the play closed with the message that "it is the nursery of life itself that is being poisoned." Reviewers objected to the play's voyeurism and the strained connection between the bombing of Hiroshima and sexual abuse.[85]

I will close by examining a novel version of *PB* created by an American community in order to move beyond the intransigence of Aeschylus's divine hero and the troubles of the twentieth century and to reimagine the reconciliation that emerged from suffering in Aeschylus's lost Prometheus trilogy. *Steelbound,* a new version of *Prometheus Bound* performed in Bethlehem, Pennsylvania in 1999, represented a communal response to the final closing of the steel plants there and became the centerpiece of "Steel Festival: The Art of an Industry." In collaboration with the Cornerstone Theater Company of Los Angeles, a group that specializes in adapting classics for community theater productions, Bethlehem's Touchstone Theatre set up interviews with former steelworkers and community members to develop a ninety-minute play that served both to memorialize past achievements and to facilitate a cathartic move to a new era; both Lehigh University and Bethlehem Steel helped make the project possible.

Written by Alison Carey and directed by Bill Rauch, both of Cornerstone, with music by Ysaye Barnwell of the gospel group Sweet Honey in the Rock and choreography by Jennie Gilrain, the cast included fifty-six people, most of them community members. The production took place in an abandoned iron foundry in the Bethlehem Steel Corporation's cavernous South Side plant; built in 1893, the ruined building, with its huge Romanesque arches, resembled an "industrial cathedral."[86] The play's Prometheus, a laid-off steelworker, refused to accept the closing of the mills; in the opening scene Brutality and Indifference, at the behest of Progress, had Prometheus (Bill George) welded in a Christ-like position to the top of a 27.5-ton pouring ladle by his reluctant fellow riggers. Prometheus was joined in succession by a chorus of curious local women who had never been allowed into the mill (Aeschylus's Oceanids); a former turner (plant supervisor) on a man lift (substituting for Ocean in the original) who failed to soften Prometheus's resistance; a chorus of local youths sizing up the past; Penny, an injured, young steelworker's daughter who lost her memory after her car crashed in the mill (this version's Io); a chorus of steelworkers; and Herman, a young historian who would like a role in the industry's new museums under development and offers both an outsider's perspective and some comic relief (Hermes in the original).

Whereas Aeschylus's play ultimately focused on the future, this production ritualized and reevaluated the past to become what Lynn Jeffries, the Cornerstone designer, called "a really good funeral."[87] As Prometheus puts it, "I'm learning that it takes/As much courage to stand in front of the past/As it used to take to stand in front of the future," and to confront "history, progress, the invisible forces of fate,/the inevitability of change" (21). "Think for one minute what it feels like to be turned into history when you're still alive," he remarks to Herman (32). Once the chorus of steelworkers arrived, they placed symbolic objects—helmets, tools—before the ladle as they recited the names of former plants and their closing dates, workers' nicknames, ethnicities, and occupations, the recipe for making good steel, and reminiscences of the excitement and the suffering produced by working in the industry, in terms of multiple injuries and false promises from steel executives. The women countered the younger people's loss of faith in trust and hard work generated by the closing ("you shouldn't count on anything . . . No room for faith in the modern economy") with "That's not the lesson/to be learned from this place" (19). Penny, a computer programmer from a steel family who initially insisted that "you can't expect a person to live without the past" (20) and lamented the loss of community her great-grandfathers shared through the mills, departed reconciled to the new community she was meeting through the web.

Prometheus's secret in this version is his certainty that a nation needs all of its people, and "progress itself will be back for me one day/To undo these chains" (30). Herman, as historian of the steel industry (1863–1998), reminded Prometheus of the workers who had it worse because they never experienced the period of economic security enjoyed by the steelworkers. Their shared recollections of worker injuries and industrial pollution partly opened the way for Prometheus's change of heart. The play celebrated the workers' pride in building America and finally made this achievement the basis for moving on: "I made the standard for what a good American life is" (10). Uz, a rigger, concluded the play with the view "We don't build America anymore because we already built it . . . and everything we built is still out there,/Wherever you look./And it's going to be out there a good long time/Because, after all, it's made of steel" (38). Above all, however, the outcome turned on the fellowship of the workers themselves. As a second rigger, Heffy, asserted, "The walls, the machines, this place was the body. But we were the soul" (38). At the conclusion, Prometheus joined the workers' festival, releasing himself from chains that his fellow union members had only pretended to make inescapable.

The production humanized Prometheus's divine tragedy—steelworkers and union members represented an embattled heroism that could span generations—and moved on to a form of reconciliation with the ambivalent powers, both industrial and historical, that controlled the workers' lives, just as in the reconciliation that may have occurred between Prometheus and Zeus at the conclusion of the original trilogy (*Prometheus Unbound*). As one member of the fire department in the audience put it, the play created a "[Vietnam] Wall for workers."[88] Although cast member Sara Brady, who played Penny, later criticized the production in *The Drama Review*, both for failing to confront the unnecessary refusal of the mills to modernize and save the workers' jobs and for compromising with Bethlehem Steel in order to use the plant's space, Touchstone and Cornerstone members responded that their production deliberately aimed to reflect the will of the community and to heal by offering a larger historical picture through which those involved could make sense of and come to terms with a conflict-ridden experience that could no longer be rectified.[89] Successful American community-based theater should in their view move beyond 1960s radicalism to engage the community in participating through art to gain a more unified and liberating experience of a shared reality.[90]

## CONCLUSION

In 1987, the first of many U.S. productions of A. R. Gurney's *Another Antigone* was staged at the Old Globe Theatre in San Diego, California, under the direction of John Tillinger. The play's classics professor, Henry Harper, had refused to grade a new version of *Antigone* by one of his students, Judy Miller, that addressed the nuclear arms race with characters based on Jane Fonda and Ronald Reagan. Henry had not invited creative assignments, since they did not in his view enhance the understanding of Greek drama. Previous versions of *Antigone* by his students had already addressed the McCarthy hearings, the civil rights movement, and the Vietnam War. "You have taken one of the world's great plays, and reduced it to a juvenile polemic on current events," he remarked (174). Judy's increasing resistance to this response ultimately leads all of the major characters into trouble and a change of heart. Neither of the two characters, as arguably in the original play, proved "right." In a sense, all ideologically and topically specific productions and versions of Greek tragedy run this same risk of offending or trivializing, as well as the reverse risk that a production that does not acknowledge in some way its place in the moment is not going to attract an audience.

Politically oriented productions of Greek tragedy in the United States, most of which have been performed since 1970, have tended to take three approaches. Some present up-to-date translations or close adaptations that avoid heavy anachronism in response to a specific context or issue and rely on timing or performance style to make the play's public statement; productions of *Trojan Women* often fall into this category. Some reimagine or rewrite the original with various degrees of anachronism and topicality; this has been a popular approach in the United States since the 1930s and represents a trend also addressed in other chapters of this book. The third approach, which has gained considerable momentum in the United States, interpolates or interweaves modern material into a production of the original play and allows the juxtaposition to make a statement. In addition, a number of new versions have pointedly violated generic boundaries between tragedy, comedy, and satire (see also chapter 5.3–4 on *Medea*) to contrast ancient and modern in a fashion that comments on the relevance of the original.[91] As noted in chapters 1 and 2, aesthetic choices have played a critical role in communicating the potentially controversial political issues posed by Greek tragedy to U.S. audiences.

Aggressively political or topical new versions have tended to fare better in Europe than in the United States, when presented in both places. Yet American productions became increasingly more responsive to war and global violence over the course of the twentieth century. Even class issues have emerged, in community-oriented productions like *Steelbound,* to complement a longer history of productions addressing gender, race, and ethnicity. Women have played an important role in the larger story from the nineteenth century on, and ethnic minorities (see especially chapter 5) have more recently joined them. In the late twentieth and early twenty-first centuries, some productions have conveyed a greater sense of pessimism and irony about public life and its corruption that is in some respect foreign to the American myths of progress, which initially resisted such ambivalent perspectives on the stage. The plays discussed in this chapter, however, largely reach a limited, educated, and primarily urban audience that might be expected to respond more favorably to them. At the same time, on the basis of sheer quantity of plays produced (this chapter has barely begun to address the full range of examples), theater makers seem to be looking more often to Greek tragedy to explore their views on public life and to make their productions of the plays more compelling from this perspective than before.

FOUR

# Reenvisioning the Hero
## American Oedipus

> *The overmastering fates that broke men and women upon the wheels of torture that destiny might be fulfilled are far away from us; the gods that lived and cast deep shadows over men's lives are turned to stone. The helpful human being who pays his way through the world finds it hard to imagine the creature kicking helpless in the traps of the gods.*
> —NEW YORK HERALD, FEBRUARY 4, 1882

> *King Oedipus certainly carries more woe to the square inch than anybody else that ever walked the stage, and it is woe of the very worst kind—without any basis of justice, without desert, without motivation, without solace, without hope.*
> —NEW YORK TRIBUNE, JANUARY 31, 1882

These two reviews of the 1882 professional version of the Harvard *Oedipus Tyrannus* (hereafter *OT*) discussed in chapter 1.1 typically assume a tension between Oedipus as an innocent victim of the gods and the ideal American citizen, who optimistically struggles to earn his or her way in the world and to be rewarded for virtue and hard work. Sophocles' hero in fact aggressively insists on discovering a fundamental civic pollution/his own human identity, reinterpreting his fate, and taking an extravagant and brutal responsibility for his unwitting crimes. American democracy has often preferred to look forward, or perhaps, like the chorus at *OT*'s conclusion, not to look at terrible truths at all—though Sophocles' chorus does not in the end avert its gaze from Oedipus. Freud's insistence that *Oedipus* is compelling to its audience because the incestuous and parricidal hero has lived out humanity's (more specifically, men's) own unconscious wishes (to kill the father and possess the mother) has sometimes compounded the problems posed by Oedipus for a reluctant American audience.

Yet paradoxically, despite this fundamental resistance to what was typically understood to be Sophocles' tragic vision, U.S. theater has preserved a significant, continuing, and evolving engagement with Oedipus. The intransigent hero unjustly trapped by an incomprehensible, divinely constructed fate gradually assumed more dimensions as the democratic yet potentially tyrannical and hubristic leader, the unwitting cause of new kinds of pollution, the child deliberately abandoned by his parents, the partner of a wife/mother who developed increasing dramatic interest in her own right. Sophocles' play sets up Oedipus as a traditional scapegoat figure only to deny his departure to exile or death promised in the play's early scenes (as well as affirmed in later plays, such as *Oedipus at Colonus*); the play separates him from his children and shuts him in his palace. Yet *OT*'s final scene apparently offers him a new sense of identity/authority through his self-destruction.[1] To the chorus's horror, Oedipus thinks he has chosen the right self-punishment for a fate that Apollo's oracle predicted; he survives to confront that destiny and seems far more certain what it should entail than Thebes' new leader, Creon. U.S. productions have taken particular advantage of the play's perhaps puzzling (given the emphasis on the plague-ridden city in early scenes) move from a public to a more personal focus but have often revised the ending (or even the beginning) to serve new interpretations of Oedipus's story and its implications for his family and social world.

As discussed earlier, Americans have been generally reluctant to invest resources in major productions of Greek tragedy on the professional, as opposed to the university, stage. Flamboyant female characters like Electra and Medea (see the introduction and chapter 5) periodically emerge as attractive vehicles for actresses, including many from abroad. Greek male heroes, however, like Orestes and Pentheus, have at certain historical moments such as the 1960s–1970s been (like Electra) more attractive for their split psyches than for their leadership and public personas.[2] The exception is *Oedipus Tyrannus*, which from its unusually public nineteenth-century debut has attracted regular substantial native productions, especially from the 1970s on, sometimes in combination with *Oedipus at Colonus* (hereafter *OC*) and *Antigone*. Despite a residual nineteenth-century reluctance on the part of critics to expose Oedipus's unwitting parricide and incest on the public stage (see chapter 1.1), *OT* was viewed from the start as the most stageworthy Greek tragedy, owing in no small part to its reputation in Aristotle's *Poetics* as the perfectly structured Greek tragedy, and to the additional luster of a plot that resonated with both Freudian theory and detective fiction (Oedipus's persistent pursuit of his identity/discovery of the murderer of Laius). Although *OT* has generated important new versions in the United States, this play offers the best chance of exploring the range of approaches taken over time on the American professional stage to producing a Greek original in translation (often supported by adequate theatrical resources). At the same time, the theatrical choices made in presenting the play raise broader questions about what the Greek male tragic hero has meant to audiences in the United States, and how the hero's complex, often ambivalent relation to the gods, fate, and the state has been represented and interpreted.

This chapter will offer a selective, thematically organized study of the U.S. reception of Sophocles' *OT* from the early 1970s to 2006, whether performed alone or in combination with related plays or reimagined in new versions. Early productions discussed in chapter 1.1, such as the Harvard *OT*, tended to be attracted to the play's formal brilliance, and many competent later productions did not offer much further interpretation or motivation for performing the play than its canonical status. From the 1970s on, however, productions developed a more self-conscious focus. Whereas a 1958 production of Albert Cook's translation at the Cleveland Play House staged by Frederic McConnell claimed in the program notes that *Oedipus* represented "a growing humanism that replaces ritual," in the 1970s and 1980s the play became a vehicle for exploring human origins or human nature in productions that put a special emphasis on ritual and on Oedipus's role as scapegoat in a fashion that may have made his story more legible, as was the case with nineteenth-century heroic melodramas discussed in the introduction, to a Christian audience (see part 1 below). More recently, a few productions and new versions have focused on Oedipus's role as the unwitting source of various new forms of social pollution and corruption (see part 2). Pairings of *OT* with other plays (see part 3) have represented in part a resistance to the spare characterization and fatal geometry of the original that was present from its earliest commercial performances, and a new interest in comparing the public styles and views of social reality represented by Oedipus or Creon as leaders, and from a different perspective, by Antigone. A number of more recent productions pointedly attempted to reimagine or reexamine Oedipus's relation to his destiny (see part 4), whether that destiny is imposed externally or subconsciously. Finally, a group of twenty-first-century plays emphasizing Oedipus's abandonment by his parents (see part 5) reflect a growing American and international interest in expanding the role of Jocasta that was promoted by the rise of feminism in this period. Despite a continuing resistance to *OT*'s overall structure and focus, these trends suggest the emergence of an evolving American identification with Oedipus's search for identity as well as an increasing willingness to confront Oedipus's role as a compelling yet potentially dangerous leader. The play, originally imagined for a democratic audience, currently resonates more with an American democracy that is beginning to observe itself from an uneasy, perhaps more "tragic" perspective.

## 1. OEDIPUS AS SCAPEGOAT

### *The 1972 Guthrie Theater* Oedipus the King

Among professional theaters in the United States, the Guthrie Theater in Minneapolis has played an important and all too distinctive role in presenting ambitious versions of Greek tragedy, featuring new translations, new music and choreography designed for its productions, and substantial rehearsal time.[3] The Guthrie's

FIGURE 22. Oedipus (Kenneth Welsh), Shepherd (Oliver Cliff), and guards (Wilberto Rosario and Douglas Hamilton) in *Oedipus the King*, adapted by Anthony Burgess, directed by Michael Langham, Guthrie Theater, St. Paul, Minnesota, 1973. Photo by Act One, Too, Ltd Photography.

1972 (revived in 1973) *OT*, staged by the British director Michael Langham, was the first of a number of productions that stressed ritual, mystical traditions, and human origins (fig. 22). This production, which drew on traditions from many ancient and primitive cultures, was designed to represent "man at the crossroads of his development" and to diverge from traditions for performing Greek tragedy established in the nineteenth century.[4] As Langham put it, "I have been groping not so much for answers that are purely Greek as for an atmosphere that is primitive in its overwhelming superstitions and timeless in its fears and meanings."[5]

The overture was set to what the adapter Anthony Burgess called "Indo-European chants."[6] Stanley Silverman's music, which accompanied both odes and parts of spoken scenes, was played on piano, trumpets, oboe, percussion, cello, bassoon, flute, piccolo, a Chinese plate cymbal, Buddhist bowls, and bamboo chimes, and included vocal drone borrowed from Pygmy, Coptic, Greek Orthodox, and Tibetan chants, as well as Middle Eastern prayer: it became "a synoptic gospel of all ancient cultures."[7] The set, designed by Desmond Heeley, placed a tall slit between two huge craggy walls of battered rusty steel that initially opened to propel Oedipus, wearing only a loincloth, onto the stage. The grays and browns of the later costumes, ragged for the populace and fur, leather, and loosely woven fabrics for the principals, suggested "a composite of primitive cultural sources," including Egypt, and in the case of the chorus, Byzantine monks or Greek Orthodox patriarchs.[8]

The published script, which followed Sophocles fairly closely, included several additions to underline its ritual logic. It opened with a polished marble altar half-obscured with the smoke of incense; following a scream, a priest plunged his hand into the body of a child, presumably sacrificed to avert the Theban plague, and drew out its heart.[9] The image also suggested birth, both the fraught birth of Oedipus and human birth. Oedipus echoed this primal scream at the moment he discovered his identity.[10] Indeed, the Sphinx's riddle about human identity deliberately framed the play. At the conclusion of Oedipus's initial dialogue with the chorus of elderly priests (one priest in the original play), a child asked for the Sphinx's story. The child cannot understand why the Sphinx's riddle was, as one priest asserts, so unanswerable. The text suggests a Eucharistic rite in which the children (whose gestures were later echoed by Oedipus) participate: "Each of them gains that way [through the sacrifice and the riddle] a little of the substance of Oedipus."[11]

At the play's conclusion, following Oedipus's onstage blinding,[12] an elderly shepherd led in children with votive offerings in gratitude for the first successful births of both animals and people since the plague began. The blind Oedipus, who in this version has been reluctantly permitted by Creon to depart for exile on his mountain mother, Cithairon, with his daughters, exits through the theater, leaning on a cane. He has become not only the double of the blind prophet Tiresias, but, as was apt for a performance that emphasized ritual so strongly, the successful scapegoat that Sophocles' play defers. Although the report of Apollo's oracle in the early scenes of the original play leads the audience to believe that the city can be saved from pollution only by removing the murderer of King Laius, Creon confines Oedipus, who continues to demand exile, against his will in the palace, awaiting further word from Apollo's oracle at Delphi, and separates him from his daughters; the play thus reentraps Oedipus within his household and refuses closure. Sir Tyrone Guthrie's own famous 1957 production of Yeats's *OT* in Stratford, Ontario, had, under the influence of the British Cambridge school, which included Jane Harrison, Gilbert Murray, and Francis Cornford, similarly interpreted Oedipus as a Christ-like scapegoat for the community under the influence of myths about the archetypal "year-spirit" whose sacrifice brought renewal and fertility.[13] In Max Reinhardt's *OT* (1910 in Munich), mentioned in chapter 1, Oedipus also famously exited through the audience. In Burgess's version, a child remains puzzled by Oedipus's fate:[14]

> CHORUS LEADER:
> Perhaps it was better to be killed by it.
> The riddle was not meant to be answered.
>
> CHILD:
> But he answered it. He saved us.

That's the story we're told.

CHORUS LEADER:
It is dangerous to answer riddles,
But some men are born to answer them.
It is the gods' doing. They hide themselves in riddles.
We must not try to understand too much.

CHILD:
Why?

Langham, in a letter to Burgess dated April 6, 1972, and included in the program, says that the play "grows with each reading and is now beginning to penetrate right into my subconscious which, I suppose, is where it belongs." Or, as the 1972 Guthrie Theater production's publicity claimed, *OT* presents "the biography of all men and this production aims to serve that end." In this self-consciously post-Freudian, poststructuralist play, man himself, the answer to the Sphinx's riddle, is unclean, a potential monster; unnatural knowledge leads to unnatural acts; the mystery of "order has both to be and not to be challenged."[15] Burgess explained: "Oedipus, seeing himself as a creature of unknown parentage, exults in being a sort of creature of nature, an animal-human member of a family which is itself the cycle of the seasons. But he ends as a kind of mutilated god who keeps that cycle alive. In both images, he is not unlike the sphinx."[16] Burgess's vision—the play was described in reviews as "the anthropologist's Sophocles" or "Oedipus as a nightmare by Jung"—was above all a response to the structuralist anthropology of Lévi-Strauss, who established the widespread connection in primitive myth between riddles and incest; in Burgess's view Tiresias's transsexuality (his mythical transformation from male to female and back) also had a comparable impact on a structuralist analysis of the play.[17]

The production publicity, however, perhaps reluctant to adopt fully Langham's take on the play, stressed instead "man's singular and questionable omniscience" in the modern world; man in this view "has not moved far from the primitive world. He brutally kills while he discusses the advanced philosophies of death.... In OEDIPUS THE KING we see man trying to deal with the forces of nature as well as the forces within himself and his gods. In this primitive context it seems there is little distinction between those forces. Man's gods are within himself, and the forces of nature are his gods." The last sentence perhaps deliberately echoes O'Neill's American reinterpretation of tragic fate mentioned in the introduction. The focus on ritual and human origins, which was generally popular in theater productions internationally in this period, derived in part from the theatrical legacy of Yeats, whose *OT* had a significant impact in its early U.S. performances.[18] Treating Oedipus as an everyman figure goes back at least as early as Jules Lacroix's version of the play, published in 1874, which was performed by Jean Mounet-Sully in New York to mixed reviews (see chapter 1.1). Yet the Guthrie program note's interest in human violence in the modern world suggests as well both a muted response to the Vietnam War and a secularizing of the Christianizing/ritualizing elements of the play, especially the ending. In this production, the more abstract perspective of the Guthrie's British directors (Langham and before him, Guthrie himself) perhaps remained in some tension with that of its local producers.

### The Guthrie's Second OT

In 2005 the Guthrie presented the American playwright Ellen McLaughlin's also close, accessible, and poetic adaptation of OT directed by Lisa Peterson. McLaughlin's modifications to the original text resembled a number of Burgess's, and in fact both director and playwright aimed in part to offer a response to the important earlier production.[19] McLaughlin's now-published play opened and closed with the Sphinx's riddle accompanied by an out-of-sequence counting of numbers and a naked child with its back to the audience;[20] the chorus struggled to make sense of an inhuman reality in part through ritual; the blinding of Oedipus again occurred on stage (in contrast to Sophocles' original), although this time the hero had his back to the audience, and the blows to his eyes took place during blackouts; the hero again departed for a desired exile at the end. In McLaughlin's version, however, the daughters were missing, as they have come to be in a number of productions that cut their final scene with the blind Oedipus, apparently to bypass familial pathos and provide a different form of closure that preserves a stronger sense of Oedipus as a public figure whose departure allows the city to forget its ills/the past.

This less-primal, stylized, and ritualistic (but without Christian coloring) production's central emphasis differed from Burgess's, however. Director Peterson, by her own report deeply influenced by Bernard Knox, who interpreted the play as a story about Athens itself, wanted to confront American identity at a historical moment also haunted by pestilence and war, and "our deep aversion to coming to terms with our own past and the consequences of our actions."[21] She observed further: "If we can manage to remain inside the present moment, we never have to answer for our actions in the past, never need to succumb to the pull of the subconscious, which is, in part, the pull of history and hence accountability."[22] For McLaughlin, the overconfident Oedipus, a political leader who is both apparent savior and actual cause of his people's suffering, learns "the true price of self-knowledge—that to be human is to be both entirely innocent and entirely guilty." The play closed far more pessimistically than the earlier Guthrie version, with the chorus's desire to forget Oedipus and their love affair with his leadership. For different reasons, then, both Oedipus and the chorus came to desire blindness; the chorus failed to confront its own human identity through the hero. By contrast, Sophocles' play includes this wish for forgetfulness but closes with the above-mentioned unresolved confrontation observed by the chorus between Creon and Oedipus over Oedipus's fate.

The spare production deployed a corrugated-metal, white circular set with one central door and an ornate marble floor punctuated only by a grand piano harp suspended above a musical "altar" at stage right (three musicians, a percussionist, bassist, and horn player worked on and around it) and a central navel-like plug that could be raised and lowered. The huge Guthrie stage was emphasized to give the impression of cold elegance and exposure: no place to hide. The plug became a "sacred space."[23] The child appeared on the central plug at the opening; a chair/throne appeared on it later. For her suicide, Jocasta stood on the chair and wrapped a rope that fell from above around her body. The chair descended. Only the rope was seen as the chair fell, and a cry was heard. Oedipus appeared on the raised plug with his back to the audience for the blinding scene.

A chorus of citizens of mixed age and gender (deliberately more democratic than Sophocles' elders) dressed in blue and black street clothes came out of the audience to sing a cappella and dance, often to African rhythms, while the rest of the cast was dressed in regal black, bronze, golds, and silvers.[24] Costume designer David Zinn aimed to create a certain level of abstraction to avoid making the performance too contemporary. The production brought the chorus close to the royal family through its emphasis on the emotional struggles of Isabell Monk O'Connor as Jocasta—especially her expanded expression of regret about having exposed the infant Oedipus.[25] Yet it also visually and spatially isolated the pointedly primal disasters of the protagonists from the citizens, who finally could not absorb the production's stark exposure of reality. Like Sophocles' play, it refused an easy closure, but, by exiling Oedipus at the specific request of the chorus, who resisted Creon's Sophoclean deferral, it augmented the play's collective refusal to know even acts visibly performed before the chorus/the audience. As one critic put it, "Do you really want to know the truth about yourself and your history?"[26] The move to develop an implicit confrontation with national identity in the second Guthrie *OT* represented an important shift from the first production's more abstract exploration of Oedipus's sacrificial role.

## Sloan and Feist's Version

Cultural amnesia can take many forms, however, and ritual and knowledge can prove disastrous in new ways. Even before the better-known 1972–73 Guthrie production, Anthony Sloan and Gene Feist's radically new version, performed at New York's Roundabout Theatre in 1970, had translated the story to a 1930s Central American presidential palace on a Caribbean island stricken by drought and built it around the "sexual rite of manhood itself," staged as a bullfight.[27] As Phil Zinkewicz noted in his review in *Show Business* (March 7, 1970),

From the beginning this is a drama of ritual. Each of the characters knows what has happened and what will happen, but each must play his part in the games within the game, the plays within the play, the ritual within the ritual. There is no discovery here, at least not in the sense of Oedipus unraveling the mysteries surrounding his guilt. There is a conscious attempt to avoid discovery, and in the process the characters lie, cheat, hurt and humiliate each other. Each character lives in a world of shadows, refusing to admit what he is, or, as in the case of Oedipus, what he has become.

For Oedipus, "facts unspoken are not truth." In a moment of passion "Jocasta verbalizes this reality of Oedipus' sins, the tragic events run their course." She blurts out what she and Oedipus have known from the start of the play: "Oedipus, listen to me. I am your mother."

This version not only denied the hero's innocence but reframed the story to reflect an increasingly corrupt political and cultural contemporary world that resists knowledge of the truth, and the powerful convergence between oracular prediction and active discovery that gives Oedipus's misfortune meaning. The *Time* magazine review (March 9, 1970, 54) saw the play as reflecting an era marked by the Kennedys, Vietnam, racial turmoil, urban carnage, generational vendetta, and the growth of drug addiction that had "moved the entire nation toward at least the beginnings of a tragic way of life. . . . The family is presented as a verbal killing ground where people prepare for real death." Oedipus was performed brilliantly by black actor Gordon Heath; the chorus was a foul-mouthed Nurse; Antigone played a teenage spitfire to a dutiful but skeptical Ismene. This pointedly un-Sophoclean play, which also imported elements from other versions of the myth, concluded, or by implication refused to reach a conclusion, as the still-surviving Jocasta asked the blinded Oedipus: "What words do you have for me, Oedipus?" He replied: "You will live, Jocasta. That is my sentence on all of you. You will live."[28] Clive Barnes (*New York Times*, February 23, 1970) viewed Oedipus and Jocasta's suppression of the truth as untragic and criticized the mixed conversational and high style and uneven acting: "Oedipus's position—and the author's—is that a fact is not a fact until that fact has been brought into the open. It is an interesting, even persuasive concept—but it is not a tragic theme." Yet the program notes to the 1972 Guthrie production asserted: "Sophocles was not concerned with individual guilt and retribution. He seems rather to be preoccupied with an overall balance to the affairs of the cosmos. . . . The point of Sophocles' work is that nothing is past and forgotten." This issue of a collective confrontation with a problematic past and the impossibility of denying it repeatedly and pointedly recurs in U.S. versions of *OT* from the 1970s to 2005.

## Abdoh's King Oedipus

In 1987, Reza Abdoh, an Iranian by birth who grew up in London and Los Angeles and died of AIDS at age thirty-two in 1995, offered an eclectic, experimental, highly visual and ritualized version of *OT* entitled *King Oedipus* at the Theater Upstairs in Los Angeles. In his production Abdoh, who once remarked that "the entire progress of our culture is based on violence and destruction,"[29] juxtaposed moments of formal, almost frozen calm and civilized grace, sometimes defined through Asian theatrical elements, with barely contained, at times explicit violence. I offer here two limited examples of the production's style, which focused above all on the hero and the destructive passion that lurks within him. In this pessimistic version, civilization collapsed under the influence of violence, and revelation and ritual failed to establish order.

The play opened in darkness punctuated by chants. Three female chorus members in Asian garb addressed Oedipus, seated alone on stage. One threw dirt (symbolic of his pollution) on him and left. Creon's ominous entrance in elaborate royal dress brought Oedipus to his feet. He put an almost violent hand on Creon, then abruptly asserted his opening of the search for Laius's killer. In their second confrontation, Oedipus spat in Creon's face, and the two wrestled. A calm, maternal Jocasta entered with a table, stool, and fruit. Oedipus sat by her and consented to her plea to stop fighting. Creon, however, threw the fruit from the table. The civilized Jocasta picked up the fruit and offered it.

Toward the conclusion, the lighting expressed Oedipus's insistence on knowing the truth by creating a huge shadow at his back that dwarfed Jocasta, who knelt stage left, then went off to die stage right. The stage darkened. Chanting was followed by choking sounds, and the chorus of three women spoke their ode about Oedipus's mysterious birth, accompanied by Asian music and a whirling dance. During the shepherd's revelation of his royal ancestry Oedipus laughed, sat, fell over, crouched. As the chorus drummed and sang he blinded himself onstage and roared. Creon arrived in an ornamental white robe and red belt. He pushed Oedipus over as if he were an embarrassment. A chorus member raised the blind Oedipus up and dropped him. The chorus rotated in dance and handed two sticks to Oedipus. Oedipus struggled to move with the sticks. The play ended with Oedipus crouched by a fire, accompanied by a pipe player and a chorus member. Darkness fell as the thumping of his stick was heard. Oedipus, now (in contrast to Sophocles) totally alone, was reduced to the level of bare survival. Civilization, apparently, is always on the verge of collapse and a renewed, but perhaps doomed, struggle to begin again. Yet the meaning of this Oedipus's struggle remained opaque.

These four productions of *OT* exploited ritual to focus on cultural difficulties in confronting the central human mysteries of birth, identity/knowledge of history, and death.[30] All four closed with an emphasis on Oedipus's final isolation and survival and his continued journey beyond Thebes. The Oregon Shakespeare Festival's 1975 *OT*, translated by Donald Sutherland and directed by Robert Loper, similarly used masks "to extend features of the actors, to suggest the ritual mystery that surrounds the play. The costumes and setting, likewise, are designed to evoke an ancient, mythical time in our collective memories" (director's note). Also influenced by Bernard Knox, the Oregon production aimed to make the play not a Freudian tragedy of fate or of all men, but to view Oedipus more positively as the symbol of the polis rising above a sea of troubles. Like the second Guthrie production, the Oregon production anticipated a growing interest in using OT to confront constructively contemporary American political and social issues. Abdoh's production, in which the civic world and its rituals (although perhaps not the arts of music and dance) apparently and significantly collapsed with the king, instead suggested the growing difficulty of reeducating a world fundamentally resistant to civilization through tragic reflection on its past.

## 2. PLAGUES

### Brustein's 1974 Oedipus Nix

As chapter 3 demonstrated, until the later 1960s Americans (like the Athenians before them) tended to be wary of productions of tragedy that were too pointedly political in their implications. The relation between Athens' democratic leader Pericles and the plague that probably occurred in the same period as OT has been hotly debated. Attic Old Comedy, however, was not shy about making fun of Pericles as the origin of Athens' troubles, including the Peloponnesian War (see, e.g., Aristophanes' *Acharnians*). U.S. productions and new versions have avoided focusing on Oedipus as the cause of his increasingly corrupt community's disaster unless similarly defended by humor. In the Watergate era of the winter of 1974 members of the Yale theater community took this risk in Robert Brustein's burlesque *Oedipus Nix*.[31] The play revealed the truth behind an episode early in the king's reign when "men broke locks upon your adversaries' doors, stole forth their papers, and overheard their private conversation" (11). Oedipus, anxious over government leaks but confident in his electoral mandate of 64 percent, foolishly disclaimed responsibility for the scandal and cursed himself, proclaiming: "The privilege of executives is holy in all things touching on security." Oedipus delegated the search for the criminals to Creon, who returned with the truth from Delphi, and was forced to resign; his smiling, supportive, and innocent wife rebelliously planned to drink and smoke in public for the first time. The lessons of the Watergate era and its president may have been soon repressed. Yet by 2000, productions of OT began to edge cautiously toward a pervasive sense of plagues that threatened the cultural and political landscape.

### The 2001 Hartford Oedipus

Several productions of Sophocles' play since 2000 have been more specific about the identity of the plague destroying Thebes and have given this plague a more central and continuous role than it had in the original (see also David Sard's

*Ballad of Eddie and Jo* below), where it becomes upstaged by Oedipus's search for the truth about his own identity. The 2001 production of Dudley Fitts and Robert Fitzgerald's translation (modified by the well-known African American playwright Adrienne Kennedy), directed by Jonathan Wilson at the Hartford Stage Company in Hartford, Connecticut, identified Thebes' plague as AIDS. A traveling troupe of actors in vivid African costumes performed Sophocles' play on a white stone platform backed by crumbling walls for a group of rural AIDS patients in an unnamed South African village. The patients, helped by their attendants, sat on a dirt floor containing one stone circular altar. The all African American cast included a speaking chorus of two (a priestess and a male elder) and young, energetic dancers from the community-based Artists Collaborative who performed to a jazz-tinged score by René McLean played on drums, a wooden xylophone, bells, pipe, and gongs. Wilson wished to comment on the refusal of some South African leaders to confront the reality of AIDS and to raise money for AIDS funds with the production (program notes).

Despite mixed (but fairly respectful) reviews of the performance, the Hartford critic Chris Rohmann criticized Wilson's interpretation for reinforcing stereotypes about sub-Saharan Africa by creating possible links between the Delphic oracle and shamanism and black magic, between dictatorship and postcolonial leadership, and between the royal incest (promiscuous sexuality) and the AIDS crisis. "Indeed, the implicit message delivered by holding 'Oedipus' up as a mirror of the AIDS crisis is one that's all too common in certain reactionary circles: 'Don't you dare think this disease has some outside cause. You've brought it on yourselves.'"[32] In a move not atypical of politically oriented American productions of Greek tragedy, setting the play in Africa also kept the audience from interpreting the AIDS crisis in the United States itself.

### The 2004 A.R.T. Oedipus

Robert Woodruff's 2004 production of *OT* translated by Stephen Berg and Diskin Clay at the American Repertory Theater in Cambridge offered, until the final scenes, an equally political, but more generalized search for the source of Thebes' illness. The set was a battered concrete rectangle with some steel spikes protruding from it and a crude altar; the platform appeared to glow, perhaps with dying flames, from below. High above the stage hung a perpetually falling man in a business suit. A curtained section at the back stage right did not conceal the space around the stage, where actors circulated before adopting their roles in Brechtian fashion. Before the play opened, the sentence "How could it have happened—it certainly happened" was announced by loud speaker over music in the background. When the chorus entered in modern dress, they carried photographs of their dead and wilted flowers to the front of the stage and left them there. The production deliberately evoked 9/11 (the falling man and the mementos). As Woodruff explained his interpretation of the play: "I think it's about a society and culture that's living with a secret and a kind of complicity with that secret—an agreement about its history that they know to be a lie.... The lies remain very deeply buried, and when they are uncovered, there's a chance of expiation and release, or perhaps the collapse of that society, which is why they kept it buried in the first place." The fifth-century Athenians "had just finished a war and gone through a plague. They were about to enter another war. The play is an inquest ... it's a society investigating itself to find the source of its sickness."[33]

John Campion's burly, often brutal Oedipus had clearly never developed the love affair with his citizens prominent in Sophocles and exploited in some other productions. In the opening scene he sat on the edge of the stage, took off his boots, and slowly washed his all-too-symbolic feet. He whispered to Creon, not the public (as in Sophocles), that he would find the murderer. The chorus made their entrance without addressing him. Oedipus eventually approached the chorus one by one but (in contrast to Sophocles) appeared as much critical as sympathetic. This play's Oedipus acted quickly throughout, without much apparent thought, with little deep concern for his people, abrupt treatment of his servants, and easy recourse to violence with Tiresias (played by a woman), Creon, and the shepherd. Even Jocasta at first failed to break up the wrestling in-laws and was pushed aside. Later Oedipus visibly made violent love to Jocasta as the chorus sang of their despair that the word of god had failed to come true.[34] Oedipus's monstrosity was not shared, as in the 1972 Guthrie production, with his fellow humanity, who appeared to be more victims than sharers in shaping the play's social world.

David Foucher's review in the *Edge Boston* objected to the play's central metaphor:[35]

> Woodruff has aligned Sophocles' tale of introspection, truth and domination with the current political climate through sheer force of will; while "Oedipus" is a valid examination of any dictatorship—and it is not a far cry to validly apply that terminology to an American administration that failed to be voted in by the majority of its constituents and then methodically implemented a worldwide campaign of oppression and aggression without just cause—it is also a morality play in which human folly brings about its own doom.... Draw your parallels to the historical arrogance of the United States on the contemporary political stage, and it's quite easy to deduce that Woodruff's metaphor is decidedly anti-American. If "Oedipus" at the A.R.T. was meant to critique a single act of a single administration (the invasion of Iraq, for example), it has been executed in a sufficiently ambiguous way so as to invite a wide range of critical interpretations; this is a dangerous mode in which to play theatre. It must be conceded to the A.R.T., however, that this type of daring, provocative theatre is rarely attempted outside their walls; and the pensive results of experiencing this production make it certainly worth the cost of admission. "Oedipus" is more crucial than comfortable—and perhaps that is a greater achievement.

The production certainly asked for a pointed political response to American leadership. But as this review concedes, the resulting performance was in fact more ambiguous and multifaceted.[36] First, a striking interpretation of Jocasta (Stephanie Roth Haberle) created a powerful contrast and complement to the representation of the hero once she appeared. The couple's relationship was intensely physical, but as they shared past stories their embraces reflected a need for reassurance and for a neutralizing of violence as much as passion. The fragile Jocasta shifted from moment to moment from maternal and fraternal (her concern for Creon) to hysterical, from laughter to agony. She laughed, leapt, tried to dance, fell down, even spoke Greek (the production's lyric language) with hysterical relief at the news brought by the Corinthian messenger (fig. 23). Moreover, the silent presence of the daughters in the scene where Jocasta and Oedipus exchanged stories gradually shifted the dramatic focus from the political to the personal even more than in Sophocles' original. Once Jocasta realized the truth, she crawled off sobbing, leaving Oedipus to kiss and dismiss his children.

Second, the chorus of this play operated in a high lyric mode, underlined by odes sung in ancient Greek with supertitles that created a powerful contrast with the speech of the principals. As I remarked in an earlier discussion of this powerful choral voice, which mixed Eastern and Western music, "The alienation produced by the incomprehensible language served to underline for the audience the different mode represented by a tragic chorus and its complex relation to the action: at the same time the supertitles permitted it to focus on the meaning of the words without being diverted from the power of the music and movement."[37] After Oedipus realized the truth and exited, the back curtain opened, and the blinded king was revealed seated before a mirror with his back to the audience like an actor at a makeup table. He shrieked, shifted to ancient Greek in a dialogue, accompanied by music, with the chorus leader. He stood up, walked blindly to center stage; the chorus simply passed by him as they moved offstage. As he knelt, then crawled, an orange cloth dropped to enclose him. The hanging figure above had now symbolically reversed its original position. Creon entered with the two daughters; Oedipus was covered in a black cloth that he threw off in a refusal to be hidden. Antigone dragged the reluctant Ismene closer. As in Sophocles, Creon stressed Oedipus's loss of political control and removed the daughters. Yet in this production Creon, like the chorus, abandoned Oedipus outside the "palace." A resisting Antigone's offstage cry then pierced Oedipus's isolation, and the orange cloth dropped to the stage; Antigone said, "Father"; the lights went out.

Apparently the hero moved, via a momentary linguistic shift to Greek in his blinding (sung in Sophocles' original), from a political to more personal fate. ART's Oedipus regained no mysterious Sophoclean authority from confronting his downfall; any connection between the plague-stricken Thebes' past and

FIGURE 23. Oedipus (John Campion) mistakenly celebrates his apparent release from guilt with Jocasta (Stephanie Roth Haberle) in Sophocles' *Oedipus,* directed by Robert Woodruff, American Repertory Theater, Cambridge, Massachusetts, 2004. Photo by Richard Feldman. Courtesy of the A.R.T.

its political future was left open to interpretation, as was Oedipus's own future. Indeed, although aspects of the final scene led the audience to expect Oedipus's departure, he neither returned to the palace as in Sophocles nor departed as in the productions focused on ritual. In an ART website interview the play's composer, Evan Ziporyn, remarked: "Performance is a structured ritualistic act, which has replaced religion for many of us." In this production the audience was left to interpret a powerful and silent physical image conditioned by the hero's recent joining of the lyric register of the chorus, and the political plagues lurking in the opening scene were left behind.

## 3. THEBAN CYCLES

From at least the 1930s, Americans, and not just Eugene O'Neill in *Mourning Becomes Electra,* have been interested (as have Europeans) in creating new trilogies or other pairings from the original Greek plays. The motives for these new combinations or versions vary. Paired plays permit an audience less familiar with the myths to follow and begin to understand patterns in family life and political shifts that are harder to grasp from the elliptical, often spare originals. Even in antiquity this may explain the postclassical popularity of plays like Euripides' somewhat overstuffed *Phoenician Women,* which certainly do not attempt an Aristotelian rigor of action (featuring necessity and probability).[38] Regardless of the violence that this conflation of plays can inflict on the originals, pairings and combinations also permit a director to modify or expand on the characters' motivation for action and psychological place in the family drama and to observe the development of character and theme over time. Aside from new combinations or versions revolving around the house of Atreus,[39] plays linking the descendants of Laius over time have been particularly attractive for these purposes. We have already observed how performances of *OT* have tended to end with a stronger hint of what comes afterward (or before, in the case of the riddle of the Sphinx) than we find in the original play. This expansion of *OT* can range from extravagantly inventive new pieces that amalgamate scenes from a wide range of plays along with new material to combinations such as the three Theban plays *OT, OC,* and *Antigone.* The tradition in the United States goes back at least to the 1931 blank-verse play *Teiresias* by Henry Bertram Lister, directed by Frederic Smith under the aegis of the La Boheme Club at the Fairmont Hotel in San Francisco. Lister used the figure of Teiresias to unify a Theban family saga that drew on a range of Greek originals and extended from the courtship of Laius and Jocasta to the fall of Creon. Probably under the influence of the International Theosophical Society at Point Loma, California, and the Greek plays of Katherine Tingley (see chapter 1.2), Lister focused on Teiresias in part because he aimed to uncover allegorical dimensions of the Greek myths lost with the demise of the Eleusinian mysteries. In Lister's version, Teiresias originally knows only that he will be able to transfer his blindness to a third king "who shall have offended the Gods, more than any other mortal." The ambitious Creon proves to be that third king, and the play ends with this dramatic transfer of blindness. The following discussion offers three examples of productions from 1980–99 that linked Sophocles' plays in order to confront issues that American productions of *OT* itself often found difficult to address: leadership (already central in Lister's play), the tragic inseparability of family and state (despite the rupture between them at the conclusion of Sophocles' play), and Oedipus's problematic fate.

### *The 1980 Theban Cycle at Classic Stage Company*

In 1980 New York's Classic Stage Company presented together for the first time on the professional stage in the United States Sophocles' three Theban plays, translated by Anthony Roche and directed by Christopher Martin. The production provoked an unusually positive critical reception. From a thematic perspective, reviewers singled out three advantages to presenting the plays together: the unifying development of the character of Creon over the three plays toward tyrannical megalomania;[40] the complex motivation developed for Antigone's actions and her family loyalty; and the trilogy's success in highlighting humanity's ultimate superiority to tragic suffering inflicted by fate and the gods—the perennial problem of Oedipus's story in the United States. Holly Hill of the *Soho Weekly News* (November 12, 1980) viewed the trilogy as Sophocles' "covert rebellion against the gods" and "a triumph of psychological justice, which only exists in the mind, over earthly injustice." As she put it, "A traditional interpretation of Greek tragedy—indeed the moralistic view of life itself—is that through suffering man learns humility before the gods. Then why does the feeling persist, at the end of both Oedipus dramas and in CSC's Sophocles, that the gods are humbled?" This production was apparently the first, and in fact one of the few, staged in the United States to reflect a view of Sophoclean heroism best embodied in the studies of Bernard Knox (1957 and 1964): in particular, its focus on the tendency of Sophocles' intransigent characters to find mysterious direction in their fatal disasters and to deploy language expressing poetic individuality that both exploits and overshadows their suffering. The staging of this trilogy also appeared to reviewers to depart from that of previous U.S. productions, in part because the repertory company was able to develop the production and its thematic argument more coherently over time. For Howard Kessel (*Women's Wear Daily*, March 16, 1981), the trilogy was staged "as real plays, not serious cultural experiences." David Sterritt of the *Christian Science Monitor* (December 8, 1980) asserted that "one of the possible benefits of such fine work is that this could be the beginning of a distinctly American style of classical performance, thoughtful as well as imaginative, modern as well as ancient."

### Settle's 1999 Chicago Blood Line

The desire to show deeper motivation for the actions of *Antigone* and to underline the transition in leadership from Oedipus to Creon inspired Joanna Settle's *Blood Line: The Oedipus/Antigone Story*, a production of *OT* and *Antigone* developed with her company Division 13 Productions in a new translation by Nicholas Rudall at The Viaduct, Chicago, March–May 1999. This version used a 6,000-square-foot converted warehouse to underline the plays' powerful mix of private and public dimensions. Four ramped stairways (stepladder units) framed a carpeted performance area surrounded by twenty tons of gravel. The audience crossed this gravel to pass to seating on three sides. Settle wanted the audience "to feel beneath their own feet the deafening crunch of a society at war with its tormented conscience."[41] The ten-person eclectic chorus moved white chairs around in the space. The huge wooden warehouse doors opened to let Antigone pass to her death past barrels of fire and a stone-throwing mob that evoked a sense of an enclosed theatrical space threatened from without. Mark Messing's sound design permitted movement of sounds around and from outside the performance space. For example, *Antigone* opened with air-raid sirens, and the first ode about the war was piped in from outside the performance space. Transitions were fast to underline a sense of inevitability; Settle claimed to be inspired by the inexorable pacing of TV news.

The production's thoroughly rehearsed and deeply engaged chorus bonded intensely to the more democratic, youthful Oedipus, who treated them as individuals, and often huddled in subservience to Creon in *Antigone,* thus underlining the effect of the political transition in Thebes. Creon used a mike to communicate his manipulative public persona. By contrast, the chorus, which vividly used their bodies to respond to the action throughout, could abandon its public role; it moved into an almost fetal position in response to the shepherd's tale in *Oedipus*.[42] The production prepared for the psychological aspects of the second play by bringing in the children to hear Jocasta and Oedipus's first telling of their stories and having Oedipus, Jocasta, and Antigone's and Ismene's younger selves return as ghosts to haunt the heroine in *Antigone,* especially as she was about to go to her death. Eurydice's silent presence throughout *Antigone* embodied Creon's neglected familial side from the start. Although the production's representation of a decline in leadership permitted by contrasting Oedipus and Creon did not develop obvious connections with the contemporary Clinton presidency, it certainly explored a style of democratic leadership in an age that threatened to undermine it.

### The Whole World Is Watching: *The Theban Trilogy as Talk Show*

More experimentally, Douglas Jacobs of the San Diego Repertory Theatre (REP) and Scott Feldsher of San Diego's Sledgehammer Theatre collaborated to stage the

Theban trilogy in a talk-show format for the San Diego REP (inspired particularly by the Jerry Springer show) in their 1996 play *The Whole World Is Watching*.[43] The show was timed to respond in part to the Republican National Convention in San Diego.[44] According to Jacobs, their trilogy, which was not meant to be a political parody, investigated what leads to corrupt or viable empires and the problems of maintaining a commitment to self as opposed to society and the gods. In this version Oedipus, who insistently sacrificed power to truth, ended up heroic, whereas Creon failed by serving power. Both the populist immigrant Oedipus and Jocasta showed an increasing gift for performance that played into the talk-show format. Oedipus from the first resisted silencing by his advisers; as in Sophocles he demanded visibility for his disaster as a literally "marked man" and even broke down the set. Creon, by contrast, constantly resisted sharing matters of state with the public until his final breakdown.

This version of the trilogy occurred in a city-state of the future, the plague-ridden Calafia (a new state formed from parts of Mexico and Southern California). Costuming and video clips were contemporary (e.g., Creon's arrival from the "oracle del Apollo" in a black limo was tracked speeding down a freeway). Protestors outside the "studio" warmed up the audience for Oedipus's first appearance in response to the plague. Oedipus interacted with a fairly aggressive talk-show host, who served as chorus leader, and the audience, who served in large part as chorus. Audience members who wanted to participate were selected in the pre-show, and the performance used actors experienced in improvisation who could maintain a connection to the plot structure regardless of the audience's questions. Fictional phone lines were also opened up to a hypothetical audience outside the studio after Oedipus requested clues about the murder of Laius. Laius's royal physician, who had given the baby Oedipus up for adoption, testified by phone from Deer Lick, Montana. When Tiresias finally revealed Oedipus's future he burst into "tongues" in the form of E. H. Plumptre's Victorian translation (1865) of the play. The TV-style set had Hellenic-style columns, statues, and symbols of state; the cameras were unable to follow Oedipus and Jocasta into a locked room backstage, thus remotivating the Greek convention against displaying death and mutilation onstage. Creon's final effort to silence and confine Oedipus and his children in the palace was foiled; this part of the trilogy closed with a report that Oedipus and his daughters had escaped from the palace.

The production's increasingly serious version of *Antigone* staged the heroine, wearing an orange prison costume, in a trial before a hung jury of TV commentators; a Nightline-style flashback set the context. The third play did not follow the original texts as closely. A twenty-minute deathbed TV interview with an eighty-year-old Ismene that told the story of Oedipus's death in *OC* ended in her own death and the final release of the family from its curse in a Felliniesque epilogue that united the family in the world of the dead.

The directors saw talk shows and Greek tragedy as in some respects analogous. Jacobs observed: "Americans love to testify. They love that process . . . Oedipus and Tyresias get into mudslinging that is similar to a talk show. Also the [interpersonal] geometry in the Greeks is similar to that of a talk show, where one person tells a story, another disagrees and then a third person comes in and makes it really messy."[45] With the exception of the last part, this format permitted the directors to follow the texts of *OT* and *Antigone* beat by beat, but in a style that, according to reviews, generated a legible contemporary audience/performance relationship and context.[46] The performance style probably meshed most readily with *OT*, with its series of personal revelations, questions about the media's representation of leadership, breakdowns in control and decorum, and exploitative exposures of the truth. The show approached the problem of representing the Greek chorus by artificially creating a participating community in a known contemporary format and involving this audience, as *Blood Line* did in a different fashion, in responding to and questioning contemporary modes of performing leadership.

## 4. DECONSTRUCTING FATALITY
### *Dare Clubb's 1998 Version of* Oedipus

A number of new versions have attempted to confront or reexamine the significance of the hero's fate in a modern context more directly. Dare Clubb produced a four-hour epic version of *OT* with the Blue Light Theater Company at New York's Classic Stage Company in 1998 that pointedly inverted the story of Oedipus and his fate. Sophocles' Oedipus initially tried to avoid his fate and finally gained a certain authority from its horrific fulfillment. As Aristotle argues, tragedy is more philosophical than history. Yet for Clubb reality fails to provide the necessary and probable pattern of action so admired in the original by Aristotle. In his version the youthful Oedipus returns to Corinth after receiving the Delphic prophecy rather than trying to escape his home. In a literal-minded attempt to respect divine will and then to create his own ethics, he kills his father, Polybus, and sleeps with his mother, Merope, who has been nurturing a pointedly Phaedra-like passion for her son, only to discover that he was adopted and cannot fulfill the oracle.

Oedipus sets out on an impassioned, excessive, but repeatedly failed quest to fulfill his destiny/discover his identity, initially with his sidekick Tiresias, who has tried to convince him that gods would not impose such a fate on a man. "I am not yet who I am!" he insists. (Jean-Paul Sartre's *Les Mouches,* in which the hero Orestes freely chooses to take on his traditional destiny, may have provided some inspiration for this plot.) The claustrophobic set for Clubb's Corinth had white flats with painted-over windows; for the journey the stage was empty except for a trench upstage, from which mysterious characters sometimes emerged. On the journey, Oedipus meets a hunter who has no fate and his wife, with whom the man has refused to procreate; they kill themselves in despair. He encounters his yet-to-be-born sons Polyneices and Eteocles, mercenaries who try to recruit him for war and then kill each other. They remark to Oedipus: "Who is going forward, who is going back? How do we know?" Tiresias abandons Oedipus, shifting to an obsession with his own fate after seeing two snakes copulating.

At Thebes, Oedipus meets a pregnant Sphinx who gives him the answer, then asks him three times what the question is. Laius asks Oedipus to remain in Thebes as his son, but in order to avoid being killed he reexposes Oedipus on Cithairon bound and pierced in a Promethean or Christ-like position. Recognizing that the gods have withheld his fate, Oedipus requests blindness. Yet he also encounters Iokaste, who debunks his quest. She favors respect for love and generosity rather than a self-absorbed quest for truth, divinity, and identity. "I am violent because the world is violent," he tells his mother. "No Oedipus," she replies, "your world is violent because you are violent." "The gods don't frighten me. Men frighten me. Men with concepts." "To be lost is what it means to be human. . . . Our monstrous fate is not a nursery tale. Fate is you will kill your father and mother or you will Not."[47] In this new version, the original play's emphasis on human blindness and the hero's powerful pursuit of what emerged as his inexorable fate led Oedipus on a pseudo-epic journey to a confusing dead end. Oedipus's tragedy emerged as neither a violation of American ideals nor a mysteriously meaningful destiny.

Clubb's effort to reconfront Oedipus's fate had in fact been anticipated in Howard Moss's heavily ironic comedy of manners for the 1960s, *The Oedipus Mah-Jongg Scandal*, directed in 1968 by William C. Christian at New York's Cooperative Theatre Club, Inc. In this remaking the highly self-conscious characters instead repeatedly attempted and failed in Pirandellian fashion to escape the plot.[48] The two principals, both knowing and refusing to know, both remembering past crimes and wanting to repeat them, desiring and refusing to desire, longing for power and status and rejecting it, circled endlessly and sometimes playfully around the inevitable and exited to meet it largely with a sense of inevitable repetition.

## *Galati's* Oedipus Complex

U.S. versions of *OT* are of course conscious of, but not necessarily enamored of, Freud's interpretation of the myth.[49] But Frank Galati's *Oedipus Complex*, which he also directed, first at the Oregon Shakespeare Festival in 2004 and then at Chicago's Goodman Theatre in spring 2007, staged a confrontation between Freud himself and *OT*. In Oregon, the play was set in a nineteenth-century dark, wood Viennese surgical amphitheater (designed by James Schuette). Large double doors served as the entrance to this womblike stage. Rows of bearded, black-suited doctors, who later enacted some of Freud's own family drama and donned masks to serve as the chorus for *OT*, attended a lecture by Freud where Oedipus was a patient who arrived for psychological dissection through the doors on a gurney; at the close Freud walked through the doors into a snowy night (and his own uncertain future).

According to reviews, the play juxtaposed most of Sophocles' play translated by Stephen Berg and Diskin Clay with scenes exploring Freud's relation to his younger, loving mother and older father, who was an unsuccessful businessman, as delineated in particular in his ten-year correspondence, from 1890 to 1900, with his friend Dr. Wilhelm Fliess about psychoanalyzing himself. The play also dramatized the Freud-Fliess relationship, which ended, after growing tension, in a permanent split between the two. The relation between the ancient and modern story was not always close. The same actress played both Freud's mother and Jocasta, whereas Freud and Oedipus, despite their visual similarity and close dramatic identity, were played by different actors. At one point, Freud, as a Teiresias figure, prophetically anticipated a growing historical plague by reliving his anger at his Jewish father for not responding actively (in contrast to Oedipus with Laius) to an anti-Semitic attack on a Viennese street (fig. 24).

In the Goodman Theatre version, for which I had access to the script, Freud opened the play with a lecture to students and faculty explaining his interpretation of the Oedipus myth. As Freud moved into the role of the priest in *OT*'s opening scene, he remarked, interrupted by choral interventions, on the profoundly grievous loss of his own father and offered the audience his interpretation of *OT* (from his *Interpretation of Dreams*) as a tragedy of fate whose story is shared unconsciously by the play's audience. He discussed his anger at his father after the incident mentioned above, his own contact with the unknown through his work on dreams, and a dream in which his mother asked him to close the eyes of his dead father. Freud later, after adopting the role of chorus leader in dialogue with Oedipus, intervened in the choral ode about Apollo's mysterious Delphic oracle to examine his unconscious wish to close his father's eyes. When Jocasta exited to summon the shepherd who exposed Oedipus for further questioning, however, Freud's rumination turned to his jealous anger at his father's relation to his mother; he recalled his ambiguous relation to childhood nurses (maternal/sexual figures) and his dreams about them, and finally, after Oedipus learns the painful truth, Freud turned to his memory of seeing his father approach his naked mother on a train. His hysterical reaction made his mother come to sleep with him instead. Following this moment of psychological recognition, Freud affirmed sharing with Oedipus "an overpowering need to understand something of the riddles of the world and share my findings with *anyone who wants to learn.*"

Above all, Galati intended the play as "a meditation on narrative and how story functions in our collective consciousness, how primal stories can heal, eroticize, and unmask life."[50] But it also used the juxtaposition to consider the influence of "Freud's 'theater of the mind' ideology" on modern drama.[51] As Galati put it, "In 20th-century American and European drama, there's necessarily a tension

FIGURE 24. Teiresias (Jeffrey Baumgartner) in Frank Galati's *Oedipus Complex*, Goodman Theatre, Chicago, 2007. Photo by Liz Lauren (Rich Hein).

between psychological complexity, the hidden materials and aberrations that are brought to the surface as psychopathology, and a more consciously artificial and theatrical mode of representation. Often things are entwined—as they are so brilliantly in Bertolt Brecht's plays."[52]

Despite largely positive reviews for the Oregon production, the Chicago reviews found that the Freud sections undercut the dramatic pace of the Sophocles and that the script failed to make a compelling point through its central juxtaposition of Freud and Sophocles.[53] In the *Sunday Oregonian* (August 8, 2004) Bob Hicks also raised the following provocative question about Galati's version, which was shared in substance by some Chicago critics:

> As fascinating as the interplay between Oedipus and Freud is in "Oedipus Complex," I can't help thinking that in today's world of ascendant absolutism, the raw power of Sophocles' original play carries a more timely theme. Thebes is a fundamentalist world, with harsh solutions to complex questions—not unlike a world of suicide bombings and ethnic cleansings and lockstep thinking, all in the name of unwavering faith to this god or that. In such a world, Freud's inner wanderings can seem self-indulgent. (On the flip side, they can seem even more essential, upholding the primacy of philosophical questioning and subtlety of thought in the face of the new primitivism.) But Freud's hold on the popular imagination is loosening, as Apollo's

did long ago. Freud may still be king, but his crown is slipping. Sometimes a cigar is only a cigar.

Performing or reenvisioning *OT* in a dramatic environment where the repression of desires is no longer a comparable cultural issue, and questions concerning representing and performing identity have evolved significantly, apparently poses problems that all of these productions had difficulty confronting. At the same time, these productions expressed a previously suppressed American longing for an individual fate, even a disastrous one, denied by a world apparently ruled by arbitrary forces.

## 5. ABANDONMENT

Although the ART Oedipus made a vulnerable Jocasta vividly embody Oedipus's suppressed fears and ambivalence, Ellen McLaughlin's attempt in her Guthrie adaptation to expand more movingly on Jocasta's impassioned reaction to her unwilling exposure of her child anticipated a recent direction in performance and adaptation of the play that was also implicit in the Woodruff version. The Sophoclean Jocasta's brief rendition of the story of the exposure (*OT* 707–25) has no special emotional coloring and is aimed at demonstrating that oracles do not always prove true. In McLaughlin's version, Jocasta declares: "It is the prophecy I have to thank for my greatest sorrow;" her Jocasta describes the child torn from its mother after several days of bonding (366–67). A production of John Lewin's translation with the well-known African American actor James Earl Jones as Oedipus and Jacqueline Brookes as Jocasta that took place at New York's Cathedral of St. John the Divine in February 1977 had already adopted a similar emphasis. As Mel Gussow reported in his review (*New York Times*, February 4, 1977), "The translation, said Mr. Jones, focuses not on the damnation of being incestuous, but on the fact that Mama agreed with Daddy to kill me. Daddy says, 'The kid's got to go. Out!' The Oedipal thing is almost secondary. I wish Freud had known that. The play is the betrayal of Oedipus by his parents."

### *Sard's* Ballad of Eddie and Jo

The betrayal of Oedipus by his parents became the central issue of several new versions, which, partly because of their conventional realistic acting styles, verged on soap opera. To the degree that these versions raised political issues, they abandoned them to focus on the "tragedy" of Oedipus and Jocasta's relationship. The plays reflected an increasing cultural interest in recovering the relation between birth parents and children that developed after stringent American adoption laws insisting on anonymity began to loosen. In each case, however, the effort to update and psychologize the Oedipus/Jocasta relation from this modern sociological perspective eventuated in a conclusion that repeatedly, despite an engaging theme, failed to satisfy its audiences. David Sard, the author of a new version of *OT* in 2006, *The Ballad of Eddie and Jo,* directed by Lorca Peress at New York's Hudson Guild Theatre, is a clinical psychologist whose work with inner-city patients made *OT*'s plot seem plausible to him in a modern context (program notes). His warm, feisty Jo is obsessed with her abandonment of her newborn son; as a frightened young teenage mother she became convinced that she could not properly care for a child with a heart defect; after she changed her mind, she was unable to find the child, who disappeared into the foster care system. Jo takes an interest in Eddie partly out of guilt over her lost child, and partly because her husband, a minor gangster, treated her with an indifference that strongly contrasts with her intuitively sympathetic relation with the lonely Eddie.

Eddie's persistence in seeking restitution for the neighborhood's industrial pollution reawakens gang opposition that leads to the revelation of his identity. An industrial mafia that caused the pollution dominates the neighborhood, but Eddie's own relation to the pollution, as opposed to that of his biological father, whom he accidentally kills in a street fight, remains hypothetical. The disconnection between hero and the cultural pollution he fights against again ensures the abandonment of the play's public dimensions in favor of the mother-son relation at the conclusion of the play. In this version, when Jo herself is forced to tell Eddie of her discovery of his identity in order to explain why their children have been removed from them by local authorities and to save him from gang murder, the audience has already witnessed everything that Jo and Eddie's awkward but passionate courtship and enabling marital life have created. Yet at the conclusion, neither Jo nor Eddie, who blinds himself and leaves to become a derelict, knows what has happened to the other, and their equally central stories remain in uneasy and ultimately cryptic juxtaposition. While praising Eddie's heroic attempt to follow the dictates of his conscience Martin Denton, for example, criticized Sard for not making his motives for the new version clear.[54]

## Oedipus at Palm Springs

Jocasta's painful secret similarly governed The Five Lesbian Brothers' *Oedipus at Palm Springs,* directed by Leigh Silverman at the New York Theatre Workshop in July–August 2005. In this play two lesbian couples meet for an off-season weekend at a Palm Springs, Arizona, resort. The play shifts suddenly from a comedic investigation of lesbian sexuality to melodramatic confession and separation. The sex-starved Con and the lactating Fran have had a dysfunctional sex life since the birth of three-year-old Basil, whereas the sex life of the other butch/femme couple, a successful older woman, Prin, and her much younger lover, Terri, is barely containable. Prin had abandoned the baby she had from her one sexual encounter with a man at fifteen. The play leaves both Prin and her daughter/lover Terri alive and physically unharmed, but broken and isolated by their discovery.

The numerous reviews of this well-attended and generally fairly well-received production were divided on whether the play's shift from a mixed soap-operatic and satiric investigation of contemporary sexual mores to "high tragedy" was successful. I include reviews in more detail for this and the next production because they indicate a suggestive contemporary attraction to and doubt about the difficulties of making the play's tragic-comic mother/child relation contemporary. Among several defenders, Matthew Murray commented that the play, while un-Sophoclean, used "the familiar story as a starting point for a rigorous and raucous examination of how love and sex affect and infect today's world,"[55] and Mark Blankenship argued that "tragic fates are so much worse when they befall characters we can laugh about, care for and recognize."[56] Jeremy McCarter of *New York Magazine*, by contrast, offered a typical critical assessment: "You have to admire the guts of making such a bold swerve into high-tragic mode, but the faux-Greek twist doesn't begin to work, and achieves no resonance. After doing so much careful exploration early in the show, the Five Lesbian Brothers would have been better off, just this once, playing it straight."[57]

Some reviews criticized the Brothers' unfortunate shift to naturalistic acting from their previous "lunatic raunchiness" and "poor theatre style" in the 1990s,[58] and the plot's trivializing emphasis on the physical rather than the metaphysical and public issues central to the original.[59] Making the Oedipal story a lesbian tragedy was meant to be psychologically provocative; yet Prin and Terri's relation did not resonate with psychological studies of the mother/daughter relationship. This version was also potentially politically regressive for a group that had specialized in exploring female desire. Theater scholar Jill Dolan objected to the troupe's

> willingness to accede to the incest taboo as the final frontier of sexual transgression, after many infamous years of casting off all other strictures on sexual relating and expression. Prin's relationship to Terri seems strong, clear, and highly charged sexually; why force it to end in shame and sorrow simply because Prin turns out to be Terri's biological mother? Under the Brothers' old logic, this would be a minor detail. . . . Prin becomes another in a long line of butch lesbian characters in theater punished for their desires and left solitary and grieving.[60]

## *LaBute's* Wrecks

Dolan's remark received an unintentional if strongly apolitical reply in Neil LaBute's *Wrecks,* performed in a sold-out, extended run at New York's Public Theater in the fall of 2006. Oedipus's abandonment by his mother also became the pivotal issue of this new version, which invoked the son's perspective.[61] A monologue by

Edward Carr (Ed Harris) over the coffin of his adored wife, Jo-Jo (Mary Josephine, Mary Jo), at a funeral parlor reveals that his search for his birth mother, whose name he discovered after a rough childhood as an orphan and foster son, ultimately led him to a conscious and passionate choice to marry his mother. The original play's search for truth becomes here a question of a strictly private confession, shared only and reluctantly with the audience. On her deathbed Jo-Jo, who does not know her second husband's identity, reveals to Edward her secret suffering over the child whom she conceived after being raped by her uncle at fourteen and whom her family forced her to give up. Ed refuses to tell the audience his four last words in reply.

The couple's seemingly ideal relationship required Jo-Jo's divorce from her unhappy first marriage, which left two angry sons behind, and produced a successful vintage-car rental business and two daughters. Edward's lifelong anxieties are expressed through his addiction to smoking, which gave both members of the couple lung cancer; the Sophoclean play's plague here affects not the community, but the couple. Similarly, in this version Edward does not kill his father, although he gets into a fist fight with his wife's first husband. Instead he destroys a completely random family in a car accident; thus his capacity for violence has no discernable intent or meaning. LaBute, the well-known author of two other bleak plays based on Greek tragedy and previously staged in New York (*Medea Redux* and *Iphigenia in Orem*)[62] here exonerates or even celebrates the play's incest as a deeply therapeutic, ideally traditional, and committed form of marital relationship. Jo-Jo taught her damaged spouse to be in touch with his feelings. "Love," as Edward puts it, "is never wrong." In this enthusiasm for mother as wife, LaBute's Edward echoes the working-class Eddy of the British actor, playwright, and director Steven Berkoff's well-known 1980 play *Greek*, although Berkoff's hero did not make a conscious choice to marry his mother.[63] *Wrecks'* idealizing of a sexual/marital bond with the mother as uniquely fulfilling from another perspective could be thought to verge on misogyny.

Although New York reviews generally praised Ed Harris's performance, many responded coolly to the play. Toby Zinman (*Philadelphia Inquirer*, October 11, 2006) pronounced the play a "one-trick pony" loaded with "tedious confessions." Marilyn Stasio (*Variety*, October 10, 2006) remarked: "However eloquently Harris conveys the man's halting expressions of love, this is a guy with a moral code strategically designed for personal gratification." Jeffrey Sweet pointedly asked: "How does a string of car rental agencies specializing in leasing classics cars bring out different values than a kingdom? What does exchanging deaths by cancer for the violence in the original do to illuminate the psychology of the characters or the sexual-societal taboos they violated?"[64]

These three plays very likely responded to other earlier and more substantial U.S. versions of *OT*, which I have discussed elsewhere, that also expanded on Jocasta's agony at abandoning her child and her own search for selfhood to the point of making her the central or more powerful figure. Martha Graham's 1947 dance *Night Journey* inaugurated this trend by focalizing the story through Jocasta,[65] whereas Ethyl Eichelberger's 1980s drag version, *Jocasta or Boy Crazy*, presented Jocasta as a tormented pedophile.[66] Both Philip Freund's 1970 *Jocasta*, set in late nineteenth-century Martinique, and Rita Dove's 1996 *The Darker Face of the Earth*, set in the pre–Civil War South, made Oedipus a slave and Jocasta a rebellious, passionate plantation owner.[67] Saviana Stanescu and Richard Schechner's 2003 *YokastaS* and 2005 *YokastaS Redux* at La MaMa, E.T.C. in New York focused on multiple Jocastas. As I have argued, this new emphasis on Jocasta's perspective and the couple's sexual bond can come at the price of reducing the focus on the hero's relentless drive for the truth and his effort to preserve public authority, and privatizing a story that is deeply engaged in the relation between rulers and subjects. Nevertheless, these reexplorations of Jocasta's role retained a fundamental link to the tragic tensions of Sophocles' play that is lacking in many respects in the three remakings discussed above.

## CONCLUSION

The archetypal fatalities for which *OT* and the larger Theban family saga are famous have provoked parodic reactions that underline the way that the American imagination tends to approach the hero. The American satirical singer-songwriter Tom Lehrer's "Oedipus Rex" (released on a record in 1959) claimed to provide the theme song that the relatively unpopular film version of *OT* (the 1957 version by Yeats, directed by Sir Tyrone Guthrie and starring Douglas Campbell) lacked. The song humorously offers Oedipus's story as an example of carrying the valuable U.S. celebration of motherhood too far, "a tragic end to a loyal son/Who loved his mother." The following excerpt parodies an American tendency to focus on the hero's unfortunate personal story at the expense of his political one:

> There once was a man, oh, who it seems
> Once carried this ideal to extremes.
> He loved his mother and she loved him,
> And yet his story is rather grim.
>
> There once was a man named Oedipus Rex
> You may have heard about his odd complex.
> His name appears in Freud's index
> 'Cause he loved his mother.
>
> His rivals used to say quite a bit
> But as a monarch he was most unfit
> But still in all they had to admit
> That he loved his mother.

Peter Schickele's *Oedipus Tex*, putatively a recently discovered manuscript of a "Dramatic Oratorio or Opera in One Cathartic Act" by his alter ego, P. D. Q. Bach (1807–1842), humorously deconstructs Oedipus's tragedy for America by embedding the story of a cowboy hero in the trappings of baroque music.[68] The piece opens in oratorio style with a repeated invocation of "tragedy, T R A G E D Y." "Well Oedipus thinks he's just an easygoing kind of guy, he's going to suffer a lot before he knows the reason why. No point in warning him of T R A G E D Y." It closes in the same fashion with a new moral: "Well the moral of this story is, of course: Don't love your mother, pardner, save it for your horse; I guarantee you will be filled with great remorse If you give your mom the love you should be saving for your horse."

Cowboy stories tend to conclude with the exit of a lone and sometimes wounded outsider to further heroic wanderings (as in Sophocles' *OC*) in a world dominated by powerful natural forces and potential violence. Schickeles' Oedipus, however fast on the trigger, is undone by romance. The country-western-style Oedipus Tex, Texas brother of the better-known Oedipus Rex, introduces himself by relating his recent triumphs over the men who told him to step aside in a gulch ("Ain't no one tells this cowboy what to do") as well as his quick solution of Bigfoot's riddle. Unfortunately, he then gives in to the antiheroic urge to settle down. A romantic duet with Billie Jo Casta, queen of the rodeo, is followed at once by a plague and the revelations of the shepherdess Madame Peep, who once saved the baby Oedipus, a man whom she still admires as a "rascal" and "my kind of guy." Billie Jo's musical style becomes pseudo-operatic in her final aria, "Goodbye, Cruel World"; Oedipus Tex, by contrast, blinds himself and regrets the choice. The traditional American hero of the West, like Oedipus Tex, has no problem "justly" gunning down an unknown dad or leaving his past behind. His sustaining relation to the natural world and his defeat of violent threats to various communities are critical to his masculine identity. Settling down with women (incest at its extreme) and exercising political leadership, however, prove incompatible with this brand of American folklore. Like others, this version uncovers yet another incompatibility between American representations of heroism and the figure of Oedipus.

Overall, U.S. productions and new versions of *OT* have, like Lehrer's and Schickele's, often attempted to reinterpret Oedipus's incestuous relation to his mother and to simplify, resist, or offer a new interpretation of the hero's fate. Some versions domesticate Oedipus by focusing on his cruel abandonment by his parents and his role as foster child and outsider in circumstances bleaker than in the original myth,[69] and by expanding on Jocasta as a character of nearly equal dramatic and psychological interest (new versions do not expand on his relation to his father or his sons). Sophocles' play is tightly framed to stress the hero's catastrophic yet mysteriously liberating discovery of the truth, but it also moves from an emphasis on the sufferings of the city to those of the hero and his family. U.S.

versions tend to expand even more on the hero's personal tragedy, but also to send him into the exile Sophocles' play denies. Exile, however, can be another way of depoliticizing Oedipus's final Sophoclean conflict of authority with Creon.

Relatively few U.S. productions (in contrast to many in Europe)[70] until recently have put particular stress on either Oedipus's tyrannical potential or his powerful political bond with the chorus, who are often represented as males and females of various ages rather than the mature statesman of Sophocles' original. These elements of Sophocles' play have been interpreted by scholars as commenting implicitly on issues of leadership in Athens' democracy, especially that of Pericles, but U.S. productions frequently avoid letting the play resonate with its own democracy or emphasizing Oedipus's assertive role as a self-made leader. The 2005 Denver Center Theatre Company production, directed by Anthony Powell, pointedly displayed a poster saying: "A powerful leader fails to see that he is the cause of his country's distress . . . But that could never happen, right?" Woodruff's ART production approached but finally backed off from this issue more than the original play. Combining *OT* with *Antigone* and *OC* in a Sophoclean trilogy has often introduced a stronger political focus to the play, perhaps because it does not ask the audience to identify either Oedipus or Creon with a specific American contemporary figure. *The Whole World Is Watching*, for example, explored modern leadership as a form of public performance.

The relative popularity of Orestes in the United States, a youthful hero whose similar "Oedipal" and dynastic troubles are largely forced on him, perhaps confirms a broader U.S. urge to reinterpret or reconfigure the dimensions of the ill-deserved trap into which Greek tragic heroes have fallen.[71] U.S. attitudes to *OT* have in this respect not moved very far from the thoughts expressed in this chapter's epigraphs from 1882. Clarence Maclin (known as "Divine Eye") who played Oedipus in a 2007 performance at New York State's Sing Sing prison argued: "Oedipus didn't need to run from himself, to try and deceive the fates. Had he been brave and more honest, he would have stayed and faced the oracles down, using his intelligence and courage to fight the hurt inside. I think we do have choices. There is no way that you can say that because you were born on such-and-such a day and a prophecy came out about you, that is how it is going to be for ever and ever. . . . The key is learning to cope and deal with it, rather than deny and run away."[72] Yet despite this resistance, Sophocles' play itself has retained its original force and direction. In the end, none of the productions discussed in this chapter confirm Maclin's optimistic American view.

FIVE

# Reimagining Medea as American Other

New versions of Euripides' *Medea* were the only Greek tragedies to make a consistent mark on the nineteenth-century American professional stage, and in various incarnations the play has remained the most-performed Greek tragedy in the twentieth century. Both adaptations and new versions have again appeared with increasing regularity since the 1970s.[1] Chapter 1.2 examined important early twentieth-century performances of Euripides' original by Margaret Anglin, who made Medea a triumphant semi-barbarian who deliberately kills her children, and by Ellen Van Volkenburg, who emphasized Medea's intelligence and conviction. American actresses have continued to have some success with Euripides' heroine in the United States, although none after Anglin could compete with various actresses performing Robinson Jeffers's adaptation of the play (discussed below), which was considerably more popular in the United States than abroad, or with touring performances by Greek or British actresses. Diana Rigg (1994) and Fiona Shaw (2002) are the most recent British successes;[2] among others, the noted Greek actress Irene Papas received some good reviews in a 1973 American-generated performance at New York's Circle in the Square directed by Minos Volanakis, and, if opera were under consideration in this book, the performances of Maria Callas in Luigi Cherubini's opera version might well be considered the most memorable. Among American actresses, Brenda Wehle, in a 1991 performance at the Guthrie Theater in Minneapolis directed by Garland Wright, seems to have outshone the men in her cast; more recently, film star Annette Bening received mixed reviews for the title role in a *Medea* directed by Lenka Udovicki at UCLA's Freud Playhouse (2009).[3]

Why has a play in which a foreign heroine is betrayed by her Greek husband Jason, takes revenge on his new bride and her family, deliberately kills her own children, and escapes her crime in Corinth to lead another life in Athens been America's most popular Greek tragedy? The plot offers a compelling vehicle for actresses, lending itself to melodramatic and extravagant acting styles as early as the mid-nineteenth century. Yet, although Medea is a victim of passion and a perpetrator of horrific and self-destructive revenge, sexual jealousy—despite many performances that have (often over-) emphasized it—is a less critical issue in Euripides' original than injustice. Medea established with Jason an atypical symbolically egalitarian marriage by oath and the clasp of right hands; she was responsible for Jason's successful acquisition of the Golden Fleece from Colchis on the Black Sea and had fulfilled her role as faithful and devoted wife by giving him two sons. (Most dangerous wives in Greek tragedy are unfaithful.) Medea interprets as at least partially specious Jason's belated attempt to defend his new marriage to the Corinthian princess Creusa as advantageous for a family living in exile; both Jason and King Creon are willing to exile the heroine to a fate that both Medea's servants and King Aegeus of Athens, who offers her sanctuary, view as betrayal (see *Medea* 17, 77, 82–84, 695, 704–7). Medea has been a benefactor to the Corinthians in the past (14); although a foreigner, she has developed considerable female, even protofeminist bonds with the play's chorus of Corinthian women, who support her revenge plans until she decides to kill her children. The appearance of the winged chariot from Medea's grandfather, the Sun, in which she escapes to Athens at the play's conclusion even seems to affirm the justice of Jason's punishment.

Recognized by all as a clever, atypical woman, Medea manages men in authority—Creon, Aegeus, and ultimately Jason—deftly. Indeed, no tragic human figure comes as close as the wronged Medea to orchestrating her own plot and deliberately performing an ambiguous identity.[4] This aspect of *Medea* has left room for later playwrights and actors to develop an implicit relation between artist or performer and central character. Euripides' sane and androgynous heroine is divided between an avenging epic hero eager to preserve her honor and a mother who wishes to save her children. Her foreign and witchlike powers, though critical to her success, play a reduced role in the original in comparison to later versions of the story, such as Seneca's Roman version. The characters of this play are not victims of fate (always a problem for American audiences; see chapter 4 on *OT*); they articulate their positions, make their own deliberate choices, and face the devastating consequences of their actions. They defy (even while exploiting) traditional expectations about male and female, Greek and barbarian, and challenge clichés. Despite the public involvement of the Corinthian royal family and chorus, the play retains a domestic focus centered on lively rhetorical battles between the sexes that invite the audience to assess different characters' positions. Indeed, the very factors that make it in many respects an unusual Greek tragedy probably best begin to explain its appeal to American audiences.[5]

The play itself, including its choral odes, also poses questions to which later productions/new versions have responded. Does Medea's story, as the chorus at first believes, reverse a Greek poetic tradition that silenced female views, and provide an answer to the male sex (*Medea* 410–30)? Or does her story confirm that tradition? Are maternity and heroism (for which there is in the Greek tradition only a male model aside from self-sacrifice) incompatible, as Medea's famous monologue suggests? Is traditional marriage fundamentally exploitative of women, as Medea argues (230–51)? Can women in particular ever safely love without moderation (620–43)? What can Medea's bonds with the female chorus imply in a modern context? Can anyone truly survive in exile from his or her homeland (644–53)? Can Athens itself integrate an infanticide without devastating consequences (824–50)? Has Medea become less than human/more monstrously godlike by exacting justice, as her appearance on the winged chariot suggests? Can Medea escape the consequences of her actions if she is still suffering the loss of her children/maternal identity (1361–62)? Is her revenge justified by Greek rather than barbarian standards (1323–36)? To these questions, later European and American versions and productions began to add others. Is Medea's escape tolerable, or should she meet just punishment or commit suicide in recognition of her maternal suffering/crime in a revised version? Can modern productions make sense of Medea's use of magic and divine assistance/implicit support? Is she mad, rather than, as in Euripides, apparently sane throughout? Does her story become more tolerable if she is forced by the Corinthians to kill her children, as in some earlier Greek versions of the myth? Can the foreign Medea be rehabilitated or integrated into a civilized, and especially a democratic, world? And if she is, how can the play's modern audience retain a fundamental sense of boundaries that cannot be transgressed?

This chapter will emphasize new U.S. versions and adaptations of *Medea*, rather than performances of the original in translation, partly because the former have been consistently more numerous, and partly because they make the American response to each complex aspect of and question about *Medea* more visible and distinctive. As a whole, U.S. *Medeas* tend above all to represent the play's complex and multifaceted heroine as the wronged, if horrific, cultural "other," whether that other is black, mulatto, Native American, Asian, lesbian, a failed beauty queen, a drag queen, or an abused teenage mother.[6] The heroine's cultural isolation and her complex past often receive more emphasis than in Euripides' original; for example, many new versions begin with scenes in Colchis before Jason and Medea return to Greece with the Golden Fleece that try to develop a legible background to the events of Euripides' play. Robert Duncan's 1965 *Medea at Kolchis: The Maiden Head*, first performed at the famous Black Mountain College, North Carolina, avant-garde summer theater program, even offered a new version that stopped before

Euripides' play begins.[7] Medea's gendered self-division and ability to perform various as well as deceptive roles are often tied to a disjunction between two cultural traditions and/or social identities and modes of creative expression (including performance styles transgressing boundaries between "tragedy" and "comedy"). Medea's articulate otherness permits her to become not only a feminist critic, which she is in part in the original play, but a broader and more pointedly ironic and/or witty social critic, with American religious and cultural prejudices a major target.

Motives for turning to or recreating *Medea* shift over time and require more careful contextualization and analysis than this study of major trends can encompass. The focus on reimagining *Medea* in so many different modes requires offering summaries of an extensive variety of new versions, and hence demands considerable patience from the reader before a larger case can be made. Part 1 of this chapter examines the only new nineteenth-century American version of *Medea* in the context of the play's reception in the United States during a period in which all performances of the tragedy modified the Greek original. Despite making several standard nineteenth-century modifications to the plot, this play responds to pre–Civil War America by emphasizing themes of slavery, female oppression, and freedom. Part 2 considers three trendsetting versions from the mid-1930s through the late 1940s. All three plays establish the foreign Medea as a cultural critic and set the stage for an explosion of new versions with ethnic heroines from the 1970s to the present, which are discussed in part 3. At the risk of generalizing, these later productions confirm that America's fascination with Medea derives from her role as an outsider who is at once victimized and surprisingly empowered in a nation often speciously categorized as a melting pot. These versions permit remotivating Medea's magical/manipulative powers and her occasional escape to another realm in Euripides' final scene and create sympathy for her failure (often as an immigrant) to assimilate to another world. Finally, Medea's androgyny has also proved increasingly compelling in productions exploring gendered identity in drag or cross-dressed versions of the play, as part 4 shows. The development of Medea as ethnic outsider began in Europe with Franz Grillparzer's 1821 *Golden Fleece* and Hans Henny Jahnn's 1926 *Medea;* Jean Anouilh's gypsy Medea in postwar Europe has been followed more recently with a variety of similar international responses.[8] Nevertheless, Medea's often androgynous and multidimensional otherness has expanded enormously in the United States, and this theme defines the central trend in Medea's American reception.

1. SETTING THE STAGE:
NINETEENTH-CENTURY *MEDEA*

Although nineteenth-century versions of *Medea* performed on the commercial stage derived from Europe, articles and translations in popular journals indicate an early and independent native interest in the heroine. An article in the June 1839 *Southern Literary Messenger* represents Medea (described in this case as "Eastern") as a beautiful, intelligent, passionate, and intensely maternal soul, an innocent destroyed by unexpected mistreatment, lacking adequate moral grounding, but nevertheless worthy of pity:

> Medea's character was a strange compound of the extremes of human vice and virtue. With a soul touchingly alive to the finest sympathies of nature, and a fascinating carriage, in which grace and majesty were wildly blended, she won over all who approached her, by the ease of her manners, her insinuating address, and the radiant charms of her beauty. The high intelligence of her mind beamed in every look and word—nor would it be easy to match her endowments by those of the most celebrated females of antiquity. But it is her moral character that we intend to delineate—and its great defect, doubtless, was the unsettled basis on which it was grounded. She possessed no principle of such binding and controvertible authority, that by its decisions *alone* she was willing to test her actions. She searched for other standards—that of interest, or pleasure or passion. Her penetration was unrivalled—and while, therefore, she could not but perceive the true moral grounds of human agency, she yet blindly pursued the compassing of her ends, by any means, fair or foul. . . . But it was not without the sharpest pangs of remorse that she violated the dictates of nature and conscience. Her soul was not yet indurated by the bleak mercy of an unfeeling world. She was not yet an adept in the artifice and unblushing effrontery of crime. At the mercy of every gust of passion, she was hurried into wild excesses, of which her better judgment bitterly repented; and it was only after she had experienced a variety of injuries, that she rushed forward to that pitch of crime and infamy that defied law and scorned contrition. We imagine in ourselves that her dark, mysterious character would have offered a fit subject of delineation to the scrutinizing genius of Byron. . . . She was a mother—a devoted mother—yet she struggled to break from the endearing ties of nature. . . . The awful pathos and sublimity of Medea's sentiments strike terror to the heart. The passionate gush of her feelings stir up the fountains of sympathy. We pity, while we condemn. We weep over the sad wreck of this noble mind, containing in itself the elements of so much moral greatness, and enriched with all the treasures of thought and imagination! (386–87)[9]

American Medea has remained a figure of startling potential, both wronged and gone wrong. Yet this ambivalent, pointedly moral perspective on a volatile, passionate, and compelling heroine soon developed new dimensions. Despite a growing acquaintance with Euripides' original, in which Medea deliberately chooses to kill her children,[10] nineteenth-century theatrical *Medeas* increasingly avoided having the heroine kill her children unless forced to do so by the Corinthians to save them from a worse fate. A powerful maternity could overshadow the heroine's jealousy or preoccupation with revenge as the representation of her social oppression magnified. Among European versions, those by Johann Simon Mayr, Franz Grillparzer, and Ernest Legouvé were produced most frequently in the United States.[11] Madame Giuditta Pasta scored a great hit in Mayr's 1813 opera *Medea in Corinto* in the United States starting in 1828. This early version preserved the divided and avenging Medea of Euripides but doubled the wronged lovers by making Aegeus the betrayed suitor of the Corinthian princess Creusa. In Franz Grillparzer's 1821 Austrian version of *Medea*, the last play of his trilogy *The Golden Fleece*, Jason's new wife Creusa tries and fails to "civilize" a Hasidic, barbarian Medea, who is nevertheless exceptionally ill-treated by her father, Jason, and Creon and guiltless of her brother's death.[12] The Czech actress Francesca (Fanny) Janauschek had more success with Grillparzer in the United States starting in 1867 than in Europe; she lived out her later years with frequent American reprises of her suggestively "Oriental" interpretation of the role, at first in German and then (from 1874) in heavily accented English.[13] The resonance of Grillparzer's version during a period of massive immigration in post–Civil War America anticipated the country's later preoccupation with Medea as cultural other.

Ernest Legouvé's 1856 *Medea,* in which his deserted wife and oppressed mother killed her children to save them from the Corinthians, proved most popular, however. The Italian actress Adelaide Ristori had made Legouvé's *Medea* famous in Europe, and her American tours of this version in Italian in 1866–67 and 1875 were highly successful, in spite of having been delayed by the Civil War.[14] Among those who preceded Ristori in the United States, the American actress Matilda Heron created a sensation with her own later published translation of the play from the French, starting with a brilliant debut at New York's Wallack's Theatre with Edward A. Southern as Jason for fourteen performances from February 16, 1857, to March 14, 1857.[15] Heron performed *Medea* at least another seven times in New York from September 21, 1858 to July 1, 1876. Some critics raved over the freshness, unconventionality, and intensity of Heron's performance (despite some predictable classic poses) but disapproved of the play, especially the killing of the children. The influential critic William Winter, on the other hand, lambasted Heron's shocking display of passion: "She did not satisfy taste and judgment as to classic form; her Medea was half a prowling maniac and half a slattering gypsy . . . the only merit of it consisting in occasional gleams of fateful fury, like intermittent flickering of fire from a slumbering volcano."[16] It took Ristori's emphatic maternity, underlined by a tour including husband and children that was especially impressive to American women, to produce a less ambivalent American reaction to the play.[17] Joy Kasson argues that the American artist William Wetmore Story's famous 1866 sculpture (first exhibited in the United States in 1874) of a towering, brooding Medea holding her knife represented a direct response to Ristori's performance that aimed to quell post–Civil War anxieties about women and the family by domesticating "the demonic powers of women."[18] A Medea cruelly driven to action could in Kasson's view ultimately affirm a fundamentally stable, spiritual, and domestic conception of woman even as she compellingly challenged it.

Edith Hall and Fiona Macintosh have interpreted nineteenth-century British *Medea*s as responding first to battles over divorce and custody laws and later to concerns over actual murder trials in which children were killed by their avenging mothers; suffragettes also appropriated the wronged heroine, especially her famous first "feminist" speech to the chorus of Corinthian women, which had been omitted in earlier new versions.[19] Yet the popularity of these varied nineteenth-century *Medea*s in the United States may have often been more closely linked with debates over slavery and freedom.

America's most important native nineteenth-century "Medea" was a historical reality. In 1856 an escaped slave woman named Margaret Garner tried to kill her children and herself "rather than to return to slavery"; she also mentioned "cruel treatment on the part of their master," perhaps implying that at least some of the children, and very likely her "nearly white" baby Mary, were the fruit of an unwilling liaison with that same master.[20] After succeeding in decapitating Mary with a butcher knife and injuring two of the other three children, Garner became a political football between Ohio defenders, who wished to put her on trial for the murder as a free woman whom they hoped would be exonerated, and her master and his allies, who managed to reenslave Margaret and her surviving family under the banner of the Fugitive Slave Act. This briefly notorious event was immortalized in contemporary abolitionist literature, in political speeches, and in fiction and paintings.[21] For example, in 1867 the Kentucky painter Thomas Satterwhite Noble completed a commission that was later entitled "The Modern Medea" in a widely circulated photolithograph woodcut version (fig. 25) in *Harper's Weekly* (May 18, 1867).[22] An 1874 poem entitled "The Slave Mother: A Tale of Ohio" by Frances E. W. Harper typically interpreted the child's murder as the profoundest act of maternal love.[23]

In the twentieth century, this forgotten story became a source for Toni Morrison's Pulitzer Prize–winning novel, *Beloved,* and was revived in Richard Danielpour's opera *Margaret Garner* (with a libretto by Morrison). Even before 1856, however, the abolitionist literature of the period had repeatedly evoked the prototype of the heroic slave mother who made exactly this moral, if terrible choice either to save her children from slavery by killing them and/or to put an end to sexual exploitation by a white master. Garner's unique story simply gave body to a cliché already well known. Infanticidal slave mothers were already familiar from Harriet Beecher Stowe's 1852 *Uncle Tom's Cabin* (the mulatto slave woman Cassy); dramatic versions of the novel by C. W. Taylor (1852) and George L. Aiken (1853) were the most performed of any adaptations in U.S. theatrical history. Another piece of popular fiction, a story for children in the 1837 *American Anti-slavery Almanac,* has an uncle explaining a lithograph of a slave mother killing her sleeping children to a puzzled child as a parable of maternal sacrifice.[24] Steven Weisenburger, author of a book on Garner, argues that "by 1856 . . . , it would have been

FIGURE 25. "The Modern Medea" (Margaret Garner) by Thomas Satterwhite Noble in a photolithograph woodcut version, *Harper's Weekly*, May 18, 1867.

possible to understand Margaret Garner in terms of three different Medeas: a Southern version in which abolitionists goad her to child murder..., a bourgeois Northern view of her as murdering from an altruistic mother love..., and an abolitionist view of her as a wronged woman of color wreaking vengeance on her white husband for his sexual and racial betrayal of her."[25]

## *Harriette Fanning Read's* Medea

Harriette Fanning Read apparently produced the only new American version of *Medea* in the nineteenth century. Typically of the period, her highly maternal Medea sacrifices her children to save them from being killed by others and commits suicide. Yet slavery and freedom, along with questions relating to women's status, characterized as another form of potential slavery, are central to the whole play.[26] Read was born at Jamaica Plain, near Boston. Her father was a bookseller and publisher, and her mother's family had emigrated to the United States during the "disturbances in Ireland under Cromwell." Both parents were "very desirous that their daughter should be a literary woman, and nature seemed to second their views. At four years of age she had read *Guy Mannering*, at five she had made good progress in the study of Latin, and at eight showed a decided taste for poetry."[27] Some women of this period were trained in Latin and occasionally even in Greek at (especially female) seminaries and academies. Read published translations in French, German, and Spanish, but it seems doubtful that she knew Greek.[28] Her father died when she was young, and her formal schooling was cut short by illness. She and her mother went to live with her uncle, A. C. W. Fanning, who was a colonel in the U.S. Army. They settled in the Washington area and then moved to New York after her uncle's death.

Read wrote a volume of verse plays between the ages of twenty and twenty-three and published a novel, *The Haunted Student*, in 1860. Her journalistic pieces confirm both her feminism and her sympathy for the plight of both slaves and American Indians.[29] Published in 1848 with two other verse dramas, her *Medea* was probably presented in some kind of production or reading in a private household (a common venue in this period) in Washington in 1842.[30] The book's flyleaf has a facsimile of a letter (dated March 19, 1842) from former First Lady Dolley Madison saying: "[I] listened to your Play with deep interest. . . . I think very highly of your production and wish it all success."[31] Read, who made a successful debut as an actress in Boston and later performed in Washington, was also definitely known to have done solo public readings from Shakespeare.[32]

Caroline May, from whose 1848 selection of the best poetry by American female poets much of Read's brief biography derives, declared that her plays (*Medea* is the only verse play in May's collection) were "written with classic taste and a masculine strength of expression."[33] Other journal reviews were similarly laudatory, although verse plays like Read's *Medea* appear to have been thought better absorbed on the page than the stage.[34] Other laudatory reviews remarked on the play's "masculine vigor and . . . rare dramatic fire" and its characterization, management of the plot, dramatic unity, graceful execution, and treatment of passion.[35] The *Union Magazine of Literature and Art* noted:

> We took up the book with an illiberal prejudice, from a deep-sated opinion of ours that women have not quite strength to write tragedies. These dramas are of action rather than of sentiment. . . . But there is a good deal of nerve; great correctness of versification; great purity of sentiment; no absurdities of action, no *fadaises* in the way of ornament, and if this seem but meager praise . . . we can only wish we could often say as much, with a clear conscience, of the so-called dramatic poetry of the day.[36]

Read's *Medea* contains much Euripidean material. Translations of very small sections of the original by Robert Potter (1781), generally but not always quoted and sometimes with slight modifications, are marked in the text by Read, but some other scenes paraphrase Euripides quite closely, especially Medea's debates with Jason.[37] Yet the play begins with an extensive prelude in Colchis that might have been inspired either by Grillparzer's as-yet untranslated 1821 trilogy *The Golden Fleece* or the Hellenistic Greek poet Apollonius's *Argonautica*.[38] As with Grillparzer, the prelude serves partly to increase sympathy and respect for Medea. But in

Read's version Medea's virtue is established above all by her treatment of her Greek slaves.

Read's play blurs the line between Greek and barbarian, slave and free, by establishing a powerful relation of gratitude, respect, and even symbolic sisterhood between Medea's devoted young Greek slave Ianthe and herself. (Ianthe and her fellow slave Lycus take over the roles of Nurse, Pedagogue, and chorus in Euripides' play.) Indeed, although Medea is later castigated by Jason for infecting their sons with "barbaric" tastes (62), in act 1, Medea herself addresses Ianthe at one point as "barbarian" (4), and the play throughout, although it does not create a specific ethnic (rather than generic barbarian) identity for the heroine, raises questions about who is in fact the ethical and cultural other. Medea initially intervenes to save Jason from her father, citing sacrilege against guests, and the play heavily stresses her hesitation to betray her family. (She kills her brother Apsyrtus only because he threatens Jason in an attempt to block their escape.) She has generously agreed to the marriage of her slaves Ianthe and Lycus before the play begins, and when the two Greeks decide to flee with Jason she liberates them both. In later acts Ianthe and Lycus choose to remain Medea's servants in Greece, and finally, as "slaves of gratitude" (69), they insist on their desire to accompany Medea into the dangers of exile from Corinth. Even Jason visibly shows remorse in this play for a wife "in whose soul/a passion ardent, pure, as this can burn" (41).

The play develops a contrast between those who are "slaves in mind" though "free of hand" (5) and those who are more genuinely "free." Though Medea becomes for a time the willing "slave" of love (8), the later scenes reestablish her fundamental "freedom." While Jason insists that the proper wife's role is silence, Medea twice asserts her role as "equal partner, not a household slave" (42). She would prefer to "dwell in poverty with slaves" than be "infected" by Jason's "perjured self" (62); once she realizes she has been betrayed, she insists that she would not have been willing to stay in Corinth if she had known:

> I have been more than woman! Can I now
> In outraged nature's agony, be less? (48)

By contrast, the Creusa of this play is loving, but constantly panic-stricken; her father pronounces her to be unfit to be a warrior's wife (67). Even Medea's meditations on love's power include a reference to the disadvantages of female status:

> The partial Gods assign no blest abode
> On Lethe's bank for woman; yet she
> Finds in love's protecting arms Elysium. (48)

In the closing scene, Medea has retreated to the temple of Juno—here explicitly a goddess of marriage—with the bodies of her children, whom she has killed in order to preserve them from slaughter by the Corinthians (see also earlier, 75). She confesses that she could not have killed them if they had been awake and offers a tender speech over the bodies of the children that is not found in Euripides. She spares Jason, who has fainted in shock over the dead children. When surrounded by Jason and the Corinthians, this Medea has no means or desire to escape. As she kills herself, she declares: "Away, Corinthian slaves! To Fate not you I yield!." She stabs herself; then, calling on Ianthe to help her to rejoin her sons, she adds:

> ... Witness that as she lived
> Medea dies,—in tameless, glorious freedom,—
> Scorning, defying mortal power! For thee,
> Ungrateful friend, false father, perjured husband,
> My curse is on thee,—live! (98)

The play's merging of the themes of slavery and oppression of women very likely represents a response to what began as a sympathetic American engagement with the Greek war of independence against Turkey (1821–29), where the Turks were thought to have enslaved Greek Christian boys and women and sold them in markets. Outrage expressed by journalists and artists, in particular in Hiram Powers's wildly popular sculpture, a nude Greek slave in an Aphrodite-like pose, with hands shackled in chains, and a cross and locket signifying her virtue, expanded in contemporary art and literature to include comparable sympathy for American slave women and women's plight in general. As Vivien Green reports, Powers's image reemerged in abolitionist stories about the beautiful, proud, and virtuous "tragic octoroon," the product of a white plantation owner and his mulatto mistress who is sold into slavery after her father's death.[39] Lydia Maria Child's publications, starting with her 1833 *An Appeal in Favor of that Class of Americans Called Africans* and her 1835 *History of the Condition of Women*, linked slavery past and present with the oppressed condition of women, and especially wives, throughout history. Her work galvanized later female abolitionists.[40] Read's Greek slaves and her courageous heroine's obsession with freedom and women's status very likely emerged from this developing historical context. Read's wronged Medea embodies the virtues of the nineteenth-century American image of Medea described at the beginning of this part of the chapter, but her self-conscious moral struggle locates her at a level far higher than those of the play's other characters.

## 2. MEDEA AS SOCIAL CRITIC FROM THE MID-1930s TO THE LATE 1940s

After the brief flowering of Greek tragedy in the early twentieth century, discussed in chapter 1.2, productions became fairly rare between the 1930s and the late 1950s except on college campuses.[41] Nevertheless, three important adaptations or new versions of Euripides' play from the mid-1930s to the 1940s by Countee Cullen,

Maxwell Anderson, and Robinson Jeffers set the stage for a long line of Medeas with a larger range of cultural identity crises. Medea becomes in both implicit and explicit ways a figure for the male artist's own ambivalent and critical perspective on and even alienation from a social and cultural world in transition during the Depression and the post–World War II era. The Greek tragic poets deployed such, often nontraditional, female figures to express a range of fraught political and social issues of great concern to men; male actors then performed these female roles for a primarily male audience. These three American writers found in Medea a comparable opportunity to "play the other" for an American audience.[42]

### Countee Cullen

In 1935 Countee Cullen, a major poet in the Harlem Renaissance movement of the 1920s and 1930s in New York, published an adaptation of Medea that included in its second edition his own original prologue and epilogue (an appendix entitled "Byword for Evil").[43] Cullen had intended the prominent Negro actress Rose McClendon to play the heroine in an integrated production. McClendon had starred in Langston Hughes's hit Mulatto, a play about mixed marriage, in the 1935–36 New York season and had performed private readings of Medea independently before Cullen finished his close adaptation.[44] Unfortunately, McClendon died unexpectedly from pneumonia before she could undertake the role, and the play had its first performance in March 1940 at Atlanta University, where it was directed by the black poet and dramatist Owen Dodson and initially starred opera singer Dorothy Ateca. Dodson was himself the author of Garden of Time, a 1939 new version of Medea performed at the American Negro Theater in Harlem in March 1945. In this Medea, John, the son of a white plantation owner, had married a black named Miranda in the postbellum South. The first production of Cullen's play already contained a prologue Dodson wrote for Medea, who delivered it dressed in a bloodred cloak, accompanied by dramatic lighting and drumrolls;[45] but major changes were made in the play after Cullen's death in 1946. Over the course of productions in 1959 and 1963 at Howard University in Washington and at the Harlem School of the Arts in 1971, Cullen's play became Dodson's own (unpublished) Medea in Africa.[46] This new version focused on the abuses of colonialism in Africa; at the end the tribal princess Medea's tribesmen beat an Afrikaans Jason to death to the beat of bongo drums.[47]

Cullen, who received a BA with Phi Beta Kappa from New York University and an MA from Harvard, studied both Greek and Latin as an undergraduate. After several fellowships, he supported his artistic life by teaching English and French in a New York junior high school. His version of Medea closely follows but cuts Euripides' play and largely transforms the choral odes, which were set to music by the well-known composer Virgil Thomson in 1935 and performed independently by a New York women's choir on December 16, 1942.[48] The poet Cullen chose to translate and adapt his *Medea* in vivid, often rhythmic, colloquial, performable prose, but a prose entirely independent of other near-contemporary translations of the original. Philip Blair Rice in *The Nation* called Cullen's version "living and utterable English. If there is to be a popular revival of interest in Greek drama, it appears that this is more likely to originate in Harlem than in the universities."[49] Although this opinion has been taken by one critic to be condescending, it is also apt,[50] as a comparison of Cullen's version of *Medea* 579–87 to that of the British scholar Gilbert Murray, whose popularity as translator of Euripides was beginning to fade in the United States at the time, demonstrates:

> MEDEA (to Jason): Careful, Jason, watch what you say—with those fine phrases: for one slip of the tongue may uncover all your treachery. If you really went into this marriage in good faith, why didn't you tell me of it in the beginning, and ask my help instead of leaving me to hear of it after it was done? (Cullen, 277)

> MEDEA (to Jason): Surely I have my thoughts, and not a few
> Have held me strange. To me it seemeth, when
> A crafty tongue is given to evil men
> 'Tis like to wreck, not help them. Their own brain
> Tempts them with lies to dare and dare again,
> Till . . . no man hath enough of subtlety.
> As thou—be not so seeming fair to me
> Nor deft of speech. One word will make thee fall.
> Wert thou not false, 'twas thine to tell me all,
> And charge me help thy marriage path, as I
> Did love thee; not befool me with a lie. (Murray, 32)

Cullen's adaptation, like many other versions before the 1970, cuts Medea's first feminist speech to the Corinthian women, reduces the speaking chorus to two companions, and characterizes Medea as a generic barbarian; race is never directly mentioned in the text.[51] The original translation and publication of the play itself, which was clearly designed for the stage and lacks "tragic grandeur,"[52] may have reflected a cautious attempt to allow McClendon to take on a controversial classical role in a context where black actors were moving into new theatrical territory; *Mulatto*'s mixed marriage had been a Broadway first. If we include Cullen's later published prologue and epilogue, however, a different picture of his version emerges. The expanded play emphasizes the heroine's unusual character, her native honesty and capacity for leadership, and her ruthlessness and deceptiveness when crossed. Cullen's Medea closes her debate over the killing of the children with the climactic "I know what a monstrous thing I have to do, but rage has mastered me through and through, and routed reason in me" (292). His longer version extravagantly expands on the fiercely divided self of this monologue.

In Cullen's added prologue, the virginal Medea responds to Jason's awe at her courage with a frank self-knowledge that Jason, obsessed with the Fleece, ignores. Even her body is frighteningly at odds with other parts of herself: "My hands are not fragile as other women's hands, Jason. They are terrible and tenacious, they are swift and strong, and sometimes they frighten me. Nor am I, in all my being, as other women are, Jason. I have the wisdom of serpents, but if trodden on, their venom too" (575). Unlike other maidens, she is frankly in touch with her desires:

> Jason, let me speak what's in my heart. Then answer me fairly. I love you, Jason. Mark with what little effort those burning words are spoken. Are maids of Greece so frank, or would they deem such an avowal forward and unmaidenly? . . . Our manners are what they are, our country being what it is. So when I say I love you, it is a truth as simple as saying I eat when hungry or sleep when weary. (577)

If Jason truly loves her, Medea adds that she will go to Greece and conform to Greek ways. She is capable of playing another more confined cultural role, but only if Jason understands whom he loves. Otherwise, Jason should escape alone.

The Elizabethan-influenced epilogue finds Medea and a blind King Aegeus in Athens on the day he will transfer power to their son, Pandion. The son is ideally virtuous, and Medea has served Aegeus as an excellent caretaker and adviser. Pandion rescues a dying sailor from the ocean who turns out to be Jason. Jason kills Pandion, who is in fact his own child. Both Jason and Aegeus, who now realizes that Medea blinded him to prevent his realizing her deception, kill themselves. Medea, observed by the chorus, takes poison and closes the play with both hideous and beautiful memories of her past. Although her suicide reinstitutes a nineteenth-century resolution to Medea's story, her choice in this context is perhaps reminiscent of defeated and transgressive female leaders such as (especially Shakespeare's) Cleopatra. Her mixture of terrible honesty and extraordinary deceptiveness mark her to the end. Greek culture cannot contain her or find a place for her extraordinary capacities.

Cullen's predilection for expanding on the myth and mixing classical and Elizabethan themes was not unique in this period. The nearly contemporary verse *Medea* by Henry Bertram Lister, a San Francisco lawyer, poet, amateur classicist, and dramatic producer, which was performed by the California Club Players on May 3, 1933, and later published by the La Boheme Club (probably in 1936), displayed some similar modifications to the text. Lister also opened with a scene in Colchis, in his case clearly drawing on Apollonius's *Argonautica;* he too cut Medea's opening "feminist" appeal to the chorus (11). The conclusion of Lister's play featured a wildly mad Medea, who imagines that she is taking the children away in the chariot of the sun, and then also drinks poison and dies.

Paradoxically, in choosing to adapt a Western classic and have the title role played by a black actress in a version that never mentions race specifically, Cullen seems, to the distress of some later critics,[53] to be reflecting ambivalence or "double consciousness" about his own artistic role as a Negro poet (a black man writing for a white country). "Yet do I marvel at this curious thing:/To make a poet black, and bid him sing!" Cullen says in his poem "Yet Do I Marvel." In 1924 he expanded on this point by asserting:

> If I am going to be a poet at all, I am going to be POET and not NEGRO POET. That is what has hindered the development of artists among us. Their one note has been the concern with their race. That is all very well, none of us can get away from it.... But what I mean is this: I shall not write of negro subjects for the purpose of propaganda. This is not what a poet is concerned with. Of course, when the emotion rising out of the fact that I am a negro is strong, I express it. But that is another matter.[54]

Cullen's education positioned him to be a poet and translator in the Western and classical tradition, but his social and cultural world posed different questions for him to confront. Gerald Early sees the choice of *Medea* as authenticating his "traditionalist and classical credentials";[55] yet there are significant similarities between *Medea* and Cullen's poem "The Ballad of the Brown Girl," which deals with the tragic marriage of an African princess and a white Kentucky aristocrat. As Houston A. Baker put it, the inconsistencies in his poetry

> can be viewed as his painful realizations that the Black man is often so scarred by his experience in America that it is difficult for him to sustain the romantic point of view that Cullen felt most conducive to poetry. The question here is not disillusionment, but having all roads blocked from the outset. A careful reading of Cullen's aesthetic dictates reveals a man with his mind set on [literary] freedom, but one who ... was confused by the relativity of the term.[56]

After McClendon's death, Cullen's expanded version of *Medea* may nevertheless have become implicitly revelatory of the potentially destructive consequences of his own self-division.[57] Though capable of "passing" effectively as Greek, Medea's inability to be true to herself in an alien cultural context proves not only contradictory, but ultimately horrific.

## Maxwell Anderson's Wingless Victory

Both Maxwell Anderson's *Wingless Victory* in 1936 and Robinson Jeffers's much-revived 1947 *Medea* used Medea's ethnic and foreign identity to raise questions about American economic rapacity, religious values, and complacent cultural preconceptions.[58] Anderson (1888–1959), a distinguished playwright of the period, as well as a newspaperman and a college professor who lost his job during World War I over his pacifism, responded to the Depression era, like many other playwrights, with pointedly political plays. His Pulitzer Prize–winning play, *Both Your Houses*, attacked congressional logrolling. Other plays dealt with romantic attitudes to war, Fascism, and the Sacco-Vanzetti case. Like Maurice Browne (see chapter 1.2), Anderson wanted to revive poetic drama in the United States, for which Greek tragedy remained a model. Despite a run of around a hundred performances in New York and good notices for Katharine Cornell as the Malaysian Medea figure, Oparre, and for Walter Abel as the Jason figure, Nathaniel McQueston, *The Wingless Victory* was not well received by critics, who generally panned it as a melodrama and avoided confronting its pointed central critique of American racial relations.[59]

Anderson set his play in 1800 at the site of the famous witch trials in Salem, Massachusetts. Nathaniel McQueston has brought back home a ship loaded with spices, a beautiful Malaysian princess, and their two daughters. His mother and minister brother Phineas insist on viewing the light-skinned Oparre, who has converted to Christianity, as black, heathen, a natural slave, and tainted. Although Faith Ingalls, a young neighbor, has always loved Nathaniel, Anderson's hero does not attempt like Jason to make another match (fig. 26). Instead, he makes the mistake of trying to buy his family's and the town's goodwill by lending money to the point where he can no longer leave when the effort fails. The town discovers from the diary of a former sailor that Nathaniel has come by his ship through possibly dubious means. Phineas and the town elders offer Nathaniel a secure place in the community if he sends Oparre and the children away. Nathaniel resists, relents, and finally decides too late to depart with Oparre, who has given herself, her nurse, and her children poison, since they have nowhere to go and the daughters no choice but a life of prostitution as half-breeds. Nathaniel and his sympathetic brother Ruel, who is also in love with Oparre, depart for exile.

Once powerful in the Celebes, the former princess Oparre frequented the battlefield and condemned men to death. Yet Oparre's rather abstract dark past, which in this play includes her own partial acknowledgment of her supposed racial inferiority, serves mainly to highlight her now feminine subservience to an all-consuming but generous love beyond "custom." In the final scene she initially rejects the returning Nathaniel with a Medea-like pride and anger but dies confessing a love that has humbled and ennobled her in an entirely un-Euripidean fashion. Yet the play's noble and nineteenth-century-style suicidal and maternal Medea figure proves less convincing than its critique of American rapacity disguised as Christianity (a reflection of Anderson's own views). Here both lovers become scapegoats of the town's vicious racism and hypocritical Christianity. The Christian women of Salem sew clothing for naked black children with whom they would not associate in reality. The men compromise their principles out of greed for Nathaniel's money. Anderson's virtuous and civilized Oparre eventually gives up her Christianity in favor of her old pagan gods, since "he came too soon,/this Christ of peace. Men are not ready yet" (249). She explains:

FIGURE 26. Nathaniel McQueston (Walter Abel), Oparre (Katharine Cornell), and Faith Ingalls (Ruth Matteson) in a scene from Maxwell Anderson's *Wingless Victory,* based on Euripides' *Medea,* Empire Theatre, New York, 1936. Photo by Vandamm Studio. Courtesy of Billy Rose Theater Division, The New York Public Library for the Performing Arts.

> When I came
> I worshipped as you worshipped, but when I knew you
> There was a kind of blackness in my heart
> For a long time. Sir, there are gods and gods,
> Each with his many faces, some of good
> And some of evil, each race with its own,
> But the most jealous are the lesser gods,
> Such as your own, of bitterness and wrath
> And eternal fire. And when I try to pray
> Then all these lesser gods go through my mind
> Angry and savage, thrusting away the Christ,
> And I pray to the unknown god. (238)

Anderson's choice to set the play in early America with an Asian,[60] rather than black, heroine (thereby avoiding a direct engagement with post–Civil War controversies) permits him to capitalize on what Caroline Winterer argues is a late nineteenth-/early twentieth-century trend in employing Greek classics, and especially selfless Greek heroines, to reassess American materialism, supported, in this case, by corrupt spirituality.[61]

### Robinson Jeffers's Medea

Robinson Jeffers (1887–1962), a native of Pittsburgh who received a solid classical education (including Greek and Latin) in both Europe and America, spent most of his life in an isolated house with a stone tower on the Pacific coast in Carmel, California. His reputation as a poet began to peak in the 1920s but declined in the 1930s and 1940s, perhaps in part because of his isolationist and more generally antiwar views,[62] his antimaterialism, and his supposed misanthropy. He espoused a philosophy of "inhumanism," which stressed contemplating the beauty of the natural world and deplored anthropocentrism.[63] Among his adaptations of Greek tragedy, *Medea*, written for the Australian actress Judith Anderson and published in 1946, has come close to or even eclipsed Euripides' original in popularity in the United States.[64] Anderson, who met Jeffers through her then-husband, University of California professor Benjamin H. Lehman, and remained a lifelong friend, collaborated through frequent discussion during the writing of the play and later performed Clytemnestra in *The Tower beyond Tragedy*, Jeffers's adaptation of the *Oresteia* and Euripides' *Electra*. After opening in New York under John Gielgud's direction on October 20, 1947, to a run of 214 performances (especially remarkable in comparison to previous performances of Greek tragedy), the Anderson production toured major cities in the United States and Europe over the next eight years. Successful New York revivals later starred Gloria Foster (1965), Minnie Gentry (1978), and Zoe Caldwell (1982, with Anderson as the Nurse), and the play continues to be performed regularly on both commercial and university stages. Anderson's performance was recorded on Decca Records and was later televised under the direction of José Quintero for WNTA-TV in New York, a show that ran for seven nights in 1959; Caldwell's performance was also televised for PBS. Both film versions are still available.

According to Jeffers,

> The story of Medea is about a criminal adventurer and his gun-moll; it is no more moral than the story of Frankie and Johnny—only more ferocious. And so with the yet higher summits of Greek tragedy, the Agamemnon series and the *Oedipus Rex;* they all tell primitive horror-stories, and the conventional pious sentiments of the chorus are more than balanced by the bad temper and wickedness, or folly, of the principal characters. What makes them noble is the poetry; the poetry, and the extreme violence born of passion.[65]

Although Jeffers expands Medea's lines, reduces the choral role, makes Aegeus into a houseguest of Creon, has the Nurse deliver the messenger speech about the death of the princess, virtually eliminates the cosmic and religious elements of the play, and tones down the magical elements, his plot follows that of Euripides fairly closely. Yet in the end, a far more ferocious if sometimes magnificent amorality prevails.

Medea's alien character is repeatedly described as "Asian" in the play, but this characterization seems largely a vehicle to contrast a figure of larger-than-life emotional scale, volatility, unconventional morality, and vivid extravagant language with the conventional attitudes of the play's three chorus women.[66] Unlike Euripides' rational, complex, and self-consciously divided heroine, who defends the justice of her position, Jeffers's once-royal Medea describes herself as rash, intemperate, and fierce (10, 19); she is humiliated by the pity of others (23); her "wisdom" is "rapid and tricky" (34). She is given to loud lamentation, to exposing, touching, and looking with gloom at her own body. Anderson and later Caldwell touched their own breasts and vaginas, Caldwell repeatedly, with a certain loathing of their larger-than-life sexuality whereas the timid, self-effacing chorus of women were covered with headdresses and long, chaste gowns and moved accordingly. Medea's language is permeated with bestial and natural imagery; one moment she is powerfully colloquial, the next strangely remote; with her eyes like "stones" (19), she delights in contemplating annihilation, fields of bones (37–38). The Greek women, "smiling chattering Greeks," as the Nurse calls them (9), believe solitude is dangerous; Medea deplores the "democratic" lack of privacy in a Greek city (17–18).

Medea is the most Sophoclean of Euripidean heroes: heroic in the style of Greek epic and intransigent.[67] Jeffers's version largely enhances the intransigence, alienation, rage, and desperation of her character. She has little real interest in survival; the Nurse's intervention is responsible for her acquiring a possible refuge in Athens with Aegeus, and she constantly gives her plans away to those who fail to notice because their imagination does not yet encompass the horrific possibility. There is no attempt, as in Euripides, to establish a common female bond with the chorus based on the cultural exploitation of women up to the point of child murder. That part of Medea's famous first speech to the chorus is missing (as in Cullen). Instead, though the chorus views her exile (27) and betrayal as wrong, they are also horrified at and frightened of Medea from the first. The conventional chorus of women deplores war and its effects on women and children (39, 63); it piously admires the exceptional gesture of giving good for evil. As the following excerpt makes clear, Medea, by contrast, "does according to nature what I have to do" (62).

> FIRST WOMAN
> But Justice
> Builds a firm house.

MEDEA
The doors of her house are vengeance.
SECOND WOMAN
I dreamed that someone
Gave good for evil, and the world was amazed.
MEDEA
Only a coward or a madman gives good for evil.—Did
You hear a thin music
Like a girl screaming? Or did I perhaps imagine it?
Hark, it is music. (63)

By delaying Medea's monologue of self-division until after the death of the princess, Jeffers reduces the chance of more than momentary sympathy for the children, whose own relation to Jason is developed in a scene that expands considerably on Euripides. Jason tries to win the boys' affection with gifts (58, 65–66), whereas Medea speaks scornfully of the ability of golden gifts to persuade Greeks (49).[68] Medea's final departing lines, as she apparently exits (not to Athens but) to an accommodating wilderness—"Now I go forth/Under the cold eyes of heaven—those weakness-despising stars:—not me they scorn" (81)—again, as with Cullen, hint at a certain alignment between the eccentric poet Jeffers in his solitary stone tower and the appalling but for many American audiences deliciously outrageous and articulate heroine he created. Jeffers saw in Euripides an alienated author like himself.[69] Medea's "barbarism," her isolation and alienation from the world around her, her forceful use of natural imagery (animals, bleak landscape, and stones), her emphasis on the oppressive aspects of democracy, which include dehumanizing Asian others, to some extent give Jeffers's own views voice.[70]

Jeffers's translation, like Cullen's, is deliberately idiomatic, almost prosaic, its vivid imagery excepted; as with Cullen's translation, reviewers contrasted it favorably with Gilbert Murray's.[71] The bleak, archaic set of the original production, with a towering Mycenaean-style palace framed against seashore and mountains, the muted blues and whites of the lighting, and the grey and black costumes closely responded to the play's imagery, as did Anderson's and later Caldwell's highly physical (in the latter case, sensual), fierce (for the period), and less naturalistic acting.[72] As Brooks Atkinson (*New York Times*, October 21, 1947) remarked, the acting "was innocent of the stuffiness peculiar to most classical productions." He noted further: "We are used to more temperate theatre. . . . But Miss Anderson's outpouring of barbaric feelings is so intelligently designed and controlled and so flaming in expression that it convinces and consumes the audience. . . . The details supply the logic, which in turn gives the character a solid foundation. But the quality that makes your scalp tingle in the theatre is the vehemence of the passion." For Atkinson, "Miss Anderson understands the character more thoroughly than Medea,

Euripides, or the scholars, and it would be useless now for anyone else to attempt the part." The now-aged Margaret Anglin, by contrast, thought the performance lacking the projection of an "awful stillness."[73]

Jeffers's exciting and volatile "Asiatic hellcat" (*Life*, November 17, 1947, 113) was and remains a powerful vehicle for actresses and has repeatedly won the admiration of critics for its modernity even as the popularity of Jeffers himself and his views were on the wane. Jeffers may have been right; his *Medea* and its success are perhaps best understood as capitalizing with particular poetic intensity on the gangster story—that popular American way of creating appealingly provocative, nakedly violent others. In contrast to the Medeas of Anderson and Cullen, Jeffers's Medea's lonely survival in a world defined as "natural" partially resonates with that of the outlaw.

### 3. MEDEA AS ETHNIC OTHER FROM THE 1970s TO THE PRESENT

As we have seen, Medea's cultural and racial otherness had already begun to make its mark on the American theatrical scene in the nineteenth century. A rash of new *Medea*s beginning in the late 1970s was provoked by the American feminist and civil rights movements. This section begins by looking at three new black Medeas who derive their magical powers from Caribbean (originally African) voodoo in plays entitled *Black Medea, Pecong,* and *Marie Christine.* Euripides' Medea came to view her passion for Jason as unwise (485); sexual involvement with white or less-black men is represented in these new plays as an inescapable curse. Like Euripides' foreign heroine, the Caribbean black Medeas escape the world that has treated them unjustly and survive their crimes, whereas the mulatto U.S. Medea can find no way out of a repressive American environment that deprives her of political and social adulthood. In Cherríe Moraga's *Hungry Woman,* however, patriarchal politics have deprived her Native American/Chicana Medea of the full legal rights to which her heritage entitles her, and she finds solace primarily in lesbian bonds.

These new Medeas generally derive their powers and their vulnerability to passion from a female line that is nonexistent in Euripides' original, even though female bonds with the chorus are central. In the 1980s, when feminists drew on world mythology to make the case for a prehistoric matriarchy that gave way to historical patriarchy, two new U.S. *Medeas—Medea: A Noh Cycle Based on Greek Myth* and *Kabuki Medea*—reflected these views through heroines who triumphantly escape patriarchal oppression by deliberately rejecting their maternity in a mythical Japanese context. By contrast, immigrant Medeas to the United States (such as the heroines in *Kokoro, wAve,* and *Pious Poetic Pie,* who are Japanese, Korean, and Dominican, respectively) confront varied problems of assimilation to a far less sympathetic modern American world that does not readily permit their survival. In many ways these more recent immigrant Medeas, who face the prospect of destroying real or symbolic offspring with immense reluctance, resemble their nineteenth-century ancestors.

*Voodoo Magic*

Numerous writers and actresses in the United States after Owen Dodson have created black Medeas. Kevin Wetmore's 2003 *Black Dionysus* offered an extensive study of important new versions, with the exception of Dodson's *Garden of Time*, Michael John LaChiusa's musical *Marie Christine*, Marianne McDonald's *Medea, Queen of Colchester*, and some recent performances of Euripides' original. Although these newly imagined black Medeas rarely serve as partial surrogates for their authors (who are generally white), they continue to facilitate exploration of a variety of issues concerning racial, cultural, and religious identity in the United States, whether the plays are set in America, the Caribbean, or Africa. These black American Medeas are not slaves but are endowed with a pagan heritage derived from Africa or the Caribbean that permits them to resist, up to a point, their legal and cultural disadvantages. As noted above, black-white intermarriage proves especially effective in "othering" them.

In this part of the chapter I will privilege the most frequent incarnation of these black heroines, a figure who relies on voodoo traditions that are often represented as handed down in a female line from mother and/or grandmother to daughter. When voodoo empowers the Medea figure to take revenge in Ernest Ferlita's 1976 *Black Medea*, Steve Carter's 1990 *Pecong*, and Michael LaChiusa's 1999 *Marie Christine*, however, each play establishes a different relation to Caribbean culture that permits a plausible version of Euripides' dramatic final escape for the Caribbean heroines in Ferlita and Carter, but not for La Chiusa's Marie Christine, who remains entrapped in the realities of her post–Civil War identity and her all-too-susceptible female sexuality. Precisely because of its heroine's confining American identity, I give detailed attention here to *Marie Christine*.

Both Ferlita's *Black Medea* and LaChiusa's musical *Marie Christine* take place in New Orleans and stage a Medea empowered by voodoo, but disadvantaged by her black blood. Ferlita's play evolves as a voodoo ceremony, punctuated by flashbacks to earlier scenes, that is performed by three women and a nurse figure, Tante Emilié. His Madeleine is a priestess of the voodoo god Damballah and daughter of an enslaved prince from Dahomey who was freed and acquired property in Haiti. She has escaped to New Orleans from a revolution in Haiti in 1810 with her white lover, Jerome, Compte d'Argonne, the son of her father's former master.[74] Once there, both Madeleine's marriage and her sons become by law illegitimate, although she remains technically free; voodoo is linked, correctly in the case of Haiti, with slave revolts. The play's Creon figure, Colonel Croydon, is here empowered by wealth rather than political office. Madeleine kills her children because their father "killed them in spirit" (see Euripides' *Medea* 1364 for a similar if belated rationale). In this play, Madeleine destroys Croydon's daughter Corinne without debasing her deeper religious powers; her gift, a golden bracelet, contains a hidden poison. At the conclusion, Madeleine escapes to hypothetical safety in southern Haiti as her powers merge with those of the god Damballah. "I am the earth, the shape of the hills/And the bend in the road. I open the night/I am Africa, I am the New World . . . I am the way to God for you!" Ferlita's play, originally performed at Loyola University in 1976, has received a number of professional performances since (up to 1990).[75] Despite its heroine's suffering and her painful confrontation with American realities, the play finally rescues her through a vision of Caribbean empowerment that resonates with that of Euripides' sane, intelligent, and resourceful heroine but might appear fragile in the case of Haiti even at the fictional date of this play.

Steve Carter's *Pecong*, written for the Victory Gardens Theater in Chicago in 1990, where Carter was a playwright in residence, has been performed in Newark (1992), San Francisco (1993), London, and New York (2009) to fairly favorable reviews.[76] Son of a white father and a West Indian mother, and a native of New York, who also taught at George Mason University in Fairfax, Virginia, Carter stressed love's power to undermine voodoo/maternal magic. "Love makes you mind go simple/and make you face swole with pimple. Is hate/should motivate/a woman's fate" (25). His play, set on imaginary West Indian "Trankey Island," makes Mediyah the daughter of Damballah. His heroine recaptures her powers, but only by renouncing a traditional female and even mortal identity. After her successful revenge, Mediyah leaves for complete isolation from humankind on the mystical and dangerous Miedo Wood Island, where she now fully replaces Granny Root, her mentor in magic even after her grandmother's death.

*Pecong* focuses more on conflicts within a black community than on race per se,[77] although Mediyah is additionally disadvantaged by being identified as blacker than some other characters. Persis and Faustina, who substitute for the Greek chorus, underline Mediyah's isolation by developing the tensions between the heroine and her (especially female) community. The womanizing, aptly named Jason Allcock defeats Mediyah's brother in the festal contest of Pecong, in which men exchange verbal insults in verse.[78] He stresses (44) that his victory in the contest (which includes Creon Pandit's daughter Sweet Bella and the rule over Carnival and Trankey Island) does not depend, as in Euripides, on Mediyah. Mediyah's humiliated brother then kills himself. In revenge, Mediyah has her twin sons poisoned and deprives Jason of his newly won status; Mediyah does not, as in Euripides, betray father or brother but avenges her mother, whom Creon Pandit impregnated but abandoned. As with Jeffers, however, survival requires reintegration into a "natural" world that operates on different principles.

*Marie Christine*, directed by Graciela Daniele in 1999 at Lincoln Center's Vivian Beaumont Theater in New York, was designed as a vehicle for the African American opera and musical star Audra McDonald. A wealthy mulatto daughter of a black West Indian voodoo (or voudon) healer and a white French father in 1894 Creole New Orleans, Marie Christine resisted her two brothers' desire for respectability and upward mobility by running off, already pregnant, with a womanizing white midwestern sailor named Dante Keyes to Chicago. (LaChiusa was inspired to write his libretto by a historical voodoo healer, Marie Leveau, whose daughter was known to have run off with a man to Chicago.) Marie Christine's resistance to a social life restricted by both her female and her racial identities initially takes the form of adopting her mother's role as voodoo healer and pursuing a pre-Fall "paradise" where men fail to control women. As a song early on in the musical puts it, "THERE'S A WAY BACK TO PARADISE./THERE IS A WAY;/BIDE YOUR TIME. BE CLEVER AND WISE. WHEN YOU LOOK AT A MAN/LOOK HIM DEAD IN THE EYES." (Caps indicate sung text, which is available on the RCA recording 09026-63593-2.)

Once in 1899 Chicago, Marie Christine's powers fail to protect her; her husband deserts his embarrassing mulatto consort for a rising political career. After having killed her brother and taken family gold to escape from New Orleans, and becoming wanted in New York for making the daughters of a man who opposed Dante poison their father, Marie Christine has no place to go. Dante demands that she depart, leaving him their two sons. Dante's racist political backer, the father of his new bride, comes with his petty gangsters to threaten Marie Christine, in part with physical humiliation. (The play realizes the gangster story implicit in Jeffers's version.) This maternal Medea kills her children less out of revenge than because they will face a humiliating life with their father as mulatto bastards.

The play takes place in a women's prison, where Marie Christine tells her story to a chorus of three tough female prisoners in flashbacks. This bleak version lacks the female solidarity of either Euripides' original or Ferlita's version, even though bonding with her mother is represented as critical to Marie Christina's sense of identity at the opening. Indeed, Marie Christine's New Orleans maid, Lisette, is the first to betray her; Magdalena, who operates a bar in Chicago, offers limited support (as the play's Aegeus figure) only because she thinks Marie Christine's magic can help her get pregnant; the female prisoners are more curious than sympathetic. The script closes in nineteenth-century style with Marie Christine's exit to death, rather than escape, as in Euripides' original.

LaChiusa's complex script, with its flashbacks within flashbacks that include family ghosts like Marie Christine's mother, offers the audience a new version of the Golden Fleece myth framed by past and future disaster. Musically, the two acts developed a contrast between the worlds of New Orleans and Chicago. New Orleans is still haunted by a pre–Civil War Southern civility that it struggles to maintain; the family servants speak incomprehensible French-Caribbean patois; the brothers, one of whom sings in French, struggle to maintain a social status inevitably compromised by race and legal disadvantages. The stifled Marie Christine clings to her mother's powers, which she confesses are largely imaginary. The brash, fast-talking Dante bursts in on this circumscribed scene and awakens in Marie Christine the doomed desire, again for a white man, of her mother, whose views are voiced in the opening scene by her ghost: "We may be able to help others and yet be powerless to help ourselves, Marie . . . SILVER MIMOSA:/CLOUDS ON A LAKE:/MORNING BIRDS SINGIN./BARELY AWAKE . . . RAIN IN SEPTEMBER: MANDOLIN STREET:/YOUR HOME:/YOUR FAMILY:/AND SOMEDAY, YOUR CHILDREN . . . /YOUR GRANDFATHER IS THE SUN/BUT YOUR MOTHER IS A WOMAN/WHO PASSES ON TO YOU/AN ALL-TOO-HUMAN HEART . . . BEAUTIFUL." Fragments of these nostalgic lyrics reappear as a lullaby sung by Marie Christine to her children just before she kills them.

The play's theme is captured in the repeated Euripidean phrase "Is love too small a pain for a woman?" For a mulatto woman, involvement with white culture or even sexuality is in this version fatal. The plot's accelerating darkness was emphasized in the production not only by subdued lighting but by the steeply raked amphitheater of the stage, which located cast members in bleachers on either side when they were not acting, and the female prisoners and a persistent percussionist, whose drums evoked both voodoo magic and doom, located above. This setting put the condemned Marie Christine on trial from both internal and external audiences from the start. In this play, class, race, gender, inherited temperament, and, in addition, "the mysteries and miracles of love" closed in on Marie Christine. In contrast to Ferlita's Madeline or Carter's Mediyah, her powers, perhaps imaginary from the start and ultimately not a source of cultural empowerment, could not stand up to the disasters produced by her attempts at assimilation. Both an exit to a mythical Caribbean world and female solidarity proved impossible.

Although Audra McDonald's performance in the challenging title role was universally praised, some critics, already skeptical about the Broadway audience's taste for musical tragedies, found that the script's elaborate and initially leisurely structure and its frequent flashbacks diffused momentum and focus, with too much explained and too little dramatized. Both Marie Christine's passion and her oppression were thought by some to be insufficiently motivated, while Dante is too obviously a cad from the start. In response, LaChiusa defended the need for musicals offering "catharsis" and engagement with central political issues.[79]

From a musical perspective, several critics categorized this ambitious piece, two-thirds of which is either sung or spoken with musical accompaniment, as an opera, or at the very least a musical in the serious vein, as composed by figures like Stephen Sondheim. Michael Feingold (*Village Voice,* December 8–14, 1999) observed more critically:

Ghosts of Puccini and Gershwin, Britten and Copeland, Kern and Sondheim and Weil and Poulenc come and go in the gloom. LaChiusa's never literal in his derivations; he just has an acute ear and a fin de siècle omnivore's taste. . . . LaChiusa's source material is as strong as is his technical range—"realized" folk songs and Caribbean chants, '90s piano rag numbers, burlesques à la Bock and Harnick or teased dissonances in the manner of Blitzstein or Jerome Moross. It seems he can do anything—except, apparently, ask himself why he does it.

Although other U.S. versions of *Medea* with black heroines, sometimes including a number of performances of Euripides' *Medea* starring black actresses, change setting and circumstance, plot patterns and themes remain similar even when the historical setting is expanded and complicated. The new black *Medea*s discussed here rely on an empowering, nurturing, but self-destructive maternal line; they locate the compelling tragedy of Medea largely in the impossibility of assimilation to a white, male-dominated, unjust, and unreliable culture. The dangers of sexual engagement per se and the devastating loss of support from a broader female community become an increasingly bleak route to isolation or death. The turn back to African origins and culture as a mode of exploring or even recapturing black identity has a long American history. These black *Medea*s reaffirm the permanent disruption of these empowering semimythical traditions. Surviving Medeas, including those discussed by Wetmore, such as the heroine of Jim Magnuson's 1968 *African Medea* or Silas Jones's Ethiopian princess in his 1995 *American Medea*, can return to unity with a supernatural world to a greater or lesser degree only outside history. In all these plays, setting the story in the past also uneasily conceals contemporary American realities, where pagan traditions and voodoo itself might appear to some American audiences as signs of suspect marginality and fantasy rather than empowerment. New Medeas confined to generally mixed marriage in America, like Marie Christine or the heroine of the 1992 *Women Are Waiting: The Tragedy of Medea Jackson*, often end up in jail or permanently marginalized.[80] Only in the case of performances of Euripides' original by black actresses such as Beah Richards, Phylicia Rashad, April Yvette Thompson, and Lisa Tharps does the heroine retain more fully the outraged authority of an angry victim of injustice in a suggestively American context.[81]

### Challenging Patriarchy: Moraga's Hungry Woman

In some now-lost alternative versions of the Medea myth, Medea was not merely an exiled foreigner but, because of her illustrious Greek heritage, was invited to serve as a legitimate queen of Corinth, before she was displaced.[82] Native American *Medea*s can also represent women deprived of their legitimate inheritance by sleeping with the enemy, initially the European invaders. Carlos Morton's 1997 *La Malinche*, directed by Abel López at the Arizona Theatre Company in Phoenix after he won their National Hispanic Playwriting Award, merged Medea's story with that of Doña Marina (La Malinche), a young Aztec translator and later, mistress of Cortés during his conquest of Mexico. Historically, Cortés left La Malinche after the birth of their son, and she married another Spaniard and gave birth to a daughter. In some legends, however, La Malinche is linked with La Llorona, a folktale figure betrayed by her husband or lover who drowned and then lamented her children.

The well-known feminist Chicana writer Cherríe Moraga's *Hungry Woman: A Mexican Medea* also drew on La Llorona and related mythology but moved Medea's story to the future in order to make a statement about gender and cultural conflicts and issues within the Chicana/o community. By focusing on the alienation of Medea from her own ethnic community and that community's lost cultural heritage from a different perspective, the play represents a later phase in U.S. identity politics than do most of the black *Medea*s. Perhaps for this reason, *The Hungry Woman* was sufficiently controversial among both Chicana/o groups and mainline theaters that it was first staged in 2000 (by the author) at the Border Festival at the Magic Theatre of San Francisco, five years after staged readings in Los Angeles in 1995.[83]

In the play's hypothetical future, Medea, her lover, Luna (Moon), and her son Chac-Mool have been exiled from Medea's homeland to a grim borderland for queers located in what is now Phoenix, Arizona, because of Medea's lesbian relation to Luna. Revolutionary forces, in which the native midwife Medea had played an important role, had previously recreated the indigenous Aztec homeland Aztlán (a popular myth in the Chicano Movement of the 1960s)[84] in the U.S. Southwest (northern Mexico before 1848). Medea's oppressive older husband, Jasón, who has remarried a young woman who turns out to be barren, wants to retrieve his son in order to bolster his otherwise illegitimate claim as a nonnative to Medea's land in Aztlán. The twelve-year-old Chac-Mool is torn between his mother's feminist critique of the patriarchal, homophobic world of Aztlán and his desire to receive his initiation into manhood at thirteen. He hopes to enlighten Aztlán by returning to his father, but Medea (ironically for a professional midwife, but not for a devotee of Aztec ritual sacrifice) poisons him with herbs to prevent him from indoctrination into misogyny and machismo. Medea is incarcerated for the crime in a prison psychiatric ward, from which flashbacks into the past are enacted, until she is liberated by Luna, who brings her poisonous herbs, and Chac-Mool, whose ghost (his name means "messenger between two worlds") leads her to another world. Here Moon and son replace Euripides' sun god but can only facilitate Medea's death. The sympathetic Chac-Mool, a major character in the play, makes Medea's killing of her son far more vivid and complex than in other versions.

As in the black *Medea*s, Medea's *curandera*, her native healer grandmother, is the source of Medea's special herbal knowledge. Yet this play's female bonds and traditions, both real and mythic, are far more developed. Moraga invokes not only the legend of La Llorona, but also the Aztec goddess Coatlicue, who gave birth to the moon and the sun; a pre-Columbian myth in which the moon goddess Coyolxauhqui is dismembered by her brother the sun; and the Aztec myth of the Hungry Woman, a being with mouths all over her body, who still cries with hunger after being split in two by the gods Quetzalcoatl and Tezcatlipoca and translated into earth and its blanket, the sky. A chorus of Aztec warrior mothers who lost their children—the Chiuatateo—and other deities reinforce the mythic dimensions of the story with music and dance. These legends create a timeless origin for the power of female fertility that is perpetually followed by female division, loss, and oppression. The Hungry Woman's desire is insatiable; the lesbian desire between Medea and Luna nearly destroys their bond as it wavers been passion and sisterhood. Yet this partially mad and divided Medea's decision to kill her son finally entails both a doomed commitment to a firm lesbian identity and a symbolic non-Euripidean reunity with Chac-Mool.[85] On the one hand, the play makes a plea against male-dominated, homophobic attitudes that refuse to recognize the diversity of Chicana/o identities, and represents female homosexuality rather than heterosexual passion as a tragically doomed condition in this context.[86] On the other hand, it attempts to restore its history to a population limited to oral tradition and to counter the American tendency to forget or repress the past.[87]

### Myths of Matriarchy: Noh- and Kabuki-Inspired Medeas

Japanese Noh and Kabuki drama can also feature vengeful mythical female figures who perform their stories as ghosts for a traveling mortal or transform into powerful monsters to exact justice. In the 1970s and 1980s both *Medea: A Noh Cycle Based on Greek Myth* and *Kabuki Medea* turned to a reimagined Japanese tradition to empower a more aggressive feminist assault on patriarchal culture than in the case of Caribbean or Native American Medeas and allowed the heroine, as in Euripides, to reclaim independence despite her suffering and humiliation. Interestingly, the nearly contemporary all-male Kabuki- and Bunraku-influenced Japanese production of *Medea* directed by Yukio Ninagawa, which toured worldwide in the 1980s, similarly aimed to mix Japanese and Western traditions to offer a feminist interpretation of Euripides' original that would empower Japanese women.[88]

UCLA professor Carol Sorgenfrei's Noh version received a number of university productions after it was published in 1975, as well as a 1984 performance directed by Yuriko Doi at San Francisco's Theatre of Yugen/Noh Space.[89] The play deliberately merges Eastern and Western traditions and myth and deploys a Japanese theatrical style and setting. The text prescribes a simple set with a Noh entrance over a bridge at stage right and a small hurry door stage left. The chorus, which serves both to narrate and to extend the actors' voices, sits to the side with musicians. The characters are to wear masklike makeup and costumes that mix

Japanese with an undefined primitive look, to move in a stylized, nonnaturalistic manner, and to sing and chant their lines.

The five-act text appropriates elements from Noh drama in the form of a god play, warrior play, woman play, frenzy or miscellaneous play, and demon play but unites them in a cycle revolving around a single theme. In god play, Medea's Nurse (as a *waki*, or foil to the principal actor) journeys to Corinth and encounters Medea (as *shite*, the principal actor who transforms from human to ghost or deity), disguised as a priestess, who justifies her past actions to the appalled Nurse and claims to have merged with the sun god as a deity in conformity with her true identity as powerful sorceress rather than wife and mother. Medea reenacts her story from Colchis on, which includes her entrapment by the Greek gods (especially Hera) into her liaison with Jason (warrior play); her rejection of her children as parasites because of Jason's betrayal; and the warning of Jason's new wife Cruesa (Euripides' Creusa) against accepting selflessness as the definition of a female role (woman play). Medea then completes her apotheosis in an onstage Kabuki-style transformation to a sun deity, which follows the infanticide.

Medea announces in god play: "Listen, woman, and I will tell you how it was. How I was trapped by the Greek gods, false gods who are a mockery to heaven. Women gods as petty as humans, envious of my freedom and power, wishing to make Jason seem wise and strong. You will learn how a woman can kill her children and yet become a god" (18). Medea's "great talents" were "hidden in the shrouds of motherhood" (52). The demon (*kyu*) play exposes Jason and his sons as demons who "suck the life from women so that 'they' might grow strong" (57). Sorgenfrei's play makes an attack on historical patriarchy that was not uncommon in this period, when feminists sought traces of an original matriarchal culture in myths and prehistoric goddess figurines. As critic Tish Dace put it in her review of the nearly contemporary play *Medea Sacrament*, Medea's experience echoes "the expulsion of the Earth Goddess cult from Western consciousness" (*Villager*, June 2, 1983, 15). Sorgenfrei's disparagement of motherhood as disempowering to women has also appeared in later feminist versions of *Medea*. *Love, Medea*, directed in 2001 by Charles Schick at New York's Bullet Space Theatre and starring Regina Bartkoff, whose journals while pregnant with her daughter, Hannah (who played the messenger) were incorporated in a script that combined Euripides and Seneca's plays and explored the subordination of a mother's priorities to her child. As the chorus of this version put it, "I, always a fighter against all forms of conformity . . . here I am in the greatest conventional role of all time."[90] Euripides' chorus, in response to the infanticide, asked a somewhat different but similarly uncomfortable question when it wondered whether having children at all is worth the struggle (*Medea* 1081–1115).

Despite the colorful and even humorous, fairy tale–like tone of *Kabuki Medea*'s early courtship scenes, Jason's final comeuppance similarly included Medea's transformation into a powerful demon who acts and speaks for all betrayed women. The production received largely stellar reviews and won awards in both Chicago and San Francisco.[91] First produced by the Wisdom Bridge Theatre in Chicago in 1984 (revived in 1993), then at the Kennedy Center in Washington, D.C. (1985), at the Berkeley Repertory Theatre (1985), and at the Hanna Theatre in Cleveland (1985), the play was directed by Shozo Sato, who studied Kabuki in Tokyo with the famous master Kanzaburo Nakamura, with a script by William Missouri Downs and Lou Anne Wright. The actors used a modified form of Kabuki movement and vocal style supported by traditional Kabuki ("jikata") music recorded by the National Theatre of Japan Music Department, mixed with electronic music by Michael Cerri of the University of Illinois at Urbana, where the play originated in 1983.

The brilliantly colorful act 1 opens in the islands of Yamato (Okinawa), where Medea is daughter of the king of the Ryukyus. The warrior prince Jason arrives searching for the imperial symbol of the Golden Dragon in order to reclaim his throne. Jason and Medea fall in love, swear allegiance, and after a magnificently staged underwater encounter with a puppet dragon, the couple escape. Act 2 begins where Euripides' play does. In a scene that conflates two Euripidean encounters between Medea and Jason, Medea goes from an angry denouncement of Jason's divorce decree—"Being a man is a disease"—to a pretend subservience. Jason—Jasons are exceptionally negative figures in both these plays—forces Medea to humiliate herself before the Princess. Medea loses control, and the Princess gloatingly demands her banishment. Medea then enlists the help of the Nurse and the chorus of women to sew a golden robe. The Nurse contributes her only treasure, a gold coin from her dying mother. "Here I place the vengeance of all betrayed women," says Medea, following a choral weaving dance. Significantly, the rebonding with her own sex pointedly marks this Medea's reempowerment, in contrast to the black Medeas discussed earlier. The poisoned cloak later bursts into what appear to be tongues of enveloping fire whirled by stagehands. Act 2 closes with a loosely Euripidean/Senecan echo: "Let no man think me weak or insignificant, for I am Medea."

Act 3 doubles the now-avenging Medea as a defeated puppet who then opens her gown to reveal a masked face and a wild demon wig. Jason enters after the miming of the destruction of the Princess to confront the demon Medea with a scene that departs from Euripides by offering an updated feminist slant on the play's battle of the sexes:

> JASON: Stop you demon woman.... The Princess was merely in love with me. Just as you were at one time. Or do you remember that? No, you must not. Mad women have no memories.

MEDEA: My memory of the past is crystal clear. Only yesterday, I loved you. I loved you for what you were and what you were to become. But, like all men, you loved me for what I was at that moment, never thinking of what I could become.

J: It is the woman who is afraid of what she will become! It is the woman who fears that the future may not be kind to her and holds out for an iron contract of fidelity and loyalty. You say "love." If you really loved me you would have seen I needed to be free.

M (laughs): You want freedom? I accept your divorce and she is dead. There, Jason, I have proven my love. I have set you free.

J: FREE FOR WHAT? You don't know what it is like to want a kingdom.

M: Don't I! Where are those promises you made so passionately? "Come with me to Yamato Court and I will make you a Queen?" What am I queen of? Queen of an empty bed in a foreign land and now even that is to be denied me. You do not know what it is like to be used and discarded by a simple creature that cannot control its animal lust.

J: This talk is pointless. Give me my children and I will leave.

Medea mockingly denies that the children exist because their marriage did not exist. She performs a *mie* (a Japanese theatrical gesture that heightens character, adds emphasis, or marks a key moment) that paralyzes Jason, who is then forced to watch her internal debate and the vivid destruction of his two Bunraku-style puppet children on stage. In the blood dance that follows, streamers of "blood" are pulled from the childrens' decapitated bodies. Medea refuses to give the children to Jason and exits with a (traditionally Japanese) great laugh. Jason departs as the chorus meditates on the effects of love. This stylized revenge scene and the novel guilt acquired by the onstage Princess invites the audience to enjoy Medea's fully dramatized revenge and vivid rejection of maternity. The play closes with a return to its beginning as a beautiful Medea enters in wedding costume to marry the King of Korea (played by the actor who played Jason). The monstrous puppet version of Medea remains onstage to prefigure a possible repetition of the cycle. This conclusion builds on that of Euripides' play, which also sends Medea to another marriage with Aegeus in Athens that ends when she attempts to kill his son Theseus. By translating Medea's story to a fairy-tale Japanese past, these plays enable Medea to become a monstrous but empowered figure of feminist rage.

### Medea as Immigrant

Euripides' play explicitly addresses the foreign Medea's need to assimilate to Greek culture. Despite having quite self-consciously withdrawn into relative isolation and conformity to Greek ways, she finds herself feared for her foreign powers and intelligence (*Medea* 38, 214–24, 285–86, 303–5, 314–23), rejected, and then exiled.

From the early twentieth century, however, U.S. theater critics often, though inaccurately, linked Medea's story with that of Puccini's Madame Butterfly (see, e.g., Alexander Woollcott, *New York Times,* March 23, 1920). Several recent new versions set in the United States, Velina Hasu Houston's *Kokoro* (True Heart) and *House of Chaos* and Sung Rno's *wAve*, echo this association by envisioning their Medea figures as naive, initially helpless, and isolated Asian immigrants. Devoted mothers and skilled housewives, these heroines attempt and fail to enact a traditional domestic role in an America that has no secure place for it. Houston exonerates her heroines and allows them to move forward once they begin to understand American culture; the final recognition and escape of Rno's M recalls that of Euripides' heroine, but her future in Korea remains uncertain. Yubelky Rodriguez's pessimistic *Pious Poetic Pie,* on the other hand, represents Medea as a struggling Dominican immigrant and artist whose assertive temperament and ultimately self-destructive talents (for both domestic and creative life) more closely resemble those of Euripides' heroine despite her concluding suicide.

### Houston's Kokoro *and* The House of Chaos

In Houston's feminist transnational drama *Kokoro,* a Japanese bride, Yasako, married to Hiro, the owner of a Japanese restaurant, has failed to adjust to San Diego. Living in total isolation and a state of economic and cultural dependence, Yasako cares for her adored daughter, Kuniko, and manages a home presided over by the spirit of Japanese rural tradition in the form of the ghost of her mother, Fuyo. (The play's atmosphere of magical realism and references to the supernatural here serve largely to mark a cultural divide.) Hiro has begun an affair with an assimilated Japanese woman, Shizuko, at his restaurant. Yasako, distressed by her loss of honor, eventually decides to commit mother-child suicide (*oyako-shinju*) in the Pacific Ocean. (The play was based on a historical event in Santa Monica in 1985.)[92] Since she views her child as inseparable from herself, she must take her with her to another world. She is rescued, but the daughter dies. The still-suicidal Yasako is arrested for murder, faces a defense from a highly ambivalent Catholic female lawyer, and is labeled a Medea by the newspapers.[93] Eventually her half-Japanese female neighbor, joined by a repentant Hiro, persuades the court that she did not intend murder. Both Yasako and Shizuko (pregnant with Hiro's illegitimate child) begin to put dependence on patriarchy and disabling cultural traditions behind them. Yasako finally chooses punishment (a year in jail and psychiatric treatment) over suicide.[94] Yasako's innocence by the standards of her own culture justifies a move to partial rehabilitation unique among American Medeas.

Houston, the offspring of a Japanese mother and a Native and African American father who has herself suffered "cultural displacement,"[95] followed *Kokoro* with a second feminist revision of Euripides' plot. In her 2007 version of *Medea, The House of Chaos,* directed by Peter Cirino at the San Diego Asian American

Repertory Theatre (SDAART), a Japanese expatriate Medea, Mina Takahashi, is exiled by her white husband and his boss from their international fashion design business, the House of Chaos. Instead of killing her daughter, Kaoko, however, Mina destroys the business and enables her daughter's move to self-reliance. Houston's plays deliberately challenge Medea's myth, both by remotivating the plot and its immigrant heroine and by providing through female bonds an alternative feminist reconfiguration of her maternal identity.

*Sung Rno's wAve*

Survival in America proves impossible for the Korean American playwright Sung Rno's new Medea in his tragic-comic *wAve*. Directed by Will Pomerantz under the auspices of the Ma-Yi Theater Company, the play premiered in March–April 2004 at New York's Ohio Theatre. *wAve's* highly domestic Korean heroine, M, has also chosen cultural isolation as her mode of dealing both with the United States and with her guilt over betraying her family. She stole the Golden Chi that permitted the making of powerful computer chips in the United States, and killed her brother for love of the Korean American Jason. Rno described his plot as "Japanese anime meets the Simpsons." The paralyzed M stays at home cooking and trying to communicate with her distracted husband, who shoots the TV when the Knicks lose (as Elvis did), and with her son, who plays violent video games constantly in order to feel empowered and prefers Big Macs to his mother's Korean cooking.

The play's satirical treatment of the problems of assimilation and its fluid shifts from humor to tragic intensity become increasingly fantastic, however. Jason, a computer techie who runs Argonaut Systems Services, has been offered a part in a film version of *Miss Saigon* called *Mr. Phnom Penh*. (His father had once saved the life of the director during the Korean War.) Jason begins an affair with Marilyn Part II, a computer-generated replica of Marilyn Monroe reengineered from her DNA. M, defined as a "fractured remnant of Medea," frustrates the psychiatrist her husband has hired to deal with her refusal to exit the house and her obsessive guilt over the past, and relates only to a Korean TV talk show starring Chinky and Gooky, which satirizes U.S. myths about Asians, especially in American films, with fake Korean accents. This show, with its deliberately failed attempt at political correctness, substitutes for the Greek chorus.

M visits the Chinky and Gooky show; her recognition of its deliberate satire ultimately enables her to act and appropriate technology for her own ends. She presents her husband with a gun that turns Marilyn into a CD-ROM disk and, in a new version of Euripides' deus ex machina conclusion, she departs in a helicopter with her son, whom the audience has just seen her killing in a (dream?) replica of the original crime enacted against her brother. This scene echoes Jason's fictional abandonment by Marilyn in a helicopter in *Mr. Phnom Penh* (yet another Medea-style story). Jason, the man of technology, is left in darkness.

This deliberately confusing, nonnaturalistic, and overloaded ending fits in with the play's dreamlike tone, which Rno intended to have the logic of music.[96] Korea, says M, is a country tragically "sandwiched between China and Japan. So we were always getting invaded." Junior responds: "Mmmm. Is that why it's always war at home?" In Rno's view, endurance, humor, and a reconnection to broader patterns in nature have been traditional tools with which Koreans addressed their complex cultural status. The country's sense of its traditional spiritual wholeness is represented as already fragmented before the characters in *wAve* struggle with their loss of it in America. Jason's and Junior's obsession with the future attempts to mask a history mired in tragedy, as does M's entrapment in a past and in a new media-dominated present where everyone is an outsider. M asserts about the United States: "No one's from here. There's no here to speak of, for one thing" (57). Assimilation proves impossible in this play. The United States fails to offer M a culture that she can join, but her final escape to Korea with her Americanized son remains a fantastic alternative.[97]

### Yubelky's Pious Poetic Pie

*Pious Poetic Pie,* the Dominican American slam poet Yubelky Rodriguez's version of *Medea,* performed for Fluid Motion Theater and directed by Denyse Owens at New York's Hudson Guild Theatre May 21–30, 2009, used Medea's story to explore failed immigration for the female artist. This play's formerly Dominican heroine Melinda, once a national poetry slam star in the United States, has become a cop to support her economically marginal life with her ex-Dominican partner, Jerome. (Slam poetry involves poetry contests for original work judged by selected audience members.) Melinda now writes slam poems for the increasingly successful Jerome, who has recently married his wealthy landlord's daughter, Gladys, without Melinda's knowledge. The lyric dimensions of this version emerge in slam poems, largely improvised by the talented Melinda, whose words have become the children she miscarried because of overwork. During a performance at the Poetic Pie Café, Melinda, a former Café founder, outshines both the puerile Gladys and Jerome, who recites a poem of Melinda's as his own.

The volatile Melinda, who had accidently killed both her brother in the Dominican Republic and several others during her police work and is about to lose her job, then tempts Jerome with copies of her poems that he could recite and serves poisoned pecan pie to the pregnant Gladys. She rips up her poems, stabs herself, and throws the knife toward Jerome, who picks it up just as Melinda's police buddy Diaz enters. Melinda points silently at, and thus incriminates, Jerome. Melinda's autobiographical poetry captures her life as both a talented immigrant/artist and a woman typical in the play's world as a whole, who is tied to laboring for a man who offers little but sex yet is unfaithful to her. Her signature poem, "Poetic Pecan Pie," originally proudly linked her female domestic and poetic creative powers: "Dreamt I was a poetic pie maker/Baking super power delectable pies/Robustly breaking through socio-economic-emotional-physical barriers." But that hopeless attempt to play a traditional domestic role while failing to adapt to a challenging role in the American economy proved a dead end for Melinda, who finally poisons her pie and destroys her creative progeny.

### 4. MEDEA'S DIVIDED SELF: DRAG AND CROSS-DRESSED PERFORMANCES

Drag and cross-dressed performances and new versions of *Medea* responding to the heroine's original highly dramatized self-division between mother and wronged hero and exploiting the classical Greek performance tradition of male actors performing female roles generally develop a complex sympathy for Medea as a sort of bisexual outcast/other. Even Jason, who loses his heroic status and is reduced to a lamenting woman at the Euripidean conclusion, has to face his female side. Theater Mitu's 2010 *Medea* staged Euripides' text adapted and directed by Rubén Polendo at New York's Access Theater, with Medea played by a bearded nude male and Jason played by a woman, who also served as the female chorus leader. The Nurse was also played by a man, and Creon by a woman. The actor playing Medea exploited his nudity largely to project shame and vulnerability rather than to offer a release from convention. Whenever the other chorus members removed the actress's sleeve (in Asian style) to reveal a white arm and a glimpse of breast, she began to speak and gesture as the male Jason. The performance persistently demanded that the audience examine the play's conflicts through the players' bodies, as it watched a vulnerable male body subjected to and attempting to challenge Medea's humiliating situation and female role, and observed Jason positioned as female from the start. Marianne McDonald's *Medea, Queen of Colchester*, directed by Kirsten Brandt and David Tierney for San Diego's Sledgehammer Theatre in 2003, on the other hand, made the heroine a black South-African drag queen who served as a tragically devoted foster parent to her lover's white children in Las Vegas.

Nevertheless, new versions of *Medea* involving cross-dressing have more closely resembled Rno's *wAve* by being playful and satirical, and in their exploration of Medea's otherness, they perhaps self-consciously reproduced some of the tone of nineteenth-century British burlesques of this and other tragedies. Although cross-dressed versions of *Medea* have been generated independently on both East and West coasts, the most important and deliberately continuous trend began with the 1984 *Medea* by Charles Ludlam, first performed in 1987 by his New

York Ridiculous Theatrical Company, the slightly earlier performances of Ethyl Eichelberger, a former member of Ludlam's company, who represented Medea as a drag queen, and Bradford Louryk's 2001 *Klytaemnestra's Unmentionables*, in which he performed Medea as a mad housewife along with other tragic heroines. Burlesque performances that satirized standard gender roles, such as John Fisher's celebrated West-Coast 1995 *Medea the Musical* and John Epperson's *My Deah* took off from Ludlam to offer broader social satire. Since I (and several others) have discussed a number of *Medea*s in this category elsewhere, I will consider only the pathbreaking *Medea* of Charles Ludlam and John Epperson's *My Deah* here.[98]

## Ludlam's Medea

Although Ludlam's Medea was played alternately by two members of his company, Everett Quinton and Black-Eyed Susan (Susan Carlson), his heroines were generally designed to be played by men, and Quinton played Medea's Nurse (a part expanded by Ludlam), when he was not Medea.[99] Ludlam's shortened version of *Medea* takes the heroine's difference to a deliberate extreme reminiscent, according to *New York Times* critic Frank Rich (November 9, 1987), of gleeful B-movie sensationalism and Hollywood melodramas of the 1930s and 1940s popular with the gay community.[100] "You know my motto: all or nothing!" (805). His Medea, who humorously exploits and comments on Jeffers's popular and familiar version with her Mae West swagger and Barbara Stanwyck rage, was pointedly foreign, antidemocratic, antifatalistic, ironic, maniacal, and unapologetically passionate in a fashion that deconstructs traditional tragic clichés as well:

MEDEA: You Greeks are idiots with your fatalism and your democracy! You institutionalize mediocrity and make a virtue of it! We don't accept fate so easily where I come from, nor do we consider it an advantage to be in the majority!

NURSE: What's the use of struggling against something that was destined before you were born?

MEDEA: Destined? I am not so sure it's destined. The stars impel, but they do not compel. . . .

NURSE: . . . Great people have great tempers! They think they're free to do what they please, but they're slaves of every mood. (802–3)

Medea's outsize shrieks and gestures (she even kisses Creon's foot and puts it on her head), evil laughs, caustic repartee, self-conscious playacting, and rapid shifts in mood invite the audience to take pleasure in her virtuosic revenge and her sheer control of the stage, including the demise of her children (played by large baby dolls) and her escape in a dragon chariot pulled across the stage. As the Nurse announces to the audience at the opening, "Go and watch, if you wish. You won't shame her! She'll play out her tragedy in public if need be!" (802). By bringing the diction down to a colloquial level (even to the point of crude insults to Jason), but closely following the gist of the original, Ludlam makes Medea, as she describes herself, both "a comedian on the stage of life" (811) and a suffering object of laughter to the gods that she also denies. As Medea says in her first appearance before the chorus, "I married for love! I didn't buy my husband. And now I've lost him for love! Marriage is not an easy thing for a woman. A man takes his pleasure where he will, and a woman must take it lying down! . . . I only ask you one thing, women: help me to get even!" (803).

### *Epperson's* My Deah

Along deliberately similar lines, John Epperson, who is known professionally as Lypsinka, a famous master of cross-dressed performance, offered several staged readings in New York of his absurdist (his term) play *My Deah* before the Off-Broadway Abingdon Theatre Company gave it full-fledged productions, which were directed by Mark Waldrop in 2005 and 2006. In Epperson's version, My Deah is played by a woman, but men cross-dressing as female help keep the play's gender issues center stage. Set in Northeast Jackson, Mississippi, Gator Hedgepeth (Jason), a former college football star, is deserting My Deah, a former college beauty queen and aging TV weather girl, for the white trash Simplicity Bullard, the daughter of the governor, in order to secure his vulgar arriviste lifestyle and avoid bankruptcy. An outspoken housekeeper (Lillie V., played by the same actress who plays My Deah) replaces the Nurse figure, and a (secretly gay) football coach replaces the Pedagogue for the couple's two sports-obsessed teenage boys. The actors who play the boys also play two of the four bridge-playing chorus women who lurk around the household with prurient fascination. My Deah, threatened with incarceration in a mental hospital after her harassing phone calls to Simplicity, turns to poisoning a Chanel dress for the bride with the help of a local voodoo Hermaphrodite, kills the boys onstage with a baseball bat, and leaves in a driving rainstorm (a darkening stage) for New Orleans in her purple and gold convertible. "Now hurry sundown! I am ready to be one of the fugitive kind!/ Interstate 55, here I come!" (85). A loud crash is heard, and Medea screams.

Double casting alone, along with local dialects, semicomic and exaggerated demises (Simplicity falls writhing into the seat of a baby stroller that My Deah gave her, and two chorus members drown in the swimming pool), and satire of Southern social life and its pretensions, much of it provided by the clever My Deah and her maid, transform the tone, but, as in Ludlam's play, the script actually adapts the original quite closely throughout and assumes a degree of audience familiarity with Euripides' text. Both Epperson and Ludlam pointedly exploit the heroine's long tradition as a manipulative performer of multiple identities, including gender identity, present in the original. Self-division between roles, in the case of both ethnic and gender roles, can enable considerable generic ambiguity, especially in late twentieth-century versions of the play where interest in identity as a mode of performance has become fashionable. These tonal shifts can also, as in *Kabuki Medea*, invite an audience to enjoy Medea's vengeance in a fashion that less-distancing versions do not.

Euripides' original, especially the first debate scene between Medea and Jason, comes close to being humorous in many performances as the spouses trade jabs in a rhetorical boxing match or Medea makes fools of her enemies, and in a country where domestic comedy has been a dominant theatrical mode from the nineteenth century to twentieth-century television dramas and sitcoms, this play proves more susceptible than many others to this development, including in performances of Euripides' play in translation.[101] For example, *Medea* has even served as the basis for a skewed straight domestic comedy, as in A. R. Gurney's 1967 *Golden Fleece*, in which a married suburban couple, Bill and Betty, have marshaled an audience to show off the Golden Fleece.[102] Bill defends his old Navy buddy Jason and is tempted by Jason's sexy new girlfriend, while Betty projects her own views about women onto her new best friend Medea. Jason and Medea fail to appear, and the infanticide occurs offstage, much to the shock and horror of their naive defenders, whose own marriage begins to collapse under the strain. Gurney's play suggests that the Jason-Medea story lurks uncomfortably behind seemingly ordinary marital relationships.

## CONCLUSION

Most U.S. treatments of *Medea* as "other" respond to the country's history as a nation of continuously and uneasily mingling peoples. U.S. versions with international settings may present a similar conflict, but that is rarer. Roger Kirby's 2004 *Medea in Jerusalem* is an example of such a conflict, between a Palestinian Medea and an Israeli Jason. Kirby's helpless Medea sends her children to the wedding with bombs in a backpack, thus tying the story to contemporary terrorism and religiously motivated violence. American ethnic Medeas may have their own special powers and mythical traditions from their foreign heritage to draw on, but these powers rarely permit more than a fantastic "Euripidean" escape from injustice and the consequences of infanticide. Maternal and domestic Medeas repeatedly fail to survive. Despite pointedly feminist reinterpretations and the heroine's potential to remake her story, Medea's relations with men, women, and Greece/America and its democracy often implode even more than in the original play, and her otherness acquires an increasing number of dimensions; new versions can also intensify patriarchal oppression. Female passion remains self-destructive, and Medea's Euripidean rationality and sense of justice can be diminished or lost under its influence. A number of new versions not discussed here represent a Medea resembling Andrea Yates or Susan Smith who is rendered partially insane by jealousy or a history of child abuse.[103]

A review by Jayne M. Blanchard (*Washington Times,* November 9, 2002) of Fiona Shaw's touring Irish performance as Medea echoes the description in the 1839 *Southern Literary Messenger* quoted at the beginning of this chapter: "Intelligent, self-aware, passionate, sexual and magical, Medea is a force of nature—a woman willing to look beyond the confines of gender to exact a revenge that would befit a wrathful god." Yet Blanchard goes on to express an American fascination with the heroine as "monstrous": "Her anger is godlike, divine in its unshakeable belief that this is the path to take and divine in its indifference to human law and morality. Medea has made a decision—and no one and nothing can stop her." The play's refusal to be a tragedy of fate and its focus on domestic conflict in a wider context invite productions that move into the realm of social satire often tinged with comedy and burlesque that does not dilute the provocative questions posed by the original play. Indeed, *Medea*'s generic flexibility, which resonated with melodrama in Matilda Heron's nineteenth-century performances, with high tragedy in the second decade of the twentieth century, with satire in the 1930s and 1940s, and with racial, ethnic, and gender politics in all periods, best explains the play's enduring fascination for American audiences.

# Epilogue

This book has argued that in various incarnations on the American stage Greek tragedy has frequently responded to national aspirations. Both productions of *Oedipus Tyrannus* in translation and new versions repeatedly confronted an American desire to modify tragic plots and make them conform more closely or respond more appealingly to the nation's preference for remaking both itself and the lives of individuals. This impulse converged with a concern, often influenced by a long-standing national taste for melodrama, to define and expand on moral consequences of the tragic action; from the nineteenth century to this day, for example, sympathetic Medeas have been forced into killing their children in order to prevent others from doing so, paid more extensively for their crimes than in Euripides' play, or escaped from infanticide only to future isolation. Both single plays that emphasized or expanded on the Greek plays' family tensions in a fashion that obscured larger social and political issues and new pairings of plays that "novelized" the relations among several generations of the family of Atreus or Laius have sometimes served to enhance a dramatic focus on personal or familial identity. In all periods, various performances exploited the gender and Greek/barbarian relations central to the original plays in order to address changing contemporary issues regarding gender, race, and immigration.

Since the late 1960s increasing familiarity with certain plays—*Oedipus Tyrannus, Antigone, Medea, Electra, Trojan Women*—has also enabled the deconstruction and remaking of these plays in a fashion legible to at least parts of the audience, enlarging the repertoire of Greek tragedies performed in major urban contexts, or the reconfiguration of the plays to reflect the tone of the most serious legitimate theater of the twentieth century, tragicomedy. Productions of rarely produced plays not discussed in this book—such as the popular and much-performed new version of Aeschylus's *Suppliant Women,* Charles Mee's *Big Love* (2000–2001); of Euripides' *Helen* (2002), *Phoenician Women* (2004), *Ion* (2008–9), and *Andromache* (2009); and of Sophocles' *Women of Trachis* (2007)—have uncovered or exploited tragicomic potential in plays that only sometimes, as in the case of *Ion* or *Helen,* could be described as tragicomic in the originals.[1] Finally, the turn to Greek tragedy in both the early twentieth century and the period from the late 1960s on has served, despite budget constraints in all periods, the development of ambitious new theatrical aesthetics.

What has apparently changed most since the nineteenth century, and still appears to be in the process of changing most radically, is the post-1960s interest in responding to larger public issues through Greek tragedy, which includes an expanded approach to issues of identity and a new focus on confronting the past or a dystopian future. These performances deliberately respond to the nation's long-standing dedication to American exceptionalism and to a reluctance to confront the complexity of American identity. Chapter 3 discussed some plays, such as *Persians, Ajax,* and *Prometheus,* that have received attention for a range of political reasons since the 1970s, but not others, such as the increasingly produced Iphigeneia plays of Euripides, especially *Iphigeneia in Aulis,* as well as plays involving other figures in the house of Atreus such as Clytemnestra and Orestes.[2] Euripides' *Bacchae* and *Orestes,* which deal with a youthful male's attempt to act in a radically changing world, emerged sporadically on the U.S. stage, especially during the unrest of the 1960s and early 1970s; occasional productions and new versions of Sophocles' *Philoctetes,* which include comparably beleaguered youths along with deserted soldiers, have also emerged more often since the 1960s and 1970s.

A new interest in *Iphigeneia in Aulis* (*IA*), sometimes linked with *Iphigeneia in Tauris* (*IT*), and in Euripides' *Hecuba* perhaps best articulates the implications of these shifts. *Trojan Women,* which, despite its relative neglect in this book, has been increasingly popular in the United States since before the First World War, addresses the female victims of the Trojan War and is loosely united around an expression of pity for the ever-increasing suffering of the Trojan queen Hecuba, along with her remaining family and fellow enslaved Trojan women. The play alludes to a less-than-happy future for many of the Greek victors and raises doubts about their behavior during the conquest of Troy; it allows Hecuba to challenge Helen's self-defense of her role in the war in a debate before Menelaus and to bury her grandson Astyanax with her fellow slaves as the city begins to burn around them.

Although *Hecuba* also dwells on the suffering of the defeated Trojan women, it confronts more pointedly the corrosive effects of the Trojan War on both victims and victors. The heroine's arguments concerning justice, which might have prevailed in peacetime, initially lose force with the Greek side in the play's repeated debates. The Greek democratic assembly, persuaded by the demagogic Odysseus, sacrifices the Trojan princess Polyxena at Achilles' tomb for questionable reasons; the doomed girl responds with moving nobility. The catastrophic losses experienced by Queen Hecuba explode in the bloody revenge that she takes with the help of her women against a treacherous barbarian ally, Polymestor, who destroyed her last son for gold; the play closes with a prophesy of Hecuba's metamorphosis into a dog and Agamemnon's future death at the hands of Clytemnestra. Moreover, although Hecuba remains physically bound to a world of women, she debates extensively with the male figures Odysseus and Agamemnon and publicly defends her revenge on Polymestor. Though initially broken by loss of family, status, and city, Hecuba learns to appropriate and master (perhaps dubious) male rhetoric and defend her place in history.

In two major productions of the play, translated by Timberlake Wertenbaker and directed by Carey Perloff at San Francisco's American Conservatory Theater (ACT) in 1995 and 1998, Olympia Dukakis's Hecuba moved from excruciating suffering to half-mad triumph. In the 1998 version in Washington, D.C., by the African Continuum Theatre Company (ACTCo), directed by the African American director Jennifer Nelson and using a published translation (1997) by her sister, the poet Marilyn Nelson, the play's articulate maternal heroine almost rose above the devastating slavery (both Trojan and American) that brutalized her; and in a 2004 Off-Off-Broadway performance translated by William Arrowsmith and directed by Alex Lippard at New York's Culture Project, Kristin Linklater's Hecuba put the complexities of debate and political rhetoric at the center of the performance. Through *Hecuba,* all three productions confronted in a pointed fashion the way in which war corrupts yet in some respects horrifically enables its beleaguered female victims.[3]

The increased interest since 1990 in both of Euripides' Iphigeneia plays, but especially in the *IA,* offers the most telling contrast to U.S. productions and new versions of *Electra* discussed in the introduction and chapter 1. *IA* brings the family of Agamemnon face-to-face with the violence of war rather than its aftermath, as in *Electra;* Agamemnon, Clytemnestra, Iphigeneia, Menelaus, and Achilles all vacillate in confronting the sacrifice of an innocent daughter, which is needed to inaugurate the Trojan expedition. The ambitious Agamemnon lures his daughter to Aulis with the pretext of a marriage to Achilles and regrets it too late, since his army is uncontrollably eager for war. The sacrifice shatters his marriage to Clytemnestra, who has suppressed her outrage over Agamemnon's killing of her child by her first marriage. The heartbroken Iphigeneia, betrayed by her adored father, then borrows his patriotic rhetoric to accept her sacrifice and wins the support and admiration of her fictive bridegroom, Achilles. In a final perhaps inauthentic messenger speech, the goddess Artemis has reportedly substituted a deer for the vanished girl. *IT* brings Iphigeneia's brother Orestes and his friend Pylades to the land of the Taurians on the Black Sea, where Artemis brought Iphigeneia to serve as a priestess in a barbarian cult that sacrifices Greeks. The exhausted Orestes cannot escape the Furies who hound him after his mother's death without bringing Artemis's statue back to Greece. The siblings eventually recognize each other just before Iphigeneia, embittered by her past, is slated to sacrifice her brother. Iphigeneia then actively plots their escape, and they return to Greece with some additional divine help. Iphigeneia is to become a priestess of Artemis in Attica.

Because *IA* allows the Greeks to make an active choice to engage in the Trojan War and explores the prices paid by innocent people for their leaders' changing, inconsistent, and apparently dubious reasons for undertaking the venture, it has come to seem particularly relevant in the light of U.S. military ventures of the late twentieth to early twenty-first century. Iphigeneia's conversion to accepting her sacrifice has served to confront a public rhetoric and a media that can abuse and even brainwash their victims. The 1967 *IA* directed by Michael Cacoyannis at New York's Off-Broadway Circle in the Square theater generated a renewed interest in the play that preceded his well-known and popular 1977 film version. Reviews noted the play's contemporary historical relevance to the Vietnam War, especially its exploration of duty in the face of a war one "feels to be worthless."[4]

Post–Vietnam War productions have taken an increasingly assertive stance to the public issues raised by *IA*. The WorkShop Theater's 2003 adaptation of *IA* in New York, directed by Elysa Marden, was generated by the 9/11 disaster.[5] Marden's collaborator, P. Seth Bauer, had been a survivor of the World Trade Center disaster. His adapted, colloquial script evolved to express implicit reactions to that event; the dress rehearsal took place on the eve of the Iraq invasion, and later versions of the production incorporated a response to it as well. Bauer reduced Euripides' gods to one God and developed the sacrifice theme by drawing on other famous child sacrifices in traditional religions, such as that of Isaac by Abraham; in Bauer's version the sacrifice becomes a test of faith in God and national destiny. Arguments pro- and con-war played a more extensive role throughout than in Euripides. As Greeks, says Bauer's Agamemnon, "we don't ask ourselves why we go to war. We ask ourselves why not" (39). A version of *IA* by the San Jose Repertory Theatre in May 2006, directed by Timothy Near, took a similar line in response to the Iraq War: "What you see is the hijacking of faith in order to perpetuate the problems of mankind."[6]

Bauer's Iphigeneia was a far more active participant in his version than Euripides' initially reluctant heroine. In her first scene with Agamemnon, she bubbled with insouciant, teenage enthusiasm for her father and her coming wedding; later, as Clytemnestra fixed her hair, she refused to get advice about her wedding night and interrupted with plans about capturing Troy that she wanted to share with her father. More sophisticated than her Euripidean predecessor, she wondered whether the lack of wind was a sign that God did not want the war (37). Instead of parroting her father's rhetoric, she constructed extensive, strategic arguments for her sacrifice with, as Marden put it in an interview, "the fervor of a suicide bomber." "What would be the point of saving me if you had to kill everybody?" (44), she asked Achilles. Bauer's script also developed and to some extent modernized Clytemnestra's active defense of her daughter to prepare for the events of the *Oresteia*. At the opening of the play a large spear was shown stuck in the ground. At the end, Clytemnestra took up this spear.

This production's concern with the way that powerful contemporary political and religious rhetoric corrupts innocent minds has become even more central to many productions of the original in the years since. For example, in Theodora Skipitares' 2005 *Iphigenia* at New York's La MaMa, E.T.C. Iphigenia was played by an actress surrounded by large Bunraku-style puppets manipulated by visible puppeteers in black. This device heightened the heroine's humanity, her capacity to suffer and change, in contrast to the other characters, who remained trapped in the role of puppets offering deceptive public rhetoric. Charles Mee's collaged script, *Iphigenia 2.0*, directed by Tina Landau in 2007 at the Signature Theatre Company in New York, intertwined Euripides with excerpts from war blogs, bride's magazines, and books on leadership and war psychology.[7] A dialogue between a chorus of soldiers, who meditated on war and why they went to war, and bridesmaids preoccupied with marriage ended with Iphigenia's hysterical conversion to a ghastly marriage/sacrifice enacted on stage. Whereas Euripides' play reports the divine demand for Iphigenia's sacrifice and the army's enthusiasm for the expedition, the soldiers in Mee's play, about to risk their own lives, initiated the demand for Iphigenia's sacrifice to Agamemnon onstage. As Agamemnon expressed this version's doubts at the play's opening, "Sometimes they [empires] are brought to ruin by no more than the belief that something must be done when in truth doing nothing would have been the better course."

The sisters Iphigeneia, Electra, and in some cases Chrysothemis are in different ways victims of the Trojan War and familial disaster in the Greek tragedies that include them. Yet while events force the resistant and bruised Electra to turn inward and confront her family, Iphigeneia must turn outward to respond directly to larger historical forces. Unlike Electra, Iphigeneia begins *IA* with a solid bond with both parents that she struggles to maintain. Although worried about the separation from her family that marriage to the glamorous Achilles will bring, she finally turns her sacrifice into a lethal symbolic marriage to all of Greece. By bringing Panhellenic politics and family into direct confrontation and even infusing the plot with a lost romance, *IA* moves beyond the claustrophobic focus on revenge and injustice central to *Electra* for an era in which political resistance can seem increasingly futile. Making Iphigeneia's story a prologue to productions of Aeschylus's *Oresteia*, sometimes with Sophocles' *Electra* substituted for *Libation Bearers*, has also served in some trilogies or tetralogies to humanize Clytemnestra's later murder of her husband and to link all the women in the family of Agamemnon as victims of patriarchal rhetoric or abuse and active responders to it during a period in which female bonds and mother-daughter relations were attracting increasing examination. Among major productions, both *The Clytemnestra Project,* directed by Garland Wright at the Guthrie Theater in Minneapolis in 1992, and Kelly Stuart's *Furious Blood,* a new version directed by Kirsten Brandt at San Diego's Sledgehammer Theatre in 2000, deployed *IA* as a prologue to Aeschylus's *Agamemnon* and Sophocles' *Electra* to this effect.[8]

American versions of *Electra* discussed in the introduction split and/or doubled the heroine's psyche. Productions of *IA* and *IT* have multiplied an often-traumatized Iphigeneia as a (more-commoditized) every girl who confronts and is traumatized by the dark side of history. Inaugurating this trend of multiplying the heroine in order make her representative of an era, Doug Dyer and Gretchen Cryer's *Wedding of Iphigeneia* and *Iphigeneia in Concert,* directed by Gerald Freedman at New York's Public Theater in 1971, revolved around a choral Iphigeneia played and sung by twelve talented young women. The girls sang and danced in 1970s style about Iphigeneia's rescue by Artemis and her bondage among the Taurians and questioned the heroine's noble behavior and the motivations for action offered in both plays. The Greek director Yannis Houvardas set a striking deconstructive version of *IT,* staged at New York's La MaMa Annex in 1992, in a glaringly white mental hospital designed by Dionyssis Fotopoulos; here eight Iphigeneias attempted to recover their often terrifying past in dreams "before the doors open and the fiery volcanic world crashes in on them."[9] Iphigeneia's nightmare of encountering Orestes as her next sacrificial victim bolstered the "dreamlike atmosphere" with clouds, scenes, and other events emerging from behind giant wardrobe doors.[10]

In 2004 Caridad Svich's postmodern *Iphigenia Crash Land Falls on the Neon Shell That Was Once Her Heart (A Rave Fable)* received its premiere at 7 Stages in Atlanta, Georgia, directed by Melissa Foulger, after several workshop versions in Los Angeles, New York, and Greece.[11] Svich's play draws from Euripides' *IA,* Racine, and Gluck and is set in an unnamed Latin American country mired in violence and corruption; her Iphigenia (partly inspired by Princesss Di) is divided between her mythic self, which knows of her coming sacrifice for the state, and a desire to reclaim her body/sensuality for another life. She attempts to escape from being silenced in her confining house, and from her father, General Adolfo, and his denials of reality and efforts to insure his reelection by sacrificing her. In an aircraft hangar now disco club, she becomes identified both with a chorus of three victimized Fresa girls (factory girls killed in Latin American border towns, but played by men) and an androgynous rock star Achilles, with whom she dances and trips on Ecstasy in a theatrical world defined by pulsing lights, music, and video and film images. In the concluding scene the dead Fresa girls tear off and don Iphigenia's designer clothing (and thus assume her social identity), after which Iphigenia departs with Achilles into a joint fantasy that does not in fact short-circuit either of their prescribed deaths for their country. Although the play centers on the isolated Iphigenia's own experience of entrapment by both a suffocating family and society, her attempt to find a self only results in multiplying that self and implicating it further in a nightmarish and inevitable victimization that provides a momentary illusion of expanded identity. In this play, crossing the boundaries between high and low, life and death, and male and female fails to eventuate in a meaningful version of the mythic voyage to another world offered to other Greek heroes.

Finally, *IT* effects a reconciliation between Iphigeneia and her brother, Orestes, in a fashion that partially undoes by implication the conflicts between their warring parents. The play's more mature, initially embittered Iphigeneia takes the family's history beyond its initial tragedies through imagination, strategy, and love of her brother, Orestes; she returns not to a private role in her family or marriage, but to a posttragic public role as a priestess who will be worshipped after her death. Both performing *IT* and combining *IA* and *IT* have permitted staging a move through and past tragedy.[12] JoAnne Akalaitis twice staged *The Iphigenia Cycle*, translated by Nicholas Rudall, at Chicago's Court Theatre in 1997, and in New York in 1999. Her *IA* offered a spectacle in which the unwitting and straightforward mother and daughter became trapped by an absurd, deadly, and sometimes laughable male war game; her *IT* emphasized the corrupting effects of their experience on all of the characters, including the chorus of enslaved Greek women, whose fury-like hostile energy was finally transformed into sympathy for the cause of the reunited siblings.

Ellen McLaughlin's 1995 *Iphigenia and Other Daughters*, initially directed by David Esbjornson at the Classic Stage Company in New York, framed a version of Sophocles' *Electra* with abbreviated versions of *IA* and *IT*.[13] The play's three carefully linked sisters, Iphigenia, Electra, and Chrysothemis, became the tortured eyes (and tongues) that witness the past and keep it alive. In the prologue Iphigenia was the object of the male gaze, aware of history only as it was about to sacrifice her:

>And all these eyes are on me
>Visible me
>This is a terrible place
>Something must be done
>Ah, I see.
>I was right
>Here is my husband
>This ancient stone
>And the quick shadow of the knife
>I am to marry everyone
>Every single one
>This is what it is at last. (24)

Yet she also returns this gaze: "I am like Medusa. I change men to silent stone" (20).

The epilogue, based on *IT*, following McLaughlin's new version of Sophocles' *Electra* mentioned in the introduction, opened a way past the tragedy of the violent central episode. Iphigenia and Orestes now share the status of sacrificial victim. In contrast to Euripides' play, where the siblings return Artemis's statue to Greece, McLaughlin's Iphigenia became the statue herself. Although remaining the object of the fascinated male gaze, she turned from victim to a source of salvation at the center of history:

> I am the statue you have come to find
> Take me to the city
> To the center of the city
> Build noise and life around me
> I will be silent and tall
> I will remind them
> I will seem to see everything
> I will be female and slightly terrifying
> I will be what I have always been
> Visible and mute
> You will place me at the center of something
> And you will lay your tortured head upon my cold feet.
> And you will finally sleep. (75)

The two siblings share the final insight that this "needle through the wall of history," "the part of justice which is merely/personal" is "finally/Something like/Love" (76). Iphigenia retains in a new and muted form the terrifying gaze, memory, and sense of justice that impel Electra, the sanity and benign remoteness from action of Chrysothemis, and the putative centrality to history of her mother, Clytemnestra. As in Joseph Chaikin's *Electra,* discussed in the introduction, repeated recognitions tie the parts of this play together, but the final recognition of McLaughlin's *IT* attempts to include both history and familial bonds, both the personal and the political so central to contemporary feminism at the time of the first performance of McLaughlin's play, yet recognizes the largely symbolic nature of its conclusion. Indeed, her Iphigenia assumes that her politically active mother must be dead because "no woman can afford to be *that* interesting" (63).

The assertive Clytemnestra herself, along with Medea, has of course not ceded a central place on the American stage to these victimized daughters. And important twenty-first-century performances and new versions of *IT,* such as Michi Barall's 2010 tragicomic *Rescue Me,* directed by Loy Arcenas at New York's Ohio Theatre, also gave Iphigeneia back the active role she adopts in the final scenes of Euripides' play.[14] Iphigeneia's story thus permits not only a confrontation with both personal and national identity, but a posttragic coda that can implicitly restore, if only partially, American optimism in a difficult era. In this respect, the Iphigeneia plays once again permit the United States both to reconfigure tragedy in its own, increasingly beleaguered, image and to recognize women's growing but still problematic move into the public world.

APPENDIX A

# Professional Productions and New Versions of Sophocles' and Euripides' *Electras*

*The Archive of Performances of Greek and Roman Drama (www.apgrd.ox.ac.uk/) has fuller cast lists and more information on sources in some cases. These entries are as complete as current information allowed.*

\* Discussed or mentioned in the introduction
\*\* Discussed or mentioned in chapters 1–3 or the epilogue
\*\*\* Production emphasizing a neurotic Electra
( ) Important visiting production

### SOPHOCLES' *ELECTRA*

\*\*1880–89 Hull House, Chicago, directed by Jane Addams (Addams [1910] 1967).

1887 Sophocles' or Euripides' *Electra*, Arch Street Opera House, Philadelphia.

\*\*1889 American Academy of Dramatic Arts, Lyceum Theatre, New York, March 1889; Hollis Street Theatre, Boston, April 25, 1889; and Harvard University, Sanders Theatre, May 1, 1889; directed by Franklin H. Sargent and produced by David Belasco and Henry C. DeMille, starring Grace Hamilton, Olive Gates, Edith A. Chapman, White Whittlesey, Percy West, and George F. Platt, with music by Laura Sedwick Collins (Pluggé 1938, 6; Hartigan 1995, 36, Brown 3: 424; Hains 1910; Choate 2009).

\*\*1908, revived in 1909 Hofmannstahl's *Elektra*, translated by Arthur Symons, Garden Theatre, New York, starring Mrs. Patrick Campbell and Mrs. Beerbohm Tree (*Drama News*, February 22, 1908; *New York Sun*, February 12, 1908; Choate 2009).

1910–11 Unknown venues in New York and California, directed by Raymond Duncan with Eleni Sikelianos as Clytemnestra (*Art and Archaeology* 3.5 [May 1916]: 250–63).

\*\*1913 and 1915 Hearst Greek Theater, University of California, Berkeley, translated by Edward H. Plumptre, directed by and starring Margaret Anglin, music by William Furst

(1913) and Walter Damrosch (1915), designed by Livingston Platt. In the 1913 production Ian McClaren played Orestes, and Ruth C. Boucicault, Clytemnestra; in the 1915 production Pedro de Cordoba played Orestes and Boucicault again did Clytemnestra (*San Francisco Examiner*, September 7, 1913; *Boston Evening Transcript*, September 7, 1913; Walter Anthony, *San Francisco Chronicle*, August 29, 1915; Johnson 1971; LeVay 1989; Choate 2009).

\*\*1918 Carnegie Hall, New York, translated by E. H. Plumptre, directed by and starring Margaret Anglin, music composed Walter Damrosch for the New York Symphony Orchestra, designed by Livingston Platt; Fred Eric played Orestes and Florence Wollerson Clytemnestra (Arthur Hornblow, *Theatre* 27.206 [April 1918]: 217; *Vogue*, April 1, 1918; *New York Times*, February 7, 1918; Kenneth Macgowan, *Boston Evening Transcript*, February 8, 1918; *New York Sun*, February 7, 1918; *Theatre Arts Magazine* 2 [February 1918]: 90; Heywood Broun, *New York Tribune*, February 7, 1918; *Nation* 106.28, February 28, 1918, 244; John Rafferty, *Morning Telegraph*, February 7, 1918; *Christian Science Monitor*, February 10, 1918; Arthur Hornblow, *Theatre Magazine* 28.206 [April 1918]: 217; *New York Times*, February 21, 1918; LeVay 1989, 186–87; Hartigan 1995, 26–27, 49–50, 90–92; Choate 2009; *Nation* 106, February 28, 1918, 244; *New York Tribune*, February 21, 1918).

1923 *Clytemnestra* by Henry Bertram Lister, written for and published by La Boheme Club, San Francisco, starring Maude Graves Lister, Lydia Warren Lister, and Maxine Siebrecht.

1925 Garden Theater, St. Louis, directed by and starring Margaret Anglin, composer Walter Damrosch, with John Knight as Orestes and Alma Kruger as Clytemnestra.

1926 Berkeley, California, directed by and starring Margaret Anglin with Ralph Roeder as Orestes and Olive Oliver as Clytemnestra.

\*\*1927 Metropolitan Opera House, New York, and Gallo Theater, directed by and starring Margaret Anglin, composer Walter Damrosch, Margaret Delmar as Clytemnestra and Ralph Roeder as Orestes at the Metropolitan, and Antoinette Perry as Clytemnestra at the Gallo. The Metropolitan Opera House, Philadelphia, production in the same year had music by William Furst (Frank Vreeland, *New York Telegram*, May 4, 1927; Brooks Atkinson, *New York Times*, May 15, 1927; Stark Young, *New Republic* 50, May 18, 1927, 354; *New York Herald Tribune*, May 5, 1927; Brooks Atkinson, *New York Times*, May 4, 1927; Burns Mantle, *Daily News*, May 4, 1927; *New York American*, May 5, 1927; John Anderson, *New York Evening Post*, May 4, 1927; Joseph Wood Krutch, *Nation* 124, May 18, 1927, 564; Larry Barreto, *Bookman* 65 [July 1927]: 572; and *Dial* 83 [July 1927]: 82; R. D. Skinner, *The Commonweal*, May 18, 1927; Arthur Ruhl, *New York Herald Tribune*, December 3, 1927; *New York Times*, December 2, 1927; Alexander Woollcott, *New York World*, May 4, 1927; Johnson 1971; LeVay 1989; Choate 2009).

\*\*1928 Providence, Rhode Island, outdoor theater, directed by and starring Margaret Anglin with the second 1927 New York cast (*Providence Journal*, June 27, 1928).

(1931 Hofmannstahl's *Elektra*, New Yorker Theatre, New York, starring Marika Cotopouli, with Katina Paxinou and Alexis Minotis.)

1931 *Mourning Becomes Electra* by Eugene O'Neill, directed by Philip Moeller, sets by Robert Edmund Jones, Guild Theatre, N.Y., starring Alice Brady as Lavinia, Alla Nazimova as Christine, Lee Barker as Ezra, Earle Larimore (replaced by Philip Foster) as Orin, Thomas Chalmers as Adam Brant (reviews in Berlin 1989). Film version directed by

Dudley Nicols in 1947, starring Rosalind Russell, Michael Redgrave, Raymond Massey, Katina Paxinou, Leo Genn, and Kirk Douglas; opera version by Martin David Levy, with a libretto by Henry Butler, in 1967, Metropolitan Opera House, New York; revived at Lyric Opera in Chicago in 1998–99, the Seattle Opera in 2003–4, City Opera, New York, in 2004, starring Lauren Flanaghan as Christine and Emily Pulley as Lavinia.

**1931 Jordan Hall, Boston, Massachusetts, directed by Robert Henderson, starring Blanche Yurka, choreography by Martha Graham, music by Lewis Horst (*Boston Post*, May 18, 1931; H. T. Parker, *New York Times*, May 24, 1931). This performance was also done in the same year at the University of Michigan in Ann Arbor.

**1932 Selwyn Theatre, New York, translation by J. T. Sheppard, directed by Robert Henderson, starring Blanche Yurka and Mrs. Patrick Campbell as Clytemnestra. Also presented at the Hollis Street Theatre, Boston, the Philadelphia Academy of Music, and the McCarter Theatre in Princeton. Staged in Berkeley by Morris Ankrun with Yurka and Hedviga Reicher and in New York at the Theatre Guild in 1937 (Richard Dana Skinner, *Commonweal*, January 27, 1932, 357–58; *Theatre Arts Monthly* 16 [March 1932]: 188–89; Arthur Ruhl, *Herald Tribune*, January 9, 1932; *Arts and Decorations*, March 1932, 62; *Theatre Guild Magazine*, February 1932, 12; Robert Garland, *World Telegram*, January 9, 1932; Gilbert W. Gabriel, *New York American*, January 9, 1932; Richard Lockridge, *New York Sun*, January 9, 1932; Burns Mantle, *NY Daily News*, January 8, 1932; *New York Post*, January 9, 1932; Brooks Atkinson, *New York Times*, January 9, 1932; Hartigan 1995, 28–29; Choate 2009).

1937 Bennington Theatre Guild, Theatre Studio, Bennington College, directed by Francis Fergusson, with a set by Arch Lauterer, starring Eleanor Mindling.

1945 Catholic University Theater, translated by Edward Percy, directed by Alan Schneider and Dr. Josephine McGarry Callan, starring Janet Fehm (*Washington Post*, December 4, 1945). Schneider also directed the play in 1943.

1948 Independent Players, 108 West 16$^{th}$ Street, New York.

1948 Baltimore Museum of Art, translation by Francis Fergusson, directed by N. Bryllion Fagin, starring Patti Singewald.

1949 The Janus Theatre, New York, adaptation of Francis Fergusson's translation, directed by Joel Friedman, starring Sylvia Gassel.

(1952 Mark Hellinger Theatre, translated by J. Gryparis, directed by Dimitri Rondiris, starring Katina Paxinou [see, among many reviews, William Hawkins, *New York World Telegram*, November 10, 1952; Brooks Atkinson, *New York Times*, November 20, 1952; Robert Coleman, *Daily Mirror*, November 20, 1952; John Chapman, *Daily News*, November 20, 1952; Walter Kerr, *New York Herald Tribune*, November 20, 1952; Richard Watts Jr., *New York Post*, November 20, 1952; Thomas R. Dash, *Women's Wear Daily*, November 20, 1952; John McClain, *New York Journal American*, November 20, 1952; Hartigan 1995, 30].)

1954 New School for Social Research, reading directed by Wayne Richardson.

1957 Theatre Marquee, New York, translated by Francis Fergusson, directed by Wayne Richardson, in repertory with *Trojan Women* and *Agamemnon*.

1959 Rita Allen Theatre, New York, adaptation of Francis Fergusson's translation, directed by Patricia McIlrath, starring Judith Evelyn (Walter Kerr, *New York Herald Tribune*,

February 14, 1959; Robert Coleman, *New York Mirror,* February 14, 1959; *Variety,* February 18, 1959; Brooks Atkinson, *New York Times,* February 14, 1959; Rube Dorin, *Morning Telegram,* February 16, 1959; Rowland Field, *Newark Evening News,* February 14, 1959; and Michael Smith, *Village Voice,* February 18, 1959).

1960 The Living Theatre, staged reading June 30 at the New School for Social Research, New York City.

1961 Institute for Advanced Studies in Theatre Arts, New York, translated by David Grene, starring Irene Baird and Margaret Vafiadis. Also performed in 1965, directed by Joy Dillingham.

(1961 Piraikon Theatron, City Center, New York, translated by John Gryparis, directed by Dimitri Rondiris, starring Aspasia Papathanassiou [Howard Taubman, *New York Times,* September 20, 1961; Robert Coleman, *New York Mirror,* September 20, 1961; *Time,* September 29, 1961; Joseph Morgenstern, *New York Herald Tribune,* September 20, 1961; Jim O'Connor, *New York Journal American,* September 20, 1961; *Newsday,* September 27, 1961; Hartigan 1995, 30–32]. The same group did the play in 1964 with *Medea.*)

1964 New York Shakespeare Festival, Delacorte Theater, Central Park, New York, translated by H. D. F. Kitto, directed by Gerald Freedman, starring Lee Grant, Florence Stanley, Olympia Dukakis, and Michael Basileon (Arthur Sainer, *Village Voice,* August 20, 1964; Whitney Bolton, *Morning Telegraph,* August 13, 1964; Richard F. Cooke, *Wall Street Journal,* August 17, 1964; Louis Chapin, *Christian Science Monitor,* August 15, 1964; Richard Watts Jr., *New York Post,* August 12, 1964; Lewis Funke, *New York Times,* August 12, 1964; Herbert Kupferberg, *New York Herald Tribune,* August 12, 1964; James Davis, *Daily News,* August 12, 1964; Edward Southern Hipp, *Newark Evening News,* August 12, 1964; Jack Thomson, *New York Journal American,* August 12, 1964; Norman Nadel, *New York World Telegram and Sun,* August 12, 1964; *Variety,* August 19, 1964; Lewis Funke, *New York Theatre Review,* August 1964; Faye Hammel, *Cue,* August 22, 1964; *Daily News,* August 23, 1964; Hartigan 1995, 32–33; Choate 2009).

1966 Milwaukee Repertory Theatre, directed by Tunc Yalman, music by Michael Hammond, starring Erika Slezak with a chorus of fourteen.

*1969 *Black Electra,* Mobile Theater, New York Shakespeare Festival, Washington Square and other New York parks, translation by H. D. F. Kitto, directed by Gerald Freedman, starring Olivia Cole and Josephine Premice (Choate 2009).

1972 The Theatre Asylum at the Extension, 277 Park Avenue South, New York, directed by Joel Stone (Dick Brukenfield, *Village Voice,* April 4, 1971).

1972 Translation by H. D. F. Kitto, directed by George Vafiadis, Lakewood, Ohio.

1972 La MaMa, E.T.C., New York, directed by Maxine Klein.

*1974 Public Theater and St. Clement's Theater, New York, directed by Joseph Chaikin, formerly of the Open Theater, adapted by Robert Montgomery, starring Michelle Collison, Shami Chaikin, and Paul Zimet; revival in 1976 at the Exchange Theater, followed by a national tour, with Tina Shephard replacing Collison (Mel Gussow, *New York Times,* May 24, 1974; Martin Oltarsh, *Show Business,* June 6, 1974, 7; Walter Kerr, *New York Times,* June 19, 1974; Michael Feingold, *Village Voice,* May 23, 1974; Marilyn Stasio, *Cue,* June 17, 1974; Arthur Sainer, *Village Voice,* January 19, 1976; Bernard Weiner, *San Francisco Chronicle & Examiner,* January 24, 1976; Michael Kirby, *The Drama Review* 18.3

[September 1974]: 127; Jennifer Merin, *Soho Weekly News,* June 22, 1976; Blumenthal 1974; Choate 2009).

1974 La MaMa, E.T.C., New York, part of *Fragments of a Greek Trilogy,* directed by Andrei Serban, with music by Elizabeth Swados. Revivals through 1979; also in 1987, 1999, and 2004 (Choate 2009; A. Green 1994; Menta 1995).

1974 Greek Art Theater at One Sheridan Square, New York, adapted and directed by George Arkas, starring Yula Gavala (Joseph Mancini, *New York Post,* November 27, 1974; Mike Lachletta, *Daily News,* November 28, 1974; *Show Business,* December 5, 1974; *Villager,* December 12, 1974). Typescript in the New York Public Library for the Performing Arts, Lincoln Center.

*1975 *Going Home,* Kuku Ryku Theatre Laboratory at the Construction Company Dance Studio, 542 La Guardia Place, New York, starring Sally Jones as Clytemnestra and Susan Weiser Finley as Electra (Doris Diether, *Villager,* January 23, 1975; Bonnie Marranca, *Soho Weekly News,* April 29, 1976). Revived at The Performing Garage in 1977.

1976 Intimate Theatre Company, The Second Stage, Seattle, translated by David Grene, directed by Margaret Booker, starring Megan Cole.

1976 *Electra* by Maurice Valency, HB Playwrights Foundation, New York, directed by Susan Lehman.

*1977–80 *Electra Speaks,* part 3 of *The Daughter's Cycle,* by Clare Coss, Sondra Segal, and Roberta Sklar, Women's Interart Centre, New York (Eleanor Fuchs, *Soho Weekly News,* November 15, 1979; *Soho Weekly News,* January 10, 1980; Sally R. Sommen, *Village Voice,* December 17, 1979; Marilyn Stasio, *New York Post,* November 4, 1980; Jennifer Dunning, *New York Times,* November 20, 1980; Malnig and Rosenthal 1993; Foley 2004, 99–102; Malnig 2009).

1981 Greek Theatre of New York, West 28th Street, directed by and starring Anna Makrakis with Isidore Sideris (in Modern Greek) (*New York Times,* July 3, 1981; Hartigan 1995, 37).

*1982–83 *Electra-Cution or You're Under Orestes,* La MaMa, E.T.C., New York, directed by James Milton, music by Denman Maroney, starring Erin Martin and Davidson Lloyd; revived in 1983, The Performance Company, St. Peter's Performing Arts Center, 336 West 20th Street, New York (Steven Hart, *Villager,* March 10, 1983; *Villager,* January 14, 1982).

1984 Old Globe Theatre, San Diego, translated by E. F. Watling, adapted and directed by Diana Maddox, starring Katherine McGrath.

1985 California State University, Long Beach. Tape at the New York Public Library for the Performing Arts, Lincoln Center.

*1987 *Elektra* by Ezra Pound and Rudd Fleming (Pound and Fleming [1987] 1989 and 1990), Classic Stage Company, New York, directed by Carey Perloff, starring Pamela Reed as Elektra, Joe Morton as Orestes, Nancy Marchand as Clytemnestra, and Veronica Cartright as Chrysothemis (Mel Gussow, *New York Times,* November 11, 1987; David Sheward, *Backstage,* November 27, 1987; Michael Feingold, *Village Voice,* November 17, 1987; Clive Barnes, *New York Post,* November 11, 1987; David Kaufman, *Downtown,* December 2, 1987; C. B. Coleman, *Theater,* Summer/Fall 1988, 83–86; Don Nelson, *Daily News,* November 16, 1987; Leo Seligsohn, *Newsday,* November 16, 1987; Kevin Grubb, *New York Native,* November 30, 1987, 24–25; J. Ellen Gainor, *Paideuma* 16:3 [Winter 1987]: 131; Beye 1989).

1988 Pearl Theatre, New York, translated by Theodore Howard Banks, directed by Emanuele Pagani, starring Robin Leslie Brown (Walter Goodman, *New York Times*, January 29, 1988).

1988 Intimate Theater Company, Seattle, directed by Laird Williamson.

1989 Sidewalks Theatre, New York, translated by Gary Beck and Carl Caravana, directed by Gary Beck, starring Nancy Guarino.

*1992 *Elektra* by Ezra Pound and Rudd Fleming, Roundhouse Theater, Washington, D.C., directed by Tom Prewitt, starring Sarah Marshall (Lloyd Rose, *Washington Post*, February 1, 1992; Hap Erstein, *Washington Times*, February 1, 1992; *New York Times*, February 20, 1992; Hartigan 1995, 33–34).

1992 Thick Description, South of Market Theatre, San Francisco, adapted by Karen Amano, directed by Tony Kelly, starring Sharon Omi with Ken Narasaki as Chrysothemis and Aegisthus (Steven Winn, *San Francisco Chronicle*, June 23, 1992; Hartigan 1995, 34).

1992 Twin Cities Low Income Center, Ten Thousand Things Theater Company, Minneapolis, Minnesota.

1992 Sacramento Theater Company, directed by Tim Ocel.

**1992 *The Clytemnestra Project*, Guthrie Theater, Minneapolis, directed by Garland Wright, translations of *Electra*, by Kenneth McLeish, *Iphigeneia in Aulis*, by George Dimock and W. S. Merwin, and the *Oresteia* by Robert Lowell, starring Isabell Monk as Clytemnestra and Jacqueline Kim as Electra (Mike Steele, *Minneapolis Star Tribune*, June 19, 1992 and June 22, 1992; Joan Bunke, *Des Moines Register*, June 28, 1992; Tad Simons, *Twin Cities Reader*, June 24, 1992, 20, 22; John Brandt, *Star Tribune*, August 17, 1992; Lawrence Shyer, *American Theatre* 9.9 [January 1992]: 44; David Richards, *New York Times*, August 9, 1992; Lewis 1996; Hartigan 1995, 76–79; Foley 1995, 316–19; Choate 2009). Videotape of the production at the New York Public Library for the Performing Arts, Lincoln Center.

1993 Court Theatre, University of Chicago, translated by Nicholas Rudall, directed by Mikhail Mokeiev, starring Jacqueline Williams (Lawrence Bommer, *Chicago Tribune*, February 26, 1993; Sid Smith, *Chicago Tribune*, March 5, 1993; Hedy Weiss, *Chicago Sun-Times*, March 4, 1993; Hartigan 1995, 34).

1994 *Electra* by Ellen McLaughlin, Actor's Gang Theatre, Los Angeles, directed by Oscar Eustis.

1994 New Jersey Shakespeare Festival, Drew University, Madison, New Jersey, Kenneth Cavander adaptation, *Agamemnon and His Daughters*, directed by Bonnie J. Monte, starring Laila Robins and Novella Nelson (Alvin Klein, *New York Times*, June 26, 1994).

*, **, and ***1995 *Iphigeneia and Other Daughters* by Ellen McLaughlin, Classic Stage Company, New York, directed by David Esbjornson, starring Sheila Tousey and Kathleen Chalfant (Ben Brantley, *New York Times*, February 11, 1995; Clive Barnes, *New York Post*, February 9, 1995; Michael Feingold, *Village Voice*, February 21, 1995; Greg Evans, *Variety*, February 13, 1995; Amy Reiter, *Backstage*, February 24, 1995, p. 52; Foley, *Didaskalia* 2.2 [April 1995]; Choate 2009; Malnig 2009); 1996, Penthouse Theater, Seattle, Washington production, directed Kerry Skalsky; 1996–97, Portland Stage Company, Portland, Maine, production, directed by Christopher Grabowski; 1997, Greasy Joan and Company Production, Griffin Theatre, Chicago, directed by Brad Shelton; 1999, A. E. Hotchner Studio

Theatre, St. Louis, Missouri, production, directed by Robert Neblett; 1999, Bug Theatre Company, Colorado, directed by Matthew Howard; 2006, Actor's Theater Workshop, 145 West 28th Street, New York; 2007, Chamber Theater and Washington Ensemble Theatre, Seattle.

(1996 City Center, New York, National Theater of Greece, directed by and starring Lydia Koniordou.)

***1996 *The Elektra Fugues* by Ruth E. Margraff (Margraff 2005), Here Arts Center "Opera Project"/Tiny Mythic Theatre Company, New York, directed by Tim Manner with a seven-piece orchestra; 1999, Bottom's Dream Theater in Los Angeles, directed by Kim Martin.

1997 American Theatre of Actors, directed by James Jennings at the A.T.A Outdoor Theatre, 314 West 54th Street, New York.

1998 Donmar Warehouse, McCarter Theatre, Princeton, New Jersey, and Richmond Theatre, New York, adaptation by Frank McGuiness, directed by David Leveaux, starring Zoe Wanamaker, with Claire Bloom as Clytemnestra (Peter Marks, *New York Times,* September 23, 1998; Peter Marks, *New York Times,* December 4, 1998; Vincent Canby, *New York Times,* December 13, 1998; Dinitia Smith, *New York Times,* December 29, 1998; Jesse McKinley, *New York Times,* January 8, 1999; Peter Marks, *Variety,* September 28, 1998). Recording in the New York Public Library for the Performing Arts, Lincoln Center.

***1999 *Another Elektra* (*Live Girls Do Elektra*) by Kristina Sutherland and Desiree Prewitt (Sutherland and Prewitt 2001), One World Theatre/Speakeasy, Center House Theater, Seattle, directed by Jena Cane; 2001, Chamber Theatre, Seattle, directed by Mark Fullerton; 2001, Revolutions, an International Theater Festival, Albuquerque, New Mexico.

(2000 Carnegie Hall, New York, MidAmerica Productions, opera by Mikis Theodorakis, adaptation by Spyros A. Evangelatos, translation by K. Ch. Myris, starring Revekka Evangelia Mauroviti as Elektra.)

2000 Actor's Studio Free Theater at Raw Space, New York, translated by Bill Coco, directed by Andreas Manolikakis, starring Elizabeth Kemp.

** and ***2000 *Furious Blood* by Kelly Stuart, version *of IA, Agamemnon, Electra/Libation Bearers,* and *Eumenides,* Sledgehammer Theatre, San Diego, directed by Kirsten Brandt, starring Jessa Watson as Clytemnestra, Tim West as Agamemnon (Anne Marie Welsh, *San Diego Union-Tribune,* February 13 and 15, 2000; Jennifer de Poyen, *San Diego Union-Tribune,* February 15, 2000; Jeff Smith, *San Diego Reader,* March 2, 2000; Pat Launer, KPBS-FM; Marie Oppedisano, *Marquee Arts and Entertainment,* February 2000; Joel Beers, *OC Weekly* 5.25, February 25-March 2, 2000; Charlene Baldridge, February 24, 2000, www.backstagewest.com; Foley 2005).

2001 *Agamemnon and His Daughters,* adaptation by Kenneth Cavander, Arena Stage, Washington, D.C., directed by Molly Smith, starring Gail Grate as Clytemnestra (Paul Harris, *Variety,* October 8, 2001; Nelson Pressley, *Washington Post,* September 9, 2001; Shirley J. Gregory, http://dcmdva-arts.org/shows/agamemnon.htm; Dorothy Chansky, http: ibs.theatermania.com/content/news.cfm?int_news_id = 1681; Jayne M. Blanchard, *Washington Times,* September 18 and 22, 2001; Jenn Brookland, September 21, 2001, www.thehoya.com/guide11.cfm; Foley, *Theater Journal* 54.1 [March 2002]: 143–45).

2001 *Klytemnestra's Unmentionables* (including a monologue by Electra) by Rob Grace, Here Arts Center, New York, starring Bradford Louryk, directed by Jennifer Wiseman (Foley 2004, 95–98 and 2005, 327–29).

(2001 Adaptation by Satoshi Miyagi and Tadashi Suzuki, directed by Tadashi, Yukiko Saitoh as Electra, Japan Society, New York.)

2002 Staged reading at the Tisch Center for the Arts, Unterberg Poetry Center, 92$^{nd}$ Street Y, New York, translation by Anne Carson, directed by and starring Kathryn Walker as Electra and Zoe Caldwell as Clytemnestra.

2003 Hartford Stage Company, translation by H. D. F. Kitto, directed by Jonathan Wilson, starring Mirjana Jokovic (Alvin Klein, *New York Times*, January 26, 2003; Jeff Rivers, *Hartford Courant*, January 17, 2003; Carolyn Clay, *Phoenix.com*, January 23–30, 2003; Alistair Highet, *Hartford Advocate*, January 23, 2003; Chris Rohmann, FrugalFun.com).

*2003 *Electricidad* by Luis Alfaro (Alfaro 2006), the Borderlands Theater in Tucson, Arizona, directed by Barclay Goldsmith, with Minerva Garcia as Electricidad; 2004, Goodman Theatre, Chicago, directed by Henry Godinez, starring Cecilia Suárez as Electricidad; 2004, Sledgehammer Theatre, San Diego; 2004, Mark Taper Forum, Los Angeles, directed by Lisa Peterson, starring Zilah Mendoza; 2006, Teatro Visión in San José, California (reviews of the Mark Taper production: Jim Farber, *Daily Breeze*, April 1–7, 2005; Don Shirley, *Los Angeles Times*, April 28, 2005; Daryl H. Miller, *Los Angeles Times*, April 8, 2005; Karen Weinstein, culturevulture.net/Theater/Electricidad.htm; Rob Kednt, rob kendt.com/Reviews/electrcidad. html; Mary E. Montoro, www.campuscircle.com/re view.cfm?r = 857; Joel Hirschorn, April 7, 2005, www.variety.com/review/VE1117926759 .html; Steven Leigh Morris, *Los Angeles Weekly*, April 1–7, 2005; Laura Hitchcock, www .curtainup.com/electricidad.html; Paula Jessop, *Splash Magazines*, www.lasplash.com/ publish/Los_Angeles_Performances_116/Electricidad.php [November 12, 2008]; James Taylor, *Theatre Talk*, KCRW; Melinda Powers, *Theater Journal*, Dec. 2005, 742—44).

2004 New York Public Library for the Performing Arts, Imagine '04 Festival, staged reading, translated by Anne Carson, starring Marisa Tomei, Kathleen Chalfant, David Strathairn, and Heather Tom, directed by Lawrence Sacharow. A response to the 2004 Republican Convention in New York (Edward Rothstein, *New York Times*, October 29, 2004; Verena Dobnik, *Chicago Sun-Times*, August 27, 2004).

2005 West End Players Guild, St. Louis, Missouri, translated by Frank McGuiness, directed by Steve Callahan, starring Michele Hand (Deanna Jent, *Riverfront Times*, February 9, 2005).

2007 *[The Blood] Electra*, The Classical Theatre of Harlem, adapted and directed by Alfred Preisser, starring Jainab Jah (James Svendsen, didaskalia.net/reviews/2007/2007_12_21 _03.html; Wilborn Hampton, *New York Times*, June 6, 2007; Paul Menard, *Backstage*, June 1, 2007; Linda Armstrong, *NY Amsterdam News*, June 7, 2007; Charles E. Rogers, *NY Amsterdam News*, June 14, 2007; Raven Snook, *Time Out New York*, June 22, 2007; Jenny Sandman, www.curtainup.com/electraharlem.html; Mark Blankenship, *Daily Variety*, June 4, 2007, www.variety.com/review/VE1117933812.html?categoryid = 33&cs = 1).

** and ***2007 *Elektrafire, A Modern Rock Opera*, Village Theatre, Bleecker Street, New York, LiveStage Performance, composed with libretto by Doug Thoms, starring Bridget Beirne, Kryst Hogan, and Heidi Suhr. For further details, images, and four songs, see www. livestageperformance.net/Elektrafire.htm (Tom Penketh, *Backstage.com*, September

21, 2007; Sean Michael O'Donnell, *Show Business,* August 29, 2007; Isaac Byrne, ny theatre.com/nytheatre/fr_rev2007.php?o = S&1 = 47; Jim Sullivan, *Boston Globe,* January 29, 1998; *Time Out New York,* www.timeout.com/newyork/events/theater/16529/243484/ elektrafire; Adam Hedrick, www.playbill.com/news/article/110307.html).

2008 *Yellow Electras,* an eclectic version composed and directed by Peter A. Campbell, Ontological-Hysteric Incubator, St. Mark's Church, New York, starring three Electras, Laura Heidinger, Genevieve de Gaillande, and Karen Rich, with a chorus of fifteen (Garrett Eisler, *Village Voice,* July 17, 2008).

2009 *An Oresteia* (Aeschylus *Agamemnon,* Sophokles *Elektra,* and Euripides *Orestes*), Classic Stage Company, New York, translated by Anne Carson; *Elektra* directed by Brian Kulick and Gisela Cardenas, starring Annika Boras as Elektra, Mickey Solis as Orestes, Michi Barall as Chrysothemis, and Stephanie Roth-Haberle as Cytemnestra (Claudia La Rocco, *New York Times,* April 14, 2009; Emily Wilson, *Nation,* April 27, 2009; Garry Wills, *New York Review of Books,* May 14, 2009; Lisa Jo Sagolla, *Backstage.com,* April 1, 2009; Alexis Soloski, *Village Voice,* April 8, 2009; Amy Probst, *Time Out New York,* April 9, 2009; Sam Thielman, *Variety.com,* April 2, 2009; Dan Bacalzo, www.theatermania.com/off-broadway/reviews/04-2009/an_oresteia_18355.html; Reese Thompson, www.offoffoff.com/theater/2009/an_oresteia.php; Robert Weinstein, www.nytheatre.com/ny theatre/showpage.php?t = ores8061; Elyse Sommer, www.curtainup.com/oresteiacsc09.html).

2009 *Are You There, Zeus? It's Me Electra,* a new tragicomedy written and directed by Aliza Shane, Looking Glass Theatre, New York.

*2010 Getty Villa, Los Angeles, translated by Timberlake Wertenbaker, directed by Carey Perloff, music by Bonfire Madigan Shive, starring Annie Purcell, with Pamela Reed as Clytemnestra and Olympia Dukakis as Chorus (Charles McNulty, *Los Angeles Times,* September 12, 2010; Bob Verini, *Variety,* September 12, 2010; Dany Margolies, www.backsatge.com/bso/reviews-la-theatre/la-review-sophocles-elektra-1004114539.story; Steven Leigh Morris, http://blogs.laweekly.com/stylecouncil/2010/09/stage_raw-take_me_out.php; Colin Mitchell, September 16, 2010, http://bitter-lemons.com/2010/09/elektra-getty-100-sweet/).

2010 *Electra in a One-Piece* by Isaac Oliver, Good Company at the Wild Project, 195 East 3rd Street, New York, directed by David Ruttura, starring Amanda Scot Ellis as Elle and Erika Rolfsrud as Clyt, Chris Bannow as Ore (Mitch Montgomery, November 1. 2010, www.backstage.com/bso/reviews-ny-theatre-off-off-broadway/electra-in-a-one-piece-1004125.story; Joseph Samuel Wright, www.theasy.com/Reviews/electrainaonepiece.php; Scott Brown, http://nymag.com/daily/entertainment/2010/11/theater_review_two_massively_h.html).

EURIPIDES' *ELECTRA*

**1910 Coburn Players, Hudson Theatre, New York, translation by Gilbert Murray, directed by Albert Lang, starring Mr. and Mrs. Coburn (Ivah Wills) (*Dramatic Mirror,* October 29, 1910; *Theatre Magazine,* January 1, 1911; Harrison Smith, "The Revival of Greek Tragedy in America," *Bookman* 41 [June 1915]: 410; *New York Telegraph,* July 30, 1910; *Craftsman,* August 1910; *New York Telegraph,* December 1, 1910; *Dramatic News,* December 10,

1910; *New York Daily Tribune,* December 1, 1910; *New York Times,* November 30, 1910; *New York Evening Post,* November 30, 1910; Feinsod 1992, 16; Palmer 1987, 86–90).

1911 Coburn Players, Harvard Yard, Sever Quadrangle.

\*\*1912 and 1914 "Brookside" theater on the estate of Marita Leonard in Mt. Kisco, New York (Johnson 1971, 20; Waugh 1917, 99–101).

\*\*1921 Bennett School of Applied Arts, Millbrook, New York, and Ardmore, Pennsylvania, garden of James Crosby Brown, and at other colleges, translated by Gilbert Murray, directed by Charles Rand Kennedy, choreography by Margaret Gage, music by Horace Middleton, starring Edith Wynne-Matthison as Electra (*Theatre Magazine,* December 21, 1921, 398–99, 436).

1935 Translation by Gilbert Murray, directed by Ellen Van Volkenberg, part of the Cornish School of Drama, Summer School, Seattle, starring Beryl Bigham and Irene Wright as Electra.

1951 Laughing Stock Company, Master Institute Theatre, New York, translated by Gilbert Murray, directed by Robert Alan Bernstein, starring Sheila Berger as Electra.

1954 New School for Social Research, New York, reading directed by Wayne Richardson.

1957 *Greek Scene* (*Agamemnon, Elektra,* and *OT*), musical composition by Harold Faberman, Jordan Hall, Boston, sung by Corinne Curry.

1958 Jan Hus Auditorium, New York, translated by Gilbert Murray, directed by Milton Miltiades, starring Tresa Hughes and Lee Henry (Lewis Funke, *New York Times,* May 10, 1958; Hartigan 1995, 61–62).

1962 Shakespearewrights Production, Players Theatre, 115 MacDougal Street, New York, translated by Gilbert Murray, directed by Philip Lawrence, starring Laura Stuart and Byrne Piven with a chorus of seven (Joseph Morgenstern, *New York Herald Tribune,* March 22, 1962; Arthur Gelb, *New York Times,* March 22, 1962; Arthur Alpert, *New York World Telegram,* March 22, 1962; Jim O'Connor, *New York Journal American,* March 22, 1962; Frances Herridge, *New York Post,* March 22, 1962; Whitney Bolton, *Morning Telegraph,* New York, March 23, 1962; *Villager,* March 29, 1962; James Davis, *Daily News,* March 22, 1962; *Village Voice,* March 29, 1962; *Cue,* March 31, 1962).

1973 Chichi Castenango, directed Jon Mazza (*Show Business,* September 20, 1973; Hartigan 1995, 62).

1981 *Electra* and *Oreste*s, one-act versions, translated by Adrienne Kennedy (A. Kennedy 1988, 105–71), Juilliard Theatre, New York, directed Michael Kahn (Marilyn Stasio, *New York Post,* April 16, 1981; Wayne Lawson, *Soho Weekly News,* April 22, 1981; Robert Massa, *Village Voice,* April 22, 1981).

1999 *Greek Fest: Electra,* Tinfish Theatre, Chicago, directed by Dejan Avramovich, starring Sabrina Lloyd as Electra and Jeffrey D. Klein as Orestes (www.tinfish,org/Electra.htm).

2004 A Noise Within Theater Company, 234 South Brand, Masonic Temple Building, Glendale, California, translated by Elizabeth Seydel Morgan, directed by Sabin Epstein, starring an all-male cast with the exception of a small girl, including Donald Sage Mackay as Electra, Stephen Rockwell as Orestes (Jana Monji, www.curtainup.com; Stephen Mikulan, *LAWeekly,* March 19–25, 2004).

(2005 *Elektra,* according to Euripides, Gardzienice Center for Theater Practices [Poland], La MaMa, E.T.C., New York, directed by Wlodzimierz Staniewski [Phoebe Hoban, *New York Times,* April 13, 2005].)

APPENDIX B

# Professional Productions and New Versions of *Antigone*

*The Archive of Performances of Greek and Roman Drama (www.apgrd.ox.ac.uk/) has fuller cast lists and more information on sources in some cases. These entries are as complete as current information allowed. (Only occasional productions of Anouilh's popular Antigone are included.)*

\* *Discussed or mentioned in chapters 1–4 of this book (including brief mentions)*
( ) *Important visiting production*

\*1845 Palmo's Opera House, New York, W. Dinneford producer, directed by George Vandenhoff, music by Felix Mendelssohn, starring Miss Clarendon as Antigone, George Vandenhoff as Creon; preview in 1844, Arch Street Theatre, Philadelphia (R. Sherman 1944, 31); accompanied by a farce, "Mischief Making"; two farces presented with it after the first performance (Johnson 1971, 15; Odell 5: 134) (*New World*, April 12, 1845; *New York Herald*, April 8, 1845; *Anglo-American* 4.25, April 12, 1845, 594–95; *New York Evening Post*, April 8, 1845; "The Drama," *Albion, British, Colonial, and Foreign Weekly Gazette*, April 5, 1945, 164–68; *Albion*, April 19, 1845, 192; Poe 1845; Odell 5: 134–35; Ireland (1866–67) 1968, 2: 445; Brown 1: 340–41; Vandenhoff 1860, 243–45).

\*1845 Mitchell's Olympic Theatre, New York, burlesque of the 1845 Palmo's *Antigone* ("Things Theatrical," *Spirit of the Times*, April 12, 1845, 92, and April 19, 80; *Albion*, April 5, 1845, 168, and April 19, 192; Odell 5: 128–29; Ireland (1866–67) 1968, 2, 442).

\*1890 The Saturday Morning Club of Boston, Bumstead Hall, Boston, translated by E. H. Plumptre, music by Felix Mendelssohn, starring Mrs. Caroline C. Burlen as Antigone and Mrs. Alice Kent as Creon (*Boston Evening Transcript, Boston Daily Advertiser, Boston Post, Boston Herald, Boston Daily Globe*, all March 13, 1890; Howe 1899, 157).

\*1891 Hyperion Theatre, New Haven (*Boston Transcript*, April 13, 1891), Mrs. H. Grant Thompson as Antigone, Mrs. S. Hartwell Chapman as Creon, and Miss Anna Richards as Haemon.

(1894 Abbey's Theater, New York, Comédie Française, French translation by Jules Lacroix, starring Jean Mounet-Sulley and Mme Second-Weber, music by Camille Saint-Saëns [*New York Daily Tribune*, March 28, 1894; *New York Times*, April 4, 1894; *New York Herald*, April 4, 1894; *Critic* 24.634, April 14, 1894, 260].)

*1910 Berkeley Greek Theater, translated by E. H. Plumptre, music by Felix Mendelssohn, directed by George Riddle, starring Margaret Anglin as Antigone, Eugene Ormonde as Creon, and Howard Hull as Haemon (Montgomery Phister, *Cincinnati Commercial*, July 10, 1910; *New York Times*, July 1, 1910; *San Francisco Call*, July 1, 1910; Burns Mantle, *New York Evening Post*, July 1, 1910; James O'Donnell Bennett, *Chicago Record Herald*, July 3, 1910; Ralph Renaud, *Sunset* 25 (September 1910): 331–36; *Theatre Magazine* 12.114 (August 1910): 48; Clayton Hamilton, *Vogue*, August 1910, reprinted in Hamilton 1920; LeVay 1989, 122).

*1923 Equity Players, Forty-Eighth Street Theater, New York, choreographed by Margaret Gage, Edith Wynne Matthison as Antigone and Charles Rand Kennedy as Creon (May 25, 1923 in *New York Sun, New York Herald, New York World, New York Telegraph; Theater Magazine*, August 8, 1923).

*1928 Berkeley Greek Theater, directed by Margaret Anglin as Antigone.

*1930 *Tiresias* by Henry Bertram Lister (Lister 1931), La Boheme Club of San Francisco, Travers Theatre, Fairmont Hotel, directed by Frederic Smith, starring Alton Wood as Tiresias, Lister as Oedipus, and his wife as Priestess (George C. Warren, *San Francisco Chronicle*, December 2, 1930; Templeton Peck, *San Francisco News*, December 3, 1930; O. E. Jones, *San Francisco Call Bulletin*, December 3, 1930).

(1930 Jean Cocteau's *Antigone*, American Laboratory Theatre, starring Marjorie Bretnall as Antigone [reviewed on April 25, 1930, in *New York World, New York Sun*, and *New York Times*].)

1931 Cleveland Playhouse, translated by Robert Whitelaw, designed by Arch Lauterer with group direction, starring Irene Tedow as Antigone, Ainsworth Arnold as Creon.

1933 Modern Greek American Progressive Association, A.W.A. Club, 361 West 57th Street, New York.

1944 Rollins Studio Players, East Hampton, Long Island, directed by Leighton Rollins with an all-female cast, starring Helen Hackett as Antigone and Suzanne Buch as Creon.

1945 *Antigone* by Alfred J. Brenner, staged reading in New York City by Hallie Flanagan Davis, the former director of the Federal Theater Project (folder in the New York Public Library for the Performing Arts, Lincoln Center).

1946 Cort Theatre, New York, Jean Anouilh, *Antigone*, directed by Guthrie McClintic, starring Katharine Cornell as Antigone (Hartigan 1995, 112–14, 127; John Chapman, *Daily News*, February 19, 1946; *Life*, March 18, 1946; Wolcott Gibbs, *New Yorker*, March 2 and 4, 1946; Stark Young, *New Republic*, March 4, 1946).

1954 Staged reading at The New School by Wayne Richardson, with Kit Merriman as Antigone and Richard Wayne as Creon.

1960 Staged reading by The Living Theatre, New School for Social Research, New York.

1961 Colorado Shakespeare Festival, Flagstaff Amphitheatre, Boulder Mountain Park, Colorado, directed by Robert Cohen, with Sally Mitchell as Antigone and K. Lype O'Dell as Creon.

1962 McCarter Theater, Princeton, New Jersey, with Gubi Mann as Antigone and Gwyllum Evans as Creon (Norman Nadel, *New York World Telegram and Sun,* January 5, 1962).
1965 Group for Ancient Drama, East River Amphitheatre, translated by Paul Nord, directed by Ted Zarpas, starring Marcha Shevness as Antigone.
1967 Young People's Repertory Theatre, Sheridan Square Playhouse, translated by Dudley Fitts and Robert Fitzgerald, directed by Therese Hayden, starring Sima Gelbart as Antigone and Gregory Reese as Creon (Herbert Kupferberg, *New York World Journal Tribune,* January 14, 1967; Dan Sullivan, *New York Times,* January 14, 1967).
1967 Caedmon Records Theater Recording Society recorded Dorothy Tutin as Antigone and Max Adrian as Creon in the Dudley Fitts and Robert Fitgerald translation. TRS320M and TRS 320S.
1967 *A Time to Die,* a new version by Eric Bentley, New York.
1967–68 Hartford Stage Company, Hartford, Connecticut, directed by Michael Murray, starring Judith McCauly as Antigone and Frank Savino as Creon.
1968–69 Tour of The Living Theatre, Bertolt Brecht's *Antigone,* New York, Brooklyn Academy of Music, 1968, starring Judith Malina as Antigone and Julian Beck as Creon (Jerry Tallmer, *New York Post,* October 11, 1968; Thomas Brennan, *Villager,* October 17, 1968; Lewis Funke, *New York Times,* October 11, 1968; Julius Novick, *Village Voice,* January 9, 1968; Henry Hewes, "The Theater: Orphans Dissenting," *Saturday Review,* October 5, 1968, 43; Neff 1970; Colakis 1993, 50–55; Hartigan 1995, 111, 116–17; Dan Sullivan, *Los Angeles Times,* March 1, 1969).
1969 *Four No Plays* by Tom Eyen, La MaMa, E.T.C., New York (Molly Haskell, *Village Voice,* February 13, 1969).
1970 Berkeley Repertory Theatre, California.
1971 Vivian Beaumont Theater, Lincoln Center, New York, translated by Dudley Fitts and Robert Fitzgerald, directed by John Hirsch, starring Martha Henry as Antigone and Philip Bosco as Creon (Clive Barnes, *New York Times,* May 14, 1971; Richard Watts, *New York Post,* May 14, 1971; Douglas Watt, *Daily News,* May 14, 1971; John Beaufort, *Christian Science Monitor,* May 14, 1971; Edward Southern Hipp, *Evening News,* May 14, 1971; George Oppenheimer, *Newsday,* May 14, 1971; *Variety,* May 19, 1971; Leo Mishkin, *Stage Review,* May 17, 1971, 3; Virginia Woodruff, *Daily Mirror,* May 17, 1971; Walter Kerr, *New York Times,* May 23, 1971; S. K. Oberbeck, *Newsweek,* May 24, 1971; T. E. Kalem, *Time,* May 24, 1971; Martin Gottfried, *Women's Wear Daily,* May 14, 1971; Brendan Gill, *New Yorker,* May 22, 1971; Martin Washburn, *Village Voice,* May 20, 1971; John Simon, *New York,* May 23, 1971, 50; Hartigan 1995, 114–15).
1971 Little Church around the Corner at the Donnell Library Center of New York Public Library, directed by Cathryn Roskam, starring Sally Gordon as Antigone, Ronald Lane as Creon, and Tazewell Thompson as Tiresias (*Backstage,* November 26, 1971, 15).
1973 *Antigone,* translated by Friederich Hölderlin, opera by Meyer Kupferman, Lenox Arts Center, Stockbridge, Massachusetts.
1974 A radically new version by Steven Lydenburg at the MDC Amphitheatre, Brighton (Carolyn Clay, *Boston Phoenix,* September 17, 1974).
1975 New York Society for Ethical Culture, translated and directed by Theo Barnes, with Mila Conway as Antigone.

1975–76 *Antigone Prism,* Berkeley, California, by the Women's Ensemble of the Berkeley Stage Company.

1978 Studio Tangerine, New York, a new version by Percy Johnston, starring Barbara Miller and Lorraine Lu (Barbara Lewis, *New York Amsterdam News,* September 16, 1978).

1980 Richard Allen Center for Culture and Art, New York, directed by Micah Whitaker, with Trazana Beverly as Antigone, Arthur Burkhardt as Creon (Sara Laschever, *Village Voice,* March 24, 1980; Maureen Clarke, *Village Voice,* April 4, 1980; Jennifer Dunning, *New York Times,* March 19, 1980; Curt Davis, *Other Stages,* March 20, 1980; Lionel Mitchell, *New York Amsterdam News,* March 15, 1980).

1980 Newfoundland Theatre, New York, directed by Martha Cooney, using the Dudley Fitts and Robert Fitzgerald translation.

*1980 *Theban Plays,* Classic Stage Company, New York, translated by Anthony Roche, directed by Christopher Martin, starring Robert Stattel as Oedipus and Karen Sunde as Antigone and Jocasta (Holly Hill, *Soho Weekly News,* November 12, 1980; David Sterritt, *Christian Science Monitor,* December 8, 1980; Howard Kessel, *Women's Wear Daily,* March 16, 1981; Thomas Ryan, *Villager,* November 20, 1980; Glenn Loney, *Other Stages,* December 18, 1980, 6; Clive Barnes, *New York Post,* December 3, 1980; Eileen Blumenthal, *Village Voice,* November 19, 1980; Hartigan 1995, 106–7).

*1982 Joseph Chaikin, New York's Public Theatre, translated by John Chioles, Lisa Barnes as Antigone and F. Murray Abraham as Creon (Howard Kissel, *Women's Wear Daily,* April 28, 1982; Gordon Rogoff, *Village Voice,* May 4, 1982; Frank Rich, *New York Times,* April 28, 1982; Sy Syna, *News World,* April 29, 1982; John Simon, *New York,* May 10, 1982; Douglas Watt, *Daily News,* April 28, 1982; Leah D. Frank, *Villager,* May 6, 1982; Clive Barnes, *New York Post,* April 30, 1982; David Sterritt, *Christian Science Monitor,* May 12, 1982; Rosette C. Lamont, *Other Stages,* May 6, 1982; Hartigan 1995, 116).

*1983 *Antigone Too* by Martha Boesing, performed at the ATA Women's Theater Festival in Minneapolis, Minnesota (Eleanor Fuchs, *Village Voice,* September 13, 1983).

1983–84 *Yu'pik Antigone,* Perseverance Theatre, Toksook Bay, Alaska, La MaMa, E.T.C., New York and other venues, directed by Dave Hunsaker (Jennifer Dunning, *New York Times,* June 29, 1984; discussed by Hunsaker in Mee and Foley 2011).

1983–84 Court Theatre, Chicago, translated by David Grene and Wendy O'Flaherty (*Chicago Tribune,* October 5, 1986).

*1984 Brecht's *Antigone* by The Living Theatre, Joyce Theater, New York, starring Judith Malina as Antigone and Julian Beck as Creon (Mel Gussow, *New York Times,* January 27, 1984; Julius Novick, *Village Voice,* February 7, 1984; Sy Syna, *New York Tribune,* January 27, 1984; Clive Barnes, *New York Post,* January 26, 1984; John Beaufort, *Christian Science Monitor,* January 31, 1984; Paul Bertram, *Stages,* March 1984; Michael Sommers, *New York Native,* February 13, 1984; Michael Feingold, *Village Voice,* January 31, 1984; Jim Theobald, *Villager,* January 26, 1984; and Ron Cohen, *Theater,* January 25, 1984).

1984 Round House Theater, Washington, D.C., directed by Mark Jaster, starring Sarah Marshall as Antigone and Dan Diggles as Creon (Lloyd Grove, *Washington Post,* January 20, 1984; David Richards, *Washington Post,* January 17, 1984; Hartigan 1995, 117).

1985–86 Pearl Theatre, New York.

1986 Chicago Actors Project, directed by Susan Padveen (*Chicago Tribune,* June 12, 1986).

1987 *Another Antigone* by A. R. Gurney, Old Globe Theatre, San Diego, California, directed by John Tillinger (Allan Wallach, *Newsday,* January 15, 1989; Sylvie Drake, *Los Angeles Times,* March 24, 1987; *Times Mirror Company,* March 24, 1987; *Nation,* February 6, 1988; *Christian Science Monitor,* February 5, 1988; *Playwrights Horizons*); 1991, Center Theater Chicago, in the Studio Theater directed by John Carlisle (*Chicago Tribune,* January 27, 1991); 1991, the Jewish Community Center of Greater Washington, Rockville, Maryland, directed by John Carlisle (*Washington Times,* January 6, 1991); 1990, Foundation Theatre at Burlington County College, New Jersey (*New Jersey Star Ledger,* April 25, 1990).

*1989 *Oedipus Requiem,* Chicago's Blind Parrot Productions, adapted from seven translations by David Perkins, music by Robert Ian Winston, starring Larry Newmann Jr. as Oedipus, Palmar Hardy as Jocasta, Jill Daly and Peggy Burr as Antigone, and Wayne Brown as Creon (Hedy Weiss, *Chicago Sun Times,* March 23, 1989; Lawrence Bommer, *Windy City Times,* March 30, 1989; Hartigan 1995, 128).

1989 Stage Left Theatre, staged by Dennis McCullough (Lawrence Bommer, *Chicago Tribune,* April 28, 1989).

*1990 *Antigone: Rites of Passion (Rites for the Dead),* film of dance version by Amy Greenfield with Bertram Ross and Janet Eilber, later distributed by Mystic Fire Video (1991); premiered in New York at the Modern Museum of Art, followed by a run at Anthology Film Archives, before being shown in other venues; Eclipse Production, Phoenix Films (Laurie Horn, *Miami Herald,* September 21, 1990; Marianne McDonald, *Hellenic Times,* October 31, 1990; David Sterritt, *Christian Science Monitor,* November 27, 1990; Jennifer Dunning, *New York Times,* November 1, 1990).

1991 Boston Conservatory Theater, directed by Phoebe Wray, starring Jane Thompson as Antigone and Rogelio Chicas as Creon (Nic Kelmar, *Tech* 111.54, November 26, 1991, 9).

1992 Irondale Ensemble Project, The House of Candles, Lower East Side, New York, directed by Jim Niesen, choreography by Annie B. Parson, and Janet O'Hair as Antigone (Stephen Holden, *New York Times,* February 16, 1992; Jack Anderson, *New York Times,* March 2, 1992; Lisa Kennedy, *Village Voice,* January 11, 1992).

1992 Northern Sign Theater, Minneapolis, adapted by Peter Cook, directed by Wendy Knox (Mike Steele, *Star Tribune,* September 22, 1992; Hartigan 1995, 117).

1992 Los Angeles, Farnsworth Park, Charmed Life Productions (Hartigan 1995, 128).

1993 The American Conservatory Theater, Stage Door Theater, San Francisco, translated by Timberlake Wertenbaker, directed by Carey Perloff, starring Elizabeth Peña as Antigone, Ken Ruta as Creon, and Vilma Silva as Ismene (Robert Hurwitt, *San Francisco Examiner,* February 19, 1993; Judith Green, *San Jose Mercury News,* February 9, 1993; Dennis Harvey, *Variety,* March 8, 1993; Jeanette Borzo, *Contra Costa Times,* February 19, 1993; Steven Winn, *San Francisco Chronicle,* February 19, 1993; Hartigan 1995, 117–18). I thank Carey Perloff of ACT for an opportunity to see a tape of the performance.

1993 Janusz Glowacki, *Antigone in New York,* Arena Theater in Washington, D.C.; 1994, Yale Repertory Theatre, directed by Liz Diamond; 1996, New York's Vineyard Theatre, directed by Michael Mayer with Ned Eisenberg, starring Priscilla Lopez as Anita, Steven Skybell as Sasha, Ned Eisenberg as Flea, and Monti Sharp as Policeman (Anna Krajewska-Wieczorek, "Two Contemporary *Antigones,*" *New Theatre Quarterly* 10, no. 40 [1994]: 327–30; Jenmba Starbuck, *Slavic and East European Performance: Drama,*

*Theater, Film* 16.3 [Fall 1996]: 94–99; *Washington Times,* March 12 and 25, 1993; *Time Magazine,* March 29, 1993; Alvin Klein, *New York Times,* November 6, 1994; *Westport News,* November 2, 1994; D. J. R. Brickner, *New York Times,* April 24, 1996; Alexis Greene, *Theater Week,* July 1–7, 1996, 17). Video recording at the New York Public Library for the Performing Arts, Lincoln Center.

1993 Gorilla Theater Productions, Kansas City, Missouri.

1995-96 Pearl Theatre, New York, translation by Dudley Fitts and Robert Fitzgerald, directed by Shepard Sobel, with Robin Lesley Brown as Antigone and Robert Hock as Creon.

1996 Missouri Repertory Theatre, Helen Spencer Auditorium, Kansas City, Mo., directed by George Keathley.

*1996 *The Whole World Is Watching,* a new version of the Oedipus trilogy by Douglas Jacobs and Scott Feldsher, Lyceum, San Diego Repertory Theatre, starring Wayne Tibbetts as Host, Lamont D. Thompson as Oedipus, Darla Cash as Jocasta, Douglas Roberts as Creon, Karola Forman as Antigone, and Linda Castro as Ismene (Anne Marie Welsh, *San Diego Union-Tribune,* February 13 and September 14, 2000; *Playbill,* July 9, 1996; Laurie Winer, *Los Angeles Times,* July 29, 1996).

1998 Sidewalks Theatre of New York, directed by Gary Beck, with Nancy Guarino as Antigone and Mark C. Hunt as Creon.

*1998 *Antigone through Time,* Gloria Maddox's Madwoman of the Woods Productions, directed by Richard S. Bach, Connelly Theater, New York, starring Christina Fanizzi as Antigone and Michael Fawcett as Creon as well as a Greek bishop and the Fascist Christo (Anita Gates, *New York Times,* August 29, 1998; Les Gutman, www.curtainup.com/fringe98.html). The performance was part of a Lower East Side Fringe festival that according to Gutman also included an *Antigone* in the studio at the Educational Alliance.

1999 Classic Greek Theatre of Oregon, directed by Rebecca Becker, Reed College, Portland.

*1999 *Blood Line: The Oedipus/Antigone Story,* a production of *OT* and *Antigone* by Joanna Settle, Division 13 Productions, translation by Nicholas Rudall, starring Anne DeAcetis as Antigone, James Stanley as Oedipus, Mark Ulrich as Creon, and Maggie Doyle as Jocasta, The Viaduct, Chicago (*Chicago Tribune,* March 24, 1999; *Chicago Sun-Times,* March 19 and 24, 1999; www.division13.org/work/bloodline.html and www.division13.org.press/rev_bloodline.html).

1999 Pocket Opera Company, Harold Washington Library Center, Chicago, opera version by John Eaton, directed by Curt Columbus and Nicholas Rudall, starring Julia Bentley as Antigone and Jeffrey McCollum as Creon.

2000 *An Antigone Story: A Greek Tragedy Hijack,* adapted and directed by Shishir Kurup for Cornerstone Theater Company, Hill Street Terminal Subway Building, Los Angeles, commissioned by the J. Paul Getty Museum, starring Page Leong as Antigone, Gracy Brown as Ismene, Joseph Grimm as Hayman, Bernard White as Krayon, and Gezel Nehmadi as Fanny (Victoria Looseleaf, *LA Downtown Times,* August 14, 2000; Laura Weinert, *Backstage,* August 3–9, 2000; Michael Phillips, *Los Angeles Times,* August 1, 2000; Steven Leigh Morris, *LA Weekly,* August 18–24, 2000; Foley 2011).

2000 American Repertory Theatre, Cambridge, Massachusetts, directed by François Rochaix and translated by Robert Fagles, starring Aysan Celik as Antigone and John

Douglas Thomson as Creon (Robert Nesti, *Boston Herald,* December 1, 2000; Patti Hartigan, *Boston Globe,* December 2, 2000; Scott Cummings, *Boston Phoenix,* November 23–30, 2000; and Cate McQuaid, *Boston Globe,* November 19, 2000).

*2001 *Becoming Antigone,* adapted from Brecht and Anouilh, Serious Play Theatre Ensemble, directed by Sheryl Stoodley, starring Toby Bercovici and Julissa L. Rodrigues as Antigone and Keith Bailey as Creon at the Third Floor Artspace, Thornes Marketplace, Northampton, Massachusetts.

*2001 *The Oedipus Plays,* Shakespeare Theatre, Washington, D.C., translated by Nicholas Rudall, directed by Michael Kahn, music by Baikida Carroll, choreography by Marlies Yearby, starring Avery Brookes as Oedipus, Michael Genet as Creon, Cynthia Martells as Antigone, Patronia Paley as Jocasta/Eurydice. Tape at the Washington Area Performing Arts Video Archive (Paul Harnes, *Variety,* October 8, 2001; *Backstage,* March 28, 2003; J. Wynn Rousuck, *Baltimore Sun,* September 5, 2001; Bob Mondello, *Washington City Paper,* September 13, 2001; Nelson Pressely, *Washington Post,* September 5, 2001, http://mason.gmu.edu/-egero/Resources/PostOedipusReview.html; Derek Gatopoulos, *Washington Times,* September 11, 2003).

2002 *Antigone,* written and adapted by Eric Parness, and *Ismene,* written by and starring Celia Montgomery, directed by Maxwell Zener, Pelican Studio Theatre, New York (Steven Boone, *Show Business,* May 15, 2002).

2002 *Antigone, The Tin Can Tied to Her Own Tail,* by Mac Wellman, Dance Theatre Workshop, New York, by Big Dance Theater, choreographed by Annie B. Parson, songs by Cynthia Hopkins, directed by Paul Lazar, starring Didi O'Connell as Antigone and Molly Hickock, Rebecca Wiscocky, Tricia Brouk, and Leroy Logan in combined roles. Also performed 2002, The Yard, Martha's Vineyard; 2004, Classic Stage Company, New York; On the Boards, Seattle, Washington; Riot Act, Inc. in Jackson, Wyoming; and MCA, Chicago; 2007, Women's Will at the Temescal Arts Center, Oakland, California, directed by Erin Merritt (*Theater* 32.2 [Summer 2002]: 62–69; Una Chaudhuri, *Village Voice,* December 11–17, 2002; Bruce Weber, *New York Times,* December 16, 2002; Elyse Sommer, www.curtainup.com/antigone.html; and http://katherinecrocker.blogspot.com/2008/03/antigone-paper.html. On the California production, see Robert Hurwitt, *San Francisco Chronicle,* October 22, 2008; Ken Bullock, *Berkeley Daily Planet,* October 19, 2007; Rachel Swan, www.eastbayexpress.com/artsculture/my_big_fat-deconstrustion/Content?oid = 522613; and http://womanswill.blogspot.com/2007/10/whose-line-is-it-anyway.html. There are several versions of this play, including the revised web version at www.macwellman.com/images/antigone.pdf. Wellman 2002 represents an earlier version; the most recent is Wellman 2005).

(2002 City Center, New York, National Theatre of Greece, directed by Nikaiti Kontouri, starring Lydia Koniordou as Antigone and Sophoklis Peppas as Creon.)

2003 *2 Lives,* Huntington Theatre Company, Lyric Stage of Boston (*Backstage,* March 28, 2003, 15). DVD available.

2004 National Asian American Theatre Company, Intar 53, New York, adaptation by Brendan Kennelly, directed by Jean Randich, starring Eunice Wong as Antigone and Mia Katigbak as Creon (D. J. R. Bruckner, *New York Times,* July 30, 2004; Dorothy Tso, *Show Business,* September 18, 2004, 14).

2004 *Antigone Falun Gong* by Cherylene Lee (based on Anouilh's *Antigone*), directed by David Furumoto, Aurora Theatre, Berkeley, California, choreography by Peter Kwong, music by Mark Izu, starring Bonnie Akimoto as A, Keiko Shimosato as I and dancer, Michael Cheng as H, David Furumoto as C, and Frances Cachapero and Raul Kacson as dancers (Robert Hurwitt, *San Francisco Chronicle*, April 17, 2004; Michael Scott Moore, *S.F. Weekly*, May 5, 2004; Sam Hurwitt, *Berkeley Express*, April 28, 2004; Nirmala Nataraj, www.sfstation.com/antigone-falun-gong-a28; *Pacific Sun*, May 4, 2004; Richard Connema, www.talkinbroadway.com/regional/sanfran/s473/html; Foley 2011).

2004 South Coast Repertory, Costa Mesa, California, adaptation by Brendan Kennelly, directed by Kate Whoriskey, starring Alyssa Bresnahan as Antigone and Randle Mell as Creon (Paul Hodgins, *Orange County Register*, January 30, 2004; Anne Marie Welsh, *San Diego Union-Tribune*, February 4, 2004; and Melinda Schupmann, *Commercial Property News*, February 9, 2004).

2004 Orphan Girl Productions, Butte Center for the Performing Arts, Butte, Mont.

2004 Greasy Joan & Company, Loop Theatre, Chicago, translated by Brendan Kennelly, directed by Julieanne Ehre, starring Nicole Burgund as Antigone and Ed Dzialo as Creon (Jonathan Arbanel, *Windy City Times*, September 22, 2004; Mary Houlihan, *Chicago Sun-Times*, September 10, 2004; Albert Williams, *Reader* 23.51, September 17, 2004, 40).

*2004 *Antigone Project*, Julia Miles Theater, New York: Karen Hartman, *Hang Ten*, directed by Anne Kaufman; Tanya Barfield, *Medallion*, directed by Dana Iris Harrell; Caridad Svich, *Antigone Arkhe*, directed by Annie Dorsen; Lynn Nottage, *A Stone's Throw*, directed by Liesl Tommy; and Chiori Miyagawa, *Red Again*, directed by Barbara Rubin (Phoebe Hoban, *New York Times*, October 27, 2004; Adam Feldman, *Time Out New York*, October 28–November 4, 2004; Alisa Solomon, *Village Voice*, November 3, 2004; Kurt Levett, *Backstage*, November 12, 2004; Helen Shaw, *New York Sun*, October 13, 2004; Linda Winer, *Newsday*, November 1, 2004; Celia McGee, *Daily News*, December 29, 2004; Martin 2009).

2004 La MaMa, E.T.C., New York, a new version drawn from a wider range of Greek myth, directed by Ellen Stewart, music by Elizabeth Swados (Margo Jefferson, *New York Times*, May 27, 2005).

2004 *The Antigone Congress*, Epic Theatre Ensemble. The result of Antigone-in-Progress, a collaborative project between schoolchildren who saw the company's *Antigone* and professional actors; students wrote choral components and scenes, and the final result was presented at The Duke at 42nd Street, New York.

2004 *Antigua* by Paula Alprin, George Washngton Masonic National Memorial, Alexandria, Virginia, Natural Theatricals, USA, directed by Cody Jones, with Thembi Duncan as Antigua.

*2005 *Hillbilly Antigone* by Rick Sims and Heidi Stillman, Lookingglass Theatre Company, Chicago, starring Mattie Hawkinson as Antigone Flick, Philip R. Smith as Preacher Creon Waller, Matt Ziegler as Harmon, Chris Mathews as Amos, and Cynthia Baker as the grandmother; Sims, Christine White, and Mary Dunford performed the music; cast members trained by Chicago's Old Town School of Folk Music (Jack Helbig, *Daily Herald*, June 10, 2005; Dan Zeff, *Copley News Service*, June 6, 2005; Brandon Hayes, www

.chicagocritic.com/html/hillbilly_antigone.html; Jonathan Abarbanel, *Windy City Times*, June 15, 2005; Chris Jones, *Chicago Tribune*, June 6, 2005; Betty Mohr, *Daily Southern Theater Critic*, June 10, 2005; Hedy Weiss, *Chicago Sun-Times*, June 6, 2005; Jenn Q. Goddu, *Chicago Tribune*, May 20, 2005; centerstagechicago.co,/theatre/articles/hillbilly-antigone.html; Christopher Platt, *Time Out Chicago*, June 8, 2005; Nick Harkin, *REVUE Chicago*, June 20, 2005; Mary Houlihan, Sunday *Chicago Sun-Times*, May 29, 2005; Novid Parsi, *Time Out Chicago*, May 26–June 2, 2005, 105; www.lookingglasstheatre.org/news/wbez061005.html). As of December 1, 2008, lookingglasstheatre.org/content/explore/image/category/162 had images and copies of many reviews.

2006 *Burial at Thebes* by Seamus Heaney, Handcart Ensemble, Theatre 315, Salvation Army, directed by J. Scott Reynolds, starring Jane Petersen as Antigone and Adam Houghton as Creon.

2006 *Antigone*, adapted by Jeremy Menekseoglu, and *Ismene*, New World Arts, Goshen, Ind., directed by Laura Gouin.

2007 *I Kreon*, adapted and directed by Aole T. Miller, Roust Theatre Company and New Moon Rep, Walkerspace, New York.

2007 *Burial at Thebes* by Seamus Heaney, directed by Alexander Harrington at La MaMa E.T.C., New York (Sam Thielman, *Backstage.com*, February 8, 2007).

2007 *Antigone* by Mac Wellman, performed by Big Dance Theater, Classic Stage Company, New York.

2008 Classic Greek Theatre of Oregon, Reed College, Cerf Amphitheatre, directed by Keith Scales, starring Christy Bigelow as Antigone and Daniel Shaw as Creon.

2008 *Oedipus Cycle*, Pearl Theater Company, New York, translated by Peter Constantine, directed by Shepard Sobel, starring Jay Stratton and T. J. Edwards as Oedipus, Jolly Abraham as Jocasta and Antigone, Dominic Cuskern as Tiresias, and John Livingston Rolle as Creon (Rachel Saltz, *New York Times*, November 3, 2008; Garrett Eisler, *Time Out New York*, October 30, 2008; Karl Levett, *Backstage.com*, October 29, 2008; Mark Blankenshop, *Daily Variety Gotham*, October 28, 2008; Jonathan Warman, *New York Blade*, November 14, 2008).

2008 *Too Much Memory*, a version of Anouilh's *Antigone* by Keith Reddin and Meg Gibson, directed by Meg Gibson for The Rising Phoenix Repertory and Piece by Piece Production, Fourth Street Theatre, New York, starring Laura Heisler as Antigone and Peter Jay Fernandez as Creon (Anita Gates, *New York Times*, 13 December 2008; Elyse Sommer, www.curtainup.com/toomuchmemory.html; Dan Bacalzo, www.theatermania.com/content/news.cfm/story/16556; Gwen Orel, www.backstage.com/bso/news_reviews/nyc/review_display.jsp?vnu_content_id=1003921081; Sam Thielman, www.variety.com/review/VE1117939185.html?categoryid=33&cs=1; Pete Boisvert, August 11, 2008, www.nytheatre.com/nytheatre/frnyc08_rev.php?o=S&1=538; Matthew Murray, www.talkinbroadway.com/ob/12_09_08a.html; Amy Freeman, offoffonline.com/reviews.php?id=1515; and news.yahoo.com/s/ap/20081210/ap_en_re/theater_review_too_much_memory_1; Foley 2011).

2009 *Fire Throws*, dance theater version of *Antigone*, 3LD Art & Technology Center, New York, directed by Rachel Dickstein for Ripe Time, score by Jewlia Eisenberg, performed by Charming Hostess, starring Erica Berg and Laura Butler as Antigone, John Campion as Creon, Jorge Jubio as Haemon/Chorus (Claudia La Rocco, *New York Times,* March 3, 2009; see www.ripetime.org/index.php/history/fire_throws/).

2009 *Gone (w.t.)* by Katori Hall, staged reading, Fluid Motion Theater, directed by Tlaloc Rivas, Theatre Row Studios, New York, starring Sameerah Luqmann-Harris as Antwonette and Felipe Bonella as Creon.

APPENDIX C

# Professional Productions and New Versions of Aeschylus's *Persians,* Sophocles' *Ajax,* and Aeschylus's *Prometheus Bound*

*The Archive of Performances of Greek and Roman Drama (www.apgrd.ox.ac.uk/) has fuller cast lists and more information on sources in some cases. These entries are as complete as current information allowed.*

\* Discussed or mentioned in chapters 1–2 of this book
( ) Important visiting production

### PERSIANS

1939 Dance version by Ted Shawn, with music by Eva Palmer Sikelianos, filmed in New York. Film at the New York Public Library for the Performing Arts, Lincoln Center.
1960 New School for Social Research, staged reading by the Living Theatre.
1970 *A Ceremony for Our Time,* St. George's Church, New York City, Phoenix Theatre, adapted by John Lewin, directed by Gordon Duffy, starring Jacqueline Brookes as Jocasta, David Spielberg as Darius, Stephen McHattie as Xerxes (Clive Barnes, *New York Times,* April 16, 1970; Walter Kerr, *New York Times,* April 26, 1970; Hartigan 1995, 102–3).
1974 Circle Repertory Theatre, New York, directed by Rob Thirkield, starring Henrietta Bagley as Atossa, Ron Seka as Darius, Jim Enzel as Xerxes, and Ken Kliban as the Messenger (Joseph Mancini, *New York Post,* May 20, 1974; Arthur Sainer, *Village Voice,* May 30, 1974; Debbie Wasserman, *Show Business,* May 23, 1974; Linda Lawrence, *Chelsea Clinton News,* June 6, 1974; Hartigan 1995, 103).
\*1993 Mark Taper Forum, adapted by Robert Auletta (Auletta [1993] 2006), directed by Peter Sellars, music by Hamza El Din, starring Cordelia González as Atossa, Howie Seago as Darius, and John Ortiz as Xerxes (Sylvie Drake, *Los Angeles Times,* October 2, 1993; John Lahr, *New Yorker,* October 18, 1993, 103–6; Hall 2004, 176–85; Hartigan 1995, 104).

*2003 Pace University, Michael Schimmel Center for the Arts, New York, translated by Ellen McLaughlin, directed by Ethan McSweeny for Tony Randall's National Actors Theatre, with Roberta Maxwell as Atossa, Len Cariou as Darius, and Michael Stuhlberg as Xerxes; 2004, Aurora Theatre Corporation, Berkeley, directed by Barbara Oliver; 2006, Shakespeare Theatre, Washington, D.C., directed by Ethan McSweeny, starring Helen Carey as Atossa, Ted van Griethuysen as Darius, Erin Gann as Xerxes, and Scott Parkinson as the Herald (Margo Jefferson, *New York Times*, June 11, 2003; Michael Feingold, *Village Voice*, June 25–July 1, 2003, 65; Jerry Talmer, *Villager* 73.7, June 18–24, 2003; Erik Piepenburg, *Gay City News*, June 19, 2003; Alexis Soloski, *Time Out New York*, June 19–26, 2003; Gordon Cox, *Newsday*, June 12, 2003; Charles Isherwood, *Variety*, June 16, 2003; Elyse Sommer, www.curtainup.com/persians.html; Nina daVinci Nichols, www.theatrescene.net/ts/articles.nsf/OBP/35FB1CB89243C14885256D4800626867; Phillp Kennicott, *Washington Post*, April 9, 2006; Peter Marks, *Washington Post*, April 13, 2006; Jayne M. Blanchard, *Washington Times*, April 12, 2006). Also directed by Jade King Caroll at People's Light and Theatre, Philadelphia, September 24–October 19, 2008.

2004 Pearl Theatre, New York, translated by Janet Lembke and C. J. Herington, directed by Shepard Sobel, starring Joanne Camp as Atossa and Sean McNall as Xerxes.

*2005 *The Persians . . . A Comedy about War with Five Songs*, Waterwell, Under St. Marks, New York, moved to Perry Street Theater, New York, July 13–August 20, 2005, written by Arian Moayed, directed by Tom Ridgely, also starring Hanna Cheek and Rodney Gardiner, music by Laura Gregor. Revived at the Abron Arts Festival, New York, 2007 (Miriam Horn, *New York Times*, July 18, 2005; Helen Shaw, *Time Out New York*, July 28–August 3, 2005, 137; Catherine Rampell, *Village Voice*, July 27–August 2, 2005; Kenneth Jones, www.playbill.com/news/article/93959.html; Barbara and Scott Siegel, www.theatermania.com/content/news.cfm/story/6375; Marion Hurt, www.offoffonline.com/archiveprinterfriendly.php?id=459; Jenifer Braun, www.theatrescene.net/ts/articles/nsf/OBMus/8056860CA7E37838525701400203C89?OpenDocument).

(2006 City Center, New York, Ancient Theatre of Epidauros, National Theater of Greece, translation by Nikoletta Frintzila, directed by Lydia Koniordou and starring Lydia Koniordou as Atossa, Ioannis Kranas as Dareios, and Christos Loulis as Xerxes [*New York Times*, September 18, 2006; Howard Stein, *Arion* 14.3 [Winter 2007]: 155–73].)

## AJAX

*1903 Hull House, Chicago, starring Georgios Metalas (Addams [1910] 1967, 388–89; Elizabeth C. Barrows "The Greek Play at Hull House," *Commons* 9 [January 1904]: 6–10).

*1904 Clinton Hall, East Side, New York, directed by Mabel Hays Barrows, music by Willys Peck Kent (*New York Dramatic Mirror*, April 2, 1904; *New York Tribune*, March 18, 1904; *New York Daily Mirror*, March 24, 1904; Hartigan 1995, 118–19).

1960 New School for Social Research, staged reading, The Living Theatre.

1972 Section of *Ajax* composed for baritone and orchestra by John Eaton, libretto by John Moore, University of Washington, Seattle.

*1986 American National Theater, La Jolla, California, and National Theater in Washington, D.C., adapted by Robert Auletta (Auletta 1986–87), directed by Peter Sellars, staging by

W. D. King, starring Howie Seago as Ajax, Aleta Mitchell as Athena, Charles Brown as Odysseus, Brent Jennings as Agamemnon, Lauren Tom as Tecmessa, and Ben Halley Jr. as chorus leader and messenger (D. Larry Steckling, *Drama-Logue*, September 11, 1986; Jack Kroll, *Newsweek*, June 23, 1986; Dan Sullivan, *Los Angeles Times*, September 2, 1986; Sylviane Gold, *Wall Street Journal*, July 2, 1986; *Variety*, June 25, 1986; *Theater* 18.1 [Fall/Winter 1986]: 9–15, 16–18, 19–35; McDonald 1992, 75–87; Hartigan 1995, 119–20). For European productions in Vienna, Amsterdam, Antwerp, and Brussels, see www.apgrd.ox.ac.uk/.

1991–92 London Small Theater Company (later Aquila Theater Company), directed by Peter Meineck, with a video available from Insight Media.

1999 The Pangea Theater, Hennepin Center for the Arts in Minneapolis, directed by Dipankar Mukherjee, David Ward as Ajax (Peter Ritter, www.citypages.com/databank/20/949/print7159.asp).

*2001 Hypocrites Theater, The Viaduct in Chicago, staged by Sean Graney, with Michelle Moe as Edith Hamilton, John Byrnes as Ajax, and Ryan Bolletino as Odysseus and others (Chris Jones, *Chicago Tribune*, June 2001; Lucia Mauro, www.chicagotheater.com/rev Ajax.html; Kevin Heckman, www.performink.com/Archives/reviewroundup/2001/5-25 ReviewRoundup.html).

*2004 Teatro LaTea, Lower East Side, Clemente Solo Valez Cultural and Education Center, New York, directed by Peter Campbell, Bennette Pologe as Ajax and Carin Murphy as Tecmessa (Jessica Slote at www.theater2k.com/Ajax_Slote_111704.html).

2005 American Indian OIC, Open Book, and Minnesota Opera, Minnesota, Ten Thousand Things, adaptation by Emily Mann.

*2005 Culture Project, New York, *Ajax: 100% Fun*, directed by Ellen Beckerman, starring Shawn Fagan as Ajax, Melody Bates as Tecmessa, Margot Ebling as Athena, Robert M. Johanson as Odysseus, Brian Deneen as Teucer, and Christopher Oden as Menelaus (www.curtainup.com review by Les Gutman, February 24, 2006; Madeleine George, *The Brooklyn Rail*, March 2006, www.brooklynrail.org/2006/03/theater-of-war-lightboxs-ajax; both appeared on the company website www.lightboxtheatre.org).

2006 6$^{th}$ at Penn Theatre, San Diego, translated by Marianne McDonald and directed by Forrest Aylsworth, starring Lawrence Brown as Ajax, (www.6atpenn.com/AJAX%20by%Sophocles.htm and Pam Kragen, www.nctimes.com/articles/2006/01/14/entertainment/theater/11106114837.txt).

2007 Outdoor theater of the New York American Theater of Actors, directed by James Jennings, starring Moti Margolin.

2007 *Ajax: A Furious Study on Humanity*, Target Margin Theater, New York, directed by Gisela Cardenas.

*2008 *Ajax in Iraq*, by Ellen McLaughlin, directed by Scott Zigler, American Repertory Theater, Cambridge, Massachusetts.

(2008 *Antigona* by José Watanabe, Getty Villa, Malibu, California, by Grupo Yuyachkani, Peru, starring Teresa Ralli.)

*2010 Theater of War Project, translated by Brian Doerries (http://theater-of-war.com/about.html,; see Clyde Haberman, *New York Times*, September 19, 2008; Meineck 2009).

2011 *Ajax in Iraq* by Ellen McLaughlin (forthcoming from Playscripts, Inc), directed by August Schulenburg, Flux Theatre Ensemble, Clemente Solo Velez Cultural and Education Center, New York, set by Will Lowry, starring Stephen Conrad Moore as Ajax, Chitistina Sharp as A.J., Raushanah Simmons as Athena (Anita Gates, *New York Times*, June 17, 2011; Helen Shaw, *Time Out New York*, June 13, 2011; Clifford Lee Johnson III, www.backstage.com/bso/reviews-ny-theatre-off-off-broadway/ajax-in-iraq-10005225852.story; Danny Bowes, www.nytheatre.com/showpage.aspx?s = ajax11859; Haytham Ellwary, www.theasy.com/Reviews/2011/A/ajaxiniraq.php).

### PROMETHEUS BOUND

1929 Ted Shawn, solo dance version, Lewisohn Stadium, New York (Michelakis 2010).

*1930 Heckscher Theatre, New York, translated by Edith Hamilton, directed by Richard Hale and C.J. Kraemer Jr., starring Hale and Sophie Bernsohn with a chorus of eleven (*Evening Post Review*, January 6, 1930).

*1957 New York, directed by James Elliott, with costumes by Eva Palmer Sikelianos, starring Blanche Yurka and Clarence Derwent (Gonda A.H. van Steen, *International Journal of the Classical Tradition* 8.3 [Winter 2002]: 375–93).

1958 *Prometheus Tempted* by John Wexley, New York.

1958 *Prometheus Found* by George Hitchcock, The San Francisco Actor's Workshop (Prometheus as a figure for the artist).

1960 Staged reading by The Living Theatre at New School for Social Research, New York.

1964 Group of Ancient Drama, New York's East River Amphitheater.

1964 *Prometheus Rebound*, one-act version by Lawrence Wunderlich (Colakis 1993, 29).

*1967 Yale Drama School, New Haven, adapted by Robert Lowell, directed by Jonathan Miller, starring Irene Worth as Io and Kenneth Haigh as Prometheus (*New York Review of Books* 9, August 3, 1967, 30–32; John Simon, *Hudson Review* 20 [1967]: 559; Walter Kerr, *New York Times*, May 11, 1967; Elenore Lester, *New York Times*, May 21, 1957; Richard Gilman, *Newsweek*, May 22, 1967; John Chadwick, *Saturday Review* 52, May 3, 1969; *Newark Evening News*, May 12, 1967; *Reporter*, June 15, 1967; Raizis 1969; Colakis 1993, 21–29; Hartigan 1995, 132–33).

*1970 Group of Ancient Drama, *Black Titan*, John McCurry as Prometheus (*Show Business*, May 2, 1970; Hartigan 1995, 132 and nn. 3–4).

1973 Theatre of the Artist's League of the Playwright's Workshop Club, Bastiano's Studio, 14 Cooper Square, New York (*Village Voice*, February 8, 1973, 63).

1978 Manhattan School of Music, New York, opera by Meyer Kupferman.

1984 New York, La MaMa, E.T.C., Shadow Theater Company, translated by Peter Arnott, directed by Bill Reichblum, starring Mohammad B. Ghaffari as Prometheus (Erika Munk, *Village Voice*, December 18, 1984: Ronn Mullen, *Backstage*, December 28, 1984; Sy Syna, *New York City Tribune*, December 14, 1984; Arnott 1987, 375).

1984 *Prometheus 84* by Barry Plumlee, directed by Bob McGrath, Pink at Zero Beach, New York (Erika Munk, *Village Voice*, April 17, 1984, 105).

1985 Richard Morse Theater, New York, new translation and staging by Jonathan Nossiter with Robert Moriano.

*1985 *The Prometheus Project: Four Movements and a Coda,* by Richard Schechner, New York Performance Garage, choreographed by Terry Beck, featuring Mahmoud Karimi-Hakak, Annie Sprinkle, and Becke Wilenski (Walter Goodman, *New York Times,* December 27, 1985; Alisa Solomon, *Village Voice,* December 31, 1985, 83 and 93; Marilyn Stasio, *New York Post,* January 31, 1986; Tish Dace, *New York Native,* January 20, 1985, 43; and Richard F. Shephard, *New York Times,* December 14, 1985; Hartigan 1995, 133–34).

1991 New York, Quirk Productions.

1997 Gorilla Theater, Nelson Atkins Museum of Art, Kansas City, Missouri, directed by David Luby, with Tom Moriarty as Prometheus and Gail Bronfman as Io; http://www.gorillatheatre.org/.

1999 The Tinfish Theater, directed by Dejan Avramovich, Chicago, starring Jeff Klein as Prometheus and Jennifer Savarirayan as Io (Richard Christiansen, *Chicago Tribune,* January 6, 1999).

1999 *Steelbound,* new version, Bethlehem, Pennsylvania, part of "Steel Festival: The Art of an Industry," Touchstone Theater Company, in collaboration with the Cornerstone Theater Company of Los Angeles, written by Alison Carey and directed by Bill Rauch, music by Ysaye Barnwell of the gospel group Sweet Honey in the Rock, choreography by Jennie Gilrain, designed by Lynn Jeffries, with Bill George as Prometheus and a cast of fifty-six people, most of them community members (Jan Cohen-Cruz, *American Theatre* 17 [March 2000]: 17–19, 68–69; Douglas J. Keating, *Philadelphia Inquirer,* September 7, 1999; Paul Willistein, *Morning Call,* September 9–11, 1999; Karen Feege, *Express Times,* September 14, 1999; and Geoff Gehman, *Morning Call,* March 7, 1999 and September 5, 1999; Gerard Stropnicky, www.communityarts.net/readingroom/archivefiles/1999/10/courting_cathar.php; Brady 2000 with extensive responses in *The Drama Review* 43.3 T171 [Fall 2001]: 8–23).

2001 *Io, Princess of Argos,* Exit Stage Left, San Francisco, directed by Mark Jackson, starring Kevin Clarke as Prometheus and Beth Wilmurt as Io (Michael Scott Moore, *SF Weekly,* March 14, 2001).

*2002 Studio Theatre in Washington, D.C., adapted by Sophy Burnham and directed by Joy Zinoman, starring William Hulings as Prometheus, Ted van Griethuysen as Zeus, and Sarah Marshall as Io (*Washington Post,* April 5 and 19, 2002). Video of the performance at the Washington Area Performing Arts Video Archive.

2003 Grand Marais Theatre, Minnesota, performed on rocks by a lighthouse, Arrowhead Center for the Arts, directed by Diane Mountford.

2003 *Scripture: Prometheus Bound,* Clemente Solo Vélez Cultural Center, New York, Casa Cruz de la Luna, directed by Aravind Enrique Adyanthaya (*Time Out New York,* July 24–31, 2003).

2004 Classic Greek Theatre of Oregon, Cerf Amphitheatre, Reed College and Portland State University, adapted and directed by Keith Scales, Kevin Connell as Prometheus and Melissa Whitney as Io.

2007 Classic Stage Company, New York, directed and translated by James Kerr, starring David Oyelowo as Prometheus, Julie McNiven as Io and Violence, and George Bartenieff as Hephaestus/Oceanus; a British-derived production with additional U.S. actors (Wilborn Hampton, *New York Times,* March 27, 2007; Adam Feldman, *Time Out New York,* March 29–April 4, 2007).

APPENDIX D

# Professional Productions and New Versions of *Oedipus Tyrannus*

*The Archive of Performances of Greek and Roman Drama (www.apgrd.ox.ac.uk/) has fuller cast lists and more information on sources in some cases. These entries are as complete as current information allowed.*

\* Discussed or mentioned in chapters 1–4 of this book
( ) Important visiting production

\*1834 *Oedipus or the Riddle of the Sphinx*, Bowery Theater, New York, starring Tom Hamblin as Oedipus, Mrs. McClure as Jocasta, and Mr. Gale as Tiresias, with a cast including a Mr. Ingersoll and Mrs. Flynn (Davis 2008; *New York Transcript*, October 21, 1834; *Peabody's Parlour Journal*, November 1, 1834, 141; Odell 4: 28; Ireland (1866–67) 1968, 1: 119; Levine 1988, 41–42; Brown 1: 112; *New York American* advertisement, November 20, 1834; *New York Clipper*, February 4, 1882).

\*1881 Sanders Theatre, Harvard University, directed by John Williams White, music composed by John Knowles Paine, designed by Charles Eliot Norton, starring George Riddle as Oedipus and L. E. Opdyke as Jocasta (Norman 1882; Hains 1914, 190–94; *New York Herald*, May 18, 1881; Julia Ward Howe, *Critic* 1, May 21, 1881, 130).

\*1882 Globe Theater, Boston and Booth Theater, New York, producers Daniel Frohman and F. H. Ober, directed by Daniel Frohman, with George Riddle as Oedipus and Georgia Cayvan as Jocasta (*Spirit of the Times*, April 4, 1882; *New York Tribune*, January 31, 1882; *New York Mail and Express*, February 2, 1882; *New York Times*, January 24, 1882; January 31 and February 1, 1882; *New York World*, January 31, 1882; *New York Clipper*, February 4, 1882; *New York Herald*, January 31, 1882; *New York Sun*, January 31, 1882; *Chicago Daily Tribune*, February 5, 1882; *Critic* 2.29, February 11, 1882, 46–47; *New York Dramatic Mirror*, February 4, 1882; Odell 11: 455).

\*1889 Unity Club of Cleveland, Unity Church (Hains 1910, 35).

*1893 American Academy of the Dramatic Arts, scenes from *Antigone* and *OT* (Odell 4: 467).
*(1894 Broad Street Theatre, Philadelphia, and Abbey's Theater and the Knickerbocker, New York, Comédie Française, French translation by Jules Lacroix, starring Jean Mounet-Sully as Oedipus and Mme Second-Weber as Jocasta [*New York Times*, March 28, April 4, April 8, 1894; *New York Herald*, March 28, 1894; *Critic* 24, April 7, 1894, 242; *New York Daily Tribune*, March 28, 1894; Hartigan 1995, 12–13 n. 6; Rogers 1986, 30–31; Odell 7: 345; Brandes 1945, 117–28].)
(1907 Lyric Theatre, New York, Ernete Novelli, Italian language production [Benjamin de Casseres, *Theatre Magazine* 7.74 (April 1907): 6; *Harper's Weekly* 51, April 6, 1907, 512; Winter (1913) 1969, 1: 419; Brandes 1945, 139–41].)
*1911 Irving Place Theatre, New York, starring John E. Kellerd as Oedipus and Lillian Kingbury as Jocasta, Eric Blind as Tiresias, and Charles James as Creon (*Theater Magazine*, October 1911; *New York Evening Post*, August 22, 1911; *New York Daily Mirror*, August 23, 1911; *New York Tribune*, August 22, 1911; *New York Times*, February 4, 1913; *New York Evening Post*, February 4, 1913; Johnson 1971, 19–20; Brandes 1945, 153–58; Hartigan 1995, 10–11; Arnott 1987, 358). Revived with Keller as Oedipus, Amelia Gardner as Jocasta, and Ernest Rowan as Tiresias at the Garden Theater, New York in 1913.
*1914 Irving Place Theatre at the Metropolitan Opera House, adapted by Adolph Wilbrandt into German, starring Rudolph Christians and Agathe Barcescu, with Heinrich Marlowe as Tiresias (*New York Dramatic Mirror*, May 6, 1914; *New York Tribune*, April 28, 1914; *New York Evening Post*, April 28, 1914; *New York Times*, April 28, 1914; *New York Press*, April 28, 1914).
*1915 Century Opera House, translation by Gilbert Murray, directed by and starring Augustin Duncan with Margaret Wycherly as Jocasta, Oswald Yorke as Creon, and Ivan Simpson as Tiresias and danced with choreography by Isadora Duncan, accompanied by Irma Duncan, Helen Freeman, Sarah Whitford, and Margherita Sargeant (*New York Times*, April 17, 1915; Sigmund Spaete, *New York Mail*, April 17, 1915; *New York Telegraph*, April 17, 1915).
*(1923 Century Theatre, New York, translation by Gilbert Murray, British production starring John Martin Harvey and Miriam Lewes, originally based on the production of Max Reinhardt, Munich 1910 [*Theater Arts Monthly* 8 (1924): 74–76; Arthur Hornblow, *Theater Magazine* 38 (December 1923): 15; Ranken Towse, *New York Evening Post*, October 26, 1923; *New York Evening Telegram*, October 26, 1923; Stark Young, *New Republic* 36, November 7, 1923, 282–83; Ludwig Lewisohn, *Nation*, November 7, 1923, 532; John Corbin, *New York Times*, October 26, 1923; *New York Times*, October 18, 1923; *New York Daily Tribune*, October 26, 1923; L. S., *New York World*, October 26, 1923; *Time*, November 5, 1923; *Town and Country*, December 1, 1923; *Theatre* 38, December 1, 1923; *Judge*, November 17, 1923; *Vogue*, December 16, 1923; *Outlook* 138, November 7, 1923, 388].)
1930 First production of *Oedipus Rex* by Jean Cocteau, composed by Igor Stravinsky, conducted by Leopold Stokowski, Philadelphia Orchestra, starring Paul Althouse and Margaret Matzenauer.
*1930 (published 1931) *Tiresias*, by Henry Bertram Lister, La Boheme Club of San Francisco, Travers Theatre, Fairmont Hotel, directed by Frederic Smith, starring Alton Wood as

Tiresias, Lister as Oedipus, and his wife as Priestess (George C. Warren, *San Francisco Chronicle*, December 2, 1930; Templeton Peck, *San Francisco News*, December 3. 1930; O. E. Jones, *San Francisco Call Bulletin*, December 3, 1930).

1930 *OT* by W. B. Yeats, Boston's Symphony Hall.

(1933 *OT* by W. B. Yeats, Abbey Players, Martin Beck Theatre, starring E. J. McCormick as Oedipus and Eileen Crowe as Jocasta [*New York Herald Tribune*, January 22, 1933; *New York Evening Post*, January 13, 1933].)

1945 *OT* by W. B. Yeats, Majestic Theatre, New York, The Reader's Theater, supervised by Eugene O'Neill Jr., directed by James Light on December 16, 1945, starring Blanche Yurka and Frederick Tozere (Robert Garland, *New York Journal American*, December 17, 1945; Robert Sylvester, *Daily News*, December 17, 1945; Burton Roscoe, *New York World Telegram*, December 17, 1945).

*(1946 Century Theater, New York, London Old Vic, starring Laurence Olivier as Oedipus, Eva Burrill as Jocasta, and Ralph Richardson as Tiresias [Lewis Nichols, *New York Times*, May 21, 1946; Herrick Brown, *New York Sun*, May 21, 1946; Robert Coleman, *New York Daily Mirror*, May 22, 1946; *Time*, June 3, 1946; Edgar Price, *Brooklyn Citizen*, May 1946; Hartigan 1995, 40].)

*1947 *Night Journey* by Martha Graham, composer William Schuman, designer Isamu Noguchi, starring Erick Hawkins as Oedipus and Martha Graham as Jocasta, Cambridge High School, Cambridge, Mass.

(1947 Broadway Theatre, Habimah National Theatre, translated into Hebrew by Saul Chernikovsky, directed by Tyrone Guthrie.)

(1952 Mark Hellinger Theatre, New York, National Theatre of Greece, starring Alexis Minotis as Oedipus and Katina Paxinou as Jocasta [Wolcott Gibbs, *New Yorker*, December 6, 1952; Richard Hayes, *Commonweal*, December 19, 1952; Brooks Atkinson, *New York Times*, November 25, 1952; Hartigan 1995, 41].)

*1952 Harry Partch, Mills College, California, set by Arch Lauterer, with Alan Louw as Oedipus and Rudolphine Radil as Jocasta, released on Gate Five LP records and now on CD, Enclosure 5: Harry Partch, Innova: American Composers Forum 1998, revived 1954 at Shell Beach, Sausalito, California, and in 1967 (Gilmore 1998 and Blackburn 1997).

1954 The Menninger School of Psychiatry Fellows Association, dramatic reading of *OT*, Dudley Fitts and Robert Fitzgerald translation, directed by Narda Stokes, starring Konstantin Geocaris with Ann Wilkins as Jocasta, Topeka Civic Theatre, Topeka, Kansas.

1954 Actor's Workshop, San Francisco, Herbert Blau director, starring Joseph A. Miksaki as Oedipus and Beatrice Manley as Jocasta.

1957 *Greek Scene*, composed by Harold Faberman for mezzo-soprano, piano, and percussion, singer Corinne Curry, Jordan Hall, Boston.

1958 Cleveland Playhouse, Albert Cook translation, staged by Frederic McConnell, starring Thomas Hill as Oedipus and Edith Owen as Jocasta.

1959 Catholic University of America, National Players, with a tour including Carnegie Hall Playhouse, New York, adapted by Leo Brady, directed by Father Gilbert V. Hartke, starring Robert Milli as Oedipus and Dolores Viola as Jocasta (Brooks Atkinson, *New York Times*, May 12, 1959; Walter Kerr, *New York Herald Tribune*, April 30, 1959; John McClain, *New York Journal American*, April 30, 1959; Frank Aston, *New York World Telegram and*

Sun, April 30, 1959; Frances Herridge, *New York Post*, April 30, 1959; Thomas R. Dash, *Women's Wear Daily*, April 30, 1959; Whitney Bolton, *Morning Telegraph*, May 1, 1959; Charles McHarry, *Daily News*, April 30, 1959). Revived in 1963, directed by William H. Graham, starring David Little as Oedipus and Marilyn Morton as Jocasta (*Ottawa Journal*, October 28, 1963; *Post-Standard*, Syracuse, New York, October 14, 1963).

1960 Staged Reading by The Living Theatre at the New School for Social Research, New York.

1960 Westside YWCA, New York, translated by C. A. Trypanis, directed by Athan Karras, starring Athan Karras as Oedipus and Paula Manny as Jocasta (Louis Calta, *New York Times*, April 4, 1960).

1965 *OT* by W. B. Yeats, The American National Theater and Academy, Beverly Hills Auditorium, Los Angeles, California, directed by Theo Marcuse, starring Edmund Gilbert as Oedipus.

1965 Actors Company, USA, translated by Bernard Knox, directed by John Thorburn Hall, unknown location in Washington, D.C., starring David Riddick as Oedipus and Jo Carpenter as Jocasta.

1968 Missouri Repertory Theatre, directed by Alexis Minotis, with music by Katinou Paxinou, starring Alvah Stanley as Oedipus and Patricia Trescott Ripley as Jocasta.

*1968 *Oedipus Wrecks* by Tony Kessick, New York Theater Ensemble at Millennium Theater, directed by Jerry Lee (Molly Haskell, *Village Voice*, November 14, 1968).

*1968 *The Oedipus Mah-Jongg Scandal* by Howard Moss, Cooperative Theatre Club, Inc., New York, directed by William C. Christian. Later performed and published as *The Palace at 4 a.m.* in 1968, Playwrights Unit, Theater Vandam, New York, directed by Charles Guys, and in 1972, John Drew Theater in East Hampton, Long Island, N.Y., directed by Edward Albee and starring Chistopher Walken and Beatrice Straight (Mel Gussow, *New York Times*, August 16, 1972).

1968–69 *OT* by W. B. Yeats, McCarter Theater, Princeton, directed by Arthur Lithgow, starring Ed Bernard as Oedipus and Eve Johnson as Jocasta.

1970 American Conservatory Theatre, San Francisco, directed by William Ball, adapted by William Ball and Dennis Powers, starring Paul Shenar as Oedipus and Carol Mayo Jenkins as Jocasta (Hartigan 1995, 41–42).

*1970 Roundabout Theatre, New York, new version by Anthony Sloan and Gene Feist, starring Gordon Heath as Oedipus and Elizabeth Owens as Jocasta (Phil Zinkewicz, *Show Business*, March 7, 1970; *Time*, March 9, 1970; Clive Barnes, *New York Times*, February 23, 1970; Daphne Kraft, *Newark Evening News*, February 16, 1970; Alan Bunce, *Christian Science Monitor*, February 27, 1970; Donald J. Mayerson, *Villager*, March 19, 1970; Dick Brukenfeld, *Village Voice*, February 19, 1970; Hartigan 1995, 42).

1970 Bucks County Playhouse in Pennsylvania, directed by Lee R. Yopp.

*1972 Guthrie Theater, Minneapolis, adapted by Anthony Burgess (Burgess 1972), directed by Michael Langham, music by Stanley Silverman, set by Desmond Heeley, starring Len Cariou as Oedipus and Patricia Connolly as Jocasta; revived in 1973, starring Kenneth Welsh and Pauline Flanaghan (*Christian Science Monitor*, November 6, 1972; Melvin Maddox, *Time*, November 13, 1972, 82; Nick Baldwin, *Des Moines Register*, June 30, 1973; *Boston Phoenix*, January 9, 1972; *Variety*, November 8, 1972; *Women's Wear Daily*, April 10, 1973, 17; Sonkowsky 1973; Hartigan 1995, 42–43; Freiert 1991).

*1974 Yale Theater Community, Robert Brustein, burlesque *Oedipus Nix*. See *Yale/Theater* 5.1 (Fall 1973): 131–38.
*1975 The Oregon Theater Festival, translated by Donald Sutherland, directed by Robert Loper, starring Ted D'Arms as Oedipus.
1976 The Actors Theatre of Louisville, directed by Jon Jory, starring Michael Gross as Oedipus and Adale O'Brien as Jocasta.
1976 Alvin Theater, New York, *Kings* (a dance version), choreographed by Emily Fraenkel, starring John Collum as Oedipus (Anna Kisselgoff, *New York Times*, September 29, 1976; Bill Zakariasen, *Daily News*, September 29, 1976; Jennie Shulamn, *Backstage*, October 15, 1976, 55).
*1976 *Oedipussy* by Max E. Verga, New York's 18th Street Playhouse, directed by Eric Neilson (Tony del Valle, *Show Business*, April 22, 1976).
*1977 St. John's Cathedral, New York, translated by John Lewin, starring James Earl Jones as Oedipus and Jacqueline Brookes as Jocasta (Mel Gussow, *New York Times*, February 4, 1977).
1978 Impossible Ragtime Theater, New York, directed by John Sumakis, starring Donald Smith as Oedipus.
*1980 *Theban Plays*, Classic Stage Company, New York, translated by Anthony Roche, directed by Christopher Martin, starring Robert Stattel as Oedipus and Karen Sunde as Antigone and Jocasta (Holly Hill, *Soho Weekly News*, November 12, 1980; David Sterritt, *Christian Science Monitor*, December 8, 1980; Howard Kessel, *Women's Wear Daily*, March 16, 1981; Thomas Ryan, *Villager*, November 20, 1980; Glenn Loney, *Other Stages*, December 18, 1980, 6; Clive Barnes, *New York Post*, December 3, 1980; Eileen Blumenthal, *Village Voice*, November 19, 1980; Hartigan 1995, 106–7).
1981 Brooklyn Academy of Music, New York, translated by Stephen Berg and Diskin Clay, directed by Emily Mann, starring Joe Morton as Oedipus and Sheila Allen as Jocasta (Frank Rich, *New York Times*, April 24, 1981; Eileen Blumenthal, *Village Voice*, April 29, 1981; David Sterritt, *Christian Science Monitor*, June 4, 1981; Walter Kerr, *New York Times*, May 3 and May 28, 1981; Victor Gluck, *Wisdom's Child*, May 4–10, 1981; Marilyn Stasio, *New York Post*, April 29, 1981; Christopher Sharp, *Women's Wear Daily*, April 27, 1981; John Simon, *New York*, May 4, 1981; Douglass Watt, *Daily News*, April 24, 1981).
1981–82 Upstart Crow Theater Company, Dairy Center for the Arts, Boulder, Colorado.
1982 *Jocasta, or Boy Crazy*, Ethyl Eichelberger, Café S.N.A.F.U., New York.
(1984 Vivian Beaumont Theatre, New York, directed by Minos Volonakis, starring Nikos Kourkoulos as Oedipus and Katerina Helmi as Jocasta [*New York Times*, July 19, 1984; Benedict Nightingale, *New York Times*, August 15, 1984; *Village Voice*, July 3, 1984; Marilyn Stasio, *New York Post*, July 20, 1984; Ronn Millan, *Backstage*, August 3, 1984; Don Nelson, *Daily News*, July 19, 1984; Sy Syna, *New York Tribune*, July 20, 1984].)
1986 Classic Greek Theater of Oregon, translated by Peter Montgomery, directed by Keith Scales (a Jungian version).
*1987 Theater Upstairs in Los Angeles, directed by Reza Abdoh, Artson Hardison as Oedipus and Ruth Cameron as Jocasta.
1988 People's Light and Theatre Company, Malvern, Pennsylvania, directed by Abigail Adams (Cary Mazer, *Philadelphia City Paper*, October 14–21, 1988).

1988 Quirk Productions, New York City.

*1988 *Oedipus Tex*, by P.D.Q. Bach (Peter Schickele), performed in Minneapolis, Minnesota, from March 15. The score was published in 1989 by Theodore Presser Company, King of Prussia, Pennsylvania. The 1990 CD, *Oedipus Tex and Other Choral Calamities*, is available from Telarc (B000003CWP).

*1989 *Oedipus Requiem*, Chicago's Blind Parrot Productions, adapted from seven translations by David Perkins, music by Robert Ian Winston, starring Larry Newmann Jr. as Oedipus, Palmar Hardy as Jocasta, Jill Daly and Peggy Burr as Antigone, and Wayne Brown as Creon (Hedy Weiss, *Chicago Sun Times*, March 23, 1989; Lawrence Bommer, *Windy City Times*, March 30, 1989).

1992 Westside Repertory Theatre, New York, directed by James Jacobus (Irene Backalenick, *Backstage*, June 19, 1992).

1993 Wilma Theatre, Philadelphia, translated by Stephen Berg and Diskin Clay, directed by Blanka Zizka, starring Olek Krupa as Oedipus and Ching Valdes Aran as Jocasta (Toby Zinman, *Variety*, May 3, 1993). A video is available at the New York Public Library for the Performing Arts, Lincoln Center.

1993 Pearl Theatre, New York, translated by Stephen Berg and Diskin Clay, directed by Ted Davis, starring Timothy Wheeler as Oedipus.

1994 Gorilla Theatre, Kansas City, Missouri.

*1996 *The Whole World Is Watching*, new version of the Oedipus trilogy by Douglas Jacobs and Scott Feldsher, Lyceum, San Diego Repertory Theatre, starring Wayne Tibbetts as Host, Lamont D. Thompson as Oedipus, Darla Cash as Jocasta, Douglas Roberts as Creon, Karola Forman as Antigone, and Linda Castro as Ismene (Anne Marie Welsh, *San Diego Union-Tribune*, February 13 and September 14, 2000; *Playbill*, July 9, 1996; Laurie Winer, *Los Angeles Times*, July 29, 1996).

*1996 *Darker Face of the Earth* by Rita Dove, Angus Bowner Theatre, Ashland, Oregon, directed by Ricardo Kahn.

1997 Missouri Repertory Theatre, Helen Spencer Auditorium, Kansas City, Missouri, directed by George Keathley.

1997 Metropolitan Museum of Art, *Oedipus* by Harry Partch, staged by Tom O'Horgan and conducted by Dean Drummond with Joe Garcia as Oedipus (Alan Shaw at www.prosoidia.com/om.html; and John Chalmers, didaskalia.open.uk/issues/vol3no1/Chalmers/htm).

1998 Classic Greek Theatre of Oregon, Reed College Amphitheater, Portland, Oregon, directed by Keith Scales, starring Scott Coopwood and Susan Johnsson.

1998 *Jocasta* (version of Hélène Cixous, *Le Nom d'Oedipe*), Cornelis Connelly Center for Education, New York, Voice and Vision, directed by Marya Mazor, music by Ruth Schonthal, choreography by Theresa P. Cheung with Mary Magdelena Hernandez, Wilma Wever, and Dawn Akemi Saito as Jocasta and Russel Hornsby and Thomas Meglioranza as Oedipus (Anthony Tommasini, *New York Times*, June 11, 1998; Foley 2004).

*1998 Classic Stage Company, New York, Blue Light Theater Company, new version by Dare Clubb, starring Billy Crudup as Oedipus, Carolyn McCormack as Iocaste, and Frances McDormand as Merope and the Sphinx. A videotape of the production, which won an

Obie Award in 1999, is available at the New York Public Library for the Performing Arts, Lincoln Center (Alisa Solomon, *Village Voice,* October 21–27, 1998; Ben Brantley, *New York Times,* October 12, 1998; Vincent Canby, *New York Times,* October 18, 1998; Jeffrey Donovan, *Newsday,* jeffreydonovanfans.com/filmography/oedipus.html; Tamsen Wolff, *Theatre Journal* 51.3 [1999]: 333–34; Jonathan Kalb, *Theater* 9.2 [1999]: 138–39; Glenn Loney, nytheatre-wire.com/lont1124.htm#6; and Elyse Sommer, www.curtainup.com/oedipus.html, who summarizes other reviews).

*1999 *Blood Line: The Oedipus/Antigone Story,* a production of *OT* and *Antigone* by Joanna Settle, Division 13 Productions, translation by Nicholas Rudall, starring Anne DeAcetis as Antigone, James Stanley as Oedipus, Mark Ulrich as Creon, and Maggie Doyle as Jocasta, The Viaduct, Chicago (*Chicago Tribune,* March 24, 1999; *Chicago Sun-Times,* March 19 and 24, 1999; www.division13.org/work/bloodline.html and www.division13.org.press/rev_bloodline.html).

1999 Theater Schmeater, Seattle, Washington, Free Classic in the Park.

(2000 City Center, New York, National Theatre of Greece, translated and directed by Vassilis Papavassileiou, starring Grigoris Valtinos as Oedipus and Jenny Gaitanopoulou as Jocasta [Ben Brantley, *New York Times,* October 6, 2000; Donald Lyons, *New York Post,* October 6, 2000; Victor Gluck, *Backstage,* October 13, 2000; Gordon Cox, *Newsday,* October 6, 2000].)

2000 Aquila Productions, translated by Peter Meineck and Paul Woodruff, directed by Robert Richmond, starring Kenn Sabberton as Oedipus and Lisa Carter as Jocasta. Tour included Baylor University, Waco, Texas.

2000 *The Oedipus Trilogy,* Cincinnati Shakespeare Festival, Cincinnati, Ohio (*Cincinnati Enquirer,* April 20, 2000).

(2001 Suzuki Tadashi and the Shizuoka Theatre Company, at Japan Society, New York [*The Drama Review* 47.3 (Fall 2003): 157; Daniel Mendelsohn, *New York Review of Books,* March 28, 2002, p. 37].)

*2001 Hartford Stage Company, Hartford, Connecticut, translation by Dudley Fitts and Robert Fitzgerald, modified by Adrienne Kennedy, directed by Jonathan Wilson, score by René McLean, starring Reg Flowers as Oedipus, Stephanie Berry as Jocasta, Novella Nelson and Jernard Burks as the Chorus, and Lou Ferguson as Tiresias (Chris Rohmann, http://www.aislesay.com/CT-OEDIPUS.html; Alvin Klein, *New York Times,* January 14, 2002; Bruce Weber, *New York Times,* January 30, 2001; Larry Parnass, *Daily Hampshire Gazette,* February 1, 2001; Carolyn Clay, www.bostonphoenix.com/boston/arts/theater/documents/00408547.htm). A videotape of the performance is located at the New York Public Library for the Performing Arts, Lincoln Center.

*2001 *The Oedipus Plays,* Shakespeare Theatre, Washington, D.C., translated by Nicholas Rudall, directed by Michael Kahn, music by Baikida Carroll, choreography by Marlies Yearby, starring Avery Brookes as Oedipus, Michael Genet as Creon, Cynthia Martells as Antigone, Patronia Paley as Jocasta/Eurydice (Paul Harnes, *Variety,* October 8, 2001; *Backstage,* March 28, 2003; J. Wynn Rousuck, *Baltimore Sun,* September 5, 2001; Bob Mondello, *Washington City Paper,* September 13, 2001; Nelson Pressely, *Washington Post,* September 5, 2001, http://mason.gmu.edu/~egero/Resources/PostOedipusReview.html; Derek Gatopoulos, *Washington Times,* September 11, 2003).

2001 Jean Cocteau Repertory Theater, translated by Robert Fagles, directed by Eve Adamson, starring Mark Riner as Oedipus and Elise Stone as Jocasta (D. J. R. Bruckner, *New York Times,* January 27, 2001).

2001 Metropolitan Playhouse, New York, adapted by Alex Rose, directed by Ian Marshall, starring Andrew Stewart-Jones as Oedipus.

2001 *OT* by W. B. Yeats, Daryl Roth Theater, New York, The Actors Studio, New York, directed by Estelle Parsons, starring Al Pacino as Oedipus and Dianne Wiest as Jocasta.

2001 or 2002 Upstart Crow Theater Company, Dairy Center for the Arts, Boulder, Colorado.

*2003–5 *YokastaS* by Saviana Stanescu and Richard Schechner, directed by Schechner, La MaMa, E.T.C., New York, starring Tracey Huffman, Suzi Takamashi, Kilbane Porter, and Rachel Bowditch as the Yokastas (*Village Voice,* March 19, 2003). Revived as *YokastaS Redux* at La MaMa, E.T.C. in 2005, starring Rachel Bowditch, Jennifer Lim, Daphne Gains, and Phyllis Johnson as the Yokastas (Miriam Horn, *New York Times,* February 22, 2005).

2003 The Shotgun Players, Berkeley, California, translated by Nicholas Rudall, directed by Patrick Dooley, starring Clive Worsley as Oedipus and Bella Warda as Jocasta (see www.shotgunplayers.org, with references to reviews).

2003 6th@Penn Theatre, San Diego, translated by Marianne McDonald, directed by George Ye, starring Matt Scott as Oedipus and Cristina Soria as Jocasta (Jennifer de Poyen, *San Diego Union-Tribune,* October 18, 2003).

*2004 American Repertory Theatre, Cambridge, translated by Stephen Berg and Diskin Clay, directed by Robert Woodruff, music by Evan Ziporyn, starring John Campion as Oedipus and Stephanie Roth-Haberle as Jocasta (Robert Nesti, *Boston Herald,* May 14, 2004; Iris Fanger, *Patriot Ledger,* May 21, 2004; Louise Kennedy, *Boston Globe,* May 9, 2004; Bill Marx, May 27, 2004, www.publicbroadcasting.net/wbur/arts.artsmain?action = viewArticle&id = 637903&ptd = 30&sid = 13; David Foucher, *Edgeboston,* May 22, 2004, www.edgeboston.com/index.php?ch = entertainment&sc = theatre&sc2 = reviews &sc3 = &id = 1179; Sally Cragin, www.bostonphoenix.com/boston/events/theater/documents/03820854.asp; *ART News* 2.4 [April 2004], www.amrep.org/oedipus/index.html #links).

*2004 *Oedipus Complex,* by Frank Galati, first directed by Galati at the Oregon Shakespeare Festival, starring William Langan as Freud, Jonathan Haugen as Oedipus, and Judith Marie Bergan as Jocasta, and then at the Goodman Theatre, Chicago, spring 2007, starring Nick Sandys as Freud, Ben Viccellio as Oedipus, Susan Hart as Jocasta, and Jeffrey Baumgartner as Tiresias (Bob Hicks, *Sunday Oregonian,* August 8, 2004 (bobhicks@news.oregonian.com); Richard Connema, www.talkinbroadway.com/regional/sanfran/s530,html; Jeff Barnard, *Associated Press,* September 14, 2004 (www.osfashland.org). For Chicago reviews, see Steve Oxman, www.variety.com; Don Hall, http://blogcritics.org/archives/2007/05/09/165803.php; Joe Stead, www.steadstylechicago.com/oedipuscomplex.htm; Jennifer Berg, http://htm.centerstage.net/theatre/articles/oedipus.html; Albert Williams, http://www.chicagoreader.com; Berson 2004).

2004 *Oedipus Text* (version of Hélène Cixous, *Le Nom d'Oedipe*), City Garage, Los Angeles, directed by Frédérique Micel, Simon Bursynski, and Maureen Byrnes.

2004 Gorilla Theatre Productions, Kansas City, Missouri.

*2005 Guthrie Theater, Minneapolis, adapted by Ellen McLaughlin (McLaughlin 2005), directed by Lisa Peterson, starring Isabell Monk O'Connor as Jocasta and Peter Macon as Oedipus (Rohan Preston, *Minneapolis Star Tribune*, January 23 and 30, 2005; Peter Ritter, www.variety.com/review/VE1117926012?categoryid+33&cs = 1; Michelle Pett, www.talkinbroadway.com/regional/minn/minn106.html, www.guthrietheater.org).

*2005 Denver Center Theater Company, directed by Anthony Powell, with masks and music by Gary Grundel, starring Bill Christ as Oedipus and Annette Heide as Jocasta (John Moore, *Denver Post*, September 26, 2004, and February 19, 2005; Juliet Wittman, *Denver Westward*, February 10, 2005; Lisa Bornstein, *Rocky Mountain News*, January 31 and February 18, 2005).

2005 Rising Phoenix Theatre, Middletown, Ohio, directed by Christine Brunner, music by Jay Brunner, starring Martin Andrews as Oedipus and Lauren Skirbunt as Jocasta (Terry Morris, *Dayton Daily News*, March 10, 2005).

2005 Leland and Gray Players, Brattleboro, Vermont, translated by Robert Fagles, directed by Ann Landenberger, starring Gordon Landenberger as Oedipus and Farrin Sofield as Jocasta (*Brattleboro Reformer*, January 27, 2005).

*2005 *Oedipus at Palm Springs* by The Five Lesbian Brothers (Babs Davy as Joni [Tiresias], Peg Healey as Terri, Lisa Kron as Con, Maureen Angelos as Fran, and Dominique Dibbell as Prin), directed by Leigh Silverman, New York Theater Workshop, New York (Charles Isherwood, *New York Times*, August 5, 2005; Charles McNulty, *Village Voice*, August 9, 2005; Hilton Als, *New Yorker*, August 22, 2005; Miriam Felton-Dansky, www.curtainup.com/oedipuspalmsprings.html; Dan Bacalzo, www.theatermania.com/content/news.cfm/story/6459; Christopher Byrne, gaycitynews.com/gcn_432/dumbstruckandstruck.html; Gerard Robinson, www.newyorkblade.com/2005/8-5/arts/theater/nudity.cfm; Cheryl B., theblist.blogspot.com/2005/08/must-see-five-lesbian-brothers-in.html; Matthew Murray, www.talkinbroadway.com/ob/08_03_05.html; Mark Blankenship, www.variety.com/VE1117927829?categoryid = 33&cs = 1; Jeremy McCarter, *New York Magazine*, newyorkmetro.com/nymetro/arts/theater/reviews/12370/; Charlotte Stoudt, *Village Voice*, August 2, 2005; Dolan 2006; http://feministspectator.blogspot.com/2005_08_01_feministspectator_archive.html, pp. 2 and 7).

2006 *OT* by W. B. Yeats, Pittsburgh Public Theater, Pittsburgh, Pennsylvania, directed by Ted Pappas, starring Jay Stratton as Oedipus and Helena Ruoti as Jocasta.

*2006 *The Ballad of Eddie and Jo* by David Sard, directed by Lorca Press, Hudson Guild Theatre, New York, starring Angelo Rosso as Eddie and Ana Mercedes Torres as Jo (Kessa de Santis, www.eljnyc.com/Offbwy.html and www.eljallartsannex.com//The%20Ballad%20of%20Eddie%20and%20Jo.htm; Martin Denton, September 14, 2006, www.theatre.com/nytheatre/archshow.php?key = 402).

*2006 *Wrecks* by Neil LaBute (LaBute 2007), Public Theater, New York, starring Ed Harris. First staged in 2005 at the Everyman Palace Theatre in Cork, Ireland (Ben Brantley, *New York Times*, October 11, 2006; Eric Grode, *New York Sun*, October 11, 2006; Boris Kachka, *New York Magazine*, October 9, 2006; John Lahr, *New Yorker*, October 23, 2006; Linda Winer, *Newsday*, October 11, 2006; Michael Feingold, *Village Voice*, October 23, 2006; Jacques le Sourd, *Journal News*, October 13, 2006; Michael Kuchwara, *Pioneer Times Journal*, October 2006; Elyse Sommer, www.curtainup.com/wrecks

.html; Matthew Murray, www.talkinbroadway.com/ob/10_10_06.html; Malcolm Johnson, www.ctnow.com; Barbara and Scott Siegel, www.theatermania.com/content/news.ofm/story/9200; John Simon, quote.bloomberg.com/apps/news?pld=20601093&sid=al_lapPqzui&refer=spend; Leonard Jacobs, www.backstage.com; Robert Simonson, www.playbill.com/news/article/102421/html; Andy Probst, www.americantheaterweb.com/news/ind.asp?id=144657; Christopher Byrne, *Gay City News*, October 26, 2006; William Wolf, www.wolfentertainmentguide.com/pub/theater.asp; Margo Channing, http://margochanning.broadwayworld.com/wrecks.htm; David Toussaint, www.edgenewyork.com/index.php?ci=&ch=entertainment&sc=theatre&sc2=review&sc3=performance&id=5234; Toby Zinoman, *Philadelphia Inquirer*, October 11, 2006; Jeffrey Sweet, http://backstage.blogs.com/cues/2006/10/wrecks_and_adap.html; Marilyn Stasio, *Variety*, October 10, 2006).

*2006 *The Darker Face of the Earth* by Rita Dove (Dove 1996), American Theater of Actors, directed by Trezana Beverley for Take Wing and Soar Productions, Inc., starring Michael Chenevery as Augustus and Kittson O'Neill as Amalia (Linda Armstrong, *NY Amsterdam News*, March 19, 2006). Beverley also directed the play at the Crossroads Theater Company, New Brunswick, New Jersey, November 1997 (Alvin Klein, *New York Times*, October 19, 1997); see also the Guthrie Theatre, Minneapolis production in March 2000.

2006 *Oedipus for Kids*, with a book by Kimberly Patterson and Gild Varod, music by Robert J. Saferstein, and directed by Dan Fields (*New York Times*, September 25, 2006).

*2006 *Jocasta* by Philip Freund (Freund 1970), directed by Gregory Stuart, George Washington Masonic National Memorial, starring Paula Alprin as Catherine de la Célianne.

2007 Gene Frankel Theatre, 24 Bond Street, New York, directed by Tom Keener (*Time Out New York*, October 25–31, 2007).

2008 *Oedipus Cycle*, Pearl Theater Company, New York, translated by Peter Constantine, directed by Shepard Sobel, starring Jay Stratton and T. J. Edwards as Oedipus, Jolly Abraham as Jocasta and Antigone, Dominic Cuskern as Tiresias, and John Livingston Rolle as Creon (Rachel Saltz, *New York Times*, November 3, 2008; Garrett Eisler, *Time Out New York*, October 30, 2008; Karl Levett, *Backstage.com*, October 29, 2008; Mark Blankenshop, *Daily Variety Gotham*, October 28, 2008; Jonathan Warman, *New York Blade*, November 14, 2008).

2008 *Oedipus Loves You* by Pan Pan, Performance Space 122, New York, directed by Gavin Quinn, starring Bush Moukarei as Oedipus, Gina Moxley as Jocasta, Aoife Duffin as Antigone, Dylan Tighe as Creon, and Ned Dennehy as Tiresias/Sphinx (Ben Brantley, *New York Times*, May 24, 2008).

2009 Getty Villa, Malibu, California, Troubadour Company, Los Angeles.

*2010 *What She Knew*, written and directed by George Hunka, Manhattan Theater Source, New York, a monologue by Jocasta (Gabriele Schafer) (Rachel Saltz, *New York Times*, December 10, 2010).

2010 *Blind* by Craig Wright, Rattlestick Playwrights Theater, New York, directed by Lucie Tiberghien, starring Seth Numrich as Oedipus and Veanne Cox as Jocasta (Ken Jaworowski, *New York Times*, March 9, 2010).

*Related Reception*

"Oedipus, The Story of Oedipus, in 8 minutes, performed by vegetables," www.Oedipusthemovie.com on youtube.com.

2004 *Small Tragedy* by Craig Lucas, Playwrights Horizons, New York, directed by Mark Wing-Davy, featured characters who are performing *OT*.

2004 *Exits and Entrances* by Athol Fugard, Fountain Theatre, Los Angeles (*Los Angeles Times,* May 28, 2004).

APPENDIX E

# Professional Productions and New Versions of Euripides' *Medea*

*The Archive of Performances of Greek and Roman Drama (www.apgrd.ox.ac.uk/) has fuller cast lists and more information on sources in some cases. These entries are as complete as current information allowed.*

\* *Discussed or mentioned in chapters 1, 2, or 5 of this book*
\*\* *Black Medeas*
\*\*\* *Drag or cross-dressed Medeas*
\*\*\*\* *Mad or abused Medeas*
( ) *Important visiting production*

*1798 *Medea and Jason,* a pantomime, first performed on June 12, 1798, at Boston's Haymarket Theatre.
*1800 *Medea and Jason,* Mount Vernon Gardens, New York, September 17, 1800, starring a Mr. and Mrs. Barrett.
*1801 *Medea and Jason,* New York (Seilhamer (1891) 1968, 3: 358; Odell 2: 97; *Weekly Museum,* May 16, 1801).
*1805 *Medea and Jason,* performed again "in Benefit" on June 21, 1805, New York's Bedlow Street Theatre (Odell 2: 97 and 236).
*(1828 Mme Pasta on tour in Johann Simon Mayr's 1813 opera *Medea in Corinto* [*Yankee and Boston Literary Gazette,* August 6, 1828, 255; August 27, 1828, 275; and 2.3, September 1829, 146–56; *Philadelphia Album and Ladies Literary Portfolio,* September 24, 1831, 310].)
*Early 1840s Performance or reading of Harriette Fanning Read, *Medea* in *Three Dramatic Poems* (Read 1848, actually published in 1847) in Washington, D.C. (book reviews: *Union Magazine of Literature and Art* 2.3 [March 1848]: 143; *Spirit of the Times,* April 14, 1849, 85; November 18, 1848, 468; November 25, 1848, 480; *Christian Register,* Boston, December 25, 1847, 207; *Literary World,* January 22, 1848, 614; *Merchant's Magazine and*

*Commercial Review* 18.3 [March 1848]: 348; *Christian Examiner and Religious Miscellany* 44.2 [March 1848]: 311; and the notice in *Albion*, October 23, 1847, 516).

1850s Fifth Avenue Theatre, New York.

1850s? Undated New York performance of Robert Brough's 1856 contemporary burlesque of Legouvé, *The Best of Mothers, with a Brute of a Husband* (Burkhard 1961, 33 n. 6, reports from archives at Yale).

*1857 Wallack's Lyceum, New York, E. Legouvé's *Medea*, translated and adapted by and starring Matilda Heron (Heron 1857) as Medea and Edward A. Southern as Jason. The play premiered in St. Louis in 1856 (*Missouri Republican*, September 15, 1856). A revival starting September 21, 1857, included two female (rather than the expected male) children, Misses O. and A. Grattan (Odell 6: 535; Brown 1: 491, 494). Heron performed *Medea* at least another seven times in New York, September 21, 1858–July 1, 1876 (Odell 7: 159; Brown 2: 37), including Boston Theatre, May 14, 1857 (American Antiquarian Society, Ephemera Theat 0067); Niblo's Garden, 1859 (Brown 1: 188; Odell 7: 249) and 1863 (Brown 1: 96); Academy of Music, June 29, 1858 (Brown 2: 34), and December 18, 1859 (Odell 7: 159; Brown 2: 37); Bowery Theatre in 1865–66 (Odell 8: 44; Brown 2: 217); Booth's, June 1876 (Brown 3: 119); also at Walnut Street Theatre, Philadelphia, in January 1860; the Worcester, Massachusetts Theatre in March 29, 1860 (American Antiquarian Society, Ephemera Worc Theat 0195); and a premiere in St. Louis in 1856 (*Missouri Republican*, September 15, 1856; *Ballou's Pictorial Drawing-Room Companion*, June 13, 1857, 181; *Spirit of the Times*, October 18, 1856, 432; *New York Times*, February 17, 1857; *New York Herald*, February 17, 1857; *Albion*, February 21, 1857, 92; Odell 6: 535; Winter 1913, 71).

1857 *Medea and My Deary*, burlesque of Heron's *Medea*, Chatham Theatre, New York, starring G. L. Fox as Medea and Miss Hathaway as Jason, March 2, 1857 (Odell 6: 559).

1858–59 Walnut Street Theatre, Philadelphia, adaptation by Oliver C. Wyman, directed by Peter Richings, starring J. M. Davenport as Medea and H. A. Perry as Jason; Davenport again played Medea at this venue in October 1859.

1858–59 Walnut Street Theatre, Philadelphia, Legouvé version in December 1858 and October 1859 (The Philadelphia Theatre Index [1855–2000], Free Library of Philadelphia).

1859 New Metropolitan Theatre (formerly Tripler Hall), O. C. Wyman's version of Legouvé's *Medea* starring a British Miss J. M. Davenport on May 7 or 9, 1858 (Odell 7: 118; Brown 1: 445; *New York Herald*, May 7, 1858; *New York Leader*, May 14, 1859, 5; *Albion*, May 14, 1859, 235).

(1860 Italian Cortesi Company, Niblo's Garden, New York; Mlle. Cortesi performed Pacini's *Medea* in New York on September 27, 1860 [Brown 1: 189; Odell 7: 322].)

1860 Old Bowery Theatre, New York, a version of *Medea* starring Misses Charlotte Crampton and Susan Denin (Odell 8: 237; *New York Herald*, May 22, 1860).

1862 Olympic Theatre, New York, starring Mary Provost (*New York Herald*, June 27, 1862; *New York Times*, June 27, 1862; Odell 7: 418; Brown 1: 511).

1863 Grillparzer's *Medea*, Stadttheatre, New York, starring Frau Becker-Grahn (Odell 7: 587; Leuchs 1966, 56).

1863–64 Chestnut Street Theatre, Philadelphia, in November, and April 13–15 and May 2, 1864, Winter Garden Theatre, New York, Legouvé's *Medea* translated by Matilda Heron, starring the British actress Avonia Jones (Odell 7: 556–57; *Spirit of the Times*, April 23, 1864, 128; *New York Times*, April 13, 1864; *New York Herald*, April 16, 1864; *Albion*, April 23, 1864, 199).

1864 Mary Provost's Theatre, New York (Brown 1: 511).

*(1866 *Medea*, adaptation by Ernest Legouvé, Théâtre Français, New York, directed by Jacob Grau, starring Adelaide Ristori as Medea [*World*, September 12, 1866; *New York Times*, September 12, 1866; *New York Herald*, September 21, 1866; Odell 8: 345; Brown 2: 57]. After another performance in Brooklyn, Ristori traveled 18,000 miles across country to thirty cities with 170 performances. Four tours followed; see 1875, Lyceum, New York; 1884, Chestnut Street Opera House, Philadelphia. On her cross-country tour, see Giorcelli 1992 and Brandes 1945, 73–82.)

1867 Broadway Theatre, New York, June 26–27; Julia Dean Hayne played a version of *Medea* (Brown 1: 517; *New York Times*, July 26, 1867; *New York Herald*, July 26, 1867).

*1867 Academy of Music, New York; Chestnut Street Theatre, Philadelphia; Academy of Music, Philadelphia (1868) as part of an extensive tour (Burkhard 1961, 22) for the adaptation by Franz Grillparzer, starring Francesca Janauschek as Medea; repeat performances in New York in 1868, 1869, and 1871; in 1873 and 1874 at the Walnut Street Theater in Philadelphia; in 1874 and 1881 at Booth's Theatre, New York; in 1877, 1879, and 1884 at New York's Thalia Theatre; in 1877, 1878, and 1881 at the Walnut Street Theatre in Philadelphia; and in 1886, Chestnut Street Opera House, Philadelphia (Odell 11: 76 and 12: 271; Burkhard 1961; Leuchs 1966; and Brandes 1945, 83–94).

1868 Banvard's Opera House, New York, Mrs. E. V. Proudfoot starred in a *Medea* on February 12 (Odell 8: 319; *New York Times*, February 13, 1868).

1872 Lyceum, New York, a "Yankee" (American) Miss Bateman starred in a version of Legouvé (*Every Saturday: A Journal of Choice Reading*, August 24, 1872, 215).

1877 Broadway Theatre, New York; Mrs. J. H. Hackett starred in a version of *Medea*.

*1879, 1880, and 1884 Thalia, New York, Magda Irschik in Grillparzer's *Medea*, and in 1884 at the Germantown Theater Guild, Philadelphia (Burkhard 1961; Leuchs 1966; and Brandes 1945, 83–94).

1897 Yiddish version of Grillparzer by Gordin, located during the reign of Antiochus IV, responding to Jewish oppression in New York (Mimoso-Ruiz 1978, 125).

1909 Bryn Mawr Club of Boston performance of Euripides' *Medea* in Boston, New York, and Philadelphia, directed by George Riddle with Anne S. T. Howe as Medea and Donal M. Payson as Jason (Hains 1910).

*1914 Chicago Little Theatre, Fine Arts Building, Chicago, Illinois, translated by Gilbert Murray, directed by Maurice Browne, starring Ellen van Volkenburg as Medea, Ernest Rowan as Jason, and Vera White as the Nurse (*Theater Arts Magazine* 1.3 [May 1920]: 403). Performed in the Arts and Crafts Theater in Michigan in 1917 (*Detroit Sunday News*, November 25, 1917; Hartigan 1995, 23).

1915 The touring theatrical group production by Mitchell and Peters' Art Drama Players, August 2, 1915 (Johnson 1971, 19–20, 49, 242).

*1915 Hearst Greek Theatre, University of California, Berkeley, translated by Gilbert Murray, directed by and starring Margaret Anglin, music by Walter Damrosch, set by Livingston

Platt, with W. Lawson Butt as Jason (*San Francisco Call*, August 23, 1915; *Christian Science Monitor*, August 28, 1915; *Theatre* 22.175 [September 1915]: 116; LeVay 1989; Johnson 1971).

1915 Legouvé *Medea*, Art Drama Players at New York University and the People's Theatre in the Bowery, directed by Ada Dow Currier, starring Mme Agathe Barcescu and Thomas Mitchell (New York Times, August 4, 1915).

*1918 Carnegie Hall, New York, translated by Gilbert Murray, music by Walter Damrosch, starring Margaret Anglin as Medea and Fred Eric as Jason (*New York Daily Mirror*, May 127, 1920; Arthur Hornblow, *Theatre Magazine* 28 [April 1918]: 217; *New York Times*, February 21, 1918; *Nation* 106, February 28, 1918, 244; *New York Tribune*, February 21, 1918; *Brooklyn Eagle*, February 21, 1918; LeVay 1989, 186–87; Hartigan 1995, 26–27, 49–50, 90–92).

1919 Actor's Fidelity League, Century Theatre, New York, a version by Thomas Broadhurst.

*1920 Garrick Theatre, New York, translated by Gilbert Murray, Chicago Little Theatre, directed by Maurice Browne, starring Ellen van Volkenburg as Medea and Maroni Olsen as Jason (J. Ranken Towse, *New York Evening Post*, March 23, 1920; *New York World*, March 23, 1920; *New York Evening Sun*, March 23, 1920; Arthur Hornblower, *Theatre Magazine* May 20, 1920, 403; Ludwig Lewisohn, *Nation* April 17, 1920, 525–26; Oliver Sayler, *New Republic*, May 12, 1920, 355; *World*, March 23, 1920; *New York Sun-Herald*, March 23, 1920; *New York Evening Mail*, March 23, 1920; Patterson James, *Billboard*, April 4, 1920; Agnes Smith, *New York Morning Telegraph*, March 23, 1920; *Dramatic Mirror*, March 27, 1920, 576; *Spectator*, April 14, 1920; Alexander Woollcott, *New York Times*, March 23, 1920; Kenneth Macgowan, *Globe*, March 3, 1920; G. W. Firkins, *Review*, April 3, 1920; Hartigan 1995, 50–51; Arnott 1987, 358).

*1927 Bennett School of Liberal and Applied Arts, Millbrook, New York, directed by Charles Rann Kennedy and Edith Wynne Hamilton, music by Horace Middleton, choreography by Margaret Gage.

*1933 California Club Players, San Francisco, new version by Henry Bertram Lister, directed by and starring Lydia Warren Lister with Mr. Alton Wood as Jason, published in 1936 by the La Bohème Club, San Francisco.

**1935 Adaptation by Countee Cullen, published 1935. A New York performance starring Rose McClendon planned for 1936 was cancelled because of the actress's death. First produced in March 1940 at Atlanta University, directed by Owen Dodson, starring Dorothy Ateca. Over the course of productions in 1959 and 1963 at Washington's Howard University and the Harlem School of the Arts in 1971, the play became Dodson's own (unpublished) *Medea in Africa* (Hatch and Abdullah 1977, 57; Hatch 1993, 61, 81–82, 96, 122, 310).

*1935 Bennett School of Applied Arts, Millbrook, New York, directed by Charles Rann Kennedy and Edith Wynne Hamilton, music by Horace Middleton, choreography by Margaret Gage (*New York Times*, May 9, 1935).

*1936 *The Wingless Victory* by Maxwell Anderson (Anderson 1936), directed by Guthrie McClintic, Empire Theatre, New York, starring Katharine Cornell as Oparre and Walter Abel as Nathaniel (Brooks Atkinson, *New York Times*, December 24, 1936; *New York Sun*, January 9, 1937; *New York Times*, January 3, 1937; and other critics cited by Corti 1998).

**1945 *Garden of Time,* 1939 version of *Medea* by Owen Dodson (now published in an electronic edition by Alexander Street Press, 2000), performed at the American Negro Theater in Harlem in March 1945.
*1946 *Cave of the Heart,* choreographed by and starring Martha Graham with Erick Hawkins as Jason, music by Samuel Barber, set by Isamu Noguchi, Columbia University, New York; 1965, 54$^{th}$ Street Theatre, New York; 1982, City Center, New York.
*1947 Adaptation by Robinson Jeffers, McCarter Theater, Princeton; Locust Street Theatre, Philadelphia; and American National Theater, New York, directed by John Gielgud, produced by Robert Whitehead, music by Tibor Serly, starring Judith Anderson as Medea, Florence Reed as the Nurse, and John Gielgud (later Dennis King) as Jason (Brooks Atkinson, *New York Times,* October 21, 1947; William A. Henry, *Time,* April 25, 1994; Hartigan 1995, 51–52 and 55–57; Corti 1998, xix). Production traveled across the country and worldwide. A film adaptation of Robinson Jeffers's adaptation, directed by José Quintero, was made in 1959, now on Ivy Classics Video, Asheville, North Carolina.
*1948 Le Petit Théâtre du Vieux Carré, New Orleans, translated by Frederick Prokosch, directed by Robert Hyde Wilson, starring Mildred Fossier as Medea and Harry Carr as Jason.
*1949 City Center, New York, adaptation by Robinson Jeffers, directed by Guthrie McClintic, starring Judith Anderson as Medea, Henry Brandon as Jason, and Hilda Vaughn as the Nurse. The production traveled to Hanna Theatre in Cleveland and Forrest Theatre in Philadelphia among many other places.
1951 *Medea,* dance-theater version, choreographed by Lester Horton, music by Audree Covington, Dance Theater Company, Ojai Music Festival, Los Angeles, California.
1953 *Medea,* dramatic monologue for contralto (or soprano) and orchestra, composed by Ernst Krenek, using Robinson Jeffers's text, Ojai Music Festival, Los Angeles, California.
1958 City Center, New York, ballet by Birgit Cullberg, based on Robinson Jeffers's *Medea,* music by Herbert Sandburg from piano pieces by Bela Bartok, starring Jacques d'Amboise and Melissa Hayden.
*1956 *Medea at Kolchis: The Maiden Head* by Robert Duncan (R. Duncan 1965), Black Mountain College, North Carolina (see further Corti 1998, 183–84).
**1959 *Medea in Africa,* new version of the adaptation of *Medea* by Countee Cullen, directed by Owen Dodsen, Howard University, Washington, D.C., 1963, starring Shirley Sadler/ Judith Eason as Medea and Joseph C. D. Mello as Jason.
1960 Staged reading by The Living Theatre, New School for Social Research, New York.
1961 Boston Conservatory of Music, Boston, Massachusetts, chamber opera version by William Van Lennep and composed by Harold Faberman, starring Corinne Curry.
1961 Channel 13, television version starring Eartha Kitt, directed by Louis Freiman.
**1963 *Medea in Africa,* adapted from Medea by Countee Cullen, directed by Owen Dodson at Howard University, starring Shirley Sadler and Judith Eason, with music by William Madden and choreography by Charles Davis (Coe 1963).
(1964 City Center, New York, The Greek Tragedy Theatre, Elsa Vergi and Aspasia Papathananassiou alternated as Medea and A. Xenakis as Jason [Lewis Funke, *New York Times,* September 1, 1964; Edward Southern Hipp, *Newark Daily News,* September 1, 1964; Whitney Bolton, *Morning Telegraph,* September 2, 1964; Arthur Sainer, *Village*

*Voice*, September 10, 1964; Jack Thomson, *New York Journal American*, September 1, 1964; George Oppenheimer, *Newsday*, September 1, 1964; Walter Kerr, *New York Herald Tribune*, September 1, 1964; Richard Watts Jr., *New York Post*, September 1, 1964; Louis Chapin, *Christian Science Monitor*, September 4, 1964].)

*1965 Martinique Theatre, New York, adaptation by Robinson Jeffers, directed by Cyril Simon, starring Gloria Foster as Medea and Michael Higgins as Jason (Howard Taubman, *New York Times*, November 30, 1965; *Village Voice*, December 4, 1965; Arnott 1987, 364).

*1968 *The Golden Fleece*, an adaptation by A. R. Gurney (Gurney 1995), first produced in the Albee-Bart-Wilder Playwrights unit at the Van Daur Theatre, directed by Jered Barclay, and at the Mark Taper Forum in Los Angeles in 1968 and revived frequently since.

**1968 *Medea in Africa* by Jim Magnuson, directed by Mikal Whitaker, New York, East River Players, James Weldon Johnson Theatre Arts, starring Detra Lambert as Medea (A. D. C., *Village Voice*, June 13, 1968; Wetmore 2003, 149–63). Re-performed 1969, Hudson's Guild, New York; and 2001, San Diego Black Ensemble Theater.

1969 Riverside Theatre Workshop, St. John's Episcopal Church, New York, adapted by Richard Ronan, starring Joanna Wilkowski as Medea.

1970 Opera by Alva Henderson based on Robinson Jeffers's *Medea*, San Francisco.

1970 Todd Wehr Theater, Milwaukee, Wisconsin, translated by Philip Vellacott, directed by Tunc Yalman, starring Sirin Devrim as Medea and Alan Zampese as Jason.

1970 Opera composed by Jonathan Elkus, University of Wisconsin Opera Theatre, Milwaukee.

**1970–71 *Deafman Glance*, adapted and directed by Robert Wilson, University Theatre, Iowa City; Brooklyn Academy of Music, New York; 1987, Alice Tully Hall, Lincoln Center, New York, starring Sheryl Sutton (Deborah Jowett, *Village Voice*, March 4, 1971; Arthur Sainer, *Village Voice*, March 4, 1971; Frank Rich, *New York Times*, July 20, 1987; Bill Marvel, *National Observer*, May 3, 1971).

1971 Forest Theatre Guild, Carmel by the Sea, California, staged reading of Robinson Jeffers's *Medea*, directed by Bernald Szold, starring Ruth Warshawsky with Lloyd Jenkins as Jason and Betty Fowlston as the Nurse.

*1972 La MaMa, E.T.C., New York, adapted and directed by Andrei Serban, with music by Elizabeth Swados, starring Priscilla Smith as Medea and Jamil Zakkai as Jason (Clive Barnes, *New York Times*, January 25, 1972; Menta 1995; Arnott 1987, 772–73, Hartigan 1995, 45–46, 52–53). Revived in 1974, 1986, 1999, and 2004.

1973 Circle in the Square, New York, adapted and directed by Minos Volonakis, starring Irene Papas as Medea and John P. Ryan as Jason (Clive Barnes, *New York Times*, January 18, 1973; John Beaufort, *Christian Science Monitor*, January 22, 1973; Kim Friedman, *Variety*, January 24, 1973; Richard Watts, *New York Post*, January 18, 1973; Douglas Watt, *Daily News*, January 18, 1973; Walter Kerr, *New York Times*, January 28, 1973; Martin Gottfried, *Women's Wear Daily*, January 19, 1973; John Simon, *New York*, February 5, 1973; T. E. Kalem, *Time*, January 29, 1973; Brendan Gill, *New Yorker*, January 27, 1973; Hartigan 1995, 53–55).

1973 Players Theatre, New York, adapted from Rex Warner's translation, directed by George Arkas, Greek Art Theatre, starring Yula Gavala as Medea and Joseph Corral as Jason (Margaret Kay, *Villager*, November 8, 1973; Richard Watts, *New York Post*, October 30,

1973; Clive Barnes, *New York Times,* October 30, 1973; Martin Oltarsh, *Show Business,* November 8, 1973; Douglas Watt, *Daily News,* October 31, 1973; *Village Voice,* November 15, 1973; John Simon, *New York,* November 19, 1973; Albert Bermel, *New Leader,* March 5, 1973).

1973 New version, directed by Samy Shmuel, Primitive Theater Company, starring Erk Bjornstad as Medea.

1973 Court Theatre, Chicago.

*1974 La MaMa, E.T.C., New York, *Medea* in *Fragments of a Trilogy,* adapted and directed by Andrei Serban, with music by Elizabeth Swados, starring Priscilla Smith as Medea, Jamil Zakkai as Jason, and Natalie Grey as the Nurse (*New York Times,* November 17, 1974; Hartigan 1995, 45–46, 52). Revived in 1986, 1999, and 2004.

1974 *Medea and Jason,* adapted from Robinson Jeffers's version and directed by Eugenie Leontovich, Little Theater, New York, starring Maria Aho as Medea and Richmond F. Johnson as Jason (David Sterritt, *Christian Science Monitor,* October 7, 1974; Douglass Watt, *Daily News,* October 4, 1974; Martin Gottfried, *New York Post,* October 4, 1974; Clive Barnes, *New York Times,* October 4, 1974).

1975 Dume Spanish Theatre, New York, directed by Herberto Dume, starring Virginia Arrea as Medea and Enrique Gomez as Jason (Edmund Newton, *New York Post,* March 17, 1975).

*1975 Westbeth Playwrights Feminist Collective, New York, adapted by Gloria Albee, directed by Patricia Carmichael. Script available at the New York Public Library for the Performing Arts, Lincoln Center (*Villager,* January 1, 1975). Also produced at Western Washington State College in 1975.

1976 St. Peter's Episcopal Church, New York, directed by Donald Brooks, starring Maria Amsell as Medea and Michael Parrish as Jason (*Show Business,* April 24, 1976).

1976 *Medea,* dance drama, choreographed by Norman Walker, Alvin Theatre, New York, starring Emily Frankel as Medea (*New York Times,* September 29, 1976; *Daily News,* September 29, 1976; *Backstage,* October 15, 1976).

1976 Uris Theatre, New York, American Ballet Theatre, choreographed by John Butler with music by Samuel Barber, starring Carla Fracci and Mikhail Baryshnikov. Also at the Spoleto Festival, Charleston, South Carolina.

*1976 *Black Medea,* adaptation by Ernest J. Ferlita, S. J. Marquette Theatre, Loyola University, New Orleans; 1977, Dock Street Theatre, Charleston, at the Spoleto Festival, U.S.A.; 1978–79, New Federal Theatre, Harry DeJur Playhouse, New York City, directed by Glenda Dickerson; at Loyola again in 1984 and 1987; Actor's Outlet Theatre, New York, twice in 1987 and again in 1990. The New York Public Library for the Performing Arts, Lincoln Center, has a partial tape; New York's Schomberg Center for Research in Black Culture has a copy of the script (Wetmore 2003, 164).

1977 San Francisco, California, ballet choreographed by Michael Smuin, music by Samuel Barber. See further productions below.

1977 Adaptation by Robinson Jeffers, directed by Bruce Caro, Stage 73, New York, starring Anita Lobel as Medea.

*1978 Adaptation by Robinson Jeffers, Daragon Associates, Basketball Court at Manhattan Plaza, New York, directed by Darryl Croxton, starring Minne Gentry as Medea and

Peter Flint as Jason (Mary Sheeran, *Show Business,* July 7, 1978; Townsend Brewster, *New York Amsterdam News,* August 19, 1978).

1979 New England Conservatory, Boston, Massachusetts, opera composed by Ray Edward Luke, libretto by Carveth Osterhaus.

1979 Kent, Ohio, version by Jean-Claude van Italie.

1980 Helen Spencer Auditorium, Kansas City, Missouri, Missouri Repertory Theatre, directed by Erik Vos.

1980 Juilliard School of Music, New York, cantata for soprano and twelve musicians by Ronald Caltabiano.

\*\*\*1980 Club S.N.A.F.U., adapted and played by Ethyl Eichelberger, New York (Duncan Scott McLaren, *Villager,* December 25, 1980; Bethany Haye, *Soho Weekly News,* July 9, 1980; Jeffreys 1996; Parnes 1998).

1980–81 Adaptation by Robinson Jeffers, Denver Center Theatre Company, Colorado.

1980–81 Adaptation by Robinson Jeffers, The Enid Jackson Center for the Performing Arts, Kansas City, Missouri, Missouri Repertory Theatre, starring Juliet Randall as Medea.

1981 Studio Theatre, Washington, D.C.

1982 *Cave of the Heart,* choreographed by Martha Graham, music by Samuel Barber, City Center, New York (see premiere in 1946).

\*1982 Adaptation by Robinson Jeffers, directed by Robert Whitehead, starring Zoe Caldwell as Medea, Judith Anderson as the Nurse, and Mitchell Ryan as Jason, opened at the Clarence Browne Theatre at the University of Tennessee, moved to the Eisenhower Theater at Washington's Kennedy Center in March, then in May to New York's Cort Theatre for sixty-five performances (William A. Henry, *Time Magazine,* April 25, 1994; Walter Kerr, *New York Times,* May 16, 1982; Frank Rich, *New York Times,* May 13, 1982; Sy Syna, *News World,* May 4, 1982; Eileen Blumenthal, *Village Voice,* May 16, 1982; T. E. Kalem, *Time,* May 31, 1982; *Variety,* May 5, 1982; Clive Barnes, *New York Post,* May 31, 1982; Howard Kissel, *Women's Wear Daily,* May 4, 1982; Jack Kroll, *Newsweek,* May 17, 1982; John Beaufort, *Christian Science Monitor,* May 18, 1982; Brendan Gill, *New Yorker,* May 17, 1982; John Simon, *New York,* May 17, 1982; Hartigan 1995, 55–56). WQED television version in 1983, directed by Mark Cullingham at the Kennedy Center, Washington, D.C., by Q. Productions and available from Films for Humanities.

1983 Playhouse in the Park, Cincinnati, Ohio, directed by Amy Saltz.

\*1983 *Kabuki Medea* by William Missouri Downs (Bill Streib) and Lou Anne Wright, directed by Shozo Sato, kabuki ("jikata") music recorded by the National Theatre of Japan mixed with electronic music by Michael Cerri, Hope Alexander Willis as Medea, University of Illinois, Champaign, Illinois; 1984 (revived in 1993), Wisdom Bridge Theater, Chicago, Illinois, starring Barbara Robertson as Medea; 1985, Hanna Theatre in Cleveland; 1985 Kennedy Center in Washington, D.C., starring Barbara Robertson and Dean Fortunato; 2001, Berkeley Repertory Theatre, starring Hope Alexander Willis and David Booth. Video available at the New York Public Library for the Performing Arts, Lincoln Center (Richard Christiansen, *Chicago Tribune,* January 12, 1984 and October 23, 1993; Rick Kogan, *Chicago Sun-Times,* January 11, 1984; Robert Finn, *Cleveland Plain Dealer,* January 6, 1985; Marianne Evett, *Cleveland Plain Dealer,* January 9, 1985; Tony Mastroianni, *Akron Beacon Journal,* January 10, 1985; Jae-Ha Kim, *Chicago Sun-Times,*

October 20, 1993; Steve Winn, *San Francisco Chronicle,* June 12, 1984; David Richards, *Washington Post,* July 15, 1985; Megan Rosenfeld, *Washington Post,* July 8, 1985; Louise Sweeny, *Washington Post,* August 15, 1985; Hartigan 1995, 57). Also performed at the International Theatre Festival, Israel (1987), the Durban Performing Arts Center in South Africa (1994), University of South Dakota (1994), and Memphis State University (1994).

*1983 Public Theater, New York, "Medea" from *Orgasmo Adulto Escapes from the Zoo,* one-act mime by Dario Fo and Francesca Rame, Public Theater, New York, starring Estelle Parsons as Medea.

*1983 *Medea Sacrament,* adaptation by Conrad Bishop and Elizabeth Fuller, starring Elizabeth Fuller, Classic Stage Company, New York, and Theatre Project, Baltimore, Maryland (Alisa Solomon, *Village Voice,* June 21, 1983; Pamela Hunt, *Other Stages,* June 2, 1983, 8; Tish Dace, *Villager,* June 2, 1983, 15).

*1983 *Medea in Sodom,* Theater for a New City (*Village Voice,* January 12, 1993).

1983–84 Adaptation by Robinson Jeffers, Repertory Theatre of St. Louis, Missouri.

*1984 *Medea: A Noh Cycle Based on Greek Myth* by Carol Sorgenfrei (Sorgenfrei 1975), Department of Dramatic Art, directed by Yuriko Doi at San Francisco's Theatre of Yugen/Noh Space; 1975, U.C. Santa Barbara and American College Theatre Festival, Los Angeles, and Kennedy Center for the Arts, Washington, DC.; 1987, University of Denver, directed by Margaret Mancinelli; August 1991, St. Mary's College of Maryland.

** and ****1984 *Medea and the Doll,* adaptation by Rudi Gray, directed by Randy Frazier, Frank Silvera Writers Workshop, Harlem, New York, and Samuel Beckett Theater, New York, starring Maria E. Ellis as Nilda and Morgan Freeman/Juney Smith as Winston (*New York Amsterdam News,* March 3, 1984; Stephen Holden, *New York Times,* October 14, 1984; Sy Syna, *New York Tribune,* October 16, 1984). The two scripts are available at the Schomberg Center for Research in Black Culture in New York; the play was revived by the North Carolina Black Repertory Company in 1996, starring Dan Martin and Ella Joyce (Von H. Washington, *Black Masks,* April 30, 1996, 4).

1985 Directed in ancient Greek by Peter Steadman, New York Greek Drama Company, Triplex II Theater, New York, starring Lavinia Lorch as Medea and Peter Steadman in all the male roles. Video distributed in 1986.

1986 Pan Asian Repertory Company, Susan Bloch Theatre, New York, adapted by Claire Bush and Alkis Papoutis, starring Ching Valdes-Aran as Medea and Ismail Abou-El-Knater as Jason (*New York Times,* February 23, 1986; Alisa Solomon, *Village Voice,* March 11, 1986).

1986 *A Medea, Requiem for a Boy with a White Toy,* written and directed by Reza Abdoh, starring Jessica Peterson as Medea, Eric Marx as Jason, Hollywood Recreation Center, Los Angeles, California. Videotape at the New York Public Library for the Performing Arts, Lincoln Center.

(1986 Toho Company, in Japanese, directed by Yukio Ninagawa, Delacorte Theater, Central Park, New York, Mikijiro Hira as Medea [Jennifer Dunning, *New York Times,* August 31, 1986; Smethurst 2002].)

***1987 Adaptation by Charles Ludlam, Ridiculous Theatre Company, Charles Ludlam Theater, New York, directed by Lawrence Kornfeld, music by Peter Golub, Medea and the Nurse played alternately by Black-Eyed Susan and Everett Quinton. Videotape at the

New York Public Library for the Performing Arts, Lincoln Center (Frank Rich, *New York Times*, November 9, 1987; David Lidov, *Women's Wear Daily*, November 9, 1987; Don Nelson, *Daily News*, November 11, 1987; David Sterritt, *Christian Science Monitor*, January 15, 1988; Allan Wallach, *Newsday*, November 10, 1987; Marilyn Stasio, *New York Post*, November 13, 1987; David Kaufam, *Downtown*, November 18, 1987; Michael Feingold, *Village Voice*, November 17, 1987; Ludlam 1989, 802–13; Corti 1998, 187–89).

1989–90 *Medea Speaks* by Lawrence Addeo and Peter Daito, Quirk Productions, New York, starring Maria Ranaldi.

1990 St. Mark's Church in the Bowery, New York, dance theatre, based on Heiner Müller, *Medeamaterial*, choreographed by Ann Papoulis, Danspace project.

**1990 *Pecong*, new version by Steve Carter (Carter 1993), directed by Dennis Zacek, Victory Gardens Theater, Ruth Page Dance Center, Chicago, starring Celeste Williams as Mediyah and Daniel Oreskes as Jason; 1992, American Theater Festival, Symphony Hall, Newark, New Jersey, starring Tonia Rowe and Earl Whitted; 1993, American Conservatory Theatre, San Francisco, California (Hedy Weiss, *Chicago Sun-Times*, January 1, 1990; Alvin Klein, *New York Times*, April 26, 1992; Steven Winn, *San Francisco Chronicle*, October 22, 1993; Calvin Ahlgren, *San Francisco Chronicle*, October 17, 1993); 2009, Take Wing and Soar productions, National Black Theater in Harlem, directed by Arthur French and Timothy J. Stickney and starring Lorna Houghton (Rachel Saltz, *New York Times*, March 25, 2010).

1990 Pearl Theater Company, New York, translated by E. P. Coleridge, directed by Shephard Sobel, starring Joanne Camp as Medea (Stephen Holden, *New York Times*, February 8, 1990; Katherine Dieckmann, *Village Voice*, February 6, 1990).

*1991 Guthrie Theater, Minneapolis, Minnesota, translated by Philip Vellacott, directed by Garland Wright, starring Brenda Wehle as Medea and Stephen Yoakam as Jason (Tad Simons, *Twin Cities Reader*, June 24, 1992, 20, 22; Mike Steele, *Minneapolis Star Tribune*, January 11 and 14, 1991; Hartigan 1995, 58–59).

1991 Adaptation by Beverly Smith-Dawson, directed by Wendy Knox, Frank Theatre, Minneapolis, Minnesota.

1991 Gorilla Theatre, Kansas City, Missouri.

***1992 New version, directed by Keenan Hollahan, Greek Active, USA, Tugs Bar, Seattle, Washington, starring Mark Mitchell as Medea (Sue-Ellen Case, *Theatre Journal* 45.2 [1993]: 246–49).

**1992 *Women Are Waiting: The Tragedy of Medea Jackson*, adaptation by Eldris Cooper for the Medea Project: Theatre for Incarcerated Women, San Francisco, directed by Rodessa Jones (Fraden 2001, 56–64; Wetmore 2003, 198–202).

1992 Ballet by Michael Smuin, music by Samuel Barber, "Medea Suite," Op. 23, Dance Theater of Harlem, State University of New York Performing Arts Center, Purchase, starring Lisa Attles as Medea, and City Center, New York, starring Leonore Pavlakos. Videotape at New York Public Library for the Performing Arts, Lincoln Center (Jack Anderson, *New York Times*, May 7, 1992; Janice Berman, *Newsday*, March 25, 1993).

***1993 *Medea in Sodom*, by Exavier Wardlow Muhammed, starring Thresher Pace, Theater for the New City, New York (Pamela Penna, *Village Voice*, January 12, 1993).

*1994 *Kokoro* by Velina Hasu Houston (Houston 1997), Theatre of Yugen, San Francisco, directed by Yuriko Doi after a special presentation at Japan Society in New York; 1995, Tina Chen directed the play at New York's 28th Street Theatre; 1998, The Perseverance Theatre Company, Alaska; 1999, Hiroshima University; 2000, Sacramento Theatre Company; 2003, Morgan Wixon-Theatre; 2004, The Actors Workshop (Usui 2000 cites reviews).

1994 *Medea* by Christopher Durang and Wendy Wassterstein (Durang 1995, 195–202), Juilliard School, New York, April 25, 1994, directed by Gerald Gutierrez, choreographed by Christopher Chadman, starring Harriet Harris as Medea and Kevin Spacy as Jason.

(1994 Longacre Theatre, New York, translated by Alistair Elliott, directed by Jonathan Kent, starring Diana Rigg as Medea and Tim Woodward as Jason. Videotape at the New York Public Library for the Performing Arts, Lincoln Center [Vincent Canby, *New York Times*, April 17, 1994; William A. Henry, *Time*, April 25, 1994; Edwin Wilson, *Wall Street Journal*, April 13, 1994; Marianne McDonald, *Didaskalia* 1.3 [1994]; Hartigan 1995, 49, 59].)

(1994 *Medée*, opera by Marc-Antoine Charpentier, directed by Jean-Marie Villégier, Brooklyn Academy of Music, New York. Video at the New York Public Library for the Performing Arts, Lincoln Center).

***1995 *Medea the Musical*, adapted and directed by John Fisher, with choreography by Jan Paik for Sassymouth USA, Lorraine Hansberry Theatre; 1996, Stage Door Theatre, San Francisco, California; 1999, Hudson Mainstage Theater, Hollywood, California; 2000, Arts West Theatre, Seattle, Washington; first performed at University of California Berkeley in 1994 (Robert Hurwitt, *San Francisco Examiner*, July 14, 1995; Steven Winn, *San Francisco Chronicle*, July 21, 1995; *San Jose Morning News*, August 9, 1996; *American Theatre* 13.10 [1996]: 7; Daedalus Howell, *Sonoma Country Independent*, November 19–24, 1998; Sandra Ross, *LA Weekly*, July 16–22, 1999; Foley 2004, 108–10).

1995 Walnut Street Theatre, Philadelphia, Pennsylvania, directed for Red Heel Theatre by Jacqueline Yancey, starring Elizabeth H. Piccio as Medea and Amani Gethers as Jason (*Philadelphia Inquirer*, May 23, 1995).

***1995 Planet Earth Multi-Cultural Theatre, Phoenix, Arizona, Arawak *Medea*, directed by Peter James Cirino, starring Mollie Kellogg Cirino as Medea and David Akin as Jason (www.phoenixnewtimes.com/issues/1995-04-20/stages.html).

**1995 *American Medea*, adaptation by Silas Jones, workshop production at the Mark Taper Forum, Los Angeles; 1996, workshop production at the Arena Stage Theatre, Washington, D.C.; 2002, Northwest Asian-American Theatre, Seattle Washington (Wetmore 2003, 187–98).

1996 Theater Schmeater, Seattle, Washington (Joe Adcock, *Seattle Post-Intelligencer*, May 29, 1996).

1997 *Cave of the Heart*, choreographed by Martha Graham, music by Samuel Barber, Fairbanks, Alaska.

1997 *Medeamaterial*, adaptation by Heiner Müller, translated by Mark von Henning, directed by Stephan Suschke, Castillo Theater, New York.

*1997 *La Malinche by* Carlos Morton, directed by Abel Lopez at the Arizona Theatre Company, Center Stage at Herberger Theatre Center in Phoenix, Arizona, starring Dawnnie

Mercado as La Malinche and Christopher Michael Bauer as Cortés (Robert L. Pela, *Phoenix New Times,* February 13, 1997, www.phoenixnewtimes.com/issues/1997-02-13/stages.html).

**1997–98 Ensemble Theatre of Cincinnati, Ohio, adapted and directed by Michael Blankenship, Deborah Brock-Blanks as Medea, with a white Southern Jason, Jeff Roper (Jerry Stern, *Cincinnati Post,* January 8, 1998, http://www.cincypost.com/living/1998/medea010898.html).

(1998 City Center, New York, National Theatre of Greece, translation by Giorgos Chaeimonas, directed by Niketi Kontouri, music by Savina Gianattou, starring Karofyllia Karabeti [Peter Marks, *New York Times,* September 25, 1998; Michael Sommers, *Star Ledger,* September 25, 1998; Jan Stuart, *Newsday,* September 26, 1998; Glenda Frank, *Backstage,* October 9, 1998; Clive Barnes, *New York Post,* September 25, 1998].)

***1998 Adaptation by Jennifer Spahr with a male Medea, Expanded Arts, New York, 85 Ludlow Street (Randy Gener, www.nytheatre-wire.com/gene925b.htm).

**1998 Woodruff Arts Center, Alliance Theatre Company, Atlanta, Georgia, directed by Kenny Leon, starring Phylicia Rashad as Medea and Curt Hotstetter as Jason (Wetmore 2003, 145–49; Dan Hulbert, *Atlanta Journal and Constitution,* May 6 14, 1998).

*1999 *Medea* (*Fragments of a Trilogy*), adapted and directed by Andrei Serban, with music by Elizabeth Swados, La Mama, E.T.C., New York. See 1972 and 1974; revived again in 2004.

****1999 *Medea Redux* (*Bash*), version by Neil LaBute (LaBute 1999), directed by Joe Mantello, Douglas Fairbanks Theater, New York, starring Callista Flockhart.

***1999 *Medea,* adapted from Charles Ludlam by Ryan Landry, Gold Dust Orphans, Dollhouse Theatre, Boston (*Boston Herald,* October 14, 1999).

1999 *Not Medea* by Yuriy Tarnawsky, directed for Mabou Mines/Suite by Gregory Hlady, starring Tania Mara Miller, 122 Community Center, Toronada Theater, New York (www.ukrweekly.com/Archive/1998/229823.shtml).

1999 Moonwater Theatre Company, University Drive Theatre, Dallas, Texas, starring Deborah Kirby as Medea and Chuck Huber as Jason (*Dallas Observer,* February 4, 1999, www.dallasobserver.com/issues/1999-02-04/stage.html)

**1999–2000 *Marie Christine, A New Musical,* adaptation by Michael John LaChiusa, directed by Graciela Daniele, Vivian Beaumont Theater, Lincoln Center, New York, starring Audra McDonald as Marie Christine and Anthony Crivello as Dante; lighting by Jules Fisher and Peggy Eisenhauer; set by Christopher Barreca (David Johnson, http://www.findarticles.com/p/articles/mi_mOCVQ/is_334/ai_60058651; Michael Feingold, *Village Voice,* December 8–14, 1999; Charles Isherwood December 3, 1999, http://www.variety.com/review/VE1117907426.html?categoryid = 31&cs = 1; Terry Teachout, *New York Times,* January 2, 2000; John Simon, nymag.com/nymetro/arts/theater/reviews/1652; David Finkle, http://bmi.com/musicworld/features/199912/mjlachiusa.asp; Elyse Sommer, http://curtainup.com/mariechristine.html; Ben Brantley, *New York Times,* December 3, 1999; Russell Bouthiller, www.broadwaybeat.com/russell/rumarie.htm; Jonathan Frank, www.talkinbroadway.com/cabaret/lachiusa.html; Barry Singer, *New York Times,* August 31, 1997; Robin Pogrebin, *New York Times,* November 5, 1999; Russell Bouthiller, www.broadwaybeat.com/russell/rosmarie.htm).

***2000 *All about Medea* (play within a play about a drag performance of *Medea*), Re-bar, Seattle, Washington, directed by Ilya Perlman, written by Mark Mitchell (www.thestranger.com/2000-07-13/theater_listings.html).

2000 Jean Cocteau Repertory, New York, translated by Philip Vellacott, directed by Eve Adamson, starring Elise Stone as Medea and Jolie Garrett as Jason (Wilborn Hampton, *New York Times,* May 24, 2000; Irene Backalenick, *Backstage,* April 21, 2000, 64).

(2000 New York Fringe Festival, August, *Die Ungarische Medeia,* adapted by Apad Gantz, Westentache Theater Company of Ulm, Germany, directed by Thomas Dentler.)

2000 Solo dance-drama by Celeste Miller, La MaMa, E.T.C., New York; Women in Theatre Conference, Washington, D.C.; 2002, Washington, D.C. (Sarah Kaufman, *Washington Post,* January 14, 2002).

*2000 *The Hungry Woman: A Mexican Medea by* Chérríe Moraga, the Border Festival, Magic Theater of San Francisco, directed by Chérríe Moraga; staged readings by Tony Kelly, Berkeley Repertory Company and at the Mark Taper Forum's New Works Festival in Los Angeles in 1995 among others. There have been several productions on college campuses since: Stanford University, 2002, directed by Chérríe Moraga and Adelina Anthony; Brown University, April 2006, directed by Patricia Ybarra; University of Massachusetts, Amherst, May 2008; Stanford University, May 15, 2005 (see Nicole Eschen, *Theatre Journal* 58.1 [March 2006]: 103–6; Straile-Costa 2010).

2000 *Medea in Exile* by Douglas Anderson, American Chamber Opera Theatre, New York.

2000 Sacramento Ballet, Community Center Theater, dance version created by Ron Cunningham, starring Kirsten Bloom.

2000 *Medeamaterial* by Heiner Müller, City Garage, Los Angeles, directed by Frédérique Michel.

2000 Philadelphia Fringe Festival, The Theater Cooperative, starring Lili Beta.

Ca. 2000? Medea, directed by Frank Silvestra, Theatre of Being, Los Angeles, starring Beah Richards as Medea (no date in Wetmore 2003, 147 or in S. Pearl, *Black Masks* 14, March 31, 2001).

2001 *Love, Medea,* adapted from Euripides and Seneca, directed by Charles Schick, starring Regina Bartkoff, Bullet Space, New York City.

*2001 *Medea Bali,* Green Tea Productions, directed by Kathy Welch, Old Arizona Studio, Minneapolis, Minnesota, with Virginia Haggart as Medea and Brian Stemmler as Jason (Rohan Preston, *Star Tribune,* October 7, 2001; Max Sparber, *Performing Arts,* October 10, 2001).

2001 Seattle Center House, Seattle, Washington, translated by Paul Roche, directed for Next Step Theater group by Rachel Rutherford, composed by John W. Bartley.

2001 Adaptation by Robinson Jeffers, directed by Heidi Helen Davis, Will Geer Theatricum Botanicum, Los Angeles, starring Ellen Geer as Medea (Carl R. Mueller, *Didaskalia* 5.2 [2001]).

2001 *By the Bogs of Cats* (a new Irish version) by Marina Carr, directed by Timothy Near, San Jose Repertory, San Jose, California.

***2001 Here Arts Center, New York, *Klytaemnestra's Unmentionables* (includes a monologue by Medea), script by Rob Grace, directed by Jennifer Wiseman, performed by Bradford Louryk (Foley 2004, 93–98).

2001–2 Pittsburgh Public Theater, directed by Ted Pappas, starring Lisa Harrow.

\*\*\*2001–2 *My Deah,* adaptation by John Epperson (Epperson 2007), directed by David Schweizer, Workshop Reading, New York Theatre Workshop, January 2002, starring Betty Buckley as Mydeah; May 2003, Zipper Theater, New York, The Art Party at the Belt Theater and Bar, starring Patty Lupone as Mydeah and T. Scott Cunningham as Gator; performances at the Abingdon Theatre Company, September 2005 and 2006, directed by Mark Waldrop, starring Nancy Opel with Maxwell Caulfield as Gator (Charles Isherwood, *New York Times,* October 25, 2006; Michael Feingold, *Village Voice,* October 31, 2006; Rob Kent, *Newsday,* October 18, 2006; Jerry Talmer, *Villager,* November 1–7, 2006; Adam Feldman, *Time Out New York,* November 2–6, 2006; and Dan Bacalzo, www.theatermania.com/content/news.cfm/story/9308).

\*2002 *The Hungry Woman: A Mexican Medea* by Cherrie Moraga, Northwest Asian-American Theatre, Seattle, Washington.

\*\*\*\*2002 *MedeaMachine* adapted and directed by Ian Belton, The Present Company Theatorium, New York International Fringe Festival (Jonathan Mandell, *New York Times,* August 21, 2002).

\*\*2002 and 2005 Classical Theatre of Harlem, New York, adapted and directed by Alfred Preisser, starring April Yvette Thompson as Medea, Lawrence Winslow as Jason, and Earle Hyman as Creon (D. J. R. Bruckner, *New York Times,* April 16, 2002; David Finkle, *Village Voice,* April 23, 2002; Hilton Als, *New Yorker,* October 3, 2005, 104; Mark Dundas Wood, *Backstage,* May 3, 2002; Neil Genzlinger, *New York Times,* September 27, 2005; *Time Out New York,* September 29, 2005, 187; Linda Armstrong, *NY Amsterdam News,* September 29, 2005; David Rosenberg, *Backstage,* October 20, 2005, 41).

2002 *Bad Women* (including Medea as a character) by Talking Band, written and directed by Sidney Goldfarb and Tina Sheperd, Here Arts Center, New York (Foley 2004).

2002 Theater de la Jeune Lune, Minneapolis, Minnesota, directed by Steven Epp, Barbra Berlovitz as Medea (Rohan Preston, *Star Tribune,* March 5, 2002).

2002 Vortex Repertory Company, Austin, Texas, Liz Lochhead's translation, directed by Lorelia Loftus, with four Medeas/chorus: Paula Gilbert, Wendy Goodwin, Betsy McCann, Regina Yonker (www.austinchronicle.com/issues/dispatch/2002–11–29/arts_exhibitionism2.html).

2002 *Medea/Macbeth/Cinderella,* adapted and directed by Bill Rauch and Tracy Young, music by Shishir Kurup, choregraphy by Sabrina Peck, and Caroline Stephanie Clay as Medea and Jennifer Griffin as Jason, Yale Repertory Theatre, New Haven, Connecticut. Videotape at the New York Public Library for the Performing Arts, Lincoln Center (*Yale Bulletin & Calendar* 31.2, 9/13/2002, www.rnh.com/news/triple.html, yaledailynews.com/article.asp?AID = 19865).

2002 Adaptation by Robinson Jeffers, The Shotgun Players, Berkeley, California, directed by Russell Blackwood, starring Beth Donohue as Medea and Jason Frazier as Jason (Ben Barron, www.dailycal.org/article.php?id = 8661; Lisa Drostova, *East Bay Express,* May 15, 2002, www.eastbayexpress.com/issues/2002–05–15/theater2.html/1/index.html; Michael Scott Moore, www.sfweekly.com/issues/2002–05–08/stage.html).

2002 Adaptation by Robinson Jeffers, Culver City Public Theatre, California, directed by Kenneth Macfarlane, starring Andrea Westby as Medea and James Lunsford as Jason.

2002 *Medea Noir* by Arthur Meiselman, Talos Ensemble, an American traveling company, a multimedia production first commissioned for Ancient Theater Alive Festival in Greece, starring Lia Beachy (www.talosensemble.com/html/medeanoir.html).
(2002 Brooklyn Academy of Music, New York, translation by Kenneth McLeish and Fredric Raphael, National Theater of Ireland, directed by Deborah Warner, starring Fiona Shaw as Medea and Jonathan Cake as Jason; part of a cross-country tour.)
2003 Adaptation by Robinson Jeffers, Tor House, Pacific Repertory Theatre, Carmel by the Sea, California.
2003 The Warehouse Theatre, Greenville, South Carolina, The Mythmakers.
**2003 Ghetto Ghost Girl Productions from Jersey City, National Black Theater Festival, August 2003, Winston Salem, N.C. (*New York Times,* August 8, 2003).
2003 *The Medea Monologue,* adaptation by Laylage Courie, Access Theater, New York.
2003 Translated by Kenneth McLeish and Frederic Raphael, directed by Sharon Lee Glassman, music by Steve Reisteter, Civic Theatre, Allentown, Pennsylvania.
2003 Classic Greek Theatre of Oregon, adapted and directed by Keith Scales, Reed College, Portland, Oregon, and Portland State University, music by Rebecca Becker, starring Quigley Provost-Landrum as Medea and Jason Connell as Jason.
** and ***2003 *Medea, Queen of Colchester,* adaptation by Marianne McDonald, directed by Kirsten Brandt and David Tierney, Sledgehammer Theater, St. Cecilia's Playhouse, San Diego, starring George Alphone Walker as Medea and Robert MacAulay as James Elliot (Tiffany Lee-Youngren, *San Diego Union Tribune,* August 21, 2003).
2003–4 *Greek Shards: Medea,* Thunder River Theatre Company, Roaring Fork Valley, Colorado, directed and designed by Lon Winston, starring Valerie Haugen, Richard Lyon, Kelley Mauldin, Michael Miller, and Linda White.
*2004 *wAve,* new version by Sung Rno (Rno 2011), directed by Will Pomerantz, Ma-Yi Theater Company, The Ohio Theatre, New York, starring Michi Barall as M and Ron Domingo as Jason (Margo Jefferson, *New York Times,* March 23, 2004; Helen Shaw, *New York Sun,* March 23, 2004; David Ng, *Village Voice,* March 24–30, 2004; Alexis Soloski, *Time Out New York,* March 25–April 1, 2004; Martin Denton, www.newtheatre.com/ny theatre/archweb/arch2004_w.htm; Les Gutman, www.curtainup.com/wave.html; Nizhen Hsieh, www.tribes.org/cgi-bin/form.pl?karticle=385). Originally commissioned by Center Theater Group/Mark Taper Forum, *wAve* received readings at Northwest Asian-American Theatre, Seattle, Washington (the artistic director Chay Yew proposed the project to the Mark Taper Forum) and staged readings at Mark Taper Forum, Ma-Yi Theater, New Work Now! at the Public Theater, Arena Stage, Asian American Theater Company, and Fluid Motion Theatre at the Public Theatre, directed by Christine Simpson.
2004 Adaptation by Robinson Jeffers, directed by Jim Lawer, Teen Theatre, Ferndale Repertory Theatre, Ferndale, California.
**2004 *M'Dear,* The Venue @ St. James, 409 West 141$^{st}$ Street, New York, written and directed by Ron Beverly, music by Ron Beverly and Christophe Pierre; M'Dear is a singer, and JaShaun is in the music business (Linda Armstrong, *NY Amsterdam News,* July 22–28, 2004).
2004 Tampa Bay Performance Center, Shimberg Playhouse, Tampa, Florida, translated by Kenneth McCleish and Frederic Raphael, Stageworks Theatre Company, directed by

Anna Brennan, starring Dawn Truax as Medea and Eric Davis as Jason (Mark E. Leib, *weekly planet* 17.4, April 21–27, 2004; Marty Clear, *St. Petersburg Times*, April 22, 2004; Joanne Milani, *Tampa Tribune*, April 20, 2004).

*2004 *Medea in Jerusalem,* adapted by Roger Kirby, directed by Steven Little, Rattlestick Theater, New York, starring Rebecca Wisocky as Medea and Sean Haberle as Jason (D. J. R. Bruckner, *New York Times*, August 11, 2004; Adam Feldman, *Time Out New York*, August 19–26, 2004, 137; Helen Shaw, *New York Sun*, August 13, 2004; Frank Scheck, *New York Post*, August 10, 2004; Celia McGee, *Daily News*, August 10, 2004; Charles McNulty, *Village Voice*, August 11, 2004; Irene Backalenick, *Backstage*, September 10, 2004).

2004 Theatre Works, New Milford, Connecticut.

2004 Staten Island, New York, Midland Beach, Theater San Greal, directed by Bill Conte as part of a "City Dionysia" (including *Prometheus Bound* and *Antigone*), starring Marie Abbatiello as Medea and Mike Baver as Jason.

2005 Jean Cocteau Repertory, Bouwerie Lane Theatre, New York, translated and adapted by Joseph Goodrich, directed by Ernest Jones, starring Ramona Floyd as Medea and Pascal Beauboeuf as Jason (Jason Zinoman, *New York Times*, November 2, 2005).

****2005 Washington Shakespeare Company, translation by Alistair Elliot, directed by Jose Carrasquillo and Paul MacWhorter, starring Delia Taylor as a pathological Medea (Jayne Blanchard, *Washington Post*, June 13, 2005).

2005 *Medead* (*Medea in Corinth* and *Medea on the Argo*) by Fiona Templeton, Mabou Mines Suite, 9$^{th}$ Street, New York, starring Clarinda Maclow.

2005 New version based on Euripides and Seneca, Club at La MaMa, E.T.C., New York, adapted and directed by Jay Scheib, music by Margaret Kammerer, Actors Without Borders, starring Zishan Ugurlu and Dan Illian as Jason (Jason Zinoman, *New York Times*, January 20, 2005; Helen Shaw, *New York Sun*, January 17, 2005; Jordy Yager, *Show Business*, February 2, 2005, 12; Adam Feldman, *Time Out New York*, January 27, 2005, 139; Campbell 2010).

**2005 Boston Court, Pasadena, California, translated by Paul Roche, directed by Stefan Novinski, Lisa Tharps as Medea and Andrew Borba as Jason (Kathleen Foley, *Los Angles Times*, February 25, 2005; Amy Nicholson, *Pasadena Star News*, February 25, 2005; Arian Mufson, *A Curtain Up* Los Angeles review, February 26, 2005; Terry Morgan, *Backstage*, February 23, 2005; Tom Sime, *Dallas Morning News*, March 16, 2005; all quoted at www.aldrichpr.com/MedeaReviews.htm).

2005 *Purgatorio* by Ariel Dorfman, Seattle Repertory Theatre, Seattle, Washington, directed by David Esbjornson, starring Charlayne Woodard and Dan Snook as Medea and Jason figures (Brendan Kiley, *Stranger*, November 10, 2005, 29).

2006 The Looking Glass Theatre, New York, directed by Candace O'Neil Cihocki, starring April Grace Lowe as Medea and Dain Geist as Jason.

2007 Producer's Club Theatre, New York, directed by Hilary Krishan.

2007 Nebunele Theater, Seattle, Washington, advised by Ruby Blundell.

2007 *Medea* by Eddie Kim, Here Arts Theatre, New York.

(2007 La MaMa, E.T.C., New York, Company East, choreographed and directed by Kanji Kawarasaki, starring Hiroshi Jin as Medea and Sho Tohno as Jason (Jennifer Dunning, *New York Times*, January 6, 2007.)

*2007 *The House of Chaos* by Velina Hanu Houston, directed by Peter Cirino, San Diego Asian American Repertory Theatre, AART, starring Elise Prosser as Mina Takahashi and Tony Perez as Tillman (Michael L. Greenwald, *Union Tribune*, July 16, 2007, www.signonsandiego.com/news/features/20070716-9999-lz1c16chaos.html). The play will reportedly be published in a volume in process, *The Myth Strikes Back: Medea Plays by Women*, edited by Houston and Marianne McDonald.

2008 La MaMa, E.T.C., Theodora Skiptares' puppet *Medea;* Nicky Paraiso operated the Medea puppet (Caryn James, *New York Times*, March 19, 2008; Andy Probst, *Backstage.com*, March 17, 2008; Rayhane S. Sanders, *Show Business*, March 3, 2008).

**2008 National Black Theatre, 2301 Fifth Avenue at 125th Street, New York, musical version, Take Wing and Soar Productions, directed by Petronia Paley and starring Trezana Beverley as Medea and Dathan Williams as Jason (Linda Armstrong, *NY Amsterdam News*, March 6-12, 2008).

(2008 *MedEia* by Dood Paard, P.S. 122, New York, starring Kuno Bakker, Manja Topper, and Oscar van Woensel [Tom Sellar, *Village Voice*, October 10, 2007; Caryn James, *New York Times*, March 19, 2008; Andy Probst, *Backstage.com*, March 17, 2008].)

*2009 UCLA's Freud Playhouse, translated by Kenneth McLeish and Frederic Raphael, directed by Lenka Udovicki, starring Annette Bening as Medea and Angus Macfadyen as Jason (Steven Leigh Morris, http://www.laweekly.com/2009-10-01/stage/me-and-my-shadows/).

*2009 *Pious Poetic Pie* by Yubelky Rodriguez, directed by Denyse Owens, Fluid Motion Theatre, Hudson Guild Theatre, New York, starring Athena Colón as Melinda and Darian Dauchan as Jerome.

***2010 Access Theater, New York, adapted and directed by Rubén Polendo for Theater Mitu, starring Justin Nestor as Medea and Aysan Celik as Jason and the Chorus leader, with Nathan Elam as the Nurse, and Nikki Calonge as Creon.

APPENDIX F

# Professional Productions and New Versions of Euripides' *Iphigeneia in Aulis* and *Iphigeneia in Tauris*

*The Archive of Performances of Greek and Roman Drama (www.apgrd.ox.ac.uk/) has fuller cast lists and more information on sources in some cases. These entries are as complete as current information allowed.*

Full listings for productions that combined IA and IT appear under IA.
\* Discussed or mentioned in the epilogue
\*\* Discussed in chapter 1
\*\*\* Productions and new versions emphasizing Iphigeneia's split or doubled psyche, some discussed or mentioned in the epilogue
( ) Important visiting production

*IPHIGENEIA IN AULIS*

\*\*1915 Hearst Greek Theater, Berkeley, California, translation by Robert Potter, directed by and starring Margaret Anglin, Ruth Holt Boucicault as Clytemnestra, Fuller Mellish as Agamemnon, with music by Walter Damrosch (*Munsey's,* July 1915; *Boston Evening Transcript,* August 26, 1915; *San Francisco Call,* September 8, 1915; *New York Times,* August 29, 1915; Walter Anthony, *San Francisco Chronicle,* August 15, 1915; *Christian Science Monitor,* August 28, 1915; LeVay 1989, 168; Johnson 1971, 304).

\*\*1921 Manhattan Opera House, Oratorio Society of New York, directed by Maurice Browne, starring Margaret Anglin as Clytemnestra, Mary Fowler as Iphigenia, and Eugene Powers as Agamemnon, with music by Walter Damrosch (Mr. Hornblow, *Theatre Magazine,* June 1921, 415; *New York Daily Mirror,* April 16, 1921; Alexander Woollcott, *New York Times,* April 9, 1921; Ludwig Lewisohn, *Nation,* April 8, 1921; Hartigan 1995, 67, 90–92).

1951 *Iphigenia,* part of *Beyond the Mountains* by Kenneth Rexroth (1951), The Living Theatre, Cherry Lane Theatre, New York (see chapter 3.2).

1960 New School for Social Research, New York, staged reading by The Living Theatre.

*1967–68 Circle in the Square, New York, translated by Minos Volonakis, directed by Michael Cacoyannis, starring Irene Papas as Clytemnestra (later replaced by Jane White), Jenny Leigh as Iphigenia, and Mitchell Ryan as Agamemnon (Clive Barnes, *New York Times*, November 22, 1967; Sonkowsky, *Arion*, Summer 1968, 309–10; Martin Gottfried, *Women's Wear Daily*, January 22, 1967; Clive Barnes, *New York Times*, April 6, 1968; Walter Kerr, *New York Times*, December 1, 1967; Richard Watts Jr., *New York Post*, November 22, 1967; Michael Smith, *Village Voice*, November 30, 1967; Whitney Bolton, *Morning Telegraph*, November 23, 1967; James Davis, *Daily News*, November 23, 1967; and Daphne Kraft, *Newark Evening News*, November 22, 1967; Hartigan 1995, 92–93).

(1968 Felt Forum, Madison Square Garden, the Dallas Theater Center, New York, Piraikon Theatre, directed by Dimitrios Ronditis, starring Elsa Vergi as Clytemnestra, Karmen Roungeri and Miranda Zafeiropoulou as Iphigenia [Clive Barnes, *New York Times*, November 13, 1968; Whitney Bolton, *Morning Telegraph*, November 14, 1968; Richard Watts Jr., *New York Post*, November 13, 1968; Edward Southern Hipp, *Newark Evening News*, November 13, 1968; Hartigan 1995, 94].)

*1968 Williamstown Theatre, Williamstown, Massachusetts, translated by Kenneth Cavander, directed by Nikos Psacharopoulos, with music by Marvin David Levy, starring Laurie Kennedy as Iphigenia and Olympia Dukakis as Clytemnestra.

1969 Ford's Theatre, Circle in the Square, New York, translated by Minos Volonakis, directed by Randall Brooks. Revival of the 1967–68 Cacoyannis production with Patricia Bower as Iphigenia, Jane White as Clytemnestra, and Harris Yulin as Agamemnon.

***1971 *The Wedding of Iphigeneia* and *Iphigeneia in Concert* by Gretchen Cryer and Doug Dyer, Martinson Hall, The Public Theater, New York, directed by Gerald Freedman, music by Peter Link and the band Goatleg (Douglas Watt, *Daily News*, December 17, 1971; Martin Gottfried, *Women's Wear Daily*, December 17, 1971; George Oppenheimer, *Newsday*, December 17, 1971; Richard Watts Jr., *Theater*, December 17, 1971; Walter Kerr, *New York Times*, December 26, 1971; Clive Barnes, *New York Times*, December 17, 1971; *Variety*, November 29, 1971; John Beaufort, *Christian Science Monitor*, December 20, 1971; Edith Oliver, *New Yorker*, December 25, 1971; Marjorie Gunner, *Bronx Home News*, January 7, 1972, 7; Sege, *Variety*, December 29, 1971; Julius Novick, *Village Voice*, December 23, 1971; Lillian Africano, *Villager*, December 30, 1971; Richard Watts, *New York Post*, December 17, 1971).

1981–82 McCarter Theater, Princeton, New Jersey, and University of Pennsylvania, Philadelphia, translation by W. S. Merwin and George Dimock Jr., directed by Spryos A. Evangelatos, starring Monique Fowler, Holly Barron, Tom Klunis, and Drew Keil.

1991 *Iphigeneia at the Bay of Aulis* (a musical), Thick Description, direction and text by Tony Kelly, Intersection for the Arts, San Francisco, California, starring Karen Amano as Iphigenia, Velina Braun as Clytemnestra, and Rhonnie Washington as Agamemnon (www.thickdescription.org).

1991 *The Sacrifice of Iphigeneia*, adaptation and direction by Dennis Landi, Rock Creek Park, Washington, D.C., starring Vanina Archawski as Iphigeneia, Brooke Kidd as Clytemnestra, and Steve Wilhite as Agamemnon.

*1991 *IA* and *IT*, translated by Nicholas Rudall, directed by Tazewell Thompson, Huntington Theater Company, Boston, Massachusetts, starring Shari Simpson as *IA* Iphigenia, Karen Evans-Kandel as *IT* Iphigenia, Lizen Mitchell as Clytemnestra, Francis Ruivivar as Agamemnon, David Patrick Kelly as Orestes (Arthur Friedman, *Boston Herald*, March 8, 1991; Kevin Kelly, *Boston Globe*, March 7, 1991; Hartigan 1995, 94).

*1992 *The Clytemnestra Project: Iphigeneia*, translated by W. S. Merwin and George Dimock; *Agamemnon*, translated by Robert Lowell; *Elektra*, translated by Kenneth McCleish; Guthrie Theater, Minneapolis, Minnesota, Kristin Flanders as Iphigenia, Isabell Monk as Clytemnestra, and Stephen Pelinski as Agamemnon. Video Available at the New York Public Library for the Performing Arts, Lincoln Center (Mike Steele, *Minneapolis Star Tribune*, June 19 and 22, 1992; Joan Bunke, *Des Moines Register*, June 28, 1992; Tad Simons, *Twin Cities Reader*, June 24, 1992, 20, 22; David Richards, *New York Times*, August 9, 1992; Lewis 1996; Robert Sonkowsky, *Arion* 4.1 [Spring 1996]: 225–34; Hartigan 1995, 76–79; Foley 2005, 317–19).

(1993 Park Slope Armory, Brooklyn, New York, *Les Atrides* [*IA* translated by Jean Bollack], Théâtre du Soleil, directed by Ariane Mnouchkine, music by Jean-Jacques Lemêtre.)

1993 Classic Greek Theatre of Oregon, Reed College, Cerf Amphitheatre, Portland, Oregon, starring Livia Newman as Iphigenia, Vana O'Brien as Clytemnestra, and Ted Roisum as Agamemnon.

1994 Jean Cocteau Repertory, Bouwerie Lane Theatre, New York, translated by W. S. Merwin and G. E. Dimock Jr., directed by Eve Adamson, starring Monique Kukovic as Iphigenia, Adrienne D. Williams as Clytemnestra, Craig Smith as Agamemnon, and John Lenartz as Achilles (David Sider, *Didaskalia* 1.2 [May 1994], www.didaskalia.net/journal.html; Julius Novick, *Newsday*, April 1, 1994; D. J. R. Bruckner, *New York Times*, March 30, 1994; Jonathan Slaff, *New York Times*, March 30, 1994; Irene Backalenik, *Backstage*, April 22, 1999, 38; Hartigan 1995, 95).

1994 *Impossible Things before Breakfast* by Debbie Falb, Telluride Drama Festival, Sheridan Opera House, Telluride, Colorado (Marianne MacDonald, *Didaskalia* 1.3, 1994, www.didaskalia.net/journal.html; and *Hellenic Chronicle*, June 30, 1994).

1994 New Jersey Shakespeare Festival, Drew University, Madison, New Jersey, Kenneth Cavander adaptation, *Agamemnon and His Daughters*, directed by Bonnie J. Monte, starring Laila Robins (Alvin Klein, *New York Times*, June 26, 1994).

***1995 *Iphigeneia and Other Daughters* by Ellen McLaughlin, Classic Stage Company, New York, directed by David Esbjornson, starring Sheila Tousey as Electra, Kathleen Chalfant as Clytemnestra, Susan Heimbinder as Iphigenia, Seth Gilliam as Orestes (Foley, *Didaskalia* 2.2 [April 1995], www.didaskalia.net/journal.html; Ben Brantley, *New York Times*, February 11, 1995; Greg Evans, *Variety*, February 13, 1995; Michael Feingold, *Village Voice*, February 21, 1995; Amy Reiter, *Backstage*, February 24, 1995, 52); 1996, Penthouse Theater, Seattle, Washington, production, directed by Kerry Skalsky; 1996–97, Portland Stage Company, Portland, Maine, production, directed by Christopher Grabowski; 1997, Greasy Joan and Company Production, Griffin Theatre, Chicago, directed by Brad Shelton; 1999, A. E. Hotchner Studio Theatre, St. Louis, Missouri, production, directed by Robert Neblett; 1999, the Bug Theatre Company, Colorado, directed by Matthew

Howard (Jim Lillie, www.westward.com/issues/1999-05-06/theater.html); 2006, Actor's Theater Workshop, 145 West 28<sup>th</sup> Street, New York; 2007, Chamber Theater and Washington Ensemble Theatre, Seattle (Richard Morin, *Seattle Weekly,* May 1, 2007).

1997 Hyperbolic Players, Kraine Theater, New York, directed by Amy Bennett and James Ford, starring Heather Rogers as Iphigeneia, Alexandra Grey as Clytemnestra, and Chris Libenson as Agamemnon (John Attanas, www.oobr.com/top/volFour/seven/iphi.html).

***1997 *The Iphigenia Cycle,* Euripides' *IA* and *IT,* translated by Nicholas Rudall, directed by Joanne Akalaitis, starring Anne Dudek as Iphigenia, Ora Jones as Clytemnestra and Athena, Taylor Price as Achilles and Orestes, Jack Willis as Agamemnon, and Eddy Saad as Menelaus, Court Theatre, Chicago, Illinois. Video available at the New York Public Library for the Performing Arts, Lincoln Center; 1999, Theatre for a New Audience, American Place Theater, New York (Peter Marks, *New York Times,* January 26, 1999; Les Gutman, www.curtainup.com/iphigeni.html; Michael Feingold, *Village Voice,* January 27–February 2, 1999; Nancy Hass, *New York Times,* January 24, 1999; Jonathan Kalb, *New York Press,* February 3, 1999, 49; Charles Isherwood, *Variety,* February 1, 1999, 70; Donald Lyons, *New York Post,* January 25, 1999 and February 18, 1999; David Kaufman, *Daily News,* January 26, 1999; Victor Gluck, *Backstage,* January 29, 1999; Amy Gamerman, *Wall Street Journal,* February 3, 1999; John Simon, *New York Magazine,* February 8, 1999, nymag.com/mymetro/arts/theater/reviews/220/).

1999 *Iphigenia in Orem* by Neil LaBute, Douglas Fairbanks Theater, New York, directed by Joe Mantello, with Ron Eldard as the Agamemnon figure. Also taped for Showtime cable TV (Charles Isherwood, *Variety,* June 25, 1999; Steve Winn, *San Francisco Chronicle,* August 28, 2000).

***2000 *Furious Blood,* adaptation of *IA* and the *Oresteia* by Kelly Stuart, directed by Kirsten Brandt, Sledgehammer Theatre, San Diego, California, starring Jessa Watson as Clytemnestra and Tim West as Agamemnon (Anne Marie Welsh, *San Diego Union-Tribune,* February 13 and 15, 2000; Jennifer de Poyen, *San Diego Union-Tribune,* February 15, 2000; Jeff Smith, *San Diego Reader,* March 2, 2000; Pat Launer, KPBS-FM; Marie Oppedisano, *Marquee Arts and Entertainment,* February 2000; Joel Beers, *OC Weekly* 5.25, February 25–March 2, 2000; Charlene Baldridge, www.backstagewest.com, February 24, 2000; Foley 2005).

2001 *Iph* by Colin Teevan, An Irish Theatre, Acoma Center, Denver, Colorado.

2001 Shotgun Players, John Hinkel Park, Berkeley, California, directed by Patrick Dooley, starring Amaya Alonos Hallifa, as Iphigenia, Mary Eaton Fairfield as Clytemnestra, and Jeff Elam as Agamemnon (www.shotgunplayers.org; Robert Hurwitt, *San Francisco Chronicle,* June 28, 2001; Karen Ahn, *Urban View,* July 3, 2001; Karen D'Souza, *San Jose Mercury News,* June 24 and 27, 2001; Erin Blackwell, *SF Frontiers,* July 27, 2001; Michael Scott Moore, *sfweekly,* July 11, 2001; Joe Mader, *San Francisco Examiner,* August 15, 2003).

2001 Pearl Theatre, New York, translated by W. S. Merwin and G. E. Dimock Jr., directed by Shepard Sobel, starring Sue Jin Song as Iphigenia, Carol Schultz as Clytemnestra, and Dan Daily as Agamemnon (Anita Gates, *New York Times,* December 15, 2001; Irene Backalenick, *Backstage,* December 7, 2001, 40; Matthew Murray, www.talkinbroadway. com/ob11 19 01.html; David Lohrey, www.curtainup.com/iphigineiaofaulis.html).

*2001 *Agamemnon and His Daughters,* adaptation by Kenneth Cavander drawing on *IA,* Aeschylus's *Agamemnon,* an *Electra* based on Aeschylus, Sophocles, and Euripides, and *IT,* directed by Molly Smith, Arena Stage Company, Washington, D.C. (Foley, *Theater Journal* 54.1 [March 2002]: 143–45; Nelson Pressley, *Washington Post,* September 9, 2001; Shirley J. Gregory, http://dcmdva-arts.org/shows/agamemnon.htm; Dorothy Chansky, http:ibs.theatermania.com/content/news.cfm?int_news_id = 1681; Jayne M. Blanchard, *Washington Times,* September 18 and 22, 2001; Jenn Brookland, September 21, 2001; www.thehoya.com/guide11.cfm).

2001 *Tantalus* (third play in the cycle) by John Barton, Denver Center for the Performing Arts, Colorado, directed by Sir Peter Hall.

2002 Yale Repertory Theater, New Haven, Connecticut, adapted by Kenneth Cavander, directed by Rebecca Bayla Taichman, starring Julyanna Soelistyo as Iphigeneia, Ching Valdes Aran as Clytemnestra, and Christopher McHale as Agamemnon (Alvin Klein, *New York Times,* May 12, 2002).

2003 *Iphigenia* (both *IA* and *IT*), Poet's Theater, Theatre 4, Seattle Center House, Seattle, Washington, directed by M. J. Sieber, Katie McKee as Iphigenia, Kerry Christianson as Clytemnestra, and Joseph Osier as Agamemnon (Chris Jensen, *Seattle Weekly,* July 2, 2003; Joseph E. Boling, tpsonline.org/discus/messages/2538/5439.html?1056277950).

*2003 The Workshop Theater (www.theworkshoptheater.org) at the Main Stage Theater, New York, adapted by P. Seth Bauer (Bauer 2006), directed by Elyssa Marden, starring Pauline Tully as Iphigenia, Brian Homer as Achilles, Marinell Madden as Clytemnestra, and Mark Hofmaior as Agamemnon; June 2005 at the Samuel Beckett Theatre by Epic Theatre Center and by Powerhouse Theatre Company at Vassar College with Emily Mendelsohn as director; 2005, a staged reading for Algonquin Productions, St. Clements Theater, New York, starring Pauline Tully as Iphigenia, Jennifer Kathryn Marshall as Clytemnestra, and Laurence Feeney as Agamemnon (Matthew Murray, www.talkinbroadway.com/ob/03_26a03.html; Jenny Sandman, www.oobr.com/top/vol Nine/twentynine/0405Iphigenia.htm; Nick Brandt, www.nytheatre.com/nytheatre/arch 2003_i.htm; www.brettsingr.com/clients/3-27-03-iphigenia-postshowdiscussion.htm).

2004 American Theatre of Actors, 314 West 54th Street, New York, directed by James Jennings.

***2004 *Iphigeneia Crash Land Falls on the Neon Shell That Was Once Her Heart (A Rave Fable)* by Caridad Svich (Svich 2005, 239–74 and Svich, *Theatre Forum* 25, Summer/Fall 2004: 27–51, 7 stages, Atlanta Georgia, directed by Melissa Foulger, starring Adam Fristoe and Heather Starkel; 2004, a Lida Project production, Denver, Colorado, directed by Brian Freeland; 2006, Son of Semele Ensemble, Los Angeles, California, directed by Matthew McCray; 2006, One Year Lease, Walkerspace, New York, directed by Ianthe Demos and Danny Bernardy, starring Brina Stinehelfer as Iphigenia, Danny Berhardy as Achilles and a Fresa Girl, and Gregory Walker, Nick Flint, and Susannah Malone in multiple roles (Deidre McFadyen, www.offoffonline.com/archives.php?id = 858; Chiori Miyagawa, *Brooklyn Rail,* September 2006; Ali Rohrs, *American Theatre 23.7,* September 2006, 24).

2004 A Lida Project production, Denver Colorado, directed by Brian Freeland.

2005 The Ten Thousand Things Theater Company, Minneapolis, directed by Theodora Skiptares.

*2005 La MaMa, E.T.C., New York, puppet version by Theodora Skiptares, translated by Philip Vellacott, music by Tim Schellenbaum and Yukio Tsuji and puppets by Skiptares and Cecilia Schiller, with Sonya Perryman as Iphigenia, Carolyn Goelzer as Clytemnestra, and John Bennett as Agamemnon. Developed at the Ten Thousand Things Theater Company, Minneapolis, 2005 (Phoebe Hoban, *New York Times,* March 23, 2005; Gordon Cox, *Newsday,* March 24, 2005; Andy Probst, *Backstage.com,* March 31, 2007, 42; Steve Luber, March 19, 2005, www.offoffline.com/archive printerfriendly.php?id = 353).

2006 San Jose Repertory Company, artistic director Timothy Near (Karen D'Souza, *American Theatre* 23.5 [May/June 2006]: 21).

2006 *Three by Mee* (Part 1, *Agamemnon;* Part 2, *The Bacchae;* Part 3, *Iphigenia*), City Garage, Los Angeles, California, directed by Frédérique Michel.

2006-7 *Trilogy,* an eclectic work that included parts of *IA,* directed by Theodora Skiptares, La MaMa, E.T.C., New York (Honor Moore, *New York Times,* March 22, 2006, March 28, 2007).

(2007 Gardzienice in Association with the National Theater Stary in Kraków [Poland], La MaMa E.T.C., New York, adapted and directed by Wiodzimierz Staniewski, with music by Zygmunt Konieczny and starring Mariusz Goiaj as Agamemnon [Rachel Saltz, *New York Times,* October 12, 2007; Tom Sellar, *Village Voice,* October 17–23, 2007; Andy Probst, *Backstage.com* October 9, 2007].)

***2007 *Iphigenia 2.0* by Charles Mee (www.charlesmee.org.html/iphigenia.html), Signature Theatre Company, New York, directed by Tina Landau, starring Louisa Krause as Iphigenia, Kate Mulgrew as Clytemnestra, and Tom Nelis as Agamemnon (David Cole, *Time Out New York,* August 9–15, 2007; Adam Feldman, *Time Out New York,* August 30-September 5, 2007; Joe Dziemianowicz, *Daily News,* August 30, 2007; Jason Zinoman, *New York Times,* August 27, 2007; Hilton Als, *New Yorker,* September 3, 2007, 141; Terry Teachout, *Wall Street Journal,* August 3, 2007; Leonard Jacobs, *New York Post,* August 29, 2007; Adam Perlman, *Backstage East,* September 13, 2007, 11; Matt Windman, *AM New York,* August 28, 2002; Frank Scheck, *New York Post,* August 27, 2007; Marilyn Stasio, *Variety,* September 3, 2007; John Helpern, *New York Observer,* September 17, 2007, C14; Linda Winer, *Newsday,* August 27, 2007; Eric Grode, *New York Sun,* August 27, 2007; Diana Barth, *Epoch Times,* September 6, 2007, B6; Jeremy McCarter, *New York Magazine,* September 17, 2007; Simon Salzman, www.curtainup.com/iphigeniameeny. html; Michael Feingold, *Village Voice,* August 28, 2007; Matthew Murray, www.talkin broadway.com/ob/08_26_07.html; and Dan Bacalzo, www.theatermania.com/content/news.cfm/story/11440).

2008 Voorness Theater, Brooklyn, New York, directed by Helen Richardson.

*IPHIGENEIA IN TAURIS*

**1913 Coburn Players, outdoors at Columbia University, New York, translated by Gilbert Murray, starring Mr. and Mrs. Coburn (Ivah Wills) (*Dramatic Mirror,* August 6, 1913; Hartigan 1995, 21).

**1915 Translated by Gilbert Murray, directed by Harley Granville Barker, starring Lillah McCarthy and Ian Maclaren as Orestes, Yale University, Harvard University, College of the City of New York, University of Pennsylvania, Princeton University, Piping Rock Country Club (*New York Times*, May 16 and 30 and June 1, 1915; *Theatre* 21, June 15, 1915; *Bookman* 41 [June 1915]: 409–16; *Nation*, May 20, 1919, 577; *Independent*, June 7, 1915, 394 and 396; *New Republic*, June 5, 1915, 127, 633–34; Hartigan 1995, 15, 18).

1925 Forest Theater Guild, Carmel-by-the-Sea, California, Forest Theater Summer Festival, translation by Gilbert Murray, produced by Herbert Heron, starring Blanche Tolmie as Electra and Ralph Geddes as Orestes.

(1931 Goethe's *IT*, Athenian Players, New Yorker Theatre; 1954, John Hall Players, New York; 1959, Jan Hus Theater, New York.)

1960 Staged reading by The Living Theatre, New School for Social Research, New York.

***1971 *The Wedding of Iphigeneia* and *Iphigeneia in Concert* by Gretchen Cryer and Doug Dyer (full listing under *IA*).

*1991 *IA* and *IT*, translated by Nicholas Rudall, directed by Tazewell Thompson (full listing under *IA*).

***1992 La MaMa, E.T.C., Annex, New York, adapted by M. Houvardas from Richmond Lattimore's translation, music by Genji Ito, set and costumes by Dionyssis Fotopoulos, starring Alyssa Breshnahan as Iphigeneia (D. J. R. Bruckner, *New York Times*, May 13, 1992; Victor Gluck, *Backstage*, June 5, 1992, 40; Roderick Mason Faber, *Village Voice*, June 2, 1992).

1994 New Jersey Shakespeare Festival, Drew University, Madison, New Jersey, Kenneth Cavander adaptation, *Agamemnon and His Daughters*, directed by Bonnie J. Monte, starring Laila Robins (Alvin Klein, *New York Times*, June 26, 1994).

*1995 *Iphigeneia and Other Daughters* by Ellen McLaughlin (full listing under *IA*).

*1997 *The Iphigenia Cycle*, Euripides' *IA* and *IT*, translated by Nicholas Rudall, directed by Joanne Akalaitis (full listing under *IA*).

1997 Classic Greek Theatre of Oregon, Cerf Amphitheatre, Reed College, directed by Keith Scales, music by John Vergin, starring Kathryn Alexis Crump as Iphigenia, Kam Sisco as Orestes, Brad Goodman as Pylades.

*2001 *Agamemnon and His Daughters*, adaptation by Kenneth Cavander, directed by Molly Smith (full listing under *IA*).

2002 Word of Mouth Theatre, Here Arts Center, New York, translated by Witter Bynner, directed by Veronica Newton, starring Susanna Macintosh as Iphigenia, Rolando Morales as Orestes, and Ron Scott as Pylades.

2003 *Iphigenia* (both *IA* and *IT*), Poet's Theater, Seattle, directed by M. J. Sieber (full listing under *IA*).

***2007 *iph.then*, written and created by Peter A. Campbell, Ontological-Hysteric Incubator, St. Mark's Church, New York, starring Amanda Boekelheide as Iphigeneia, David Gordon as Orestes, and Peter Clark as Pylades. This version also drew on Goethe and Gluck and contained video clips.

*2008 *If/Then among the Taureans*, by Michi Barall, a staged reading at The Milagro Theater, Clemente Solo Vélez Cultural Center, New York, March 30, 2008, by Second Generation, directed by Kim Weild, starring Maria Elena Ramirez as Iphigenia and Julian Barnett as Orestes.

*2010 *Rescue Me,* by Michi Barall, directed by Loy Arcenas, starring Jennifer Ikeda as Iphigenia, Julian Barnett as Orestes, Ryan King as Pylades, David Greenspan as Artemis/Athena, and Leon Ingulsud as Thoas, Ohio Theatre, New York, the Ma-Yi Theater Company (Paul Menard, March 20, 2010, www.backstage.com/bso/reviews-ny-theatre-off-broadway/ny-review-rescue-me-a-postmodern-classics-1004079355.story; Deidre Donovan, www.curtainup.com/rescueme.html; Jason Zinoman, *New York Times,* April 5, 2010; Alexis Soloski, *Village Voice,* April 10–May 16, 2010; Diane Snyder, *Time Out New York,* April 6, 2010; Heather J. Volanti, March 26, 2010, www.nytheatre.com/ny theatre/showpage.php?t = resc9664; Patrick Lee, www.theatremania.com/off-broadway/reviews/03-2010/rescue-me_26142.html).

APPENDIX G

# Other Professional Productions and New Versions

*The entries listed below represent productions discussed in chapters 1–3 or the epilogue that are not included in other appendices.*

1820 Talfourd's *Alcestue* (misspelling of *Alcestis*?), Boston, starring George E. Brown, Boston (R. Sherman 1944, 20).
1836 Talfourd's *Ion*, Walnut Street Theatre, Philadelphia, starring Ms. Ternan as Ion, and in New York, starring G. Jones.
1836–37 Talfourd's *Ion*, New York's National Theatre, starring Charles Burke as Ion.
1837 Talfourd's *Ion*, Park Theatre, New York, starring Ellen Tree as Ion.
1837 *Ion Travestie*, burlesque, perhaps derived from the British version by Frederick Fox Cooper, Walnut Street Theatre, Philadelphia. *Ion Travestie* also appeared at the Walnut Street Theatre in Philadelphia with a Mr. Walton as Ion.
1840 Talfourd's *Ion*, Bowery Theatre, New York, starring Mrs. Shaw as Ion.
1845 Talfourd's *Ion*, revived in New York with Ellen Tree, with a rival New York production, Bowery Theatre, starring Mrs. Shaw as Ion (Odell 4: 124).
1850 Burlesque of F. Talfourd's *Alcestis, or the Original Strong-Minded Woman*, at both Burton's Olympic Theater and Brougham's Theatre, New York (Brown 1: 287; Odell 6: 148 and 5: 57).
1852 Talfourd's *Ion*, New York, with Anna Mowatt as Ion.
1853 Talfourd's *Ion*, Buffalo, New York (*Buffalo Commercial*, May 23, 1853).
1857 Talfourd's *Ion*, Arch Street Theatre, Philadelphia.
1857 Talfourd's *Ion*, a theater in New York, with Mrs. J. W. Wallack Jr. as both Shakespeare's Romeo and Ion.
1858 and 1862 Talfourd's *Ion*, Walnut Street Theatre, Philadelphia.
1858 Version of *Electra* without a chorus that included a character called Arcas, presented by Fred Widdows, starring Cordelia Cappell as Electra, Mrs. Jm Taylor as Clytemnestra,

and Isaac C. Pray as Orestes, New York's Academy of the Drama, six performances opening on June 30, 1858 (*Albion* 36.27, July 3, 1858, 320; *New York Leader* 4.21, July 3, 1858, 5; *New York Times,* June 30, 1858; Brandes 1945, 62–63).

1859 Talfourd's *Ion,* Arch Street Theatre, Philadelphia, with Mrs. James W. Wallack; in 1866 with Jean Hosmer as Ion; and in 1867 at the same theater with Julia Dean.

1867 and 1869 Goethe's *Iphigenie auf Taurus,* Academy of Music in Philadelphia and in New York in 1867, starring Francesca Janauschek (Brown 2: 60; Odell 8: 347 on the December 28, 1867, production).

1876 *Helen in Egypt,* directed by William Daly, Chestnut Street Theatre, Philadelphia.

1877 Talfourd's *Ion,* Walnut Street Theatre, Philadelphia, with Mary Anderson as Ion; Anderson also played the part in Boston in 1877 and 1881.

1887 Version of *Electra,* Arch Street Opera House, Philadelphia (Philadelphia Theatre Index, Free Library of Philadelphia, 1855–2000).

1898 Aeschylus's *Eumenides,* produced by Katherine Tingley, Music Hall, Buffalo, New York (*Musical America II,* November 19, 1898, 12; *New York Tribune,* November 19, 1898; *Buffalo Evening News,* December 2, 1898; *Buffalo Express,* December 4, 1898; *Theosophical Path* 27 [July 1924]: 86, cited in Greenwalt 1955, 43).

1911 *Hippolytus* by Julia Ward Howe (Howe 1941), Tremont Theatre, Boston, starring Margaret Anglin as Phaedra and Walter Hampden as Hippolytus (Philip Hale, *Boston Herald,* March 25, 1911; *Boston Globe,* March 25, 1911; *New York Times,* March 25, 1911; Mrs. S. C. Williams, *Boston Advertiser,* March 25, 1911; *Christian Science Monitor,* March 18, 1911; William E. Sage, *Cleveland Leader,* March 28, 1911).

1933 Aeschylus's *Libations Bearers,* dance version by Doris Humphreys, drawing on music from Darius Milhaud and a text by Paul Claudel; studio performances of this work, entitled *Orestes,* occurred earlier (Bannermann 2010, 257–58).

1934 and 1935 Euripides' *Bacchae,* directed by Eva Palmer Sikelianos at Smith and Bryn Mawr colleges (*New York Times,* June 2, 1934; *Springfield Union,* June 16, 1934; *Smith College Weekly,* June 20, 1934; *College News,* February 20, 1935, March 6, 1935, June 5, 1935; *New York Herald Tribune,* June 2, 1935; Prins, forthcoming).

1938 *Trojan Incident,* a Federal Dance Theatre Project version of Euripides' *Trojan Women,* adapted by Philip H. Davis, St. James Theater on 44th Street, New York, directed by Helen Tamiris and Harold Bolton, choreography by Helen Tamiris, music by Wallingford Riegger, setting by Howard Bay, starring Isabel Booner as Hecuba and Helen Tamiris as Cassandra (Gervaise Butler, "Tamiris and a Tale of Troy," *Dance Observer,* May 5, 1938, 60; Brooks Atkinson, *New York Times,* April 22, 1938; John Martin, *New York Times,* May 1, 1938; Grant Code, *Dance Observer,* June 9, 1939; Paul Douglas, *New Theater,* November 1935, 26–27; Burns Mantle, *Daily News,* April 22, 1938; Robert Coleman, *Daily News,* April 22, 1938; Richard Lockridge, *New York Sun,* April 22, 1938; John Anderson, *New York Journal-American,* April 22, 1938; Arthur Pollock, *Brooklyn Daily Eagle,* April 22, 1938; Richard Watts Jr., *New York Herald Tribune,* April 22, 1938; John Mason Brown, *New York Post,* April 22, 1938; L. B., *New York World,* April 22, 1938; *Variety,* April 22, 1938; Tish 1994).

1951 Kenneth Rexroth (Rexroth 1951), *Beyond the Mountains* (*Phaedra, Iphigenia at Aulis,* and *Berenike*), staged by The Living Theatre, Cherry Lane Theater, New York (S. Brecht 1969).

1954 Sophocles' *Women of Trachis,* translated and adapted by Ezra Pound, staged reading by The Living Theatre, New School University, starring James Dean as Hyllus, with Anne Jackson, Adelaide Klein, Earle Montgomery, and Joseph Sullivan.

1958 *Clytemnestra,* based on Aeschylus's *Oresteia,* choreographed by Martha Graham, music by Halim El-Dabh, Adelphi Theatre, New York (John Martin, *New York Times,* April 2, 1958; Clive Barnes, *New York Times,* November 7, 1965); 2008–9, Graham's original version of *Clytemnestra* revived, Skirball Center, New York University (www.clytemnestra project.com).

1960 Sophocles' *Women of Trachis,* translated and adapted by Ezra Pound, performed by The Living Theatre, Living Theatre Playhouse, 560 6th Avenue at 14th Street, New York (Jerry Tallmer, *Village Voice,* July 7, 1960; Brooks Atkinson, *New York Times,* June 23, 1960; Colakis 1993, 50; Tytell 1995, 164; Robert Brustein, "History Now: A Discussion with the Becks," *Yale/Theater* 2.1 [1969]: 20).

1960 *Alcestis,* based on Euripides' play and Theodore Morrison's poem *The Dream of Alcestis,* choreographed by Martha Graham, music by Vivian Fine, 54$^{th}$ Street Theater, New York (Stodelle 1984, 218–22).

1962 *Phaedra,* based on Euripides' *Hippolytus* and Racine's *Phaedra,* choreographed by Martha Graham, music by Robert Starer, Broadway Theater, New York. A related late piece, *Phaedra's Dream,* was performed in 1983 (McDonagh 1973, 262–63; Stodelle 1984, 228–31; Anna Kisselgoff, *New York Times,* October 13, 1988).

1967 *Cortege of Eagles,* based on Euripides' *Trojan Women* and *Hecuba,* choreographed by Martha Graham, music by Eugene Lester, Mark Hellinger Theatre, New York.

1974 Euripides' *Trojan Women,* directed by Andrei Serban, music by Elizabeth Swados, starring Priscilla Smith as Andromaca, Valois Mickens as Cassandra, and Joana Peeled as Helen (Clive Barnes, *New York Times,* October 20, 1974; Mel Gussow, *New York Times,* June 25, 1974; Julius Novick, *New York Times,* November 18, 1974 and January 18, 1976; Menta 1995, 21–32; A. Green 1994; Hartigan 1995, 45–46, 52). Excerpts available from Insight Media, with a complete videotape at the New York Public Library for the Performing Arts, Lincoln Center (reviews of the 1996 La MaMa revival: Peter Marks, *New York Times,* December 17, 1996; Justin Davidson, *Newsday,* December 23, 1996; Linda Winer, *Newsday,* December 24, 1996; Ted Lambert, *New York Times,* December 8, 1996; Jon Pareles, *New York Times,* December 17, 1996).

1977 *Agamemnon,* New York Shakespeare Festival, translated by Edith Hamilton, adapted by Andrei Serban, music by Elizabeth Swados, at the Vivian Beaumont Theater, Lincoln Center, starring Priscilla Smith as Clytemnestra and Cassandra and Jamil Zakkai as Agamemnon and Aegisthus, and at the Delacorte Theater, Central Park, starring Gloria Foster as Clytemnestra, Dianne Wiest as Cassandra, Jamil Zakkai as Agamemnon, and Ron O'Neal as Aegisthus (Margaret Croyden, *New York Times,* May 8, 1977; Bernard Knox, *New York Review of Books,* July 14, 1977, reprinted in Knox 1979, 70–78; Foley 2005, 310; Hartigan 1995, 45–46, 52–53, 72–74, 151; Menta 1995, 32–38).

1983 *The Gospel at Colonus,* a musical version of Sophocles' *Oedipus at Colonus* by Lee Breuer and Bob Telson, Brooklyn Academy of Music, starring Morgan Freeman and Clarence Fountain and the Five Blind Boys of Alabama as Oedipus, Isabel Monk and Jevetta Steele as Antigone, Robert Earle Jones as Polyneices, as well as Carl Lumbly, the J. D. Steele Singers, and J. J. Farley and the Original Soul Stirrers. Later presented on Public Television in its Great Performance series in 1985, currently available on DVD, New Video NYC; revived 1988, Broadway Lunt-Fontaine Theatre, and 2004, Apollo Theater, Harlem, New York (Wetmore 2003, with extensive bibliography; A. Green 1994, 58–66; Koger 1997; McDonald 2001, 159–77; Foley 2007, 370–72; Goff and Simpson 2007, 178–218).

1986 Adaptation of Euripides' *Alcestis,* translated by Dudley Fitts and Robert Fitzgerald, with added text by Heiner Müller (Fuchs and Marranca 1986), directed by Robert Wilson, American Repertory Theater, Cambridge, Massachusetts, movement by Suzushi Hanayagi, designed by Tom Kamm, sound by Hans Peter Kuhn, lighting by Jennifer Tipton, starring Diana D'Aquila as Alcestis, Paul Rudd as Admetus, and Harry Murphy as Heracles. Workshop performance in 1985; later performances in Paris and Stuttgart (Mel Gussow, *New York Times,* March 21, 1986; Fuchs 1986; Fuchs and Marranca 1986; Rouse 1986–87; Arnott 1987, 377–81; A. Green 1994, 66–68; Holmberg 1996. Photos: Quadri, Bertoni and Stearns 1998).

1987 *Revelation in the Courthouse Park,* a version of Euripides' *Bacchae* by Harry Partch, conducted by Partch's disciple Danlee Mitchell with the assistance of Alfred Blatter, directed by Jiri Zizka, commissioned by Eric Salzman, choreography by George Faison, starring Obba Babatunde, Dion/Dionysus, Suzanne Costallos, Mom/Agave, Christopher Durham, Pentheus/Sonny, Gene Anthony Ray (John Rockwell, *New York Times,* October 10, 1987; Leighton Kerner, *Village Voice,* November 3, 1987; *Commonweal,* November 6, 1987). Recorded on Tomato Music Works TOM-3004, with a tape at the New York Public Library for the Performing Arts, Lincoln Center that also demonstrates the twenty instruments in the production (Original Illinois Production, *Enclosure 5,* Harry Partch, Innova, American Composers Forum 1998).

1995 Euripides' *Hecuba,* Yerba Buena Center, American Conservatory Theater, San Francisco, translated by Timberlake Wertenbaker, directed by Carey Perloff, music by David Lang for the Eastern European a cappella group KITKA, starring Olympia Dukakis as Hecuba, Elisabeth Imboden as Polyxena, Ken Ruta as Odysseus, James Carpenter as Agamemnon, Gerald Hiken as Talthybius, and Stephen Markle as Polymestor. Revived at the Geary Theatre in 1998 ( also performed at the Williamstown Theatre Festival in Williamstown, Massachusetts) with Olympia Dukakis as Hecuba, Roxanne Raja as Polyxena, Marco Barricelli as Odysseus, L. Peter Callender as Agamemnon, Steven Anthony Jones as Polymestor, and Apollo Dukakis as Talthybius (Robert Hurwitt, *San Francisco Examiner,* October 22, 1998; Stephen Winn, *San Francisco Chronicle,* October 23, 1998; Michael Scott Moore, *San Francisco Weekly,* October 28–November 3, 1998; Brad Rosenstein, *San Francisco Bay Guardian,* October 28, 1998; Judy Richter, *Aisle Say San Francisco,* October 24, 1998; Karen D'Souza, *Bee Theater Critic,* October 23, 1998; Mark de la Vina, *San Jose Mercury News,* October 23, 1998; Chad Jones, *Oakland Tribune,* October 20 and 23, 1998; and *San Mateo Co. Times,* October 3, 1998; Lee Brady,

*Pacific Sun,* October 28–November 8, 1998; Pat Craig, *Contra Costa Times,* October 16 and 24, 1998; Robin Pogrebin, *New York Times,* September 29, 1998; and Carol Benet, *Ark,* Tiburon, California, November 18, 1998). A video of the first production is available at the New York Public Library for the Performing Arts, Lincoln Center.

1998 Euripides' *Hecuba,* The African Continuum Theater Company, (ACTCo), Washington, D.C., translated by Marilyn Nelson (1997), directed by African American Jennifer Nelson, starring Cheryl Collins as Hecuba, Lisa Biggs as Polyxena, Addison Switzer as Odysseus and Polymestor, and Jefferson A. Russell as Agamemnon (Pamela Sommers, *Washington Post,* November 11, 1998; Sarah Kaufman, *Washington Post,* November 20, 1998; and Bob Mondello, *City Paper,* November 13, 1998). A video of the performance is available at the Washington Area Performing Arts Video Archive.

2000 *Big Love,* a version of Aeschylus's *Suppliant Women,* by Charles Mee (http://charlesmee.org), Actor's Theatre of Louisville, staged by Les Waters.

2001 *Big Love,* a version of Aeschylus's *Suppliant Women,* by Charles Mee (http://charles mee.org), Long Wharf Theater, New Haven, Connecticut; Berkeley Repertory Theatre; Goodman Theatre, Chicago; BAM Next Wave Festival, Brooklyn, New York; ACT Seattle, staged by Brian Kulik; Rude Mechanicals, Austin, Texas, staged by Darron West.

2002 *Helen* by Ellen McLaughlin (1995), directed by Tony Kushner, The Public Theater, New York, starring Donna Murphy as Helen, Marian Seldes as Servant, Johanna Day as Io, Phylicia Rashad as Athena, and Dennis O'Hare as Menelaus (Ben Brantley, *New York Times,* April 9, 2002; Charles McNulty, *Village Voice,* April 16, 2002).

2004 Euripides' *Hecuba,* Culture Project, 45 Bleecker Street, as part of the Hellenic Festival at the New York Public Library, translated by William Arrowsmith, directed by Alex Lippard, starring Kristin Linklater as Hecuba, Curzon Dobell as Odysseus, Mike Genovese as Agamemnon, Christopher McCann as Polymestor, and Heather Tom as Polyxena (Charles McNulty, *Village Voice,* October 19, 2004; Charles Isherwood, *New York Times,* October 15, 2004; Gwen Orel, www.theatrescene.net/ts%5Carticles.nsf/0/E82DE4E)CD D2B4B985256F3900271D44?OpenDocument, Gyda Arber, nytheatre.com/nytheatre/he cuba564.htm; Dan Bacalzo, www.theatermania.com/content/news.cfm/story/5217).

2004 Euripides' *Phoenissae,* version by Steven Gridley (2006), directed by Steven Gridley and Jacob Titus, starring Erin Treadway as Jocasta, Andrew Bloch as Oedipus, Tara Gibson as Antigone, Carid Bridger as Polyneices, Shawn J. Davis as Eteocles, Karen Allen as Ismene, and Brandon Bales as Messenger, Flamboyan Theater, Clemente Solo Velez Cultural and Educational Centre, New York (Foley 2010, 149–50).

2005 Euripides' *Children of Heracles,* American Repertory Theater, Cambridge, Massachusetts, sponsored by A.R.T. and the Ruhr Triennial Arts Festival, Germany, translated by Ralph Gladstone, directed by Peter Sellars, starring Jan Triska as Iolaus, Brenda Wehle as Demophon, Julyana Soelistyo as Macaria and Alcmene, Elaine Tse as Copreus, Cornel Gabara as Eurytheus; also performed at Lichthof, Bottrop, North-Rhine-Westphalia, Germany, September 19–29, 2002; Teatro Vale, Rome, Italy, Romaneuropa Festival, November 2002; unknown venue, Paris, France; Beurs van Berlage, Amsterdam, Netherlands, June 4–9, 2004 (*Dioniso* n.s. 2 [2003]: 211; articles, reviews, interviews with Sellars, and other material can be found on the American Repertory Theatre website, www.am rep.org/herakles/; Daniel Mendelsohn, *New York Review of Books,* February 13, 2003).

2006 *Seven,* adaptation of Aeschylus's *Seven against Thebes* by Will Power, New York Theater Workshop, choreographed by Bill T. Jones, starring Edwin Lee Gibson as Oedipus/Laius, Benton Greene as Eteocles, and Jamyl Dobson as Polyneices. Tape of the 2002 version (Robert Hurwitt, *San Francisco Chronicle,* August 28, 2001) at the New York Public Library for the Performing Arts, Lincoln Center (Jeremy McCarter, http://newyork metro.com/arts/theater/reviews/16020; Amanda Cooper, www.curtainup.com/seven .html; Stan Richardson, www.nytheatre.com/nytheatre/archweb/arch2006_22.htm#531; Jennifer Dunning, *New York Times,* February 10, 2006; Elizabeth Zimmer, *Village Voice,* January 4–10, 2006; John Lahr, *New Yorker,* March 6, 2006; Michael Feinhold, *Village Voice,* February 22–28, 2006; Sean O'Donnell, www.showbusinessweekly.com/archive/374/Seven.shtml; David Spencer, http://www.aislesay.com/NY-SEVEN.html; Ron Kendt, www.broadway,com/gen/Buzz_Story.aspx?ci = 525051; David Cote, *Time Out New York,* February 16–22, 2006; Charles Isherwood, *New York Times,* February 13, 2006; Meineck 2006; Mee 2006).

2007 *The Rockae,* a rock opera version of Euripides' *Bacchae,* by Prospect Theater Company, music and lyrics by Peter Mills, choreography by Marlo Hunter, and directed by coauthor Cara Reichel, Hudson Guild Theatre, New York, September 14–October 14, starring Michael Cunio as Dionysus, Michael Jarvis as Pentheus, Meghan McGeary as Agave, and Gordon Stanley as Cadmus (John Beer, *Village Voice,* September 25, 2007; Matthew Murray, www.talkinbroadway.com/ob/09_17_07.html; Amy Krivohlavek, www.show businessweekly.com/archive/456/The_Rockae.shtml; Jerry Portwood, www.backstage .com/bso/news_reviews/nyc/review_display.jsp?vnu_content_id = 1003645250; Edward Karam, www.offoffonline.com/archives.php?id=1190; Jenna Tesse Fox, www.broadway world.com/article/The_Rockae_I_Am_A_Golden_God_20071009; Dan Bacalzo and Andy Probst, www.theatermania.com/content/news/cfm/story/11669; Rachel Saltz, *New York Times,* October 8, 2007).

2007 *Women of Trachis,* adapted by Kate E. Ryan, directed by Alice Reagan, Target Margin Theater, Ohio Theater, New York, starring Hedi Schrek as Deianeira, Debargo Sanyal as Hyllus and Lichas, and Todd d'Amour as Heracles (Jonathan Kalb, *New York Times,* January 24, 2007).

2008 *Love Child,* a version of Euripides' *Ion* written and performed by Daniel Stratton and Robert Stanton, directed by Carl Forsman, Primary Stages, New York (Neil Genzlinger, *New York Times,* October 30, 2008).

2009 Euripides' *Ion,* Shakespeare Theatre Company, Washington, D.C., translated by David Lan, directed by Ethan McSweeny, starring Keith Eric Chappelle as Ion, Lisa Harrow as Creusa, and Sam Tsoutsovouvas as Xuthus (Peter Marks, *Washington Post,* March 18, 2009).

2009 Euripides' *Andromache,* directed by Jesse Alexander Myerson for fullofnoises.org, Workman's Circle/Arbeter Ring, 45 E. 33rd Street, New York, starring Vella Lovell as Andromache, Sol Marina Crespo as Hermione, Garry Goodrow as Peleus, Jose Jaoquin Garcia as Menelaus, Omar Perez as Orestes, and Reyna Bonaparte as the Nurse.

NOTES

INTRODUCTION

1. Chapter epigraphs: Bigsby and Wilmeth 1999, 20; second epigraph quoted in Wharton 1990, 894. Bigsby and Wilmeth 1999,19.
2. Winterer 2002, 4, 20, 66–68.
3. Felski 2008, 4; Steiner 1961 and 2008.
4. Bigsby and Wilmeth 1998, 19; McConachie 1998, 138; Williams 1998, 305.
5. McConachie 1998, 131.
6. McDermott 1998, 191; Richardson 1998, 254, 266–72, 284, 298; Williams 1998, 312; Miller 1999, 233.
7. See Levine 1988.
8. The term "opera" could refer to any kind of musical performance (John Kasson 1990, 217).
9. McConachie 1998, 147; and McDermott 1998, 191.
10. McConachie 1992, 200.
11. McConachie 1992, 252–53.
12. McConachie 1998, 123, 138, 161; McDermott 1998, 191; Postlewait 1999, 132, 170.
13. Murphy 1999, 298; Postlewait 1999, 141–48.
14. McConachie 1998, 113.
15. McConachie 1992, ix.
16. Richardson 1998, 258–62; Bigsby and Wilmeth 1999, 2–3.
17. McConachie 1992, 1.
18. Postlewait 1999, 158; McConachie 1992, 157–58, 194–95, 199.
19. McConachie 1992, 77–81, 97–98, 119–225.
20. *Express,* May 23, 1866, 2, quoted in McConachie 1992, 227.

21. See Marra 2006, xv, on era of the woman in the 1890s.
22. Postlewait 1999, 115.
23. Foster 2004, 117. See further Foley 2010 and Aronson 2000, 89, 95, 97, 100.
24. McConachie 1998, 148–50, 165–66; Williams 1998, 312; McConachie 1992, 75; Marra 2006, 9.
25. McConachie 1998, 165–66.
26. Williams 1998, 305; Frick 1999, 198–201.
27. Frick 1999, 200–205, 215–16, 222.
28. John Kasson 1990, 248.
29. Postlewait 1999, 150; Frick 1999, 197.
30. Bigsby and Wilmeth 1999, 6–7.
31. Frick 1999, 218.
32. Bigsby and Wilmeth 1999, 10–12; Fearnow 1999, 348–49; Chansky 2004.
33. Bigsby 1985, 19.
34. Bigsby and Wilmeth 1999, 21; Postlewait 1999, 165–66; Aronson 2000, 100.
35. Aronson 2000, 107, 126, 139; Baumol and Bowen 1966; Bigsby 1985, 23–29.
36. For a discussion of this phenomenon more broadly, see Hall et al. 2004.
37. See chapter 1 for important productions in this period of Euripides' *Iphigeneia in Aulis* and *Iphigeneia in Tauris* and one of Aeschylus's *Eumenides*. The range of plays in colleges and universities was larger; see Pluggé 1938; and chapter 1.1.
38. Bigsby 1985, 67; and, more generally, Marvin Carlson 2004.
39. Bigsby 2000a, 13; Aronson 2000, 94, 105; Lomonaco 2000, 227.
40. Aronson 2000, 149.
41. McConachie 1998, 157; Williams 1998, 331; Bigsby and Wilmeth 1999, 8; Postlewait 1999, 141–43.
42. See Foley 1999.
43. It was the task of surviving males to enact vendettas and of female relatives to promote justice through lamentation (Foley 2001, chap. III.2).
44. On productions that doubled Clytemnestra in order to juxtapose her character before and after Iphigeneia's sacrifice, see Foley 2005 and Colakis 1993, 66–78; Saviana Stanescu and Richard Schechner's 2003 *YokastaS* and 2005 *YokastaS Redux* multiplied the character of Jocasta from Sophocles' *Oedipus Tyrannus*.
45. For productions and new versions of *Iphigeneia in Aulis* and *Iphigeneia in Tauris* that multiplied or split Iphigeneia, see the epilogue.
46. See chapter 4, Charles Mee's *Orestes* (1998), and further discussion in Foley 2005.
47. Other important exceptions include the 1969 *Black Electra* and the much-revived 1974 *Elektra* directed by Andrei Serban with music by Elizabeth Swados. See further Choate 2009 and Laks 1995.
48. Appendix A notes important U.S. productions that emphasized neurotic Electras.
49. Quoted in Cargill et al. 1961, 111.
50. Bigsby 1982, 44, 82, and 85.
51. For other related new versions of *Electra*, see the 1982–83 *Electra-Cution or You're under Orestes*, and the 1996 and 1999 productions of *The Elektra Fugues* by Ruth E. Margraff (Margraff 2005).

52. From Young's 1931 review (*New Republic*, November 11, 1931), reprinted in Berlin 1989, 35. For a more complex view, see Nugent 1988.

53. Berlin 1989, 21. Major reviews reprinted in the Berlin volume largely recognize the importance of O'Neill's play and the production but are mixed on its move toward melodrama.

54. Greek tragedies such as Euripides' *Iphigeneia in Tauris* can also represent an attempt to move past previous family tragedies, however (see the epilogue).

55. After many revivals, the play was made into a film directed by Dudley Nicols in 1947, and an opera by Martin David Levy, with a libretto by Henry Butler, in 1967.

56. See further Blumenthal 1974 and Choate 2009. The 1975 and 1977 *Going Home* by the Kuku Ryku Theater Laboratory similarly reduced the myth to a two-person, partially improvised conflict on a bare stage with role reversals between Clytemnestra and Electra in which Clytemnestra communicated with the dead Iphigeneia, and Electra with the dead Agamemnon.

57. Blumenthal 1974, 103.
58. Walter Kerr, *New York Times*, June 19, 1974.
59. Jennifer Merin, *Soho Weekly News*, June 22, 1976, 19, speaking of the 1976 production.
60. Parts of this discussion are revised and repeated from Foley 2004, 99–102.
61. Coss et al. (1980) 1985 and 1983.
62. Malnig and Rosenthal 1993, 207. See now Malnig 2009.
63. Canning 1996, 180.
64. Coss et al. 1983, 241.
65. Eleanor Fuchs, *Soho Weekly News*, November 15, 1979, 56.
66. See especially Chodorow 1978.
67. Fleming, reported by Reid in Pound and Fleming (1987) 1989, xiii.
68. I quote from Reid's 1989 edition. My own views are similar to those in Carey Perloff's introduction to the 1990 edition and to Beye 1989. See also Choate 2009.
69. Xie 1999, 214–16.
70. See appendix A for the premiere in 2003 and other productions.
71. See further Foley 2001, chap. III.2.
72. McLaughlin 2005. For further discussion, see Foley 1995, Choate 2009, Malnig 2009, and the epilogue.
73. See Foley 2011.

## 1. GREEK TRAGEDY FINDS AN AMERICAN AUDIENCE

1. See, for example, Cheney 1914, 97–100, 116.
2. Quoted in Moses and Brown 1934, 61. See further Wilmeth and Bigsby 1998, 12–13.
3. See appendix G.
4. Hall and Macintosh 2005, 287.
5. Felton 1837, 486.
6. Odell 4: 467 (Odell's fourteen-volume *Annals of the New York Stage*, originally published in 1927–49, is cited throughout by volume and page number).
7. Odell 4: 467; Johnson 1971, 11; Hains 1910, 34; 1914, 197.

8. Addams (1910) 1967, 388–89; Chansky 2004, 57, cites the exact date as 1892.
9. See Hall and Macintosh 2005,
10. Hall and Macintosh 2005.
11. Odell 5: 134.
12. Brown 1: 341 (Thomas Allston Brown's three-volume *History of the New York Stage*, published in 1903, is cited throughout by volume and page number).
13. Poe 1845; see also Vandenhoff 1860, 243–45, esp. 245 on the "goat-bearded" chorus.
14. Odell 5:128–29.
15. See further Rogers 1986, 10–14; Hall and Macintosh 2005, chap. 12 and 337–41. The burlesque adapted a British version parodying the Covent Garden production (*Albion*, April 19, 1945).
16. Davis 2008 suggests that the play was a new American version based on the British John Savill Faucit's 1821 *Oedipus, A Musical Drama in Three Acts*; the American version added the story of the Sphinx and deleted Faucit's characters Creon and Eurydice.
17. Davis 2008.
18. Carson (1932) 1965, 254. The English verse translation was presented together with a Spanish play, *El Sitio de Colchester*, on the occasion of the students' eight annual examination.
19. Norman 1882 provides extensive documentation.
20. Norman 1882, 62; Pluggé 1938, 4; Reinhold 1984, 332.
21. Norman 1882, 55.
22. Norman 1882, 18–19.
23. Norman 1882, 65.
24. Norman 1882, 120–21.
25. Norman 1882, 49, 64, 72, 94. The Smith College Sophocles' *Electra* in 1889, with set, costumes, singing, and movement similar in style, is equally well documented in Tyler 1891; see also Fairclough 1903 on a 1902 production of *Antigone* at Stanford.
26. F. D. Millett was the costume designer; see his article in *Century Magazine*, November 1881, cited in Norman 1882; and also *Frank Leslie's Illustrated Newspaper*, June 4, 1881, 237. The Harvard and Smith 1889 productions used colorful costumes, in contrast to the white cheesecloth of many later college productions.
27. The play opened January 30. Its reception is documented in Norman 1882, 58–60, 104–12, 128–29; and Hains 1914, 190–94; the *New York Herald*, May 18, 1881, was critical of Riddle's performance.
28. *New York Mirror*, February 4, 1882; the same issue offered a parody by its "Giddy Gusher."
29. See *New York Dramatic Mirror*, February 4, 1882, as well as *New York World*, January 31, 1882, and Alexander 1960, 417–21. The *New York Times* review, January 31, 1882, defended the play against this interpretation.
30. Winter (1913) 1969, 1: 419.
31. Odell 12: 135 for 1883.
32. *New York Dramatic Mirror*, May 6, 1914.
33. *Theater Arts Monthly* 8, 1924, 74–76, for example, admired aspects of the production, especially the traces of Reinhardt in the opening scene, but pilloried the acting, Miriam

Lewes's Jocasta partially excepted. Arthur Hornblow, *Theatre Magazine* 38 (December 1923): 15, invoked Mounet-Sully as far superior.

34. Brandes 1945, 162.
35. Hapgood 1901, 143–49.
36. Harvard did so in 1886, and other schools and colleges followed (Reinhold 1984, 332–33; Winterer 2002, 101–2); by 1905, most colleges no longer required Greek for admission (see Hains 1910, 24, 26; Rogers 1986, 16–17).
37. Hofstadter et al. 1959, 302–7; Tyler, 1891, 63.
38. Johnson 1971, 10, 12.
39. See Hall and Macintosh 2005 on earlier school productions, however.
40. Norman 1882, 17.
41. Norman 1882, 108–10.
42. Pluggé 1938, 14, 148; Rogers 1986, 15–16.
43. Pluggé 1938, 17.
44. Pluggé 1938, 30. Pluggé sent detailed questionnaires to colleges and universities around the country.
45. Pluggé 1938, 30. See the forthcoming study by Yopie Prins.
46. Before 1926, speech departments had produced 18 out of 141.
47. Pluggé 1938, 108–10.
48. Pluggé 1938, 20, 110, 148–50.
49. On Wilamowitz, see Wiley 1999, 38–42. Wilamowitz believed in fidelity to the text, but both his translations and productions aimed to make Euripides available to a modern audience; Murray supported Barker (see below) and corresponded with Wilamowitz.
50. Pluggé 1938, 87.
51. Pluggé 1938, 85, 148–50.
52. Wiley 1999, 93. Wiley suggests (94, 100) that both the rise of public universities, with their interest in civic functionality, and the 1896 Olympic Games played a role here as well.
53. Review, *Boston Evening Transcript,* May 29, 1893.
54. See Pearcy 2008.
55. *Old Penn,* April 25 and May 2, 1903.
56. See, generally, Cheney 1918.
57. Macintosh 2009b, 161–64, esp. 161.
58. Germany, perhaps influentially, had adopted the practice of outdoor performance both in order to differentiate its theater practice from what it viewed as ornate and sophisticated performances in France and Italy and to create a site for plays and pageants expressing national ideals that included folk drama, plays dealing with Teutonic mythology, Shakespeare, and Greek drama in a beautiful, natural setting. See Cheney 1918, 65–81.
59. Cheney 1918.
60. Cheney 1918, 131–32, 159.
61. Cheney 1918, 130–31.
62. Waugh 1917, 5 and 24.
63. Cheney 1918, 148–49, defends the acoustics of outdoor settings that are naturally well-located and use bowl-shaped construction.

64. Arthur Row, "California's Outdoor Theater," *Illustrated World of Recreation*, September 1912.

65. Johnson 1971, 11; Palmer 1965, 132; Greenwalt 1955, 46.

66. Cheney 1918, 112–15.

67. See Hains 1910, 27; 1914, 192–94; Pluggé 1938, 73, 83; Foley 2005, 308. As in many places in Europe, early college performances in the United States often reflected recent literature on historical reconstructions of Greek theater (Macintosh 1997, 292).

68. Rogers 1986, 44.

69. Cheney 1918, 76, 128–29.

70. Johnson 1971, 17–18.

71. In contrast to the *Theatre Magazine* review (13 [January 1, 1911]) and other attributions of amateurism to the company, a number of reviews compared this production favorably with the British actress Mrs. Patrick Campbell's New York production of Hugo von Hofmannsthal's *Electra* in 1908 and criticized the "morbid Teutonic imagination" of Hofmannsthal in contrast to the simplicity, skepticism, and realism of Euripides (Smith 1915, 410). Feinsod (1992, 16) and Palmer (1987, 86–90) rely too much on the *Theatre Magazine* review.

72. See Pluggé 1938, 6, on *Electra*.

73. Johnson 1971, 19–20, 49, 242; Brandes 1945, 153–58.

74. D. Kennedy 1985, 182.

75. See D. Kennedy 1985, 44, 49, and 182.

76. On Murray as the most popular translator of the period under discussion in this chapter, see Pluggé 1938, 110.

77. D. Kennedy 1985, 181.

78. For further detail, see Richard C. Beacham, "Tragedy in the Bowl!" 48–51 (full reference for this article, accessible in the Archive of Performances of Greek and Roman Drama at Oxford, is not yet available), which drew on the Archives of the Yale Dramat at Yale University for local detail; and D. Kennedy 1985, 180–85. For a summarizing review, see "Revitalizing Greek Tragedy for American Consumption," *Current Opinion* 59, no. 1, July 1915, 28–29, which approved the production's modernity along with that of Isadora Duncan's recent *Oedipus* at the Century Opera House.

79. Mary Fanton Roberts saw Barker's *Trojan Women* as a response to German militarism (*Craftsman* 9, 1916, 431).

80. Smith 1915, 416.

81. The text remains in the Yale Music Library and is reproduced in Elberson 1968, 300–324.

82. See Smith 1915, 412; and Roberts, *Craftsman* 9, 1916, 440–41 n. 91; Rogers 1986, 57–58, defended Wilkinson's modern, innovative art nouveau costumes. The costumes for *Trojan Women* were more muted and received largely favorable responses.

83. Maria Carlson 1993; Deak 1993; Gerould and Kosicka 1980.

84. A point emphasized by Lingan's immensely helpful dissertation (2005); see also his web presentation at http://www.newmedialab.cuny.edu/PSM/e1s3.htm.

85. These productions are cited in the issues of the *Theosophical Path* for 1922, 1925, and 1927, Theosophical Library Center Archives.

86. Johnson 1971, 11; Palmer 1965, 132; and Greenwalt 1955, 46.

87. J. H. Fussell, "The School of Antiquity: Its Meaning Purpose, and Scope," *Sunrise* 47, April/May 1998, 139.

88. Maria Carlson 1993, 114–25.

89. R. Baker 1907, 238.

90. Waterstone 1995, esp. 156–58.

91. Waterstone 1995, 158, 174–75.

92. Greenwalt 1955, 107.

93. Program at New York Public Library for the Performing Arts, Lincoln Center.

94. Lecture, Bridgeport Art Club, November 15, 1898 (some members of the club attended the New York performance of *Eumenides*); letter from Katherine Tingley to Miss Elizabeth Whitney, New York, August 11, 1898, Theosophical Library Center Archives.

95. Blavatsky 1909; see further Lingan 2005, 45–47; Katherine Tingley to Elizabeth Whitney, August 11, 1898, 1–2, Theosophical Library Center Archives. Deak 1993, 117–19, cites French theater artists who also interpreted Wagner's works as occult texts.

96. Swanwick 1873.

97. See Hardwick 2000, 32–36.

98. Lecture, Bridgeport Art Club, November 15, 1898; and Joseph E. Fussell, "The Eumenides of Aeschylus—A Mystery Drama," *Theosophical Path*, 1922, 19, Theosophical Library Center Archives.

99. Greenwalt 1955, 99.

100. Tingley, lecture Bridgeport Art Club, November 15, 1898, Theosophical Library Center Archives.

101. Greenwalt 1955, 101; R. Baker 1907, 232.

102. Katherine Tingley, notes on *Eumenides*, November 8, 1898, Theosophical Library Center Archives. See also Fussell, "*Eumenides* of Aeschylus," *Theosophical Path*, 1922, 19, Theosophical Library Center Archives.

103. Fussell, "*Eumenides* of Aeschylus," *Theosophical Path*, 1922, 20–21, Theosophical Library Center Archives..

104. Lingan 2005, 69–72.

105. Photo in Theosophical Society Archives. See http://www.newmedialab.cuny.edu/PSM/e1s3.htm for photos.

106. Katherine Tingley to Elizabeth Whitney, New York, August 11, 1898, Theosophical Library Center Archives.

107. R. Baker 1907, 235.

108. "The Aroma of Athens—Athenian Flower Festival," *Century Path—Supplement*, Point Loma, Calif., vol. 14, no. 22, April 2, 1911.

109. *A Promise: A Greek Symposium by a Student of Esotero*, Issued by the Approval of Katherine Tingley, Official Head of the Universal Brotherhood and Theosophical Society (Point Loma, Calif.: Theosophical Publishing Company, 1901), 8, Theosophical Library Center Archives.

110. *Promise*, 11–12.

111. Lingan 2005, 57–58.

112. LeVay 1989, 17; Johnson 1971, iii and 82–83.

113. LeVay 1989, 209. On her versatility, see Johnson 1971, iv, 3, 154, and 227. On her revision of scripts, including changing the order of scenes, altering dialogue, and cutting choral odes, see Johnson 1971, 65; and Choate 2009.

114. Walter Prichard Eaton, *American Magazine* 76, October 1913, 47, gave her credit for being the first U.S. scenic reformer; Cheney 1914, 171, calls her one of the first to revolt against naturalism.

115. Johnson 1971, 192–98.

116. Johnson 1971, 48; LeVay 1989, 121.

117. *Harper's Bazaar*, June 1915, 24; and LeVay 1989, 228.

118. Isadora Duncan also visited Greece; see chapter 2.1.

119. LeVay 1989, 234, 229.

120. Johnson 1971, iii, 4.

121. *New York Evening World,* February 21, 1918; *New York Herald,* April 8, 1921; *New York Telegram,* August 4, 1921.

122. *University of California Chronicle* 17.4, 1915.

123. James O'Donnell Bennett, *Chicago Record-Herald*, December 2, 1913.

124. *New Jersey American,* June 1915.

125. LeVay 1989, 65–66; Johnson 1971, 47, 58–59. The critic was James O'Donnell Bennett (1906 letter to Johnson); see also John Webber, *Canadian Magazine*, December 1906, quoted by LeVay, 89.

126. LeVay 1989, 50, 61; and *San Francisco Wave,* July 8, 1900.

127. LeVay 1989, 124; Johnson 1971, 93–94; *Hearst's International Magazine* 28, July 1915.

128. *Hearst's International Magazine* 28 (July 1915).

129. See Arthur Inkersley, "*Oedipus Tyrannus* at the University of California," *Overland Monthly* 56, July 1910, 230.

130. Row, "California's Outdoor Theatre."

131. *Hearst's International Magazine* 28 (July 1915).

132. LeVay 1989, 122. She lost $5,000 on the production, expending $9,500 with a take of $4,500 for 8,000 attendees.

133. Cheney 1918, 161–63. Bright lights burning calcium carbonate replaced candles and oil lamps in the first third of the nineteenth century; indoor electric lights began to be used in the 1880s.

134. *Theatre Magazine* 22.175 (September 1915): 114.

135. Montgomery Phister, *Cincinnati Commercial,* July 10, 1910.

136. *Vogue,* August 1910, cited in Hamilton 1920, 212.

137. Johnson 1971, 17–18.

138. See Johnson 1971, 243.

139. James O'Donnell Bennett, one of a number of critics who journeyed to Berkeley to report on the play, *Chicago Record-Herald,* July 3, 1910.

140. Johnson 1971, 114.

141. Johnson 1971, 82–83.

142. Anglin, *Theatre Magazine* 24 (December 16, 1916): 352.

143. Anglin, quoted in *Providence Journal,* June 5, 1928 (cited in Johnson 1971, 79).

144. *New York Sun,* February 3, 1918; *New York Evening Post,* April 27, 1927; Johnson 1971, 84–85.

145. Johnson 1971, 5–6, 88, and 258; Le Vay 1989, 124, 252, and 265. In both 1911 and 1913 the Harvard Greek Department demanded too much historical correctness. Yale insisted on a student cast. In Anglin's view Henderson lacked feeling for the "religious" quality of Greek tragedy. Anglin arrived to play in Neumayer's *Antigone* on the day of the performance, and she was completely unsympathetic to Henderson's production. In a later interview Anglin also pronounced Riddle "too tenacious of the academic" (*New York Post,* March 2, 1918; Johnson 1971, 96).

146. LeVay 1989, 14. A 1916 survey listed David Belasco, George M. Cohan, Mrs. Fiske, and Anglin as America's best directors (Choate 2009, 49).

147. Ada Patterson, *Harper's Bazaar,* June 1915, 24; see also *New York Dramatic Mirror,* June 1913.

148. *Hearst's International Magazine* 28, July 1915, 44.

149. Review of *Electra,* August 29, 1915, preceded by reviews of *IA* and *Medea* on August 15 and August 2.

150. *New Jersey Star,* June 14, 1913.

151. *Harper's Bazaar,* June 1915, 24.

152. Johnson 1971, 69, 72–73, 133, 208. The *New York Dramatic Mirror,* June 1913, noted her American casts.

153. "Margaret Anglin Plays "Iphigenia" in California," August 21, 1915, source illegible in clipping from the Robinson Locke Collection, Margaret Anglin, vol. 21, p. 35, New York Public Library for the Performing Arts, Lincoln Center, New York; Walter Anthony, *San Francisco Chronicle,* August 8, 1915.

154. Frank Vreeland, *Evening Telegram* (New York), May 4, 1927; and Johnson 1971, 148.

155. Johnson 1971, 237; *San Francisco Examiner,* September 7, 1913; *Detroit Journal,* January 20, 1916; LeVay 1989, 143.

156. *Detroit Journal,* January 20, 1916; Ada Patterson, "A Greek Revival in the Drama," *Cosmopolitan* 59, August 1915, 358; and Johnson 1971, 241–42.

157. Johnson 1971, 245.

158. Johnson 1971, 231.

159. *Theatre Magazine* 19.160 (June 1914): 290; the *Sioux City Journal,* July 4, 1914, makes it three hundred seats and $600.

160. LeVay 1989, 166–67. See Choate 2009, 153–57, on Anglin's creation of a villainous Clytemnestra.

161. Johnson 1971, 144–46; Walter Anthony, *San Francisco Chronicle,* August 29, 1915; *San Francisco Examiner,* September 15, 1913.

162. Johnson 1971, 78, quoting Anglin.

163. A. S., "Anglin Cheered in *Electra,*" *New York American,* December 2, 1927 (cited in Johnson 1971, 124). For further discussion of Anglin's voice and delivery, which did not please all critics, see Johnson 1971, 125–30.

164. Johnson 1971, 122.

165. Walter Anthony, "Margaret Anglin Stages Euripides," *Chicago Evening Post*, August 26, 1915 (cited in Johnson 1971, 122).
166. Johnson 1971, 118.
167. *Theatre Magazine* 19.160 (June 1914): 290.
168. *Theatre Magazine* 19.160 (June 1914): 290.
169. Hamilton 1920, 211–12.
170. On Electra as the dominant force in propelling the production's revenge theme, see *New York Times*, February 7, 1918, 9; and Choate 2009, 103–4.
171. Frank Vreeland, *Evening Telegram* (New York), May 4, 1927.
172. LeVay 1989, 168; Johnson 1971, 304.
173. LeVay 1989, 162. She was criticized in the *New York Call*, September 4, 1921, for lack of appropriately Greek austerity.
174. *Munsey's*, July 1915.
175. *New York Times*, August 29, 1915; Walter Anthony, *San Francisco Chronicle*, August 15, 1915.
176. Johnson 1971, 255.
177. *Munsey's*, July 1915. On the virtues of Potter's translations, see Walton 2006; see Choate 2009 on Anglin's revisions of the script of *Electra*.
178. See Johnson 1971, 137–44, on critical responses to the music of Anglin's productions.
179. Johnson 1971, 213–16. The promptbook for *IA* with musical notation was available to Johnson.
180. Johnson 1971, 218.
181. Johnson 1971, 217, 221.
182. LeVay 1989, 162.
183. Johnson 1971, 89–90, 112–16, 204, 213–19, 250.
184. Johnson 1971, 115, 216, 251–52.
185. *San Francisco Call*, August 23, 1915; see also *Christian Science Monitor*, August 28, 1915; *Theatre Magazine* 22 (September 1915): 116.
186. LeVay 1989, 166. Johnson 1971, 102, 306.
187. Ada Patterson, *Theatre Magazine* 23 (June 1916): 340–41.
188. LeVay 1989, 165; Johnson 1971, 246.
189. See Hall and Macintosh 2005, 391–429, on British *Medea*s. Some reviews described Anglin's Medea as mad.
190. A total of three for *Electra*, five in all, due to popular demand (Brandes 1945, 187.)
191. For further discussion of the April 7–8, 1921, production of *IA*, with Anglin as Clytemnestra, see Le Vay 1989, 199–201; and Browne 1955, 254–56.
192. LeVay 1989, 186.
193. Arthur Hornblow, *Theatre Magazine* 27.206 (April 1918): 217; *Vogue*, April 1, 1918.
194. Johnson 1971, 148–49, 235–38.
195. Johnson 1971, 149, 240–41.
196. *New York Times*, April 29, 1915.
197. *New York Times*, February 7, 1918.
198. Hiram K. Moderwell, "New York Approves Play by Sophocles, in Which Margaret Anglin Plays the Role," *Indiana News*, date illegible, 1918, Robinson Locke Collection,

Margaret Anglin, vol. 21, p. 81, New York Public Library for the Performing Arts, Lincoln Center, New York; see similar point in *Christian Science Monitor,* February 10, 1918.

199. Frank Vreeland, *Evening Telegram* (New York), May 4, 1927.

200. *Providence Journal,* June 27, 1928.

201. Anglin inaugurated the outdoor Garden Theater with twelve evening performances in St. Louis that played to 29,000 (Johnson 1971, 27, 68).

202. F. Vreeland, *Evening Telegram* (New York), May 4, 1927.

203. Brooks Atkinson, *New York Times,* May 15, 1927.

204. R. D. Skinner, *Commonweal,* May 18, 1927, called it "the only momentous and truly great performance I have seen on the English stage."

205. *Philadelphia Sun,* December 17, 1927.

206. *New York Times,* May 4, 1927. See Johnson 1971, 109–10, for negative academic views.

207. Johnson 1971, 107–10; Le Vay 1989, 209.

208. Johnson 1971, 263–65.

209. Johnson 1971, 222; LeVay 1989, 235, 248.

210. Johnson 1971, 265–72; LeVay 1989, 235.

211. Johnson 1971, 211.

212. Johnson 1971, 275–80; LeVay 1989, 285, 295–96, 298–99.

213. Johnson 1971, 274.

214. Browne 1955, 251–56.

215. LeVay 1989, 38.

216. LeVay 1989, 268, is uncertain of the date of this encounter. His source for both points is a letter from Jerome Collamore, October 28, 1985.

217. Although the Chicago Little Theatre was not technically the first of its kind, Browne was generally acknowledged as founder of the movement, and, ultimately, of New York's Off Broadway (Rogers 1986, 99; Wiley 1999, 118; Dukore 1957, 126).

218. On the Little Theatre audience, see Dukore 1957, 14–16; Edwards 1987, 54; and, more generally, Chansky 2004, esp. 14–16.

219. Wiley 1999, 59–65. As Wiley notes, Yeats himself was inspired by a production at Notre Dame in 1911 (63); the Irish Players also had a profound influence on O'Neill (65).

220. Program to the 1915 *Trojan Women,* New York Public Library for the Performing Arts, Lincoln Center, New York.

221. Browne 1955, 118–19.

222. Wiley 1999, 29.

223. Program note written by Browne's friend John Cowper Powys.

224. See further Browne 1913 and 1914–15 and Feinsod 1992, 84.

225. Browne 1955, 188; Dukore 1957, 25–26, 126.

226. Edwards 1987, 81.

227. Browne 1955, 180–81.

228. Wiley 1999, 138, 143–45.

229. Edwards 1987, 66, 80, 90; Duffey 1954, 29, 243; Wiley 1999, 145.

230. Edwards 1987, 79–80.

231. Feinsod 1992, 92.

232. Feinsod 1992, 79, 83. Wagner was also an influence.
233. Floyd Dell, *Harper's Weekly*, November 29, 1913, 22; Feinsod 1992, 85–86.
234. Feinsod 1992, 89–90, 90.
235. On the acting, see further Feinsod 1992, 85.
236. Dukore 1957, 54–57; Browne 1955, 159.
237. Feinsod 1992, 91.
238. Browne 1955, 159.
239. Dukore 1957, 99.
240. Browne 1955, 384. Dukore 1957, 101–2, offers a sample of the music for *Medea*, which is modal rather than tonal, with one note per syllable in a fashion that suits folk song.
241. Browne 1914–15, 617 and 625; see also Browne 1955, 159.
242. James O'Donnell Bennett, "Art of Stage Management versus Millinery," *Record-Herald,* March 22, 1914, part II, 1–2.
243. Floyd Dell, *Harper's Weekly*, November 29, 1913, 22.
244. Dell, *Harper's Weekly*, November 29, 1913, 24; Browne and Barker shared these goals.
245. Wiley 1999, 19. The group also went to Milwaukee, St. Louis, and Kansas City.
246. Dukore 1957, 14–15, 46.
247. See Browne 1955, 252–56.
248. Kenneth Macgowan, *Globe*, March 3, 1920.
249. See further on *Medea*'s stagecraft Dukore 1957, 74–101.
250. Rogers 1986, 102–6.
251. Browne 1955, 246.
252. Browne 1955, 189.
253. Browne 1955, 245–46.
254. Johnson 1971, 35.
255. Feinsod 1992, 16.
256. The play was also presented at a dramatic festival at Ann Arbor, Michigan.
257. Richard Dana Skinner, *Commonweal*, January 27, 1932, 357–58. See also Hartigan 1995, 28–29. Only Mrs. Patrick Campbell as Clytemnestra maintained the formal stately style often thought to be appropriate to Greek tragedy, but failed to excite several critics. See further Choate 2009.
258. See above all *Commonweal,* January 27, 1932.
259. Gilbert W. Gabriel, *New York American,* January 9, 1932, who preferred a visiting production of Hofmannsthal's *Electra* starring the Greek actress Mme Marika Kotopouli in 1931.
260. Hamilton 1920, 208, 210.
261. Richard Lockridge, *New York Sun*, January 9, 1932; *Commonweal,* January 27, 1932.
262. See Browne 1955, 200–201, on his relation to Cook; he found American plays disappointing.
263. Wiley 1999, 170–71.
264. Glaspell (1927) 1941, 224–25.

265. Bigsby 1982, 10.
266. Glaspell (1927) 1941, 47–48.
267. Sarlós 1982, 35–36.
268. Sayler 1923, 73–74.
269. Nietzsche's important influence on Cook also played a role here (Wiley 1999, 153–56).
270. Glaspell (1927) 1941, 249–5.
271. Glaspell (1927) 1941, 414.
272. Cook 1926; see also the preface to this book; Glaspell (1927) 1941, 271.
273. Bigsby 1982, 7.
274. Bigsby 1982, 39, 42, 118–19.
275. See Cargill et al. 1961, 111.
276. Letter to Arthur Hobson Quinn, 1925, quoted in Bigsby 1982, 45.
277. Gelb and Gelb (1973) 1987, 5.
278. Letter to Arthur Hobson Quinn, 1925, quoted in Bigsby 1982, 45.
279. Törnqvist 1969, 13–14.
280. Berlin 1989, 46, 59, 62, 63.
281. Manheim 1998, 1–2.
282. Eugene O'Neill, "On Masks," Yale Collection.
283. Jones 1962, esp. 45–46 and 270.
284. See Bigsby 1982, 10.
285. "Trojan Women Comes to Columbus," *Columbus Citizen*, May 11, 1915; Feinsod 1992, 90, 93; Dukore 1957, 125.
286. Macgowan 1921, 13, 26.
287. Macgowan 1921, 66, 216–18.
288. Wiley 1999, 178–80, argues that the revolution in stagecraft in fact predated the writings of Craig, Appia, and others and suggests something similar for the role of the independent theater movement, but I would interpret this trend more broadly and include outdoor, club, and academic theater.
289. Macgowan 1921, 198. Reinhardt was in Macgowan's view overly theatrical and trivialized the stage in favor of the "orchestra."
290. Macgowan 1921, 264.
291. Macgowan 1921, 279–80.
292. Macgowan 1921, 283.
293. Productions fell by a third (Watermeier 1998, 49); see further the introduction.
294. Pluggé 1938, 116, 158–59, 163.

## 2. MAKING TOTAL THEATER IN AMERICA

1. For ancient sources, see Csapo and Slater 1995. There is some evidence that the tragic chorus danced in rectangular formations, but these passages may refer only to entrances (see Csapo 2008, 280–84). Although vase paintings and sculpture depict dancing, we cannot, with the likely exception of plays with Dionysiac choruses, link up the visual

representations with specific movements that were named but insufficiently described in ancient sources. Several papyrus scraps and inscriptions have musical notation; its interpretation remains controversial; see especially West 1992.

2. See P. Brown 2004, McDonald 2001, and Brown and Ograjensek 2010. On some American operatic versions of the *Oresteia*, see Foley 2005.

3. Daly 1995, 122–31. From 1909, the Viennese Émile Jaques-Dalcroze's system of eurythmics, developed for learning and experiencing music through movement, also attracted American enthusiasts in Switzerland, where he moved from Germany.

4. See Banta 1987, 638–54, for further examples and discussion.

5. Banta 1987, 643, 647.

6. Banta 1987, 641.

7. Pluggé 1938, 97–102, 106, 113, 125–26, 140, 151, 159, 161. More ambitious productions, such as Euripides' *Alcestis* at the University of New Mexico, began to adopt new techniques (Pluggé 1938, 106–7).

8. See Choate 2009, 208–10, for further discussion.

9. Daly 1995, 19.

10. On the tour (which included Philadelphia, Chicago, St. Louis, Brooklyn, Boston, and Washington) and Duncan's collaboration with Walter Damrosch, see Kay Bardsley, *Ballet Review* 19.3 (Fall 1991): 86–96.

11. As a whole this discussion relies heavily on Daly 1995.

12. Influences on Duncan included Darwin, Walt Whitman, Plato, Wagner, Nietzsche, and her lover Gordon Craig, as well as Greek art and the U.S. physical culture movement. She worked briefly with the dancer Loie Fuller, who used fabric and colored lights to produce striking visual images.

13. I. Duncan 1928, 131.

14. Daly 1995, 140.

15. See "Boston Is Bacchic Says Miss Duncan," *Boston Sunday Herald*, November 28, 1909, Isadora Duncan Clippings, Washington, D.C. (cited in Daly 1995, 145, 246 n. 101); and I. Duncan, 1927b, 592.

16. I. Duncan 1927a, 45. On Duncan's views of the Greek chorus, see further Franko 1995, 17–20.

17. Daly 1995, 220.

18. "Boston Is Bacchic Says Miss Duncan," *Boston Sunday Herald*, November 28, 1909, Isadora Duncan Clippings, Washington, D.C. (cited in Daly 1995, 145, 246 n. 101).

19. I. Duncan 1928, 84.

20. I. Duncan 1928, 87.

21. I. Duncan 1927a, 136.

22. She attempted at one point to portray all fifty maidens of Aeschylus's *Suppliants* in solo dance (I. Duncan 1927a, 136).

23. Folder 107, Irma Duncan Papers, Washington, D.C. (quoted in Daly 1995, 147–48); F. Blair 1986, 191–92; Loewenthal 1993, 133–35.

24. Daly 1995, 150.

25. Daly 1995, 151, 184.

26. Daly 1995, 153.

27. Daly 1995, 151–52; Kurth 2001, 336.

28. See *Art and Archaeology* 3.5 (May 1916): 250–63. Raymond Duncan's New York production cut Chrysothemis; the actresses, including his wife, Eleni Sikelianos, as Clytemnestra, were better reviewed than the actors.

29. Plato's *Laws*, perhaps too tendentiously, repeatedly represents this ideal. See especially Winkler 1990.

30. *Classical Journal* 19 (1924): 514.

31. *Theatre Magazine*, December 1921, 398–99. Scores of his music are currently inaccessible at the New York Public Library for the Performing Arts, Lincoln Center, New York.

32. Kennedy and Kennedy 1921, 398; see also Gage 1929, 573.

33. Margaret Gage, interview by Betty White, August 6, 1979, recording and transcript, New York Public Library for the Performing Arts, Lincoln Center, New York.

34. John Corbin, *New York Times*, May 25, 1923, praised Kennedy's acting but thought Matthison's 1923 Antigone lacked "the keen steel of resolution"; *Theatre Magazine*, August 8, 1923, 16, also praised Kennedy's acting and thought Matthison effective but too fanatical and insufficiently tender.

35. *New York Times*, May 24, 1931, and May 28, 1933. In his earlier review of the *Trojan Women* (*New York Times*, May 29, 1932), Martin criticized the open-air setting for diffusing the focus on Gage's "a little fragile and a little ladylike" chorus, which unlike Isadora Duncan, aimed at "moving simplicity" and certainly "grasps the form of a choric ode."

36. Selden 1929, 18–19 and 49, who also comments on Eva Sikelianos' *Bacchae*. See also Donnelly 1930, 57–63.

37. Margaret Gage, interview by Betty White, August 6, 1979, recording and transcript, New York Public Library for the Performing Arts, Lincoln Center, New York; "Reminiscences of Mary Wigman," by Margaret Gage, August 8, 1979, New York Public Library for the Performing Arts, Lincoln Center, New York; Gage 1932.

38. Gage 1929, 575.

39. Gage 1929, 575, 577, 578, 566.

40. Gage 1929, 577, 578.

41. Gage 1929, 573–74.

42. Donnelly 1930, 60 and 62, with quotations from Gage.

43. Pluggé 1938, 83.

44. Lawrence E. Davis, *New York Times*, June 2, 1935, counted nine hundred in the audience and a chorus of forty-two; the production in his view aimed at Plato's unity of "poetry, music, and gymnastics." Local reviews had a mixed response to the music and the prose translation. See further the forthcoming discussion by Yopie Prins.

45. See Palmer-Sikelianos 1993, 114–15; and further discussion in Albright 2010 and Michelakis 2010.

46. See especially Spackman 1985 and Goldman 1950 on Riegger's music.

47. Spackman 1985, 441–42.

48. Flanagan (1940) 1965, 435.

49. Press release, WPA Theatre Project, "Government and the Arts in America" exhibition, December 1993–May 1994, New York Public Library for the Performing Arts, Lincoln Center, New York,.

50. Lloyd 1949, 133. On Tamiris's dance generally, see further Schlundt 1972, Tish 1994, and Cooper 1997.

51. The *New York Journal* thought the play "bunk," while the *Daily News* thought it "arresting and dignified." Among other mixed reviews, Howard Bay's set received the most frequent praise.

52. "Dance Theater of the WPA: A Record of National Accomplishment, Part II," *Dance Observer*, June 9, 1939, 281.

53. Tish 1994, 354–55, 339.

54. New York Public Library for the Performing Arts, Lincoln Center, New York.

55. Davis, unpublished "Theatre Notebook," 4, Hallie Flanagan Collection, New York Public Library for the Performing Arts, Lincoln Center, New York.

56. Martin, *New York Times*, May 1, 1938, particularly praised the performance of this ode.

57. Graham, quoted in Armitage (1937) 1966, 100. For a useful discussion of Graham's political and formal development, see Franko 1995.

58. See further Foley 2004 and 2005.

59. Graham, quoted in Louis Horst Manuscripts, New York Public Library for the Performing Arts, Lincoln Center, New York. See Franko 1995, 54.

60. Franko 1995, 55 and 64.

61. See Schlundt 1962 and J. Sherman 1983.

62. Terry 1976. Another important close contemporary, Doris Humphrey, developed a fully choreographed version of Aeschylus's *Libation Bearers* by 1933, drawing on Darius Milhaud's *Les Choéphores* with a text by Paul Claudel. The energetic choral work included, as did ancient choreography, the use of vivid hand gestures. See Bannermann 2010, 257–58.

63. Stodelle 1984, 15.

64. Stodelle 1984, 101, 106–7, 145.

65. A number of works, especially Stodelle 1984, offer good basic discussions. See also Chioles 1993, de Mille 1956, Horosko (1981) 2002, Leatherman 1966, McDonagh 1973, Foley 2004 and 2005, Bannerman 2010, and Zajko 2010. In addition, Graham's own *Notebooks* (1973) offer insights into her creative process.

66. *New York Times*, April 3, 1944; Stodelle 1984, 169.

67. See Helpern 1994 and Horosko (1981) 2002.

68. For further description, see Stodelle 1984, 251–55.

69. *Cave* and *Night Journey* are recorded and remain a regular part of the Graham company's repertory. See also McDonagh 1973, 190; Stodelle 1984, 141–45, 156. I rely for *Phaedra* on the description of McDonagh, 262–63; Stodelle, 228–31; and a review by Anna Kisselgoff, *New York Times*, October 13, 1988, since, in contrast to the other dances I mention, I have been unable to see any version of this dance.

70. See further Graham 1991, 212–18; Stodelle 1984, 155–60; Foley 2004, 84–85, with further bibliography; and McDonagh 1973, 200–201.

71. See further McDonagh 1973, 249–51; Chioles 1993; Stodelle 1984, 193–99; and Foley 2005, 314–16, with further bibliography.

72. Graham 1991, 11.

73. The discussion of Serban/Swados's general approach repeats but adapts my discussion in Foley 2007. On Schechner's important *Dionysus in 69*, see especially Schechner 1970, Zeitlin 2004, Brian De Palma's film version, and Foley 2007 (on choreography).

74. Menta 1995; A. Green 1994, 46–52.

75. Elizabeth Swados, quoted in a WNYC-TV documentary on Ellen Stewart, September 21, 1990 (A. Green 1994, 48 n. 21); Bartow 1988, 294; and Menta 1995, 16.

76. See Menta 1995, 21–32; and Hartigan 1995, 45–46, 52.

77. See especially Bernard Knox, *New York Review of Books*, July 14, 1977, reprinted in Knox 1979, 70–78; Foley 2005, 310; Hartigan 1995, 45–46, 52–53, 72–74, 151; and Menta 1995, 32–38. Knox objected to the reversal of the order of the final scenes, where Aegisthus confronted the chorus before Clytemnestra; the play then ended with the silent appearance of Orestes and Electra as witnesses and future avengers.

78. Margaret Croyden, *New York Times*, May 8, 1977.

79. Menta 1995, 34.

80. The Delacorte version, which is the one I saw myself, received much better reviews (see Menta 1995).

81. Knox 1979, 73.

82. For further documentation, see Menta 1995.

83. Partch 1991, 218; and Sheppard 2001, 187.

84. Partch 1991, 219.

85. Partch was aware of Graham's work, however.

86. See Partch 1991, esp. 240. See further Sheppard 2001, 183–85.

87. Partch 1991, 194. See further Sheppard 2001, 182–83.

88. See Partch 1974 and further, 1991, 220. See Wolff 2010 and Chalmers 1996 on Partch's music and his Greek music-dramas; Gilmore's biography (1998, esp. 198–205 on the 1952 production and 222–26 on the 1954 production at the Sausalito Art Festival and KPFA recording) gives, along with Blackburn 1997, 142–44, 486–87, and 491, helpful details about the production and reviews of *Oedipus*.

89. Partch 1991, 244. Another revival of the 1967 version occurred in 1997 at the Metropolitan Museum in New York.

90. Partch 1991, 213. See further Sheppard 2001, 186–88.

91. Partch 1991, 214.

92. Partch 1991, 214; see also 270.

93. See Partch 1991, 244, for his hostility to contemporary recitations of Greek choruses in unison.

94. Partch 1991, 239 and 182. Gilmore 1998, 203, notes that some critics found the speaking voices monotonous. *Revelation in the Courthouse Park* had more continuous musical accompaniment.

95. See further Partch 1991, 216–17.

96. Partch 1991, 244. Partch originally planned to transfer *Bacchae* entirely into an American setting (Sheppard 2001, 210).

97. See Sheppard 2001, 209 and 308 n. 16, for a full reference to this unpublished text.

98. See Partch 1991, 322–24, for detailed descriptions of the production; and Peter Yates in Blackburn 1997, 302–6, for an eloquent eyewitness description.

99. Partch 1991, 246; "Religious rituals with a strong sexual element are not unknown to our culture" (245).

100. Partch 1991, 246.

101. Partch 1991, 245.

102. Partch 1991, 246.

103. See further Sheppard 2001, 222–24, who notes the similarities to Richard Schechner's vision of Dionysus in *Dionysus in 69*.

104. Partch 1991, 246.

105. Stiller 1992, 895–96; see also Sheppard 2001, 208–9.

106. Sheppard 2001, chap. 13, sees Partch as part of a trend in American musical theater to use ritual and references to popular music for social criticism, especially of the relation between individual and society.

107. Partch 1991, esp. 222–23, 233; see also Blackburn 1997, 501–2.

108. Mee 2006, 32.

109. Mee 2006, 32; Meineck 2006, 153–54. Meineck notes that Bill T. Jones was thought by some to lack hip-hop credibility (158).

110. Mee 2006, 31. A mix of speech and song, rap's accentual meter preserves the same number of strong beats (not total beats) per line, which permits shifts in tempo and syncopation, or "flow" that persists regardless of the music accompanying it.

111. Mee 2006, 32.

112. Meineck 2006, 149, notes this.

113. Mee 2006, 29–31. Power (Mee, 31) saw a parallel with the generations of the Bush family in the presidency.

114. Mee 2006, 70.

115. Mee 2006, 28–30; Meineck 2006, 150.

116. Among many positive and mixed reviews (see appendix G), John Lahr, *New Yorker*, March 6, 2006, 80–81, praised Power's intelligence and wordplay but thought hip-hop too untheatrical—"It's all tell and no show" (81). Sean O'Donnell, www.showbusinessweekly.com/archive/374/Seven.shtml, thought the first half "meandered," but the second half "crackled"; the music was "forgettable" and "derivative," and the two brothers miscast.

117. Meineck 2006, 151, has a mixed view on this question. Michael Feinhold, *Village Voice*, February 22–28, 2006, praised the production's ambition, energy, and choreography but diagnosed a gap between Aeschylus's ritualistic, public original and hip-hop's alienated, colloquial, profane, satiric, and individual style. David Spencer, http://www.aislesay.com/NY-SEVEN.html, preferred the lighter first half but found the play's politics unconvincing. Charles Isherwood's fairly positive review (*New York Times*, February 13, 2006) agreed, finding the play successful as long as it lampooned its urtext.

118. See especially Wetmore 2003 (with extensive bibliography); A. Green 1994, 58–66; Koger 1997; McDonald 2001, 159–77; and Goff and Simpson 2007, 178–218. Koger and McDonald discuss the play's music in detail. Foley 2007, 370–72, includes and expands on some of the points I make here. The 1985 production is currently available on DVD, New Video NYC.

119. See Edmunds 1996 and Wilson 1997.

120. See Breuer, quoted in William Harris, "Mabou Mines Set Lear on a Hot Tin Roof," *New York Times*, January 21, 1990.

121. As Breuer was aware, however, *The Gospel*'s metatheatre makes contradictions between Sophocles and Pentecostal Christianity legible. See Cody 1999, 458; and Goff and Simpson 2007.

122. Breuer 1989, ix. As Wetmore 2003, 103, points out, however, Greek tragedies did not always forge communal bonds in any simple sense.

123. Burton 1980, 240.

124. Taplin 1984–85 (1988).

125. Goff and Simpson 2007, 191.

126. See especially D'Aponte 1991, 102; Koger 1997; and Wetmore 2003, 104–5.

127. Wetmore 2003, 110.

128. Critics sympathetic to *The Gospel* generally agree on this point. See especially Wetmore 2003; D'Aponte 1991, 109; A. Green 1994; McDonald 2001.

129. Reviews criticized its condescending representation of Appalachian stereotypes, its cluttered and meandering plot, weak dialogue in a love scene between Antigone and Harmon, interludes concerning the Amos, still alive in act 1, and revelations about Antigone's mother, Mama Virginia in act 2.

130. Christopher Platt, *Time Out Chicago*, June 8, 2005. Creon's drawl apparently evoked George W. Bush. Platt criticized the play's overly fast-paced direction.

131. Andy Probst, www.theatermania.com/content/news/cfm/story/11669, thought the show made the case that "this is what you're missing if you think the rock revolution only thrives on Broadway"; and Jenna Tesse Fox, www.broadwayworld.com/article/The_Rockae _I_Am_A_Golden_God_20071009, called it "the best combination of rock and theatre in recent memory." Aside from complaints of unevenness, the only mixed review was that of Rachel Saltz, *New York Times*, October 8, 2007.

132. See Foley 1985, 205–58.

133. See Cornerstone Theater's 2000 *Antigone Story, A Greek Tragedy Hijack,* a multimedia rock musical in Los Angeles (Foley 2011) and LiveStage Performance's 2007 *Elektrafire: A Modern Rock Opera* by Doug Thoms at New York's International Fringe Festival (Village Theatre), after earlier versions that played at a rock club in Cambridge, Massachusetts, in 1998.

134. For valuable discussion, see especially Fuchs 1986; Fuchs and Marranca 1986; Rouse 1986–87; Arnott 1987, 377–81; A. Green 1994, 66–68; and Holmberg 1996. For photos, see Quadri et al. 1998.

135. Holmberg 1996, 53.

136. See Smith 1986, 89.

137. Fuchs and Marranca 1986, 88.

138. Wilson, quoted in Fuchs and Marranca 1986, 102.

139. Fuchs and Marranca 1986, 82.

140. Smith 1986, 88.

141. Müller's text is published in Fuchs and Marranca 1986.

142. The designer Tom Kamm, quoted in Fuchs and Marranca 1986, 89–90.

143. Rouse 1986–87, 59, thought the energetic confrontation of this scene the dramatic high point. Fuchs 1986, by contrast, found the Alcestis-Admetus bedroom scene banal.

144. Fuchs 1986 sees a feminist theme throughout in a descent from a prehistoric femaleness or androgyny to masculine patriarchal culture and industrialism, then back to the vagina-like final eye. Rouse 1986–87, 58, interprets the play as torn between depicting the patriarchal sacrifice demanded by the powerful and a nostalgic yearning for preindustrial innocence.

145. Hans Peter Kuhn, quoted in Fuchs and Marranca 1986, 102–3.

146. Wilson, quoted in Fuchs and Marranca 1986, 86.

147. Actress Diane D'Aquila, Alcestis, quoted in Fuchs and Marranca 1986, 97–100.

148. Quoted from Wilson's script in the Houghton Library's Theatre Collection at Harvard.

## 3. DEMOCRATIZING GREEK TRAGEDY

1. Chapter epigraphs: Sartre, quoted in Contat and Rybalka 1974, 188; Robbe-Grillet 1965, 38 and 41.

2. For a useful summary of recent views, see Saïd 1998.

3. K. Blair 1994, 146.

4. See Foley 2005.

5. Chansky 2004, 107; and K. Blair 1994, 145, who notes the active role of women as actors, donors, and founders.

6. Secretary's Report, Saturday Morning Club archive, Schlesinger Library, Radcliffe College. See Choate 2009 on the Sargent and Belasco *Electra*.

7. *Boston Daily Advertiser*, March 13, 1890.

8. The Saturday Morning Club archive contains detailed accounts for the production.

9. Howe 1899, 157.

10. Richards and Elliot (1915) 1990, 203–5; Howe 1899, 238, 240; and Foley, forthcoming.

11. See the review in *New York Times*, March 24, 1911.

12. Morrison, "Memories," 1890, Saturday Morning Club papers, Schlesinger Library, Radcliffe College. Some newspaper clippings preserved in the club's archives are without date or attribution. Rachel Lesser investigated these papers on my behalf and offered comments on this section of this chapter.

13. See Banta 1987, 654.

14. Morrison preferred the anonymous review in the *Boston Daily Advertiser*, March 13, 1890, which she attributes to Heloise E. Hersey.

15. Anonymous review, *Boston Daily Advertiser*, March 13, 1890.

16. *Boston Daily Advertiser, Boston Post, Boston Herald*, all March 13, 1890. The *Boston Evening Transcript*, March 13, 1890, was somewhat more critical.

17. *Boston Daily Advertiser*, March 13, 1890.

18. Banta 1987, 659–60; and *Boston Daily Globe*, March 13, 1890.

19. Winterer 2001, 77.

20. Winterer 2001, 80.

21. A. Murray 1903, 7–18.

22. Winterer 2001, 71.

23. My source is an unattributed newspaper clipping dated June 3, 1909, from the New York Public Library for the Performing Arts, Lincoln Center (Antigone clippings file).

24. Johnson 1971, 20, cites her as Marita Howard; Waugh 1917, 99–101, with illustrations, gives her name as Marcia Howard and thinks the play was Sophocles' *Electra*. Such private performances were not uncommon in this period. William Faversham presented Euripides' *Orestes* in 1916 at the Rosemary Theatre in Huntington, Long Island, on the private estate of Roland Conklin (Johnson 1971, 23). The cast included Faversham, Julie Opp, Julia Arthur, and Nijinsky performing Greek dances. *Oedipus* was performed at the Unity Club of Cleveland, the Unity Church, 1889; the Twentieth Century Club's Drama and Music Committee did Gilbert Murray's translation of Euripides' *Andromache* starring Vivian Cameron with music by Hugh Archibald Clarke at Jordan Hall, Boston, in 1909, and the Bryn Mawr Club of Boston did a *Medea* in 1909 (Hains 1910, 35).

25. *Boston Daily Advertiser,* March 13, 1890.

26. Flanagan (1940) 1965, 5–6; Davis 2010–11.

27. See Bigsby 1985, 19, on economic issues.

28. Folder on Brenner's *Antigone,* New York Public Library for the Performing Arts, Lincoln Center, without further details.

29. See Bigsby 1985, 4–7.

30. For useful overviews of The Living Theatre, see Tytell 1995 and Bigsby 1985.

31. Rexroth 1951; Tytell 1995, 32.

32. S. Brecht 1969, 47.

33. S. Brecht 1969, 47.

34. See Colakis 1993, 50–51. Their later production of Jean Cocteau's *Orphée* (1954) was more successful.

35. B. Brecht 1984.

36. Neff 1970, 235.

37. Neff 1970, 124.

38. For discussions of the production, see Colakis 1993, 50–56; Hartigan 1995, 111, 116–17; Neff 1970, 123–28; Biner 1972, 145–58. See further Richard Schechner's interview with the Becks (1969, 40–41).

39. See S. Brecht 1969, 52–53.

40. Beck (c. 1972) 1986, 119. On the play's original reception in Germany, see Malina in "Letters from the Becks," *Yale/Theatre* 2.1 (1969): 14–15.

41. On this shift, see Amitin 1981, 34.

42. Colakis 1993, 54.

43. Schechner 1969, 37 and 43.

44. S. Brecht 1969, 48–49.

45. McDermott 1969, 80. Brustein 1969, 102, thinks Norman O. Brown influenced the group's concern with pleasure and freedom from morality; see also S. Brecht 1969, 67; and Silber 1969.

46. Brustein 1969, 103.

47. New York reviews of the 1968 performance at BAM recognized the anti-Vietnam dimension but complained of its length, pretentiousness, and repetition. Only Julius

Novick, *Village Voice,* January 9, 1968, expressed excitement over its "ritualistic stylization." Kostelanetz (1994, 74 and 78–79) and S. Brecht (1969, esp. 58–59, 66–67, 70–71) offer considerably more positive assessments of The Living Theatre's theatrical work in this period as a whole but view *Antigone* as the weakest of the four major productions because The Living Theatre's acting was strongest on the nonverbal side. Rogoff 1969, 96, thinks the problem with *Antigone* was that the theatrical argument was more interesting than the political one. See also Rogoff 1969, 99, summary: "The Becks's theatre offers precious little fun, and it can be tendentious, insistent, selfish, and boring. But from inside the mounting hysteria of a nation-state that accommodates itself with such dexterity to the crushing choice of lesser evil, it is possible to say their contradictions are better than most."

48. "Interview with Eric Bentley," *Yale/Theatre* 2.1 (1969): 105–8; and Bentley in *New York Times,* October 20, 1968. For other discussions of the play's reception, see Colakis 1993, 51–56; and Hartigan 1995, 111, 116–17.

49. See Bigsby 1985, 90 and 95–96, on the group's growing rigidity as its mode was outflanked by historical change. New York reviews of the Joyce Theater production in 1984 viewed the production as follows: "mired in the 60s," badly acted" (Mel Gussow, *New York Times,* January 27, 1984), an "ordeal of stupid sincerity" (Julius Novick, *Village Voice,* February 7, 1984), "pseudo-intellectual" (Sy Syna, *New York Tribune,* January 27, 1984), "too often confuses eccentricity with originality" (Clive Barnes, *New York Post,* January 26, 1984), as "anti-audience as anti-war" (John Beaufort, *Christian Science Monitor,* January 31, 1984), with a sexist Creon who gropes women (Paul Bertram, *Stages,* March 1984).

50. Howard Kissel, *Women's Wear Daily,* April 28, 1982.

51. Gordon Rogoff, *Village Voice,* May 4, 1982.

52. For this much discussed production, which I will not address in this book, see especially Schechner 1970 and more recently Zeitlin 2004.

53. Arnott 1987, 367, reports on an Off-Broadway production of *Persians,* about which I have no further information, in the late 1960s or early 1970s designed to respond to the Vietnam War.

54. Hall 2004, 176–85.

55. It was revived at New York's Abron Arts Festival, 2007. See Moayed in Denton 2006. Waterwell's website (www.waterwell.org) contains excerpts of the songs and dances discussed below.

56. For bibliography on *Persians,* see Hall 1996 and Garvie 2009.

57. Auletta 1993 and 2006.

58. The production drew on Kabuki, Kathakali, and rock, using low-level spotlights and hand-held microphones; see further Hall 2004, 176–85.

59. McLaughlin 2005, 255.

60. Atossa's failure to reappear occurred because the same actor (out of two available) played Xerxes and Atossa, because the actor playing Darius remained on stage hidden in his tomb, or simply because Aeschylus did not want to mitigate Xerxes' disaster with parental care and sympathy (see Garvie 2009, xxxiv, 338).

61. Although Michael Feingold, *Village Voice,* June 25–July 1, 2003, 65, found the play too staid and distant, Nina daVinci Nichols, www.theatrescene.net/ts/articles.nsf/OBP/35

FB1CB89243C14885256D4800626867, offered a rave review. Despite the changed historical context, the Washington reviews largely echoed those in New York.

62. Addams (1910) 1967, 388–89.

63. Sellars 1992. On the production, see further McDonald 1992; Hartigan 1995, 118–20; and Winterer 2002, 147; the script is published in *Yale/Theater* 18.1 (Fall/Winter 1986–87): 9–35, with an introduction that closely describes the staging by W. D. King.

64. Sellars 1992, 94.

65. Sellars 1992.

66. Sellars 1992, 91.

67. Sellars 1996, 226.

68. See appendix C for other productions of *Ajax*.

69. Latea's version, directed by Peter Campbell, used texts from soldiers in Vietnam and Afghanistan; the chorus was female, however. Athena watched the action as a video from the sidelines.

70. This is the actor's own story. The production was developed collaboratively; the main deviation from Sophocles' text involved substituting for Ajax's suicide speech parts of a speech from Charles Mee's *Big Love* in which a character discusses the problems of being a male soldier.

71. Mackey and Miller 2004.

72. Etkind 1997.

73. Madeleine George, *Brooklyn Rail,* March 2006, emphasized the physical precision and sharp jump cuts that made the collage approach work effectively.

74. http://www.theater-of-war.com/about.html; see Meineck 2009.

75. See *Dioniso* n.s. 2 (2003): 211.

76. For discussion, see especially articles, reviews, interviews with Sellars, and other material on the American Repertory Theater website (www.amrep.org/herakles/) and the review by Daniel Mendelsohn in *New York Review of Books,* February 13, 2003.

77. See the article by William Allen on the American Repertory Theater website (www.amrep.org/herakles/).

78. Louise Kennedy, *Boston Globe,* January 3, 2003; "The Balm of Ancient Words," ARTicles 1.2 (December 1, 2002), http://www.americanrepertorytheater.org/inside/articles/articles-vol-1-i2-balm-ancient-words.

79. The 1930 production (translated by Edith Hamilton) at New York's Heckscher Theatre was directed by Richard Hale and C. J. Kraemer Jr.; the *Evening Post Review,* January 6, 1930, praised Hale and Hamilton's translation for a production reminiscent of an oratorio. The dancer Ted Shawn performed a solo version in 1929, which is discussed in chapter 2.1; see Michelakis 2010.

80. See Hartigan 1995, 132 and nn. 3–4; and *Show Business,* May 2, 1970. Colakis 1993, 29, discusses Lawrence Wunderlich's one-act new version, *Prometheus Rebound.*

81. Elenore Lester, *New York Times,* May 21, 1957, pronounced the play "a fundamental misconception of Greek tragedy." See Price 1968 and Brustein 1968 for valuable discussions of the production.

82. For a valuable discussion with further references, see Colakis 1993, 21–29. Walter Kerr (*New York Times*), Richard Gilman (*Newsweek,* May 22, 1967), and Colakis all discuss

the play's "death of god" theme. John Simon, *Hudson Review* 20 (1967): 559, criticizes the play's misogyny, with its acquiescent Io and Prometheus's indifferent wife, who has abandoned her spouse to his troubles, and its uncourageous chorus. Raizis 1969, 165 n. 34, sees a possible comment on Lyndon Johnson's betrayal of the liberal intellectuals who had helped him; Brustein 1968,18, also viewed the play as a commentary on some aspects of L. B. J.'s America.

83. On Lowell's political theater, see Bigsby 1985, 297–310, 318–21.

84. Walter Goodman, *New York Times*, December 27, 1985.

85. My source for this production is detailed newspaper reviews. In the 1973 Theatre of the Artist's League of the Playwright's Workshop Club, New York, production, Prometheus was "attired in an American flag made by blood that issued from his chest wound (doubtless an ultimate in patriotic gore). . . . Whatever else can be said about this production, it did not fear hubris" (*Village Voice*, February 8, 1973, 63). Professional productions of *PB* have been staged more frequently since the 1990s. The most pointedly political was the TinFish Theatre's 1999 Chicago production by Dejan Avramovich, which set the action in future Yugoslavia; Ocean became a fussy diplomat who arrived in a helicopter, and Hermes "a suave emissary from headquarters." The play ended in a blast of modern-day gunfire (Richard Christiansen, *Chicago Tribune*, January 6, 1999). See appendix C for further productions.

86. Gerard Stropnicky, www.communityarts.net/readingroom/archivefiles/1999/10/courting_cathar.php.

87. Gerard Stropnicky, www.communityarts.net/readingroom/archivefiles/1999/10/courting_cathar.php.

88. *The Drama Review* 43.3 (T171) (Fall 2001): 22.

89. Brady 2000 with extensive responses in *The Drama Review* 43.3 (T171) (Fall 2001): 8–23.

90. A 2002 performance of Aeschylus's play at the Studio Theatre in Washington, D.C., adapted by Sophy Burnham and directed by Joy Zinoman, also offered a new conclusion to the lost trilogy that incorporated our fragmentary knowledge about the original.

91. See further Foley 2010.

### 4. REENVISIONING THE HERO

1. See further Knox 1957.

2. See Foley 2005; and chapter 2.

3. See appendix D for professional native productions of *OT* before 1972 not mentioned in chapter 1.1.

4. Play publicity. See chapter 1.1 for nineteenth-century approaches to staging Greek tragedy.

5. Interview, quoted in *Christian Science Monitor*, November 6, 1972.

6. Burgess 1972, 88.

7. Burgess 1972, 87.

8. Burgess 1972, 86; Sonkowsky 1973.

9. See Melvin Maddox, *Time*, November 13, 1972, 82. Sonkowsky 1973, 29, thinks Pasolini's 1969 film *Medea* influenced the opening sacrifice.

10. See Macintosh 2009b, 150, on Laurence Oliver's famous scream in the 1945–46 productions of Yeats's *OT*.

11. Burgess 1972, 14; Sonkowsky 1973, 30.

12. Burgess 1972, 3, argues that a post-Senecan and Elizabethan tradition demands this violation of Greek tradition.

13. See Macintosh 2009b, 163–68.

14. Burgess 1972, 80. The play also does not explain why Creon insists on separating Oedipus from his daughters. Revermann 2003, 799, suggests that the poet wishes Oedipus to fall on his return into the palace, thus embodying the image of the crawling child of the Sphinx's riddle. On the problems posed by Sophocles' conclusion, see Foley 1993 and Burian 2009; on Sophocles' tendency to avoid dramatic closure, see Roberts 1988. The Jean Cocteau/Stravinsky *Oedipus* also had Oedipus exit at the conclusion, and that choice may have influenced Burgess.

15. Burgess 1972, 6.

16. Burgess 1972, 4–5.

17. Burgess 1972, 5, 27, 87. Burgess wrote a novel called *MF* in which a young puzzle-solver had incest with his sister. See Hartigan 1995, 42–43; Freiert 1991; and Sonkowsky 1973 for further comments on the production. Reviews were largely positive. Len Cariou as Oedipus and Patricia Conolly (1972) received strong notices, Kenneth Welsh and Pauline Flanagan in the 1973 production less so. Nick Baldwin, *Des Moines Register*, June 30, 1973, objected to the quasi-primitive music and dance, but most others liked it; the *Christian Science Monitor*, November 6, 1972, found the onstage blinding too Elizabethan and thought that Burgess's blank verse clashed anachronistically with Oedipus's characterization as a "self-aware savage"; see also *Time*, November 13, 1972, 82, which detected English repertory accents lurking behind the Neanderthal animal skins.

18. Yeats's play was first performed in the United States at Boston's Symphony Hall in 1930, followed by Yeats's own Abbey Players in 1933 at New York's Martin Beck Theatre; the London Old Vic's version with Laurence Olivier made an enormous impression at New York's Century Theatre, May 20, 1946. See appendix D for additional productions.

19. Interview with Ellen McLaughlin (2008).

20. McLaughlin 2005, 333. Stephen Spender's *Oedipus* trilogy (Spender 1985), performed at the Oxford Playhouse in 1983, also reintroduced the riddle.

21. See www.guthrietheater.org for McLaughlin's comments about Knox; McLaughlin 2005, 313.

22. McLaughlin 2005, 319. See Jocasta's speech at 376.

23. Program notes, www.guthrietheater.org.

24. Program notes, www.guthrietheater.org.

25. Reviews stressed the cerebral quality of the production, its missing sense of primal transgression, and the power of Monk O'Connor's performance and McLaughlin's text.

26. Rohan Preston, *Minneapolis Star Tribune*, January 23, 2005.

27. *Time*, March 9, 1970; Hartigan 1995, 47.

28. Hartigan 1995, 42, to the contrary, the sometimes puzzled reviews of this melodramatic production ranged from mixed to fairly positive, especially for acting and direction.

29. Mufson 1999, 24, from an interview with Abdoh.
30. Director's notes and study guide for the Oregon Shakespeare Festival's 1975 *OT*.
31. *Yale/Theater* 5.1 (Fall 1973): 131–38.
32. Rohmann, http,//www.aislesay.com/CT-Oedipus.html. Critics generally singled out the musical score and incantatory delivery of chorus members and felt that the youthful Reg Flowers as Oedipus, Stephanie Berry as Jocasta, and Michael Early as Creon lacked sufficient authority.
33. www.bostonphoenix.com/boston/events/theater/documents/03820854.asp. See also Woodruff's interview with James Leverett, *Theater* 35.1 (March 2005): 56–65.
34. Abdoh's production also put the mother-son incest on stage.
35. David Foucher, *Edge Boston*, May 22, 2004, www.edgeboston.com/index.php?ch = entertainment&sc = theatre&sc2 = reviews&sc3 = &id = 1179.
36. The ART website (www.amrep.org) was exceptionally helpful to students of this production and included extensive citation of reviews.
37. Foley 2007, 359.
38. For the development of Oedipus's story as a bildungsroman in Europe, see Macintosh 2008.
39. See Foley 2005 on U.S. productions that mix parts of the *Oresteia* with other plays based on the house of Atreus myths.
40. A new Theban trilogy translated by Peter Constantine and directed by Shepard Sobel and performed at New York's Pearl Theatre in October 2008 also gave Creon's changed leadership a central role, whereas the 2001 *Oedipus Plays*, translated by Nicholas Rudall and directed by Michael Kahn at the Shakespeare Theatre, Washington, D.C., which set the trilogy in an "Africa of the Imagination," explored the changing relation between divine and human law.
41. For interviews with the director and a list of reviews that responded above all to the setting, direction, and Anne DeAcetis's stellar performance as Antigone, see www.division13.org/work/bloodline.html and www.division13.org.press/rev_bloodline.html.
42. The 1989 *Oedipus Requiem* by Chicago's Blind Parrot Productions also offered a version of the Oedipus cycle that staged much of the *OT* as a flashback at the moment of Antigone's death.
43. The play received eleven Los Angeles Drama-Logue Awards.
44. See *Playbill*, July 9, 1996.
45. Quoted in *Playbill*, July 9, 1996.
46. Laurie Winer, *Los Angeles Times*, July 29, 1996, criticized the show's radical shifts in tone.
47. Though reviewers' reactions, with the exception of their responses to some of the acting, were largely negative, Alisa Solomon (*Village Voice*, October 21–27, 1998) defended the play's effort to examine what constitutes moral behavior, and whether it is possible: "Language itself is a subject in Clubb's play. Naming and confessing and cursing and vowing—all inexorably call action into being. Clubb shows how cruel or even thoughtless words can slaughter and maim."
48. It was later published and performed as *The Palace at 4 a.m.* in 1968 (Playwrights Unit, Theater Vandam, New York, directed by Charles Guys) and in 1972 (John Drew

Theater in East Hampton, NY, directed by Edward Albee and starring Christopher Walken and Beatrice Straight).

49. For other related versions, see the 1968 *Oedipus Wrecks* and Max E. Verga's *Oedipussy*, 1976.
50. Berson 2004, 120.
51. Berson 2004, 117.
52. Berson 2004, 119.
53. Bob Hicks, *Sunday Oregonian*, August 8, 2004 (bobhicks@news.oregonian.com).
54. September 14, 2006, www.theatre.com/nytheatre/archshow.php?key=402. Other Internet reviews (see appendix D) were mixed, but several praised the acting, the script's moments of raw emotion, and the quirky neighborhood chorus.
55. www.talkinbroadway.com/ob/08_03_05.html.
56. www.variety.com/VE1117927829?categoryid=33&cs=1.
57. newyorkmetro.com/nymetro/arts/theater/reviews/12370/. Others criticized the play's adherence to butch-femme stereotypes that the group had previously debunked, the gratuitous degree of nudity, and the uneven acting.
58. Jill Dolan, http,//feministspectator.blogspot.com/2005_08_01_feministspectator_archive.html, pp. 2 and 7.
59. Charles McNulty, *Village Voice*, August 9, 2005.
60. See note 57 above; and Dolan 2006. The *New Yorker*, August 22, 2005, 82–84, took a somewhat similar view on generic grounds.
61. LaBute 2007.
62. LaBute 1999.
63. See Macintosh 2009b, 173–81; and Berkoff (1980) 1994.
64. http://backstage.blogs.com/cues/2006/10/wrecks_and_adap.html.
65. See Foley 2004, 85.
66. See Foley 2004, 95. More recently, *What She Knew*, written and directed by George Hunka and performed at Manhattan Theatre Source in December 2010, offered a monologue by Jocasta.
67. See Freund 1970 (production in 2006) and Dove 1996 (productions in 1997, 2000, and 2006).
68. See appendix D, 1988.
69. For other versions of Oedipus as outsider in twentieth-century European theater, see Macintosh 2008.
70. See Macintosh 2007 and 2008.
71. See Foley 2005 on Orestes in U.S. versions of *Agamemnon*.
72. Renner 2007, 120.

## 5. REIMAGINING MEDEA AS AMERICAN OTHER

1. On the basis of the Archive of Performance of Greek and Roman Drama database (www.apgrd.ox.ac.uk), this is often true in Europe.
2. Mme Agathe Barcescu (sometimes spelled Barsescu) also did an outdoor professional version of E. Legouvé's *Medea* with the Art Drama Players in 1915 at New York University

and at the People's Theatre in the Bowery, directed by Ada Dow Currier. The first modern British performance of Euripides in translation, directed by Granville Barker and translated by Gilbert Murray in 1907, slightly antedated that of Anglin, Barcescu, and others (Hall and Macintosh 2005, 391).

3. On the Volanakis and Wright productions, see Hartigan 1995, 53–54 and 58–59.

4. Gods such as Dionysus in *Bacchae* also orchestrate plots. See Macintosh 2000, 2–3, on Medea's role as performer.

5. See further Rabinowitz 1993, 125, on the unusual features of the play.

6. Wetmore 2003 has already explored black Medeas as American "others."

7. See further R. Duncan 1965; and Corti 1998, 183–84.

8. See Macintosh 2000, 19–23 and 27. Jahnn's version was first performed in Berlin starring the black actress Agnes Straub.

9. "The Character of Medea," *Southern Literary Messenger* 5.6 (June 1839): 383–92. As a whole, the article tries to make a case for studying the classics in the original languages and for the moral value of Greek tragedy as a source of civic education. See also "The Beauties of Greek Tragedies," *American Monthly Magazine* 1.4, June 1, 1833, 193–202. Translations of passages from *Medea* appeared regularly in popular magazines.

10. Translations by Robert Potter (1781–83), Michael Woodhull (1782), T. C. W. Edwards (1821), and the prose translation by D. Spillan in Richard Porson's edition (1825) were probably available (see further Walton 2006). As one of the few Greek tragedies read by school or college students (Winterer 2002, 32), it was more familiar than many other plays and provoked the kind of response, including magazine translations, mentioned above.

11. Brandes 1945, 51–100, offers additional evidence and further reviews of all New York performances of versions of *Medea* until 1881. Burkhard 1961, 33 n. 6, also reports an undated New York performance at the Fifth Avenue Theatre of Robert Brough's 1856 contemporary burlesque of Legouvé, *The Best of Mothers, with a Brute of a Husband*.

12. A lengthy description of the play, which highlights the superiority of contemporary German tragedy to British, appeared as early as 1823 in *North American Review*, April 1823, 7, 11.

13. Hall and Macintosh 2005, 424, suggest that British audiences did not respond to Janauschek's "Orientalism." Burkhard (1961), Leuchs (1966), and Brandes (1945, 83–94) document our full evidence on Janauschek and other German actresses who performed Grillparzer's *Medea* from as early as 1862 throughout the United States, most notably the less-successful Magda Irschik (Odell 11, 76 and 12, 271). A Yiddish version of Grillparzer by Jacob Gordin located during the reign of Antiochus IV responded to Jewish oppression in New York in 1897 (Mimoso-Ruiz 1978, 125).

14. On the four tours, see Giorcelli 1992; Brandes 1945, 73–82.

15. Heron's translation (published in 1857) in fact represented a revised version of Legouvé's French for an American audience; rhetoric and mythological references were reduced, as was the children's oscillation between Medea and Creusa, the attacks of the populace on Medea, the emphasis on Medea's barbarism, and Orpheus's role in Medea's defense.

16. Winter 1913, 71. Despite Winter, who also disliked Heron's wildly successful *Camille*, the reception of Heron's Medea was generally more positive than Hall and Macintosh 2005,

423, suggest. See also *Every Saturday: A Journal of Choice Reading*, 2.8, August 24, 1872, 215, for a review of the "Yankee" (American) Miss Bateman's performance of Legouvé at New York's Lyceum in 1872, which echoes Winter's suggestive language by noting the heroine's "racial" inferiority to the Greeks.

17. Giorcelli 1992, 33, 36.

18. Joy Kasson 1990, 218-36. Though Story's Medea is contemplative, her fierce, rational expression appears to me to reinforce rather than dampen anxieties.

19. Hall and Macintosh 2005, 391-429, 488-89.

20. Weisenburger 1998, 89. He links the first of these Medeas with Mayr's Medea and the last with Legouvé's.

21. Weisenburger 1998, chap. 5.

22. See Furth 1998, 37-57.

23. Weisenburger 1998, 286.

24. Weisenburger 1998, 254; see also 246, 253, 255, and 258. For additional pre-Garner examples from as early as 1848, see Winterer 2007, 185-86.

25. Weisenburger 1998, 228.

26. Read 1848.

27. May 1848, 429.

28. See Kelley 2006, esp. 39; and Winterer 2007, 142-64, on female education in the period.

29. See, e.g., *Spirit of the Times* 25.8, April 7, 1855, 87, on the plight of American Indians and our "African kin"; or her defense of Lady Macbeth in *Spirit of the Times* 22.17, June 12, 1852, 199.

30. On genteel performance in private mansions or town houses, see McConachie 1998, 124.

31. Although we do not know to which of her three plays Madison refers, *Medea* seems more likely, since it immediately won a continuing reputation. See Weisenburger 1998, 228.

32. *Spirit of the Times* 19.8, April 14, 1849, 408; 26.14, May 17, 1856, 168; and 20.2, March 2, 1850, 24, which remarks on her successful readings in Cincinnati. Washington's one or two professional theaters in this period largely hosted theater companies from Philadelphia; newspapers offered notices rather than reviews of theatrical performances until toward the end of the period. See Mudd 1902, 64-86; and 1903, 222-66, which lists no version of Greek drama performed in Washington until 1850 other than Ellen Tree in Talfourd's *Ion* (1838).

33. May 1848, 429, who selected two sections of *Medea* for the anthology (430-35). See also Melanie Young in Mainiero 1979-94, 1:447-49, who singles out *Medea* as Read's best work and notes her interest in women's issues, exemplified in *The Haunted Student* as well as the plays. Blain et al. 1990, 888-89, also note Read's stress on individual freedom and women's equality with men.

34. *Literary World* 51, January 22, 1848, 614, notes that most new verse plays were "intended rather for the closet than the stage"; Read's volume proves in this review an exception to that criticism.

35. Reviews are listed in appendix E.

36. *Union Magazine of Literature and Art* 2.3 (March 1848): 143.

37. Two marked quotations on pp. 53 and 95 in Read 1848 are not from Potter; quotations on pp. 62, 63, 75, 85 are not from *Medea;* but Read does quote Potter's lines 425, 928, 956, 988–1001, 1460–61, 1470–71 (modified), 1489–90 (modified), 1509 (modified), and 1529 (modified).

38. *North American Magazine,* October 1854, 409, summarizes the epic, suggesting that it was of interest during the period.

39. See V. Green 1982, 31–39; and Winterer 2007, 64.

40. Winterer 2007, 169–75.

41. Edwards 1987, 101–2.

42. See especially Zeitlin 1996 and Foley 2001, with relevant bibliography on *Medea.*

43. Cullen 1935 and 1991; I quote from the second, complete version of *Medea* in Cullen 1991. Cullen had intended both *Medea* and the new prologue and epilogue to be published in Cullen 1947, but the contents were changed when his death in 1946 intervened. If Henri Lenormand's new version of *Medea* at the Théâtre Antoine in 1931, *Asie,* where a French colonel brings back an Indo-Chinese princess to France (Corti 1998, 190–91) influenced Cullen when he was in Paris in 1926–28, his play does not make ethnicity an explicit issue.

44. Wetmore 2003, 145; see also Gill 2000, 23.

45. Hatch and Abdullah 1977, 81–82.

46. See Hatch and Abdullah 1977, 57; and Hatch 1993, 61, 81–82, 96, 122, 310.

47. See Coe 1963.

48. Published by G. Schirmer (46641) in 1942. A 1967 version by Daniel Pinkham with a mixed chorus premiered on June 13, 1967, in Cambridge, Massachusetts (Early's introduction to Cullen 1991, 67).

49. "Euripides in Harlem," *Nation* 141 (1935): 336. See also Peter Munro Jack, *New York Times,* January 12, 1936.

50. Wetmore 2003, 146, views it as condescending in the context of the rest of the review.

51. See Macintosh 2000, 18, on the tradition of omitting this speech before the feminist movement took it up in the later nineteenth century. See Cook and Tatum 2010, 148–52, for a negative reading of Cullen's version.

52. H. Baker 1974, 50, also finds Medea's famous soliloquy "maudlin" and the final scene with the children "too sentimental."

53. See Shucard 1987, 26; Corti 1998, 191.

54. Margaret Sperry, "Countee P. Cullen, Negro Boy Poet, Tells His Story," *Brooklyn Daily Eagle,* February 10, 1924.

55. Introduction to Cullen 1991, 67.

56. H. Baker 1974, 30; see also 14, 26–27, 52.

57. See Early's introduction to Cullen 1991, 59, with an emphasis on Cullen's engagement with lying and deception; Corti 1998, 191–93, also interprets Cullen's *Medea* in the light of his personal and poetic biography, but for different reasons.

58. During this period, college performances continued with some regularity along with Martha Graham's 1946 dance version, *Cave of the Heart,* discussed in chapter 2.1, and a 1948 production of the original in New Orleans at the Petit Théâtre du Vieux Carré, directed by Robert Hyde Wilson.

59. Corti 1998, 195. I quote Anderson's 1936 play from Sanderson and Zimmerman 1957.
60. One critic (*New York Times*, January 3, 1937) thought Cornell insufficiently Eastern as well.
61. Winterer 2002, esp. 3–5, 65–68, 95, 125. Oparre clearly voices some of Anderson's own views, though he does not link his own artistic role to hers.
62. Corti 1998, 203.
63. Corti 1998, 201.
64. I quote from the 1948 acting edition, which contains useful material on the original staging. See further Edwards 1987, 101–2; and Griffith 2003.
65. *New York Times Book Review*, January 18, 1948.
66. The main exception is Jason's speech on the benefits that rational Greece conferred on Medea, whose Asia is mired in dirt and superstition (35). On whether Jeffers is "Orientalist" or a proponent of Nietzsche and Schopenhauer and a freely chosen morality, see Griffith 2003, 23, 34, 38.
67. See Knox 1977.
68. On materialism, see Jeffers's poem "The Trap" (Jeffers 1988–2001, 2: 415).
69. Quoted in Bennett 1966, 217.
70. Edwards 1987, 109, 112–14, 121; and Griffith 2003, 27, 32–34. Edwards, 141, also sees a postwar fear of nuclear catastrophe in the play's stress on annihilation.
71. Edwards 1987, 137–41.
72. For the extensive and generally ecstatic reviews of both the Anderson and the Caldwell performances, see Edwards 1987, 134–58.
73. LeVay 1989, 314.
74. See Wetmore 2003, 166–67, on Damballah and the Louisiana Code Noir.
75. For performances from 1977 to 1990, see Wetmore 2003, 164; and appendix E. The New York Public Library for the Performing Arts, Lincoln Center, New York has a partial tape, and I am grateful to New York's Schomburg Center for Research in Black Culture for a copy of the script.
76. Carter 1993.
77. The original director, Dennis Zacek, wanted the end of act 1 to link the sexual relationship of Jason and Mediyah on Miedo Wood Island to suggest that of "the first couple" on earth (director's note in Carter 1993).
78. See further Wetmore 2003, 178.
79. Interview with LaChiusa by Jonathan Frank, www.talkinbroadway.com/cabaret/lachiusa.html.
80. Fraden 2001, 56–64; and Wetmore 2003, 198–202.
81. All black and Caribbean Medeas are starred in appendix E. Beah Richards's performance at the Theatre of Being in Los Angeles directed by Frank Silvestra is undated. See Wetmore 2003, 145–49; and S. Pearl, *Black Masks* 14, March 31, 2001.
82. Eumelos, *Korinthiaka* 2.3.10–11 = Eumelus frag. 5PEG, Simonides 545 PMG. See further Gantz 1993, 368.
83. There have since been several productions on college campuses: Stanford (2005), Brown (2006), and University of Massachusetts (2008); see Nicole Eschen, *Theatre Journal*

58.1 (March 2006): 103–6; and Straile-Costa 2010's detailed discussion of the production by the Stanford Drama Department.

84. Straile-Costa 2010, 213.

85. Moraga 2001 and 2004.

86. On U.S. plays that similarly explore doomed lesbian sexuality, see Love 2008.

87. Straile-Costa 2010, 211, cites Moraga on this point.

88. Smethurst 2002. See Corti 1998, 179, for Yeats's influence on the modernist appropriation of Noh drama for performing Greek tragedy.

89. Sorgenfrei 1975. Thomas Sturge Moore's Noh/Yeatsian-inspired *Medea*, published in the 1920 *Tragic Mothers*, anticipated Sorgenfrei (see further Macintosh 2000, 6). Gloria Albee's 1975 *Medea*, performed by the Westbeth Playwrights Feminist Collective in New York, also exonerated Medea across the board in a fashion characteristic of the period.

90. Wren 2002, 25. European versions of the same period also performed in the United States, such as the Italian tongue-in-cheek "Medea Prologue" and "Medea" by Dario Fo and Franca Rame (published in translation in 1982), make a similar point.

91. Reviews especially praised the visual elements of the production and the performance of Barbara E. Robertson as Medea in Chicago and Washington and occasionally criticized the slower first act and the feminist dimensions of the script.

92. Usui 2000, 173.

93. Houston's play includes an inaccurate version of Medea as a foreign woman who not only kills her children but feeds them to her husband (123). *Kokoro* is published in Houston 1997, 89–130.

94. *Kokoro* had its premiere at the Theatre of Yugen, San Francisco, in June 1994, directed by Yuriko Doi, after a special presentation at the Japan Society in New York the previous month, and was restaged in 1995, 1998, 1999, 2000, 2003, and 2004. Usui 2000 cites reviews; see also the review of Houston's book of plays by Gregory Choy, *Journal of Asian American Studies* 1.3 (1998): 303–8.

95. Usui 2000, 178–79.

96. Reviews of this production, including the acting (especially the stellar performance of Michi Barall as M) and directing, were unusually positive.

97. The play also includes a mysterious character called the Wavemaker, whose perspective on reality, its mix of waves and particles that create light, echoes M's divided sense of self. Science, enhanced in this play by satiric distance on the immigrant experience, offers a new form of liberating mythology. Other Asian versions include the 1986 *Medea*, adapted by Claire Bush and Alkis Papoutsis for the Pan Asian Repertory Theatre Company, and the 2001 *Medea Bali*, performed by Green T Productions and directed by Kathy Welch in Minneapolis.

98. See Foley 2004, Case 1993, and Blundell et al. 1999, as well as Macintosh 2000, 5, on some cross-dressed Medeas in the nineteenth century.

99. Ludlam himself declined to play Medea because of the infanticide (see the introduction to Ludlam 1989, xviii, by Steven Samuels). Marilyn Stasio, *New York Post*, November 13, 1987, comments on the "mythological references scattered like hairpins on the floor of a wig shop." My discussion is based on Black-Eyed Susan's taped performance at the New York Public Library for the Performing Arts, Lincoln Center.

100. See Ludlam 1989, 802–13. Corti 1998, 187–89, offers a different interpretation of Ludlam from that of most reviewers.

101. See Foley 2010.

102. Gurney 1995; first produced in 1968, it has been revived frequently across the country.

103. Starred in appendix E.

## EPILOGUE

1. See appendix G.
2. See, e.g., Foley 2005.
3. *Hecuba* has been revived on the British stage for similar reasons.
4. A second American Vietnam War-era *IA*, directed by Nikos Psacharopoulos at the Williamstown Theatre in Williamstown, Massachusetts, in 1968 again made precisely this point.
5. Bauer 2006. I wish to thank Bauer and Marden for the now-published script, photographs, and discussion of the performance.
6. Quoted by Karen D'Souza, *American Theatre* 23.5 (May/June 2006): 21.
7. www.charlesmee.org.html/iphigenia.html.
8. See Foley 2005.
9. D. J. R. Bruckner, *New York Times*, May 13, 1992.
10. Victor Gluck, *Backstage*, June 5, 1992, 40.
11. In an article by Ali Rohrs (*American Theatre* 23.7 [September 2006]: 24) Svich claims to have wanted to give Iphigenia the voice she was denied by Euripides, but at the same time to reclaim the original myth. See Svich 2005, 239–74; 2004.
12. The African American director Tazewell Thompson's production with the Huntington Theatre Company at the Boston University Theatre in 1991 anticipated Akalaitis.
13. McLaughlin 2005.
14. All recent versions of the play cited in appendix F take a version of this position.

REFERENCES

Addams, Jane. (1910) 1967. *Twenty Years at Hull House*. New York: Macmillan.
Albright, Daniel. 2010. "Knowing the Dancer, Knowing the Dance: The Dancer as Décor." In *The Ancient Dancer in the Modern World*, edited by Fiona Macintosh, 297–312. Oxford: Oxford University Press.
Alexander, Doris M. 1960. "Oedipus in Victorian New York." *American Quarterly* 12.3: 417–21.
Alfaro, Luis. 2006. "Electricidad." *American Theatre* 23.2: 63–85.
Alvarez, Al. 1965. "A Talk with Robert Lowell." *Encounter*, February: 39–43.
Amitin, Mark. 1981. "The Living Theater Abroad: Radicalizing the Classics; Interview with Julian Beck and Judith Malina." *Performing Arts Journal* 14, vol. 5.2: 26–40.
Anderson, Maxwell. 1936. *The Wingless Victory*. Washington, D.C.: Anderson House.
Armitage, Merle. (1937) 1966. *Martha Graham*. Reprint, Brooklyn: Dance Horizons.
Arnott, Peter D. 1987. "North America." In *Living Greek Theatre: A Handbook of Classical Performance and Modern Production*, edited by J. Michael Walton, 355–81. New York: Greenwood Press.
Aronson, Arnold. 2000. "American Theatre in Context: 1945–The Present." In *The Cambridge History of American Theatre*, vol. 3, *Post–World War II to the 1990s*, edited by Don B. Wilmeth and Christopher Bigsby, 87–162. Cambridge: Cambridge University Press.
Auletta, Robert. 1986–87. "*Ajax*, adapted from Sophocles." *Yale/Theater* 18.1: 18–35.
———. 1987. *Ajax, adapted from Sophocles*. Amsterdam: International Theatre Bookshop.
———. 1993. *The Persians by Aeschylus: A Modern Version*. With an introduction by Peter Sellars. Los Angeles: Sun and Moon Press.
———. 2006. *The Persians by Aeschylus*. New York: Broadway Play Publishing Inc.
Baker, Houston A. 1974. *A Many-Colored Coat of Dreams: The Poetry of Countee Cullen*. Broadside Critics Series. Detroit: Broadside Press.

Baker, Ray Stannard. 1907. "An Extraordinary Experiment in Brotherhood: The Theosophical Institution at Point Loma, California." *American Magazine* 63.3: 227–40.

Bannerman, Henrietta. 2010. "Ancient Myths and Modern Moves: The Greek-Inspired Dance Theater of Martha Graham." In *The Ancient Dancer in the Modern World: Responses to Greek and Roman Dance*, edited by Fiona Macintosh, 255–74. Oxford: Oxford University Press.

Banta, Martha 1987. *Imaging American Women: Idea and Ideals in Cultural History*. New York: Columbia University Press.

Barrows, Elizabeth C. 1904. "The Greek Play at Hull House." *Commons* 9 (January): 6–10.

Bartow, A. 1988. *The Director's Voice: 21 Interviews*. New York: Theater Communications Group.

Bauer, P. Seth. 2006. *Iphigenia*. New York: Dramatists Play Service Inc.

Baumol, William J., and William G. Bowen. 1966. *Performing Arts: The Economic Dilemma*. New York: Twentieth Century Fund.

Beck, Julian. (c. 1972) 1986. *The Life of the Theatre: The Relation of the Artist to the Struggle of the People*. San Francisco: Limelight Editions; later distributed by Harper and Row.

Bennett, Melba Berry. 1966. *The Stone Mason of Tor House: The Life and Work of Robinson Jeffers*. Los Angeles: Ward Ritchie Press.

Berkoff, Steven. 1982. *Greek*. Published privately in 1980. Reprint, London: John Calder Ltd.

———. 1994. *Greek*. In *Collected Plays*, 1: 95–140. London and Boston: Faber and Faber.

Berlin, Normand, ed. 1989. *Eugene O'Neill: Three Plays; Mourning Becomes Electra, The Iceman Cometh, Long Day's Journey into Night; A Casebook*. Basingstoke and London: Macmillan Education Ltd.

Berson, Misha. 2004. "Dr. Freud, I Presume?" *American Theatre* 21.8: 117–22.

Beye, Charles. 1989. "Pound and Sophocles." *Parnassus: Poetry in Review* 15.1: 83–98.

Bigsby, C. W. E. 1982. *A Critical Introduction to Twentieth-Century American Drama*. Vol. 1, *1900–1940*. Cambridge: Cambridge University Press.

———. 1985. *A Critical Introduction to Twentieth-Century American Drama*. Vol. 3, *Beyond Broadway*. Cambridge: Cambridge University Press.

———. 2000a. Introduction to *The Cambridge History of American Theatre*, vol. 3, *Post–World War II to the 1990s*, edited by Don B. Wilmeth and Christopher Bigsby, 1–23. Cambridge: Cambridge University Press.

———. 2000b. *Modern American Drama: 1945–2000*. Cambridge: Cambridge University Press.

Bigsby, Christopher, and Don. B. Wilmeth. 1998. Introduction to *The Cambridge History of American Theatre*, vol. 1, *Beginnings to 1870*, edited by Don B. Wilmeth and Christopher Bigsby, 1–19. Cambridge: Cambridge University Press.

———. 1999. Introduction to *The Cambridge History of American Theatre*, vol. 2, *1870–1945*, edited by Don B. Wilmeth and Christopher Bigsby, 1–23. Cambridge: Cambridge University Press.

Biner, Pierre. 1972. *The Living Theatre: A History without Myths*. Translated by Robert Meister. New York: Avon.

Blackburn, Philip. 1997. *Enclosures 3: Harry Partch*. St. Paul, Minn.: American Composers Forum.

Blain, Virginia, Patricia Clements, and Isobel Grundy, eds. 1990. *The Feminist Companion to Literature in English: Women Writers from the Middle Ages to the Present*. New Haven, Conn.: Yale University Press.
Blair, Fredrika. 1986. *Isadora: Portrait of the Artist as a Woman*. New York: McGraw-Hill.
Blair, Karen J. 1994. *The Torchbearers: Women and Their Amateur Arts Associations in America, 1890–1930*. Bloomington: Indiana University Press.
Blavatsky, H. P. 1909. *The Secret Doctrine: The Synthesis of Science, Religion, and Philosophy*. Point Loma, Calif.: Aryan Theosophical Press.
Blumenthal, Eileen. 1974. "The Presence of the Character: The Robert Montgomery/Joseph Chaikin *Electra*." *Yale/Theater* 6: 98–108.
———. 1984. *Joseph Chaikin: Exploring the Boundaries of Theater*. Cambridge: Cambridge University Press.
Blundell, Ruby, Bella Zweig, Nancy Sorkin Rabinowitz, and Mary-Kay Gamel. 1999. *Women on the Edge: Four Plays by Euripides*. New York and London: Routledge.
Bosher, Kathryn, Fiona Macintosh, Justine McConnell, and Patrice Rankine, eds. Forthcoming. *Oxford Classical Handbook to Greek Drama in the Americas*. Oxford: Oxford University Press.
Brady, Sara. 2000. "Welded to the Ladle: *Steelbound* and Non-radicality in Community-Based Theatre." *The Drama Review* 44.3 (T167): 51–74.
Brandes, Paul Dickerson. 1945. "Greek Tragedy in New York." Master's thesis, University of Wisconsin.
Brecht, Bertolt. 1949. *Antigonemodell 1948*. Berlin: Gebr. Weiss.
———. 1984. *Antigone: A Version by Bertolt Brecht*. Translated by Judith Malina. New York: Applause: Theatre Book Publishers.
Brecht, Stefan. 1969. "Revolution at the BAM." *The Drama Review* 13.3: 46–73.
Breuer, Lee. 1989. *The Gospel at Colonus*. New York: Theatre Communications Group.
Brown, Peter. 2004. "Greek Tragedy in the Opera House and Concert Hall of the Late Twentieth Century." In *Dionysus since 69*, edited by Edith Hall, Fiona Macintosh, and Amanda Wrigley, 285–310. Oxford: Oxford University Press.
Brown, Peter, and Suzana Ograjensek, eds. 2010. *Ancient Drama in Music for the Modern Stage*. Oxford: Oxford University Press.
Brown, Thomas Allston. 1903. *A History of the New York Stage from the First Performance in 1732 to 1901*. 3 vols. New York: Dodd, Mead and Co.
Browne, Maurice. 1913. "The Temple of a Living Art." *Drama* 3, November: 160–78.
———. 1914–15. "The New Rhythmic Drama, Parts I and II." *Drama* 4–5: 616–30, 146–60.
———. 1955. *Too Late to Lament: An Autobiography*. Bloomington: University of Indiana Press.
Brustein, Robert. 1968. "No More Masterpieces." *Yale/Theatre* 1.1: 10–19.
———. 1969. "An Interview with Robert Brustein." *Yale/Theatre* 2.1: 102–3.
Burgess, Anthony. 1972. *Sophocles, Oedipus the King, Translated and Adapted by Anthony Burgess*. Minneapolis: University of Minnesota Press.
Burian, Peter. 1997. "Tragedy Adapted for Stages and Screens: The Renaissance to the Present." In *The Cambridge Companion to Greek Tragedy*, edited by P. E. Easterling, 228–83. Cambridge: Cambridge University Press.

———. 2009. "Inconclusive Conclusion: The Ending(s) of *Oedipus Tyrannus*." In *Sophocles and the Greek Tragic Tradition*, edited by Simon Goldhill and Edith Hall, 99–118. Cambridge: Cambridge University Press.

Burkhard, Arthur. 1961. *Franz Grillparzer in England and America*. Vienna: Berland Verlag.

Burton, R. W. B. 1980. *The Chorus in Sophocles' Tragedies*. Oxford: Oxford University Press.

Campbell, Mrs. Patrick. 1922. *My Life and Some Letters*. New York: Dodd, Mead and Co.

Campbell, Peter. 2010. "Jay Scheib's *The Medea* as Postdramatic Performance." In *Unbinding Medea: Interdisciplinary Approaches to a Classical Myth from Antiquity to the 21$^{st}$ Century*, edited by Heike Bartel and Anne Simon, 176–85. London: Legenda.

Canning, Charlotte. 1996. *Feminist Theaters in the U.S.A.: Staging Women's Experience*. New York and London: Routledge.

Cargill, Oscar, N. Bryllion Fagin, and William J. Fisher. 1961. *O'Neill and His Plays: Four Decades of Criticism*. New York: New York University Press.

Carlson, Maria. 1993. *"No Religion Higher than Truth": A History of the Theosophical Movement of Russia, 1875–1922*. Princeton, N.J.: Princeton University Press.

Carlson, Marvin. 2004. *Performance: A Critical Introduction*. New York and London: Routledge.

Carson, William G. B. (1932) 1965. *The Theatre on the Frontier: The Early Years of the St. Louis Stage*. New York: Benjamin Blom. Reprint, Chicago: University of Chicago Press.

Carter, Steve. 1993. *Pecong*. New York: Broadway Publishing Inc.

Case, Sue-Ellen. 1993. "Medea by Euripides Ferreira, Greek Active, Tugs, Seattle, 6 July, 1992." *Theater Journal* 45.2: 246–49.

Chalmers, John. 1996. "Radical Reworkings: *Oedipus* and *Revelation in the Courthouse Park*: Harry Partch's Two Music-Dramas on Classical Greek Themes." *Didaskalia* 3.1. http://didaskalia.open.uk.

Chansky, Dorothy. 2004. *Composing Ourselves: The Little Theatre Movement and the American Audience*. Carbondale: Southern Illinois University Press.

Chapman, John, and Garrison P. Sherwood. 1955. *The Best Plays of 1894–1899*. New York: Dodd, Mead and Co.

Cheney, Sheldon. 1914. *The New Movement in the Theatre*. New York: M. Kennerley.

———. 1918. *The Open-Air Theater*. New York: M. Kennerley.

Chioles, John. 1993. "The *Oresteia* and the Avant Garde: Three Decades of Discourse." *Performing Arts Journal* 45 (15.3): 1–28.

Choate, E. Teresa. 2009. *Electra USA: American Stagings of Sophocles' Tragedy*. Madison and Teaneck, N.J.: Fairleigh Dickinson University Press.

Chodorow, Nancy. 1978. *The Reproduction of Mothering: Psychoanalysis and the Sociology of Gender*. Berkeley and Los Angeles: University of California Press.

Cody, Gabrielle. 1999. "Interculturalism and Performance." In *Conversations on Art and Performance*, edited by Bonnie Marranca and Gautam Dasgupta, 452–48. Baltimore: Johns Hopkins University Press.

Coe, Richard. 1963. "The New Negro Dramatist." *Transition* 11: 29–30.

Colakis, Marianthe. 1993. *The Classics in the American Theater of the 1960s and Early 1970s*. Lanham, Md.: University Press of America.

Contat, Michel, and Michel Rybalka, eds. 1974. *Writings of Jean-Paul Sartre*. Translated by Richard C. McCleary. Evanston, Ill.: Northwestern University Press.

Cook, George Cram. 1926. *The Athenian Women (Hoi Athenaies)*. Athens: H. F. Kauffmann.

Cook, William W., and James Tatum. 2010. *African American Writers of Classical Tradition*. Chicago: University of Chicago Press.

Cooper, Elizabeth. 1997. "Tamiris and the Federal Dance Theatre, 1936–1939: Socially Relevant Dance amidst the Policies and Politics of the New Deal Era." *Dance Research Journal* 29.2: 23–48.

Corti, Lillian. 1998. *The Myth of Medea and the Murder of the Children*. Westport, Conn.: Greenwood Press.

Coss, Clare, Sondra Segal, and Roberta Sklar. (1980) 1985. "Separation and Survival: Mothers, Daughters, Sisters—The Women's Experimental Theater." In *The Future of Difference*, edited by Hester Eisenstein and Alice Jardine, 193–235. Boston: G. K. Hall. Reprint, New Brunswick: Rutgers University Press.

———. 1983. "Notes on the Women's Experimental Theatre." In *Women in Theater: Compassion and Hope*, edited by Karen Malpede, 235–44. New York: Drama Book Publishers.

Csapo, Eric. 2008. "Star Choruses: Eleusis, Orphism, and New Musical Imagery and Dance." In *Performance, Iconography, Reception: Studies in Honour of Oliver Taplin*, edited by Martin Revermann and Peter Wilson, 262–90. Oxford: Oxford University Press.

Csapo, Eric, and William J. Slater. 1995. *The Context of Ancient Drama*. Ann Arbor: University of Michigan Press.

Cullen, Countee. 1935. *The Medea and Some Poems*. New York and London: Harper and Brothers.

———. 1947. *On These I Stand*. New York: Harper and Row.

———. 1991. *My Soul's High Song: The Collected Writings of Countee Cullen*. Edited with an introduction by Gerald Early. New York and London: Anchor Books.

Daly, Ann. 1995. *Done Into Dance*. Middletown, Conn.: Wesleyan University Press.

D'Aponte, Mimi Gilsofi. 1991. "The *Gospel of Colonus* and Other Black Morality Plays." *Black American Literature Forum* 25: 101–13.

Davis, Robert. 2008. "The Riddle of the *Oedipus*: Practicising Reception and Antebellum American Theatre." *New Voices in Classical Reception Studies* 3. www2.open.ac.uk/classical receptions.

———. 2010–11. "Is Mr. Euripides a Communist? The Federal Theater Project's 1938 *Trojan Incident*." In *Translation, Performance, and Reception of Greek Drama, 1900–1960: International Dialogues*, special issue, *Comparative Drama* 44.4 (Winter 2010)/45.1 (Spring 2011): 457–76.

Deak, Frantisek. 1993. *Symbolist Theater: Formation of an Avant-Garde*. Baltimore: Johns Hopkins University Press.

de Mille, Agnes. 1956. *Martha: The Life and Work of Martha Graham; A Biography*. New York: Random House.

Denton, Martin. 2006. *Playing with Canons*. New York: New York Theatre Experience.

Dolan, Jill. 2006. Review of *Oedipus at Palm Springs*. *Journal of Gay and Lesbian Studies* 12.3: 494–506.

Donnelly, Francis P., SJ. 1930. "The Millbrook Greek Play and Its Choral Dance." *Art and Archaeology* 29: 57–63.
Dove, Rita. 1996. *The Darker Face of the Earth*. Brownville, Ore.: Story Line Press.
Duffey, Bernard. 1954. *The Chicago Renaissance in American Letters: A Critical History*. East Lansing: Michigan State College Press.
Dukore, Bernard Frank. 1957. "Maurice Browne and the Chicago Little Theatre." PhD diss., University of Illinois, Urbana.
Duncan, Isadora. 1927a. *Ecrits sur la danse*. Paris: Editions du Grenier.
———. 1927b. "Dancing in Relation to Religion and Love." *Theatre Arts Monthly* (August): 592.
———. 1928. *The Art of the Dance*. Edited by Sheldon Cheney. New York: Theatre Arts.
Duncan, Robert. 1965. *Medea at Kolchis: The Maiden Head*. Berkeley: Oyez.
Dunn, Francis, ed. 1996. *Sophocles' "Electra" in Performance*. Stuttgart: J. B. Metziersche Verlagsbuchhandlung und Carl Ernst Poeschel Verlag für Wissenschaft und Forschung.
Durang, Christopher. 1995. *Christopher Durang, 27 Short Plays*. Lyme, N.H.: Smith and Kraus.
Durham, Weldon B., ed. 1987. *American Theatre Companies, 1888–1930*. Westport, Conn.: Greenwood Press.
Eaton, Walter Prichard. 1908. "Sophocles in the Backyard." In *The American Stage of Today*, 83–95. Boston: Small, Maynard and Company.
Edmunds, Lowell. 1996. *Theatrical Space and Historical Place in Sophocles' "Oedipus at Colonus."* Lanham, Md., and London: Rowman and Littlefield.
Edwards, Paul. 1987. "'Putting on the Greeks': Euripidean Tragedy and the Twentieth-Century American Theatre." PhD diss., University of Colorado.
Elberson, Stanley Denton. 1968. "The Nature of Harvey Granville Barker's Productions in America in 1915." PhD diss., University of Oregon.
Epperson, John. 2007. *My Deah*. New York: Samuel French.
Etkind, Mark 1997. *. . . Or Not to Be: A Collection of Suicide Letters*. New York: Riverhead Books.
Fairclough, H. Rushton. 1903. *Antigone: An Account of the Presentation of the "Antigone" of Sophocles*. San Francisco: Paul Elder and Co.
Fearnow, Mark. 1999. "Theatre Groups and Their Playwrights." In *The Cambridge History of American Theatre*, vol. 2, *1870–1945*, edited by Don B. Wilmeth and Christopher Bigsby, 343–77. Cambridge: Cambridge University Press.
Feinsod, Arthur. 1992. *The Simple Stage: Its Origins in the Modern American Theater*. Westport, Conn.: Greenwood Press.
Felski, Rita, ed. 2008. *Rethinking Tragedy*. Baltimore: Johns Hopkins University Press.
Felton, Cornelius C. 1837. "*Ion*, a Tragedy in Five Acts." Review article no. 8. *The North American Review* 44: 485–503.
Flanagan, Hallie. (1940) 1965. *Arena: The History of the Federal Theatre*. New York: Duell, Sloan and Pearce. Reprint, New York: Benjamin Blom.
Fo, Dario, and Franca Rame. 1982. *Female Parts: One Woman Plays*. London: Pluto Press.
Foley, Helene P. 1985. *Ritual Irony: Poetry and Sacrifice in Euripides*. Ithaca, N.Y.: Cornell University Press.

———. 1993. "Oedipus as Pharmakos." In *Nomodeiktes: Essays in Honor of Martin Ostwald*, edited by Ralph Rosen and Joseph, 525-38. Ann Arbor: University of Michigan Press.

———. 1995. Review of Ellen McLaughlin's *Iphigeneia and Other Daughters*, performed by the CSC Repertory Company, January 31-March 5, 1995. *Didaskalia* 2.2. http://www.didaskalia.net/issues/vol2no2/foley.html.

———. 1999. "Modern Performance and Adaptation of Greek Tragedy." *Transactions and Proceedings of the American Philological Association* 129: 1-12. Presidential Address for 1998. Also available at www.apaclassics.org.

———. 1999-2000. "Twentieth-Century Performance and Adaptation of Euripides." *Illinois Classical Studies* 24-25: 1-13.

———. 2001. *Female Acts in Greek Tragedy*. Princeton, N.J.: Princeton University Press.

———. 2003. "Reimagining Euripides' *Hippolytus*." *Dionsio* n.s. 2: 178-89.

———. 2004. "Bad Women: Gender Politics in Late Twentieth-Century Performance and Revision of Greek Tragedy." In *Dionysus since 69*, edited by Edith Hall, Fiona Macintosh, and Amanda Wrigley, 77-112. Oxford: Oxford University Press.

———. 2005. "The Millennium Project: *Agamemnon* in the United States." In *"Agamemnon" in Performance*, edited by Fiona Macintosh et al., 307-42. Oxford: Oxford University Press.

———. 2007. "Envisioning the Chorus on the Modern Stage." In *Visualizing the Tragic: Drama, Myth, and Ritual in Greek Art and Literature*, edited by Chris Kraus et al., 353-78. Oxford: Oxford University Press.

———. 2010. "Generic Ambiguity in Modern Productions and New Versions of Greek Tragedy." In *Theorizing Performance: Greek Drama, Cultural History, and Critical Practice*, edited by Edith Hall and Stephe Harrop, 137-53. London: Duckworth.

———. 2011. "Millennial *Antigone* in the U.S.: Anouilh Revisited." In *"Antigone" on the Contemporary World Stage*, edited by Erin Mee and Helene P. Foley, 373-91. Oxford: Oxford University Press.

———. Forthcoming. "Julia Ward Howe's *Hippolytus*." In *Oxford Classical Handbook to Greek Drama in the Americas*, edited by Kathryn Bosher, Fiona Macintosh, Justine McConnell, and Patrice Rankine. Oxford: Oxford University Press.

Foster, Verna A. 2004. *The Name and Nature of Tragicomedy*. Aldershot, U.K.: Ashgate.

Fraden, Rena. 2001. *Imagining Medea: Rhodessa Jones and Theater for Incarcerated Women*. Chapel Hill and London: University of North Carolina Press.

Franko, Mark. 1995. *Dancing Modernism/Performing Politics*. Bloomington and Indianapolis: Indiana University Press.

Freiert, William K. 1991. "Timeless Oedipus: 'The Primitive' in Three Modern Adaptations." *Text and Presentation* 11: 19-24.

Freund, Philip. 1970. *Jocasta*. In *Three Poetic Plays*, 94-70. London: W.H. Allen.

Frick, John. 1999. "A Changing Theatre: New York and Beyond." In *The Cambridge History of American Theatre*, vol. 2, *1870-1945*, edited by Don B. Wilmeth and Christopher Bigsby, 196-232. Cambridge: Cambridge University Press.

Fuchs, Elinor. 1986. "Robert's Wilson's *Alcestis*: A Classic for the '80s." *Village Voice*, July 2, 1986.

Fuchs, Elinor, and Bonnie Maranca, eds. 1986. "The PAJ Casebook: *Alcestis*." *Performing Arts Journal* 5.28: 78–115.
Furth, Leslie. 1998. "'The Modern Medea' and Race Matters: Thomas Satterwhite Noble's Margaret Garner." *American Art* 12.2: 37–57.
Gage, Margaret. 1929. "The Greek Choral Drama." *Theatre Arts Monthly*, August: 569-78.
———. 1932. "A Study in American Modernism." *Theatre Arts Monthly*, March: 299–32.
Gantz, Timothy. 1993. *Early Greek Myth: A Guide to Literary and Artistic Sources*. Baltimore and London: Johns Hopkins University Press.
Garvie, A. F. 2009. *Aeschylus, Persae*. Oxford: Oxford University Press.
Gelb, Arthur, and Barbara Gelb. (1973) 1987. *O'Neill*. New York: Perennial Library. Reprint, New York: Harper and Row.
Gerould, Daniel, and Jadwiga Kosicka. 1980. "The Drama of the Unseen—Turn-of-the-Century Paradigms for Occult Drama." In *The Occult in Language and Literature*, edited by Hermione Riffaterre, 3–42. New York: New York Literary Forum.
Gill, Glenda E. 2000. *No Surrender! No Retreat! African-American Pioneer Performers of Twentieth-Century American Theatre*. New York: St. Martin's.
Gilmore, Bob. 1998. *Harry Partch: A Biography*. New Haven, Conn.: Yale University Press.
Giorcelli, Cristina. 1992. "Ristori on the American Scene." *Voices in Italian Americana* 3.1: 29–40.
Glaspell, Susan. (1927) 1941. *Road to the Temple*. Reprint, New York: Frederick A. Stokes Co.
Goff, Barbara, and Michael Simpson. 2007. *Crossroads in the Black Aegean: "Oedipus," "Antigone," and the Dramas of the African Diaspora*. Oxford: Oxford University Press.
Goldman, Richard F. 1950. "The Music of Wallingford Riegger." *Musical Quarterly* 36.1: 39–61.
Graham, Martha. 1973. *The Notebooks of Martha Graham*. New York: Harcourt, Brace, Jovanovich, Inc.
———. 1991. *Blood Memory*. New York: Doubleday.
Green, Amy S. 1994. *The Revisionist Stage: American Directors Reinvent the Classics*. Cambridge: Cambridge University Press.
Green, Vivien M. 1982. "Hiram Power's 'Greek Slave': Emblem of Freedom." *American Art Journal* 14.4: 31–39.
Greenwalt, Emmett A. 1955. *The Point Loma Community in California, 1897–1942*. Berkeley and Los Angeles: University of California Press.
Gridley, Steven. 2006. *Post-Oedipus*. New York: Playscripts, Inc.
Griffith, Mark. 2003. "Robinson Jeffers and Greek Tragedy." *Jeffers Studies* 7.1: 19–50.
Gurney, A. R. 1995. *Nine Early Plays, 1961–1973*. Lyme, N.H.: Smith and Kraus.
———. 2000. *Collected Plays*. Vol. 3, *1984–1991*. Hanover, N.H.: Smith and Kraus.
Hains, D. D. 1910. "Greek Plays in America." *Classical Journal* 6.1: 24–39.
———. 1914. "The Presentation of Classical Plays, Part I." *Classical Journal* 9.5: 189–98.
Hall, Edith. 1996. *Aeschylus, Persians*. Warminster, UK: Aris and Phillips, Ltd.
———. 2004. "Aeschylus, Race, Class, and War in the 1990s." In *Dionysus since 69*, edited by Edith Hall, Fiona Macintosh, and Amanda Wrigley, 169–98. Oxford: Oxford University Press.

Hall, Edith, and Fiona Macintosh. 2005. *Greek Tragedy and the British Theatre, 1660–1914.* Oxford: Oxford University Press.
Hall, Edith, Fiona Macintosh, and Oliver Taplin, eds. 2000. *"Medea" in Performance, 1500–2000.* Oxford: Legenda.
Hall, Edith, Fiona Macintosh, and Amanda Wrigley, eds. 2004. *Dionysus since 69: Greek Tragedy at the Dawn of the Third Millennium.* Oxford: Oxford University Press.
Hamilton, Clayton. 1920. *Seen on the Stage.* New York: H. Holt and Co.
Hapgood, Norman. 1901. *The Stage in America: 1897–1900.* New York: Macmillan.
Hardwick, Lorna. 2000. *Translating Words, Translating Cultures.* London: Duckworth.
Hartigan, Karelisa. 1995. *Greek Tragedy on the American Stage: Ancient Drama in the Commercial Theatre, 1882–1994.* Westport, Conn. and London: Greenwood Press.
Hatch, James V. 1993. *Sorrow Is the Only Faithful One: The Life of Owen Dodson.* Urbana and Chicago: University of Illinois Press.
Hatch, James V., and Omani Abdullah. 1977. *Black Playwrights, 1823–1977: An Annotated Anthology.* New York: R. R. Bowker.
Helpern, Alice. 1994. *The Technique of Martha Graham.* Dobbs Ferry, N.Y.: Morgan & Morgan.
Henderson, Mary. 1998. "Scenography, Stagecraft, and Architecture in the American Theatre: Beginnings to 1870." In *The Cambridge History of American Theatre,* vol. 1, *Beginnings to 1870,* edited by Don B. Wilmeth and Christopher Bigsby, 373–423. Cambridge: Cambridge University Press.
Heron, Matilda. 1857. *Medea, a Tragedy in Three Acts, Translated from the French of M. Legouvé by Matilda Heron.* New York: Samuel French.
Hofstadter, Richard, William Miller, and Daniel Aaron. 1959. *The American Republic.* Vol. 2, *From Reconstruction.* 2nd ed. Englewood Cliffs, N.J.: Prentice Hall.
Holmberg, Arthur. 1996. *The Theater of Robert Wilson.* Cambridge: Cambridge University Press.
Horosko, Marian. (1981) 2002. *Martha Graham: The Evolution of Her Dance Theory and Training.* Rev. ed. Gainesville: University Press of Florida.
Houston, Velina Hasu, ed. 1997. *But Still, Like Air, I'll Rise: New Asian American Plays.* Philadelphia: Temple University Press.
Howe, Julia Ward. 1899. *Reminiscences, 1819–1899.* Boston and New York: Houghton Mifflin.
———. 1941. *Hippolytus.* In *"Monte Cristo" and Other Plays.* Princeton, N.J.: Princeton University Press. Electronic edition by Alexander Street Press, 2010.
Ireland, Joseph N. (1866–67) 1968. *Records of the New York Stage, 1750–1860.* New York: T. H. Morrell. Reprint, New York: Benjamin Blom.
Jeffers, Robinson. (1946) 1948. *Medea: Freely Adapted from the "Medea" of Euripides.* New York: Samuel French.
———. 1988–2001. *The Collected Poetry of Robinson Jeffers.* Edited by Tim Hunt. 5 vols. Stanford, Calif.: Stanford University Press.
Jeffreys, Joe E. 1996. "An Outré Entrée into the Para-ridiculous Histrionics of Drag Diva Ethyl Eichelberger: A True Story." PhD diss., New York University.
Johnson, Arnold G. 1971. "The Greek Productions of Margaret Anglin." PhD diss., Case Western Reserve University.

Jones, John. 1962. *On Aristotle and Greek Tragedy.* London: Chatto & Windus.
Kasson, John. 1990. *Rudeness and Civility: Manners in Nineteenth-Century Urban America.* New York: Hill and Wang.
Kasson, Joy S. 1990. *Marble Queens and Captives: Women in Nineteenth-Century Sculpture.* New Haven, Conn., and London: Yale University Press.
Kelley, Mary. 2006. *Learning to Stand and Speak: Women, Education, and Public Life in America's Republic.* Chapel Hill: University of North Carolina Press.
Kennedy, Adrienne. 1988. *In One Act.* Minneapolis and London: University of Minnesota Press.
Kennedy, Dennis. 1985. *Granville Barker and the Dream of Theatre.* Cambridge: Cambridge University Press.
Knox, B. M. W. 1957. *Oedipus at Thebes: Sophocles' Tragic Hero and His Time.* New Haven, Conn.: Yale University Press.
———. 1964. *The Heroic Temper: Studies in Sophoclean Tragedy.* Berkeley and Los Angeles: University of California Press.
———. 1977. "The *Medea* of Euripides." *Yale Classical Studies* 25: 193–225. Reprinted in B. M. W. Knox, *Word and Action: Essays on Ancient Theater* (Baltimore and London: Johns Hopkins University Press, 1979), 292–322.
———. 1979. *Word and Action: Essays on Ancient Theater.* Baltimore and London: Johns Hopkins University Press.
Koger, Alicia Kae. 1997. "Dramaturgical Criticism: A Case Study of *The Gospel at Colonus*." *Theatre Topics* 7.1: 23–35.
Kostelanetz, Richard. 1994. *On Innovative Performance(s): Three Decades of Recollections on Alternative Theater.* Jefferson, N.C., and London: McFarland and Co., Inc.
Kurth, Peter. 2001. *Isadora: A Sensational Life.* Boston and London: Little, Brown and Co.
LaBute, Neil. 1999. *Bash: Latterday Plays.* Woodstock, N.Y.: Overlook Press.
———. 2007. *"Wrecks" and Other Plays.* New York: Faber and Faber.
Lacroix, Jules. 1874. *Oeuvres de théâtre.* Vol. 3. Paris: M. Lévy Frères.
———. 1892. *Oedipe roi, tragédie de Sophocle.* Paris: Calmann Lévy.
Lahr, John. 1993. "Inventing the Enemy." *New Yorker,* October 18, 103–6.
Laks, Batya Casper. 1995. *Electra: A Gender-Sensitive Study of the Plays (Aeschylus' "Oresteia" through Sam Shephard's "Curse of the Starving Class").* Jefferson, N.C., and London: McFarland and Co., Inc.
Leatherman, LeRoy. 1966. *Martha Graham: Portrait of the Lady as an Artist.* New York: Alfred A. Knopf.
Leuchs, Fritz A. H. 1966. *The Early German Theatre in New York, 1840–1872.* New York: AMS Press.
LeVay, John. 1989. *Margaret Anglin: A Stage Life.* Toronto: Simon and Pierre.
Levine, Lawrence W. 1988. *Highbrow/Lowbrow: The Emergence of Cultural Hierarchy in America.* Cambridge, Mass.: Harvard University Press.
Lewis, Jim. 1996. "*The Clytemnestra Project* at the Guthrie Theater." In *The Production Notebooks: Theater in Process,* edited by Mark Bly, 1–62. New York: Theatre Communications Group.

Lingan, Edmund B. 2005. "The Theatre of the New Religious Movements of Europe and America from the Nineteenth Century to the Present." PhD diss., CUNY.

Lloyd, Margaret. 1949. *The Borzoi Book of Modern Dance*. New York: Alfred Knopf.

Loewenthal, Lillian. 1993. *Isadora: The Legend and Legacy of Isadora Duncan*. Pennington, N.J.: Princeton Book Company.

Lomonaco, Martha. 2000. "Regional/Resident Theatre." In *The Cambridge History of American Theatre*, vol. 3, *Post-World War II to the 1990s*, edited by Don B. Wilmeth and Christopher Bigsby, 224–48. Cambridge: Cambridge University Press.

Love, Heather K. 2008. "Spectacular Failure: The Figure of the Lesbian in *Mulholland Drive*." In *Rethinking Tragedy*, edited by Rita Felski, 302–18. Baltimore: Johns Hopkins University Press.

Lowell, Robert. 1969. *Prometheus Bound*. New York: Farrar, Straus and Giroux.

Ludlam, Charles. 1989. *The Complete Plays of Charles Ludlam*. New York: Harper and Row.

Macgowan, Kenneth. 1921. *The Theatre of Tomorrow*. New York: Boni and Liveright.

Macintosh, Fiona. 1997. "Tragedy in Performance: Nineteenth- and Twentieth-Century Productions." In *The Cambridge Companion to Greek Tragedy*, edited by P. E. Easterling, 284–323. Cambridge: Cambridge University Press.

———. 2000. "Introduction: The Performer in Performance." In *"Medea" in Performance, 1500–2000*, edited by Edith Hall, Fiona Macintosh, and Oliver Taplin, 1–31. Oxford: Legenda.

———. 2007. "Parricide versus Filicide: *Oedipus* and *Medea* on the Modern Stage." In *Tragedy in Transition*, edited by Sarah Annes Brown and Catherine Silverstone, 192–211. Oxford: Blackwell.

———. 2008. "Performance Histories." In *A Companion to Classical Receptions*, edited by Lorna Hardwick and Chris Stray, 247–58. Oxford: Blackwell.

———. 2009a. "The French Oedipus of the Inter-war Period." In *Sophocles and the Greek Tradition*, edited by Simon Goldhill and Edith Hall, 158–78. Cambridge: Cambridge University Press.

———. 2009b. *Sophocles: Oedipus Tyrannus*. Cambridge: Cambridge University Press.

———, ed. 2010. *The Ancient Dancer in the Modern World: Responses to Greek and Roman Dance*. Oxford: Oxford University Press.

Macintosh, Fiona, Pantelis Michelakis, Edith Hall, and Oliver Taplin, eds. 2005. *"Agamemnon" in Performance, 458 BC–AD 2004*. Oxford: Oxford University Press.

Mackey, Chris, with Greg Miller. 2004. *The Interrogators: Inside the Secret War against Al Qaeda*. London: Murray.

Mainiero, Lina. 1979–94. *American Women Writers: A Critical Reference Guide from Colonial Times to the Present*. 5 vols. New York: Ungar.

Malnig, Julie. 2009. "All Is Not Right in the House of Atreus: Feminist Theatrical Renderings of the *Oresteia*." In *Feminist Theatrical Revisions of Classic Works*, edited by Sharon Friedman, 21–41. Jefferson, N.C., and London: McFarland and Co., Inc.

Malnig, Julie, and Judy C. Rosenthal. 1993. "The Women's Experimental Theatre: Transforming Family Stories into Feminist Issues." In *Acting Out: Feminist Performances*, edited by Peggy Phelan and Lynda Hart, 201–14. Ann Arbor: University of Michigan Press.

Manheim, M., ed. 1998. *The Cambridge Companion to Eugene O'Neill.* Cambridge: Cambridge University Press.
Mantle, Burns, and Garrison P. Sherwood. 1934a. *Best Plays of 1899–1904.* New York: Dodd, Mead and Co.
———. 1934b. *Best Plays of 1909–1919.* New York: Dodd, Mead and Co.
Margraff, Ruth. 2005. "The Elektra Fugues." In *Divine Fire: Eight Contemporary Plays Inspired by the Greeks,* edited by Caridad Svich, 163–208. New York: Back Stage Books.
Marra, Kim. 2006. *Strange Duets: Impresarios and Actresses in American Theatre, 1865–1914.* Iowa City: University of Iowa Press.
Martin, Carol. 2009. "The Political Is Personal: Feminism, Democracy, and *Antigone Project.*" In *Feminist Theatrical Revision of Classic Works,* Sharon Friedman, 79–96. Jefferson, N.C.: McFarland and Co., Inc.
Mattison, Edith Wynne, and Charles Rann Kennedy. 1921. "Production of Greek Plays." *Theatre Magazine* 34 (December): 398–99, 436.
May, Caroline. 1848. *The American Female Poets with Biographical and Critical Notices.* Philadelphia: Lindsay and Blakiston.
McConachie, Bruce A. 1992. *Melodramatic Formations: American Theatre and Society, 1820–1870.* Iowa City: University of Iowa Press.
———. 1998. "American Theater in Context, from the Beginnings to 1870." In *The Cambridge History of American Theatre,* vol. 1, *Beginnings to 1870,* edited by Don B. Wilmeth and Christopher Bigsby, 111–82. Cambridge: Cambridge University Press.
McDermott, Douglas. 1998. "Structure and Management in the American Theatre from the Beginnings to 1870." In *The Cambridge History of American Theatre,* vol. 1, *Beginnings to 1870,* edited by Don B. Wilmeth and Christopher Bigsby, 182–215. Cambridge: Cambridge University Press.
McDermott, Patrick. 1969. "Portrait of an Actor, Watching." *The Drama Review* 13.3: 74–85.
McDonagh, Don. 1973. *Martha Graham: A Biography.* New York and Washington, D.C.: Praeger.
McDonald, Marianne. 1992. *Ancient Sun, Modern Light: Greek Drama on the Modern Stage.* New York and Oxford: Columbia University Press.
———. 2001. *Sing Sorrow: Classics, History, and Heroines in Opera.* Westport, Conn., and London: Greenwood Press.
McLaughlin, Ellen. 2005. *The Greek Plays.* New York: Theatre Communications Group.
Mee, Charles L. 1998. *History Plays.* Baltimore and London: Johns Hopkins University Press.
———. 2006. "Hip Hop Visions of an Ancient World: Will Power and Company Turn Aeschylus Everyway but Loose." *American Theatre* 23.3: 28–32, 70.
Mee, Erin, and Helene P. Foley, eds. 2011. *"Antigone" on the Contemporary World Stage.* Oxford: Oxford University Press.
Meineck, Peter. 2006. "Live From New York: Hip Hop Aeschylus and Operatic Aristophanes." *Arion* 41.1: 145–67.
———. 2009. "'These are the men whose minds the Dead have raised'": Theater of War/The Philoctetes Project." *Arion* 17.1: 173–91.
Menta, Ed. 1995. *The Magic World behind the Curtain: Andre Serban in the American Theatre.* New York: Peter Lang.

Michelakis, Pantelis. 2010. "Dancing with Prometheus: Performance and Spectacle in the 1920s." In *The Ancient Dancer in the Modern World*, edited by Fiona Macintosh, 224–35. Oxford: Oxford University Press.

Miller, Tice L. 1999. "Plays and Playwrights: Civil War to 1896." In *The Cambridge History of American Theatre*, vol. 2, *1870–1945*, edited by Don B. Wilmeth and Christopher Bigsby, 233–61. Cambridge: Cambridge University Press.

Mimoso-Ruiz, Duarte. 1978. *Médée antique et moderne: Aspects rituels et socio-politiques d'un mythe.* Paris: Edition Orphys.

Moraga, C. L. 2001. *The Hungry Woman.* Albuquerque, N.M.: West End Press.

———. 2004. "Queer Atzlán: The Re-formation of Chicano Tribe." In *Queer Cultures*, edited by Deborah Carlin and Jennifer di Grazia, 224–38. New York: Prentice Hall.

Moses, Montrose J., and John Mason Brown, eds. 1934. *The American Theatre as Seen by Its Critics, 1752–1934.* New York: Norton.

Moss, Howard. 1980. *Two Plays.* New York: Sheep Meadow Press/Flying Point Books.

Mudd, A. I. 1902. "Early Theatres in Washington." *Records of the Columbia Historical Society* 5: 64–86.

———. 1903. "The Theatres of Washington from 1833–1850." *Records of the Columbia Historical Society* 6: 222–66.

Mufson, Daniel. 1999. *Reza Abdoh.* Baltimore and London: Johns Hopkins University Press.

Murphy, Brenda. 1999. "Plays and Playwrights: 1915–1945." In *The Cambridge History of American Theatre*, vol. 2, *1870–1945*, edited by Don B. Wilmeth and Christopher Bigsby, 289–342. Cambridge: Cambridge University Press.

Murray, A. T. 1903. "Antigone: A Dramatic Study." In *Antigone: An Account of the Presentation of the "Antigone" of Sophocles*, edited by H. R. Fairclough, 5–21. San Francisco: Paul Elder and Company.

Murray, Gilbert. 1906. *The Medea of Euripides.* New York: Oxford University Press.

Neff, Renfreu. 1970. *The Living Theatre: USA.* Indianapolis and New York: Bobbs Merrill Company.

Nelson, Marilyn. 1997. Hecuba. In *Euripides*, vol. 1, edited by D. R. Slavitt and P. Bovie, 71–146. Philadelphia: University of Pennsylvania Press.

Norman, Henry. 1882. *An Account of the Harvard Greek Play.* Boston: J. R. Osgood.

Nugent, S. Georgia. 1988. "Masking Becomes Electra: O'Neill, Freud, and the Feminine." *Comparative Drama* 22: 37–55.

Odell, George C. D. (1927–49) 1970. *Annals of the New York Stage.* 14 vols. New York: Columbia University Press. Reprint, New York: AMS Press.

O'Neill, Eugene. 1958. *Three Plays: Desire under the Elms, Strange Interlude, and Mourning Becomes Electra.* New York: Vintage Books, Random House.

Palmer, Richard. 1965. "The Outdoor Theater Movement in the United States from 1900 to 1920." PhD diss., University of Iowa.

———. 1987. "Coburn Players"; "Ben Greet Players." In *American Theatre Companies, 1888–1930*, edited by Weldon B. Durham, 86–90, 197–203. Westport, Conn.: Greenwood Press.

Palmer-Sikelianos, Eva. 1993. *Upward Panic: The Autobiography of Eva Palmer-Sikelianos*, edited by J. P. Anton. Amsterdam, Chur, and Philadelphia: Harwood Academic Publishers.

Parnes, Uzi. 1998. "Pop Performance, Four Seminal Influences: The Work of Jack Smith, Tom Murrin—the Alien Comic, Ethyl Eichelberger, and the Split Britches Company." PhD diss., New York University.

Partch, Harry. 1974. *Genesis of a Music*. 2nd ed. New York: Da Capo Press.

———. 1991. *Bitter Music: Collected Journals, Essays, Introductions, and Librettos*. Edited by Thomas Geary. Urbana and Chicago: University of Illinois Press.

Pearcy, Lee T. 2008. "In the Shadow of Aristophanes: The 1903 *Iphigeneia in Tauris* in Philadelphia." In *In Pursuit of Wissenschaft: Festschrift für William M. Calder III zum 75. Geburtstag*, edited by Stephen Heilen, Robert Kirstein, R. Scott Smith, Stephen M. Trzaskoma, Rogier L. van der Wal, and Matthias Vorwerk, 327–40. Zurich and New York: Georg Olms Verlag Hildesheim.

Pluggé, Domis E. 1938. "History of Greek Play Production in American Colleges and Universities from 1881 to 1936." PhD diss., Columbia University.

Poe, Edgar Allen. 1845. "The *Antigone* at Palmo's." *Broadway Journal* 1.15, April 12: 236–37. Reprinted in James A. Harrison, ed., *The Complete Works of Edgar Allen Poe* (New York: AMS Press, 1965), 12: 130–35.

———. (1902) 1965. *The Complete Works of Edgar Allen Poe*. Edited by James A. Harrison. 17 vols. New York: Crowell. Reprint, New York: AMS Press.

Postlewait, Thomas. 1999. "The Hieroglyphic Stage: American Theatre and Society, Post–Civil War to 1945." In *The Cambridge History of American Theatre*, vol. 2, *1870–1945*, edited by Don B. Wilmeth and Christopher Bigsby, 107–95. Cambridge: Cambridge University Press.

Potter, Robert. 1781. *Medea*. In *The Tragedies of Euripides, Translated in Two Volumes*, 1: 239–312. London: J. Dodsley, Pall-Mall.

Pound, Ezra. 1957. *Sophokles, Women of Trachis: A Version by Ezra Pound*. New York: New Directions.

Pound, Ezra, and Rudd Fleming. (1987) 1989. *Elektra: A Play by Ezra Pound and Rudd Fleming*. Edited and annotated by Richard Reid. Princeton, N.J.: Princeton University Press.

———. 1990. *Sophokles Elektra: A Version by Ezra Pound and Rudd Fleming*. With an introduction and notes by Carey Perloff. New York: New Directions Books.

Price, Jonathan. 1968. "Jonathan Miller Directs Robert J. Lowell's PROMETHEUS." *Yale/Theatre* 1: 40–50.

Prins, Yopie. Forthcoming. *Ladies Greek: Translations of Tragedy*. Princeton, N.J.: Princeton University Press.

Psacharopoulos, Nikos. 1968. "Directing Greek Drama: A Comment." *Yale/Theatre* 1: 32–39.

Quadri, Franco, Franco Bertoni, and Robert Stearns. 1998. *Robert Wilson*. New York: Rizzoli.

Rabinowitz, Nancy Sorkin. 1993. *Anxiety Veiled: Euripides and the Traffic in Women*. Ithaca, N.Y.: Cornell University Press.

Raizis, M. Byron. 1969. "Robert Lowell's *Prometheus Bound*." *Papers on Language and Literature* 5 (Supplement, Summer 1969): 154–68.

Read, Harriette Fanning. 1848. *Dramatic Poems*. Boston: Wm. Crosby and H. P. Nichols.

Reinhold, Meyer. 1984. *Classica Americana: The Greek and Roman Heritage in the United States*. Detroit, Mich.: Wayne University Press.

Renner, Pamela. 2007. "Oedipus at Sing Sing." *American Theatre* 24.1: 34–36, 120.

Revermann, Martin. 2003. "Spatio-Temporal Dynamics in Sophocles' *Oedipus the King.*" *University of Toronto Quarterly* 72: 789–800.
Rexroth, Kenneth. 1951. *Beyond the Mountains.* Direction 20. Brattleboro, Vt.: The Belgrave Press.
Richards, Laura E., and Maud Howe Elliot, assisted by Florence Howe Holt. (1915) 1990. *Julia Ward Howe, 1819 to 1910.* Vol. 1. Reprint, Boston and New York: Houghton Mifflin.
Richardson, Gary A. 1998. "Plays and Playwrights: 1800–1865." In *The Cambridge History of American Theatre*, vol. 1, *Beginnings to 1870*, edited by Don B. Wilmeth and Christopher Bigsby, 250–302. Cambridge: Cambridge University Press.
Rno, Sung. 2011. *wAve.* In *Version 3.0: Contemporary Asian American Plays,* edited by Chay Yew, 131–200. New York: Theatre Communications Group.
Robbe-Grillet, Alain. 1965. *For a New Novel: Essays on Fiction.* Translated by Richard Howard. Freeport, N.Y.: Grove Press.
Roberts, Deborah. 1988. "Sophoclean Endings: Another Story." *Arethusa* 21: 177–96.
Robinson, Marc. 1994. *The Other American Drama.* Baltimore and London: Johns Hopkins University Press.
———. 2009. *The American Play: 1787–2000.* New Haven, Conn., and London: Yale University Press.
Rogers, Priscilla S. M. 1986. "Greek Tragedy in the New York Theatre: A History and Interpretation." PhD diss., University of Michigan.
Rogoff, Gordon. 1969. "The Theater Is Not Safe." *Yale/Theatre* 2.1: 89–101.
Rouse, John. 1986–87. "Structuring Stories: Robert Wilson's *Alcestis.*" *Theater* 18: 56–59.
Russak, John Ben, ed. 1941. *Monte Cristo, as Played by James O'Neill, & Other Plays by Julia Ward Howe, George C. Hazelton, Langdon Mitchell, William C. De Mille.* Princeton, N.J.: Princeton University Press.
Saïd, Suzanne. 1998. "Tragedy and Politics." In *Democracy, Empire, and the Arts in Fifth-Century Athens,* edited by Deborah Boedeker and Kurt A. Raaflaub, 275–96. Cambridge, Mass., and London: Harvard University Press.
Sanderson, James L., and Everettt Zimmerman. 1957. *Medea: Myth and Dramatic Form.* Boston: Houghton Mifflin.
Sarlós, Robert Károly. 1982. *Jig Cook and the Provincetown Players.* Amherst: University of Massachusetts Press.
Sayler, Oliver. 1923. *Our American Theatre.* New York: Brentano's.
Schechner, Richard. 1969. "An Interview with the Becks." *The Drama Review* 13.3: 24–44.
———, ed. 1970. *The Performance Group: Dionysus in 69.* New York: Farrar, Straus and Giroux.
Schlundt, Christena L. 1962. *Professional Appearances of Ruth St. Denis & Ted Shawn: A Chronology and an Index of Dances, 1906–1932.* New York: New York Public Library.
———. 1972. *Tamiris: A Chronicle of Her Dance Career, 1927–1955.* Studies in Dance History 1.1. New York: New York Public Library.
Seely, Hart, ed. 2003. *Pieces of Intelligence: The Existential Poetry of D. H. Rumsfeld.* New York: Free Press.
Seilhamer, George. (1888–91) 1968. *History of American Theatre.* 3 vols. Philadelphia. Reprint, Grosse Pointe, Mich.: Scholarly Press.

Selden, Elizabeth S. 1929. "The Greek Drama Revived: Margaret Gage at the Bennett School Gives New Impetus to the Interest in Greek Choral Work." *Dance Magazine,* December: 18–19 and 49.

Sellars, Peter. 1992. "Sellars Talk at Carnuntum." In *Ancient Sun, Modern Light: Greek Drama on the Modern Stage,* by Marianne McDonald, 89–95. New York: Columbia University Press.

———. 1996. "Conversation with Michael Billington, 18.11.1994." In *In Contact with the Gods? Directors Talk Theatre,* edited by Maria M. Delgado and Paul Heritage, 224–38. Manchester: Manchester University Press; New York: St. Martin's Press.

Shay, Jonathan. 1994. *Achilles in Vietnam: Combat Trauma and the Undoing of Character.* New York: Maxwell Macmillan International.

Sheppard, W. Anthony. 2001. *Revealing Masks: Exotic Influences in Modernist Music Theater.* Berkeley and Los Angeles: University of California Press.

Sherman, Jane. 1983. *Denishawn: The Enduring Influence.* Boston: Twayne.

Sherman, Robert L. 1944. *Drama Cyclopedia, a Bibliography of Plays and Players.* Chicago: Self-published.

Shucard, Allan. 1987. "Countee Cullen." In *Dictionary of Literary Biography,* vol. 51. Detroit: Bruccoli Clark.

Silber, Irwin. 1969. "Open Letter to the Living Theatre." *The Drama Review* 13.3: 86–89.

Smethurst, Mae. 2002. "Ninagawa's Production of Euripides' *Medea.*" *American Journal of Philology* 123.1: 1–18. An earlier version appeared in Edith Hall, Fiona Macintosh, and Oliver Taplin, eds., *"Medea" in Performance, 1500–2000* (Oxford: Legenda, 2000), 191–216.

Smith, Harrison. 1915. "The Revival of Greek Tragedy in America." *Bookman* 41, June: 409–16.

Smith, Ronn. 1986. "Wilson Weaves Classical Magic: *Alcestis* at ART." *Theatre Crafts,* November: 30–31, 88–92.

Sonkowsky, Robert. 1973. "Classical Theater and the Burgess-Langham Production of 'Oedipus the King' at the Guthrie." In *Miscellaneous Papers of the Bell Museum of Pathobiology,* 27–33. Minneapolis: University of Minnesota Medical School.

Sorgenfrei, Carol. 1975. *Medea: A Noh Cycle Based on Greek Myth.* New York and Hollywood: Samuel French.

Spackman, Stephen. 1985. "Wallingford Riegger and the Modern Dance." *Musical Quarterly* 71.4: 437–67.

Spender, Stephen. 1985. *Oedipus Trilogy: A Version by Stephen Spender.* New York: Random House.

Steiner, George. 1984. *Antigones: The Antigone Myth in Literature, Art, and Thought.* Oxford: Oxford University Press.

———. 2008. "Tragedy Reconsidered." In *Rethinking Tragedy,* edited by Rita Felski. 29–44. Baltimore and London: Johns Hopkins University Press.

Stiller, Andrew. 1992. "Harry Partch." In *The New Grove Dictionary of Opera,* edited by Stanley Sadie, 3: 895–96. London: Macmillan.

Stodelle, Ernestine. 1984. *Deep Song: The Dance Story of Martha Graham.* New York: Schirmer Books; London: Collier Macmillan.

Straile-Costa, Paula. 2010. "Myth and Ritual in *The Hungry Woman: A Mexican Medea*; Cherríe Moraga's Xicana-Indigena Interpretation of Euripides' *Medea*." In *Unbinding Medea: Interdisciplinary Approaches to Classical Myth from Antiquity to the 21$^{st}$ Century*, edited by Heike Bartel and Anne Simon, 209–23. London: Legenda.
Sutherland, Kristina, and Desiree Prewitt. 2001. *Live Girls Do Elektra*. Seattle: Rain City Projects.
Svich, Caridad. 2004. "Euripides' Children" and "Iphigenia Crash Land Falls on the Neon Shell That Was Once Her Heart (A Rave Fable)." *Theater Forum* 25: 27–51.
———, ed. 2005. *Divine Fire: Eight Contemporary Plays Inspired by the Greeks*. New York: Back Stage Books.
Swanwick, Anna. 1873. *The Dramas of Aeschylus*. London: Bell & Daldy.
Swofford, Anthony. 2003. *Jarhead: A Marine's Chronicle of the Gulf War and Other Battles*. New York: Scribner's.
Taplin, Oliver. 1984–85 (1988). "Lyric Dialogue and Dramatic Construction in Later Sophocles." *Dioniso* 55: 115–22.
Terry, Walter. 1976. *Ted Shawn: Father of American Dance*. New York: Dial Press.
Tish, Pauline. 1994. "Remembering Helen Tamiris." *Dance Chronicle* 17.3: 327–60.
Törnqvist, Egil. 1969. *A Drama of Souls: Studies in O'Neill's Super-Naturalistic Technique*. New Haven, Conn.: Yale University Press.
Tyler, Henry M. 1891. *A Greek Play and Its Presentation*. Springfield, Mass.: Clark W. Bryan and Company.
Tytell, John. 1995. *The Living Theatre: Art, Exile, and Outrage*. New York: Grove Press.
Usui, Masami. 2000. "Creating a Feminist Transnational Drama: *Oyako-Shinju* (Parent-Child Suicide) in Velina Hasu Houston's *Kokoro* (True Heart)." *Japanese Journal of American Studies* 11: 173–98.
Vandenhoff, George. 1860. *Leaves from an Actor's Note-book*. New York and London: D. Appleton and Co.
Walton, J. Michael. 2006. *Found in Translation: Greek Drama in English*. Cambridge: Cambridge University Press.
Watermeier, Daniel J. 1998. "O'Neill and the Theater of His Time." In *The Cambridge Companion to Eugene O'Neill*, edited by M. Manheim, 33–50. Cambridge: Cambridge University Press.
Waterstone, Penny Brown. 1995. "Domesticating Universal Brotherhood: Feminine Values and the Construction of Utopia, Point Loma Homestead, 1897–1920." PhD diss., University of Arizona.
Waugh, Frank A. 1917. *Outdoor Theaters: The Design, Construction, and Use of Open-Air Auditoriums*. Boston: Richard G. Badger.
Weisenburger, Steven. 1998. *Modern Medea: A Family Story of Slavery and Murder in the Old South*. New York: Hill and Wang.
Wellman, Mac. 2002. *Antigone* in *Miniature*. New York. Roof Books.
———. 2005. *Antigone*. Electronic ed. Alexandria, Va.: Alexander Street Press.
West, M. L. 1992. *Ancient Greek Music*. Oxford: Oxford University Press.
Wetmore, Kevin J., Jr. 2003. *Black Dionysus: Greek Tragedy and African American Theatre*. Jefferson, N.C., and London: McFarland and Co., Inc.

Wharton, Edith. 1990. *A Backward Glance*. In *Novellas and Other Writings*, 767–1064. New York: Library of America.

Wiley, Eric. 1999. "Hellenism and the Independent Theatre Movement in America." PhD diss., Louisiana State University.

Williams, Simon. 1998. "European Actors and the Star System in American Theatre, 1752–1870." In *The Cambridge History of American Theatre*, vol. 1, *Beginnings to 1870*, edited by Don B. Wilmeth and Christopher Bigsby, 303–37. Cambridge: Cambridge University Press.

Wilmeth, Don B., and Christopher Bigsby, eds. 1998. *The Cambridge History of American Theatre*. Vol. 1, *Beginnings to 1870*. Cambridge: Cambridge University Press.

———. 1999. *The Cambridge History of American Theatre*. Vol. 2, *1870–1945*. Cambridge: Cambridge University Press.

———. 2000. *The Cambridge History of American Theatre*. Vol. 3, *Post–World War II to the 1990s*. Cambridge: Cambridge University Press.

Wilson, Joseph P. 1997. *The Hero and the City: An Interpretation of Sophocles' "Oedipus at Colonus."* Ann Arbor: University of Michigan Press.

Winkler, J. J. 1990. "The Ephebe's Song." In *Nothing to Do With Dionysus? Athenian Drama in Its Social Context*, edited by J. J. Winkler and F. I. Zeitlin, 20–62. Princeton, N.J.: Princeton University Press.

Winter, William. 1913. *Vagrant Memories: Being Further Recollections of Other Days*. New York: Moffat, Yard, and Co.

———. (1913) 1969. *The Wallet of Time, Containing Personal, Biographical, and Critical Reminiscences of the American Theatre*. 2 vols. New York: Moffat, Yard and Co. Reprint, Freeport, N.Y.: Books for Library Press.

Winterer, Caroline. 2001. "Victorian Antigone: Classicism and Women's Education in America, 1840–1900." *American Quarterly* 53.1: 70–93.

———. 2002. *The Culture of Classicism: Ancient Greece and Rome in American Intellectual Life, 1780–1910*. Baltimore and London: Johns Hopkins University Press.

———. 2007. *The Mirror of Antiquity: American Women and the Classical Tradition*. Ithaca, N.Y., and London: Cornell University Press.

Wolff, Christian. 2010. "Crossings of Experimental Music and Greek Tragedy." In *Ancient Drama in Music for the Modern Stage*, edited by Peter Brown and Suzana Ograjensek, 285–304. Oxford: Oxford University Press.

Wren, Celia. 2002. "In Medea Res." *American Theatre* 19.4: 22–25, 60–61.

Wright, Evan. 2004. *Generation Kill: Devil Dogs, Iceman, Captain America, and the New Face of American War*. New York: G. Putnam's Sons.

Xie, Ming. 1999. "Pound as Translator." In *The Cambridge Companion to Ezra Pound*, edited by Ira B. Nadel, 204–23. Cambridge: Cambridge University Press.

Zajko, Vanda. 2010. "Dance, Psychoanalysis, and Modern Aesthetics: Martha Graham's *Night Journey*." In *The Ancient Dancer in the Modern World: Responses to Greek and Roman Dance*, edited by Fiona Macintosh, 330–46. Oxford: Oxford University Press.

Zanobi, Alessandra. 2010. "From Duncan to Bausch with Iphigenia." In *The Ancient Dancer in the Modern World: Responses to Greek and Roman Dance*, edited by Fiona Macintosh, 236–54. Oxford: Oxford University Press.

Zeitlin, Froma I. 1996. *Playing the Other: Gender and Society in Classical Greek Literature.* Chicago: University of Chicago Press.

———. 2004. "Dionysus in 69." In *Dionysus since 69: Greek Tragedy at the Dawn of the Third Millennium,* edited by Edith Hall, Fiona Macintosh, and Amanda Wrigley, 49–75. Oxford: Oxford University Press.

# INDEX

Abbey Theatre (Dublin), 61, 68
Abdoh, Reza, 168–69
Abel, Walter, 205, 206*fig.*
acting styles, 4–5, 7, 22, 47, 51, 61, 64, 67, 77, 80, 84–85, 110, 155, 168, 191, 312, 323, 330, 333–35, 340; realistic, 6, 183, 185; non-naturalistic, 2, 10, 209
Addams, Jane, 30, 62, 146, 147
Aeschylus, 46, 93; *Agamemnon*, 38, 79, 98–99, 234; *Eumenides*, 38, 43–46, 45*fig.*, 46*fig.*, 122; *Libation Bearers*, 233–34; *Persians*, 60, 122, 124, 139–46, 143*fig.*, 145*fig.*, 149, 151; *Prometheus Bound*, 93, 124, 154–58; *Seven against Thebes*, 79, 99, 104–7, 134; *Suppliant Women*, 230
aesthetic, theatrical, 3, 10–11, 13, 26, 28, 38, 61, 63, 69, 73, 75, 85, 100, 116, 120–21, 124–25, 127, 132, 159, 204, 230
*African Medea* (Magnuson), 215
AIDS, 168, 171
Aiken, George L., 196
*Ajax* (Sophocles), 124, 146–52; as deaf and native American, 147; as immigrant, 146–47
*Ajax: 100% Fun* (Beckerman), 147, 149–52, 150*fig.*
*Ajax in Iraq* (McLaughlin), 152
Akalaitis, JoAnne, 235
*Alcestis* (Euripides), 79, 116–20; Gluck's version of, 93; Talfourd's burlesque of, 29
Alfaro, Luis, 22–25, 24*fig.*

Alfred, William, 50
*American Medea* (Jones), 215
amnesia, cultural, 166–70
Amnesty International, 149
Anderson, Judith, 61, 133, 207–9
Anderson, Laurie, 117
Anderson, Maxwell, 204–7, 206*fig.*, 210
*Andromache* (Euripides), 230
Anglin, Margaret, 28, 35, 38, 47–61, 210; *Antigone* of, 34, 35, 47, 49–51; Barker and, 41; Browne and, 64; Duncan and, 78; as Electra, 12, 14, 48, 52–53, 56, 57*fig.*, 58*fig.*, 60–61, 66–67; as Iphigenia, 48, 53–54, 55*fig.*, 66; as Medea, 48, 55*fig.*, 56–60, 190; as Phaedra, 60, 126; Reinhardt and, 51, 73; as producer and director, 47, 49, 50–52, 56; acting style of, 47, 49, 51–54, 59, 67
*Another Antigone* (Gurney), 158
Anouilh, Jean, 26, 133, 193
Anspacher, Louis, 83
Anthony, Walter, 51–52
Antigone, as nineteenth-century ideal, 129–31
*Antigone* (Sophocles), 49, 161–62, 175–79; Anglin's version of, 34, 35, 47, 49–51; Anouilh's version of, 26, 133; Brecht's version of, 9, 124, 131–38; Brenner's version of, 132; Chaikin's version of, 138; college productions of, 36, 124; film versions of, 51, 96; Gurney's version of, 158; "hillbilly," 79, 110;

363

364  INDEX

Antigone (continued)
  nineteenth-century performances of, 30–31, 34, 125–31, 128fig., 129fig.; parodies of, 30–31; Settle's version of, 177
Antigone through Time (Maddox), 131
Antigone Too (Boesing), 131
Apollonius of Rhodes, 198, 203
Appia, Adolphe, 47, 63, 72
Argonautica, 198, 203
Aristophanes: Birds, 38; Lysistrata, 48, 68–70
Aristotle, 95, 161, 175
Armes, William Dallam, 48
Aroma of Athens: Athenian Flower Festival, The, 44, 46–47
Arrowsmith, William, 231
Artaud, Antonin, 98, 135, 137
Art Drama Players, 40
Ashbery, John, 133
Aspasia, 44, 46, 70
Asquith, H. H., 40
Ateca, Dorothy, 201
Athenian Women, The, 68, 70
Atkinson, Brooks, 67, 89–90, 209
Auletta, Robert, 139–41, 147–49
Aurora Theatre Company, 139
avant-garde theater, 9, 43, 98, 132–38, 192–93
Awakening of Helena Richie, The, 49, 56

Bacchae (Euripides), 88, 102, 114; Dionysus in 69 as, 9, 96, 138; Revelation in the Courthouse Park as, 102–4, 103fig.; The Rockae as, 79, 110–16, 115fig.
Bach, Richard S., 131
Baibussynova, Ulzhan, 153
Baker, George Pierce, 40
Baker, Houston A., 204
Baker, Ray Stannard, 46
Balinese theater, 97
Ballad of Eddie and Jo (Sard), 170–71, 183–84
Barall, Michi, 236
Barker, Harley Granville, 28, 38; antiwar productions of, 62–63, 132; Eastern college tour of, 40–42
Barnes, Clive, 168
Barnwell, Ysaye, 156
Barrows, Elizabeth C., 147
Barthkoff, Regina, 218
Bartholemew, W., 30
Bauer, P. Seth, 232–33
Baumgartner, Jeffrey, 182fig.

Bay, Howard, 90
Beck, Julian, 132–38
Beckerman, Ellen, 147, 149–52
Beer, John, 115–16
Belasco, David, 29, 125
Benchley, Robert, 71
Bening, Annette, 190
Bennett School of Liberal and Applied Arts, 76–78, 84, 86fig., 87fig.
Bentley, Eric, 138
Berg, Stephen, 171, 181
Berkoff, Steven, 186
Bernhardt, Sarah, 38, 59
Bethlehem Steel Corporation, 156–58
Big Love (Mee), 230
Bigsby, C.W.E., 9, 71
Bird, Robert Montgomery, 5
Birdcatcher in Hell, The, 117
Black Dionysus (Wetmore), 211
Black Medea (Ferlita), 211–12
Black Mountain College, 192–93
Black Titan, 154
Blanchard, Jayne M., 227–28
Blankenship, Mark, 185
Blatter, Alfred, 104
Blavatsky, Helena, 38, 43, 44
Blood Line: The Oedipus/Antigone Story, 177, 179
Bloom, Claire, 8
Boesing, Martha, 131
Bolton, Harold, 88
Bonney, Jo, 104
Booth, Edwin, 126
Both Your Houses (Anderson), 204–5
Bowery Theatre, 4, 31
Bracale Opera Company, 89
Brady, Alice, 16fig.
Brady, Sara, 157–58
Brandt, Kirsten, 224, 234
Brecht, Bertolt, 171, 182; Antigone of, 9, 124, 131–38; Modellbuch of, 135
Brecht, Stefan, 133, 137
Breuer, Lee, 79, 108–9
Brook, Peter, 98
Brookes, Jacqueline, 183
Browne, Maurice, 7, 28; Anderson and, 205; Anglin and, 60; antiwar productions of, 62–63, 132; Barker and, 41; Chicago Little Theatre and, 61–66; on Greek chorus, 64; influences on, 63, 73; lighting innovations by, 73

Brustein, Robert, 137–38, 155, 170
Bulwer Lytton, Edward, 5
Bunraku puppets, 217, 220, 233
Burgess, Anthony, 163–65
Burlen, Caroline C., 127, 128*fig.*
Burton, Richard, 108
Butler, Gervaise, 89
Bynner, Witter, 83

Cacoyannis, Michael, 8, 232
Caldwell, Zoe, 207, 208
Callas, Maria, 190
Campbell, Douglas, 187
Campion, John, 172–73, 174*fig.*
Carey, Alison, 156–58
Carey, Helen, 143*fig.*
Carlson, Susan, 225
Carnegie Peace Foundation, 62
Carroll, Jade King, 139
Carter, Steve, 211, 212
catharsis, tragic, 106, 109, 214
*Cave of the Heart* (Graham), 93, 94
Cayvan, Georgia, 32
Century Opera Company, 81
Cerri, Michael, 219
Chaikin, Joseph: *Antigone* of, 138; *Electra* of, 17–19, 236; Open Theater of, 132
Chapin, Alice, 62
Cheney, Sheldon, 37
Cherubini, Luigi, 190
Chicago Little Theatre, 7, 61–67, 65*fig.*; Living Theatre and, 132; touring company of, 28. *See also* Little Theatre movement
Chicanas, 210, 216–17
Child, Lydia Maria, 200
*Children of Heracles* (Euripides), 124, 152–54; and refugee problem, 152–54
Chinese opera, 77
choice, tragic, 2, 12, 95, 186, 188–89, 191, 203, 205, 232
*choreia*, 78–79, 90, 104–5, 120
choreography, 54–55, 64, 66, 76–99, 87*fig.*, 120–21; of *Ajax*, 146; of *Alcestis*, 116–20; of *The Seven*, 104–5, 107; of *Steelbound*, 156; of *The Rockae*, 111, 115*fig.*; of *Trojan Incident*, 78, 88–92; of *Trojan Women*, 85, 86*fig.*; of Waterwell's *Persians*, 144
chorus, performance of, 9, 20, 25, 30–32, 34, 41, 45*fig.*, 50, 52–54, 56, 67, 78, 80, 89–91, 94, 96–99, 101–05, 114–15, 117, 127, 129*fig.*, 130–31, 134–36, 140–42, 144, 147–48, 156–57, 163–64, 167–69, 171–73, 175, 177–81, 202, 207–08, 213, 217–20, 224, 233–35; Browne on, 64; Isadora Duncan and, 82–84; Gage on, 76–77, 86–87; in *Oedipus at Colonus*, 108–9
Christian, William C., 180
Christianity and Greek tragedy, 103–04, 108–10
Christians, Rudolph, 34, 35
civil rights movement, 158, 210; Julian Beck and, 134; protest songs of, 89. *See also* race
Clarke, H. A., 37
class, social, 4–5, 7, 31, 61, 71, 73, 80–82, 105, 124–25, 137, 159, 186, 214
Clay, Diskin, 171, 181
Cliff, Oliver, 163*fig.*
closure, dramatic, 2, 166–67, 333
Clubb, Dare, 179–80
*Clytemnestra* (Graham), 93, 95–96
*Clytemnestra Project, The*, 234
Coburn, Charles Douville, 39–40
college performances, 36–42, 75, 84–85, 124, 125, 130; avant-garde, 192–93; after Great Depression, 132, 200
Collison, Michelle, 18
Conway, Henry J., 5
Cook, Albert, 162
Cook, George Cram, 28, 61, 68–71
Copeau, Jacques, 63
Copeland, Charles, 125
Corbin, John, 12, 59
Cornell, Katharine, 133, 205, 206*fig.*
Cornford, Francis, 68, 164
*Cortege of Eagles* (Graham), 93–95
Coss, Clare, 18–19
costumes in performances, 22, 30, 32, 36–37, 42, 45, 50, 52, 54, 56, 59, 64, 77, 83, 86, 88, 99, 110, 125, 129, 131, 133, 142, 146, 153–55, 163, 167, 169–71, 178, 209, 217, 220
Craig, Gordon, 47, 52, 63, 72
cross-dressing, 187, 224–27
Cryer, Gretchen, 234
Cullen, Countee, 200–204, 210
Culture Project, 231; *Ajax: 100% Fun* of, 149–52, 150*fig.*
Cushman, Charlotte, 6, 126

Dace, Tish, 218
Daly, Ann, 82
Daly, Augustin, 5
Damrosch, Walter, 47, 52, 54, 60, 81

Danielpour, Richard, 196
*Darker Face of the Earth, The* (Dove), 187
Davis, Philip H., 88, 91–92
*Death of a Salesman* (Miller), 132
Debussy, Claude, 52
Delsarte System of Expression, 80–82; in *Antigone*, 127, 128*fig.*, 129*fig.*
De Mille, H. C., 29
Denishawn dancers, 80–81, 93
Dennie, Ellen M., 126
Denton, Martin, 184
Derwent, Clarence, 154
*Diana and Endymion* (Denishawn), 93
Dinneford, William E., 30
Dionysian inspiration, 9, 69, 82
Dionysus, 211; in *The Bacchae*, 102; in Brecht's *Antigone*, 135; in *The Rockae*, 111–14
*Dionysus in 69* (Schechner), 9, 96, 138
*Dithyrambic* (Graham), 93
Dodson, Owen, 201, 211
Doerries, Brian, 152
Doi, Yuriko, 217–18
Dolan, Jill, 185
Douglas, Paul, 90–91
Dove, Rita, 187
Downs, William Missouri, 219
drag performers, 187, 192–93, 224–27
drama, poetic, 8, 28, 62, 64, 66, 75, 133, 205
*Dream of Alcestis* (Graham), 93
Dukakis, Olympia, 231
Duncan, Augustin, 39, 81, 83
Duncan, Irma, 83
Duncan, Isadora, 56, 78, 81–84; Anglin and, 78; daughter of, 67; Gage and, 78; Graham and, 92–94; as Iphigenia, 60; *Oedipus* of, 81; Serban and, 99
Duncan, Raymond, 83
Duncan, Robert, 192–93
Dunnock, Mildred, 8
Dyer, Doug, 234

Early, Gerald, 204
Eichelberger, Ethyl, 187, 224
Electra, 11–26, 16*fig.*, 23*fig.*, 24*fig.*, 161; Anglin as, 12, 14, 48, 52–53, 56, 57*fig.*, 58*fig.*, 60–61, 66–67; Yurka as, 12, 14, 51, 60, 66–67; as everywoman, 18; doubling of, 18; self-division of, 13–14, 18, 20–21, 26
*Electra* (Sophocles), 14; Hofmannsthal's version of, 14, 52; *Iphigenia and Other Daughters* and, 235–36; *Libation Bearers* and, 233–34; nineteenth-century performances of, 29–30, 125, 127; Pound's version of, 20–22, 23*fig.*; Strauss's version of, 13, 14
*Electra Speaks*, 18–20
*Electricidad* (Alfaro), 22–25, 24*fig.*
Ellington, Justin, 104
Epperson, John, 225–27
ethnicity, 159, 210, 220–24. See also race
*Eumenides* (Aeschylus), 38, 43–46, 45*fig.*, 46*fig.*, 122
Euripides: *Alcestis*, 79, 93, 116–20; *Andromache*, 230; *Bacchae*, 9, 79, 88, 96, 102–4, 110–16, 138; *Children of Heracles*, 124, 152–54; *Hecuba*, 97, 230–31; *Helen*, 230; *Hippolytus*, 47, 60, 68, 93, 95, 126; *Ion*, 29, 230; *Iphigenia in Aulis*, 48, 53–55, 60, 66, 133, 230–37; *Iphigenia in Tauris*, 36–37, 230–37; *Phoenician Women*, 175, 230. See also *Medea*; *Trojan Women*
exceptionalism, American, 1, 230

Fagan, Shawn, 150*fig.*
fate, tragic, 2, 11, 14–15, 23, 30, 32, 53, 62, 70–72, 95, 105, 108, 110, 118, 126–27, 135–36, 142, 152, 155, 157, 160–61, 164–65, 167, 170, 173, 176, 179–81, 185, 188–89, 195, 200, 212, 225, 228
Fanning, A. C. W., 198
Federal Dance Theatre (FDT), 89
Federal Theatre Project (FTP), 8, 75; *Trojan Incident* of, 8, 78, 88, 89, 132
Feingold, Michael, 214–15
Feldsher, Scott, 177–79
Felton, Cornelius C., 29
feminism: 2, 9, 13–14, 18, 25, 124, 131, 328; Antigone and, 126–27, 129, 131; Electra and, 18, 23; Jocasta and, 162; Medea and, 66, 191, 193, 196, 197, 202, 210–11, 216–22, 227, 328; suffrage and, 126, 196; transnational, 221. See also gender
Ferlita, Ernest, 211–12
film versions, 110, 148, 152–53, 207; of *Antigone*, 51, 96; of *Iphigenia at Aulis*, 232; of *Oedipus*, 104, 187
Firkins, G. W., 66
Fisher, John, 224–25
Fitts, Dudley, 118
Fitzgerald, Robert, 118, 171
Five Lesbian Brothers, 184–85
Flanagan, Hallie, 88, 132
Fleming, Rudd, 20

Fliess, Wilhelm, 181
*FLOW* (Power), 104
Fokine, Michael, 89
Fonda, Jane, 158
Forrest, Edwin, 6
Foster, Gloria, 207
Foster, Philip, 16*fig.*
Fotopoulos, Dionyssis, 234
Foucher, David, 172
Fountain, Clarence, 109
*Fragments of a Greek Trilogy* (Serban & Swados), 96–99
*Fragments: Tragedy and Comedy* (Graham), 93
Freedman, Gerald, 234
Freeman, Helen, 83
Freeman, Morgan, 109
Freud, Sigmund, 8, 34, 68, 92; Oedipus complex and, 160, 161, 180–83, 187; Freudian interpretations, 9, 15, 103
Freund, Philip, 187
Frohman, Charles, 34, 81
Frohman, Daniel, 7, 32
*From a Grecian Vase* (Denishawn), 93
Fugitive Slave Act, 196
Fuller, Loie, 322
*Furious Blood* (Stuart), 234
Furst, William, 52

Gage, Margaret, 75–78, 84–88, 87*fig.*; *Trojan Women* of, 86–88, 86*fig.*
Galati, Frank, 180–83, 182*fig.*
*Garden of Time* (Dodson), 201, 211
Garner, Margaret, 196–97, 197*fig.*
Gayley, Charles, 50
gay theater, 9, 225–26
gender: 9, 10, 18–19, 121–22, 131, 159, 167, 214, 216, 224, 226, 228–29; Medea's androgyny and, 191, 193; *Oedipus at Palm Springs* and, 184–85; transsexuality and, 165. *See also* feminism
genre, tragic, 1, 5, 11; crossing genre boundaries, xiv, 10, 144–46, 158, 180, 193, 225–29, 236
Gentry, Minnie, 207
George, Bill, 156
*Gesamtkunstwerke*, 100. *See also* total theater
Gielgud, John, 207
Gildersleeve, Basil, 37
Gilrain, Jennie, 156
Gladstone, Ralph, 152
Glaspell, Susan, 68, 70

Gluck, Christoph Willibald, 52, 54, 81–83, 93, 234
Goethe, Johann Wolfgang von, 29
Goff, Barbara, 109
*Golden Fleece* (Grillparzer), 193, 195, 198
*Golden Fleece* (Gurney), 227
Goodell, Thomas D., 40
*Gospel at Colonus* (Breuer & Telson), 79, 108–9
Graham, Martha, 78–79, 92–96; at Dance Repertory Theatre, 89; *Electra* dance interlude by, 66; Gage and, 85; *Cave of the Heart* of, 93–95; *Clytemnestra* of, 95–96, 98; *Night Journey* of, 93, 95, 187; *Phaedra* of, 95; focalization through women, 85; total theater of, 93–94
Great Jones Repertory Company, 99
*Grecian Suite* (Denishawn), 93
*Greek* (Berkoff), 186
Greek, ancient, use of in productions, 21, 31–32, 35–37, 48, 173
Greek war of independence (1821–29), 200
Green, Vivien, 200
Greenfield, Amy, 96
Greet, Philip Ben, 38, 84
Griethuysen, Ted van, 143*fig.*
Grillparzer, Franz, 193, 195, 198
Gurney, A. R., 158, 227
Gussow, Mel, 17
Guthrie, Tyrone, 164, 187
Guthrie Theater (Minneapolis): *Clytemnestra Project* of, 234; *Medea* of, 190; *Oedipus Tyrannus* of, 162–70, 163*fig.*, 183

Haberle, Stephanie Roth, 173, 174*fig.*
Haeckel, Ernst, 68
Haigh, Kenneth, 155
Haiti, 211–12
Hall, Edith, 196
Hamblin, Tom, 31
Hamilton, Clayton, 49, 67
Hamilton, Douglas, 163*fig.*
Hamilton, Edith, 50, 98
Hammond, Will, 104
Hampden, Walter, 126
Harper, Frances E. W., 196
Harper, Henry, 158
Harris, Ed, 186
Harrison, Jane, 68, 164
Hartigan, Karelisa, xii
Harvey, Martin, 35

Hawkins, Erick, 93
Heath, Gordon, 168
*Hecuba* (Euripides), 97, 230–31
Heeley, Desmond, 163
*Helen* (Euripides), 230
Henderson, Robert, 51
Henry Street Settlement House, 89
Hepburn, Katharine, 67
Herne, Chrystal, 42
Heron, Matilda, 6, 195, 228
Herreshoff, Constance Mills, 131
Hicks, Bob, 182–83
Hill, Holly, 176
*Hillbilly Antigone* (Sims & Stillman), 79, 110
hip-hop theater, 79, 104–6, 223
*Hippolytus* (Euripides): Graham's version of, 93, 95; Howe's version of, 60, 126; music for, 47; O'Neill's version of, 68
Hiroshima, 156
Hofmannsthal, Hugo von, 14, 52
Hölderlin, Friedrich, 134
Homer, 8, 14, 52, 70, 146
Horatio Alger mythology, 1, 11
*House of Chaos, The* (Houston), 221–22
Houston, Velina Hasu, 220–22
Houvardas, Yannis, 234
Howard, Marita, 131
Howe, Julia Ward, 60, 126
Howe, Maud, 126
Hughes, Langston, 201
Hull, Howard, 48, 49
Humphrey, Doris, 85, 89
*Hungry Women: A Mexican Medea* (Moraga), 210, 215–17
Hunter, Marlo, 110–11
"Hymn to Apollo," 45
Hypatia, 43

identity: national, 3, 26, 43, 167, 237; identity politics, 3, 9, 26, 122, 215–16
International Theosophical Society. *See* Theosophical Society
*Ion* (Euripides), 29, 230
*Iphigeneia in Concert*, 234
*Iphigenia and Other Daughters* (McLaughlin), 26, 235–36
*Iphigenia Cycle, The*, 235
*Iphigenia in Aulis* (Euripides), 230–37; Anglin's version of, 48, 53–54, 55*fig.*, 60, 66; Cacoyannis's version of, 232; Racine's version of, 234; Rexroth's version of, 133; Skipitares' version of, 233; Svich's version of, 234–35; splitting and multiplying of Iphigeneia in, 26, 234–35
*Iphigenia in Orem*, 186
*Iphigenia in Tauris* (Euripides), 36–37, 230–37
*Iphigénie en Aulide* (Gluck), 82–83, 234
*Iphigénie en Tauride* (Gluck), 82–83
Iran-Iraq War, 144
Iraq conflict: *Ajax* and, 149–52; *Children of Heracles* and, 124, 152–54; *Iphigenia at Aulis* and, 232; *Oedipus* and, 172; *Persians* and, 139–41, 144–46
Isis Theatre, 43
Ito, Genji, 99

Jacobs, Douglas, 177–79
Jahnn, Hans Henny, 193
Janauschek, Francesca, 29, 195
Jaques-Dalcroze, Émile, 63, 64
Jebb, Richard, 50
Jeffers, Robinson, 61, 133, 190, 207–10, 212; inhumanism in, 207
Jefferson, Margo, 143
Jeffries, Lynn, 156
*Joan of Arc*, 60
Jocasta, American re-interpretations of, 95, 162, 167–78, 172, 177–78, 183–84, 187–88
*Jocasta* (Freund), 187
*Jocasta or Boy Crazy*, 187
Jones, Bill T., 76, 79, 104
Jones, James Earl, 183
Jones, Silas, 215
Jonson, Raymond, 63, 66
Judge, W. Q., 43
Jung, Carl Gustav, 68, 92, 165

Kabuki, 77, 97, 210, 217–20, 226
Kahn, Otto, 81
*Kassandra*, 134
Kasson, Joy, 195
Kathakali, 77, 97
Kauser, Alice, 47
Kellerd, John, 40
Kelly, Tony, 104
Kennedy, Adrienne, 171
Kennedy, Charles Rann, 84
Kent, Willys Peck, 146
Kessel, Howard, 176
Kimbrough, Emily, 53–54
Kincaid, Jean, 127–29
King, Martin Luther, Jr., 154

INDEX    369

King, Mary Perry, 80
King, Rodney, 144
*King Oedipus* (Abdoh), 168–69
Kirby, Roger, 227
*Klytaemnestra's Unmentionables* (Louryk), 224
Knowles, Sheridan, 4, 5
Knox, Bernard M. W, 99, 166, 176
*Kokoro* (Houston), 220–22
Korean War, 10
Kruger, Alma, 41

La Boheme Club, 175–76
LaBute, Neil, 185–86
LaChiusa, Michael John, 107, 211, 213–15
Lacroix, Jules, 34, 165–66
La Mama, E.T.C., 79, 96, 99, 187, 233, 234
*Lamentation* (Graham), 93
Landau, Tina, 233
Lang, B. J., 125
Langham, Michael, 163–65
Lauterer, Arch, 101
leadership, as tragic theme, 151, 161–62, 171, 175–79, 188–89, 202–03, 233, 334
Legouvé, Ernest, 6, 195
Lehman, Benjamin H., 207
LeVay, John, 51
Lévi-Strauss, Claude, 165
Lewin, John, 183
Lewisohn, Irene, 89
*Libation Bearers* (Aeschylus), 233–34
lighting techniques, 52, 63–64, 73, 93, 117, 136, 153, 316
Linklater, Kristin, 231
Lippard, Alex, 231
Lister, Henry Bertram, 47, 175–76, 203
Little Theatre movement, 7; Provincetown Players and, 68; stage sets of, 73–74; Toy Theatre of Boston and, 52, 66. *See also* Chicago Little Theatre
Living Theatre, 123–24; acting style of, 134–36, 138; anarchism of, 134, 137; antiwar movement and, 134, 136–38; and versions of Greek tragedy, 133–34; Brecht's *Antigone* by, 9, 124, 131–38; Pound's *Women of Trachis* by, 133; Racine's *Phèdre* by, 133; Rexroth's *Beyond the Mountains* by, 133
Lookingglass Theatre Company, 79, 110
Loper, Robert, 169–70
López, Abel, 215–16
Louryk, Bradford, 224
*Love, Medea*, 218

Lowell, Robert, 155
Ludlam, Charles, 224–26
Lydon, Christopher, 152
*Lysistrata* (Aristophanes), 48, 68–70

Mabou Mines theater group, 9
MacCrae, Wendell, 86
Macgowan, Kenneth, 72–75
Macintosh, Fiona, 196
MacKaye, Percy, 83
MacKaye, Steele, 80
Maclaren, Ian, 41
Maclin, Clarence, 189
Macready, William C., 6
*Madame Butterfly* (Puccini), 220
Maddox, Gloria, 131
Madison, Dolley, 198
Magnuson, Jim, 215
Malina, Judith, 132–38
*Malinche, La* (Morton), 215–16
Marchand, Nancy, 22
Marden, Elysa, 232, 233
*Marie Christine* (LaChiusa), 107, 211, 213–15
Martin, Christopher, 176
Martin, John, 85, 90
masks, 77, 148; in *Alcestis*, 118; O'Neill on, 72, 135; puppets and, 217, 220, 233; in *Revelation in the Courthouse Park*, 102, 103*fig.*
Matteson, Ruth, 206*fig.*
Matthison, Edith Wynne, 42, 84
May, Caroline, 198
Mayr, Johann Simon, 195
McCarter, Jeremy, 185
McCarthy, Lillah, 40–42
McCarthyism, 10, 158
McClendon, Rose, 201, 202
McClure, Michael, 134
McConachie, Bruce, 4
McConnel, Frederic, 162
McCurry, John, 154
McDonald, Audra, 213–14
McDonald, Marianne, 211, 224
McLaughlin, Ellen: *Ajax in Iraq* of, 152; *Iphigeneia and Other Daughters* of, 26, 235–36; *Oedipus Tyrannus* of, 166–67, 183; *Persians* of, 139, 141–43, 143*fig.*
McLean, René, 171
McSweeny, Ethan, 139, 143*fig.*
Medea, 26, 161, 194, 236; androgyny of, 191, 193; controversial fate of, 191–93, 212, 214, 226; cross-dressing of, 224–27; as ethnic other,

Medea (*continued*)
  210–24; feminism and, 66, 191, 193, 196, 202, 210–11, 216–22, 227; intermarriage and, 211, 215; as lesbian, 216–17; racialized, 196–97, 210–24; relation to female chorus, 191–92, 212–13; as social critic, 193, 200–210
*Medea* (Euripides), 62, 66, 190–93, 227–29; Anderson's version of, 204–7, 206*fig.*, 210; Anglin's version of, 48, 55*fig.*, 56–60, 190; Anouilh's version of, 193; Cullen's version of, 200–204, 210; Dodson's version of, 201; Epperson's version of, 225–27; Ferlita's version of, 211–12; Graham's dance version of, 93–94; Houston's versions of, 220–22; Jeffers's version of, 61, 133, 190, 207–10, 212; Jones's version of, 215; Kirby's version of, 227; LaChiusa's version of, 107; Lister's version of, 203; Ludlam's version of, 224–26; Magnuson's version of, 215; McDonald's version of, 211, 224; Moraga's version of, 210, 215–17; nineteenth-century performances of, 190, 193–200, 197*fig.*; Read's version of, 125, 197–200; Rno's version of, 221–23; Rodriguez's version of, 221, 223–24; Seneca's version of, 191, 218; Van Volkenburg version of, 56, 190
*Medea and Jason* (pantomime), 29
*Medea at Kolchis* (Duncan), 192–93
*Medea in Corinto* (Mayr), 195
*Medea Redux* (LaBute), 186
Mee, Charles, 13, 149; *Big Love* of, 230; *Iphigenia 2.0* of, 233
melodrama, 4–6, 12–13, 22, 54, 71, 110, 123, 184, 191, 205, 225, 228; apocalyptic, 5; heroic, 5, 29, 67, 162; Hollywood, 225; sensation, 5–6
memory, collective, 166–70
Mendelssohn-Bartholdy, Felix, 30, 50, 125
Mendoza, Zilah, 24*fig.*
Messing, Mark, 177
metatheater, 108, 144, 327. *See also* total theater
Middleton, Horace, 84
Miller, Arthur, 10, 132
Miller, Jonathan, 155
Miller, Judy, 158
Mills, Peter, 110–16
*Minotaur, The* (Denishawn), 93
Misch, Robert, 48
Mitchell, Danlee, 104
Mitchell, Thomas, 40
Moayed, Arian, 139, 144, 145*fig.*
Moeller, Philip, 14–15, 16*fig.*
Monk, Isabell, 109
Montgomery, Robert, 17–19
Moraga, Chérríe, 210, 215–17
Morrison, Lewis, 32
Morrison, Mary Gray, 126, 127, 130
Morrison, Toni, 196
Morton, Carlos, 215–16
Morton, Joe, 22
Moss, Howard, 180
Moulton, Richard G., 64
Mounet-Sully, Jean, 34, 165–66
*Mourners, The* (Sharon), 13
*Mourning Becomes Electra* (O'Neill), 9, 12–17, 16*fig.*, 28, 60–61, 67–68, 71
*Mulatto* (Hughes), 201
Müller, Heiner, 117, 118
Murray, A. T., 130
Murray, Gilbert, 35, 36, 40, 68, 84, 164; Cullen and, 202; Jeffers and, 209; as World War I supporter, 63
Murray, Matthew, 185
music in performances, 5, 28, 30–32, 34, 37, 40–41, 45, 47, 50, 52, 54, 60, 78–84, 88–94, 97–101, 103–05, 107, 109–10, 112–15, 125, 131, 139, 144, 146–47, 151, 155–56, 162–63, 167, 169–71, 172, 188, 201, 213–14, 217, 219, 234
musical theater, 107–16, 115*fig.*, 213–14
Mussey, Mabel Kay Barrows, 131, 146
*Mystères Dionysiaques, Les* (Denishawn), 93
mystery cults, 46–47

National Actors Theatre, 139
Nazimova, Alla, 16*fig.*
Near, Timothy, 232
Neff, Renfreu, 138
Nelson, Jennifer, 231
Nelson, Marilyn, 231
Neumayer, Charles von, 51
New School for Social Research, 133
Nietzsche, Friedrich, 68
*Night Journey* (Graham), 93, 95, 187
Ninagawa, Yukio, 217
9/11 attacks, 171, 232, 233
nineteenth-century performances, 28–37; of *Antigone*, 30–31, 34, 125–31, 128*fig.*, 129*fig.*; of *Electra*, 29–30, 125, 127; of *Medea*, 190, 193–200, 197*fig.*; of *Oedipus*, 29–35, 33*fig.*, 160–62, 165–66; of *Philoctetes*, 31
Nixon, Richard, 137, 170
Noble, Thomas Satterwhite, 196, 197*fig.*
Noguchi, Isamu, 93–95

Noh drama, 77, 97, 210; *Medea* as, 217–18; Rexroth's use of, 133
Novelli, Ermete, 34
Novick, Julius, 97–98
Noyes, Florence Fleming, 85
nuclear weapons, 155–56, 158

Ober, F. H., 32
O'Connor, Isabell Monk, 167
Odell, George, 29, 30
*Odyssey* (Homer), 14
Oedipus, 160–62, 187–89; exit of, 164, 166–67, 169, 188; Freud and, 160, 161, 180–83; onstage blinding of, 164, 166; as scapegoat, 161–70; in Theban cycles, 175–79; Tiresias and, 164, 165, 179–80
*Oedipus at Colonus* (Sophocles), 46, 161, 178, 188; gospel version of, 79, 108–9
*Oedipus at Palm Springs*, 184–85
*Oedipus Complex* (Galati), 180–83, 182*fig.*
*Oedipus Mah-Jongg Scandal, The* (Moss), 180
*Oedipus Nix* (Brustein), 170
*Oedipus or the Riddle of the Sphinx*, 31
*Oedipus Tex* (Schickele), 188
*Oedipus Tyrannus* (Sophocles), 38; Abdoh's version of, 168–69; A.R.T.'s version of, 171–75, 174*fig.*, 189; censorship of, 32–34; Dare Clubb's version of, 179–80; Duncan's version of, 81, 83; film versions of, 104, 187; Guthrie Theater production of, 162–70, 163*fig.*, 183; Hartford Stage Company's version of, 170–71; nineteenth-century performances of, 29–35, 33*fig.*, 160–62, 165–66; Oregon Shakespeare Company's version of, 169–70; parodies of, 32, 170, 180, 187; Partch's version of, 79, 99–102; Reinhardt's version of, 34–35, 40, 48, 51, 164; Sard's version of, 170–71, 183–84; Settle's version of, 177; Sloan-Feist version of, 167–68; Yeats's version of, 133, 164
Olcott, Henry S., 43
Oliver, Barbara, 139
Olivier, Laurence, 133
Olympic Games, 82
O'Neill, Eugene, 14, 70–72, 165; Cook and, 68; on masks, 72, 135; Nobel Prize for, 71; *Desire under the Elms*, 28, 68, 71; *The Emperor Jones*, 74; *The Great God Brown*, 74; *Mourning Becomes Electra*, 9, 12–17, 16*fig.*, 28, 60–61, 67–68, 71
O'Neill, James, 60

opera, 81–83, 99–100; of Gluck, 52, 54, 81–83, 93, 234; *Margaret Garner*, 196; *Marie Christine*, 214; *Medea in Corinto*, 195; *Oresteia*, 79; of Strauss, 13, 14; of Wagner, 44, 54, 68, 72, 100
Oregon Shakespeare Festival: *Oedipus Complex* at, 180; *Oedipus Tyrannus* at, 169–70
Orestes, 13, 161, 207, 233–37; in *Odyssey*, 14; in Sartre's *Les Mouches*, 179
*Orestes* (Mee), 13
*Orpheus* (Denishawn), 93
Oshima, Mark, 117
outdoor performances, 37–38, 39*fig.*, 75, 86*fig.*, 87*fig.*, 131
Owens, Denyse, 223

Paine, J. K., 32
Panama-Pacific International Exposition (1915), 53–54
*Pan and Syrinx* (Denishawn), 93
pantomime, 29, 78, 125
Papas, Irene, 190
Parker, H. T., 37, 67
Partch, Harry, 99–104, 103*fig.*
Pasta, Giuditta, 195
Pater, Walter, 61
Payne, John Howard, 4
*Pecong* (Carter), 211, 212
Pentheus, 102–04, 103*fig.*, 111–14, 161
People's Light & Theatre, 139
Peress, Lorca, 184
Performance Group, The, 132; *Dionysus in 69* by, 9, 96, 138
Pericles, 44, 46, 70, 189
Perloff, Carey, 26; *Hecuba* by, 231; *Elektra* by, 20, 22, 23*fig.*
Persian Gulf War. *See* Iraq conflict
*Persians* (Aeschylus), 60, 122, 124; McLaughlin's version of, 139, 141–43, 143*fig.*; Sellars-Auletta version of, 139–41, 149; Waterwell's version of, 139, 144–46, 145*fig.*, 151; Atossa's changed role in, 142, 144; Xerxes' psychology in, 141
Peters, Frank, 40
Peterson, Lisa: *Electricidad* by, 22–25, 24*fig.*; *Oedipus* of, 166–67
*Phaedra*, 47, 68, 126; Graham's version of, 93, 95; Racine's version of, 38, 60, 93, 133; Rexroth's version of, 133; Seneca's version of, 60
Phelps, Elizabeth Stuart, 130
Phillips, Charles, 48
*Philoctetes* (Sophocles), 31, 152, 230
*Phoenician Women* (Euripides), 175, 230

Phrynichus, 122
Pindar, 84
*Pious Poetic Pie* (Rodriguez), 221, 223–24
Pirandello, Luigi, 180
plague, 164, 170–75, 178
Plato, 44, 83
Platt, Livingston, 52, 56–59, 64, 73
Pluggé, August, 36, 75
Plumptre, E. H., 50, 52, 125, 130, 178
Poe, Edgar Allan, 27, 30
Polendo, Rubén, 224
Pomerantz, Will, 222
post-traumatic stress disorder, 2, 152
Potter, Robert, 54, 198
Pound, Ezra: *Elektra*, 20–22, 23*fig.*; *Women of Trachis*, 20, 22, 133
Powell, Anthony, 189
Powell, Colin, 147
Power, Will: *FLOW*, 104; *The Seven*, 79, 104–7, 106*fig.*
Powers, Hiram, 200
Prewitt, Tom, 20
*Prometheus Bound* (Aeschylus), 93, 124, 154–58; and exploitation of women, 154–55; and imperialism, 154–55; and nuclear weapons, 154–56
*Prometheus Project, The* (Schechner), 155–56
*Promise, The*, 46–47
Provincetown Players, 28, 61, 68–70; Cook and, 68–71; Macgowan and, 72–73; manifesto of, 69
Puccini, Giacomo, 220
puppets, 217, 220, 233. *See also* masks
Puritans, 3
*Pyrrhic Dance* (Denishawn), 83, 93

Quintero, José, 207
Quinton, Everett, 225

Rabkin, Gerald, 98
race: 121–23, 171, 202, 229; in *Ajax*, 147–48; Cullen on, 204–06; in *Medea*, 196–97, 210–24; slavery and, 193, 196–97, 199–200. *See also* civil rights movement
Racine, Jean: *Iphigénie en Aulide*, 234; *Phèdre*, 38, 60, 93, 133
Rage Against the Machine, 13
Rains, Claude, 41
Randall, Tony, 139
Rashad, Phylicia, 215
Rauch, Bill, 156–57

Read, Harriette Fanning, 198; *Medea* of, 125, 197–200; feminism of, 198–200
Reagan, Ronald, 147, 158
Reboch, Wenzel A., 44–45
recognition, tragic, 15, 17–99, 22, 26–27, 67, 95, 101, 103, 113, 181, 221–22, 236
Reed, Pamela, 22, 23*fig.*
Reichel, Cara, 110–16
Reinhardt, Max, 47, 69; Anglin and, 51–52; Browne and, 63; influence of, 73; *Oedipus* of, 34–35, 40, 48, 51, 164
Repertory Theatre (San Diego), 177–79
*Rescue Me* (Barall), 236
*Revelation in the Courthouse Park* (Partch), 79, 102–4, 103*fig.*
Rexroth, Kenneth, 133
Reznikov, Hanon, 134
Rice, Philip Blair, 202
Rich, Frank, 225
Richards, Beah, 215
Riddle, George, 32, 33*fig.*, 34; Anglin and, 48, 49, 51
Ridgely, Tom, 139, 144–46, 145*fig.*, 151
Riegger, Wallingford, 88–89, 90
Rigg, Diana, 190
Ristori, Adelaide, 195
ritual: 9, 62, 69, 75, 79, 83, 92–93, 95–100, 102, 106, 108, 118, 120, 134, 136–38, 162–70, 175; dance and, 120; Living Theatre and, 134; of mystery cults, 46–47; in *Oedipus Tyrannus*, 162–70; Partch on, 99, 100
Rivers, H. Fletcher, 45
Rno, Sung, 221–24
Robbe-Grillet, Alain, 122, 124
Roche, Anthony, 176
*Rockae, The*, 79, 110–16, 115*fig.*
Rodriguez, Yubelky, 221, 223–24
Rohmann, Chris, 171
Rosario, Wilberto, 163*fig.*
Rosenthal, Jean, 93
Ross, Alex, 101
Rudall, Nicholas, 235
Rumsfeld, Donald, 151

Sacco-Vanzetti trial, 205
Salzman, Alexander von, 63
*Sappho*, 93
Sard, David, 170–71, 183–84
Sargeant, Margherita, 83
Sargent, Franklin H., 29–30, 125, 127
Sartre, Jean-Paul, 122, 179

Sato, Shozo, 219
Saturday Morning Club (Boston), 80, 125–30, 128*fig.*, 129*fig.*
satyr plays, 77, 117
Saunders, Charles H., 5
scapegoating, 161–70
Schechner, Richard, 132; *Dionysus in 69* of, 96, 138; *Prometheus Project* of, 155–56; *YokastaS* of, 187
Schick, Charles, 218
Schickele, Peter, 188
Schlesinger, Kathleen, 101
Schopenhauer, Arthur, 68
Schuette, James, 180
Schulenburg, August, 152
Scriabin, Alexander, 93
scripts for performances: collaged, 233, 331; fragmentation of, 117–20; interpolated, 149–51, 158; pastiche in, 10, 147
Seago, Howie, 148
Seely, Hart, 151
Segal, Sondra, 18–19
Selden, Elizabeth, 85
Sellars, Peter, 123–24; *Ajax of,* 147–49; *Children of Heracles* of, 152–54; *Persians* of, 139–41, 149
Seneca: *Medea* of, 191, 218; *Phaedra* of, 60
Serban, Andrei, 79, 96–99
set designs in performances, 32, 34, 39–41, 50, 52, 56, 56*fig.*, 63–64, 67, 72–74, 88, 90, 93, 97, 99, 110–11, 116–18, 135, 142, 163, 167, 169–71, 177–80, 209, 214, 217, 234
*Seven, The* (Power), 79, 104–7, 106*fig.*
*Seven against Thebes* (Aeschylus), 79, 99, 104–7, 134
Shakespeare, William, 4, 43, 149; *Antony and Cleopatra,* 203; *King Lear,* 51; *Twelfth, Night,* 38
Sharon, Yuval, 13
Shaw, Fiona, 190, 227–28
Shawn, Ted, 80–81, 93
Shay, Jonathan, 151
Sheppard, J. T., 67
Shubert brothers, 7, 59
Sikelianos, Angelos, 88, 154
Sikelianos, Eva Palmer, 75, 78, 88, 154
Silverman, Leigh, 184
Silverman, Stanley, 163
Simpson, Michael, 109
Sims, Rick, 110
Sirotta, Michael, 99
Skipitares, Theodora, 233

Sklar, Roberta, 18–19
slam poetry, 79, 104–6, 223
slavery, 193, 196–97, 199–200. *See also* race
Sledgehammer Theatre (San Diego), 177–79, 224, 234
Smith, David Stanley, 40
Smith, Frederic, 175
Smith, Priscilla, 99
Smith, William H., 5
Sorgenfrei, Carol, 217–18
Sondheim, Stephen, 214, 215
Sophocles: *Ajax,* 124, 146–52; *Electra,* 14, 29–30, 125, 127, 233–36; *Oedipus at Colonus,* 46, 79, 108–9, 161, 178, 188; *Philoctetes,* 31, 152, 230; *Women of Trachis,* 20, 22, 133, 230. *See also* *Antigone; Oedipus Tyrannus*
Southern, Edward A., 195
Spartacus, 5
Sphinx's riddle, 164–66
Springer, Jerry, 178
Stanescu, Saviana, 187
Stasio, Marilyn, 186
St. Denis, Ruth, 93
*Steelbound* (Carey), 156–58; community theater and, 156–58
Steiner, George, 2
Steiner, Rod, 8
Stewart, Ellen, 79, 99
Stillman, Heidi: *Hillbilly Antigone,* 110
Story, William Wetmore, 195
Stowe, Harriet Beecher, 5, 196
Strauss, Richard, 13, 14
Stuart, Kelly, 234
suffragists, 126, 196
*Suppliant Women* (Aeschylus), 230
Sutherland, Donald, 169–70
Swados, Elizabeth, 79, 96–99
Swanwick, Anna, 44
Sweet, Jeffrey, 186
Swofford, Anthony, 150
*Symposium* (Plato), 44
Synge, John, 61

tableaux, 5, 64, 125
Talfourd, Thomas Noon, 29
Tamiris, Helen, 78, 85, 88–92
Taylor, C. W., 196
television, reality, 144, 179
Telson, Bob, 79, 108–9
Tharps, Lisa, 215
Theater of War project, 152

Theatrical Syndicate, 7, 34
Theban cycles, 175–79, 189, 207
Theosophical Society, 28, 38, 39*fig.*, 43–46, 45*fig.*, 46*fig.*, 175
Thompson, April Yvette, 215
Thomson, Virgil, 201
*Three Choric Dances for an Antique Greek Tragedy* (Graham), 93
Thucydides, 46, 70
Tierney, David, 224
Tillinger, John, 158
Tingley, Katherine, 28, 42–47, 125, 175
Tinkham, Julian R., 131
Tiresias, 164, 165, 175–76, 179–80
Tish, Pauline, 90
total theater, 28, 76–80, 99–108, 103*fig.*, 106*fig.*, 144; as *Gesamtkunstwerke*, 100; Graham's contributions to, 93–94; Partch on, 100; Serban's influence on, 98; sound techniques for, 135
Toy Theatre (Boston), 52, 66
*Tragic Patterns* (Graham), 93
*Trojan Incident* (Davis), 8, 78, 88–92, 132
*Trojan Women* (Euripides), 9–10, 36, 124, 131, 138, 158, 229–30; antiwar productions of, 8, 28, 40–42, 60–63, 132, 158; Barker's production of, 28, 40–42; Cacoyannis's production of, 8; Chapin's version of, 62; at Chicago Little Theatre, 61–66, 65*fig.*; choreography for, 85, 86*fig.*; Gage's version of, 86–88, 86*fig.*; Graham;s *Cortege of Eagles*, 93, 95; Serban-Swados version of, 96, 97
Tzavellas, George, 51

Udovicki, Lenka, 190
*Uncle Tom's Cabin* (Stowe), 5, 196

Vandenhoff, George, 30, 31
Van Volkenburg, Ellen, 28, 61–64; as Medea, 56, 66, 190
Vellacott, Philip, 106
Vietnam War, 10, 158, 232; *Ajax* and, 147, 149; *Antigone* and, 136–38; *Trojan Women* and, 8, 158
Volanakis, Minos, 190
voodoo, 211–15

Wagner, Richard, 44, 54, 68, 72, 100
Wagstaff, Blanche Shoemaker, 39
Waldrop, Mark, 226

*Waste*, 134
Watergate scandal, 170
Waterwell theater group, 139, 144–46, 145*fig.*, 151
Waugh, Frank, 37
*wAve* (Rno), 221–24
*Wedding of Iphigeneia* (Cryer), 234
Wehle, Brenda, 190
Weidman, Charles, 85, 89
Weingartner, Felix von, 34
Weisenburger, Steven, 196–97
Welsh, Kenneth, 163*fig.*
Wertenbaker, Timberlake, 231
Wetmore, Kevin, 109, 211, 215
Wheatcroft, Nelson, 47
Wheeler, Benjamin, 50
White, John Williams, 125
Whitford, Sarah, 83
Whitman, Walt, 68, 89
*Whole World Is Watching, The* (Jacobs & Feldsher), 177–79, 189
Wigman, Mary, 85
Wilamowitz-Moellendorff, Ulrich von, 36
Wilbrandt, Adolf, 34
Wilde, Oscar, 61
Wilkinson, Norman, 41
Williams, Raymond, 71
Williams, Tennessee, 10, 132
Wilson, Jonathan, 171
Wilson, Robert: *Alcestis* of, 79, 116–20
*Wingless Victory, The* (Anderson), 204–7, 206*fig.*, 210
Winter, William, 195
Winterer, Caroline, 129–30, 206–7
Woman's Peace Party, 62, 63, 68
*Women Are Waiting: The Tragedy of Medea Jackson*, 215
*Women of Trachis* (Sophocles), 20, 22, 133, 230
Women's Experimental Theatre (WET), 18–20
women's suffrage, 126
Woodruff, Robert: *Oedipus* of, 171–75, 183, 189
Woollcott, Alexander, 66, 220
Worth, Irene, 155
World Trade Center. *See* 9/11 attacks
World War I: *Athenian Women* and, 70; Chicago Little Theatre and, 62; German-US theater and, 35; touring companies during, 28, 40–42
World War II, 74–75; *Antigone through Time* and, 131; *Trojan Women* and, 60, 132

*Wrecks* (LaBute), 185–86
Wright, Evan, 150
Wright, Garland, 190, 234
Wright, Lou Anne, 219

Xie, Ming, 22

Yeats, William Butler, 61, 68, 101; *Oedipus* of, 133, 164, 187
*YokastaS* (Schechner and Stanescu), 187, 310
Young, Stark, 14

Yurka, Blanche: as Electra, 12, 14, 51, 60, 66–67; in *Prometheus Bound,* 154

Zakkai, Jamil, 99
Zane, Arnie, 104
Zigler, Scott, 152
Zinkewicz, Phil, 167–68
Zinman, Toby, 186
Zinn, David, 167
Ziporyn, Evan, 175
Zizka, Jiri, 104

www.ingramcontent.com/pod-product-compliance
Lightning Source LLC
Chambersburg PA
CBHW020329240426
43665CB00043B/161